THE MADISONIAN TURN

NEW COMPARATIVE POLITICS

Series Editor
Michael Laver, New York University

Editorial Board
Ken Benoit, Trinity College, Dublin
Gary Cox, University of California, San Diego
Simon Hix, London School of Economics
John Huber, Columbia University
Herbert Kitschelt, Duke University
G. Bingham Powell, University of Rochester
Kaare Strøm, University of California, San Diego
George Tsebelis, University of Michigan
Leonard Wantchekon, Princeton University

The New Comparative Politics series brings together cutting-edge work on social conflict, political economy, and institutional development. Whatever its substantive focus, each book in the series builds on solid theoretical foundations; uses rigorous empirical analysis; and deals with timely, politically relevant questions.

Curbing Bailouts: Bank Crises and Democratic Accountability in Comparative Perspective
    Guillermo Rosas

The Madisonian Turn: Political Parties and Parliamentary Democracy in Nordic Europe
    Edited by Torbjörn Bergman and Kaare Strøm

Political Survival of Small Parties in Europe
    Jae-Jae Spoon

Veto Power: Institutional Design in the European Union
    Jonathan B. Slapin

The Madisonian Turn

Political Parties and
Parliamentary Democracy in
Nordic Europe

Edited by
TORBJÖRN BERGMAN *and* KAARE STRØM

The University of Michigan Press ♦ *Ann Arbor*

First paperback edition 2013
Copyright © by the University of Michigan 2011
All rights reserved

This book may not be reproduced, in whole or in part, including illustrations, in any form (beyond that copying permitted by Sections 107 and 108 of the U.S. Copyright Law and except by reviewers for the public press), without written permission from the publisher.

Published in the United States of America by
The University of Michigan Press
Manufactured in the United States of America
⊗ Printed on acid-free paper

2016 2015 2014 2013   5 4 3 2

A CIP catalog record for this book is available from the British Library.

Library of Congress Cataloging-in-Publication Data

The Madisonian turn : political parties and parliamentary democracy in Nordic Europe / edited by Torbjorn Bergman and Kaare Strom.
    p. cm. — (New comparative politics)
  Includes index.
  ISBN 978-0-472-11747-5 (cloth : alk. paper) — ISBN 978-0-472-02550-3 (ebook)
  1. Cabinet system—Scandinavia. 2. Political parties—Scandinavia. 3. Legislative bodies—Scandinavia. 4. Scandinavia—Politics and government—1945–
  5. Comparative government. I. Bergman, Torbjorn. II. Strom, Kaare.

JN7066.M33   2011
324.20948—dc22   2010043127

ISBN 978-0-472-03529-8 (pbk. : alk. paper)

Contents

List of Abbreviations
vii

Acknowledgments
ix

THEORY AND BACKGROUND

1 ♦ Parliamentary Democracies under Siege?
Kaare Strøm and Torbjörn Bergman
3

2 ♦ Nordic Europe in Comparative Perspective
Torbjörn Bergman and Kaare Strøm
35

THE FIVE NORDICS

3 ♦ Change and Challenges of Danish Parliamentary Democracy
Erik Damgaard
67

4 ♦ Finland
Moving in the Opposite Direction
Tapio Raunio
112

5 ♦ Iceland
Dramatic Shifts
Svanur Kristjánsson and Indridi H. Indridason
158

6 ✦ Norway
From Hønsvaldian Parliamentarism Back to Madisonian Roots
Hanne Marthe Narud and Kaare Strøm
200

7 ✦ Swedish Democracy
Crumbling Political Parties, a Feeble Riksdag,
and Technocratic Power Holders?
Torbjörn Bergman and Niklas Bolin
251

COMPARATIVE CONCLUSIONS

8 ✦ Parties and Party Systems in the North
Nicholas Aylott
297

9 ✦ East-West Conflict and Europeanization
International Effects on Democratic Politics
in the Nordic States
Cynthia Kite
329

10 ✦ The Nordics
Demanding Citizens, Complex Polities
Torbjörn Bergman and Kaare Strøm
356

Contributors
389

Name Index
393

Subject Index
399

Abbreviations

EC	European Community
ECO	European Consultative Organ
ECSC	European Coal and Steel Community
EEA	European Economic Area
EEC	European Economic Community
EFTA	European Free Trade Agreement
EMU	European Monetary Union; Economic and Monetary Union
EP	European Parliament
ESDP	European Security and Defense Policy
ESS	European Social Survey
EU	European Union
GDP	gross domestic product
MDS	multidimensional scaling
MP	member of parliament
MPs	members of parliament
NATO	North Atlantic Treaty Organization
NPM	New Public Management
OECD	Organization for Economic Cooperation and Development
PM	prime minister
PR	proportional representation
SEA	Single European Act
UK	United Kingdom
USSR	Union of Soviet Socialist Republics; the Soviet Union

Acknowledgments

As editors and contributors to this volume, we have over the past several years accumulated a great number of debts to the many individuals and institutions who have helped us make this study possible or improved its quality. Besides our respective home institutions, the first main sponsor of this research was the Nordiska samarbetsnämnden för humanistisk och samhällsvetenskaplig forskning, NOS-HS, through its grant to the project Nordic Parliamentary Democracy (Nordisk parlamentarisk demokrati, Ref. NOS-S 20084 Bergman). And through its grant to the project Constitutional Reform 2010: Political Parties and the Rules of the Game (P2007-0370:1-E Bergman), the Swedish Riksbankens Jubileumsfond helped us complete the project and the book.

Both the individual contributors and the editors have been very fortunate in having excellent research assistance. The contributors are pleased to acknowledge these contributions in their respective chapters. We unfortunately cannot here thank all those who have helped us centrally or locally, but we do want to acknowledge that at different times during the past few years Emelie Lilliefeldt, Erik Svedman, and Marcus Holmström at Umeå University and Jens Nilsson at Luleå University of Technology have through their hard work and long hours helped us tremendously in the central coordination and execution of this study.

During the final months of our project, Emily O. Matthews has meticulously and efficiently reviewed the entire manuscript, including all the tables and figures, for consistency and clarity of presentation. She was also instrumental in proofreading the text and in preparing the manuscript for submission. In effect, at this critical juncture she managed the editors, and she did so to our great satisfaction.

We are endlessly grateful also to all those colleagues who have read various parts of this manuscript and provided constructive comments. We especially want to express our gratitude to Robert Harmel and Jo Saglie, who a couple of years back read the entire manuscript and gave us detailed suggestions that helped us rethink and improve the book. Not least, we want to express our gratitude to our contributors, who, even though most have had previous experience of working with us, have stood by the editors in a long research process. Their positive attitudes and commitments have made our job a lot easier. The responsibility for any remaining errors rests with us, the editors. We are also most grateful to Melody Herr and the production staff at the University of Michigan Press for their efficient, professional, and cheerful collaboration in turning this manuscript into a traditional as well as an electronic book. Finally, we thank our respective families, and especially Cindy and Digna, for their invaluable patience and support.

The text discusses Nordic politics up through early 2010. The tables report data available at that time. With the publication of this book, we will release additional tables containing a variety of useful data on the parliamentary institutions of the Nordic countries. The interested reader will find these in the Nordic Parliamentary Democracy Data Archive at the following Internet address: www.erdda.se.

Torbjörn Bergman ♦ Kaare Strøm

✦ **THEORY AND BACKGROUND** ✦

1 ✦ Parliamentary Democracies under Siege?

KAARE STRØM AND TORBJÖRN BERGMAN

There is increasing concern across the advanced industrial democracies about the health of two essential democratic institutions: legislatures and political parties.[1] As Russell Dalton argues, citizens "have grown distrustful of politicians, skeptical about democratic institutions, and disillusioned about how the democratic process functions" (2004, 1). Most of those that have been concerned with the health of representative democracies have worried about presidential systems in particular (Linz 1994; Lijphart 1999). Yet, the parliamentary regime-type characteristic of most European countries has its own share of challenges (Strøm, Müller, and Bergman 2003), and these polities have not been immune from international events and turmoil, such as the financial and economic crisis that has recently hit the capitalist world.

In this book, we focus on the health of parliaments and parties in democracies in a particular set of European parliamentary democracies—those in the Nordic or Scandinavian region.[2] This region is not an obvious political trouble spot. On the contrary, many observers of the Nordic countries have praised their well-functioning democracies and attributed their health to the efficiency with which they operate (Damgaard 1992; Esaiasson and Heidar 2000) and the esteem in which they are held by their citizens (Norris 1999). In addition to serving as examples of stable, well-functioning parliamentary democracies, the Nordics have often been singled out as affluent, peaceful, and remarkably successful across a variety of policy areas (including poverty reduction, public health, and gender equality).

Nonetheless, many of the challenges that face democratic societies elsewhere in the world are currently relevant in the Nordic region as well. The Nordic model evolved during a period of social peace and robust (though perhaps not spectacular) economic growth, and doubts have arisen concerning its ability to deliver in more turbulent times. Among the most important political pillars of this model are well-functioning parliaments and cohesive and powerful political parties. Indeed, the specter of parliamentary and/or party decline should be particularly troubling to citizens of the Nordic democracies because they rely so much on both of these political institutions. Moreover, the fact that party government is both strongly entrenched and critical to the democratic process makes the Nordic countries a particularly intriguing region in which to examine the changes that contemporary parliaments and parties are undergoing. In short, simultaneous parliamentary and party decline can be more challenging in Nordic Europe than in just about any other democratic region.

While this book is primarily an examination of contemporary parliaments and parties and the challenges they face, it is also a study of the Nordic region. As such, our book has a particular thesis: the Nordic combination of strong parties and strong parliaments is a function of specific social, historical, and institutional factors; and this constellation of conditions that has fostered strong parliaments and parties in the past is increasingly under challenge from developments among voters, politicians, and European states. But these forces of change are not affecting parties and parliaments equally, nor are the Nordic states all equally impacted. On the contrary, the Nordic region is far less politically homogenous than many outsiders believe, and in recent decades the changes that have taken place in the region's parliamentary and party systems have not been uniform. This heterogeneity is grounded in the history of the region, and it has important—indeed essential—ramifications for the ways in which parliaments and political parties operate and for the challenges they currently face.

In the rest of this chapter, we discuss the nature of parliamentary government and parliamentary democracy and the role that political parties play in such regimes. Parliamentary democracy, we shall argue, is a particular way to structure political delegation from ordinary citizens to political decision makers. In this context, we will introduce two models of representative democracy: the Westminster model and the Madisonian model. Though in no way confined to such regimes, these models can both be found under parliamentary government. Yet they imply radically different roles for political parties and for the policy-making role of parliament. Toward the end of the chapter, we discuss three contemporary challenges to parties and parliaments in parliamentary systems stemming from changes in the electorate, changes in politicians, and changes in the political environment, respectively. The chapters that follow will examine the implications of these challenges for the Nordic countries.

Democracy and Parliamentary Government

Any discussion of the challenges to contemporary parliaments and parties in democracies must begin with a proper understanding of the essential properties of democracy itself. To us, democracy is a matter of citizen sovereignty. Democracy is a form of governance that allows ordinary citizens to be the ultimate political stakeholders.[3] The scope of democracy, that is, what decisions the majority of citizens should be able to control, is a more contested matter. For present purposes, it suffices to say that democratic governance should be important and influential, but also limited. It should also be *liberal*, which means that citizens have inalienable rights upon which governments cannot legitimately encroach.

Early democratic polities began as direct democracies, with citizens participating directly in the making of important political decisions. As Robert A. Dahl (1971) has argued, however, in contemporary societies direct democracy is often infeasible for reasons of capacity, competence, or coordination. Representative democracy implies that citizens therefore delegate the vast majority of political decisions to legislators or executive officeholders. These politicians then delegate to one another or to civil servants.

There are many forms of representative democracy, but in the contemporary world the most common type is parliamentary government. Parliamentary government vests parliament with the critical power to dismiss the chief executive, and, in practice, the levers are pulled by the leaders of the relevant political parties.[4] In addition, one of the hallmarks of parliamentary government is that the key political officeholder, the prime minister, is not elected directly by the people. In stark contrast to presidential systems, in a pure parliamentary system only the national legislature (the parliament) is a direct agent of the citizens in the sense that it is elected by those citizens (Strøm, Müller, and Bergman 2003). Thus, parliament has a central and unique place in the constitutional make-up of such polities, and any challenge to the authority or effectiveness of parliament goes to the heart of popular governance.

Parliamentary Democracy and the Chain of Democratic Delegation

As explained above, *parliamentary government* is a regime type defined most minimally by the cabinet's responsibility to the parliamentary majority. The dismissal power vested in parliament means that it can, by majority vote, force the prime minister and his or her cabinet to resign at any moment. The broader concept of *parliamentary democracy*, in our usage, refers to an ideal-typical way to organize the political delegation of citizen sovereignty. Any representative democracy can be understood as a *chain of political delegation* that runs from citizens to their elected representatives, from those elected representatives to officials with chief executive authority, and from these officials to public administrators and all the way down to the street-level civil servants who ultimately implement public policy. In any chain of delegation, those authorized to make political decisions (*principals*) conditionally designate others (*agents*) to act in their name and place. A delegation chain thus consists of a series of agency relationships. Note that the same person or organization can be an agent in one link of the chain and a principal in the next. For example, in parliamentary systems, the prime minister is both the agent of the parliamentary majority and the principal of the members of his or her cabinet.

Under parliamentary democracy, the chain of delegation includes four discrete steps or links (Strøm 1997; Bergman and Damgaard 2000; Bergman, Müller, and Strøm 2000; Strøm, Müller, and Bergman 2003):

1. from voters to elected representatives (legislators);
2. from legislators to the chief executive (prime minister) and his or her cabinet;
3. from the cabinet and the chief executive to the "line ministers" (typically individual cabinet members) who head the different executive departments; and
4. from cabinet members, in their capacity as heads of different executive departments (ministries), to civil servants within their agencies.

Parliamentary democracy is thus a particular ideal-typical chain of political delegation with a singular and hierarchical chain of command. In its pure type, all agents report to only one principal. For example, all civil servants in a particular ministry serve one particular master, their senior minister. To a large extent, principals also delegate to singular or noncompeting agents rather than to a set of competing ones. Thus, ministerial jurisdictions are supposed to be mutually exclusive, and each minister controls only the civil servants in his or her own ministry. These features differ from those of presidentialism, in which agents often report to multiple principals (for example, in the United States, many civil servants report to the president as well as to the House of Representatives and the Senate), and in which principals often delegate to many competing agents (see fig. 1.1).

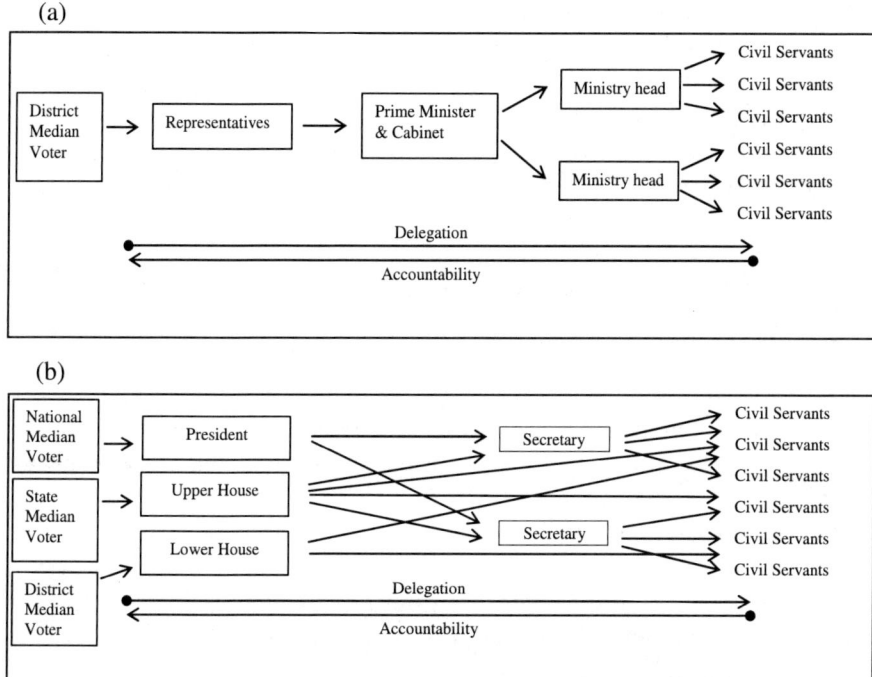

Fig. 1.1. Delegation and accountability under parliamentary and presidential government. (Data from Strøm 2003; Strøm, Müller, and Bergman 2006.)
(a) Single-chain delegation model of a parliamentary system
(b) Multiple-chain delegation model of a U.S.-style presidential system

In its pure form, parliamentarism is thus a particularly simple and efficient design for democratic delegation.

Accountability

Even though the need for political delegation may be obvious, it is no simple matter. Indeed, for more than two thousand years political observers have commented on the dangers of representation and delegation, as well as on the need for politicians to be under popular control and to keep each other in check. Picking agents is far from easy. As Manin, Przeworski, and Stokes (1999, 40) put it, "politicians may want to pursue their own ideas even if these differ from those of citizens. Some may care most about advancing their careers against fellow politicians, within the government or the same party. Some may seek perks. Some may want to get rich at the expense of citizens, while in office or after leaving it. Some may be most concerned about recognition by foreigners. In all these cases politicians will want something whose pursuit is injurious to citizens."

In technical terms, the problem is that delegation can easily lead to agency loss, which is the difference between the actual policy outcome and the feasible outcome that the principal would have most preferred (see Lupia 2003). All public-spirited citizens would presumably like to find candidates for office who are both capable and driven by a true concern to serve their constituents. But the problem is how to tell who will act effectively in the public interest and who will not. Alas, the candidates' own representations of their motivations will rarely reveal the "rotten apples." Nor is the scrutiny of an electoral campaign always sufficient. As Schumpeter (1943, 288) put it, "the qualities of intellect and character that make a good candidate are not necessarily those that make a good administrator, and selection by means of success at the polls may work against the people who would be successes at the head of affairs."

Perhaps the rotten apples are even disproportionately drawn to politics. The force of political competition may perversely favor the most ruthless and self-interested politicians because only such individuals survive in the electoral rough and tumble. This is the problem of adverse selection in democratic politics—which, in more technical terms, means that political candidates (potential agents) have private information about their aptitude and that some incentive schemes may perversely favor the candidates that are least likely to act in the principal's best interest.

Selecting good political candidates, however, is not enough to ensure that the voters' desires will be satisfied. Even if the elected politicians are fully capable of making the "right" decisions, they may nevertheless behave contrary to the voters' preferences. If oversight is sufficiently lax and the chance of getting caught is small, public officials may shirk their obligations in favor of junkets, receptions, and other opportunities for leisure and pleasure. Alternatively, they may pursue policy interests not shared by their voters or, even worse perhaps, pursue their own personal enrichment. This is the problem of moral hazard, the risk that political agents once selected may take hidden action contrary to the interest of the principal.

Agency problems such as adverse selection and moral hazard are an inevitable risk in representative democracy. To counteract these dangers, the democratic chain of delegation needs to be coupled with political accountability mechanisms by which, if their behavior or performance in office is unsatisfactory, politicians can be checked or removed. In the words of

Manin, Przeworski, and Stokes, "governments are accountable if citizens can discern representative from unrepresentative governments and can sanction them appropriately . . . An 'accountability mechanism' is thus a map from the outcomes of actions of public officials (including messages that explain these actions) to sanctions by citizens" (1999, 10). Or, more concretely, an accountability mechanism is a "device by which a principal (a) can get information about an agent's intentions, skills, and behaviour or (b) can sanction or reward the agent" (Bergman et al. 2003, 110).

Accountability mechanisms must convey information to the principal and permit him or her to impose sanctions on the agent. Principals can accomplish these objectives through such means as (1) contract design, (2) screening and selection mechanisms, (3) monitoring and reporting requirements, and (4) institutional checks (Lupia 2003; see also Aghion and Tirole 1997; Kiewiet and McCubbins 1991). The first two are mechanisms by which principals seek to contain agency losses ex ante, that is, before entering any agreement. The latter two (numbers 3 and 4) operate after the fact of delegation (ex post facto). The ex post mechanisms are often institutionally (if not constitutionally) defined.

Screening and selection are classical ways in which principals can obtain important information about the agent before any delegation takes place. *Screening* means that the principal undertakes costly action to learn more about the qualifications of the agent. *Selection* means that the agent demonstrates her suitability in a way that is costly to herself, for example, by running for a hopeless seat or holding a minor office.

Other important mechanisms of political accountability operate after delegation has taken place, in the form of constraints such as the vote of no confidence and the threat (or promise) of future elections. In their study of congressional delegations in the United States, Epstein and O'Halloran (1999, 100) identify 14 different types of constraints, "procedural mechanisms that Congress writes into legislation to constrain the bureaucracy." Among these are contract design features (e.g., time limits, spending limits), veto provisions, reporting requirements, direct oversight, hearings, and appeals procedures. As we will discover in the five Nordic country chapters, some of these mechanisms are also heavily featured in parliamentary democracies.

All accountability mechanisms are costly, and none are universally effective (Lupia 2003). The choice between them depends on the relevant agency problems as well as on the resources of the principal. Briefly stated, ex ante mechanisms such as screening tend to be more effective against problems of adverse selection, whereas ex post oversight is more likely to be helpful in combating moral hazard. To the extent that real-world polities face both adverse selection and moral hazard, we should therefore expect to see greater unresolved problems of adverse selection in polities that rely heavily on ex post controls, and more severe issues of moral hazard where ex ante accountability devices predominate.

Parliamentary Democracy and Political Parties

Democracies have fostered organizations that specialize in the containment of political agency problems. The most important of them are political parties, which are groups or organizations that run political candidates for office under their label. One important difference between a classical parliamentary regime and a presidential one lies in the greater role and cohesion of political parties in the former. Yet even among parliamentary democracies there is significant variation in the role that parties play. Thus, we distinguish between a Westminster model and a Madisonian version of parliamentary democracy. The Westminster model relies heavily on political parties for political delegation and accountability. This model obviously derives its name from the British experience, and especially the form that the emergent British democracy took from the late nineteenth century on. Around that time, British parliamentary democracy evolved into a form that relied on cohesive political parties and cabinet dominance of the policy process. The term Westminster democracy has also been used in a broader sense in Arend Lijphart's (1984, 1999) influential work to designate a form of representative governance that features a series of majoritarian and power-concentrating provisions.

Our conception, however, will be narrower. Briefly stated, as we use the term in this book, the Westminster model maximizes the power of a winning coalition of members of parliament (MPs).[5] It features unitary and centralized government, winner-take-all elections, minimal popular and constitutional constraints on parliamentary power (parliamentary sovereignty), and no institutions designed to foster minority influence or require supermajority decision making. Its lines of accountability are all vertical and hierarchical, not horizontal, which is to say that political agents are not set up to check or compete with one another but are rather given sole authority to serve their principals within their respective competencies.

The accountability device that underpins this system is the political party. Parties are key features of most contemporary governments. In principle, democracy is possible without political parties; indeed, most constitutions (at least those drafted before World War II) read as if parties did not exist. Nevertheless, political parties have become a ubiquitous feature of democracies as we know them. Part of the explanation, no doubt, is their ability to promote popular policy choice and accountability. The Westminster model in particular relies on political parties to mobilize and control a winning coalition of parliamentarians. All important decision makers are recruited through political parties and screened and vetted by these organizations. And where competition among a small number of (ideally two) cohesive and policy-oriented parties is high, as in the ideal-typical Westminster model, citizens have clear policy choices. Political parties can thus enhance citizen control of public policy-making as well as impose discipline on politicians.

This is an efficient form of delegation. It features a radically simple and effective mechanism of political accountability: the next election. Ideally, the leaders of political parties know that they are subject to the voters' judgment at the next electoral crossroads, and hence the fear of losing the voters' confidence will keep party leaders on their toes and motivate them to keep discipline within their ranks. Therefore, the parties in power should serve as efficient mechanisms of delegation for the winning coalition of voters.

The classical embodiment of Westminster democracy is the form that it took in the United Kingdom between approximately 1911 and 1973. (It is also a form from which the British system has since departed in several ways.) The crux of this model is that parliamentary institutions are combined with centralized, cohesive, and policy-oriented political parties in a format that fosters single-party government, alternation in executive office, and robust electoral competition. As Cox (1987) has demonstrated, party government and parliamentary government evolved simultaneously and symbiotically into the "efficient secret" of British government (Bagehot [1867] 1963)—political organizations that align the preferences of the occupants of the most important political offices and subordinate them to centralized control. As Palmer describes it, "the Westminster model of government similarly involves the holding of a competition (an election) between competing organizations (parties) for the virtually unconstrained right to exercise a monopoly power (by government, over legitimate coercion). The electorate seeks competing bids from parties in terms of promises to govern according to particular policy preferences and leadership characteristics. By appointing one disciplined party as its agent, the electorate accepts, by majority vote, what it judges to be the best bid" (Palmer 1995, 168). The Westminster model is thus the polity that most effectively enables citizens to control the policy process by choosing between a set of programmatic political parties. This form of democratic control has also been referred to as the party mandate model or the responsible-party model (see, e.g., Ranney 1962).

Within the Westminster model, political parties control delegation from voters to representatives, as well as from representatives to the chief executive (Müller 2000). Party control means extensive screening of prospective parliamentarians as well as potential cabinet members. Before candidates gain access to higher office, they must acquire the proper party credentials and prove themselves in lesser offices. However, the effects of party attenuate as we move downstream in the policy chain. Their reach into administrative agencies is either tenuous or controversial, since partisanship in the civil service often conflicts with cherished values such as competence, neutrality, or simply "clean government" (Müller 2000, 330).

Westminster parties serve politicians and voters alike. By aligning the preferences of the occupants of the most important political offices (parliament, the cabinet, and the heads of the different executive agencies), they are beneficial to voters under three conditions:

1. partisanship is associated with systematic and transparent differences in the bundles of goods and policies that governments produce (the party platforms);
2. these party platforms reflect salient policy preferences among the voters, who can therefore make informed partisan choices;
3. political parties also provide a way in which elected representatives can later be held responsible for their performance in office.

These three conditions spell out the circumstances in which it makes sense for voters to attach themselves to partisan labels.

Parties must also serve the purposes of politicians. Politicians will submit to party discipline and invest in partisan brand names only if partisanship offers them tangible and predictable benefits. Parties help politicians control the flow of governmental decisions and dispersals (Aldrich 1995), and they help politicians get reelected (or, perhaps, elevated to higher office) (Cox and McCubbins 1993; Schlesinger 1991). Parties are particularly strong under Westminster democracy in part because the rewards controlled by party leaders are so valuable to rank-and-file politicians. These rewards include ballot access, access to executive office, campaign finance, and positions of authority within the legislature. Indeed, in a pure Westminster system, the governing party has monopoly control of all important legislative and executive offices.

When parties are useful to voters as well as to politicians, citizens can rely on parties to screen and sanction candidates for political office, and politicians can count on citizens to support them. Party leaders can present voters with a package of candidate agents whose policy preferences are well understood and whose behavior will be strictly policed by this semi-public organization. Moreover, even though the voter can directly influence only the selection of parliamentarians, the downstream consequences of a victory for one team or another are straightforward and predictable.

Political parties thus have a privileged place in parliamentary systems because of the important functions they perform as mechanisms of delegation and accountability. In short, parliamentary democracy rests on parliaments and parties to a greater extent than does any other form of democracy, and the role of parties is particularly critical in the Westminster model. Among parliamentary systems, the more a political system resembles this classic Westminster model, the greater the role of parliaments and parties and, therefore, the more serious any weakness in those institutions is likely to be.

We juxtapose the Westminster world with an alternative model of representative democracy: Madisonianism.[6] There is nothing new about Madisonianism—many of the key ideas were formulated by the U.S. founders in the *Federalist Papers* more than two hundred years ago. Yet, in an earlier study of parliamentary delegation and accountability in Western Europe, we found a growing convergence between these ideas and the structure of contemporary parliamentary democracies. We thus noted that a major cross-national trend seemed to "strengthen ex post controls and weaken ex ante screening devices" (Strøm et al. 2003, 701). We also noted "that the decline of political parties, especially in electoral and membership terms, entails a serious challenge to traditional parliamentary democracy and especially the Westminster model" (Strøm, Müller, and Bergman 2003, 736). In this study, we build on these conclusions and establish an alternative parliamentary model—the Madisonian one—that we ultimately (in chapter 10) flesh out by drawing on our empirical examination of the Nordic democracies.

Even though it need not take the presidential form that we know from the United States, Madisonianism is characterized by complex delegation schemes, institutional constraints, and checks and balances. The key features of a Madisonian parliamentary democracy is that political authority is dispersed and that different branches of government are made to check one another such that ambition counteracts ambition (*Federalist* No. 51, 322). The pure Westminster model means that citizens have only one direct agent and that the power of that agent is maximized. In contrast, Madisonianism implies that citizens are served by several directly elected agents. And it implies a principle of minimizing the power of the strongest of these (partisan) agents.

The Westminster model implies strong parties that align the incentives of the politicians that join them. The Madisonian model is skeptical about parties and the "mischiefs of faction" (*Federalist* No. 10, 78), and its operating principle is that political incentives and ambitions should conflict, rather than align. The Westminster model, when it works, means that citizens can efficiently and predictably delegate authority. The Madisonian model at its best means that, due to constraints that are external to the parliamentary chain of governance, citizens have broad-based, reliable protections against political agency loss. While external constraints may under some circumstances exacerbate rather than reduce democratic agency loss, they play a critical role in the Madisonian model mainly because they limit the threat of majority tyranny. For the U.S. founders, federalism was a particularly prominent and credible constraint on democratic politicians. For federalism, according to Madison (*Federalist* No. 10, 84), can be a "republican remedy for the diseases most incident to republican government," namely parochialism and "the violence of faction" (*Federalist* No. 10, 77).[7]

Deparliamentarization?

Democracies thus come in many forms and they differ among themselves in the roles played by national legislatures in the representation of citizen preferences. This role tends to be larger in parliamentary systems than in presidential systems, larger in unitary systems than in federal systems, larger in systems with relatively few veto gates than in those with many, and larger in states with a permissive (perhaps unwritten) constitution and weak judicial review than in systems with a restrictive constitution and strong institutions of judicial review. Similarly, political parties play a more critical role in Westminster than in Madisonian systems.

All democracies are in flux, as political institutions such as parliaments evolve and as organizations such as political parties wax and wane in their effectiveness. Across a broad range of contemporary democracies, however, parties as well as parliaments seem to be increasingly under pressure. Peter Mair (2006) thus speaks of a "hollowing" of Western democracy, in which the roles of voters as well as elected representatives are under challenge. The thesis of deparliamentarization suggests that parliamentary influence in the democratic policy process has weakened. This is not a new argument. At least since Bryce (1921), scholars have argued that parliaments have been losing authority, including the capacity to oversee executive decision making.

To judge whether democratic parliaments have in fact suffered a loss of power, we must consider the functions that legislatures ideally or typically serve. Wheare's (1963) classic analysis follows just such an approach when it focuses on the tasks performed by parliaments. The most obvious role of legislatures is to legislate. Yet, as crafters of detailed legislation, parliamentarians have long been eclipsed by the politicians of the executive branch and the bureaucrats who serve them. Parliament has thus delegated much of its law-making function to the executive branch. Much the same can be said for decisions on the government budget. The effectiveness of such delegation depends on parliament's ability to formulate and to withdraw or reformulate its mandate. A parliament that is *unable* to legislate or budget, or even to define the terms on which it delegates these functions to the executive, is therefore in a much weaker position than a parliament that is *capable* of legislating and budgeting but that prefers to leave the initiative to the executive branch. In our case studies, we seek to assess not only the activity levels of the various Nordic parliaments, but also their capacity for key democratic decisions.

As Bagehot ([1867] 1963) observed well over a century ago, however, actually making laws does not necessarily rank among the most prominent functions of modern parliaments. Instead, the preeminent task of modern parliaments, according to Bagehot, is the elective function. In the classic Westminster model, the cabinet emerges from the parliamentary majority; indeed, all members of the cabinet simultaneously have to be members of parliament. Thus, parliament not only "elects" (albeit not formally) the cabinet, it also does so from among its own members and in such a way that these members remain parliamentarians and can be recalled from the executive by parliament at any time.

In contemporary parliamentary democracies, however, this elective function has been attenuated. Institutionally, many parliamentary constitutions do not require cabinet members to retain their membership in the legislative branch; in fact, some constitutions, including those of Norway and Sweden, specifically prohibit such overlapping memberships (Andeweg and Nijzink 1995). And in many cases, past or present membership in the legislative branch is no prerequisite for appointment to the cabinet. Thus, in some European countries, in recent decades only about 50 to 60 percent of all cabinet members have had any parliamentary background; moreover, several of the Nordic democracies rank close to or at the very bottom of this scale in European comparison (Andeweg and Nijzink 1995, 160). To the extent that the overlap between parliamentary and cabinet service has thus weakened, we might expect the elective function of parliament to be eroded.

A third function of parliament is to oversee policy formulation and implementation in the executive branch. As parliaments have become less directly involved in legislation, their oversight role has arguably become more important. However, over time this activity has also become steadily more difficult as government responsibilities have expanded and the executive branch has grown increasingly large and specialized. The literature that seeks to judge whether parliaments are in fact facing more severe obstacles in their attempts to oversee the executive focuses in large part on the volume of parliamentary activity devoted to oversight functions. The results are ambiguous. Indeed, some Nordic scholars report that parliamentary activity has increased and that parliament has gained greater control over the national executive (for example, Christensen, Lægreid, and Roness 2002). Thus, as Elgie and Stapleton (2006) suggest, the thesis of declining parliamentary influence may not apply equally well in all domains or polities. However, although increased parliamentary activity might mean more effective oversight, as we shall see in later chapters, the inference is not always straightforward. As Christensen, Lægreid, and Roness suggest, parliaments may in fact have gotten "more control over less"(2002, 37).

Yet, legislative activity levels may not in themselves give us a reliable read on the contemporary status of European parliaments. Parliamentary influence requires not only effort, but also skill. A decline in parliamentary influence may therefore be due to an erosion of the competence of the individuals who fill its seats. As Bryce (1921) observed in the early twentieth century, legislators are no longer as socially and intellectually exclusive as they once were. In addition, due to cognitive and social mobilization, citizens are less likely to defer to parliamentarians based on the latter's perceived status or competence. As a result, what Bagehot called the teaching function of parliament has been attenuated. Similarly, parliament's "informing function" (Bagehot [1867] 1963), its role in hearing and expressing the grievances of individual citizens against the government, has declined. This may be a result in part of the greatly increased political access that ordinary citizens have come to enjoy, and in part of such institutional innovations as the creation of ombudsmen (parliamentary commissioners) authorized to hear and act upon such grievances.

In this volume, we shall examine the deparliamentarization thesis by scrutinizing parliamentary activity and recruitment in our five countries. In so doing, we will focus on the defining feature of parliamentary democracy, namely the relationship between the legislature and the executive. As Anthony King (1976) has famously pointed out, however, it is critical to recognize that parliamentary democracy hinges on the relationship between the political party (or parties) in government and those in opposition.[8] But since parliamentary influence requires competence as well as activity, we shall also examine the credentials of all the politicians who have held four of the most important cabinet portfolios in each country. Thus, to understand parliamentary democracy and its alleged contemporary predicament, we must study both the institutions of the policy process and the parties and individuals that come to occupy these institutions.

Political Parties in Decline?

Among students of European politics, concerns about the health of political parties have been just as prominent as, if not more so than, worries about the decline of parliament. It has long been argued that political parties are on the wane in both parliamentary and presidential systems. As Dalton and Wattenberg (2000, 3) put it, "Today, mounting evidence points to a declining role for political parties in shaping the politics of advanced industrial democracies. Many established political parties have seen their membership rolls wane, and contemporary publics seem increasingly skeptical about partisan politics." In their survey of parties in 16 advanced industrial democracies, Webb, Farrell, and Holliday (2002, 441) similarly report that in all but one of their countries, "there is evidence of a significant level of disaffection with, or cynicism towards, parties." For two countries (Italy and Belgium), they report, the level of popular dissatisfaction must be understood as "a full-blown crisis of the political system." These results are, at least in part, also a consequence of what aspects of political parties are under scrutiny.

Dalton and Weldon (2005) thus summarize the prevailing status of political parties in Western representative democracies: "citizens today express widespread skepticism about political parties as institutions, and the process of representative government based on political parties. Most citizens believe that parties do not care what they think, are not sufficiently responsive to public interest, and cannot be trusted to represent the public's interest. Such sentiments have also become more common in the past generation" (947).

In this book, we shall focus on the roles that parties play in the democratic chain of delegation in the Nordic countries. In order to do so, we need to understand that political parties are multifaceted. In his influential work, V. O. Key (1964) identified three aspects of political parties: the party in the electorate, the party organization, and the party in government.[9] The thesis of party decline concerns all of these aspects of parties.

The *party-in-the-electorate* aspect has to do with the attachment of voters to political parties and the willingness of these voters to exchange their support for the kind of programmatic packages that the parties offer. This support is a critical condition for the parties to develop such policy platforms and for the politicians within these parties to submit themselves to the discipline of party loyalty.

In recent decades, the cross-national literature has suggested serious challenges to the party-in-the-electorate in advanced industrial democracies. In their comprehensive study of OECD nations, Dalton and Wattenberg (2000) provide striking evidence of decline in the electoral party. In virtually all advanced industrial democracies, party identification has declined over the second half of the twentieth century, often substantially. These trends are particularly noticeable among younger and more educated voters. At the same time, particularly since the 1980s, citizens have become more fickle in their voting choices, as reflected in increased electoral volatility. Moreover, surveys of voting behavior show that in many countries voters make up their minds later, often late in the election campaign.

Finally, voter turnout has been declining across most of the democratic world, and in some countries this decline has been dramatic. Moreover, it appears that decreased turnout has been particularly great in the most recent decades. Findings revealed in Webb, Farrell, and Holliday (2002) support this development. Important indicators such as party identification (ID) and party membership generally show a downward trend.

The second aspect of political parties identified by Key (1964), extra-parliamentary *party organization*, structures the selection of activists and candidates into political parties, helps keep parties close to their grassroots, and maintains internal communication. There is strong evidence of decline here, too. Some variation notwithstanding, Europe has seen a massive decline in party membership, whether measured as a share of the electorate or in absolute numbers (Mair and van Biezen 2001). The latter have dropped dramatically, particularly since the 1980s (Scarrow 2000). In the early twenty-first century, many European parties reported membership numbers that were only a fraction, in many cases only 20 or 30 percent, of what they were just a couple of decades earlier.

Finally, there are challenges to the *party in government*, which is the organization that maintains discipline among the parties' elected representatives and ensures that the policy packages they promise can be delivered. The party in government is a *sine qua non* for Westminster democracy.

While we could imagine parties in government functioning without strong parties in the electorate, the converse is a much more difficult proposition. In other words, parties may well act cohesively in the governmental arena even if voters are not strongly attached to them, but voters (at least rational ones) will hardly make strong commitments to political parties if they provide no governmental cohesion or policy consequences.

Decline in the party in government is more difficult to measure than decline in the electoral party or the membership organization, but it may be reflected in parliamentary voting cohesion and in the proportion of nonpartisans appointed to public office. There is no strong cross-national evidence of declining legislative party cohesion, but there is some evidence that parties are losing their tight grip on the recruitment of parliamentarians. This is reflected in the proportion of independent or nonpartisan legislators. While this proportion is generally very low, it began rising in several countries in the 1990s (Strøm 2000; see also Strøm, Müller, and Bergman 2003, esp. chap. 23). Political parties might also be losing control over the selection of government ministers, though the evidence here is sparse. It is still rare in most parliamentary systems for nonpartisans to be appointed to cabinet office, yet the data show an upward trend for several countries for the 1990s (Strøm 2000, 207). Overall, the challenges to the party in government have been less obvious and dramatic than those that have affected the electoral party or the party organization. Yet, in our survey of Nordic parties, we shall scrutinize all three aspects of parties.

Strong Parliaments, Strong Parties?

As we have observed, the Nordic region has been noted for its coincidence of strong parliaments and strong parties. This is by no means an obvious or ubiquitous coincidence. Strong parties and strong parliaments are not always found together, nor does a weakening of parliaments necessarily imply a similar attenuation of the influence of political parties. In fact, when parliament is strong, parties are often weak, and vice versa.

Even if their legislatures have considerable powers of deliberation and oversight, Madisonian parliamentary democracies often feature weak and fractionalized parties. The Italian parliament has many features of institutional strength, but Italian parliamentary parties have often been fragile and factionalized. And in the (admittedly presidential) United States in the 1970s, the weak cohesion of the political parties indeed helped bolster Congress as a decision-making institution. On the other hand, as Cox (1987) argues, the formation of strong and cohesive parties in Britain caused the

House of Commons to decline as an arena of deliberation. Thus, parliamentary democracies commonly show an inverse relationship between legislative and party strength.

Yet, with their traditionally strong parties and transformational parliaments, the Nordic states seem to defy this regularity. Why has this been so? One reason is that the Nordics have tended to avoid some institutional dynamics that often come with strong parties and that result in weak parliaments. The Westminster model implies not only a particular type of party, but also an *alternational* party system (Bergman et al. 2003, 181–83). In alternational systems, two parties (or two blocs of parties) compete for the voters' favor and alternate in power. Policy decisions are effectively made by the voters in general elections, and parliament is marginalized in the policy-making process.

Even multiparty systems may feature fierce electoral competition and the same alternational dynamics of turnover between, say, governments of the right and governments of the left. Electoral institutions such as the French double ballot, the Single Transferable Vote, or the German second vote may drive multiparty systems toward the alternational format. Some of the Nordic states, and especially Norway and Sweden (and to some extent Denmark), have long exhibited such competitive two-bloc politics. But as it has happened, competitive two-bloc politics coupled with party system fragmentation has often resulted in "hung" parliaments (minority situations) and minority governments, during which parliament has become a critical arena for accommodations between government and opposition.

An alternative type is the pivotal party system, in which there is a single party (or occasionally a bloc of smaller parties) that forms the core of the governing coalition, often because it controls the median legislator on the dominant policy dimension. The pivotal party may sometimes rule with one set of partners (e.g., the left) and sometimes with others (e.g., the right). Thus, the pivotal party may change coalition partners, but there is no wholesale alternation in power as a result of electoral contests.[10] Whereas alternational politics tends toward strong parties and weak parliaments, pivotal party systems often foster strong parliaments but weak parties. The toxic effects of pivotal politics are twofold: the quasi-permanent parties of government are beset with factionalism, intrigue, and often corruption, whereas the quasi-permanent opposition, in its frustration, has a tendency to turn to extremism and political irresponsibility (Sartori 1976).

Among the Nordic countries, Finland and Iceland have tended to be closest to the pivotal model, but even the Social Democrats in Sweden and Norway and the Radicals in Denmark have at times come close to pivotal status. Yet, with the partial exception of Iceland, they have escaped most of the ill effects of pivotal party systems, and specifically clientelism. This may be due in part to the early professionalization of public administration under Scandinavian monarchies (see Shefter 1994); in part to the segmental, interest-based nature of Nordic parties, which may have kept them from becoming vehicles of rampant personalistic ambition; and in part to the transparency and social capital of Nordic societies, which have helped contain abuses of power (Rothstein 1998). Whether these or other forces are still sufficient to protect Nordic parties is a different question, and one that we shall have to confront.

Contemporary Political Transformations

There is thus a large body of evidence that parliaments as well as parties are facing a cold and unpleasant season in contemporary Europe. But is there a specifically Nordic chill? And what might lie behind this predicament of contemporary parliaments and parties? If parliaments as well as political parties in many contemporary democracies are under siege, what are the forces responsible for this situation? In this section, we identify current trends in Western and Nordic societies that might affect support for these democratic institutions. Such a list of contemporary changes could be very long and still not exhaustive because democratic institutions are complex and because challenges are coming from many different quarters. Hence, we choose to focus on three prominent transformations having to do, respectively, with the democratic principals, their agents, and the institutional environment in which they interact. The first challenge stems from a changing and more individualistic electorate. The second challenge, which has tended to be overlooked in the Nordic literature, has to do with the way in which party elites relate to their constituents. The third concerns the increasing complexity of contemporary politics and the dispersion of power away from the nation-state.

As regards all three transformations, the Western world, including the Nordic region, has changed greatly over the past half-century, and in particular over the past couple of decades. Voters have become more resourceful and harder to please. Politicians increasingly face incentives and temptations that might distance them from their supporters and democratic principals. And finally, the policy process has become more constrained and complex, so that parties and parliaments have greater difficulty controlling it. These developments are not mutually exclusive, and in some respects they reinforce one another.

A More Demanding Electorate

The first trend lies in the growing demands that parliamentarians and party politicians face from their political constituents, the voters. We are living in an age in which knowledge is much more easily accessible than ever before. As Robert A. Dahl notes, new information technology offers enormous opportunities for enhanced communication and dissemination of knowledge and opinions. "By means of telecommunications virtually every citizen could have information about public issues almost immediately accessible in a form (print, debates, dramatization, animated cartoons, for example) and at a level (from expert to novice, for example) appropriate for the particular citizen" (1989, 339).

In addition, the citizenries of contemporary advanced democracies are better educated than ever; in Europe, the changes over the past few decades have been remarkable. In most European societies, the 1960s and 1970s were critical decades in the expansion of educational opportunities. By the mid-1990s, the proportion of adult citizens (aged 25 to 64) who had completed at least an upper-secondary education had surpassed 50 percent in most OECD countries and 80 percent in some. Furthermore, in many countries about a fourth or a fifth of the same age group had completed a higher education (Norris 2000, 48–49). Among the youngest of these adults, the numbers were often significantly higher.

This revolution in information and education has had obvious political consequences. It is now easy for ordinary citizens to get access to an abundance of government and parliamentary papers and official information about the lives and actions of politicians. Media reports about both the public sector and politicians are also plentiful and accessible. The information-education revolution has greatly enhanced the volume of information available to voters and lessened the informational asymmetries between citizens and their political representatives.

These developments may have affected voters' sense of efficacy more than their actual understanding of political processes, since the political environment has at the same time become more complex (discussed later). But surely the empowerment of ordinary citizens has resulted in a much less deferential attitude toward politicians. Quite simply, voters are more difficult to please than ever before. Moreover, when they are not pleased, they do not necessarily give their erstwhile parties a second chance. In Hirschman's (1970) terms, voters increasingly opt for exit strategies over voice and especially over loyalty. Not only is loyalty to political parties in retreat, but the declining number of party members indicates that the same applies to "voice." In other words, an increasing number of voters behave like consumers, shopping around for the best deal without much brand-name loyalty.

We can readily observe the growing fickleness of European voters. The second half of the twentieth century witnessed a gradual rise in electoral volatility (Lane and Ersson 1999, 128) and, more specifically, an increasing tendency for incumbent (cabinet) parties to lose vote shares (Müller and Strøm 2000, 589). As Narud and Valen (2008, 379–80) show, in the average Western European election between 1945 and 1999, the governing parties suffered a net loss of 2.59 percent of the total popular vote relative to their previous vote share. These losses have increased monotonically over time. The average losses of incumbent cabinets were fairly low in the 1940s (0.10 percent) and the 1950s (1.08 percent). By the 1980s, the mean electoral setback of incumbent cabinets had reached 3.44 percent. Yet, electoral losses have continued to increase, almost doubling in the 1990s to 6.28 percent.

Contemporary politicians thus defy their restive citizenries at their own peril, and a plausible trajectory for contemporary advanced democracies is one in which it becomes progressively more difficult for elected officials to satisfy their constituents. While such a trend may be read as an ever-increasing entrenchment of short-term citizen sovereignty, it may also reflect a situation in which citizen preferences are becoming increasingly difficult to aggregate and in which politicians are given less and less latitude to do so. Politicians, it seems, are given fewer opportunities to take one step back in order to take two steps forward, and their principals have become less tolerant of concessions they might make in order to forge political compromises.

Growing Political Agency Problems

The second trend that can influence parties and parliaments in advanced industrial democracies is that politicians (party elites) may be in the process of becoming less faithful agents of their citizens. Such growing agency losses between citizens and their representatives could be due to any of several developments, including expanded opportunities for politicians to act contrary to their constituents' interests as well as increasing preference divergence between citizens and politicians. Both of these forces are likely to be at work in the Nordic region. The next section will discuss how European integration and globalization have not only restricted the discretion of national politicians, especially in economic policy, but also made the entire policy process less transparent and comprehensible for regular citizens.

The second and in some sense even more worrisome possibility is that there may be a trend toward greater preference divergence between citizens and their political representatives. While there is little academic scholarship on Nordic political parties that suggests that politicians have become less credible agents of their voters than in previous eras, we believe this possibility should not be ignored. The main reason is that sweeping social transformations over the past generation have increased the risk of adverse selection, which is to say that citizens may increasingly lack the necessary cues to pick the politicians that will best represent their interests. The same loss of social transparency may make it more difficult for ordinary voters to ascertain whether the politicians that they have placed in office truly act in the interest of their constituents. This is the problem of moral hazard.

The social conditions that once favored successful selection and control of politicians no longer exist. Many of the dominant political parties in advanced industrial democracies, including the Nordics, grew out of distinct social subcultures such as the industrial working class, the farming sector, or religious communities. Social insulation, transparency, and solidarity helped minimize agency problems between these subcultures and their political representatives. As societies have become more diverse and fragmented, however, the effectiveness of such mechanisms of control have diminished, and problems of adverse selection or moral hazard may have become more serious.

In their highly influential work, Katz and Mair (1995) suggest that such social changes have also led to a change in party organization, from mass parties to catchall parties to cartel parties. Parties used to articulate demands on behalf of particular social groups, but now have been transformed into organizations that serve as brokers between the state and civil society. Parties have made this transition partly out of necessity. As social subcultures have eroded and the attachments between ordinary citizens and political parties attenuated, parties have had to look elsewhere for resources. Katz and Mair (1995) argue that in many cases they have turned to the state, which has expanded its capacities and riches, thus enabling it to become a direct and important source of party funding. These authors single out "public subsidies" as a cause of many evils—for example, as contributing to less vital party organizations, creating a barrier against new parties, and enabling party leaders to ignore members (and membership recruitment).

Since the 1970s, public party finance has become a virtually universal feature of Western European democracies. In most of these countries, the volume of party subventions has increased steadily, and in many cases public subsidies now account for the bulk of all party incomes. One danger of public party finance is that, if it is controlled by the dominant parties themselves, it may help sustain a cartel of established parties and petrify the existing party system (Paltiel 1981, 170). Cartelization is less likely if public money is extended to parties not represented in parliament and thus unlikely to be part of any cartel. But the troubling fact is that, in some countries, a quarter of a century or more of public funding has passed without any extension of these benefits to non-parliamentary parties (Strøm, Müller and Bergman 2003).

The cartel party thesis suggests that established parties may more or less willingly let their loyalist base and extra-parliamentary organization atrophy, while maintaining a tight hold on the levers of governmental power, and especially on public-sector sources of income (Katz and Mair 1995). Such a trend could easily undermine the ability and willingness of politicians to act as faithful servants of the citizens at large. Specifically, the conditions favoring the emergence of the cartel party may also give rise to a growing risk of moral hazard among public officials.

There may be additional forces that threaten to increase agency problems and limit the control of party organizations over high-ranking politicians. Poguntke and Webb (2005) argue that parliamentary democracies are becoming more and more "presidential" largely as a result of changes in mass media and public access to information. Presidentialization means that democratic politics have become more executive-dominated and leadership-focused, to the detriment of parliament. From the perspective of party elites, such tendencies toward presidential prime ministers might further diminish the need for an extra-parliamentary mass-based party organization. At a minimum, Blyth and Katz (2005) argue, cartelization trends make politics more managerial and less ideological, and thus also less about policy differences insofar as parties all promote similar policies.

An Increasingly Constrained National Policy Process

A third sweeping transformation in contemporary democracies is the growing importance of external constraints on national policymakers. More and more, democratic politicians are bound not only by their popular mandates but also by other societal actors and institutions. *Internal* constraints are limitations on political authority that are formed within the parliamentary chain of delegation, such as the election program (manifesto) of the governing party or, in the case of multiparty governments, the coalition agreement that parties sign before taking office together. There are also constraints that are *external* to the parliamentary policy process.[11] Some are *democratic* constraints, such as abrogative referendums, federalism, and other constitutional provisions that vest critical powers in actors outside the parliamentary policy process. These are partitions of sovereignty, which disperse democratic authority. *Technocratic* constraints remove political authority from elected representatives altogether and assign it instead to non-elective institutions that are not subject to majority rule (at least in the short run), such as central banks or independent courts authorized to exercise judicial review. Finally, there are *societal* constraints, such as the mechanisms of consultation and collective decision-making inherent in corporatist or consociational institutions, which force elected politicians to share authority with civil society.

Though this volume will examine the changes that have affected a multitude of political constraints, the most critical challenge is to be found in the constraints imposed by the international environment. Globalization is commonly argued to undermine, or progressively constrain, the nation-state "not only by shrinking the resources under national control for shaping economic and social outcomes, but also by reducing government's legitimacy and authority in the eyes of the public" (Berger 2000, 45).[12]

In contemporary Europe the development of greatest importance to national governance is the challenge posed by European integration—in particular the demands of the policy-making process of the 27 countries that currently make up the European Union (EU). Since the 1957 Treaty of Rome, member states have increasingly delegated decision-making powers to the EU. The EU has thus grown substantially in geographic scope and substantive importance, particularly since the 1980s. The Single European Act of 1986, the Maastricht Treaty of 1991, and a number of subsequent reforms and treaties have set the stage for a dramatic increase in the domain of supranational decision making.

As European integration progresses, there are serious concerns about the ability of national parliaments to scrutinize their respective governments in EU affairs and about the effects of the resulting informational asymmetries. The increasing scope of supranational legislation, as well as the growing complexity and empowerment of EU institutions, pose severe challenges for national legislatures intent on scrutinizing and influencing supranational policy-making (Bergman and Damgaard 2000). The resulting "multilevel governance" features a "dispersion of authoritative decision making across multiple territorial levels" (Hooghe and Marks 2001, xi). Common wisdom and most scholarship suggest that the national parliaments have been on the losing end of these developments.

The effects of European integration on national legislatures are certainly not all negative. The loss of formal authority must be weighed against the gains flowing from a larger market, the opportunity to combat environmental and other problems, and the enhanced opportunity to solve collective action problems on the world stage (Bergman and Damgaard 2000). Thus, Raunio and Hix (2000) maintain that while there has been a transfer of legal authority away from national parliaments, these developments are not confined to the EU states, but are rather part of large-scale processes of modernization and globalization. They also argue that much of what is going on is a domestic transfer of influence from parliaments to executives, who in turn have gained authority through European decision making.

Yet, the European Union does introduce agency problems between national parliamentarians and supranational institutions. Moreover, relative to the foreign ministry, the prime minister and those ministers most involved in EU affairs have increased their power in foreign and European affairs. Thus, the presidentialization of European parliamentary politics has been significantly hastened by the forces of supranational integration (Poguntke and Webb 2005).[13] Parliaments of member states have adjusted by creating new control instruments such as European affairs committees for consultation with and scrutiny of their respective executives. It is a growing challenge for national governments to control the numerous national civil servants who serve in EU working groups and the so-called comitology of the European Union. While all national governments have worked out new systems for domestic coordination at the apex of ministries, they have little oversight over lower echelons of civil servants.

European integration may seem of limited relevance in the Nordic region, where two of five countries—Iceland and Norway—are not even EU members as of 2010. Instead, their relations with the EU are regulated by the European Economic Area (EEA). In reality, however, this relationship is among the most important constraints on the autonomy of national policymakers in both countries. Moreover, there is a striking similarity in the observed impact of European integration between, on one hand, the three member states (Denmark, Finland, and Sweden) and, on the other hand, the nonmembers (Norway and Iceland). In fact, the EEA states often find themselves obliged to implement the results of a decision-making process that they have difficulty influencing. In this sense the EU's "democratic deficit" may be most severe for EEA member states. European integration is thus a huge challenge for all Nordic parliamentarians. It can promote favorable and efficient policy-making, but it also complicates the mandate and accountability of national political agents.

The Nordic Cases

To understand the changes and challenges facing parliamentary democracy today, we look for evidence in five "least-likely" cases of party or parliamentary decline. There are two main reasons why the Nordic countries are of particular interest in this context. One is that the traditionally strong position of parties and parliaments makes it easy to understand the significance of these institutions in context. The other reason is that if the Nordic states are experiencing an erosion in the functions of these institutions, then we can safely assume that the same trend is widespread across the democratic world.

In the rest of this book we describe and analyze the changes in the roles and functions of parliaments and political parties that have taken place in the Nordic region. Our focus is primarily on the past two decades, from about 1990 to the present. This is the period during which the challenges to parliamentary and party authority have been most evident. Also, it has been close to 20 years since the most recent authoritative study of party and parliamentary power in these countries was conducted (Damgaard 1992).

As we have noted, the Nordic countries are of particular interest since they have had both strong parliaments and centralized and cohesive (strong) political parties. The region is also interesting because these intra-Nordic similarities coexist with a number of important institutional differences. While Lijphart (1984; 1999) classifies all the Nordic countries as largely consensual, the political differences between them are in fact substantial. The chapters that follow will detail how the Nordic countries break down between Westminster and Madisonian regimes, as well as between pivotal and alternational party systems. Against this background, we can assess differences in the challenges they face and the ways in which they have responded.

We investigate the current state of Nordic parliamentary democracy with the help of a set of comparative data collected by the contributors to this volume. Their chapters will show how the Nordic states have moved away from their previous resemblance to a Westminster model with consensual traits toward a form of parliamentary democracy with more separation-of-powers (Madisonian) features. These features are evident both in vertical power relations (for example, relations with the European Union and with subnational levels of government), and in horizontal ones (that is, as reflected in increasingly independent courts and central banks). However, these developments are far from uniform. Whereas Finland has shifted in the direction of classical Westminster democracy, Norway and Sweden have moved notably toward a more Madisonian model. Denmark has moved more modestly in this direction, while the Icelandic party system is more unstable than ever and basic parliamentary ground rules have come under challenge. These developments help increase our understanding of five increasingly diverse countries that have long been considered bastions of democracy and welfare. The results also show that there may be many different responses to the political challenges that so many Western democracies now face.

Following the five country-specific chapters, chapter 8 will sum up the empirical evidence on the state of Nordic parties. It compares the unique information presented in these chapters and brings together the most important developments in the five party systems. In chapter 9, we return to the international context that interacts with domestic politics. The chapter shows that without taking into consideration such developments as the end of the Cold War and the process of European integration, it is difficult to comprehend many of the trends we observe or the conditionality of the different responses to the contemporary challenges these systems face. In the final chapter, we compare the Nordic democracies with the Westminster and Madisonian models and offer our assessment of the "Madisonian turn" that has affected the parliamentary politics of much of the Nordic region.

In order to help the reader understand the background against which these forces have been working, however, we first need to place the Nordic countries in a broader European and historical context. The next chapter, therefore, examines the Nordic region and the backdrop it provides for parliamentary politics.

NOTES

1. Note that parliaments (and more generally legislatures) and political parties are both institutions and actors. Thus, parliament legislates (acts) but also constitutes a central democratic institution (a set of rules and an arena). Likewise, political parties are, in our view, the most important actors in parliamentary politics. Parties need not be unitary actors, even though the Nordic ones have a strong record of cohesive behavior in parliament.

2. The region covered in this book is most properly referred to as "the Nordic region" (or "the Nordic countries"), rather than "Scandinavia." We discuss the proper meaning of the two terms in greater detail in chapter 2.

3. By *governance* we mean "the practice of governing." Governance sometimes refers to how a form of government works in practice (democratic or parliamentary governance). At other times we use (cabinet) governance to describe how coalition governments are maintained from the time they are formed until they resign. For alternative usages of the concept see, for example, Pierre 2000.

4. By our minimalist definition, we count as systems of parliamentary government those polities in which the prime minister and his or her cabinet are accountable to and can be removed from office by a parliamentary majority for no particular cause other than "lack of confidence" (Strøm, Müller, and Bergman 2003).

5. Note again that our conceptualization of the Westminster model is different from, and less complex than, that of Arend Lijphart (1984; 1999), even though we abstract from the same empirical reality.

6. As noted, just as Lijphart's definition of Westminster democracy is broader than ours, his contrasting conception of consensus democracy shares only some of the features of our Madisonian model.

7. A key difference between the consensus model (Lijphart 1984; 1999) and Madisonianism is that while the former is conceptualized at the level of the (nation-)state, the "federal" components of the latter enable us to recognize the growing importance of supranational constraints.

8. "Government" here refers to the entire set of executive offices controlled by the ruling party or parties, including but not limited to the cabinet.

9. Katz and Mair (1993) instead refer to party on the ground, the party in the central office, and the party in public office. Here we make no further distinctions between these concepts and the ones proposed by Key (1964).

10. The distinction between alternational and pivotal multiparty systems reflects, in part, the cohesion of interparty coalitions. There is an analogy at the party level. In his analysis of the United States Congress, Krehbiel (1998) defines pivotal politics as a situation in which partisanship has no constraining effect on the voting behavior of legislators. In Krehbiel's model of individual legislative behavior, all bargaining power rests with the pivotal legislator on the critical policy dimension. Parties cannot credibly commit politicians to joint action, either across issues or over time.

In a world in which the players are cohesive political parties instead of individual legislators, the analogy to Krehbiel's model is a bargaining situation in which there are no credible pre-electoral coalitions, because parties have no capacity to make binding commitments to one another. In this kind of pivotal party system, parties cannot commit themselves to stable coalitions. Instead, the pivotal party, typically the one holding the median legislator on the most important policy dimension, dominates the policy process through ad hoc and often alternating majorities with parties in its immediate policy neighborhood (often those of the center-right or center-left).

The distinction between pivotal and alternational systems also corresponds to a difference in cabinet types. Pivotal systems tend to feature broad majority or supermajority coalitions, whereas alternational multiparty systems tend toward minimum winning pre-electoral bloc coalitions. When no pre-electoral coalition obtains a parliamentary majority, alternational systems often experience minority governments formed by the bloc that can most easily negotiate ad hoc majorities. As we shall see, the distinction between pivotal and alternational politics cuts right across the Nordic region.

Finally, the contrast between pivotal and alternational party politics has implications for democratic delegation and accountability. Pivotal party politics promotes efficient democratic delegation, since the median voter is presumably well represented in the pivotal party and central to the governing coalition. Alternational party systems may feature governments whose point of gravity is further away from the median voter, since the latter is typically at the "centrist" end of a coalition that may extend to the extreme of the relevant policy dimension. The advantage of such coalitions, however, is that they promote accountability because voters can more easily punish or dismiss coalitions with which they are dissatisfied.

11. External constraints are thus contextual forces that can enable and/or constrain the players in the democratic policy process. They influence politics through their effects on the choice sets, information sets, or preferences of these players.

12. The extent to which globalization undermines national decision-making capacity is certainly contested. While most scholars agree that globalization is a major contemporary challenge to nation-state politics, the "national varieties of capitalism" literature insists that different institutional and political settings meet these challenges in varying ways (Berger 2000, 56).

13. For a more skeptical view of the "decline of parliament" thesis, see Riddell 2006.

REFERENCES

Aghion, Phillipe, and Jean Tirole. 1997. "Formal and Real Authority in Organizations." *Journal of Political Economy* 105 (1): 1–29.
Aldrich, John A. 1995. *Why Parties? The Origin and Transformation of Political Parties in America.* Chicago: University of Chicago Press.
Andeweg, Rudy, and Lia Nijzink. 1995. "Beyond the Two-Body Image: Relations Between Ministers and MPs." In Herbert Döring, ed., *Parliaments and Majority Rule in Western Europe.* Frankfurt am Main: Campus; New York: St. Martin's Press.
Bagehot, Walter. [1867] 1963. *The English Constitution.* London: Fontana/Collins.
Berger, Suzanne. 2000. "Globalization and Politics." *Annual Review of Political Science* 3:43–62.
Bergman, Torbjörn, and Erik Damgaard, eds. 2000. *Delegation and Accountability in European Integration: The Nordic Parliamentary Democracies and the European Union.* London: Frank Cass. (Also available as a special issue of *Journal of Legislative Studies* 6 (1).)
Bergman, Torbjörn, Wolfgang C. Müller, and Kaare Strøm, eds. 2000. "Parliamentary Democracy and the Chain of Delegation." Special issue, *European Journal of Political Research* 37 (3): 255–429.
Bergman, Torbjörn, Wolfgang C. Müller, Kaare Strøm, and Magnus Blomgren. 2003. "Democratic Delegation and Accountability: Cross-National Patterns." In Kaare Strøm, Wolfgang C. Müller, and Torbjörn Bergman, eds., *Delegation and Accountability in Parliamentary Democracies.* Oxford: Oxford University Press.
Blyth, Mark, and Richard S. Katz. 2005. "From Catch-all Politics to Cartelisation: The Political Economy of the Cartel Party." *West European Politics* 28 (1): 33–60.
Bryce, James. 1921. *Modern Democracies.* New York: MacMillan.

Christensen, Tom, Per Lægreid, and Paul G. Roness. 2002. "Increasing Parliamentary Control of the Executive? New Instruments and Emerging Effects." *Journal of Legislative Studies* 8 (1): 37–62.
Cox, Gary W. 1987. *The Efficient Secret: The Cabinet and The Development of Political Parties in Victorian England.* Cambridge: Cambridge University Press.
Cox, Gary W., and Mathew D. McCubbins. 1993. *Legislative Leviathan: Party Government in the House.* Berkeley: University of California Press.
Dahl, Robert A. 1971. *After the Revolution?* New Haven: Yale University Press.
Dahl, Robert A. 1989. *Democracy and Its Critics.* New Haven: Yale University Press.
Dalton, Russell J. 2004. *Democratic Challenges: Democratic Choices. The Erosion of Political Support in Advanced Industrial Democracies.* Oxford: Oxford University Press.
Dalton, Russell J., and Martin P. Wattenberg, eds. 2000. *Parties without Partisans: Political Change in Advanced Industrial Democracies.* Oxford: Oxford University Press.
Dalton, Russell J., and Steven A. Weldon. 2005. "Public Images of Political Parties: A Necessary Evil?" *West European Politics* 28 (5): 931–51.
Damgaard, Erik, ed. 1992. *Parliamentary Change in the Nordic Countries.* Oslo: Scandinavian University Press.
Elgie, Robert, and John Stapleton. 2006. "Testing the Decline of Parliament Thesis: Ireland, 1923–2002." *Political Studies* 54 (3): 465–85.
Epstein, David, and Sharyn O'Halloran. 1999. *Delegating Powers: A Transaction Cost Politics Approach to Policy Making under Separate Powers.* Cambridge: Cambridge University Press.
Esaiasson, Peter, and Knut Heidar, eds. 2000. *Beyond Westminster and Congress: The Nordic Experience.* Columbus: Ohio State University Press.
The Federalist Papers. [1787–1788] 1982. Alexander Hamilton, James Madison, and John Jay. New York: Bantam Dell.
Hirschman, Albert O. 1970. *Exit, Voice, and Loyalty: Responses to Decline in Firms, Organizations, and States?* Cambridge, MA: Harvard University Press.
Hooghe, Liesbet, and Gary Marks. 2001. *Multi-Level Governance and European Integration.* Lanham, MD: Rowman & Littlefield.
Katz, Richard S., and Peter Mair. 1993. "The Evolution of Party Organizations in Europe: Three Faces of Party Organization." *American Review of Politics* 14: 593–617.
Katz, Richard S., and Peter Mair. 1995. "Changing Models of Party Organization and Party Democracy: The Emergence of the Cartel Party." *Party Politics* 1 (1): 5–28.
Key, V. O. 1964. *Politics, Parties, and Pressure Groups.* New York: Crowell.
Kiewiet, D. Roderick, and Mathew D. McCubbins. 1991. *The Logic of Delegation.* Chicago: University of Chicago Press.
King, Anthony. 1976. "Modes of Executive-Legislative Relations: Great Britain, France, and West Germany." *Legislative Studies Quarterly* 1 (1): 11–36.
Krehbiel, Keith. 1998. *Pivotal Politics: A Theory of U.S. Lawmaking.* Chicago: University of Chicago Press.
Lane, Jan-Erik, and Svante Ersson. 1999. *Politics and Society in Western Europe.* 4th ed. London: Sage.

Lijphart, Arend. 1984. *Democracies: Patterns of Majoritarian and Consensus Government in Twenty-one Countries.* New Haven: Yale University Press.
Lijphart, Arend. 1999. *Patterns of Democracy: Government Forms and Performance in Thirty-six Countries.* New Haven: Yale University Press.
Linz, Juan J. 1994. "Presidential or Parliamentary Democracy: Does It Make a Difference?" In Juan J. Linz and Arturo Valenzuela, eds., *The Failure of Presidential Democracy.* Baltimore: Johns Hopkins University Press.
Lupia, Arthur. 2003. "Delegation and Its Perils." In Kaare Strøm, Wolfgang C. Müller, and Torbjörn Bergman, eds., *Delegation and Accountability in Parliamentary Democracies.* Oxford: Oxford University Press.
Mair, Peter. 2006. "Ruling the Void: The Hollowing of Western Democracy." *New Left Review* 42 (Nov–Dec): 25–51.
Mair, Peter, and Ingrid van Biezen. 2001. "Party Membership in Twenty European Democracies, 1980–2000." *Party Politics* 7 (1): 5–21.
Manin, Bernard, Adam Przeworski, and Susan Stokes. 1999. "Elections and Representation." In Adam Przeworski, Susan Stokes, and Bernard Manin, eds., *Democracy, Accountability, and Representation.* Cambridge: Cambridge University Press.
Müller, Wolfgang C. 2000. "Political Parties in Parliamentary Democracies: Making Delegation and Accountability Work." *European Journal of Political Research* 37 (3): 309–33.
Müller, Wolfgang C., and Strøm, Kaare. 2000. *Coalition Governments in Western Europe.* Oxford: Oxford University Press.
Narud, Hanne Marthe, and Henry Valen. 2008. "Coalition Membership and Electoral Performance." In Kaare Strøm, Wolfgang C. Müller, and Torbjörn Bergman, eds., *Cabinets and Coalition Bargaining: The Democratic Life Cycle in Western Europe.* Oxford: Oxford University Press.
Norris, Pippa, ed. 1999. *Critical Citizens: Global Support for Democratic Governance.* Oxford: Oxford University Press.
Norris, Pippa. 2000. *A Virtuous Circle: Political Communications in Postindustrial Societies.* Cambridge: Cambridge University Press.
Palmer, Matthew. 1995. "Toward an Economics of Comparative Political Organization: Examining Ministerial Responsibility." *Journal of Law, Economics, and Organization* 11 (1): 164–88.
Paltiel, Khayyam Z. 1981. "Campaign Finance: Contrasting Practices and Reforms." In David Butler, Howard R. Penniman, and Austin Ranney, eds., *Democracy at the Polls: A Comparative Study of Competitive National Elections.* Washington, DC: American Enterprise Institute.
Pierre, Jon, ed. 2000. *Debating Governance: Authority, Steering, and Democracy.* Oxford: Oxford University Press.
Poguntke, Thomas, and Paul Webb, eds. 2005. *The Presidentialization of Politics: A Comparative Study of Modern Democracies.* Oxford: Oxford University Press.
Ranney, Austin. 1962. *The Doctrine of Responsible Party Government: Its Origins and Present State.* Urbana: University of Illinois Press.
Raunio, Tapio, and Simon Hix. 2000. "Backbenchers Learn to Fight Back: European Integration and Parliamentary Government." *West European Politics* 23 (4): 142–68.

Riddell, Peter. 2006. "Books on Parliament." *Journal of Legislative Studies* 12 (1): 110–14.
Rothstein, Bo. 1998. *Just Institutions Matter.* Cambridge: Cambridge University Press.
Sartori, Giovanni. 1976. *Parties and Party Systems: A Framework for Analysis.* Cambridge: Cambridge University Press.
Scarrow, Susan E. 2000. "Parties without Members: Party Organization in a Changing Electoral Environment." In Russell J. Dalton and Martin P. Wattenberg, eds., *Parties without Partisans: Political Change in Advanced Industrial Democracies.* Oxford: Oxford University Press.
Schlesinger, Joseph A. 1991. *Political Parties and the Winning of Office.* Ann Arbor: University of Michigan Press.
Schumpeter, Joseph A. 1943. *Capitalism, Socialism and Democracy.* London: George Allen & Unwin.
Shefter, Martin. 1994. *Political Parties and the State: The American Historical Experience.* Princeton: Princeton University Press.
Strøm, Kaare. 1997. "Democracy, Accountability, and Coalition Bargaining: The 1996 Stein Rokkan Lecture." *European Journal of Political Research* 31 (1–2): 47–62.
Strøm, Kaare. 2000. "Parties at the Core of Government." In Russell J. Dalton and Martin P. Wattenberg, eds., *Parties without Partisans: Political Change in Advanced Industrial Democracies.* Oxford: Oxford University Press.
Strøm, Kaare. 2003. "Parliamentary Democracy and Delegation." In Kaare Strøm, Wolfgang C. Müller, and Torbjörn Bergman, eds., *Delegation and Accountability in Parliamentary Democracies.* Oxford: Oxford University Press.
Strøm, Kaare, Wolfgang C. Müller, and Torbjörn Bergman, eds. 2003. *Delegation and Accountability in Parliamentary Democracies.* Oxford: Oxford University Press.
Strøm, Kaare, Wolfgang C. Müller, and Torbjörn Bergman. 2006. "The (Moral) Hazards of Parliamentary Democracy." In Dietmar Braun and Fabrizio Gilardi, eds., *Delegation in Contemporary Democracies.* London: Routledge.
Strøm, Kaare, Wolfgang C. Müller, Torbjörn Bergman, and Benjamin Nyblade. 2003. "Dimensions of Citizen Control." In Kaare Strøm, Wolfgang C. Müller, and Torbjörn Bergman, eds., *Delegation and Accountability in Parliamentary Democracies.* Oxford: Oxford University Press.
Webb, Paul D., David Farrell, and Ian Holliday, eds. 2002. *Political Parties in Advanced Industrial Democracies.* Oxford: Oxford University Press.
Wheare, K. C. 1963. *Legislatures.* Oxford: Oxford University Press.

2 ✦ Nordic Europe in Comparative Perspective

TORBJÖRN BERGMAN AND KAARE STRØM

Few readers will be surprised at our treatment of Denmark, Finland, Iceland, Norway, and Sweden as one region. There is in fact widespread agreement among students of politics, social life, history, and culture that these countries share many commonalities, and that it is for a variety of purposes meaningful and interesting to study them jointly. While the Nordic countries make up a plausible and familiar region, they are not historically or geographically indistinguishable. Two countries (Norway and Sweden) are located on the geographically and culturally cohesive Scandinavian Peninsula (which takes its name from Skåne, the southernmost part of Sweden). Denmark lies on the other side of the strait of Öresund, but is seen as part of Scandinavia for historical, political, and cultural reasons. In strictly geographic terms and in our analysis, Finland and Iceland are considered to be Nordic countries, but not Scandinavian ones.

Many observers argue that the political similarities between the five countries outweigh the differences. For this reason, they are often seen as suitable for "most similar system" comparisons (see, for example, Miles 1996; Arter 1999, 147–49). Indeed, Einhorn and Logue (2003, xii) argue that with the impact of globalization and the collapse of the Soviet Union, "the commonalities [in the region] have grown while the differences have lessened." The research presented in this book will allow us to assess such judgments as they apply to contemporary Nordic parliaments and parties.

Background and Overview

Some readers will be familiar with the region while others might need more of an introduction. In what follows, we provide a brief historical-geographical background and examine the early history of Nordic representative democracy. This short overview is necessarily sketchy, but it provides a basis for a discussion of some distinctive cultural and organizational characteristics, such as Scandinavian consensus and compromise, democratic corporatism, and the welfare state(s). The chapter then goes on to explain how we structure the book with its focus on representative democracy as a chain of delegation from voters to political decision makers. In doing so, we begin with the citizens and move on to the subsequent policy-making process of parliamentary democracy. After that, we place this policy process in the context of the constraints (domestic and international) that are external to the parliamentary chain of delegation itself. In the final section of this chapter, we detail the contents of the chapters that follow and explain how we examine the recent trajectories of parliaments and political parties in Nordic Europe.

Historical Origins

The Nordic region as a whole is one of the few parts of Western Europe that was never subject to Roman rule or civilization, and in cultural as well as political terms it remains somewhat apart from the rest of the continent. Most of the region was never effectively integrated into the feudal Europe of the Middle Ages. The Protestant Reformation led to internal conflicts, but these were not quite as furious and bloody as those that plagued much of continental Europe. In the nineteenth century, the area was influenced as much by developments in the United States and Russia as by Western Europe. Indeed, the Nordic region remains the least integrated part of Western Europe. Until 1995, only Denmark had joined the European Union (EU), and even today (as of 2010) the Nordics account for two (Norway and Iceland) of the four West European states that have chosen to remain outside the EU (the other two are Switzerland and the Principality of Liechtenstein).

Apart from their historical distinctness from the rest of Europe, the Nordics have surely changed. The peoples of the region used to be poor and uncivilized, at least in the view of people further south on the European continent. Today, they are more likely to be considered rich and successful. Likewise, the region was an area of troublesome and unrelenting conflict in the sixteenth and seventeenth centuries. However, for the past century (with some notable exceptions related to the two world wars) it has in general been a remarkably peaceful corner of Europe. In the seventeenth century, it was a region where monarchs were quite successful (at least for a while) in establishing absolutist rule. Today, the region is widely known for its egalitarianism and strong commitment to democracy.

The Nordic region is geographically large, although it is difficult to establish exactly where it begins and ends. Due to the seafaring prowess of the Vikings (and other qualities that are today less publicly praised), the area of Nordic settlement ranged from the East Coast of North America to the Black Sea, and Viking influence was well entrenched as far south as Ireland and France and as far north as Greenland. Some of this vast area remains under Scandinavian influence today. Greenland, though geographically closer to North America, is a part of the Danish realm (albeit with a significant and recently increasing measure of home rule). Indeed, much of the Arctic area, including Spitsbergen, is politically and culturally integrated into Scandinavia. Large parts of the region are rugged, very sparsely populated, and, for most people's tastes, desperately cold. Although indigenous peoples such as Inuits and Samis make up only a small percentage of the inhabitants, they are more noticeably a part of the populations of these countries than they are anywhere else in Western Europe.

In political terms, the Nordic region begins in the lowlands just south of the North Sea and is bordered by the Baltic Sea and Russia in the east, the Atlantic Ocean (and more specifically, the Davis Strait) in the west, and the Arctic region in the north. Culturally, of course, such boundaries are arbitrary. Large parts of the Baltic region have had and retain close ties to the Nordic region, while most of the population of Greenland has more in common with inhabitants of Northern Canada than with Scandinavia. And the Greenland population is certainly less Nordic, or for that matter Scandinavian, than the inhabitants of Shetland or the Hebrides.

As shown in table 2.1, the total population of the five Nordic countries is about 25 million. In contrast to other northern European countries such as Germany and Russia, it continues to grow, albeit slowly in recent years. Growth has been fueled not only by immigration, but also by relatively healthy native fertility rates. Nonetheless, the population is hardly large by world or even European standards—the total Nordic population is less than one-third of that of Germany, less than half of France or Italy, and not much more than half of Spain.

In territorial terms, however, the region is vast. Sweden is the third largest country in Western Europe, surpassed only by France and Spain. Finland and Norway are also quite large by Western European standards. Greenland is enormous—four times the size of France. This territory of the region stretches a long way from north to south—so far in fact that a person standing at the southern border of Scandinavia is closer to North Africa than to the region's northernmost limits. Within each of the five countries, the population is overwhelmingly concentrated in the south (in

Iceland, the southwest). Except for Sweden, this is also where the capital cities are located. Finally, each of the Nordic countries is notably monocephalic, in the sense that the capital city greatly dominates all other urban centers.

The Emergence of National Representative Democracy

The Nordic countries have long and interdependent histories. Denmark, Norway, and Sweden emerged as something resembling nation-states about a thousand years ago. Iceland did as well, although most of its population was initially made up of settlers from elsewhere in Scandinavia or from Ireland. Finland's history was different, but by the thirteenth century the evolution of its national history became bound up with that of Sweden. Iceland lost its independence in the thirteenth century—first falling under Norwegian and later Danish rule. Norway suffered the same fate after the

TABLE 2.1. The Nordic Countries

	Territory, in Square Kilometers[a]	Population, 2006	GDP per Capita in PPS (Euro), 2006[b]	Foreign-Born Population, 2006 (%)
Denmark	43,098	5.4 million	29,600	6.5
Finland	338,145	5.3 million	27,500	3.6
Iceland	102,928	0.3 million	30,600	9.9
Norway	385,191	4.7 million	43,800	8.3
Sweden	450,295	9.1 million	29,300	12.9

Source: Data on territory from *Encyclopedia Britannica Online*, s.v. "World Data," http://search.eb.com/ (accessed February 7, 2008).

Data on population and foreign-born population from the following sources: Statistics Iceland, "Citizenship and Country of Birth" (2007), http://www.statice.is (accessed February 7, 2008); *Statistikbanken*, "BEF3: Folketal pr. 1. januar efter commune/amt, køn, herkomst, oprindelsesland og statsborgerskapsgruppe" (2006), http://www.statistikbanken.dk/bef3 (accessed February 13, 2008); *Statistikcentralen*, Offentliggörande "Finlands befolkning 2006" (2007), http://www.stat.fi/til/vaerak/2006/vaerak_2006_2007-03-23_tie_001_sv .html (accessed February 7, 2008); *Statistisk Sentralbyrå*, "Folkemengde og invandrerbefolkningen etter landbakgrunn 1970–2007 Absolute tall og prosent" (2007), http://www.ssb.no/emner/02/01/10/innvbef/ tab-2007-05-24-07.html (accessed February 7, 2008); *Statistiska Centralbyrån*, "Befolkningsstatistik i sammandrag 1960–2006" (2007), http://www.scb.se/templates/tableOrChart____26040.asp (accessed February 7, 2008).

Data on GDP per capita in PPS from *Eurostat*, "Gross Domestic Product at Market Prices" (2007), http://epp.eurostat.ec.europa.eu/ (accessed February 13, 2008).

[a]Conversion of territory into square miles is as follows: Denmark, 16,640 sq. mi. (excluding Greenland: 840,000 sq. mi.); Finland, 130.559 sq. mi.; Iceland, 39,741 sq. mi.; Norway: about 148,726 sq. mi.; Sweden, 173,860 sq. mi. (data from *Encyclopedia Britannica Online* [2006]).

[b]GDP (gross domestic product) is an indicator of the size of a nation's economy. It is a measure of the total value of all goods and services produced minus the value of goods and services used for intermediate consumption in their production. Expressing GDP in PPS (purchasing power standards) eliminates differences in price levels between countries. Calculations of GDP on a per head basis make it possible to compare economies significantly different in absolute size.

Black Death in the fourteenth century. By the time of the formation of the Kalmar Union in 1397, Scandinavia had been loosely integrated under Danish hegemony.

By the 1520s, a new Swedish dynasty rebelled against this awkward integration, especially when it implied the ruthless slaughter of large portions of the Swedish nobility, as infamously happened in Stockholm in 1520. The next two centuries were marked by polarization and seemingly unending conflict between Denmark and Sweden, with a gradual shift in the balance of power toward the latter. This period lasted until the downfall of Swedish King Karl XII in 1718 in the Great Nordic War. The rivalry between Denmark and Sweden bifurcated Scandinavian history, and from that point on the societies and polities of the Nordic region evolved along two distinct paths: a western tradition associated with Denmark, Iceland, and Norway, and an eastern tradition associated with Sweden and Finland. This divergence has had important implications up until the present time.

By the time of the Napoleonic Wars, Scandinavian dualism (Denmark versus Sweden) had fragmented into a more complex pattern due to the growing strength of the voices of nationalism and democratization. In addition, Scandinavian history was more and more subject to the influences of great power politics, which these countries could no longer successfully resist on their own. In 1809, Sweden was forced to surrender Finland to Russia, although the Finns gained a significant measure of home rule (see table 2.2), at least initially (and again after the aborted revolution of 1905). In 1814, Denmark found itself on the losing side of the Napoleonic Wars (indirectly due to Admiral Nelson's bombardment of Copenhagen) and was forced to cede Norway to Sweden. The Norwegians, however, hastily gathered a constitutional assembly and drew up a constitution. It served as the foundation of their home rule under the dual monarchy with Sweden that lasted until 1905, when Norway became a fully independent and sovereign state. Finland gained its independence 12 years later, when the

TABLE 2.2. Nordic Political History

	National Independence	Home Rule	Universal Adult Suffrage	Parliamentary Government	Year of Current Constitution
Denmark	10th century	n.a.	1915	1901	1953
Finland	1917	1809	1906	1917	2000
Iceland	1944	1918	1915	1904	1944
Norway	1905	1814	1913	1884	1814
Sweden	11th century	n.a.	1921	1917	1975

Source: Data from Heidar 2004, 14, 18. Year of current constitution provided by the authors.

Russian empire collapsed during World War I. Iceland gained domestic autonomy during World War I and declared independence in 1944, when Denmark was occupied by Nazi Germany.

Sweden had pioneered the evolution of parliamentary power and constitutional monarchy during its "Age of Liberty" from 1718 to 1772 (Metcalf 1977), but representative democracy in the Nordic region developed slowly. It attained a form roughly similar to today's institutions at about the same time across all five of the countries. As table 2.2 shows, universal adult suffrage was introduced around the time of World War I. Finland was in the forefront in the introduction of female suffrage, while Norway was first to extend the right to vote to lower-class males (nearly a century earlier). In most cases, parliamentary government prevailed some years earlier than universal suffrage, though in Finland the sequence was reversed. In Denmark and Norway, representative democracy was already secure at or before the turn of the century. In Sweden, after a long battle for supremacy, the king finally agreed in 1917 to stay on the political sidelines (Lewin 1988).

In the period between the world wars, developments in the Nordic states diverged dramatically. The transition to democracy took a violent turn in Finland. The country was the only part of the former Russian empire to escape forcible reincorporation into the Soviet Union, but the 1918 War of Independence was also a bloody civil war between the left (the Reds) and the right (the Whites), and it was fought with heavy international involvement from the Soviet Union (for the Reds) and Germany (for the Whites). When the Whites won the war, representative democracy was established. In Iceland, the transition to representative democracy and sovereignty also coincided with the two world wars, but it was gradual and peaceful.

The formal constitutions of the Scandinavian states were not changed until well after World War II, and the monarch remains head of state in all three. Finland and Iceland, in contrast, have popularly elected heads of state (presidents). Although significantly amended, the Norwegian constitution of 1814 remains in force to this day. Denmark enacted a significant constitutional reform in 1953. A new Swedish constitution came into effect in 1975 (Bergman 1995, 1999). Until then, Swedish kings formally appointed their prime ministers and retained other symbolic political powers. The new constitution stripped the Swedish monarch of even symbolic involvement in matters such as government formation and parliamentary dissolution. By contrast, the Danish and Norwegian monarchs retain a formal role in parliamentary politics (Bogdanor 1984).

Consensus and Compromise

Despite the early history of wars and conquest, the contemporary Nordic states are often said to share a culture of consensus and compromise. Scandinavia, and particularly Sweden, is known throughout much of the world for its consensual political culture (Ruin 1983; Sannerstedt 1987, 1989; Sjölin 1987; von Sydow 1989). The Swedish method of decision-making has long been famous for its emphasis on deliberation and thorough, lengthy treatment of political issues in government-appointed commissions. There has, of course, been historical variation in the level of consensus by which these changes have happened,[1] but the general thesis has been summed up best by Anton (1980, 158): "No image of modern Swedish politics is more widely celebrated than that of the rational, pragmatic Swede, studying problems carefully, consulting widely, and devising solutions that reflect centuries of practice at the art of compromise." From this perspective, Sweden and Scandinavia are seen as a prime example of a consensual political culture.

At the same time, an exclusive emphasis on consensus provides too narrow a conceptualization of Scandinavian politics. An alternative view emphasizes how politics and society have been shaped by struggles between influential groups and political parties associated with the traditional class struggle. Proponents of this "conflict" perspective maintain that compromise emerged from a struggle between a mobilized working class and organized capital (see Esping-Andersen 1990; Katzenstein 1985; Kenworthy and Pontusson 2005; Korpi 1983; Stephens 1979). In contrast to the consensus literature, this compromise is not portrayed as reflecting an absence of conflict. Instead, compromise is seen as an efficient solution to deep-seated class conflict. At the heart of the compromise are "national agreements" forged between labor unions and organized business in the 1930s. In each of the three Scandinavian countries, the 1930s produced "crisis agreements" between the Social Democrats and the party representing organized farmers. These compromises in the face of economic distress and major social conflict paved the way for consensus democracy. At the same time, they effectively pulled the rug out from underneath aspiring fascist movements (Lindström 1985).

Thus, some scholars see compromise as a result of a culture of consensus, while others emphasize inherent conflict and stress how powerful workers' movements, largely dominated by social democrats, succeeded in building welfare states to counterbalance market-based capitalism. Both perspectives contribute to an understanding of the politics of compromise and the simultaneous existence of consensus and conflict in the Nordic countries. The most appropriate understanding of political developments may well vary by country. Though Sweden and Norway are in many ways alike, Sweden has experienced more class conflict and Norway more divisions between the cities and the countryside (see Eckstein 1966). Denmark, in turn, has had different alignments of labor and land and much more prosperous agriculture. Finland and Iceland are even more divergent. Finland is the only Nordic country that in the twentieth century was torn by civil war, and its agrarian movement has long been among the strongest in all of Europe. In contrast, research on Icelandic society tends to emphasize southern-European style clientelism and the absence of a strong industrial working class (Indridason 2005). Thus, while the five countries are all frequently labeled "consensual democracies" (Elder, Arter, and Thomas 1982), in the coming chapters we also explore differences among them.

Democratic Corporatism

Corporatism is another notable feature of the Nordic region. It refers to the strength and organizational unity of economic producer groups, and to the ways in which these groups interact with one another and the government in economic (and other) policy-making. From the 1930s and 1940s, corporatism in its "societal" or "liberal" varieties became a complement, rather than a competitor, to parliamentary democracy in smaller European societies such as Scandinavia and Austria. Corporatist practices in these countries were in large part associated with the emergence of strong social-democratic governing parties (especially in Scandinavia) and with postwar economic compromises between capital and labor (Katzenstein 1985).

Through the mid-1980s, corporatism was widely depicted as an efficient practice in its ascendancy. Since then, however, more somber assessments have tended to dominate. In Sweden in the late 1980s and early 1990s, business associations opted out of the system of interest representation through government commissions and executive boards, and the whole remiss system (i.e., broad formal consultations by the government with domestic stakeholders) has declined in importance (Lewin 1994; Rothstein and Bergström 1999). Similar, though less dramatic, developments have taken place in Denmark (Iversen 1999; Blom-Hansen 2001). European integration has also reduced the scope for government intervention in some of the policy areas most relevant to economic producer groups.

In the rest of the Nordic region, the state of corporatism is more ambiguous. In Norway (ranked by Lijphart 1999 as the world's most corporatist country), corporatist practices in comprehensive wage bargaining and tax and social security reform declined under the nonsocialist governments of the early 1980s, but were reinforced again under the social democrats in the 1990s. At the same time, however, the number of consultative committees and boards continued to decline. In addition, the effectiveness of corporatist bargaining has been weakened by labor fragmentation linked to the growth of independent white-collar organizations at the expense of traditional blue-collar unions allied with the social democrats. In Finland and Iceland, on the other hand, corporatist practices evolved somewhat later and seem less adversely affected. In the region as a whole, however, there seems to be more evidence of decline than of further corporatist growth.

The Welfare State and Economic Performance

Nordic similarities are also reflected in the ways in which these countries allocate public resources. On average, the five Nordics spend more public money at the national level than their Western European neighbors. Yet, from 1995 to 2006 the gap between the Nordic region and non-Nordic Europe narrowed considerably.[2] Government spending as a percent of GDP declined throughout Western Europe over this period, but the average decline in the Nordic states was significantly greater than elsewhere in Europe. As table 2.3 demonstrates, between 1995 and 2006, total government spending in the Nordic countries fell quite significantly as a percentage of GDP. The central government's share of public spending shows a similar downward trend. Nonetheless, the public sectors of the Nordic countries remain large relative to the size of their economies, although those of Iceland and Norway are now smaller than the European average.

There are a number of explanations for the shrinking size of the traditionally large public sectors of the Nordic countries. One prominent cause lies in economic developments. In Finland and Sweden, the severe economic crises of the early 1990s and the concomitant spending cuts account for much of the decline. Both countries experienced negative GDP growth rates and undertook retrenchment measures to cut public spending (Kautto 2000). More broadly, poor economic performance over a longer period of time may have influenced public sector developments. In Denmark, economic problems of the late 1970s and 1980s prompted a series of public sector retrenchment measures beginning in the 1980s (Green-Pedersen 2002). Efforts to contain costs and promote higher levels of employment continued into the 1990s and beyond. Sweden has experienced a long-term economic decline relative to other affluent countries in Europe and elsewhere. In per capita terms, the country was among the three or four richest in the world around 1970, but had dropped to fourteenth place in OECD rankings by the mid-1990s. To halt the slide, an influential government report from that time called for significant cuts in the size of the public sector (Lindbeck et al. 1994).

Whether or not Nordic economic performance has more recently been inferior to that of other affluent states depends on the time period and the indicators one chooses to study. Between 1997 and 2006/2007, the Nordic

TABLE 2.3. Public Spending

	Total General Government Expenditure (% of GDP)[a]			Central Government Expenditure (% of GDP)		
	1995	2006	Change	1995	2006	Change
Austria	56	49.3	−6.7	31.9	29.2	−2.7
Belgium	51.9	48.5	−3.4	31.1	27.3	−3.8
Denmark	59.6	51.5	−8.1	41.6	31.7	−9.9
Finland	61.6	48.8	−12.8	37.2	24.9	−12.3
France	54.4	53.4	−1.0	25.2	22.3	−2.9
Germany	54.8	45.4	−9.4	20.6	14.1	−6.5
Greece	45.5	42.3	−3.2	35.9	30.3	−5.6
Iceland	42.7	40.7	−2.0	33.7	29.5	−4.2
Ireland	41.1	34.2	−6.9	33.5	28.0	−5.5
Italy	52.5	50.1	−2.4	38.3	28.4	−9.9
Luxembourg	39.7	39.0	−0.7	27.2	27.8	0.6
Netherlands	56.4	46.1	−10.3	34.1	26.8	−7.3
Norway	50.9	40.6	−10.3	39.6	32.5	−7.1
Portugal	42.8	46.4	3.6	29.4	30.9	1.5
Spain	44.4	38.6	−5.8	25.6	14.9	−10.7
Sweden	66.3	54.3	−12.0	40.3	29.9	−10.4
United Kingdom	44.5	44.6	0.1	41.5	41.1	−0.4
Average for Western Europe	50.9	45.5	−5.4	33.3	27.6	−5.7
Average for non-Nordic Western Europe	48.7	44.8	−3.8	31.2	26.8	−4.4
Average for Nordic countries	56.2	47.2	−9.0	38.5	29.7	−8.8

Source: Data from Eurostat, "Total General Government Expenditure as % of GDP" (2007), http://epp.eurostat.ec.europa.eu/ (accessed February 9, 2008).

[a]In the European System of Accounts (ESA 95), total general government expenditure is defined by reference to a list of categories including intermediate consumption; gross capital formation; compensation of employees; other taxes on production; subsidies; payable property income; current taxes on income, wealth, and so on; social benefits; some social transfers; other current transfers; some adjustments; capital transfers; and transactions on nonproduced assets. Central government includes all administrative departments of the state and other central agencies whose purview normally extends over the whole economic territory, excluding the administration of social security funds. Also included are all nonprofit institutions that are controlled and mainly financed by the central government and whose purview extends over the whole economic territory.

states on average had slightly less unemployment and inflation than the rest of Western Europe (see indicators of change in table 2.4). Per capita income levels were also higher. It is more questionable, however, whether the region experienced a higher level of growth.

As reflected in table 2.4, Denmark and Norway had unemployment rates lower than 4 percent in 2006, something they shared with only one non-Nordic country in Western Europe (the Netherlands). Finland had the highest unemployment in the Nordic region, but given the sharp jump in unemployment rates in the early 1990s, its more recent employment record is still quite an achievement. Though the data for Iceland is not strictly comparable, it is a reliable indication that it had the lowest unemployment rate in the Nordic region (a situation that changed radically with the collapse of its financial institutions in 2008-9). Overall, the Nordic states have recently had strong employment records. Moreover, the high rate of female participation in the labor force throughout the Nordic region means that an unusually large share of the population has found paid employment.

This high rate of employment has not in recent years come at the cost of high inflation. Iceland's inflation rate has been rather high, but on average, Nordic performance on inflation over the last decade has been slightly better than that of the rest of Europe. The record of economic growth, however, has been less robust. Measured as change in GDP per capita controlling for purchasing power parity, Nordic economic growth (.46 percent per year) has been identical to the average for non-Nordic Western Europe. However, regionwide performance is pulled up by Norway, which has benefited from booming raw materials exports, especially oil and gas. Nordic growth performance minus Norway is only .36 percent annually, which is worse than non-Nordic Europe. On the whole, then, Nordic economic performance has in recent years been more or less on a par with the rest of Western Europe.

Contemporary Representative Democracy

Nordic citizens have traditionally been among the most regime-supportive and participatory in the democratic world. Table 2.5, which is based on approximately 30,000 interviews by the European Social Survey project (ESS) in 16 countries,[3] presents variation in trust and satisfaction with democracy across Western Europe. In comparison with other Europeans, Nordic citizens place more trust in their national parliaments, their legal systems, their police forces, their politicians, their national governments, and their national democracy. They also have a more favorable impression of the

TABLE 2.4. Unemployment, Inflation, and Growth

	Openly Unemployed (of active population)[a] (%)			Inflation (index = 2005)[b]			GDP per Capita in PPS[c]		
	1997	2006	Change	1997	2007	Change	1998	2006	Change (%)
Austria	4.4	4.7	0.3	88.2	103.6	15.4	22,500	30,000	7,500 (33)
Belgium	9.2	8.2	−1.0	86.5	104.2	17.7	20,800	28,200	7,400 (36)
Denmark	5.2	3.9	−1.3	85.9	103.5	17.6	22,400	29,600	7,200 (32)
Finland	12.7	7.7	−5.0	88.4	102.8	14.4	19,400	27,500	8,100 (42)
France	11.5	9.2	−2.3	87.8	103.6	15.9	19,500	26,100	6,600 (34)
Germany	8.7	9.8	1.1	90.0	104.1	14.1	20,800	26,900	6,100 (29)
Greece	9.8	8.9	−0.9	76.6	106.4	29.8	14,100	23,000[d]	8,900 (63)
Iceland	4.9	2.6	−2.3	78.4	108.5	30.1	23,800	30,600	6,800 (29)
Ireland	9.9	4.4	−5.5	76.7	105.5	28.8	20,600	34,200	13,600 (66)
Italy	11.3	6.8	−4.5	83.3	109.8	26.5	20,300	24,300	4,000 (20)
Luxembourg	2.7	4.7	2.0	82.3	105.7	23.4	36,900	65,700	28,800 (78)
Netherlands	4.9	3.9	−1.0	81.9	103.3	21.4	21,800	30,700	8,900 (41)
Norway	4.0	3.5	−0.5	86.5	103.2	16.7	23,500	43,800	20,300 (86)
Portugal	6.8	7.7	0.9	79.6	105.5	25.9	13,000	17,500	4,500 (35)
Spain	16.7	8.5	−8.2	79.4	106.5	27.1	16,200	24,700	8,500 (52)
Sweden	9.9	7.1	−2.8	89.19	103.2	14.1	20,800	29,300	8,500 (41)
United Kingdom	6.8	5.3	−1.5	89.7	104.7	15.0	19,700	27,700	8,000 (41)
Average for Western Europe	8.2	6.3	−1.9	84.1	105.0	20.8	20,948	30,576	9,629 (46)
Average for non-Nordic Western Europe	8.6	6.8	−1.7	83.5	105.2	21.8	20,517	29,917	9,400 (46)
Average for Nordic countries	7.3	5.0	−2.3	85.7	104.2	18.6	21,980	32,160	10,180 (46)

Source: Data from *Eurostat*, "Unemployment Rate—Total" (2007), http://epp.eurostat.ec.europa.eu/ (accessed February 9, 2008); *Eurostat*, "Inflation Rate" (2007), http://epp.eurostat.ec.europa.eu/ (accessed February 10, 2008); *Eurostat*, "Gross Domestic Product at Market Prices" (2007), http://epp.eurostat.cec.eu.int/ (accessed February 13, 2008). Unemployment data for Iceland is from http://www.statice.is/?PageID=1191 (accessed February 10, 2008).

[a] The average unemployment figure for the Nordic countries is based on data from Denmark, Finland, Norway, and Sweden. This is because Icelandic statistics, while reliable, are based on different definitions.

[b] Inflation was calculated by adding the inflation value for each month and then dividing by 12. Data on inflation in Ireland in December 2007 is missing, and so the figure for this country is based on 11 values.

[c] Percentage change in GDP per capita in PPS (Euro) is calculated by dividing the change in GDP per capita by the GDP per capita in the base year (1998).

[d] For Greece 2006, GDP per capita in PPS is a forecast.

TABLE 2.5. Trust and Satisfaction with Institutions, 2004–5

	Trust in Country's Parliament	Trust in the Legal System	Trust in the Police	Trust in Politicians	Trust in the European Parliament	Trust in the United Nations	How Satisfied with the National Government	How Satisfied with the Way Democracy Works in Country	Total Ranking Points[b]
Austria	4.8 (8)[a]	5.8 (6)	6.2 (9)	3.3 (14)	4.0 (13)	4.5 (15)	4.2 (14)	6.0 (6)	85 (12)
Belgium	4.7 (9)	4.8 (13)	5.8 (14)	4.2 (6)	5.0 (5)	5.1 (9)	4.7 (7)	5.6 (12)	75 (10)
Denmark	6.3 (1)	7.2 (1)	7.9 (2)	5.6 (1)	4.8 (8)	6.6 (3)	5.9 (3)	7.3 (1)	20 (1)
Finland	6.0 (2)	6.9 (2)	8.0 (1)	4.9 (4)	5.0 (5)	6.6 (3)	6.2 (1)	6.7 (2)	20 (1)
France	4.3 (13)	4.8 (13)	5.8 (14)	3.5 (12)	4.3 (11)	4.7 (13)	4.3 (12)	4.8 (15)	103 (15)
Germany	4.1 (15)	5.4 (9)	6.4 (8)	3.2 (15)	4.2 (12)	5.0 (11)	3.4 (15)	5.1 (13)	98 (13)
Greece	4.7 (9)	5.5 (8)	6.1 (10)	3.7 (10)	5.4 (1)	4.0 (16)	4.5 (9)	6.2 (4)	67 (8)
Iceland	5.9 (3)	6.0 (5)	7.3 (3)	5.0 (3)	5.3 (3)	6.7 (2)	5.0 (6)	5.9 (8)	33 (4)
Ireland	4.7 (9)	5.2 (11)	6.7 (5)	4.0 (9)	5.4 (1)	5.8 (6)	5.2 (4)	5.9 (8)	53 (6)
Luxembourg	5.8 (4)	6.1 (4)	6.5 (6)	5.2 (2)	5.1 (4)	5.4 (7)	6.2 (1)	6.6 (3)	31 (3)
Netherlands	4.6 (12)	5.4 (9)	6.0 (12)	4.6 (5)	4.5 (10)	5.4 (7)	4.4 (10)	5.7 (11)	76 (11)
Norway	5.4 (5)	6.4 (3)	7.1 (4)	4.2 (6)	4.6 (9)	6.9 (1)	4.4 (10)	6.2 (4)	42 (5)
Portugal	3.7 (16)	3.9 (16)	5.0 (16)	2.1 (16)	4.0 (13)	4.7 (13)	2.5 (16)	3.4 (16)	122 (16)
Spain	5.1 (7)	4.7 (15)	5.9 (13)	3.7 (10)	5.0 (5)	5.0 (11)	5.1 (5)	6.0 (6)	72 (9)
Sweden	5.4 (5)	5.8 (6)	6.5 (7)	4.2 (6)	4.0 (13)	6.3 (5)	4.6 (8)	5.9 (8)	58 (7)
United Kingdom	4.2 (14)	5.0 (12)	6.1 (10)	3.5 (12)	3.5 (16)	5.1 (9)	4.3 (12)	5.1 (13)	98 (13)
Average for Western Europe	5.0	5.6	6.5	4.1	4.6	5.5	4.7	5.8	65.8
Average for non-Nordic Western Europe	4.6	5.2	6.1	3.7	4.6	5.0	4.4	5.5	80.0
Average for Nordic countries	5.8	6.5	7.4	4.8	4.7	6.6	5.2	6.4	34.6

Source: Survey data from the European Social Survey, ESS Round 2 (2004–5), http://www.europeansocialsurvey.org/ (accessed September 26, 2006).

Notes: Italy was not included in the survey. In general, we use ESS Round 2 because ESS Round 3 (2006) includes fewer countries. The respondents answered the following questions:

(1)–(6) "Please tell me on a score of 0–10 how much you personally trust each of the institutions. 0 Means you do not trust an institution at all, and 10 Means you have complete trust." (7) "How satisfied are you with the way your country's government is doing its job? (0 = extremely dissatisfied, 10 = extremely satisfied)." (8) "On the whole, how satisfied are you with the way democracy works in your country? (0 = extremely dissatisfied, 10 = extremely satisfied)." The number of respondents (N) ranges from approximately 1,000 to 3,000 per country and question. The total number of respondents is about 30,000.

[a]The number on the left of the column under each survey item denotes the average response level in each country. The higher this number, the greater the level of trust or satisfaction for the given institution. The figure in parentheses shows ranking within each category.

[b]The total ranking points is the combined scores for all the columns. (Hypothetically, the smallest possible number is 8 and the highest is 128 [or 8 × 16].) For rankings, a lower score means that citizens have higher trust and satisfaction with the institution in question.

United Nations. The Nordics are relatively more satisfied with national-level than with international institutions. With the exception of the Swedes, Nordic respondents on average also trust the European Parliament somewhat more than does the rest of Western Europe.

Table 2.6 reports on the preferred level of political decision making.

TABLE 2.6. Preferred Political Decision-Making Level (scores in percentages)

	International	European	National	Regional	Don't Know / No Answer
Austria	31.9	23.2	30.7	9.3	4.9
Belgium	36.7	28.9	21.6	7.0	5.8
Denmark	25.1	23.9	38.6	5.8	6.6
Finland	24.1	18.8	45.8	9.3	2.0
France	35.0	27.1	28.8	6.6	2.4
Germany	35.6	29.1	28.2	5.1	2.0
Greece	25.1	22.0	38.3	5.9	8.7
Iceland	n.d.[a]	n.d.	n.d.	n.d.	n.d.
Ireland	16.9	17.9	48.1	10.6	6.4
Italy	25.1	23.9	32.1	11.9	7.8
Luxembourg	36.1	23.9	28.4	3.1	8.6
Netherlands	37.9	29.3	25.3	4.9	2.6
Norway	32.1	15.4	45.4	5.8	1.4
Portugal	24.6	22.0	39.1	3.8	10.6
Spain	31.8	19.0	27.5	7.0	14.8
Sweden	25.8	19.6	42.4	7.1	5.1
United Kingdom	30.1	11.9	44.2	11.1	2.3
Average for Western Europe	29.6	22.2	35.3	7.1	5.8
Average for non-Nordic Western Europe	30.6	23.1	32.7	7.2	6.4
Average for Nordic countries	26.8	19.4	43.1	7.0	3.8

Source: Survey data from the European Social Survey, ESS Round 1 (2002–3), http://www.europeansocialsurvey.org/ (accessed September 27, 2006). (The same question is not included in ESS Round 2 or Round 3.)

Notes: Respondents answered the following questions:"At which level do you think the following policies should mainly be decided?" . . . protecting the environment; . . . fighting against organized crime; . . . agriculture; . . . defense; . . . social welfare; . . . aid to developing countries; . . . immigration and refugees; . . . interest rates. The figures presented in the table are the aggregated answers from all of the eight policy categories. Each respondent answered eight questions about what he or she believed to be the most appropriate level of decision-making authority for eight different policy areas. If an individual answered that four of the eight should be decided at the international level, the individual score for that person in the international category is 50%. The table reports the average for all nationals in the survey. For example, the average score for Danish respondents is that they want to see two of the eight policy areas (25.1%) decided at the international level. The table does not indicate which these two policy areas are, but it indicates that on average, the respondents from the Nordic countries (43%) think that almost half of the policies should be decided at the national level. The number of respondents (N) ranges from approximately 1,000 to 3,000 per country and question. The total number of respondents is approximately 30,000.

[a]Iceland was not included in the survey, and so "n.d." means "no data." The average value for the Nordic countries is based only on Denmark, Finland, Norway, and Sweden.

Data for Iceland are missing, but voters in Finland, Norway, and Sweden like to have most matters decided nationally, a preference they share with voters in countries such as Ireland and the United Kingdom. It comes as no particular surprise that while voters in the North do trust the European Parliament, at the same time they put less faith in European institutions of decision-making than in their own domestic institutions, which is in keeping with the EU-skepticism for which Scandinavians are also known. For example, Norwegian voters have twice, in the referendums of 1972 and 1994, rejected membership in the European Union. The fact that Norway and Iceland's relationships with the EU are defined and regulated by the European Economic Area (EEA) agreement, which gives them access to the internal market but no formal voting rights in the EU, is a consequence of this reluctance. This association might also further EU-skepticism.[4]

Note, however, that the Danes, members since a 1972 referendum, are more positive to European political institutions than are their northern neighbors. Reluctance toward the EU has not been as vocal in Finland (or Iceland), but in the data in table 2.6, Finnish voters express as much (or more) support for national decision-making as do the other Nordics. Nordic voters are also more dubious about international decision-making forums beyond the EU. Support for the UN is strong, yet many voters are not particularly eager to transfer authority to such international institutions.

Taken together, these survey responses indicate that Nordic voters support national-level institutions and prefer to keep political authority at home. Danes and Finns are the most trusting and satisfied, with Icelanders close behind. Norwegians and Swedes are less trusting and satisfied with their societal institutions and with how democracy works. Overall, however, Nordic voters rank high in trust by West European standards.

The Parliamentary Chain of Democratic Delegation

Although two of the Nordic countries are republics and three have monarchies, all are parliamentary democracies in which the preponderant executive power rests with the prime minister (PM), who is in turn responsible to the parliamentary majority. The delegation from parliament to cabinet is governed by fairly permissive rules, such as negative parliamentarism, across the Nordic region. That is to say, none of these countries have traditionally required a new PM/cabinet to win a confirmatory majority vote in parliament in order to take office, though Finland changed its constitutional rules in March 2000 to introduce such a positive investiture vote.[5] In Sweden, an investiture vote is held, but for the new cabinet to be installed all that is required is that there is no absolute majority of MPs voting against it. Under negative parliamentarism, a new cabinet is simply appointed by the head of state, which makes cabinet transitions easier and minority governments more feasible (Bergman 1993, 1995; Strøm 1986, 1990).

The vote of no confidence is a defining feature of parliamentary democracy, in that the prime minister (and thereby also the other cabinet members) has to resign if he or she loses a vote of no confidence. In all five Nordic countries, the parliamentary majority can also dismiss individual cabinet members without necessarily also removing the prime minister, something that is not possible in France, Germany, or the United Kingdom, to name a few. The complement to the no confidence vote, the confidence vote, is an instrument used when the prime minister wants to test whether, or to prove that, he or she retains majority support in parliament. None of the Nordic countries has constitutionally codified rules and procedures for such confidence votes, but by convention the mechanism exists and is enforceable everywhere. When Nordic cabinets lose confidence votes, they resign. However, this does not mean that governments resign whenever they lose significant parliamentary votes. Under minority government especially, Scandinavian cabinets often lose important parliamentary votes but remain in power anyway. Instead of resigning, they usually try to diminish the importance of the vote they have lost. It is only if the bill has explicitly been designated as a confidence vote that the government is obliged to step down after losing.

The opportunity to call early elections is another typical feature of parliamentary democracies. Parliaments are typically elected for a maximum term, but can be dissolved, with new elections called, at virtually any time up to the end of the regular term (see Strøm, Müller, and Bergman 2003; Strøm and Swindle 2002). On this point, some of the Nordic countries are actually more restrictive than many other parliamentary democracies. Norway is the only parliamentary democracy that does not permit early elections under any circumstances, whereas in Sweden, under its current constitution, the power of parliamentary dissolution is so restricted that it has never been practiced. Denmark stands in the Westminster tradition with very permissive rules, whereas in Finland and Iceland there has been some controversy about the president's authority to intervene in the dissolution process.

Political Parties and Cabinet Governance

A look at the historical record of cabinet formation reveals that more than half of all Nordic cabinets in recent decades have been minority governments. However, the Nordic region is far from uniform. Although Finland has had its share of minority governments, mainly in the early postwar period, it is actually below the European average. Minority governments are even less common in Iceland, where they have never really been accepted as a regular part of the parliamentary repertoire. It is the strictly Scandinavian countries that are responsible for the high rate of minority governments in the Nordic region.

Thus, there are important within-region differences between the countries that tend to feature majority coalitions (Finland and Iceland) and those in which policy is often made through parliamentary bargaining (Denmark, Norway, and Sweden). The former systems rely on stable coalitions negotiated at the beginning of the parliamentary term and formally constituted by the coalition of parties holding executive office. In the latter, ad hoc majorities will more commonly emerge through ongoing bargaining, which takes place as much in the parliamentary arena as in executive quarters.

Given the greater importance of the initial bargaining process in the coalitional countries, we might also expect the cabinet formation process in these societies to be more critical and contentious. The historical record of cabinet formation is consistent with these expectations, as Finland and Iceland are indeed quite different from their Nordic neighbors. Whereas Denmark and even more so Norway and Sweden have a very low incidence of bargaining "failure," both Finland and especially Iceland are well above the European average. We see similar contrasts in the duration of the bargaining process. In Finland and Iceland, it typically takes about a month to form a new government, whereas in Scandinavia the average is only about a week (slightly longer in Denmark, somewhat shorter in Norway). It is these latter three countries, rather than Finland and Iceland, that are most different from the rest of Europe.

Constraints: Domestic and International

The national parliamentary chain is far from all that matters in contemporary governance. In this section, we look at other ways in which citizens and interest groups can hold politicians accountable, while also examining ways in which such constraints can be responsible for agency loss.

Instruments of direct democracy at the national level are one kind of constraint on the parliamentary chain. Referendums might be beneficial for all sorts of reasons and may be democratic and legitimate, but they also shift delegation and accountability away from the parliamentary chain. Table 2.7 presents comparative data on national referendums in Western

Europe between World War II and the year 2000. Collectively, the Nordic countries used this institution relatively infrequently. Within the Nordic region, however, there is considerable variation. Denmark has held the highest number of referendums—a total of 16 between 1940 and 2000. Sweden is a distant second with 4; none of the other Nordic countries com-

TABLE 2.7. External Constraints and Social-Political Context

	National Referendums, Total 1940–2000 (Strøm, Müller, and Bergman 2003, 693)	Index of Federalism and Decentralization (1–5) (Lijphart 1999, 189)	Judicial Review and Activism (Lijphart 1999, 226)	Media[a] Number of Daily Papers per Million Inhabitants, 2004[b]	Number of (sold) Copies per 1,000 Inhabitants, 2003	Corruption Perceptions Index, 2007 (higher score = lower corruption)
Austria	2	4.5	3	2.1	355	8.1
Belgium	1	5	3	2.7	173	7.1
Denmark	16	2	2	5.6	322	9.4
Finland	1	2	1	10.1	524	9.4
France	13	1.2	3	1.4	167	7.3
Germany	0	5	4	4.5	322	7.8
Greece	4	1	2	2.9	67	4.6
Iceland	2	1	2	6.9	317	9.2
Ireland	22	1	2	1.7	250	7.5
Italy	55	1.3	2.8	1.6	116	5.2
Luxembourg	0	1	1	13.4	316	8.4
Netherlands	0	3	1	2.1	319	9.0
Norway	2	2	2	17.0	684	8.7
Portugal	2	1	2	2.8	66	6.5
Spain	5	3	3	3.2	122	6.7
Sweden	4	2	2	10.0	505	9.3
United Kingdom	1	1	1	1.7	375	8.4
Average for Western Europe	7.7	2.2	2.2	5.3	294	7.8
Average for non-Nordic Western Europe	8.8	2.3	2.3	3.3	221	7.2
Average for Nordic countries	5.0	1.8	1.8	9.9	470	9.2

Source: Data from Strøm, Müller, and Bergman 2003, 693; Lijphart 1999, 189. Data for media is from World Association of Newspapers, *WAN-world Press Trends* (2005); Tidningsutgivarna, http://www.tu.se (accessed September 9, 2006); Nikkei, http://www.nikkei-ad.com/media_data/en/japan_market/j_market_papers.html (2006) (accessed September 9, 2006). Data for corruption from Transparency International, *Global Corruption Report 2007*, http://www.transparency.org (accessed February 9, 2008).

[a]Most of the data on the media comes from Tidningsutgivarna. This information was supplemented with data from Nikkei where necessary (number of daily papers/million inhabitants for Belgium, Luxembourg, and Portugal and number of copies per thousand inhabitants for Luxembourg). Although the two sources use the same database, there are minor discrepancies between them. The differences are small and have no significant effect on the overall patterns reported here. To calculate the other ratios for newspapers/population, the following sources have been used: *Eurostat*, table, "Average Population by Sex and Five-Year Age Groups" (2006), http://epp.eurostat.cec.eu.int/ (accessed September 27, 2006); Heston, Summers, and Aten, http://pwt.econ.upenn.edu/php_site/pwt_index.php (2006) (accessed September 27, 2006).

[b]The number of daily papers per million inhabitants counts papers with at least four issues a week. For Belgium, Luxembourg, and Portugal, this data is for 2003.

monly use referendums as a mechanism of national decision-making. Except for Denmark, the Nordics tend to place their faith in indirect, rather than direct, methods of popular governance.

When the other Nordic states have resorted to referendums, they have most often done so to resolve questions of European integration. Indeed, referendums on EU issues have caused numerous headaches for leading politicians in all the Scandinavian countries. Here, as on other issues, Finland (where both politicians and most voters have been EU enthusiasts) and Iceland (where citizens have not yet been asked to vote on membership) stand apart. Elsewhere in the region, voters have defied party leaders by voting against membership (as in Norway) or against efforts to deepen integration (as in Denmark and Sweden). If party elites had decided these issues, Norway would have joined the European Union in the 1970s, and both Denmark and Sweden would have been members of the Economic and Monetary Union (EMU).

Power-Sharing

Nordic skepticism toward supranational solutions coexists with a lack of constitutional entrenchment of the powers of subnational levels of government. There is no formal federalism in the Nordic countries. This might reflect their affinity for the nation-state as the appropriate level of political decision-making. Nonetheless, Lijphart's (1999) index of federalism and decentralization captures the fact that four of the Nordic states, despite being formally unitary, also are quite decentralized (a score of 2 out of 5) in terms of welfare spending and local autonomy (see table 2.7). The degree of autonomy is a matter decided by the national parliament. Iceland is the Nordic state with the least such local autonomy, which is hardly surprising given its small population.

Other similar constraints on national governments in the Nordic states are weak. For example, these countries have traditionally had only weak forms of judicial review, with Finland having the weakest (table 2.7). The country-specific chapters will suggest that the Nordic states' low degree of judicial-legal constraint is changing, but it still stands in contrast to the continental European tradition found in countries such as Austria, Germany, and Italy.

Societal Constraints

Civil society and mass media can also create important informal constraints and checks on representative political institutions. Table 2.7 suggests that the Nordic countries are more amply endowed with such informal constraints than with the more formal ones. Relative to population size, far more newspapers are published and sold in the Nordic states than in other European countries (see Milner 2002). Only Luxembourg can compete with respect to the number of newspapers per capita. To some extent, this is surely a function of population size, as countries with small populations have a larger number of newspapers relative to the number of inhabitants than do large countries. For example, opportunities for vigorous public debate may not require Britain to have 200 times as many newspapers as Iceland. Yet, the distinctive position of the Nordic countries holds up even when one measures the number of newspapers sold per 1,000 inhabitants. The pattern here is actually quite distinctly a North-South one, as people in southern Europe consult far fewer newspapers per day than do northern Europeans.

A similar North-South pattern exists with regard to a quite different measure of constraint on political rulers: political corruption. Based largely on surveys that ask businesspeople about how much corruption they encounter when they do business in different countries, the Transparency International index of perceived corruption provides a rough indication of the effectiveness of legal constraints on rulers (see table 2.7). The five Nordic states rank among the cleanest in Europe, with Denmark and Finland at the top of the Nordic league and Norway (with its sizeable oil economy) at the bottom. Other northern European countries rank about equal to the Nordics, while parts of southern Europe are perceived as distinctly more troubled by corruption.

Prior Research on the Nordic Region

In the rest of this book, we examine contemporary challenges to parliamentary and party governance in the five Nordic countries. In the case studies, we record the changes in the roles and function of parliaments and political parties that have taken place in the Nordic region in recent decades. Ours is hardly the first study of these issues. The thesis of parliamentary decline was largely refuted in studies of these countries in the late 1980s and the early 1990s (Damgaard 1992; Sjölin 1991, 1993). More recently, Rommetvedt (2003) concluded that the power of the Norwegian parliament, the Storting, actually increased during the latter part of the twentieth century.

Yet, many of the challenges that face democratic societies elsewhere in the world are surely relevant in the Nordic region, and perhaps more so than they were a decade or two ago. The severity of the challenges also seems to vary across the countries. In 2003, groups of scholars in Denmark and Norway completed in-depth investigations of power and democracy in their respective countries. A few years earlier, a smaller but similar study was completed in Sweden. When we compare these studies, the impression is that Danish democracy is largely alive and well, while developments in Norway are more troubling (Karvonen 2004; Strandberg 2006). Sweden seems to fall in between (Strandberg 2006, 537).

The diverging results of these studies may have been influenced by their relative timing. For example, decline in party membership in Denmark largely took place in the 1960s and 1970s and then leveled off. The Norwegian decline is much more recent, and therefore perhaps seen as more alarming (Christiansen and Togeby 2006, 22). Yet we are inclined to think that there is more to these findings than timing. As Strandberg (2006) rightly points out, different groups of scholars working on similar problems can come to different conclusions, but we (like him) believe that there are some real and palpable differences.

Christiansen and Togeby (2006) identify several such differences between Denmark and Norway: "Local autonomy in Norway is experiencing serious problems that do not exist in Denmark; minority parliamentarism appears to function more proficiently in Denmark than in Norway . . . ; and the relationship with the EU creates democratic problems in both Denmark and Norway, but they likely seem graver in Norway, which is not a member, but via the European Economic Community Protocol must comply with many EU decisions" (21).

The somewhat conflicting conclusions of these studies suggest that there is a need for a common framework of analysis, but also that the Nordic region may be more differentiated and complex than many observers have been inclined to believe. The fact that Nordic citizens and politicians feel a commonality of identity does not mean that these countries are guaranteed, or condemned to, a common political trajectory. Our focus in this study is primarily on the past two decades, from the late 1980s on. This is a watershed point in time, since it marked the collapse of the Communist regimes that neighbor Scandinavia to the east, and since those dramatic events were followed by severe economic crises in some of the Nordic states, as well as by new opportunities for European integration.

In order to study the fate of parties and parliaments in the Nordic region, we shall draw on the analytical models we have explicated in chapter 1. As Allern and Pedersen (2007, 84) remind us, it is important to be clear about "what model of democracy—and party function—is used as a normative standard." And as Nils Stjernquist (1995, 15) once pointed out, many comparative discussions of representative democracy take the Westminster model as an implicit starting point. We do so explicitly.

At the same time, we recognize that the Nordic countries vary substantially in the degree to which they approximate this model. In reality, few contemporary parliamentary democracies come close to the stylized features of the Westminster model. As Arter (2004) points out, such Nordic characteristics as coalition and minority governments can make democratic accountability less straightforward than in the Westminster model. Another such characteristic lies with the most celebrated of all democratic delegation and accountability mechanisms, namely free and fair elections. All the Nordic states have proportional representation (PR) electoral systems that differ from the majoritarian (single-member district plurality) elections embedded in the Westminster model. And PR electoral systems tend to result in a fragmented party system and the absence of a majority party (Duverger 1954; Cox 1997).

The Organization of This Book

The five country-specific chapters that follow provide test cases for the theses of parliamentary and party decline. Each chapter begins by examining the chain of democratic delegation as it is defined by the national constitution. Identifying these rules is not always entirely straightforward. Any serious account of these parliamentary institutions must certainly include the formal constitutions, but it cannot stop there. Here we follow Bogdanor (1988, 5), who argues that an analysis of constitutions cannot confine itself to the document called the "the Constitution" but must consider the "working constitution" as well. A typical example is electoral laws, which often are not included in the constitution itself.[6]

In order to judge the status and trajectory of the role of parliaments, we also need to understand the policy process in which it operates. These five country-specific chapters trace the policy process all the way from voters to civil servants and scrutinize the ways in which political parties and external constraints contribute to parliamentary governance. The authors begin by focusing on the constitutionally mandated national policy chain of parliamentary democracy and then expanding the scope of their analysis to the broader policy process.

The authors next turn to the status of political parties. Have the political parties declined in size and importance, as the party-decline thesis holds? Has there been any change in "partyness" (Sjöblom 1987)? If so, in what ways has this occurred? Are there countervailing trends? Each author will examine these trends with reference to the party in the electorate, the party organization, and the party in government (Key 1964). These are indeed the aspects of party politics that are most critical to the functions of parliamentary democracy.

The chapters contain a standard set of tables that relate to these questions. For the party organization, each chapter reports time-series data on party membership. For the party in the electorate, we present similar time-series data for a battery of survey-based indicators. These include a measure of class voting (the Alford index), which reflects the abiding strength of the traditionally most important social cleavage affecting party attachments. We also report the share of voters reporting party sympathies and a measure of electoral volatility. Finally, the country chapters include tables that show the share of voters making their voting decisions during the election campaign and the percentage expressing a high level of trust in parliament (which is a measure of the status of parliaments, rather than parties, but is included with the other survey measures here for simplicity of presentation). Jointly, these measures give us a rich and multifaceted picture of the strength of electoral parties in the Nordic countries.

As it turns out, even among the Nordics, some data can be scarce. In this respect, it has sometimes been more difficult to find data from the statistical offices, parliaments, and the political science communities in Finland and Iceland than it has been for the Scandinavian countries. The differences, largely due to variations in the survey traditions and the size and orientations of the respective scholarly communities, should not be exaggerated, as we have had access to some of the best country experts that are available. However, in a few cases, such as historical data on party memberships or class voting, we have had to rely on what is available rather than the indicators that we would have chosen in an ideal world. The Alford index (above) is one case in point. It is the percentage of support for the socialist (left) parties among working class voters (manual labor) minus the support for the same parties in all other classes. If left-wing party support is stronger among workers than among other classes, then the Alford index will be positive; the higher the positive number, the more class voting. Critics of the Alford index have raised important questions about (a) how to identify the parties of the left and (b) the adequacy of the two-class assumption that underlies this measure (Knutsen 2006). Yet, for comparative purposes, this is often the only measure that is available in national election surveys. Such surveys, in turn, have the critical advantage of allowing us to track changes over time. Thus, even if we note and at least partly share the scholarly reservations that have been expressed, we use the Alford index where it is available (Denmark, Norway, and Sweden). Fortunately, this index has also been found to correlate well with other measures of class voting (Knutsen 2006, 117).

We then turn our attention to the status of the Nordic parliaments. With the help of a great deal of data on governments and parliamentary activities, our country contributors scrutinize the current status of these institutions. Is the parliament more or less active today than a decade (or two) ago? What is the role of the parliament in key policy decisions? When and where have cabinets been stable and effective, and when have they not? Has there been a decline in the capacity of parliament to impose its stamp on the policy process? Are members of parliament more or less active than before in legislative activity and in scrutinizing their cabinets and individual ministers? Is the cabinet—and the entire executive branch—more powerful today, relative to the parliament? Has the prime minister gained more "presidential" powers? Are civil servants free-wheelers or are they constrained and faithful agents of the politicians? In this part of their analysis, the authors examine trends in legislative activity and parliamentary questions. Moreover, the contributors look for the weight of party and parliamentary credentials in a rich set of personal data on all individuals who have held four of the most important cabinet portfolios in each country.

In the sections that follow, the authors explain how cabinet governance by minority as well as majority cabinets works in practice and how it relates to the status of parliamentary democracy. This includes both the formation and termination stages, but also the lesser-known aspects of governance between elections and cabinet negotiations. We devote special attention to peculiarly Scandinavian features, such as the high incidence of minority governments. For minority cabinets, the authors describe how these governments have formed winning legislative (and budget) coalitions in parliament. They also discuss how and under what conditions these cabinets have been able to govern effectively. The final set of tables in each country chapter gives us the evidence that ultimately counts the most: how Nordic governments have fared when they have had to face their respective masters (the voters) in national elections.

In the conclusion of each country-specific chapter, the authors assess the status of parliament and parties in their particular country. How and to what extent has the role and power of the national parliament declined? What is happening to political parties and how are they reacting to current challenges? Are parties and parliaments losing out to other societal actors, to European and international-level developments, or other transformation in society? Is it true that national parliaments are deciding "more over less"? If so, who are the main beneficiaries of this transfer of power?

In the final three chapters of this book, we pull together the comparative lessons from our case studies. For one thing, we will show that the Nordic region contains more internal diversity than might be obvious at first glance, and that the forces that sustain parliamentary democracy are not everywhere identical. In many respects, it is meaningful and reasonable to speak of these polities as consensual, but consensual systems are not all the same. The Nordic systems share a culture of transparency, relative equality, and accommodation. Yet, politically, these shared cultural and social traits take different forms. In the next five chapters we explore the similarities and the differences within this region as we provide our best verdict on the contemporary fortunes of Nordic parties and parliaments. Are they increasingly under siege? Is there a Madisonian turn? And, if there is a decline in the functions of Nordic parties and parliaments, is it present in all of these countries in similar forms, or is the picture more complex? These are the questions that the rest of this book will consider.

NOTES

1. For a historical narrative of the ebb and flow of conflict and consensus in Swedish politics, see Stjernquist 1993.
2. For Iceland, except for 1995, data is not available from the same sources.
3. Italy was not included in the 2004/2005 survey.
4. The agreement on the European Economic Area (EEA) means that Iceland and Norway bind themselves to accept the rules of the EU-internal market while abstaining from formal participation in the EU institutions that govern this policy area. Policy areas such as agriculture and fishing fall outside of the EEA (Bergman and Damgaard 2000).
5. We count a new cabinet when *any* of the following three conditions have been met (Müller and Strøm 2003, 12): (1) any change in the set of parties holding cabinet membership (note that we count as members of the cabinet only those parties that have designated representatives with cabinet voting rights; external support parties, i.e., parties that support the cabinet in parliament without holding cabinet portfolios, are not included); (2) any change in the identity of the prime minister (by prime minister we mean the head of the cabinet, whatever title that office might have, e.g., federal chancellor, president of the council of state, etc.); (3) any general election.
6. The concept of a working constitution recognizes that constitutional practice can be an important guide for behavior (a rule), but that not all observable regularities are rule-governed. We limit the concept of rules to those practices and expectations that are well-defined and enforceable. Voters, politicians, and/or civil servants must expect such expectations to be reinforced by direct or indirect sanctions from their principals, or from courts or other third parties. Alternatively, enforceability can rest on the political actors' expectations that if they break the rules, voters will

punish them in upcoming elections, or potential coalition partners will reject them as less than trustworthy.

REFERENCES

Allern, Elin H., and Karina Pedersen. 2007. "The Impact of Party Organizational Changes on Democracy." *West European Politics* 30 (1): 68–92.
Anton, Thomas J. 1980. *Administered Politics: Elite Political Culture in Sweden*. Boston: Martinus Nijhoff.
Arter, David. 1999. *Scandinavian Politics Today*. Manchester: Manchester University Press.
Arter, David. 2004. "Parliamentary Democracy in Scandinavia." *Parliamentary Affairs* 57 (3): 581–600.
Bergman, Torbjörn. 1993. "Formation Rules and Minority Governments." *European Journal of Political Research* 23:55–66.
Bergman, Torbjörn. 1995. *Constitutional Rules and Party Goals in Coalition Formation: An Analysis of Winning Minority Governments in Sweden*. PhD diss., Department of Political Science, Umeå University.
Bergman, Torbjörn. 1999. "Trade-Offs in Swedish Constitutional Design: The Monarchy Under Challenge." In Wolfgang C. Müller and Kaare Strøm, eds., *Policy, Office, or Votes? How Political Parties in Western Europe Make Hard Decisions*. Cambridge: Cambridge University Press.
Bergman, Torbjörn, and Erik Damgaard, eds. 2000. *Delegation and Accountability in European Integration: The Nordic Parliamentary Democracies and the European Union*. London: Frank Cass.
Blom-Hansen, Jens. 2001. "Organized Interests and the State: A Disintegrating Relationship? Evidence from Denmark." *European Journal of Political Research* 39 (3): 391–416.
Bogdanor, Vernon. 1984. "The Government Formation Processes in the Constitutional Monarchies of North-West Europe." In Denis Kavanagh and Gillian Peele, eds., *Comparative Government and Politics: Essays in Honour of S. E. Finer*. London: Heinemann.
Bogdanor, Vernon. 1988. *Constitutions in Democratic Politics*. Aldershot: Gower.
Christiansen, Peter Munk, and Lise Togeby. 2006. "Power and Democracy in Denmark: Still a Viable Democracy." *Scandinavian Political Studies* 29 (1): 1–24.
Cox, Gary W. 1997. *Making Votes Count*. Cambridge: Cambridge University Press.
Damgaard, Erik, ed. 1992. *Parliamentary Change in the Nordic Countries*. Oslo: Scandinavian University Press.
Duverger, Maurice. 1954. *Political Parties: Their Organization and Activity in the Modern State*. London: Methuen.
Eckstein, Harry. 1966. *Division and Cohesion in Democracy: A Study of Norway*. Princeton: Princeton University Press.
Einhorn, Eric S., and John Logue. 2003. *Modern Welfare States: Scandinavian Politics and Policy in the Global Age*. 2nd ed. Westport, CT: Praeger.

Elder, Neil, David Arter, and Alastair H. Thomas. 1982. *The Consensual Democracies? The Government and Politics of the Scandinavian States.* Oxford: Martin Robertson.

Esping-Andersen, Gøsta. 1990. *The Three Worlds of Welfare Capitalism.* Princeton: Princeton University Press.

Green-Pedersen, Christoffer. 2002. *The Politics of Justification: Party Competition and Welfare-State Retrenchment in Denmark and the Netherlands from 1982 to 1988.* Amsterdam: Amsterdam University Press.

Heidar, Knut, ed. 2004. *Nordic Politics: Comparative Perspectives.* Oslo: Universitetsforlaget.

Indridason, Indridi H. 2005. "A Theory of Coalitions and Clientelism: Coalition Politics in Iceland, 1945–2000." *European Journal of Political Research* 44 (3): 439–64.

Iversen, Torben. 1999. *Contested Economic Institutions.* Cambridge: Cambridge University Press.

Karvonen, Lauri. 2004. "Review of Scandinavian Power Studies." *Scandinavian Political Studies* 27 (4): 423–27.

Katzenstein, Peter. 1985. *Small States in World Markets: Industrial Policy in Europe.* Ithaca: Cornell University Press.

Kautto, Mikko. 2000. *Two of a Kind? Economic Crisis, Policy Responses and Wellbeing During the 1990s in Sweden and Finland.* Stockholm: Fritzes offentliga publikationer.

Kenworthy, Lane, and Jonas Pontusson. 2005. "Rising Inequality and the Politics of Redistribution in Affluent Countries." *Perspectives on Politics* 3 (3): 449–71.

Key, V. O. 1964. *Politics, Parties, and Pressure Groups.* New York: Crowell.

Knutsen, Oddbjørn. 2006. *Class Voting in Western Europe: A Comparative Longitudinal Study.* Lanham, MD: Lexington.

Korpi, Walter. 1983. *The Democratic Class-Struggle.* London: Routledge & Kegan Paul.

Lewin, Leif. 1988. *Ideology and Strategy: A Century of Swedish Politics.* Cambridge: Cambridge University Press.

Lewin, Leif. 1994. "The Rise and Decline of Corporatism: The Case of Sweden." *European Journal of Political Research* 26 (1): 59–79.

Lijphart, Arend. 1999. *Patterns of Democracy: Government Forms and Performance in Thirty-Six Countries.* New Haven: Yale University Press.

Lindbeck, Assar, Per Molander, Torsten Persson, Olof Petersson, Agnar Sandmo, Birgitta Swedenborg, and Niels Thygesen. 1994. *Turning Sweden Around.* Cambridge, MA: MIT Press. First published 1993 as *Nya villkor för ekonomi och politik: Ekonomikommissionens förslag* by SOU.

Lindström, Ulf. 1985. *Fascism in Scandinavia, 1920–1940.* Stockholm: Almqvist & Wiksell.

Metcalf, Michael. 1977. *Russia, England and Swedish Party Politics 1762–1766: The Interplay between Great Power Diplomacy and Domestic Politics during Sweden's Age of Liberty.* Stockhom: Almqvist & Wiksell.

Miles, Lee, ed. 1996. *The European Union and the Nordic Countries.* London: Routledge.

Milner, Henry. 2002. *Civic Literacy: How Informed Citizens Make Democracy Work.* Hanover, NH: University Press of New England.
Müller, Wolfgang C., and Kaare Strøm, eds. 2003. *Coalition Governments in Western Europe.* 2nd ed. Oxford: Oxford University Press.
Rommetvedt, Hilmar. 2003. *The Rise of the Norwegian Parliament.* London: Frank Cass.
Rothstein, Bo, and Jonas Bergström. 1999. *Korporatismens fall och den svenska modellens kris.* Stockholm: SNS.
Ruin, Olof. 1983. "Svensk politisk stil: Att komma överens och tänka efter före." In Lennart Arvedson, Ingemund Hägg, and Bengt Rydén, eds., *Land i olag: Samhällsorganisation under omprövning.* Stockholm: Studieförbundet Näringsliv och Samhälle.
Sannerstedt, Anders. 1987. "Teorier om det svenska samförståndet." In Lars Göran Stenelo, ed., *Statsvetenskapens mångfald: Festskrift till Nils Stjernquist.* Lund: Lund University Press.
Sannerstedt, Anders. 1989. "Forskning om författningsreformer." *Statsvetenskaplig Tidskrift* 92:304–12.
Sjöblom, Gunnar. 1987. "The Role of Political Parties in Denmark and Sweden, 1970–1984." In Richard S. Katz, ed., *Party Governments: European and American Experiences.* Berlin: de Gruyter.
Sjölin, Mats. 1987. "Riksdagen och konsensusdemokratin." In Lars Göran Stenelo, ed., *Statsvetenskapens mångfald: Festskrift till Nils Stjernquist.* Lund: Lund University Press.
Sjölin, Mats. 1991. "'Decline of parliaments-tesen' och den svenska riksdagens makt under 1970 och 1980-talet." *Statsvetenskaplig Tidskrift* 94 (2): 125–48.
Sjölin, Mats. 1993. *Coalition Politics and Parliamentary Power.* Lund Political Studies 78. Lund: Lund University Press.
Stephens, John D. 1979. *The Transition From Capitalism to Socialism.* London: Macmillan.
Stjernquist, Nils. 1993. "Konflikt och konsensus i Sverige under skilda konstitutionella villkor." In Björn von Sydow, Gunnar Wallin, and Björn Wittrock, eds., *Politikens väsen: Idéer och institutioner i den moderna staten.* Stockholm: Tidens förlag.
Stjernquist, Nils. 1995. *Parlamentarismen i de nordiska länderna. En egen modell?* Stockholm: Riksbankens Jubileumsfond and Gidlunds förlag.
Strandberg, Urban. 2006. "Introduction: Historical and Theoretical Perspectives on Scandinavian Political Systems." *Journal of European Public Policy* 13 (4): 537–50.
Strøm, Kaare. 1986. "Deferred Gratification and Minority Governments in Scandinavia." *Legislative Studies Quarterly* 11 (4): 583–605.
Strøm, Kaare. 1990. *Minority Government and Majority Rule.* Cambridge: Cambridge University Press.
Strøm, Kaare, Wolfgang Müller, and Torbjörn Bergman, eds. 2003. *Delegation and Accountability in Parliamentary Democracies.* Oxford: Oxford University Press.
Strøm, Kaare, and Stephen M. Swindle. 2002. "Strategic Parliamentary Dissolution." *American Political Science Review* 96 (3): 575–91.
von Sydow, Björn. 1989. *Vägen till enkammarriksdagen: Demokratisk författningspolitik i Sverige 1944–1968.* Stockholm: Tidens förlag.

INTERNET SOURCES

Britannica Book of the Year. 2006.
  France. Accessed September 27, 2006. http://search.eb.com/eb/article-9403306
  Germany. Accessed September 27, 2006. http://search.eb.com/eb/article-9403310
  Spain. Accessed September 27, 2006. http://search.eb.com/eb/article-9403406
Compton's by Britannica. 2006.
  Greenland. Accessed September 27, 2006. http://search.eb.com/ebi/article-9274658
  Scandinavia. Accessed September 27, 2006. http://search.eb.com/ebi/article-207715
Encyclopedia Britannica. 2006.
  Denmark. Accessed September 27, 2006. http://search.eb.com/eb/article-9106173
  Finland. Accessed September 27, 2006. http://search.eb.com/eb/article-9109757
  Sweden. Accessed September 27, 2006. http://search.eb.com/eb/article-9108596
  World Data. Accessed September 20, 2006. http://search.eb.com/
Encyclopedia Britannica. 2008. "World Data." Downloaded February 7, 2008. http://search.eb.com/
European Social Survey, ESS Round 1. 2002/2003. Accessed September 27, 2006. http://www.europeansocialsurvey.org/
European Social Survey, ESS Round 2. 2004/2005. Accessed September 26, 2006. http://www.europeansocialsurvey.org/
European System of Accounts (ESA 95). Accessed September 27, 2006. http://forum.europa.eu.int/irc/dsis/nfaccount/info/data/esa95/en/titelen.htm
Eurostat. 2006.
  Growth Data. Accessed June 29, 2005. http://epp.eurostat.cec.eu.int/
  Table "DAD16144—Total general government expenditure as % of GDP." Accessed September 27, 2006. http://epp.eurostat.ec.europa.eu/
  Table "demo_ppavg Average population by sex and five-year age groups." Accessed September 27, 2006. http://epp.eurostat.cec.eu.int/
  Table eb040 "d: Inflation rate—Annual average rate of change in Harmonized Indices of Consumer Prices (HICPs)." Accessed September 21, 2006. http://epp.eurostat.ec.europa.eu/
  Table employ_t "I.7.1: Total unemployment rate—Unemployed persons as a share of the total active population." Accessed September 21, 2006. http://epp.eurostat.ec.europa.eu/
Eurostat. 2007.
  "Gross domestic product at market prices." Downloaded February 13, 2008. http://epp.eurostat.ec.europa.eu/
  "Inflation rate." Downloaded February 10, 2008. http://epp.eurostat.ec.europa.eu/
  "Total general government expenditure as % of GDP." Downloaded February 9, 2008. http://epp.eurostat.ec.europa.eu/
  "Unemployment rate—total." Downloaded February 9, 2008. http://epp.eurostat.ec.europa.eu/

Heston, Alan, Robert Summers, and Bettina Aten. 2006. *Penn World Table Version 6.2*, Center for International Comparisons of Production, Income and Prices at the University of Pennsylvania, September 2006. Accessed September 27, 2006. http://pwt.econ.upenn.edu/php_site/pwt_index.php

Ministry for Foreign Affairs. 2006. *Iceland, Basic Facts*. Accessed September 27, 2006. http://iceland.is

Nikkei. 2006. *Newspapers in Japan*. Accessed September 9, 2006, and September 27, 2006. http://www.nikkei-ad.com/media_data/en/japan_market/j_market_papers.html

Parliamentary Democracy Data Archive. Accessed September 27, 2007. http://www.pol.umu.se/ccpd

Statistics Iceland. 2006. "Citizenship and country of birth." Accessed September 21, 2006, and June 6, 2007. http://statice.is/

Statistics Iceland. 2007. "Citizenship and country of birth." Downloaded February 7, 2008. www.statice.is

Data on Unemployment. Accessed February 10, 2008. http://www.statice.is/?PageID=1191

Statistikbanken. 2006. "BEF3: Folketal pr. 1. januar efter commune/amt, køn, herkomst, oprindelsesland og statsborgerskapsgruppe." Accessed September 21, 2006, and February 13, 2008. www.statistikbanken.dk/bef3

Statistikcentralen. 2006. Public announcement "Befolkningsstrukturen 2005." Accessed September 21, 2006. http://www.stat.fi/til/vaerak/2005/vaerak_2005_2006-04-13_tie_001_sv.html

Statistikcentralen. 2007. Offentliggörande "Finlands befolkning 2006." Downloaded February 7, 2008. http://www.stat.fi/til/vaerak/2006/vaerak_2006_2007-03-23_tie_001_sv.html

Statistisk Sentralbyrå. 2006. "Folkemengde og invandrerbefolkningen etter landbakgrunn 1970–2006 Absolute tall og prosent." Accessed September 21, 2006. www.ssb.no

Statistisk Sentralbyrå. 2007. "Folkemengde og invandrerbefolkningen etter landbakgrunn 1970–2007 Absolute tall og prosent." Downloaded February 7, 2008. http://www.ssb.no/emner/02/01/10/innvbef/tab-2007-05-24-07.html

Statistiska Centralbyrån. 2006. "Befolkningsstatistik i sammandrag 1960–2005." Accessed September 21, 2006. http://www.scb.se

Statistiska Centralbyrån. 2007. "Befolkningsstatistik i sammandrag 1960–2006." Downloaded February 7, 2008. http://www.scb.se/templates/tableOrChart____26040.asp

Transparency International. 2006. *Global Corruption Report 2006*. Accessed September 21, 2006. http://www.transparency.org

Transparency International. 2007. *Global Corruption Report 2007*. Downloaded February 9, 2008. http://www.transparency.org

World Association of Newspapers. 2005. *WAN-world Press Trends 2005*. Tidningsutgivarna. Accessed September 9, 2006, and September 27, 2006. http://www.tu.se

✦ **THE FIVE NORDICS** ✦

3 ✦ Change and Challenges of Danish Parliamentary Democracy

ERIK DAMGAARD

Denmark is the oldest of the Nordic states, with a continuous history of sovereignty that goes back more than a thousand years. It also has one of the world's oldest continuous monarchies. Although Denmark experienced the longest period of royal absolutism (1660–1849) of the Nordic states, it has gradually evolved, since 1849, into a constitutional monarchy that exhibits many of the most typical features of parliamentary democracy. Today, European integration, an unrivaled tendency toward minority parliamentarism, and an increasingly vigorous form of direct democracy pose new challenges for this very old and well-established state.

The Danish constitution (1953) does not use the term *citizen sovereignty*, but it is generally recognized that "the sovereign people" is the ultimate basis of the Danish system of representative government (Sørensen 1973). Although citizens are regarded as the ultimate principal, they do not have the right to recall elected representatives. In addition, an imperative mandate is explicitly ruled out by the constitution (Section 56), which states, "The members of the Folketing shall be bound solely by their own consciences and not by any directions given by their electors."

The original constitution (of 1849) introduced a separation-of-powers political system (formally still in force) in which legislative authority was to be vested in the king and parliament conjointly, while executive authority was to rest with the king and judicial authority in the courts of justice. After a protracted political struggle, this Madisonian system was modified by the introduction of the Westminster idea of cabinet accountability to the lower chamber of parliament (Folketinget) in 1901. Since that time, a legislative majority can control lawmaking as well as cabinet formation and dismissal.

The story of Danish parliamentary democracy since World War II must necessarily include a discussion of three changes or transformations that, to some extent, are interrelated: the consolidation of minority rule, a reduction (in some respects) in the power of established parties, and greater external constraints on parliamentary actors in general. It must also include a discussion of several specific changes to the various steps, or links, of delegation and accountability in the parliamentary chain of governance.

Traditionally, the scholarly literature treated minority cabinets as abnormal or unfortunate deviations from healthier and stable majority cabinets consisting of one or more coherent parties (Herman and Pope 1973; Taylor and Laver 1973; Laver and Schofield 1990). A successful counterattack on that approach was initiated by Kaare Strøm (1990) and others (cf. Bergman 1995; Damgaard 2000b), who argued that the formation of minority cabinets can often be a sensible result of rational party behavior in competitive situations and that minority cabinets are not necessarily inferior in terms of political and economic performance compared with majority cabinets. Strøm argued that such is the case in the Scandinavian countries. This is particularly true for Denmark, which holds the world record for incidence of minority cabinets among parliamentary democracies since 1945 (Mitchell 2001). Majority coalitions were not unknown in Denmark in the 1950s and 1960s (Damgaard 1992), but since the early 1970s, there have been no such cabinets, except for a short interlude of about 18 months in the early 1990s (the first Nyrup Rasmussen cabinet of 1993–94; cf. Damgaard 2000a).

Danish minority cabinets are not only controlled by the power of noncabinet parties but also constrained by various national and international institutions and actors external to the parliamentary chain of governance. Referendums, mass media, the courts, the central bank, independent state enterprises, international actors, and, not least, the European Union (EU) have assumed increasing importance in Danish political decision making. In some instances (e.g., referendums), these developments do not reduce citizen control of the political process. However, in other cases (e.g., the EU) they clearly do, although they may simultaneously reinforce other forms of citizen control, protect human rights, or promote particular interests in some respects.

A number of changes in the parliamentary chain of delegation and accountability are also quite visible and important. Parties, despite important changes, continue to be key actors in mass politics, parliament, and executive cabinets, so the first section of this chapter will present the main features of the Danish parties and party system. The second section focuses on the actors and institutions (voters, parliament, cabinet, civil servants) in the constitutional chain of delegation and accountability. The third section looks at a number of relevant external constraints and the challenges they pose for the democratic chain of governance. However, in assessing the impact of these constraints, we should bear in mind that such "constraints" may also, in some situations, create opportunities for influence by particular interests and actors.

While the research questions relevant to this discussion have been presented in much more detail in previous chapters, one may say that they cover three main issues. The first is whether there has been a decline in "partyness" in the Nordic countries. The second is whether there has been a decline in the capacity of parliament to impose its stamp on the policy process, or whether parliamentary parties perhaps have become more active and influential compared to cabinet parties. The third main topic is the extent to which the national policy process has become increasingly constrained by actors and institutions external to the parliamentary chain of governance. If that has come to pass, the system of decision making that has emerged may combine Madisonian and Westminster elements.

Parties and the Party System

Although the political parties have changed considerably, they are still very important as instruments of representation and governance. The most significant development culminated in 1973, when Danish voters completely changed the structure of the Danish party system. The four "old" parties (the Social Democrats, Radical Liberals, Liberals, and Conservatives) and the more recently founded Socialist People's Party all lost heavily at the polls. Three very new parties (the Progress Party, Center Democrats, and Christian People's Party) entered parliament, together with two older parties (the Justice Party and Communists) that had previously lost their seats in parliament (Pedersen 1988). The voters clearly demonstrated that their votes could not be taken for granted, and the new party system had immediate effects on cabinet formation and work in the Folketing. The high level of fractionalization created in the party system by the 1973 election has since declined, but as of 2007, there are still seven parties in parliament.

The Danish party system is probably best understood in terms of five groupings of parties (see table 3.1). Between 1945 and 2005, the number and type of parties in each group has varied. First, there is a group of relatively small left-wing parties. At different times, this group has included one, two, or even three of the following parties: Communists, Left Socialists, Common Course, the Unity List, and the Socialist People's Party. The Social

Democratic Party, which was the largest party from 1924 to 2001, is in a group of its own. The third group is made up of relatively small center parties, including the old Radical Liberals, the Justice Party, and, in the mid-1960s, the Liberal Center Party. In the 1970s, the center space became increasingly crowded with the addition of two new parties: the Center Democrats and the Christian People's Party. The fourth group includes the older, moderate center-right parties, the Liberals and the Conservatives. Fi-

TABLE 3.1. Elections to the Danish Parliament (the Folketing), 1945–2008

Election Year	Com	LS/UL	CC	SPP	SD	CD	RL	CPP	JP	Con	Lib	DPP	IND/PP	NY	Others
1945	12.5				32.8		8.1		1.9	18.2	23.4				3.1
1947	6.8				40.0		6.9		4.5	12.4	27.6				1.4
1950	4.6				39.6		8.2		8.2	17.8	21.3				0.3
1953a	4.8				40.4		8.6		5.6	17.3	22.1				1.2
1953a	4.3				41.3		7.8		3.5	16.8	23.1		2.7		1.2
1957	3.1				39.4		7.8		5.3	16.6	25.1		2.3		0.4
1960	1.1			6.1	42.1		5.8		2.2	17.9	21.1		3.3		0.4
1964	1.2			5.8	41.9		5.3		1.3	20.1	20.8		2.5		0.8
1966	0.8			10.9	38.2		7.3		0.7	18.7	19.3		1.6		2.5
1968	1.0		2.0	6.1	34.2		15.0		0.7	20.4	18.6		0.5		1.5
1971	1.4		1.6	9.1	37.3		14.4	2.0	1.7	16.7	15.6		PP		0.2
1973	3.6		1.5	6.0	25.6	7.8	11.2	4.0	2.9	9.2	12.3		15.9		
1975	4.2		2.1	5.0	29.9	2.2	7.1	5.3	1.8	5.5	23.3		13.6		
1977	3.7		2.7	3.9	37.0	6.4	3.6	3.4	3.3	8.5	12.0		14.6		0.9
1979	1.9		3.7	5.9	38.3	3.2	5.4	2.6	2.6	12.5	12.5		11.0		0.4
1981	1.1		2.7	11.3	32.9	8.3	5.1	2.3	1.4	14.5	11.3		8.9		0.2
1984	0.7		2.7	11.5	31.6	4.6	5.5	2.7	1.5	23.4	12.1		3.6		0.1
1987	0.9		1.4	14.6	29.3	4.8	6.2	2.4	0.5	20.8	10.5		4.8		1.5
1988	0.8		0.6	13.0	29.8	4.7	5.6	2.0		19.3	11.8		9.0		1.4
1990			1.7	8.3	37.4	5.1	3.5	2.3	0.5	16.0	15.8		6.4		0.9
1994		3.1		7.3	34.6	2.8	4.6	1.9		15.0	23.3		6.4		1.0
1998		2.7		7.6	35.9	4.3	3.9	2.5		8.9	24.0	7.4	2.4		0.4
2001		2.4		6.4	29.1	1.8	5.2	2.3		9.1	31.2	12.0	0.6		
2005		3.4		6.0	25.8	1.0	9.2	1.7		10.3	29.0	13.3			0.3
2007		2.2		13.0	25.5		5.1	0.9		10.4	26.3	13.8		2.8	0.0

Source: Data from *Folketingets Håndbog* (1977), 296–97; *Folketinget efter valget* (2001), 269–72; *Folketinget efter valget* (2005), 216–17; *Politiken.dk*, http://politiken.dk/politik/article4277836.ece (accessed February 2, 2008).

Notes: Numbers in table represent vote shares in percentages. Party abbreviations are as follows: Com = Communists (Danmarks Kommunistiske Parti); LS = Left Socialists (Venstresocialisterne) until 1987; UL = Unity List (Enhedslisten) from 1990; CC = Common Course (Fælles Kurs); SPP = Socialist People's Party (Socialistisk Folkeparti); SD = Social Democrats (Socialdemokratiet); CD = Center Democrats (Centrum-Demokraterne); RL = Radical Liberals (Det Radikale Venstre); CPP = Christian People's Party (Kristeligt Folkeparti); JP = Justice Party (Dansmarks Retsforbund); Con = Conservatives (Det Konservative Folkeparti); Lib = Liberals (Venstre, Danmarks Liberale Parti); DPP = Danish People's Party (Dansk Folkeparti); PP = Progress Party (Fremskridtspartiet) from 1973 through 2001; IND = Independents (De Uafhængige) until 1968; NY = New Alliance, later Liberal Alliance (Ny Alliance); Others = Other parties (Andre partier). In 1945 the Danish Unity Party (Dansk Samling) received a vote share of 3.1%. In 1966 the Liberal Center (Liberalt Centrum) received a vote share of 2.5%.

[a]Two elections were held in 1953.

nally, a fifth group is the right-wing parties. This includes the Independent Party (in the early 1960s) and, from the early 1970s, the Progress Party, which obtained surprisingly strong support as a protest party in the remarkable election of 1973. In the late 1990s, the Progress Party split, and the new Danish People's Party picked up most of the former Progress voters.

The three most recent elections (2001, 2005, and 2007) produced remarkable changes in the strengths of the various parties. The Social Democrats suffered severe setbacks and lost their status as the largest Danish party. That position has instead been held by the Liberals since 2001. The Danish People's Party also gained substantial support, which enabled it to form a majority in parliament with the Liberals and Conservatives. In 2005, the Radical Liberals were the only center party to win enough votes to remain in parliament. Despite the party's electoral success in 2001 and 2005, a nonsocialist parliamentary majority was able to form without it.

It is important to note that the high level of Danish party discipline (according to standard measurements) did not decline after the transformation of the party system in 1973 (Svensson 1982; Damgaard and Svensson 1989; Jensen 2000). The parties are still as cohesive as they need to be for the parliamentary chain of delegation and accountability to work (Jensen 2002). Nonetheless, the greater number of parties in combination with minority governance implies that no distinct party or coalition of parties can normally be in full command of policy-making.

Party Members and Attachment to Parties

Important changes have also occurred at the level of party organization (Bille 1997; Hansen 2002; Bille and Elklit 2003). The introduction of public financial support for political parties in the late 1980s, with a major increase in the 1990s, has strengthened the party organizations. Public subsidies are now the main source of income for all parties. At the same time, as in most other established democracies, the number of party members has declined dramatically in recent decades (see fig. 3.1). Only about 4–5 percent of the Danish electorate currently belongs to a political party, compared to about 20 percent in the 1960s (Bille 2003). To make matters worse, it also appears that the activity level of party members declined in the late 1990s (Pedersen and Hansen 2003). Yet some parties have more members now than they did in the early 1990s.

The number of party members is only one, albeit important, indicator of voter attachment to parties. Other indicators are listed in table 3.2. Voter turnout (about 85 percent) has *not* declined in Denmark, as it has in most

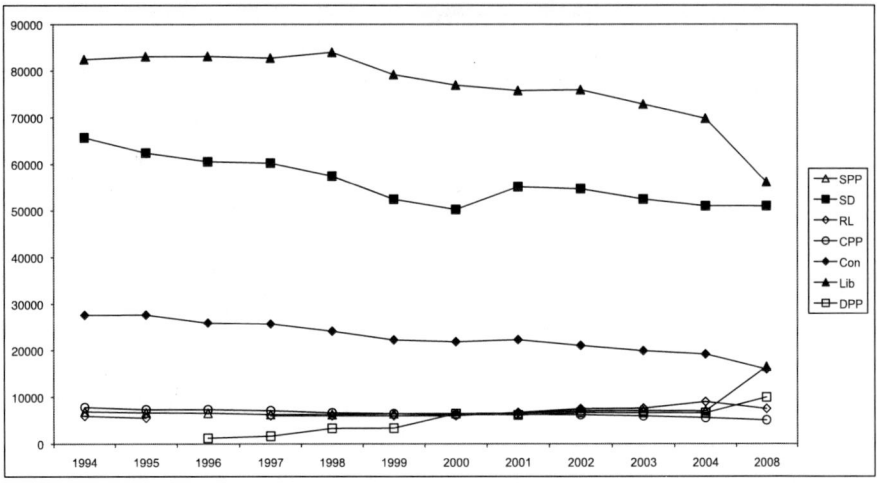

Fig. 3.1. Party membership in Denmark, 1994–2008. See table 3.1 for explanation of party labels.

other established democracies (Hague and Harrop 2001, 133). Part of the explanation might be Denmark's election system of proportional representation (PR) with a low threshold of representation (2 percent) and effective preferential voting; but a high level of party competition over government offices and a continued sense of citizen duty to participate in elections may also play a role (Elklit et al. 2005).

It is also noteworthy that the level of party identification has not declined since 1971 (the year of the first election survey in Denmark). There are some variations, of course, but throughout this period, roughly 50 percent of voters have identified with a party. However, there has been a strong decline in class voting, as measured by the Alford index. In the last few elections, it has almost entirely disappeared. Electoral volatility, measured as the share of voters changing party between elections, was high in the 1973 election (44 percent) but then gradually declined to a low of about 20 percent in 1990. It has increased again in the four most recent elections, although not to the level of 1973. The share of voters deciding which party to vote for during the election campaign has generally been about 20–30 percent, but in 2005, it jumped to 37 percent. Finally, although the distrust of politicians was high in the early 1970s, there has been a clear decline in distrust over the period. From a high of 62 in 1975, it had decreased to only 35 percent in 2005.

Thus, in Denmark we find high and stable turnout, stable party identification, a decline in class voting, variation in the share of voters changing

TABLE 3.2. Strength of Party Attachment in Denmark, 1945–2005

Election Year	Turnout (%)	Class Voting (Alford Index)[a]	Share of Voters Identifying with Party (%)[b]	Share of Voters Changing Party between Elections (%)	Share of Voters Deciding Which Party to Vote for during the Election Campaign (%)	Distrust of Politicians[c] (%)
1945	86.3					
1947	85.8					
1950	81.9					
1953	80.8					
1957	83.7					
1960	85.8					
1964	85.5					
1966	88.6					
1968	89.3					
1971	87.2	43	54	17	16	48
1973	88.7	35	45	44	32	58
1975	88.2	35	54	29	25	62
1977	88.7	27	49	27	27	54
1979	85.6	26	52	19	23	53
1981	83.2	26		18	28	51
1984	88.4	26		22	23	55
1987	86.7	23		23	23	54
1988	85.7	23		23	27	
1990	82.8	29	52	20	21	53
1994	84.3	18	49	28	28	57
1998	86.0	13	50	29	26	47
2001	87.1	6	47	34	29	43
2005	84.5	10	50	25	37	35

Source: Data on turnout in 1945–68 from Thomsen 1984, 46–47. Data on turnout in 1971–2005 from *Folketinget,* "Valg og tendenser" (2006), http://www.ft.dk/pdf/ark9.pdf (accessed February 14, 2008). Ole Borre kindly provided data based on the following sources: Share of voters changing party between elections, Nielsen and Thomsen 2003, 67. All numbers are recall data, except from 1973 and 1988, which are panel data. Share of voters deciding which party to vote for during election campaign: from 1974 to 1984, Siune 1984, 140; from 1987 to 1988, Tonsgaard 1989, 137; from 1998, Nielsen 1999, 52; from 2001, Nielsen and Thomsen 2003, 70. The numbers from 1990 to 1994 are calculated by Ole Borre.

Note: Share of voters shifting bloc is not included in table 3.2. The distinction between a socialist and nonsocialist (bourgeois) bloc does not fit well with Danish politics, in which parliamentary cooperation across such blocs is quite common. The "blocs" actually change composition over time. All the numbers from 2005 calculated by Ole Borre on the basis of the main survey, 2005.

[a] Data on class voting is from Andersen and Andersen 2003, 209. The Alford index is based on the difference between the vote share for the parties on the left (in this case the Left and Social Democratic Parties) among the working class (measured by occupation) and the vote share for the same parties among the middle class. A higher index implies that working-class voters vote for parties on the left to a greater extent than do middle-class voters.

[b] Data on share of voters identifying with party: From 1971 to 1979 and 1990 to 2001, Borre 2003b, 1977. Information from the elections of 1981–88 does not exist.

[c] Distrust of politicians: Counted as an average of two numbers, (1) percentage agreeing that "the politicians in general do not take the voters' opinion into account" and (2) percentage disagreeing that "one can in general trust that the politicians decide what is best for the country." Data from 1971 to 1984 is from Borre 1984, 158. Data from 1990 to 2001 is from Andersen and Borre 2003, 405. Data from 1987 calculated by Ole Borre. For 1988 one of the two numbers does not exist.

parties between elections, variation in the share of voters deciding which party to vote for during the election campaign (with increases toward the end of the period), and declining distrust in the three most recent elections. Apart from the low number of party members, it is hard to conclude that these developments give cause for serious concern.

The Dimensionality of the Party System

Table 3.1 on elections reflects a traditional left-right ordering of political parties. So does table 3.3, which shows the party composition of cabinets and the party of the median legislator in the Folketing. The ordering is based on expert judgments on two socioeconomic, left-right scales reported by Laver and Hunt (1992): "increase services vs. cut taxes" and "pro-public vs. anti-public ownership" (cf. Damgaard 2000a). Laver and Hunt's data refer to a specific point in time (about 1990), which means that three of the small parties were not included—the Independents, the Liberal Center Party, and the Unity List.

Even if the experts' judgments are accepted as accurate at the time when they were originally reported, party positions might have differed before as well as after that time. Parties might change policy positions for strategic or other reasons. In addition, if a policy field is crowded with parties, even minor policy changes could change their relative positions. In general, however, the socioeconomic, left-right ordering of the Danish parties is stable, as has been shown in a number of previous studies (Damgaard 2000a). Compared to most standard accounts, the only major deviation is that the Laver and Hunt (1992) study reverses the position of the Liberals and the Conservatives. This shift recorded by the experts probably occurred in the 1980s, although appropriate data to settle the issue is not available.

Some parties—the Social Democrats, Radical Liberals, Conservatives, and Liberals—have held seats in the parliament continuously since 1945. Other parties have a more mixed record. For example, the Justice Party lost its seats in the late 1950s. It reentered parliament for one period in the late 1960s and sat for several years in the mid-1970s, but it has not won any seats since 1979. The Communist Party held seats in parliament until the late 1950s and for a few years in the 1970s. Other parties that have held seats for only part of the period since 1945 include the Center Democrats and the Christian People's Party.

One of the center parties, most often the Radical Liberals, has normally controlled the median legislator on the left-right dimension. On average, the experts place the Center Democrats slightly to the left of the Radical Liberals. If the ordering of these two parties had been reversed by the experts, however, the domination of the median position by the Radical Liberals would have appeared almost crushing. Yet in four cases, none of the center parties controlled the median MP. In 1966, the Social Democrats were pivotal and formed a legislative voting majority with the Socialist People's Party. In 2001, 2005, and 2007, the Liberals and Conservatives could form a majority with the Danish People's Party.

Danish students of electoral behavior currently agree that voting behavior cannot be adequately understood in terms of one dimension alone. They claim not that the old socioeconomic, left-right dimension has disappeared but that an additional dimension has emerged (Borre and Andersen 1997; Borre 1999; Borre 2003a; Stubager 2000, 2006). They distinguish between "old" and "new" politics and argue that both dimensions must be used to properly locate voters and parties in policy space. In a study of the 2001 election, Borre (2003a) analyzes old politics in terms of attitudes toward social reform, equality of income, state intervention in business, and progressive taxation. New politics includes attitudes toward immigration, development aid, law and order, and the environment. Borre finds that the new politics dimension has gradually become an important dimension in electoral behavior. The new Danish People's Party, with its explicit anti-immigration positions, can be seen as a representative of this alternative dimension. However, the problems of the current economic crisis could possibly reinforce the traditional socioeconomic left-right dimension.

In the present context, the most interesting question is whether political conflict and cooperation at the parliamentary level has also become two-dimensional. Asbjørn Skjæveland (2005) has tried to answer this question. His analysis is based on final voting on bills in the lawmaking process during the period 1981/82 through 2002/3, and his research technique is multidimensional scaling (MDS) of the votes of cohesive parties. Skjæveland concludes that a one-dimensional scale is sufficient to locate parliamentary parties in terms of their actual voting behavior and that there are only very modest tendencies toward a two-dimensional pattern. Thus, single-dimensional ordering can still explain parliamentary voting, although a change in the policy content of the left-right dimension has probably occurred over time.

Another measure that illustrates that the Danish party system has not necessarily become more complex over time is the measure of the "effective number of parties" (see table 3.3). This measure jumped from about

TABLE 3.3. Cabinets in Denmark, 1945–2008

Cabinet Number	Prime Minister	Date (yymmdd)	Cabinet Share (%) of All Parliamentary Seats	Effective Number of Legislative Parties[a]	Median Legislator Party	Parties in Cabinet	Majority Cabinets Single-Party	Majority Cabinets Coalition[b]	Minority Cabinets Single-Party	Minority Cabinets[c] Coalition
1	Kristensen	451107	25.5	4.5	RL	Lib			X	
2	Hedtoft I	471113	38.7	3.5	RL	SD			X	
3	Hedtoft II	500916	39.7	4.0	RL	SD			X	
4	Eriksen I	501030	39.7	4.0	RL	Lib, Con				X
5	Eriksen II	530421	39.7	3.8	RL	Lib, Con				X
6	Hedtoft III	530930	41.9	3.7	RL	SD			X	
7	Hansen	550201	41.9	3.7	RL	SD			X	
8	Hansen II	570528	52.5	3.9	RL	SD, RL, JP		X		
9	Kampmann I	600221	52.5	3.9	RL	SD, RL, JP		X		
10	Kampmann II	601118	49.2	3.7	RL	SD, RL				X
11	Krag I	620903	49.2	3.7	RL	SD, RL				X
12	Krag II	640926	43.0	3.6	RL	SD			X	
13	Krag III	661122	39.1	4.1	SD	SD			X	
14	Baunsgaard	680222	54.8	4.3	RL	RL, Con, Lib		X		
15	Krag IV	711011	39.7	4.0	RL	SD			X	
16	Jorgensen I	721005	39.7	4.0	RL	SD			X	
17	Hartling	731219	12.3	7.0	RL	Lib			X	
18	Jorgensen II	750213	30.2	5.5	RL	SD			X	
19	Jorgensen III	770215	36.9	5.2	CD	SD			X	
20	Jorgensen IV	780830	49.2	5.2	CD	SD, Lib				X
21	Jorgensen V	791026	38.6	4.9	CD	SD			X	
22	Jorgensen VI	811230	33.5	5.6	CD	SD			X	

23	Schlüter I	820910	36.9	5.6	CD	Con, Lib, CD, CPP	X
24	Schlüter II	840110	43.6	5.1	CD	Con, Lib, CD, CPP	X
25	Schlüter III	870910	39.1	5.3	CD	Con, Lib, CD, CPP	X
26	Schlüter IV	880603	38.0	5.4	RL	Con, Lib, RL	X
27	Schlüter V	901218	33.5	4.4	CD	Con, Lib	X
28	Rasmussen I	930125	50.8	4.4	CD	SD, RL, CD, CPP	
29	Rasmussen II	940927	42.5	4.5	RL	SD, RL, CD	X
30	Rasmussen III	961230	39.7	4.5	RL	SD, RL	X
31	Rasmussen IV	980311	39.7	4.8	CD	SD, RL	X
32	Fogh I	011127	40.8	4.6	Con	Lib, Con	X
33	Fogh II	050208	39.1	5.1	Con	Lib, Con	X
34	Fogh III	071113	35.8	5.6	Con	Lib, Con	X

Source: Data from Damgaard 2000b; *Folketinget efter valget 8* (February 2005); *Folketinget,* http://www.ft.dk/ (accessed February 2, 2008); Keesing's Record of World Events, vol. 53 (November 2007 Denmark): 48272.

Notes: See the notes to table 3.1 for explanation of party labels. In April 2009, the 34th cabinet changed leaders when L. Løkke Rasmussen (Lib.) replaced A. Fogh Rasmussen (Lib.) as PM when the latter was appointed Secretary General of NATO.

[a] Effective number of legislative parties: Index developed by Markku Laakso and Rein Taagepera that is a measure of party system size. Both the number of parties and their relative size are taken into account. For an accessible introduction see Lijphart 1984.

[b] Majority cabinet coalitions can be either a minimal winning coalition (mwc—a coalition that cannot lose a party and still be "winning") or a surplus coalition (a coalition that can lose one or more parties and still be winning). Cabinets 8, 9, 14, and 28 are minimal winning coalitions.

[c] Minority cabinets control 50% or less of all seats in parliament.

four effective parties in the 1960s to seven in the 1973 election. Based on this measure, the party system is less complex now than it was in 1973, although it remains more complex than it was in the 1960s. This indicator therefore provides no support for a thesis of steadily growing fragmentation in the party system.

The Democratic Constitutional Chain of Governance

The first focus of this section is on the links of delegation and accountability between voters and MPs, between MPs and the cabinet, and in intra-cabinet relations. The next part of this section connects cabinets to voters and analyzes cabinet electoral performance. This is followed by a more general discussion of the parliament-cabinet relationship. The final part of this section examines the link between ministers and civil servants.

From Voters to Parliament

Denmark introduced unicameralism in 1953 through a constitutional amendment that abolished the upper chamber. As the party composition of the two chambers had become almost exactly identical, the upper chamber no longer served a useful purpose. Twenty years later, Danish voters became represented in the European Parliament (EP), and since 1979, they directly elect their representatives to this body. So far, however, voters have not been particularly interested in EP elections, and many of those who vote distribute their votes among parties differently than they do in national elections (Damgaard and Nørgaard 2000).

The constitution prescribes a national election system according to the principle of proportional representation. Although the technicalities of the system are quite complex, it basically assures proportional representation of parties that obtain at least 2 percent of the national vote (Elklit and Pade 1996). The election period is formally four years but is often much shorter than that in practice, because early elections can be called by the prime minister at almost any time. Danish voters can cast their votes for either a party or a preferred candidate within a party. The effect of preferential voting depends on the type of candidate list presented by the parties. Parties can present a "pure party list" with ranked candidates or, if they prefer, an alphabetical list of candidates in which preferential voting can be much more decisive. Individual parties thus decide how much of a choice voters have. Interestingly, most parties have presented variations of the latter type.

In all parties, the local and regional party organizations are crucial in the nomination process (Bille 1993). They can hold their elected MP accountable, which is important with regard to renomination and reelection. The local party organizations are keen, however, to propose candidates who can attract votes, which means that an individual MP has a considerable advantage if he or she is likely to be an electoral asset. Nevertheless, MPs in most parties also rely on the parliamentary party organization to be reelected or to advance within the party hierarchy (Damgaard 1995).

Studies have shown an increasing rank-and-file member influence on candidate nomination (Hansen and Pedersen 2003), as well as an increase in the effect of preferential voting on the election of candidates. However, in both respects, it is necessary to distinguish between a group of "old" parties and a group of "new" ones (Pedersen 2002, 60–61). The old or traditional parties can still function as mass parties "with an organized training of new recruits and with possibilities of genuine screening of candidates . . . In these parties the prospective and ambitious individual may still dream about—or plan—an orderly political career" (Pedersen 2002, 61). This is not possible in the smaller new parties, however. While it is relatively easy to move ahead in such parties, the final step (a seat in parliament) is a serious obstacle, and unpredictability is an important feature in these parties. Pedersen concludes that national and local leadership have lost some of their gatekeeping control to rank-and-file members in the nomination process. He also concludes that voters have gained more influence on election day due to the increasing use of preferential voting. One might add that both developments tend to weaken party organizations and their leadership. A similar conclusion is reached by Togeby and colleagues (2003) in the final report of the Danish power and democracy project.

The PR electoral system assures that the party composition of the Folketing reflects the party preferences of voters very well. However, it does not produce a membership composition that mirrors the electorate in terms of demographic and socioeconomic background characteristics (Christiansen, Møller, and Togeby 2001; Kjær and Pedersen 2004; Jensen 2004). Over time, this "descriptive representation" (Pitkin 1967) has improved on some scores (e.g., women and young people), but the MPs are still not a "mirror in miniature" of the voters electing them. If party affiliation were the only thing that mattered, such deviations would not be very interesting. However, studies have shown that, independent of party affiliation, background characteristics have some effect on MP attitudes and self-reported activities (Narud and Valen 2000; Wängnerud 2000; Esaiasson 2000; Jensen 2004). Thus, one might recommend that voters use preferential voting if they want to promote certain interests in addition to party policies (Jensen 2004, 254–55).

Another recent study is skeptical about a causal linkage between background characteristics and actual policy decisions, because it has proven impossible or very difficult to establish such a link in studies of recruitment and representation (Kjær and Pedersen 2004, 183–84).

MPs and the Cabinet

Once MPs have been elected as "agents of the people," they also become "principals of the cabinet." The mechanisms by which the cabinet members account to their parliamentary masters are implicit and complex.

Cabinet Formation

The constitutional amendments of 1953 included a codification of the informal practice of "negative parliamentarism" (developed since the early twentieth century), stating that a cabinet can stay in office as long as it is tolerated by a majority in parliament. The constitution contains no rules about how a cabinet is to be formed. It only specifies that a cabinet must resign if it receives a motion of no confidence passed by a plurality in parliament. Existing informal rules assure that a new cabinet is at least tolerated for some unspecified period of time (Damgaard 1992). Informal rules on cabinet formation require that the parties give advice, at one or more stages of the process, by publicly stating their cabinet preferences at a formal visit to the monarch (head of state). If their advice unambiguously points to a majority cabinet or a cabinet with assured support of a majority in the Folketing, the monarch is obligated to appoint such a cabinet. If no such majority emerges, the goal is to appoint the minority cabinet most likely to survive, at least in the short run. The whole process is essentially one of bargaining among parties, which sometimes prefer that a leading parliamentarian be appointed to serve as a "royal informateur" in the first stage. The head of state has no independent role in the process. If the advice given by the parties is unclear, the acting prime minister, not the monarch, is responsible for interpreting it. Table 3.3 provides information on the cabinets formed since 1945.

Single-party majority cabinets do not occur in Denmark, and only four majority coalitions have been formed in the post-1945 period (see table 3.3). This means that the dominant type of executive is a minority cabinet. Cabinets representing a single party or a coalition minority are about equally frequent over the period as a whole, 14 versus 16 respectively. However, as table 3.3 shows, parties have, over time, become more inclined to build minority coalitions. They were quite rare in the 1950s, 1960s, and 1970s but became the rule from the early 1980s. A single-party cabinet has not been formed since 1981, and there has been only one—short-lived—majority coalition (in 1993–94).

A careful reading of table 3.3 indicates that majority cabinets last longer than minority cabinets. However, if a minority cabinet has stable support from noncabinet parties (as, e.g., cabinets 7, 11, 24, and 31), it may actually match majority cabinets with respect to relative duration (not shown in table 3.3).

Twelve of the 20 coalition cabinets were formed by parties located adjacent to each other on the left-right scale presented in tables 3.1 and 3.3. The Social Democratic–Liberal coalition of 1978–79 is the only major deviation from the overall pattern. The coalition was short-lived and not very successful. The minority coalitions formed in 1982, 1984, and 1987 do not quite conform to the party locations on the scale, mainly because the Center Democrats (CD) are considered more "leftist" than the Radical Liberals. However, if the relative placement of these two parties is erroneous—i.e., if the Center Democrats were actually to the right of the Radical Liberals—then the latter should not have formed a coalition with the Conservatives and Liberals (as they did in 1988) without both the Center Democrats and the Christian People's Party.

One of the lessons from these minority coalitions is that the small center parties have usually been able to choose coalition partners to the left (Social Democrats) or right (Conservatives and Liberals) based on expediency. Since 1982, the Radical Liberals, Center Democrats, and Christian People's Party have actually participated in cabinets with, on the one hand, the Social Democrats and, on the other, the Liberals or Conservatives. They have also cooperated with each other in various combinations. The coalitions formed between 1982 and 2001 vividly illustrate this point.

The history of cabinet formation in Denmark suggests that the Danish form of negative parliamentarism facilitates the formation of minority cabinets (usually policy-connected along the left-right dimension when they are coalitions). Such cabinets can normally be formed quite rapidly, but when they lack stable external support, they are less durable than majority cabinets.

Cabinet Parties and Opposition Parties in Parliamentary Affairs

Parliament-cabinet relations also include the relationship between the parties that hold cabinet seats and the opposition parties. The next four tables present data on parliamentary activities that illuminate these interactions. Table 3.4a presents data on the number of bills and resolutions (proposed and passed) in the 1972–2008 period. This covers the era of the new party system that began with the landslide election of 1973 and the period after the establishment, in 1972, of a new committee structure with permanent, specialized committees largely mirroring the division of policy areas among cabinet ministries.

There has been a general increase in the number of cabinet bills pro-

TABLE 3.4a. Numbers of Parliamentary Bills and Resolutions, Denmark, 1972–2008

Year	Bills				Resolutions				Sitting Hours
	Cabinet Bills	Of Which Passed	Private Members' Bills	Of Which Passed	Cabinet Proposals	Of Which Passed	Private Members'	Of Which Passed	
1972–73	218	195	20	1	9	9	22	4	—
1973–74	180	119	70	5	9	4	54	2	—
1974–75	264	174	127	17	7	4	92	2	—
1975–76	180	161	102	11	6	5	72	5	—
1976–77	276	186	138	4	10	7	84	2	—
1977–78	165	146	99	5	1	1	93	3	—
1978–79	148	146	86	1	1	1	102	0	—
1979–80	170	160	71	1	8	8	127	1	—
1980–81	163	152	68	7	2	2	106	3	—
1981–82	209	153	120	11	7	6	90	2	—
1982–83	136	111	83	14	4	4	104	19	—
1983–84	240	175	78	7	5	5	171	8	—
1984–85	152	140	85	14	2	2	130	9	—
1985–86	203	179	73	11	4	3	147	20	—
1986–87	180	162	73	14	2	2	168	20	—
1987–88	220	122	80	4	0	0	147	4	—
1988–89	191	174	58	10	4	4	81	10	—
1989–90	199	181	45	6	3	3	71	5	—
1990–91	221	143	85	17	4	3	104	11	—
1991–92	244	219	59	17	3	3	89	13	—
1992–93	290	273	57	3	14	14	88	1	—
1993–94	231	226	31	5	14	14	81	2	—
1994–95	234	223	32	1	6	6	111	1	—
1995–96	231	227	41	5	14	14	119	3	—
1996–97	236	229	41	4	10	10	139	4	—
1997–98	266	191	48	1	15	11	149	4	—
1998–99	217	206	32	3	12	12	133	5	496
1999–2000	265	261	28	2	6	6	160	4	589
2000–2001	213	213	26	3	8	8	192	6	617
2001–2	229	171	41	1	10	10	178	3	616
2002–3	203	201	26	0	9	9	169	9	696
2003–4	225	224	16	4	10	10	201	1	724
2004–5	312	225	24	1	7	7	216	0	—
2005–6	227	220	16	4	5	5	132	5	—
2006–7	213	205	12	2	3	3	162	4	—
2007–8	219	184	6	0	11	10	155	3	—

Source: Data from *Folketingstidende, Årbog og registre* (2002–3); Secretariat of Law in the Danish Folketing.

posed and enacted. The number of private members' (opposition) bills jumped sharply in the beginning of the period but then declined, over time, back to about the same low level of the early 1970s. Today, opposition MPs apparently do not propose much new (technically difficult) legislation, but they actively propose new policy initiatives in the form of resolutions requesting the cabinet to take action in various policy areas. Opposition bills and resolutions were most successful in the period of 1982–92, when the cabinet was led by Poul Schlüter from the Conservative Party. His minority cabinet coalitions wanted to stay in power and therefore accepted more defeats in legislative voting than is usual in Danish politics, both before and after his time as prime minister.

The Danish Folketing may be a "working parliament" (Arter 1999, chap. 9), but it is certainly also a "talking parliament," as the available evidence on sitting hours indicates. Until the early 1970s, the Folketing was able to cope with an increasing workload without extending the total time spent on floor meetings per year, which, on average, was about 300 hours in 1963–74 (not reported in table 3.4a). The sitting hours then increased to more than 400 per year in the 1970s and 1980s (Damgaard 1977, 1992). In the mid-1990s, the number of hours was 434 (Jensen 1999). As shown in table 3.4a, the number increased again to about 600 in the late 1990s and even to around 700 in the most recent years for which data is available. The conclusion is clear. Never, even going back to the 1850s (Damgaard 1977), has there been so much talk in the Folketing as there has been in recent years.

One indicator of the strength of parliament versus the cabinet is a simple measure of how often the cabinet is on the winning side in final divisions on all bills, resolutions, and "proposals for a decision" (which conclude interpellation debates). For each governmental period, defined here by (change in) the party composition of cabinet, the number of times the governing parties were on the losing side of a vote was counted ("no" or "abstain" if a measure was adopted, "yes" or "abstain" if a measure was rejected). The results are reported in table 3.4b.

The first cabinet in table 3.4b was also the last one under the traditional party system (Arter 1999). The Social Democratic cabinet relied on support from the Socialist People's Party to form a majority in crucial divisions, but it based its defense and foreign policy on cooperation with the Liberals and Conservatives. The cabinet lost only one single final vote, confirming the traditional norms of Danish executive-legislative relations (Damgaard 1992). The Liberal cabinet that formed after the dramatic 1973 election commanded only 12 percent of the seats in parliament and had to struggle to survive. It clung onto power for roughly one year and lost five final votes (3.2 percent). The next two cabinets lost relatively few votes, but signs of change were evident again when a Social Democratic cabinet held office from 1979 to 1982. However, it was with the four-party minority coalition composed of the Conservatives, Liberals, Center Democrats, and Christian People's Party that relations between parliament and the cabinet changed markedly. Also, its two successors (1988–90, 1990–93) lost unusually many votes, whereas the four-party majority coalition (comprised of the Social Democrats, Radical Liberals, Center Democrats, and Christian People's Party) brought things back to normal. Its two successors (1994–96, 1996–2001) also lost relatively few votes. The Liberal-Conservative minority coalition that formed in 2001 with the support of the Danish People's Party did quite well in its first three years, losing less than 1 percent of final decisions. The average percentage of votes lost by cabinets during the whole period was 2.5 percent. It appears that cabinets with above-average losses were headed by Liberals or Conservatives, while those headed by Social Democrats suffered relatively fewer losses. One plausible explanation for this difference is that the Social Democrats have often been able to form legislative majorities not only with parties to the right but also with ones to the left, whereas, until recently, Liberal-Conservative cabinets have not had

TABLE 3.4b. Final Votes in the Danish Parliament in Which the Cabinet Was Not on the Winning Side, 1971–2004

Cabinet Period	Cabinet Party(ies)	Percentage not Winning[a]	(N)
1971–73	Social Democrats	0.2	423
1973–75	Liberals	3.2	155
1975–78	Social Democrats	0.5	965
1978–79	Social Democrats, Liberals	0.5	198
1979–82	Social Democrats	1.6	641
1982–88	Conservatives, Liberals, Christian People's Party, Center Democrats	8.0	1,356
1988–90	Conservatives, Liberals, Radical Liberals	4.2	574
1990–93	Conservatives, Liberals	6.5	635
1993–94	Social Democrats, Radical Liberals, Center Democrats, Christian People's Party	0.2	560
1994–96	Social Democrats, Radical Liberals, Center Democrats	0.5	666
1996–2001	Social Democrats, Radical Liberals	0.7	1,625
2001–4	Liberals, Conservatives	0.8	953
1971–2004	All	2.5	8,751

Source: Damgaard 1999, 49–70; Folketingstidende, Årbog og Registre (1996–97 through 2002–3); Folketing, archive (2003–4), http://www.ft.dk.
[a] Percentage not winning as percentage of total final votes on proposals (N).

that choice (Green-Pedersen 2001). Thus, it seems that some minority cabinets have had more bargaining power than others.

Another indicator of the strength of noncabinet parties versus cabinet parties is the degree to which cabinet bills are amended in the legislative process. A study by Damgaard and Jensen (2006) shows that both the cabinet and opposition parties try to change cabinet bills. Somewhat surprisingly, the cabinet is more active than the opposition in this respect. In fact, amendments moved by the cabinet constitute more than half of the amendments to its own bills. The study also demonstrates that the success rate of amendments moved by the cabinet is almost 100 percent, whereas it is less than 10 percent for amendments proposed by opposition parties.

These findings may be interpreted in two different ways. First, note that about every other cabinet bill is amended during its readings in the Folketing. Thus, not only before but also after it has introduced a bill, the cabinet must consider the views of opposition parties if it wants to minimize the risk of having its legislation defeated or amended. A second important observation is that more than 95 percent of the bills and amendments passed have been introduced by the cabinet. Part of the explanation is that the Folketing is unable to draft, adopt, and implement bills independently of the cabinet. It simply lacks the necessary legal expertise and insight. Such expertise and knowledge is much more readily available in cabinet ministries. That explains why executives (even minority cabinets) have the upper hand in lawmaking, although they must pay considerable attention to opposition parties to get their legislative proposals enacted.

If a minority cabinet wants to avoid defeats in parliamentary voting, it must be sure that a majority voting coalition exists before the final vote is taken. Although party competition for cabinet office is fierce, the parties that win that game do not necessarily win in the full sense of the term, and the losers have not necessarily lost everything. It is therefore interesting to examine the party composition of such legislative voting coalitions. This has been done on the basis of data collected for two recent cabinet periods (1998–2001 and 2001–4) of roughly equal length and with different cabinets and support arrangements. During 1998–2001, a Social Democratic–Radical Liberal cabinet held office with support from left-wing parties. During 2001–4, a Liberal-Conservative coalition cabinet held office with the support of the Danish People's Party. A winning voting coalition is defined as the group of parties voting "yes" if a proposal is adopted and "no" if it is rejected. All types of formal proposals are included: bills, draft resolutions, and proposed decisions. To simplify a complex world, the winning voting coalitions were reduced to five main types: all parties, cabinet parties and parties to their left and right, cabinet parties and support parties, cabinet parties without support parties, and alternative majorities (see table 3.4c).

It appears that about one-fourth of the proposals voted on were decided unanimously in the final decisions and that almost one-half of them were decided by a broad majority comprised of cabinet parties as well as parties to their left and right. These findings do not seem to leave much room for more controversial outcomes. Still, about 30 percent of outcomes were decided by other party combinations. In the periods studied, "alternative majorities" did not play a significant role at all, although they did so in previous periods when support arrangements were more complex. However, there is a clear difference between the two cabinets in terms of the extent to which their majorities were based on support parties as compared to other parties in parliament. Thus, the average percentage (about 14 percent) for the full period hides the fact that the Liberal-Conservative cabinet based its legislative winning coalitions on its support party to a higher extent than the Social Democratic–Radical Liberal cabinet—about 20 percent compared to about 10.

As already indicated, the Folketing makes three kinds of formal decisions (other than procedural matters): acts of parliament, resolutions, and decisions. Once adopted, bills are legally binding laws. Resolutions are only politically binding on ministers. The same is true of "decisions" that conclude debates on interpellations. Table 3.4d provides data on these three types of proposals and shows that there are considerable differences between winning coalitions in the three categories. All-party coalitions are more likely in voting on bills than on resolutions and decisions, and there

TABLE 3.4c. Winning Parliamentary Coalitions in Denmark by Cabinet Period and Final Votes on All Proposals

Winning Coalition	Social Democrats and Radical Liberals (1998–2001)	Liberal and Conservative (2001–2004)	Both Cabinets (1998–2004)
All parties	23.3	24.7	24.0
Cabinet and parties to its left and right	46.5	46.6	46.6
Cabinet and support parties	10.1	18.6	14.1
Cabinet without support parties	19.5	9.2	14.7
Alternative majority	0.7	0.8	0.7
N	1,073	954	2,027

Source: Data from Damgaard 1999, 49–70; Folketingstidende, Årbog og Registre (1996–97 through 2002–3); Folketing, archive, (2003–4), http://www.ft.dk.

Note: Numbers in table are percentages of total final votes on proposals (N).

is little variation between coalitions of the left versus those of the right. On the other hand, there are clear differences as regards winning coalitions composed of cabinet and support parties. This voting pattern, which can be considered a more confrontational one, is not very common in decisions about bills but is more likely on resolutions and decisions. This might help explain the findings of Kurrild-Klitgaard, Klemmensen, and Hansen (2006) that there are no major differences between the two cabinet periods in terms of "bloc politics." This result is based on their analysis of final voting on passed bills (i.e., legislation) only. Finally, table 3.4d shows that the biggest difference between the two cabinet periods concerns proposed decisions. The Liberal-Conservative cabinet relied heavily on its support party (40.8 percent), while the Social Democratic–Radical Liberal cabinet rarely did so (only 4.9 percent).

The state budget is formally treated as a normal bill, although it has actually become more important than most ordinary legislation. Simply stated, the basic difference is that the budget used to be passed as the (financial) consequences of legislative decisions already taken. From 1984, however, the procedure became "politicized."

In December 1983, the Social Democrats decided not to support the budget proposed for 1984. They did so on the grounds that they had had too

TABLE 3.4d. Winning Parliamentary Coalitions in Denmark by Type of Proposal and Cabinet Composition

Winning Coalition	Laws		Resolutions		Decisions	
	Social Democratic and Radical Liberal Cabinet	Liberal and Conservative Cabinet	Social Democratic and Radical Liberal Cabinet	Liberal and Conservative Cabinet	Social Democratic and Radical Liberal Cabinet	Liberal and Conservative Cabinet
All parties	29.0	31.0	13.1	13.3	10.9	12.5
Cabinet and parties to its left and right	46.6	49.8	42.6	45.0	50.0	35.5
Cabinet and support parties	6.9	12.5	28.4	20.6	4.9	40.8
Cabinet without support parties	17.1	6.4	14.2	17.8	33.7	10.5
Alternative majority	0.4	0.2	1.7	3.3	0.5	0.7
N	713	622	176	180	184	152

Source: Data from Damgaard 1999, 49–70; *Folketingstidende, Årbog og Registre* (1996–97 through 2002–3); Folketing, archive (2003–4), http://www.ft.dk.

Note: Numbers in table are percentages of total final votes on proposals (*N*).

little influence on the content of the bill and because there was a lack of support for the cabinet from other noncabinet parties. The budget proposal was thus rejected in parliament, and the cabinet called for a new election. Since that time, all (minority) cabinets have understood that they cannot count on budgetary support without explicit commitments from opposition parties. This means that the annual budget negotiations not only determine whether the budget bill will be passed but also involve handing out "prizes" to opposition parties in order to enlist their support in the final vote for the budget as a whole. Once concessions have been made to opposition parties and it is clear that the budget will be passed, the game is actually over. Some noncabinet parties may even give their support to the budget without agreeing on its content. In general, the cabinets of the Liberal-Conservative coalition and the Social Democratic–Radical Liberal coalition relied on budgetary support from their regular support parties. However, the finer details of interparty agreements on budgetary matters can be very complex. One interesting aspect of budgetary amendments is that the budget process does not simply sum up what has already been decided. It also sets part of the agenda for new legislation aimed at implementing the agreements already made. Therefore, the annual budget negotiations have become a battleground for parties aiming for cabinet office, policy influence, and votes.

Finally, table 3.5 provides a summary of the use of three forms of questioning in the Folketing. The figures refer to the total numbers, but all three forms are overwhelmingly used by noncabinet parties. Interpellations are the most serious form of questioning, because debate on them can conclude with the adoption of a decision criticizing a minister and/or the cabinet—ultimately in the shape of a no-confidence vote.

The number of interpellations has increased since the 1970s and particularly in the 1990s. Since the mid-1990s, the number of interpellation debates has been 60 to 70 per year. Ordinary questions (requesting either an oral or, most frequently, a written answer) have also increased substantially over time. In the most recent sessions, the number of such questions has been more than 5,000. Committee questions assumed increasing importance since 1972. The new, standing specialized committees were not limited to asking questions related to bills and resolutions under deliberation but were empowered to ask about literally any matter within the jurisdiction of a minister and committee. Formally, the committee as such asks the questions. In reality, however, the questions are asked by individual members of the committees (mainly those belonging to opposition parties; see Jensen 1995). In the early twenty-first century, the number of committee questions was 8,000 to 9,000 annually, although successful motions of no confidence are rare. There have been only two since 1945 (in 1947 and 1975), and in both cases, the cabinet resigned. However, such motions are always possible, and the right to put interpellations and other forms of questions to the cabinet are important instruments in the hands of members of parliament.

TABLE 3.5. Interpellations and Questions to Cabinet Ministers, Denmark, 1972–2007

Year	Interpellations	Questions	Committee Questions
1972–73	6	354	2,939
1973–74	6	476	2,222
1974–75	13	500	2,963
1975–76	23	804	3,357
1976–77	13	785	4,355
1977–78	28	1,231	4,290
1978–79	32	1,519	4,713
1979–80	22	1,252	5,507
1980–81	31	1,536	6,416
1981–82	27	1,469	5,892
1982–83	33	1,666	6,704
1983–84	29	1,483	5,859
1984–85	27	1,750	6,690
1985–86	33	1,775	7,443
1986–87	34	1,691	7,185
1987–88	46	1,324	6,814
1988–89	32	1,233	7,784
1989–90	33	1,231	8,356
1990–91	38	1,188	7,200
1991–92	27	1,151	6,950
1992–93	30	1,472	6,805
1993–94	43	1,878	5,470
1994–95	48	2,293	8,217
1995–96	52	3,699	8,401
1996–97	70	3,454	8,562
1997–98	65	3,078	8,417
1998–99	62	3,328	8,880
1999–2000	64	4,012	8,649
2000–2001	70	4,115	8,341
2001–2	63	3,810	7,916
2002–3	67	5,017	8,765
2003–4	60	5,635	9,478
2004–5	51	5,964	9,319
2005–6	45	7,194	8,806
2006–7	46	6,224	9,096

Source: Data from *Folketingstidende, Årbog og Registre* (2002–3); Secretariat of Law in the Danish Folketing.

Within the Cabinet

With respect to authority relationships within the cabinet, the prime minister has a small secretariat staffed by civil servants who attempt to monitor executive departments. However, the secretariat rarely interferes directly with department activities, because individual ministers are quite autonomous within their own jurisdictions. The PM chairs the weekly cabinet meeting, which deals with all important topics—if only to make sure that there is agreement on joint cabinet policy. Interministerial differences are normally sorted out before an item reaches a cabinet meeting. Agendas for cabinet meetings are set by the PM, who receives proposals from individual ministers. The decision rule applied in cabinet meetings is best described as "consensus as defined by the PM" (Damgaard 2003a). The development of European integration has affected the role of the PM in Denmark and other Scandinavian countries (Bergman and Damgaard 2000). The prevailing view is that EU membership has increased the power of the PM, reduced the power of the minister of foreign affairs (who previously was more clearly in charge of international relations), and increased the power of other affected ministers (who have obtained new international functions). The role of the PM has expanded as a result of the increasing number of meetings in the European Council (summits, intergovernmental conferences) devoted to the coordination of national policies that do not fit well into the traditional divisions of international and domestic policy.

Danish coalition cabinets are based on an expectation of coalition discipline in parliamentary voting. Members of cabinet parties always support the cabinet position in voting. Backbenchers sometimes deviate from the party line, but they are required to make their position known in advance, and they risk being sanctioned by their party leadership (Damgaard 1995). Discipline is also expected in all other important matters affecting coalition unity. Outside formal parliamentary proceedings, members of cabinet parties are freer to state views that include criticism of coalition politics and actions. In most cases, parties joining a coalition cabinet are free to appoint their own ministers once the number of positions and portfolios of each party have been agreed on. Formally, however, the prime minister must approve proposed ministers because they become members of "his" cabinet.

According to the constitution, the prime minister decides the number of ministers and the distribution of the executive duties among them. This implies that new ministries can be established and old ones abolished at any time and that the jurisdictions of ministries can be changed by executive decree. The number of ministries and jurisdictions might therefore be issues for coalition bargaining among the parties. These flexible rules facilitate agreements among the parties on portfolio distribution.

The number of ministries and cabinet members has increased over time, from about 15 to about 20. The difference between the number of ministries and of cabinet ministers is generally very small. Deviations can nonetheless occur if a cabinet member directs more than one ministry, if a ministry is somehow shared by two cabinet ministers, or if ministers without portfolios are appointed to the cabinet. The difference between the two numbers was particularly large during the Liberal single-party minority cabinet of 1973–75, which had only 22 members in parliament. The Liberal Party had a manpower shortage—it lacked "office capacity," to use Skjaeveland's (2003) expression—and several ministers were therefore put in charge of two ministries.

Denmark (like Finland and Iceland) has no junior ministers—that is, political appointees under the minister level with a formal position in the chain of command of the ministry. However, ministers can appoint people known as "special advisors" to assist them in roles that can be termed "political." In 2004, there were 14 such advisors, most of who were responsible for relations with the media (*Embedsmænds rådgivning og bistand* 2004).

Studies show that, with the exception of the Baunsgaard cabinet (1968–71), the leader of the largest coalition party is always appointed prime minister. The other parties receive a share of positions in rough proportion to their relative strength, usually with some overrepresentation of smaller parties. It is probably universally recognized that the offices of the prime minister, foreign affairs, and finance are the three most important ministries, but no uniform rank exists among the remaining (and changing) portfolios, and parties might have different preferences over the various cabinet positions. The Social Democrats, in addition to the position of prime minister, have always had the Ministry of Labor and almost always the Ministry of Social Welfare. The Liberals, with their strong links to the farming population, have always had the Ministry of Agriculture, and the Conservatives, with their ties to the business community, the Ministry of Trade and Industry. These allocations fit well with the traditional cleavages in Danish politics.

New data on the background of cabinet ministers at the time of their first appointment provide interesting information. The data refer to background characteristics of the prime minister ($N = 12$), the minister of finance ($N = 16$), the minister of foreign affairs ($N = 13$), and the minister of justice ($N = 17$) over the period 1945–2005 (see table 3.6). There is no real difference between the four types of ministers with regard to age. They

TABLE 3.6. Ministerial Background, First Appointment, by Portfolio, Denmark, 1945–2005

Portfolio within Cabinet	Age (mean years)	Female Ministers (%)	Prior Cabinet Position (%)	Parliamentary Experience (mean years)	Prior Party High-Rank Position (%)[b]	Prior Youth Party High-Rank Position (%)[c]	Major Prior Appointment within Parliament (%)[d]	Major Prior Elected Offices at Local/Regional Level (%)[e]	Formal Education Level[f]	Any Prior Employment within the Public Sector (%)[g]	Any Prior Employment within the Private Sector (%)	Any Prior Salaried Employment in Party (%)	Member of Parliament at the Time of Minister Appointment (%)[h]	N (unique number of ministers)
Prime minister	51.3	0	75	10.5	83	67	67	25	3.3	25	100	25	100	12
Finance[i] minister	48.3	0	75	7.6	56	44	31	25	3.8	44	94	19	94	16
Foreign minister	49.2	0	62	10.2	69	62	54	15	4.2	54	92	31	77	13
Justice[j] minister	51.1	24	53	8.8	47	35	53	35	4.8	71	76	18	94	17
Mean 1945–2005	50.0	6	66	9.1	62	50	51	26	4.1	50	90	22	91	58
Mean 1945–75	52.1	6	64	8.6	56	42	39	25	3.9	61	89	19	92	36
Mean 1991–2005	46.2	20	70	11.4	50	70	70	30	5.0	30	90	20	100	10

Source: Data from Kaarsted 1977, 1992; Rigsdagsårbogen (various years); Folketingsårbogen (various years); Folketinget efter valget (various years).

Note: All of the calculations presented in this section are based on a data set that contains data on ministers who got portfolios at the beginning of a new cabinet. A new cabinet is defined here as a cabinet that fulfills at least one of three conditions: any change in the set of parties holding cabinet membership, any change in the identity of the prime minister, or any general election (see Müller and Strøm 2003, 12).

[a]Prior parliamentary experience (in full years) does not include years that a person has been in cabinet. That is, for systems that allow for the holding of simultaneous cabinet and parliamentary positions, we only count "parliamentary experience" for the years that the MP does not also have a cabinet position. (The latter is coded as prior cabinet experience: yes or no.) If the total parliamentary experience (service as MP) sums to less than six months, it is counted as zero (0) years of experience.

[b]Prior party high-rank position refers to any of the following: party leader, party secretary, member of the party national board, or head of local or regional board.

[c]Prior youth party high-rank position refers to the positions in a youth organization corresponding to the prior party high-rank positions.

[d]Major prior appointment within parliament refers to any of the following: Speaker (president of parliament or chamber/subdivision), group leader, vice group leader, committee chairman, or vice committee chairman.

[e]Major prior elected offices at local/regional level refers to any of the following: head of municipality, head of region, member of local parliament, or member of regional parliament.

[f]Formal education level: 1 = primary (or less); 2 = secondary (high school, Swedish gymnasium); 3 = any enrollment in postsecondary education (such as technical college, nursing school, college, university) but no degree; 4 = any undergraduate degree at technical college, nursing school, college, or university (2–4 years in length) that is post–high school or post-gymnasium; 5 = postgraduate degree (licensiat, huvudfag, PhD).

[g]Prior employment refers to the employer, that is to say, the one paying the salary. Salary by the party does not include elected offices, only jobs (such as party ombudsman). The three categories (public, private, party) are not mutually exclusive categories (as they, in combination, speak to a minister's general career pattern). Private employment includes people employed in trade unions and other nongovernmental organizations.

[h]The coding, "Member of parliament at the time of minister appointment" only has one possible answer (yes or no).

[i]Finance minister is defined as the minister heading the ministry in control of the state budget.

[j]Justice minister is defined as the minister heading the ministry in control of the police force.

are all first appointed when they are about 50. So far, few women (to say the least) have held these positions in Denmark. The majority of ministers have had a prior cabinet position, especially the prime minister and the finance minister. The prime minister and foreign minister have had the highest seniority in parliament and the highest proportion of party positions, including positions in youth organizations. The justice minister has had the highest level of formal education, the prime minister the lowest. The same is true of prior employment in the public sector. Prior employment in the private sector is the reverse—prime ministers have had the most and justice ministers the least. We are dealing with small numbers, so these differences should not be overstated; however, the general impression from table 3.6 is that in the screening and recruitment process for these four ministerial posts, there are somewhat different qualifications in terms of education and political and administrative experience.

Table 3.6 divides information on the background of ministers into different time periods between 1945 and 2005. The first two columns show that in the second half of the post–World War II period, ministers were a bit younger when they were first appointed. There were also more female ministers appointed. Other background characteristics that become increasingly important are having a career in the youth party or in parliament. Comparing the second and third columns reveals that the former two background characteristics (young and female) remained important in the 1990s and 2000s. In the last period, the importance of previous partisan experience increased in terms of both youth party and parliamentary experience.

Cabinet Termination and Performance

If cabinet formation and governance are important phenomena in the chain of delegation and accountability, the same is true for termination and the electoral performance of cabinets. It is well known that governing parties tend to lose votes in elections. This is confirmed in table 3.7, which shows that two-thirds of the cabinets in office at the time of elections (16 of 24) lost votes, but the pattern is far from uniform.

At the polls, single-party (minority) cabinets are more often punished than rewarded (in 6 of 9 cases), but on some occasions they have made big gains (in 1947, 1974, and 1977). A remarkable finding concerning coalition cabinets is that all the participating parties are never rewarded at the same time. The result of the 1979 election appears to contradict this statement, but the two cabinet parties (Social Democrats and Liberals) had actually split up before the election. Conversely, there are cases in which all coalition parties are punished (in 1964 and 1971), but most of the time, voters reward some and punish others. Looking at individual parties, the Liberals have fared best with respect to electoral support when in cabinet (with gains in 8 out of 12 cases). Despite this, the safest bet is that a party entering the cabinet will lose votes at the next election. The three majority coalitions (facing their first elections in 1960, 1971, and 1994, respectively) all lost their majority at the polls.

TABLE 3.7. Electoral Performance of Incumbent Cabinet Parties, Denmark, 1945–2008

Cabinet Number	Cabinet Composition	Election Year following Cabinet	SD	CD	RL	CPP	JP	Con	Lib	Cabinet Total
1	Lib 1945	1947							+4.2	+4.2
2	SD 1947	1950	−0.4							−0.4
4	Lib, Con 1950	1953I						−0.5	+0.8	+0.3
5	Lib, Con 1953	1953II						−0.5	+1.0	+0.5
7	SD 1955	1957	−1.9							−1.9
9	SD, RL, JP 1960	1960	+2.7		−2.0		−3.1			−2.4
11	SD, RL 1962	1964	−0.2		−0.5					−0.7
12	SD 1964	1966	−3.7							−3.7
13	SD 1966	1968	−4.0							−4.0
14	RL, Con, Lib 1968	1971			−0.6			−3.7	−3.0	−7.3
16	SD 1972	1973	−11.7							−11.7
17	Lib 1973	1974							+11.0	+11.0
18	SD 1975	1977	+7.1							+7.1
20	SD, Lib 1978	1979	+1.3						+0.5	+1.8
21	SD 1979	1981	−5.4							−5.4
23	Con, Lib, CD, CPP 1982	1984		−3.7		+0.4		+8.9	+0.8	+6.4
24	Con, Lib, CD, CPP 1984	1987		+0.2		−0.3		−2.6	−1.6	−4.3
25	Con, Lib, CD, CPP 1987	1988		−0.1		−0.4		−1.5	+1.3	−0.7
26	Con, Lib, RL 1988	1990			−2.1			−3.3	+4.0	−1.4
28	SD, RL, CD, CPP 1993	1994	−2.8	−2.3	+1.1	−0.4				−4.4
30	SD, RL 1996	1998	+1.3		−0.7					+0.6
31	SD, RL 1998	2001	−6.8		+1.3					−5.5
32	Lib, Con 2001	2005						+1.2	−2.2	−1.0
33	Lib, Con 2005	2007						+0.1	−2.7	−1.3
Mean gains/losses			−1.9	−1.5	−0.5	−0.2	−3.1	−0.2	+1.2	−1.0

Source: Data from Damgaard 2000b; *Folketinget efter valget 8* (February 2005); *Politiken.dk,* http://politiken.dk/politik/article427836.ece (accessed February 2, 2008).

Notes: See the notes to table 3.1 for explanation of party labels. An election was called in December 1974, but the election was not held until January 9, 1975. Numbers given in table represent percentage of national vote.

General Analysis of the Parliament-Cabinet Relationship

There is clear evidence that new practices in Danish parliament-executive relationships have developed since the early 1980s (Damgaard and Svensson 1989; Damgaard 1992, 2003b). One such practice is that cabinets have stayed in office even if they were defeated in parliament on important issues, provided that a parliamentary majority did not explicitly request their resignation. A second development is that, in order to survive, cabinets have had to make sure in advance that the budget bill would not be defeated. All cabinets have been required to make deals with opposition parties to ensure the passage of their budgets. Third, the idea and practice of an "alternative majority" (not including cabinet parties) developed in the 1980s. This refers to the fact that a group of opposition parties commanding a majority can—in effect—"govern" while the cabinet is effectively in "opposition" to the noncabinet parties. Although this dual system of parliamentary government was most pronounced in the 1980s, it still occurs in less dramatic forms. The system seems to be exceptional in a comparative perspective. It does not appear to have been described or analyzed in the literature, although it is known that cabinets in several countries, including the UK, sometimes or even often lose a vote in parliament.

Motions of no confidence are rarely proposed, and only two have been adopted since 1945. Nevertheless, they are important as an omnipresent possibility and therefore function through the rule of "anticipated reaction." As a counterbalancing force to possible motions of no confidence, the cabinet has the right to dissolve parliament at almost any time and to announce any legislative decision to be a vote of confidence in the cabinet. However, the PM must pay attention to the views of possible coalition partners, because, in practice, the cabinet must agree on dissolution if its parties want to continue their cooperation. Most Danish elections are called well before the end of the four-year constitutional election period. The fact that the "agent" can dismiss the "principal" is in keeping with Westminster practice but not really with the general notion of delegation and accountability in a hierarchical ideal-typical parliamentary democracy.

The Danish parliament has a great number of ex post control instruments at its disposal, ranging from innocent questions by members of parliamentary committees to very serious interpellations with the possibility for a lethal motion of no confidence. First, the Folketing can request various kinds of reports from the cabinet. Its members can demand and expect answers to written and oral questions in parliamentary committees and plenary sessions. Committee members can also demand the presence of cabinet ministers in committees for so-called "consultations." Weekly sessions with oral questions and unprepared answers were introduced in 1997. Quasi-judicial commissions of inquiry to deal with possible "scandals" have been quite frequent since the 1980s. The Folketing can also use a number of external institutions and actors as third parties in controlling the cabinet. Two good examples are the ombudsman and the National Auditing Office, both of which are independent in the performance of their tasks but report to the Folketing. Even written or personal communication with citizens, firms, and organizations can play a role in the work of parliamentary committees, as can new forms of hearings in committees and more traditional forms of bill-drafting commissions and hearings organized by the cabinet with experts and interested parties. Finally, interest organizations and the mass media often contribute with information that can be useful to members of parliament (Damgaard 2003b, chap. 7).

Two trends are evident concerning ex post parliamentary control of the cabinet. First, the Folketing has more instruments at its disposal than previously, because of new devices like committee hearings, new forms of questions, and commissions of inquiry. Second, several control instruments are used to a greater extent than in the past, such as questions with written answers, questions in committees, committee hearings, consultation with ministers, and commissions of inquiry. All instruments of control are available at any time, although their use and potential effects are obviously greatest during periods of minority rule.

This review suggests that the relationship between parliament and cabinet in Denmark appears to be quite different from the one described in the Westminster model. Anthony King's classic analysis of different modes of executive-legislative relations can help us understand the difference. King (1976) was interested in the kind of relationship between cabinets and parliament that is most important for cabinet survival. In the UK, this is not the relationship between the cabinet and opposition parties but, rather, intraparty relations within the governing majority party. For Germany, King concluded that an interparty mode of relationship is crucial, because in that country, bargaining among political parties determines which parties will combine to form and sustain a cabinet. Interparty executive-legislative relations are also crucial in the five Scandinavian countries, although in two different ways. King (1976, 32) deliberately did not deal with minority cabinets. However, minority cabinets have become the rule in Denmark, Norway, and Sweden, and they create a situation that requires almost constant bargaining among governing and opposition parties. By contrast, Icelandic and Finnish cabinets have been based on majority coalitions that are able to rely on their own votes in policy-making (Damgaard 2000c). It remains to be seen whether the current majority coalitions in Norway and Sweden will be a more lasting phenomenon (Christiansen and Damgaard 2008).

Between the Cabinet and Civil Servants

Traditional Danish administrative philosophy states that a cabinet minister is responsible for his or her executive department. While the minister might not be personally responsible for mistakes made by civil servants, ministerial accountability is the basic norm. There is a direct line of command from the minister downward through the administrative bureaucracy. Higher-level civil servants are appointed by the minister, with the support of his or her cabinet colleagues in the cabinet's committee on appointments. Ministers are therefore in a position to control the careers of top civil servants. Civil servants are usually recruited on the basis of merit, which normally requires a university degree in law, economics, or political science, although special agencies may require more technical degrees. Promotions are also granted on the basis of merit. Civil servants are supposed to be politically neutral and to report only to their own minister.

It is unanimously agreed that ministers in the modern world need pertinent political advice and practical assistance. They must therefore delegate tasks to an agent capable of providing the services required. A device used almost universally in this regard is reliance on politically appointed secretaries of state, junior ministers, vice ministers, or similar arrangements. However, this solution has never been adopted in Denmark, despite many proposals and debates on the topic in recent decades. In fact, it seems that ministers have not really wanted the appointment of junior ministers or the like, and civil servants have consistently opposed such an idea. Hence, the services required by the ministers have had to be provided in other ways.

Two main solutions have been relied on. The first is that regular civil servants have accepted or perhaps preferred to play an expanded role in relation to their minister. Civil servants not only work, in the classic way, as neutral, nonpolitical, impartial bureaucrats giving technical and unbiased advice to the minister in their areas of expertise. They also act as advisors to the minister in what are called "political-tactical" matters (*Forholdet mellem minister og embedsmænd* 1998; *Embedsmænds rådgivning og bistand* 2004). The ministers have been quite satisfied with this development, although it has not solved all their problems of advice and assistance. There is still some debate as to whether the expanded role of civil servants has resulted in an unintended and unwanted politicization of the bureaucracy, although the dominant view is that it has not.

The second solution is the introduction of "special advisors" to ministers in staff (not line) functions—particularly with tasks relating to the management of mass media relations, which regular civil servants cannot really take care of. Despite the fact that the number of special advisors remains quite small (14 as of 2004), the development has created much debate about what is perceived to be a deplorable increase in spin-doctoring. An expert committee reviewing the experience since 1998 concluded that the debate had been dramatized compared to actual developments. It also noted that the number of politically appointed civil servants (special advisers) was significantly higher in Norway, Sweden, and the UK than in Denmark: "Whereas the number in the first three countries is between 59 and 139, there are . . . only a total of 14 special advisers in Denmark" (*Embedsmænds rådgivning og bistand* 2004, 275). But, one might add, there are also no secretaries of state or junior ministers (with authority to give instructions) in Denmark.

Both of these developments point to an important change in ministerial control of appointments and promotions of civil servants (ex ante control). Ministers have become more assertive in terms of appointments, and they use their powers much more than in the past, although high-level appointments to regular positions still have to be confirmed by a special cabinet committee. It has even been suggested that civil servants have, for career reasons, become almost subservient to the minister, which is the opposite of the traditional allegation about bureaucratic influence. It seems safe to conclude that ministerial control of appointments and promotions in the civil service has increased over the last few decades (Christensen 1999a; Damgaard 2003b, chap. 8).

Many of the ex post control instruments mentioned with regard to relations between parliament and cabinet are also important in relations between ministers and civil servants. Thus, ministerial reports and answers to questions in parliament concern civil servants with delegated powers in relevant areas, as well as the responsible ministers. This also applies to commissions of inquiry investigating "scandals" and to critical reports by the ombudsman and the National Auditing Office, as well as to complaints from interest organizations, the mass media, and so on. In sum, while ministerial control of civil servants may still involve problems, it has certainly not become weaker in recent years.

External Constraints

It can be argued that changes concerning institutions and actors external to the chain of governance are just as important for the development of parliamentary democracy as changes within the chain of delegation and accountability. This section briefly reviews several such changes. It should be kept in mind that while "constraints" might limit the scope for political action, they might also provide opportunities of influence for particular interests.

Interest Organizations

Denmark is traditionally considered to be a corporatist country in which affected interests are routinely integrated into the preparation and implementation of policies, especially within the areas of the labor market, agriculture, and industry. Another example of an influential organization is the association of local governments (Kommunernes Landsforening), which represents the components of the comparatively decentralized local government system in Denmark (Blom-Hansen 2002).

While interest organizations are still important actors, several studies and surveys of the field have found them to be somewhat less influential than they were in the first decades of the postwar period (Damgaard 2003b, chap. 3). The most comprehensive study (Christiansen and Nørgaard 2003) confirms that general development since the 1980s. Today, there is more openness and pluralism than there used to be. MPs are less concerned about the power of interest groups than they were some 20 years ago. However, Christiansen and Nørgaard note that the development has led to increased inequality among interest groups. The groups that are strong in terms of members and money are also those with the closest relations to civil servants in the central administration and to members of the Folketing. The labor unions in particular have been hurt by a decline in membership since the 1990s, whereas the unions of white-collar workers (Funktionæres og Tjenstemændenes Fællesrad) and of university graduates (Akademikernes Centralorganisation) have been able to keep their members.

There have also been interesting developments concerning the general representation of interest organizations in public committees (Christiansen and Nørgaard 2003). This kind of representation refers to the formalized integration of interest groups into national administration through membership on committees, councils, or commissions. The tasks of such committees vary from giving advice during the preparation of legislation to participation in their administrative implementation. The number of public committees increased over time, reaching a peak of about 715 around 1980. This was followed by a sharp decline in the following decade, resulting in fewer than 400 committees by the mid-1990s (although there was an upward turn around 2000 to about 500 committees). Nonetheless, interest organizations have continued to be represented in public committees. In the early period, they had members on slightly more than every second committee; more recently, the figure has been roughly three of four committees. Thus, interest groups have become better represented on fewer committees.

The EU and the International Dimension

Small countries like Denmark cannot possibly be fully "sovereign" in any meaningful sense. Therefore, the constitution (of 1953) provides for the delegation of powers to "international authorities set up by mutual agreements with other states for the promotion of international rules of law and co-operation." From a Danish constitutional point of view, the powers delegated to the European Community (EC/EU) on several occasions since 1972 are revocable, since a law can be passed that simply recalls these powers. In practice, however, that would entail enormous political, economic, and social costs. As long as unanimity was the dominant method of decision making in the Council of Ministers, delegation did not need to be a problem, provided that the Danish system of control and accountability worked as it should. With the increasing use of qualified majority voting, however, there is an increasing risk that member states could become losers in the process of voting. Yet they can also be on the winning side in the making of decisions on matters that no single country can effectively handle on their own (Damgaard and Nørgaard 2000).

The issues of EU membership and European integration have always divided Danish voters and parties (see "Referendums" following). However, the enlargement to 27 EU member states, as well as the defeat of the EU Constitutional Treaty in France and the Netherlands, has temporarily put the issue of the EU on standby. More recently, the Lisbon Treaty has also faced difficulties.

The Courts

Danish courts have traditionally been cautious about interfering in political matters (Alivizatos 1995). It was generally assumed that courts could rule on the constitutionality of specific pieces of legislation, but they hesitated to overrule a law. This behavior has changed somewhat in recent years

(Damgaard 2003b, chap. 4; Sørensen 2003). A small step in the direction of judicial activism was taken in 1996 when the Supreme Court (surprisingly) allowed a group of citizens to sue the PM for having signed the Maastricht Treaty, which, they claimed, violated the constitution. The PM was acquitted (in 1998), but the Court emphasized that it alone had the authority to decide on the constitutionality of laws. In 1999, for the first time, the Supreme Court overruled a law (in the so-called Tvind case), stating that it was not compatible with the constitutional separation of powers. Additional cases of judicial review are likely to come up in the future.

Two other developments have also tended to increase the political role of the courts. One is court involvement in matters of human rights in accordance with international conventions, not least the European Convention on Human Rights, which has been incorporated into Danish law. The other is a reform of the judicial system (effective in 1999) to buttress the independence of the courts as "the third state power." The reform introduced new rules for the appointment of judges in order to broaden the basis of recruitment and transferred the management of the courts from the Ministry of Justice to the independent Court Administration. However, some of these changes had actually been under way within the old system (Christensen 2003).

The Central Bank

Various ratings rank the independence of the Danish central bank, Nationalbanken, fairly high compared with most other central banks (Bernhard 1998; Lijphart 1999). According to Danish authors, its influence was particularly high during the 1980s (*Dansk Økonomi* 1985; Jensen 1989; Marcussen 2000; Damgaard 2003b, chap. 4). It was successful in promoting a new monetary regime, including fixed exchange rates, as well as liberalization of capital flows and a more market-oriented economy in general. Such changes had been resisted by previous Social Democratic cabinets but were welcomed by the incoming Liberal-Conservative cabinets of the 1980s. Today, there is a near consensus on the new economic regime. The central bank continues to give regular advice to cabinets on economic policies. Nationalbanken presents itself as a real "independent central bank," and it is a strong supporter of Danish membership in the European Monetary Union, which was defeated in a referendum in 2000. Thus, just as the courts have displayed a degree of "judicial activism," one might suggest that the central bank has displayed a degree of "financial activism," at least in the 1980s. Since 2008, the bank has also been an important actor in the attempts to manage the ongoing global economic crisis.

Independent State Enterprises

In keeping with the new economic regime previously mentioned, there has been a growth in the number of public corporations organized in accordance with Danish company law, with the central government owning all or part of the shares. The same is true of public enterprises with their own boards of directors. From 1975 to 1995, the number of enterprises organized in these two ways increased from 41 to 85. In addition, some genuine privatizations occurred during the same period (Christensen 1999b) and later. Overall, these developments represent a shift from hierarchical government to market governance. In the present context, it is crucial that ministers do not control the day-to-day activities of such independent state enterprises, although they are often blamed or held accountable if something goes wrong. Independent state enterprises are thus located in a gray zone between state and market, and there is an ongoing debate about how (if at all) one can get the best of both worlds (cf. Christiansen 1996; Greve 2000, 2002; Christensen and Pallesen 2001).

Referendums

Danish voters do not delegate all their power to parliament. In certain situations, they can act as a veto player through the use of referendums. The constitution requires that the electorate make the final decision concerning changes in voting age, constitutional amendments, and delegation of powers to international authorities if a bill delegating power is passed in parliament by a majority smaller than five-sixths of all MPs. In addition, decisive referendums on bills passed in parliament, with certain exceptions (including taxation), can be organized at the request of one-third of the MPs. This means that defeated parliamentary minorities can, in some cases, appeal to the electorate to veto bills that have been passed before they enter into force. Finally, parliament can order consultative referendums (not mentioned in the constitution) if a law to that effect is adopted. Danish voters, however, have no right to initiate referendums.

A total of 16 referendums have been held since 1953. In half of these cases, voters disagreed with a parliamentary majority. With only one exception, all referendums since 1972 have concerned relations to the EC/EU. These took place in 1972, 1986, 1992, 1993, 1998, and 2000. More EU referendums are to be expected in the years to come. While 16 referendums over 50 years might not seem to be very many, the very possibility of a referendum influences the behavior of parties. Even legislative majorities must consider its use in any particular situation. Today, the EU issue in particular creates problems in the representational link between voters and MPs.

The Mass Media

Journalists and the mass media have become much more independent of political parties and political institutions than they were in the first decades of the postwar period. The old four-party newspaper system (one paper for each of the four old parties in major towns) gradually broke down in the first two decades after 1945, a process that culminated toward the end of the 1990s. Newspapers directed by and loyal to a party simply do not exist anymore.

Most studies on the current role of the mass media (e.g., Krogh 1998; Hjarvard 1999; Lund, Jensen, and Marosi 2001; Lund 2002; Damgaard 2003b, chap. 3) agree that the media influence political agenda setting and the selection of individuals heard in the public debate. Politicians have to play according to the norms established by the media and generally deplore the influence of journalists. They are no longer in control of the agenda but are forced to adjust to the needs and priorities of the media if they want to be noticed and to influence political developments. The importance of the mass media is reinforced by the high level of competition among numerous political parties. As previously mentioned, ministers have tried to control news stories by employing spin doctors, although not with overwhelming success.

Summing Up

Although Denmark is a small, unitary, and fairly homogeneous state, it is well equipped with external constraints on the parliamentary chain of governance. It is important to keep in mind that external constraints not only limit the behavior of parliamentary principals and agents. Some of them may also provide benefits to such actors. For example, one study showed that MPs found interest groups to be quite useful, not least because of the information they provide. Even the mass media were given credit for raising questions and problems that parliamentarians must address (Damgaard 2003b, chap. 3). Further, the role of the courts supports the rule of law and the rights of citizens. It may also be argued that the central bank assists both parliament and cabinet with advice on sound economic policies. However, even if independent state enterprises may relieve ministers of time-consuming operational tasks, they also seem to create problems of democratic accountability. While the EU clearly limits the powers of the member states, it also creates a collective capacity to deal with issues that states cannot possibly take care of with their own resources. Finally, while referendums do not square well with the delegation and accountability that are typically found in representative democracies, they are certainly important instruments of democracy in a broader sense.

Conclusion

Deparliamentarization and party decline are well-known themes in Denmark. In fact, the suspicion that parties and parliament had declined over the past few decades was the main reason a committee in the Folketing authorized a study of Danish democracy and power (Togeby et al. 2003; Damgaard 2003b). What does the analysis presented here show about these two themes and the influence of external constraints?

The evidence is a bit mixed concerning a decline in "partyness" since the 1970s. On the one hand, parties have steadily lost members since the 1960s. On the other, several indicators of party attachment demonstrate that there is no reason for serious concern: high and stable turnout, a stable level of party identification, a decline of class voting, and declining political distrust. We do find some intraparty changes over time. These largely have to do with increased rank-and-file member influence over nominations and a concomitant weakened control by party organizations. In addition, widespread use of intraparty preference voting has clearly given voters more influence on the personal composition of the Folketing. While the old system of lists with party-ranked candidates hardly exists anymore, this does not constitute a democratic problem in a broader sense. The overall conclusion must therefore be that while there have been changes and challenges for established parties to cope with, they give no major reasons for democratic concerns. That the parties have fewer members means less income, but the introduction of generous state subsidies compensates for that. On the whole, parliamentary parties are still important actors in almost all steps of the chain of delegation and accountability.

The analysis also shows that minority cabinets continue to be "the rule" in Denmark. The Danish form of negative parliamentarism facilitates the formation of minority cabinets. It also means that, in most cases, cabinets can be formed quite rapidly, and they are less durable than majority cabinets if they lack stable external support. As a result of minority governance, parliamentary majorities must be built with the participation of noncabinet parties, as regards budget making, lawmaking, and resolutions, as well as other parliamentary decisions. Opposition parties derive strength from the minority position of cabinets, and they have several instruments available for controlling cabinet behavior. MPs have more instruments at their disposal than previously, and they use them to a greater extent than before.

Of course, there are limits to the influence of noncabinet parties. Opposition parties lack the judicial and technical expertise required to draft legislation. They are dependent on the cabinet if major policy changes are to be made. Meanwhile, any minority cabinet must anticipate the reaction of opposition parties in order to build parliamentary majorities. Finally, one should note that cabinet ministers apparently have increased their control over civil servant appointments and promotions over the past few decades.

On balance, it is reasonable to conclude that the Danish parliament has not declined relative to the executive branch in its capacity to influence policy-making. The main reason is that Danish minority cabinets need the votes of one or more opposition parties to enact their legislation. A future majority coalition could therefore change this situation.

These conclusions on the roles and influence of parties and parliament may seem rather optimistic (Christiansen and Togeby 2006). An important final question, therefore, is whether the impact of various changes in the roles of external constraints—such as interest groups, the mass media, the courts, the central bank, independent state enterprises, the EU, and referendums—might change or modify the picture. Overall, Denmark is well equipped with external constraints that clearly limit the actions of parties and parliament. However, the developments we observe as regards the salience of these constraints are not uniform. In fact, the most conspicuous finding probably is that the evolution of these constraints does not paint a homogeneous picture. In addition, what looks like increasing limitations on the actions of the people's representatives can also create opportunities for new interests without damaging the influence of parties and parliament in the democratic chain of delegation and accountability.

REFERENCES

Aarbog og registre. Various years. Copenhagen: Folketinget.
Alivizatos, Nicos C. 1995. "Judges as Veto Players." In Herbert Döring, ed., *Parliaments and Majority Rule in Western Europe.* Frankfurt: Campus Verlag.
Andersen, Johannes, and Jørgen Goul Andersen. 2003. "Klassernes forsvinden." In Jørgen Goul Andersen and Ole Borre, eds., *Politisk forandring.* Århus: Systime.
Andersen, Johannes, and Ole Borre. 2003. "Synet på den demokratiske proces." In Jørgen Goul Andersen and Ole Borre, eds., *Politisk forandring.* Århus: Systime.

Arter, David. 1999. *Scandinavian Politics Today*. Manchester: Manchester University Press.

Bergman, Torbjörn. 1995. *Constitutional Rules and Party Goals in Coalition Formation*. PhD diss., Umeå University, Department of Political Science.

Bergman, Torbjörn, and Erik Damgaard, eds. 2000. *Delegation and Accountability in European Integration: The Nordic Parliamentary Democracies and the European Union*. London: Frank Cass.

Bernhard, William. 1998. "A Political Explanation of Variations in Central Bank Independence." *American Political Science Review* 92 (2): 311–27.

Bille, Lars. 1993. "Candidate Selection for National Parliament in Denmark, 1960–1990." In Tom Bryder, ed., *Party Systems, Party Behavior, and Democracy*. Copenhagen: Copenhagen Political Studies Press.

Bille, Lars. 1997. *Partier i forandring: En analyse af danske partiorganisationers udvikling 1960–1995*. Odense: Odense Universitetsforlag.

Bille, Lars. 2003. "Den danske partimodels forfald?" In Lars Bille and Jørgen Elklit, eds., *Partiernes medlemmer*. Århus: Aarhus Universitetsforlag.

Bille, Lars, and Jørgen Elklit, eds. 2003. *Partiernes medlemmer*. Århus: Aarhus Universitetsforlag.

Blom-Hansen, Jens. 2002 *Den fjerde statsmagt? Kommunernes Landsforening i dansk politik*. Århus: Aarhus Universitetsforlag.

Borre, Ole. 1984. "Træk af den danske vælgeradfærd 1971–1984." In Jørgen Elklit and Ole Tonsgaard, eds., *Valg og vælgeradfærd*. Århus: Politica.

Borre, Ole. 1999. "Gammel og ny venstre-højre ideologi." In Jørgen Goul Andersen et al., *Vælgere med omtanke*. Århus: Systime.

Borre, Ole. 2003a. "To konfliktdimensioner." In Jørgen Goul Andersen and Ole Borre, eds., *Politisk forandring*. Århus: Systime.

Borre, Ole. 2003b. "Træk af den danske vælgeradfærd 1971–2001." In Andre Wang Hansen et al., eds., *Topforskning fra Århus Universitet—en jubilæumsantologi*. Århus: Aarhus Universitetsforlag.

Borre, Ole, and Jørgen Goul Andersen. 1997. *Voting and Political Attitudes in Denmark*. Århus: Aarhus University Press.

Christensen, Jens Peter. 2003. *Domstolene—den tredje statsmagt*. Århus: Magtudredningen, Institut for Statskundskab.

Christensen, Jørgen Grønnegård. 1999a. "Political Responsiveness in a Merit Bureaucracy." Paper, Department of Political Science, Aarhus University.

Christensen, Jørgen Grønnegård. 1999b. "Statslige selskaber og privatisering." *Nordisk Administrativt Tidsskrift* 80 (3): 175–99.

Christensen, Jørgen Grønnegård, and Thomas Pallesen. 2001. "Institutions, Distributional Concerns, and Public Sector Reforms." *European Journal of Political Research* 39 (2): 179–202.

Christiansen, Flemming Juul, and Erik Damgaard. 2008. "Parliamentary Opposition under Minority Parliamentarism: Scandinavia." *Journal of Legislative Studies* 14 (1–2): 46–76.

Christiansen, Peter Munk. 1996. "Magt uden ansvar? Offentlig institutionsdrift i nye organisationsformer." *Politica* 28 (3): 271–85.

Christiansen, Peter Munk, Birgit Møller, and Lise Togeby. 2001. *Den danske elite*. Copenhagen: Hans Reitzels Forlag.

Christiansen, Peter Munk, and Asbjørn Sonne Nørgaard. 2003. *Faste forhold— flygtige forbindelser: Stat og interesseorganisationer i det 20. århundrede*. Århus: Aarhus Universitetsforlag.

Christiansen, Peter Munk, and Lise Togeby. 2006. "Power and Democracy in Denmark: Still a Viable Democracy." *Scandinavian Political Studies* 29 (1): 1–24.

Damgaard, Erik. 1977. *Folketinget under forandring*. Copenhagen: Samfundsvidenskabeligt Forlag.

Damgaard, Erik. 1992. "Denmark: Experiments in Parliamentary Government." In Erik Damgaard, ed., *Parliamentary Change in the Nordic Countries*. Oslo: Scandinavian University Press.

Damgaard, Erik. 1995. "How Parties Control Committee Members." In Herbert Döring, ed., *Parliaments and Majority Rule in Western Europe*. Frankfurt: Campus Verlag; New York: St. Martin's Press.

Damgaard, Erik. 1999. "Parlamentarismens udvikling." In Ole Stig Andersen et al., eds., *Folketingets festskrift I anledning af grundlovens 150-års jubilæum den 5. juni 1999*. Copenhagen: Folketingets Præsidium.

Damgaard, Erik. 2000a. "Denmark: The Life and Death of Government Coalitions." In Wolfgang C. Müller and Kaare Strøm, eds., *Coalition Governments in Western Europe*. Oxford: Oxford University Press.

Damgaard, Erik. 2000b. "Minority Governments." In Lauri Karvonen and Krister Ståhlberg, eds., *Festschrift for Dag Anckar*. Åbo: Åbo Akademi University Press.

Damgaard, Erik. 2000c. "Parliament and Government." In Peter Esaiasson and Knut Heidar, eds., *Beyond Westminster and Congress: The Nordic Experience*. Columbus: Ohio State University Press.

Damgaard, Erik. 2003a. "Denmark: Delegation and Accountability in Minority Situations." In Kaare Strøm, Wolfgang C. Müller, and Torbjörn Bergman, eds., *Delegation and Accountability in Parliamentary Democracies*. Oxford: Oxford University Press.

Damgaard, Erik. 2003b. *Folkets styre: Magt og ansvar i dansk politik*. Århus: Aarhus Universitetsforlag.

Damgaard, Erik, and Henrik Jensen. 2006. "Assessing Strength and Weakness in Legislatures: The Case of Denmark." *Journal of Legislative Studies* 12 (3–4): 426–42.

Damgaard, Erik, and Asbjørn Sonne Nørgaard. 2000. "The European Union and Danish Parliamentary Democracy." In Torbjörn Bergman and Erik Damgaard, eds., *Delegation and Accountability in European Integration*. London: Frank Cass.

Damgaard, Erik, and Palle Svensson. 1989. "Who Governs? Parties and Policies in Denmark." *European Journal of Political Research* 17 (6): 731–45.

Dansk Økonomi. September 1985. Copenhagen: Akademisk Forlag.

Elklit, Jørgen, Birgit Møller, Palle Svensson, and Lise Togeby. 2005. *Gensyn med sofavælgerne*. Århus: Aarhus Universitetsforlag.

Elklit, Jørgen, and Anne Birte Pade. 1996. *Parliamentary Elections and Election Administration in Denmark*. Copenhagen: Ministry of Interior.

Embedsmænds rådgivning og bistand. 2004. Betænkning 1443. Copenhagen: Schultz Information.

Esaiasson, Peter. 2000. "How Members of Parliament Define Their Task." In Peter Easaisson and Knut Heidar, eds., *Beyond Westminster and Congress: The Nordic Experience*. Columbus: Ohio State University Press.

Folketinget efter valget. Various years. Copenhagen: Folketinget.
Folketingets årbog. Various years. Copenhagen: Folketinget.
Folketingets håndbog. Various years. Copenhagen: Folketinget.
Folketingstidende. Various years. Copenhagen: Folketinget.
Forholdet mellem minister og embedsmænd. 1998. Betænkning 1354. Copenhagen: Statens Information.
Green-Pedersen, Christoffer. 2001. "Minority Governments and Party Politics." *Journal of Public Policy* 21 (1): 53–70.
Greve, Carsten. 2000. *Statens virksomheder: Aktieselskabsdannelse og privatisering i 1990'erne.* Copenhagen: Jurist-og Økonomforbundets Forlag.
Greve, Carsten. 2002. *Privatisering, regulering og demokrati.* Århus: Department of Political Science, Magtudredningen.
Hague, Rod, and Martin Harrop. 2001. *Comparative Government and Politics.* Basingstoke, England: Palgrave.
Hansen, Bernhard. 2002. *Party Activism in Denmark: A Micro Level Approach to a Cross-Sectional Analysis of the Correlates of Party Activism.* Århus: Politica.
Hansen, Bernhard, and Karina Pedersen. 2003. "Medlemsrollen og det interne partidemokrati." In Lars Bille and Jørgen Elklit, eds., *Partiernes medlemmer.* Århus: Aarhus Universitetsforlag.
Herman, Valentine, and John Pope. 1973. "Minority Governments in Western Democracies." *British Journal of Political Science* 3:191–212.
Hjarvard, Stig. 1999. "Politik som mediemontage: Om mediernes forandring af den politiske kommunikation." In Jørgen Goul Andersen et al., eds., *Den demokratiske udfordring.* Copenhagen: Hans Reitzels Forlag.
Jensen, Henrik. 1995. *Arenaer eller aktører?* Frederiksberg: Samfundslitteratur.
Jensen, Henrik. 2002. *Partigrupperne i Folketinget.* Copenhagen: Jurist-og Økonomforbundets Forlag.
Jensen, Jesper Bo. 1989. *Liberalisering af de finansielle markeder.* Århus: Department of Political Science, Aarhus University.
Jensen, Torben K. 1999. "Dänemark: Berufspolitiker in einer egalitären politischen kultur." In Jens Borchert, ed., *Politik als Beruf.* Opladen: Leske und Budrich.
Jensen, Torben K. 2000. "Party Cohesion." In Peter Esaiasson and Knut Heidar, eds., *Beyond Westminster and Congress: The Nordic Experience.* Columbus: Ohio State University Press.
Jensen, Torben K. 2004. *De folkevalgte.* Århus: Aarhus Universitetsforlag.
Kaarsted, Tage. 1977. *De danske ministerier 1929–1953.* Copenhagen: Odense Universitetsforlag.
Kaarsted, Tage. 1992. *De danske ministerier 1953–1972.* Copenhagen: Odense Universitetsforlag.
King, Anthony. 1976. "Modes of Executive-Legislative Relations: Great Britain, France, and West Germany." *Legislative Studies Quarterly* 1 (1): 11–36.
Kjær, Ulrik, and Mogens N. Pedersen. 2004. *De danske folketingsmedlemmer.* Århus: Aarhus Universitetsforlag.
Krogh, Torben. 1998. *Farvel til partierne.* Copenhagen: Gyldendal.
Kurrild-Klitgaard, Peter, Robert Klemmensen, and Martin E. Hansen. 2006. "Blokpolitik og det 'samarbejdende folkestyres' fire gamle partier, 1953–2005." *Økonomi og Politik* 79 (1): 79–84.

Laver, Michael, and W. Ben Hunt. 1992. *Policy and Party Competition*. New York: Routledge.
Laver, Michael, and Norman Schofield. 1990. *Multiparty Government: The Politics of Coalition in Europe*. Oxford: Oxford University Press.
Lijphart, Arend. 1984. *Democracies*. New Haven: Yale University Press.
Lijphart, Arend. 1999. *Patterns of Democracy: Government Forms and Performance in Thirty-Six Countries*. New Haven: Yale University Press.
Lund, Anker Brink. 2002. *Den redigerende magt: Nyhedsinstitutionens politiske indflydelse*. Århus: Aarhus Universitetsforlag.
Lund, Anker Brink, Katrine N. Jensen, and Kalle Marosi. 2001. *Danskernes syn på medier og demokrati*. Odense: Syddansk Universitet.
Marcussen, Martin. 2000. *Ideas and Elites: The Social Construction of Economic and Monetary Union*. Ålborg, Denmark: Aalborg University Press.
Mitchell, Paul. 2001. "Coalition Membership in Parliamentary Democracies." Paper presented at the annual meeting of the American Political Science Association, San Francisco, CA, 30 August–2 September.
Müller, Wolfgang C., and Kaare Strøm, eds. 2003. *Coalition Governments in Western Europe*. 2nd ed. Oxford: Oxford University Press.
Narud, Hanne Marthe, and Henry Valen. 2000. "Does Social Background Matter?" In Peter Esaiasson and Knut Heidar, eds., *Beyond Westminster and Congress: The Nordic Experience*. Columbus: Ohio State University Press.
Nielsen, Hans Jørgen. 1999. "De individuelle forskydninger 1994–98." In Johannes Andersen et al., eds., *Vælgere med omtanke*. Århus: Systime.
Nielsen, Hans Jørgen, and Søren Risbjerg Thomsen. 2003. "Vælgervandringer." In Jørgen Goul Andersen and Ole Borre, eds., *Politisk forandring*. Århus: Systime.
Pedersen, Karina, and Bernhard Hansen. 2003. "Partimedlemmernes aktivitet." In Lars Bille and Jørgen Elklit, eds., *Partiernes medlemmer*. Århus: Aarhus Universitetsforlag.
Pedersen, Mogens N. 1988. "The Defeat of All Parties: The Danish Folketing Election 1973." In Kay Lawson and Peter H. Merkl, eds., *When Parties Fail*. Princeton: Princeton University Press.
Pedersen, Mogens N. 2002. "Denmark: The Interplay of Nominations and Elections in Danish Politics." In Hanne Marthe Narud and Henry Valen, eds., *Party Sovereignty and Citizen Control*. Odense: University Press of Southern Denmark.
Pitkin, Hanna F. 1967. *The Concept of Representation*. Berkeley: University of California Press.
Siune, Karen. 1984. "Bestemmer tv valgresultatet?" In Jørgen Elklit and Ole Tonsgaard, eds., *Valg og vælgeradfærd*. Århus: Politica.
Skjæveland, Asbjørn. 2003. *Government Formation in Denmark, 1953–1998*. Århus: Politica.
Skjæveland, Asbjørn. 2005. "Dimensionaliteten i Folketinget: Er der en ny politisk dimension?" *Politica* 37 (4): 411–22.
Sørensen, Max. 1973. *Statsforfatningsret*. Copenhagen: Juristforbundets Forlag.
Sørensen, Mette H. 2003. "Domstolenes politiske rolle—de danske domstoles udvikling siden 1990." Master's thesis, Aarhus University, Department of Political Science.
Strøm, Kaare. 1990. *Minority Government and Majority Rule*. Cambridge, MA: Cambridge University Press.

Stubager, Rune. 2000. "Ny politik i Danmark." *Økonomi and Politik* 73 (3): 15–30.
Stubager, Rune. 2006. *The Education Cleavage: New Politics in Denmark*. Århus: Politica.
Svensson, Palle. 1982. "Party Cohesion in the Danish Parliament during the 1970s." *Scandinavian Political Studies* 5 (1): 17–42.
Taylor, Michael, and Michael Laver. 1973. "Governments in Western Europe." *European Journal of Political Research* 1:205–48.
Thomsen, Søren Risbjerg. 1984. "Udviklingen under forholdstalsvalgmåden (1920–84)." In Jørgen Elklit and Ole Tonsgaard, eds., *Valg og vælgeradfærd*. Århus: Politica.
Togeby, Lise, Jørgen Goul Andersen, Peter Munk Christiansen, Torben Beck Jørgensen, and Signild Vallgårda. 2003. *Magt og demokrati i Danmark: Hovedresultater fra Magtudredningen*. Århus: Aarhus Universitetsforlag.
Tonsgaard, Ole. 1989. "Vælgervandringer og vælgerusikkerhed." In Jørgen Elklit and Ole Tonsgaard, eds., *To folketingsvalg*. Århus: Politica.
Wängnerud, Lena. 2000. "Representing Women." In Peter Esaiasson and Knut Heidar, eds., *Beyond Westminster and Congress: The Nordic Experience*. Columbus: Ohio State University Press.

INTERNET SOURCES

Folketing. Archive, 2003–4. http://www.ft.dk
Folketinget. Accessed February 2, 2008. http://www.ft.dk
Folketinget. 2006. "Valg og tendenser." Accessed February 14, 2008. http://www.ft.dk/pdf/ark9.pdf
Keesing's Record of World Events. 2007. "Nov 2007—General Election." Vol. 53 (November, 2007 Denmark): 48272. http://www.keesings.com
Politiken.dk. Accessed February 2, 2008. http://politiken.dk/politik/article427836.ece

4 ✦ Finland

Moving in the Opposite Direction

TAPIO RAUNIO

The Finnish political system is normally categorized as semi-presidential, with the executive functions divided between an elected president and a cabinet that is accountable to the parliament. However, recent constitutional reforms have transformed Finnish politics by strengthening parliamentary democracy. The new constitution, which entered into force in 2000, completed a period of far-reaching constitutional change that curtailed presidential powers and brought the Finnish political system closer to a standard version of parliamentary democracy. Cabinet formation is now based on partisan negotiations, and the president is almost completely excluded from the policy process in domestic matters. However, while political parties are now much more at the center of things than before, their ability to effectively align preferences is increasingly in doubt, as indicated by declining turnout and party memberships and the transforming cleavage structure.

In contrast to the other Nordic countries, the Finnish political system has arguably become less subject to national and international constraints over the past two decades. The end of the cold war removed the shadow of the Soviet Union from Finnish policy-making, although membership in the European Union (EU) and corporatism have set significant limits on what the parliament can do. In addition, the rights of citizens have been strengthened, with constitutional regulations covering key aspects of public policy (in addition to fundamental rights)—including the right to free basic education and to social security and health care services.[1] The introduction of direct elections for choosing the president is also a potentially destabilizing factor, as it gives the president incentives to wield his or her significant powers.

This chapter examines the development of the Finnish political system since World War II, although the main focus is on recent developments and current practices. The first section analyzes the role of political parties in connecting citizens' preferences to public policy-making. The second section explores the changing constitutional environment, tracking changes that have transformed the chain of delegation from voters to MPs, from parliament to cabinet, from prime minister to ministers, and from ministers to civil servants. The third section deals with external constraints, focusing primarily on the changing balance of power between the president and the cabinet and on the impact of European integration. The concluding section summarizes the main findings.

Political Parties

The parliamentarization of the Finnish political system and the concomitant reduction in the powers of the president have considerably strengthened the role of political parties in the policy process. Parties are no longer in the shadow of the president, and they have new opportunities and more responsibilities under the new constitution.

Table 4.1 shows the partisan distribution of votes in national parliamentary elections after World War II. Measured by the number of effective parties, the Finnish party system is the most fragmented among the West European countries, with an average of 5.1 effective parties (see table 4.3) between 1945 and 2000 (Mattila and Raunio 2004, 269). Since the declaration of independence in 1917, no party has even come close to winning a majority of parliamentary seats, and the lack of a clearly dominant party (like the Social Democrats in Sweden) has necessitated cooperation between the main parties. Indeed, in Finland, it is rare for a single party or electoral alliance to win a majority of the votes even within a single electoral district.

The years after World War II can be roughly divided into two periods (Arter 2008, 51–147). First, until about 1970, the party system remained stable: class voting was high, electoral volatility was low, and practically no new parties entered the Eduskunta, the national parliament. As the class cleavage was crucial in the emergence of Finnish parties, it is not surprising that class dealignment has contributed to increasing electoral instability, in terms of both party system fragmentation and electoral volatility. However, despite the entry into the Eduskunta of new parties such as the Green League and the Rural Party, the party system has remained rather stable, with the three main parties—the Social Democratic Party, the Center Party, and the National Coalition—largely holding on to their vote shares in recent decades (Sundberg 1996, 1999, 2002b; Paloheimo and Raunio 2008). Neither lower turnout nor increasing volatility has led to any significant support for extremist or nationalist parties (Kestilä 2006).

Turning to the linkage between parties and the electorate, the situation in Finland does not differ from that in the majority of European countries (see chapter 1). Disengagement from parties is evident in declining party membership (see fig. 4.1). Although membership rose until the 1980s, there has been a sharp decline since. In the 1960s, almost 20 percent of voters were party members; by the first years of the twenty-first century, the figure had fallen to around 7 to 9 percent (Sundberg 2002b, 196; Borg 2008).[2] Party members are less active within their organizations, with an increasing percentage not attending party meetings or taking part in campaign

TABLE 4.1. Elections to the Finnish Parliament (Eduskunta), 1945–2008

Election Year	COM	FPDU	SDP	GR	Ce	FRP/TF	LIB	CHR	SW	CON	Others
1945		23.5	25.1		21.3		5.2		7.9	15.0	2.0
1948		20.0	26.3		24.2		3.9		7.7	17.1	0.8
1951		21.6	26.5		23.2		5.7		7.6	14.6	0.8
1954		21.6	26.2		24.1		7.9		7.0	12.8	0.4
1958		23.2	23.2		23.1		5.9		6.8	15.3	2.5
1962		22.0	19.5		23.0	2.2	6.3		6.4	15.0	5.6
1966		21.1	27.2		21.2	1.0	6.5	0.5	6.0	13.8	2.7
1970		16.6	23.4		17.1	10.5	6.0	1.1	5.7	18.0	1.6
1972		17.0	25.8		16.4	9.2	5.2	2.5	5.4	17.6	0.9
1975		18.9	24.9		17.6	3.6	4.3	3.3	4.7	18.4	4.3
1979		17.9	23.9		17.3	4.6	3.7	4.8	4.2	21.7	1.9
1983		13.5	26.7		17.6	9.7		3.0	4.6	22.1	2.8
1987		13.6	24.1	4.0	17.6	6.3	1.0	2.6	5.3	23.1	2.4
1991		10.1	22.1	6.8	24.8	4.8	0.8	3.1	5.5	19.3	2.7
1995		11.2	28.3	6.5	19.8	1.3	0.6	3.0	5.1	17.9	6.3
1999	0.8	10.9	22.9	7.3	22.4	1.0	0.2	4.2	5.1	21.0	5.0
2003	0.8	9.9	24.5	8.0	24.7	1.6	0.3	5.3	4.6	18.6	2.5
2007	0.7	8.8	21.4	8.5	23.1	4.1	0.1	4.9	4.6	22.3	1.7

Source: Data from *Statistics Finland* (years 1948–75 include also votes in the Åland Islands).

Notes: Numbers given in table represent vote shares in percentages. Party abbreviations are as follows: Ce = Center Party (Suomen Keskusta, KESK), until 1962 the Agrarian Union, in 1983 including the Liberal Party; SDP = Finnish Social Democratic Party (Suomen Sosialidemokraattinen Puolue); CON = National Coalition Party (Kansallinen Kokoomus); FPDU = Left Alliance (Vasemmistoliitto), until 1987 the Democratic League of the People of Finland, in 1987 including DEVA; GR = Green League (Vihreä Liitto), in 1987 not as a party of its own; CHR = Christian Democratic Party (Kristillisdemokraatit), before 2001 Suomen Kristillinen Liitto (Christian League of Finland), CHRL; SW = Swedish People's Party (Svenska Folkpartiet/Ruotsalainen Kansanpuolue); FRP/TF = True Finns (Perussuomalaiset), was formed after the dissolution in 1995 of the Finnish Rural Party, in 1962 and 1966 the Small Holders Party and until 1995 the Finnish Rural Party (SMP); COM = Finnish Communist Party (Suomen Kommunistinen Puolue); LIB = Liberal People's Party (Liberaalinen Kansanpuolue), until 1948 the National Progressive Party, until 1966 the Finnish People's Party, until 1999 the Liberal Party; FPDU = Suomen Kansan Demokraattinen Liitto (Finnish People's Democratic Union); SDL = Sosialidemokraattinen Oppositio (Social Democratic Opposition); Others = Other parties.

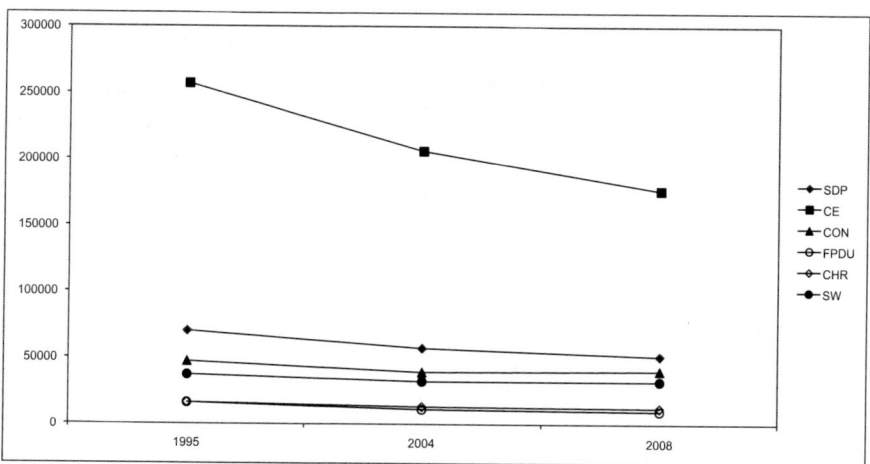

Fig. 4.1. Party membership in Finland, 1995–2008. See table 4.1 for explanation of party labels.

activities. The number of local party branches has also decreased since the early 1980s. Given the gradual aging of members, it appears that the downward trend in membership will continue in the future (Borg 2008).

Another measure of disengagement is voter turnout, which has fallen fairly consistently since the 1960s (see table 4.2). In the 1960s, on average, 85 percent of the electorate cast votes. The figure was 81 percent in the 1970s, about 79 percent in the 1980s, 71 percent in the 1990s, and below 70 percent in the first decade of the twenty-first century (the lowest figure since World War II). The share of voters who decide during the election campaign whom to support has increased from 23 percent in 1966 to 57 percent by 2003 (Wiberg 2006, 92; Borg 2006, 68–69). There are also signs of weakening party identification. While 59 percent of the voters reported identification with one of the parties in 1975, 61 percent did so in 1991. By 2003, the figure had dropped to 47 percent (Pesonen and Sänkiaho 1979, 163; Pesonen, Sänkiaho, and Borg 1993, 215–19; Grönlund et al. 2005, 100; Borg 2008, 95).

The weaker linkage between parties and citizens is also reflected in the gradually changing cleavage structure. The main cleavage has traditionally been the left-right dimension, but since the early 1990s, the rural-urban/center-periphery divide has become the second main cleavage, partly because the EU and globalization issues have emerged on the political agenda (Nousiainen 2000, 265–68; Paloheimo 2005b, 2008; Reunanen and Suhonen 2009). The integration/independence dimension is entwined with the center-periphery/rural-urban cleavage, and it may become more salient in national elections, particularly if ideological differences on the left-right dimension get smaller and because MPs and party leaders are more pro-integrationist than their voters (Mattila and Raunio 2005). A survey from 1995 showed that even on the left-right dimension, Finnish MPs were far less representative of their voters than their colleagues were of voters in the other Nordic countries (Holmberg 2000).

TABLE 4.2. Strength of Party Attachment in Finland, 1948–2008

Election Year	Turnout (%)	Class Voting (%)[a]	Party Attachment (share of those who report that they are close to a party) (%)	Share of Voters Changing Party between Elections (%)	Share of Voters Deciding Which Party to Vote for during the Election Campaign (%)[b]	Distrust of Parliament (%)
1948	78.2					
1951	74.6					
1954	79.9					
1958	75.0					
1962	85.1					
1966	84.9				23	
1970	82.2					
1972	81.4					
1975	79.7	69	59	24		
1979	81.2			20		
1983	81.0			22	35	35
1987	76.4	67		24		
1991	72.1		61	28	40	64
1995	71.9	61		30	55	67
1999	68.3			24	60	57
2003	69.7	57	47	26	57	
2007	67.9		53			

Source: Data on turnout from *Statistics Finland*. Data on class voting from Paloheimo and Sundberg 2005, 172. Data on party attachment from Pesonen and Sänkiaho 1979, 163; Pesonen, Sänkiaho, and Borg 1993, 216; Grönlund et al. 2005, 100; Borg 2008, 95. Data on share of voters changing party between elections from Paloheimo and Sundberg 2005, 198. Data on share of voters deciding which party to vote for during the election campaign from Wiberg 2006, 92. Data on distrust in parliament from Mattila and Sänkiaho 2005, 80, measured as the share of voters that had no confidence or not very much confidence in the parliament (1981, 1990, 1996, 2000).

Note: Figures for bloc voting were not available.

[a]Class voting is not measured using the Alford index. Instead, the entries in the cells report the percentage of voters who voted for the "party of their class"—for example, working-class people voting for left-wing parties and white- collar employees voting for bourgeois parties.

[b]The figures in the column for the share of voters deciding which party to vote for during the election campaign reports the share of voters who made their vote choice on election day, some days before election day, 1–2 weeks before election day, or 1–2 months before election day.

However, when we examine parties in the cabinet, the picture looks very different. With the president now firmly in the background on domestic politics, Finnish politics is more party-dominated than ever before. Indeed, free from presidential interference, cabinet formation and the passage of legislation (see the next two sections) are now more controlled by parties than at any time since the declaration of independence. The public funding of parties has also strengthened party organizations. Political parties were first legally recognized in the 1969 Party Act, which gave them a privileged status in elections and in the allocation of public funds. Both extra-parliamentary party groups (the national party organizations) and parliamentary party groups receive public funding based on the share of seats won in the most recent parliamentary election. Parties that are represented in parliament have had their national party organizations publicly funded since 1968, and parliamentary party groups (the actual MPs of a particular party) have been funded since 1967. Parties without parliamentary representation do not get public funding (Wiberg 1991). Hence the system offers the established parties protection against potential new rivals.

The Constitutional Chain of Delegation

From Voters to Parliament

Let us examine first the delegation from voters to their parliamentary representatives. With the exception of candidate selection, the main features of the electoral system have remained intact throughout the period under analysis. The 200 members of the unicameral Eduskunta are elected for a four-year term (a three-year term prior to 1954). The country is divided into one single-member and 14 multi-member electoral districts, with the Åland Islands entitled to one seat. Turning to district magnitude (excluding the single-member districts), from 1907 to 2003 the smallest district had between 6 and 9 seats while between 19 and 33 MPs were elected from the largest district. The average district magnitude is thus 13.3. Each district is a separate subunit, and there are no national adjustment seats. The formula used for allocating seats to districts is the method of largest remainders, with the d'Hondt method used in allocating seats to parties (for details, see Kuusela 1995, 37–38; Sundberg 2002a). The proportionality of the electoral system is high (Raunio 2005a). As the d'Hondt formula favors large parties, most small parties join electoral alliances, and without this option, proportionality between votes and seats would be lower.[3] The voters choose among individual candidates who are placed on the party lists in alphabetical order.[4]

This open-list system means that Finnish elections are highly candidate-centered. Voter surveys have asked citizens whether the candidate or the party is more important in guiding their voting behavior. Longitudinal data shows little change since the early 1980s. In the 1983 elections, 52 percent said the party was more important and 42 percent the candidate; in 1991, the figures were 51 and 43 percent (Pesonen, Sänkiaho, and Borg 1993, 72–74). In 1995, 37 percent reported that they based their vote choice primarily on party, while 50 percent chose based on candidate. The figures were 34 percent (party) and 56 percent (candidate) for the 1999 elections and 49 percent and 47 percent in 2003 (Paloheimo 2005b, 113). In the 2007 elections, 48 percent stated that the party was more important, while 51 percent reported that the candidate was more important (Karvonen 2009, 102).

The electoral acts of 1969 and 1975 significantly changed candidate selection. Up to this period, the lack of legal regulations gave the parties a relatively free hand in making their own arrangements, and this resulted in processes that were strongly influenced by national party executives. An important tool for parties was the right to field the same candidate in several constituencies. Since 1969, however, candidates are allowed to compete in only one constituency, thereby reducing the influence of the party leadership.

Since the 1975 reforms, candidate selection has been based on membership balloting within electoral districts (Kuitunen 2002). Membership ballots are rarely used in small parties, whereas the large parties have them in most electoral districts. After the balloting, the district party executive can replace a maximum of one-quarter of the candidates. While such list manipulation by the district party executive does occur in most districts, it is not normally a conflictual element in the process and is primarily explained by either candidate refusals or the need to form a more balanced list by correcting, for example, for geographical or occupational bias among the candidates.

The national-level party organization is almost completely excluded from the process. The party leadership has thus only "limited and theoretical possibilities" to influence candidate selection at the district level, with such interference restricted to cases of severe internal conflicts within the party (see also Kuitunen 2002, 64; Helander 1997). The weak involvement of the national party organization is also reflected in campaigning. During the campaign, the national party organization and leadership primarily act as a background resource, providing local branches with necessary campaign material and, through the party leader, giving the party a public face. The actual work of collecting funds and spreading the message is the responsibility of candidates' support groups, with private donations being important in financing candidates' campaigns (Sundberg 1995).

The candidate-centered character of the electoral system is also reflected in parliamentary work. While Finnish parties can be characterized as rather centralized between elections (Sundberg 1994, 1996), the decentralized process of candidate selection limits the disciplinary powers of party leaders vis-à-vis MPs, because representatives seeking reelection need to cultivate support among their local constituents.[5] Despite relatively high cohesion indices (Pajala and Jakulin 2007), group cohesion in the Eduskunta has been lower than in the other Nordic legislatures, with Finnish MPs also valuing group discipline much less than do their opposite numbers in the other Nordic parliaments (Jensen 2000; see also Heidar 2000; Karvonen 2004, 218–20). Indeed, when asked in 1995 about the importance attached to performing various tasks in their work, only 9 percent of the Finnish MPs thought it "most important" to promote the policies of their parties. The corresponding figures were much higher in the other Nordic countries (Esaiasson 2000). Furthermore, the share of MPs with no previous experience in party politics has increased since the early 1980s (Ruostetsaari 2000), and it may well be that these representatives do not share the same norms regarding party behavior as those held by MPs with long service in the party before entering the parliament. Nevertheless, party groups in the Eduskunta can still be characterized as rather cohesive (Wiberg 2000; Pajala and Jakulin 2007).

From Parliament to Cabinet

The Constitution Act of 1919 was virtually silent on the issue of cabinet formation. The cabinet was required to maintain the confidence of the Eduskunta, and the president was "to appoint citizens of Finland known for their honesty and ability to serve as members of the Council of State" (Section 36). In practice, cabinet formation was strongly influenced by the president. After the outgoing cabinet had submitted its resignation, the president invited the speaker of parliament and the representatives of the parliamentary parties to bilateral discussions. The fragmented party system, with no clearly dominant party, strengthened the president's hand in steering the negotiations. The president then appointed a *formateur* whose task was to continue negotiations over coalition membership, the cabinet program, and portfolio allocation. However, it was also common for the president to influence the selection of individual ministers. The process ended with the president appointing the new cabinet in the last full plenary meeting of the resigning cabinet.

While the power was not frequently used, the president did have the right to appoint a caretaker cabinet consisting of civil servants if negotiations for cabinet formation fail. The last case of strong presidential intervention in cabinet formation occurred in 1987, when President Mauno Koivisto overruled a coalition between the Center Party and the National Coalition, indicating that a coalition between the (conservative) National Coalition and the Social Democrats was preferable. Since 1945, Finland has had six caretaker cabinets, most recently the Liinamaa cabinet in 1975. In addition, about two-thirds of the remaining postwar cabinets have included nonpartisan ministers.

The new 2000 constitution (Section 61) parliamentarized cabinet formation (official Finnish sources generally translate references to "cabinet" in terms of "government"): "The Parliament elects the Prime Minister, who is thereafter appointed to the office by the President of the Republic. The President appoints the other Ministers in accordance with a proposal made by the Prime Minister. Before the Prime Minister is elected, the groups represented in the Parliament negotiate on the political program and composition of the Government. On the basis of the outcome of these negotiations, and after having heard the Speaker of the Parliament and the parliamentary groups, the President informs the Parliament of the nominee for Prime Minister. The nominee is elected Prime Minister if his or her election has been supported by more than half of the votes cast in an open vote in the Parliament. If the nominee does not receive the necessary majority, another nominee shall be put forward in accordance with the same procedure. If the second nominee fails to receive the support of more than half of the votes cast, the election of the Prime Minister shall be held in the Parliament by open vote. In this event, the person receiving the most votes is elected." Prior to a constitutional amendment in 1991, the cabinet was not obliged to present its program in the Eduskunta. A new vote of investiture was first used in 1995, when the rainbow coalition headed by Paavo Lipponen took office. Under the new constitution, the cabinet shall without delay submit its program to the parliament in the form of a statement, which is then followed by a debate and a mandatory confidence vote. The decision rule is simple majority. By approving the program, the parliamentary groups of MPs from the cabinet parties commit themselves to abiding by that document. However, one can also argue that the introduction of the investiture vote strengthens the parliament, as it enables the party groups of cabinet parties to at least set certain ex ante limits or guidelines for cabinet behavior (Paloheimo 2002, 209; Paloheimo 2003, 232; Aula 2003, 103–4).

When compared with other European and Nordic countries, Finnish cabinets are outliers in three respects: their parliamentary support, level of fragmentation, and ideological diversity. Finland used to be characterized by short-lived and unstable cabinets functioning in the shadow of the president. Between 1945 and 2000, only Italy had more cabinets than Finland among the West European countries (Nousiainen 2000). Of the 44 cabinets formed between 1945 and 1999, nearly half (46 percent) were surplus majority coalitions, 25 percent were minority cabinets, 16 percent were minimal winning coalitions, and 16 percent were caretaker cabinets. Table 4.3 provides information on the main aspects of Finnish cabinets formed after World War II.

The overwhelming majority of Finnish cabinets have been cross-bloc coalitions bringing together parties from the left and the right. Reflecting the fragmentation of the party system and the tradition of forming majority cabinets, the mean number of cabinet parties between 1945 and 2000 was 3.5, by far the highest figure among the Nordic countries (Mattila and Raunio 2002, 264). The Center Party has occupied the position of the median legislator, which, together with strong backing from presidents, has facilitated its inclusion in the majority of postwar cabinets. The Swedish People's Party, the ethnoregionalist party established to defend the interests of the Swedish-speaking minority, has participated in most cabinets, including all those formed after 1979. The near-permanent cabinet status of the Swedish People's Party can be interpreted as a mechanism for protecting minority rights, but it is also explained by the centrist and flexible ideology of the party.

Recent cabinets have, as a rule, included two of the three main parties, the Social Democrats, the Center Party, and the National Coalition. An oversized coalition cabinet, bringing together the Social Democrats, the National Coalition, the Left Alliance, the Swedish People's Party, and the Green League, took office after the 1995 election, and this so-called rainbow government renewed its mandate in the March 1999 elections (Jungar 2002). According to Nousiainen (2000, 270), the formation of this coalition indicated that "the traditional bloc boundary of the party system has lost much of its importance." Government formation after the 2007 elections is a good example of how oversized coalitions have become the dominant pattern. Immediately after the election result became clear, it seemed

TABLE 4.3. Cabinets in Finland, 1945–2008

Cabinet Number	Prime Minister	Date (yymmdd)	Cabinet Share (%) of Parliamentary Seats	Effective Number of Legislative Parties[a]	Median Legislator Party	Parties in Cabinet	Majority Cabinets Single-Party	Majority Cabinets Coalition[b]	Minority Cabinets Single-Party	Minority Cabinets Coalition	Non-Partisan Cabinets[c]
1	Paasikivi III	450417	85.5	4.78	Ce	FPDU, SDP, Ce, LIB, SW		X			
2	Pekkala	460326	81.0	4.78	Ce	FPDU, SDP, Ce, SW		X			
3	Fagerholm I	480729	27.0	4.54	Ce	SDP			X		
4	Kekkonen I	500317	37.5	4.54	Ce	Ce, LIB, SW				X	
5	Kekkonen II	510117	64.5	4.54	Ce	Ce, SDP, LIB, SW		X			
6	Kekkonen III	510920	59.5	4.78	Ce	Ce, SDP, SW		X			
7	Kekkonen IV	530709	33.0	4.78	Ce	Ce, SW				X	
8	Tuomioja	531117	0	4.78	Ce	Nonpartisan					
9	Törngren	540505	60.0	4.71	Ce	SW, SDP, Ce		X			
10	Kekkonen V	541020	53.5	4.71	Ce	Ce, SDP		X			
11	Fagerholm II	560303	66.5	4.71	Ce	SDP, Ce, LIB, SW		X			
12	Sukselainen I	570527	39.5	4.71	Ce	Ce, LIB, SW				X	
13	Sukselainen II	570702	33.0	4.71	Ce	Ce, LIB				X	
14	Sukselainen III	570902	42.5	5.59	Ce	Ce, SDL, LIB				X	
15	von Fieandt	571129	0	5.59	Ce	Nonpartisan					
16	Kuuskoski	580426	0	5.59	Ce	Nonpartisan					
17	Fagerholm III	580829	68.5	5.32	SDP	SDP, Ce, LIB, SW, CON		X			
18	Sukselainen IV	590113	24.0	5.32	SDP	Ce			X		
19	Miettunen I	610714	24.0	5.32	SDP	Ce			X		
20	Karjalainen I	620413	56.0	5.09	Ce	Ce, LIB, SW, CON		X			

#	Name	Date			PM party	Parties			
21	Lehto	631218	0	5.09	Ce	Nonpartisan			
22	Virolainen	640912	56.0	5.09	Ce	Ce, LIB, SW, CON	x		
23	Paasio I	660527	76.0	4.96	SDP	SDP, FPDU, SDL, Ce	x		
24	Koivisto I	680322	82.0	4.96	SDP	SDP, FPDU, SDL, Ce, SW	x		
25	Aura I	700514	0	5.56	Ce	Nonpartisan			
26	Karjalainen II	700715	72.0	5.56	Ce	Ce, FPDU, SDP, LIB, SW	x		
27	Karjalainen III	710326	54.0	5.56	Ce	Ce, SDP, LIB, SW	x		
28	Aura II	711029	0	5.56	Ce	Nonpartisan			
29	Paasio II	720223	27.5	5.51	Ce	SDP		x	
30	Sorsa I	720904	53.5	5.51	Ce	SDP, Ce, LIB, SW	x		
31	Liinamaa	750613	0	5.51	Ce	Nonpartisan			
32	Miettunen II	751130	76.0	5.31	Ce	Ce, FPDU, SDP, LIB, SW	x		
33	Miettunen III	760929	29.0	5.31	Ce	Ce, LIB, SW	x		
34	Sorsa II	770515	76.0	5.31	Ce	SDP, FPDU, Ce, LIB, SW			x
35	Sorsa III	780302	71.0	5.31	Ce	SDP, FPDU, Ce, LIB	x		
36	Koivisto II	790526	66.5	5.21	Ce	SDP, FPDU, Ce, SW	x		
37	Sorsa IV	820219	66.5	5.21	Ce	SDP, FPDU, Ce, SW	x		
38	Sorsa V	821231	51.0	5.21	Ce	SDP, Ce, LIB, SW	x		
39	Sorsa VI	830506	61.5	5.14	Ce	SDP, Ce, FRP, SW	x		x

(continues)

TABLE 4.3—(Continued)

Cabinet Number	Prime Minister	Date (yymmdd)	Cabinet Share (%) of Parliamentary Seats	Effective Number of Legislative Parties[a]	Median Legislator Party	Parties in Cabinet	Majority Cabinets Single-Party	Majority Cabinets Coalition[b]	Minority Cabinets Single-Party	Minority Cabinets Coalition	Non-Partisan Cabinets[c]
40	Holkeri I	870430	65.5	4.86	Ce	CON, SDP, FRP, SW					
41	Holkeri II	900828	61.0	4.86	Ce	CON, SDP, SW		X			
42	Aho I	910426	57.5	5.23	Ce	Ce, CD, SW, CON		X			
43	Aho II	940628	53.5	5.23	Ce	Ce, SW, CON		X			
44	Lipponen	950413	72.5	4.88	Ce	SDP, CON, SW, FPDU, GR		X			
45	Lipponen II	990415	70.0	5.14	Ce	SDP, CON, SW, FPDU, GR		X			
46	Lipponen III	020531	64.5	5.14	Ce	SDP, CON, SW, FPDU		X			
47	Jäätteenmäki	030417	58.5	4.92	Ce	Ce, SDP, SW		X			
48	Vanhanen	030624	58.5	4.92	Ce	Ce, SDP, SW		X			
49	Vanhanen II	070419	63.0	5.12	Ce	Ce, CON, GR, SW		X			

Source: Data from Nousiainen 2003, updated from 1999 onward by Tapio Raunio; Sundberg 2004, 1001; Zárate's Political Collections (ZPC), http://www.terra.es/personal2/monolith/ooeuropa.htm (accessed May 17, 2008); *Keesing's Record of World Events,* vol. 49 (June 2003 Finland): 45478; *Statsrådet,* http://www.vn.fi/hallitus/sv.jsp (accessed February 2, 2008); *Eduskunta,* http://www.eduskunta.fi/triphome/bin/tixhaku.sh?lyh=hex81102kieli=ru?lomake=tix5050_ru (accessed February 2, 2008).

Note: See the notes to table 4.1 for explanation of party labels.

[a] Effective number of legislative parties: index developed by Markku Laakso and Rein Taagepera that measures party system size. Both the number of parties and their relative size are taken into account. For an accessible introduction, see Lijphart 1984.

[b] Majority cabinet coalitions can be either minimal winning (mwc—a coalition that cannot lose a party and still be "winning") or a surplus coalition (can lose one or more parties and still be winning).

[c] Minority cabinets control 50% or less of all seats in parliament.

that the likeliest coalition alternative was a center-right cabinet formed by the Center Party, the National Coalition, and the Swedish People's Party. However, Matti Vanhanen, who, as prime minister and the leader of the largest party, would be responsible for forming the new cabinet, announced that his new cabinet should control around 120 of the 200 seats. Vanhanen justified this by referring to the need to ensure the smooth functioning of the cabinet. Soon afterward, Vanhanen declared that the new cabinet would be a coalition between the Center Party, the National Coalition, the Swedish People's Party, and the Green League, commanding a comfortable majority in the Eduskunta with 126 seats (63 percent).

Despite their size and ideological heterogeneity, the cabinets formed since 1983 have been surprisingly stable and free from major internal conflicts. The only exception was the short-lived coalition between the Center Party, the Social Democrats, and the Swedish People's Party that took office after the elections in March 2003. Anneli Jäätteenmäki was forced to resign from the position of prime minister in June of that year after allegations concerning her use of secret documents from the foreign ministry during the election campaign. The same three parties formed a new cabinet immediately after Jäätteenmäki had resigned (Arter 2006, 217–37). Another caveat is that on three occasions, a small party has resigned from the governing coalition: the Rural Party in 1990 over budgetary disagreements, the Christian Democrats in 1994 due to the cabinet's pro-EU stance, and the Green League in 2002 because of the decision to build a fifth nuclear reactor. None of these defections led to the prime minister's resignation or threatened the overall stability of the relevant cabinet.

Not surprisingly, the oversized coalitions that have held government power since 1983 have ruled without much effective opposition from the Eduskunta. The fragmented nature of the opposition has been particularly important. With the exception of the bourgeois coalition that governed in 1991–95, cabinets have brought together parties from both the left and the right, which has left the opposition both numerically weak and ideologically fragmented. For example, after the 2003 elections, in respect to the cabinet led by Vanhanen, the main opposition parties were located to both the right (the National Coalition) and the left (the Green League and Left Alliance). Considering such ideological fragmentation, the opposition could hardly sustain a coherent strategy of criticizing the cabinet.[6]

From the perspective of democratic representation, the formation of multiparty cabinets is a double-edged sword. Parties and their leaders are engaged in an almost constant process of negotiation, and the art of making compromises and logrolls is an essential feature of daily politics. In order not to exclude themselves from cabinet formation negotiations, parties do not present voters with preelection alliances, nor do they make public statements ruling out power sharing with particular parties. While partisan cooperation in multiparty cabinets and in the Eduskunta may enhance parties' abilities to defend the interests of their constituents, it also makes it more difficult for voters to assess the performance of their representatives, particularly given the lack of transparency that characterizes coalition-cabinet decision making. Thus, in recent years, Finland has scored high on parliamentary stability and accommodation but markedly lower on prospective and retrospective accountability.

Nevertheless, there is now a more direct link between election results and cabinet formation than existed in the past (Mattila and Raunio 2002). This follows from three factors: the president can no longer effectively intervene in cabinet formation; prerogatives of foreign policy are no longer that relevant (the conservative National Coalition was excluded from the cabinet between 1966 and 1987 owing to the need to anticipate Moscow's reactions) (see also chapter 9); and, whereas ideological differences between the left and the right were sharp and highly salient in cabinet formation until the 1970s, the moderation of ideological tensions has led to a situation where practically all coalitions are possible.

The role of party leaders has become particularly important in electoral campaigns, with parliamentary elections seen more and more as elections about the future prime minister. This reflects the fact that electoral competition between the three biggest parties—the Social Democrats, the Center Party, and the National Coalition—is increasingly also a competition for the next PM. Each party seeks to present its leader as the most suitable next PM. This constrains party leaders from adopting strong political stances or engaging in confrontational discourse, privileging instead the quality of "statesmanship" and the (perceived) ability to manage a coalition cabinet. There is also some evidence to suggest that leadership effects have generally become more important for Finnish voters, especially after the 1995 elections (Paloheimo 2005a, 2005b; Karvonen 2009).

Turning to relations between the Eduskunta and the cabinet, there is unfortunately no sufficiently representative roll-call data on coalition politics, from either the plenary or the committee stage. Annually, between 50 and 70 percent of all recorded plenary votes have dealt with the government budget, which further reduces the informational value of the existing roll-call data. These recorded budget votes enable the MPs to show that they defended constituency interests. The spike in recorded votes in the 1970s (see table 4.4) was due to the tactics of the Rural Party, whose leader Veikko Vennamo demanded a formal vote on basically all issues (Pajala

2006). The budgetary process takes place almost exclusively outside of the Eduskunta. Interministerial bargaining—dominated by the Ministry of Finance—is obviously influenced by political parties, but the ability of the Eduskunta to actually guide the negotiations in the ministries is estimated to be fairly low. Examining the differences between the cabinet's proposal for the state budget and the final bill as approved by the parliament, Wiberg (2006, 193, 234) shows that only in 1947 and 1953 did the Eduskunta manage to raise the total budget more than 10 percent. Since 1960, the differences have been minimal, usually below 1 percent.

The bluntest tool for controlling the cabinet while it is in office is the vote of no confidence, of which there are three types (Helander and Isaksson 1994). First, the cabinet can, in practice, introduce a confidence motion by making it known that a defeat will lead to its downfall. The last cabinet resignation caused by such a cabinet-initiated confidence motion occurred no more recently than in 1953. Second, the opposition can, without prior warning and in connection with any policy issue, propose a no-confidence vote during a plenary session. So far, such a motion of no confidence has never forced any cabinet to resign. Third, a confidence vote may follow from a parliamentary debate over an interpellation. Under any of these procedures, decisions are made by simple majority.

In recent decades, interpellations have become the standard form of no-confidence vote. Although an individual MP can initiate an interpellation, they are usually put forward by opposition party groups. A minimum of 20 signatures (10 percent of MPs) is needed for an interpellation to be presented to the cabinet or an individual minister. The most recent cabinet resignation caused by a vote of no confidence following an interpellation occurred in 1958. Yet the number of interpellations has increased steadily (Raunio and Wiberg 2008, 594), and their main objective is to raise the profile of the opposition and perhaps also to stimulate debate on topical issues. When tabling the interpellation, the opposition basically knows that it will not result in the cabinet being voted out of office (Nousiainen 2006, 311–12).

The role of parliamentary questions has also become more important over time (Wiberg 1994). Originally, MPs could table only written questions (introduced in 1906), but oral questions were introduced in 1966, and questions to the Council of State (i.e., the cabinet) were introduced in 1989. The first two options were available to individual MPs, while questions to the Council of State had to be signed by at least four representatives, and they had to be on matters both "current" and "of consequence." The procedure for tabling oral questions was initially quite favorable for the cabinet. The minister replied to a written question submitted by an MP, who was then entitled to ask two additional questions during the question time. In

TABLE 4.4. Parliamentary Activities, Finland 1945–2008

Year	Government Bills	Government Reports	U-Matters[a]	E-Matters[b]	Private Members' Bills[c]	Petitionary Initiatives[d]	Budgetary Initiatives[e]	Recorded Votes	Plenary Hours
1945	147				53	327	147	159	
1946	156				67	449	142	341	
1947								616	
1948	95				87	475	363	302	
1949	172				140	673	366	531	
1950	230							682	
1951	58				119	266	413	371	
1952	111				212	526	465	603	
1953	182				286	739	713	697	
1954	123				189	583	609	521	
1955	179				258	924	707	581	
1956	163				292	1,042	562	495	
1957	223				338	1,172	521	720	
1958	88				133	451	438	299	
1959	162				205	697	444	465	
1960	172				289	965	532	473	
1961	179				414	1,430	614	573	
1962	149				336	1,010	643	515	
1963	198				456	1,322	726	556	
1964	235				540	1,480	583	450	
1965	256				692	1,917	729	672	
1966	140				385	1,309	455	189	
1967	196				480	1,823	462	240	
1968	197				520	2,147	581	371	
1969	283				607	2,593	828	457	
1970	199	1			415	2,233	957	726	
1971	246	1			549	3,104	1,319	1,077	
1972	247	1			563	2,880	1,312	1,152	
1973	297	1			735	3,585	1,294	2,128	
1974	302				979	4,107	1,533	2,829	
1975	166				1,069	4,746	604	967	
1975II	198				585	1,637	1,402	1,355	
1976	329				678	2,103	1,019	1,984	
1977	288	2			763	2,549	801	1,736	
1978	361	3			836	3,140	1,103	2,399	
1979	191				457	1,999	1,235	1,847	
1980	256	2			590	2,881	1,513	1,587	
1981	285	1			602	3,493	1,484	1,412	
1982	340	3			632	4,005	1,557	1,841	
1983	221				192	1,867	1,300	598	273
1984	294	4			253	2,400	1,881	506	424
1985	301	4			330	3,010	2,091	902	473
1986	306	4			413	3,945	2,703	1,251	571
1987	218				146	1,337	2,827	1,003	316
1988	286	3			227	2,376	3,138	1,249	441
1989	307	1			188	3,021	3,554	1,172	462
1990	375	5			358	4,041	3,559	1,272	578

TABLE 4.4—(Continued)

Year	Government Bills	Government Reports	U-Matters[a]	E-Matters[b]	Private Members' Bills[c]	Petitionary Initiatives[d]	Budgetary Initiatives[e]	Recorded Votes	Plenary Hours
1991	237	2			110	1,796	1,290	621	521
1992	415	4			149	2,111	467	834	614
1993	385	5			179	2,285	447	897	539
1994	419	6		38	248	2,378	669	974	747
1995	221	3	65	18	70	351	364	273	355
1996	302	7	145	152	139	580	441	311	601
1997	290	8	211	251	237	898	705	279	598
1998	327	2	307	370	394	1,131	931	372	759
1999	198	4	49	72	196	607	1,042	249	425
2000	215	3	82	106	195	37/273	1,127	253	519
2001	251	5	92	145	169	294	1,341	271	496
2002	273	5	85	165	187	209	1,523	481	661
2003	181	5	70	112	166	97	908	491	367
2004	282	8	79	145	152	118	1,069	722	536
2005	232	6	53	140	161	118	1,269	815	492
2006	280	8	80	178	186	167	1,580	1,002	542
2007	181	3	52	138	145	64	1,069	668	446
2008	236	8	86	137	137	78	1,088	722	471

Source: Data from Information service of the Eduskunta. Data on recorded votes from Pajala 2006 and data kindly supplied by Antti Pajala.

Note: This table does not include questions and interpellations.

[a]U-matters = usually legislative proposals from the Commission of the European Union that fall within the competence of the parliament.

[b]E-matters = other EU matters, typically commission's legislative initiatives that fall outside the jurisdiction of the Eduskunta and nonlegislative documents published by the EU institutions or the Finnish government.

[c]Private members' bills = an individual MP can propose a new law or the amendment or repeal of an existing law.

[d]Petitionary initiatives = a proposal by an individual MP concerning either legislation or other measures.

[e]Budgetary initiatives = an individual MP can propose that an appropriation in the government's budget proposal be increased or reduced or that a new appropriation is added to the budget. These initiatives are handled during the annual budget debate.

1987, the procedure was reformed to give other MPs the chance to put forward additional questions. The monthly questions to the Council of State were televised live and were introduced in order to enable the parliament and the cabinet to engage in a more open dialogue on topical issues. In 1993, the procedure for oral questions was again redesigned so that any MP could put questions to the cabinet ministers present in the chamber. In 1999, oral questions and questions to the Council of State were merged into a question time, during which MPs can spontaneously put questions to the ministers on topics of their own choice. These sessions are also shown live on the main state-owned TV channel. While the impact of questions is hard to measure, their steady increase shows that members find them worthwhile (see table 4.5).

TABLE 4.5. Parliamentary Questions in the Finnish Parliament (Eduskunta), 1945–2008

Year	Written Questions	Written Questions per Decade (annual average)	Oral Questions	Oral Questions per Decade (annual average)	Questions to the Council of State	Questions to the Council of State per Decade (annual average)
1945	69					
1946	77					
1947	152					
1948	37					
1949	86	421 (84)				
1950	154					
1951	49					
1952	100					
1953	159					
1954	68					
1955	100					
1956	82					
1957	174					
1958	35					
1959	90	1,011 (101)				
1960	152					
1961	168					
1962	129					
1963	146					
1964	196					
1965	276					
1966	78		78			
1967	177		214			
1968	216		274			
1969	301	1,839 (184)	445		1,011 (253)	
1970	226		436			
1971	316		396			
1972	331		362			
1973	302		420			
1974	383		463			
1975	210		291			
1975 II	101		132 (EEDB)/ total 555			
1976	382		332			
1977	431		287			
1978	664		462			
1979	323	3,669 (367)	327		4,040 (404)	
1980	617		432			
1981	507		431			
1982	549		755			
1983	341		360			
1984	495		462			
1985	468 (EEDB)/ 460 (EKLIBR)		411/410 (EKLIBR)			

TABLE 4.5—(Continued)

Year	Written Questions	Written Questions per Decade (annual average)	Oral Questions	Oral Questions per Decade (annual average)	Questions to the Council of State	Questions to the Council of State per Decade (annual average)
1986	564		728			
1987	493		224			
1988	715		229			
1989	697	5,446 (545)	149	4,181 (418)	102	
1990	841		200		133	
1991	443 (EEDB)/ 441 (EKLIBR)		190		64	
1992	765		261		126	
1993	731		72		95	
1994	907		292		74	
1995	445		138		75	
1996	1,011		165		107	
1997	1,357		195		98	
1998	1,745		296		50	
1999	993	9,238 (924)	191	2,000 (200)		924 (92)
2000	1,071		264			
2001	1,440		212			
2002	1,254		259			
2003	723		151			
2004	1,068		236			
2005	1,101		180			
2006	1,206		213			
2007	637		124			
2008	1,066	9,566 (1 063)	207	1,846 (205)		

Source: Data from Information service of the Eduskunta. EEDB = according to Eduskunta's electronic database; EK-LIBR = according to Eduskunta's library.

Note: Originally MPs could table only written questions (introduced in 1906), with oral questions introduced in 1966 and questions to the Council of State introduced in 1989. The first two options were available to individual MPs, but questions to the Council of State had to be signed by at least four MPs, and they had to be on matters that were both "current" and "of consequence." In 1999 the oral questions and questions to the Council of State were merged into a question time, during which MPs can spontaneously put questions to the ministers on topics of their own choice.

The Eduskunta has attempted to make plenary debates a more central aspect of its work. The amount of time devoted to debates has increased from around 300 hours annually in the 1970s to the current level of approximately 500 hours. Reforms carried out in the 1990s gave the cabinet and MPs (either as a group or as individual parliamentarians) the right to propose debates on topical matters (Nousiainen 2006, 293–94). In addition, the streamlining of the various reporting requirements of the cabinet and the increase in the number of such reports has improved the quality of information received by the Eduskunta (Nousiainen 2006, 293–94, 313–15). This applies particularly to cabinet reports and announcements by the prime ministers, which have become routine tools of parliamentary debate. The cabinet has submitted about five such reports per year since the early 1990s, and the number of announcements has been about three during the first years of the twenty-first century. While these reforms have undoubtedly elevated the status of the plenary debates (as illustrated by the regular presence of the PM in the chamber), it is very difficult to evaluate their impact on parliament's ability to control the cabinet. Nonetheless, it is clear that the cabinet is now required to publicly explain and defend its actions and policies to a much greater extent than before.

Like the other Nordic legislatures, the Eduskunta can be categorized as a "working parliament," with emphasis on work carried out in parliamentary committees. Committee consideration of laws is mandatory and precedes the plenary stage. A committee has a quorum when at least two-thirds of its members are present (unless a higher quorum is specifically required). Committees meet behind closed doors, and ministers do not hold seats on committees. According to the constitution, in each electoral term, the Eduskunta appoints the Grand Committee (the EU committee), the Constitutional Law Committee, the Foreign Affairs Committee, the Finance Committee, and other standing committees. In addition, the Eduskunta can appoint ad hoc committees. The number of committees has remained quite stable, with an increase of only two after 1945. More important, a major reform of the committee system was carried out in 1991. Two committees were abolished, and three new ones were established. Committee jurisdictions were also reshuffled. As a result of these reforms, the competencies of individual standing committees largely mirror the jurisdiction of the respective ministries (Forsten 2005, 67). It also appears that the frequency and duration of committee meetings have risen over time.

A crucial element in holding the government accountable is access to information, and in this sense, the Eduskunta's powers have traditionally been very strong. According to the constitution, the parliament and its committees have access to all information in the possession of public authorities that they need in the consideration of relevant matters (Section 47). These strong information rights are complemented by the right to receive information on matters relating to the EU (Section 96); reports from the cabinet (Section 44); the government's annual reports on its activities, measures undertaken in response to parliamentary decisions, state finances, and adherence to the budget (Section 46); and information on international affairs (Section 97). The right to receive information on EU matters and international affairs, introduced in connection with Finland's joining the EU, has improved the Eduskunta's capacity to control the government.

Turning, finally, to the dissolution of the parliament, until the 1990s, the president alone had the right to dissolve the Eduskunta and order new elections, and he was not obliged to consult the cabinet or parliament before doing so. The president exercised this right four times during the postwar era (in 1953, 1962, 1971, and 1975). A constitutional amendment in 1991 altered the situation in favor of the cabinet, by requiring the explicit consent of the PM for parliamentary dissolution. Section 26 of the new constitution consolidated this practice: "The President of the Republic, in response to a reasoned proposal by the Prime Minister, and after having heard the parliamentary groups, and while the Parliament is in session, may order that extraordinary parliamentary elections shall be held. Thereafter, the Parliament shall decide the time when it concludes its work before the elections."

Within the Cabinet

There are no constitutional regulations about the number of ministers or how they are to be selected. The new constitution states, "The Government consists of the Prime Minister and the necessary number of Ministers. The Ministers shall be Finnish citizens known to be honest and competent" (Section 60). The number of ministers has remained fairly constant since World War II, although there has been a slight increase, with recent cabinets having 18 ministers. The current cabinet, formed after the 2007 elections, has an all-time high of 20 ministers, 12 of whom are women. The number of ministries has also remained about the same and is currently 12.

Table 4.6 reports background information about those who have occupied the four key ministerial portfolios between 1945 and 2005—PM, finance minister, foreign minister, and justice minister (the ministry in charge of the police). Most prime ministers have had prior cabinet experience and high-ranking posts in both the party and parliament. Party experience has been less important for foreign ministers, while cabinet experience and prior employment in the public sector have been more prevalent. Finance ministers are most likely to have had prior employment in the private sector as well as a background in the party and parliament. Prior high-ranking positions in the party and parliament are the least common among those appointed to the position of foreign minister. Justice ministers, on the other hand, are the least likely to have prior cabinet experience, they are slightly younger than other ministers, and more likely to have held important office at local or regional levels.

TABLE 4.6. Ministerial Background, First Appointment, by Portfolio, Finland, 1945–2005

Portfolio within Cabinet	Age (mean years)	Female Ministers (%)	Prior Cabinet Position (%)	Parliamentary Experience (mean years)[a]	Prior Party High-Rank Position (%)[b]	Prior Youth Party High-Rank Position (%)[c]	Major Prior Appointment within Parliament (%)[d]	Major Prior Elected Offices at Local/Regional Level (%)[e]	Formal Education Level[f]	Any Prior Employment within the Public Sector (%)[g]	Any Prior Employment within the Private Sector (%)	Any Prior Salaried Employment in Party (%)	Member of Parliament at the Time of Minister Appointment (%)[h]	N (unique number of ministers)
Prime minister	51.9	4	78	6.2	65	26	65	52	4.1	83	74	30	48	23
Finance minister[i]	49.5	0	57	8.5	57	13	60	57	3.7	70	83	30	73	30
Foreign minister	51.1	5	67	4.8	43	19	48	33	4.3	86	62	24	48	21
Justice minister[j]	47.5	0	42	6.8	55	6	52	77	3.4	81	74	23	65	31
Mean 1945–2005	50.0	2	61	6.6	55	16	56	55	3.9	80	73	27	58	105
Mean 1945–75	50.7	0	65	6.0	53	10	49	50	3.8	81	75	26	54	80
Mean 1991–2005	48.9	13	47	10.2	67	20	87	80	3.9	80	73	27	87	15

Source: Data compiled from the information services of the Eduskunta and the Council of State.

Note: All of the calculations presented in this section are based on a data set that contains data on ministers who got portfolios at the beginning of a new cabinet. A new cabinet is defined here as a cabinet that fulfills at least one of three conditions: any change in the set of parties holding cabinet membership, any change in the identity of the prime minister, or any general election (see Müller and Strøm 2003, 12).

[a] Prior parliamentary experience (in full years) does not include years that a person has been in cabinet. That is, for systems that allow for the holding of simultaneous cabinet and parliamentary positions, we only count "parliamentary experience" for the years that the MP does not also have a cabinet position. (The latter is coded as prior cabinet experience: yes or no.) If the total parliamentary experience (service as MP) sums to less than six months, it is counted as zero (0) years of experience.

[b] Prior party high-rank position refers to any of the following: party leader, party secretary, member of the party national board, or head of local or regional board.

[c] Prior youth party high-rank position refers to the positions in a youth organization corresponding to the prior party high-rank positions.

[d] Major prior appointment within parliament refers to any of the following: Speaker (president of parliament or chamber/subdivision), group leader, vice group leader, committee chairman, or vice committee chairman.

[e] Major prior elected offices at local/regional level refers to any of the following: head of municipality, head of region, member of local parliament, or member of regional parliament.

[f] Formal education level: 1 = primary (or less); 2 = secondary (high school, Swedish gymnasium); 3 = any enrollment in postsecondary education (such as technical college, nursing school, college, university) but no degree; 4 = any undergraduate degree at technical college, nursing school, college, or university (2–4 years in length) that is post–high school or post-gymnasium; 5 = postgraduate degree (licensiat, huvudfag, PhD).

[g] Prior employment refers to the employer, that is to say, the one paying the salary. Salary by the party does not include elected offices, only jobs (such as party ombudsman). The three categories (public, private, party) are not mutually exclusive categories (as they, in combination, speak to a minister's general career pattern). Private employment includes people employed in trade unions and other nongovernmental organizations.

[h] The coding "Member of parliament at the time of minister appointment" only has one possible answer (yes or no).

[i] Finance minister is defined as the minister heading the ministry in control of the state budget.

[j] Justice minister is defined as the minister heading the ministry in control of the police force.

Recently appointed cabinet ministers (those who were first appointed to their respective posts between 1991 and 2005) have been slightly younger and more likely to be female than the average for the whole post-1945 period. In addition, recent cabinet members have more experience from parliamentary work and are more likely to have held high-ranking positions both in parliament and in their parties. After 1991, 87 percent of the key ministers were MPs at the time of their appointment to the cabinet, compared to only 58 percent over the entire postwar period. Interestingly, however, fewer key ministers have prior experience from cabinet work, although this finding is probably partly explained by increased cabinet duration since the early 1980s. The most recent cabinet, appointed after the 2007 elections, includes also a high proportion of senior politicians, measured in terms of both previous parliamentary and cabinet experience and positions within their parties.

While recent constitutional developments have undoubtedly strengthened the position of the prime minister (Paloheimo 2002, 2003, 2005a), the bargaining involved in forming and sustaining coalition cabinets significantly constrains the executive powers of the PM. This is particularly true as regards his or her ability to hire and fire line ministers. Apart from ministers from the PM's own party and with the possible exception of the two most important sectoral portfolios, finance and foreign ministers, the PM has hardly any influence on the selection of cabinet members, which is the prerogative of coalition partners. The same applies to dismissal powers. Since 1991, the PM has had the right to ask the president to fire an individual minister.[7] Although the PM can put pressure on coalition partners, he or she cannot, in practice, appoint or dismiss individual ministers without the consent of the cabinet parties. However, if the PM resigns, the whole cabinet is dissolved. In addition, the office of the prime minister has risen in stature in recent decades. It coordinates decision making in the ministries and operates as a broker in case of disputes within or between ministries. The PM's office had a staff of 70 in 1970, 192 in 1980, 124 in 1990, 227 in 2000 (Paloheimo 2002, 213), and 243 in late 2007.

There are two kinds of government plenaries (meetings of the cabinet), those chaired by the PM and those chaired by the president. In the latter, there is no voting, as the president alone makes decisions on the basis of a presentation by the minister to whose portfolio the item belongs. In plenaries chaired by the PM, voting is used (with a simple majority decision rule), but decisions are taken collegially (Paloheimo 2003, 226). In addition to plenary meetings, the work of the cabinet is coordinated through four statutory ministerial committees: the Cabinet Committee on Foreign and Security Policy, the Cabinet Finance Committee, the Cabinet Committee on Economic Policy, and, since 1995, the Cabinet Committee on European Union Affairs. All committees are chaired by the PM. In addition, recent governments have set up issue-specific working groups to improve horizontal coordination within the executive. The full plenary session is seldom the place where decisions are actually made; hence the work carried out in the ministerial committees or at the level of individual ministers has become increasingly relevant in terms of understanding where power lies within the cabinet.

However, the most important decisions are made in discussions between the leaders of the coalition parties, including planning the cabinet's agenda (Paloheimo 2002, 2003; Tiili 2008). Since postwar cabinets have tended to be broad coalitions, the PM needs good bargaining skills, because decisions are usually based on deals among the coalition partners. In addition to meetings of the coalition leaders, an increasingly important conflict-resolution mechanism—or a way to preempt conflicts—is the cabinet program. These programs have become longer and more detailed over the decades, with coalition partners investing a lot of resources in bargaining over them.[8] The length of the programs is primarily explained by the high number of parties forming the cabinet and the need to commit them (and their party groups) to established rules and policies. Whereas the program of the Sorsa VI cabinet, appointed in 1983, contained 1,788 words, the program of the Vanhanen cabinet from 2007 contained 15,304 words. There was a major leap at the turn of the millennium, with the cabinets appointed since the turn of the century drafting programs in excess of 12,000 words.

It is commonly accepted among the cabinet parties that the program forms the backbone of the cabinet and that it binds all the parties (Nousiainen 2000; Paloheimo 2003).[9] The cabinet parties also monitor their party groups to ensure that they support these programs. The rules in use since the early 1980s concerning cooperation between the governing parties' parliamentary groups effectively prevent any public expression of disagreement or conflict between the cabinet and the party groups. The only exceptions are matters that are clearly "local" in nature and certain questions of conscience (Nousiainen 2006, 308–10; Wiberg 2006, 191–93).

Individual ministers have become more autonomous actors in recent decades, and they wield stronger influence in their fields of competence than previously. Since 1970, all ministers have had their own special political advisors, distinct from civil servants in the ministries. Since 2005, ministers may also have their own state secretaries. In the Vanhanen cabinet appointed after the 2007 elections, just over half of the ministers had one. This delegation of authority from the PM and the cabinet to the individual ministers is primarily explained by the increasing workload of the government and the resulting need to divide labor and delegate power to the line ministers (Nousiainen 2000, 89–92; Paloheimo 2002, 211–14; Paloheimo 2003). Nevertheless, individual action by ministers is strongly constrained by the cabinet program and the agreements between the leaders of the coalition parties, at least in politically significant matters. It has been argued that Finnish line ministers have little autonomy compared to their European counterparts (Nousiainen 2000, 270).

Examining the electoral performance of cabinet parties, we can clearly see the impact of multiparty coalitions and a fragmented party system (see table 4.7). The cabinet almost always contains both parties that won and parties that lost votes in the most recent election. However, the party holding the position of the PM tends to lose votes in the subsequent election, while the share of votes cast for the biggest opposition party has increased in nearly all elections. With the exception of the 1983 elections, cabinet parties have collectively lost votes in all elections held since the mid-1960s.[10]

Constitutional reforms have also impacted on cabinet termination. With the president and the Kremlin no longer intervening in government work, either recent cabinets have stayed in office for the full four-year period, or cabinet termination has been explained by disputes among cabinet parties (rather than disputes between the cabinet and president). In the past, it was customary for the cabinet to resign when a presidential election was held. However, this has not happened since 1982. Foreign policy imperatives have brought down two cabinets, in 1959 (Fagerholm III) and 1962 (Miettunen I). In both cases, a crisis in the relationship with the Soviet Union was the cause.

Turning to relations between the cabinet and the opposition, recent constitutional reforms have widened the gap between the ruling majority and the opposition. Finland has traditionally been categorized among countries in which the impact of opposition parties on government policy is higher than average, not least through the committee system (Laver and Hunt 1992; Strøm 1990). More specifically, the instrument of the deferment rule empowered the opposition. According to the deferment rule, one-third of MPs (67 of 200) could postpone the final adoption of an ordinary law until the next election, with the proposal adopted if a majority in the new parliament supported it. In 1987, the period of postponement was shortened to the next annual parliamentary session, and the whole mechanism was abolished in 1992. This deferment rule partially explained the propensity to form oversized coalitions and contributed to the practice of inclusive, consensual decision making that reduced the gap between cabinet and opposition (Mattila 1997; Forestiere 2008). It was expected that the abolition of the deferment rule would result in minimum winning coalitions or in cabinets with narrower majorities in the parliament, but this has clearly not taken place (see table 4.3).

Given the abolition of the deferment rule and other constitutional changes, it is not surprising that since the early 1990s, Finland has become a strongly executive-dominated polity (Nousiainen 2006; Raunio and Wiberg 2008). However, it is still fair to argue that Finland operates largely according to consensual practices, especially in decision making on foreign

TABLE 4.7. Electoral Performance of Incumbent Cabinet Parties, Finland, 1946–2008

Cabinet Number	Cabinet Composition	Election Year following Cabinet	FPDU	SDL	GR	SDP	CE	FRP	LIB[a]	CHR	SW	CON	Cabinet Total
2	FPDU, SDP, CE, SW 1946–48	1948	−3.5			+1.2	+2.9				−0.2		+0.4
5	CE, SDP, LIB, SW 1951	1951				+0.2	−1.0		+1.8		−0.1		+0.9
19	CE 1961–62	1962					−0.1						−0.1
22	CE, LIB, SW, CON 1964–66	1966					−1.8		+0.2		−0.4	−1.2	−3.2
24	SDP, FPDU, SDL, CE, SW 1968–70	1970	−4.4	−1.2		−3.8	−4.1				−0.4		−13.9
35	SDP, FPDU, CE, LIB 1978–79	1979	−1.0			−1.0	−0.3		−0.6				−2.9
38	SDP, CE, LIB, SW 1982–83	1983				+2.8	+0.3				+0.4		+3.5
39	SDP, CE, FRP, SW 1983–87	1987				−2.6	0	−3.4			+0.7		−5.3
41	CON, SDP, SW 1990–91	1991				−2.0					+0.2	−3.8	−5.6
43	CE, SW, CON 1994–95	1995					−5.0				−0.4	−1.4	−6.8
44	SDP, FPDU, GR, SW, CON 1995	1999	−0.3		+0.8	−5.4					0	+3.1	−1.8
46	SDP, FPDU, SW, CON 2002	2003	−1.0			+1.6					−0.5	−2.4	−2.3
48	CE, SDP, SW 2003	2007				−3.1	−1.6				0		−4.7
	Mean gain/loss		−2.0	−1.2	+0.8	−1.2	−1.1	−3.4	+0.5		−0.1	−1.1	−3.2

Source: Data from Nousiainen 2003; from 1999 onward compiled by Tapio Raunio from data of *Statistics Finland*.
Notes: See the notes to table 4.1 for explanation of party labels. Numbers in table represent percentage of national vote.
[a] In the 1983 elections the Liberal party (LIB) merged with the Center party (CE). There are no separate numbers reported for the Liberal party in that election.

policy and EU matters. The Finnish political system is often characterized as both consensual and elitist (Ruostetsaari 2003). This applies particularly to foreign policy, in which maintaining amicable relations with the Soviet Union was of overriding importance during the cold war. Even though the range of actors involved in making foreign and security policy has broadened, the same logic largely continues to guide decision making, with emphasis on achieving national unity and avoiding public dissent.

These consensual arrangements are further enhanced by the system used to formulate national integration policy. The most important purpose of the national EU coordination system is to manufacture national unanimity or at least broad consensus, which can arguably be translated into additional influence in EU level bargaining (Raunio 2006a). While the overall aim "is to speak with one voice on all levels of decision shaping in Brussels" (Stubb, Kaila, and Ranta 2001, 306), the importance attached to achieving such consistency varies between policy areas and individual legislative initiatives. In general, the coordination system is based on wide consultation among both public and private actors, including the parliament and the relevant interest groups. Decision making in other policy domains is also broadly inclusive and based on extensive consultation with key interest groups.

Between Cabinet and Civil Servants

Finnish public administration is divided into three levels: national, regional, and municipal. The national-level administration consists of ministries and other central state agencies. Since the preparation of issues and actual decision making is often delegated downward from the minister to the civil servants, the leading bureaucrats in the ministries are especially influential players.

Ministers directly control the agencies under their jurisdiction, but their steering authority is constrained by a lack of effective appointment and dismissal powers and by the legalistic tradition of the state bureaucracy. It is particularly noteworthy that the top civil servants in the ministries, the permanent secretaries, are appointed not by the ministers but by the president. However, party politics does penetrate most levels of administration. For example, party membership can facilitate access to influential, well-paid positions. This applies particularly to top jobs in state-owned companies, central state agencies, and ministries but also to regional and local levels. Patronage is therefore not unknown, although it is not a core element of the political system or a major factor in the relationship between the cabinet and supporting parties. The political culture is primarily legalistic, and the spoils system has never been very characteristic of the Finnish public administration (Nousiainen 1996, 123).

Legislation and public policy reforms have traditionally been prepared within ministries in committees where both politicians and civil servants are represented. The number of such committees has dwindled since their peak in the 1970s. There were 178 such committees in 1972, while there were only 11 in 2000. They have been replaced with reports produced by nonpartisan policy advisors or working groups consisting primarily of civil servants appointed by the ministries. There were 113 working groups in 1972, but the number had risen to 368 by 1994. The first two reports produced by nonpartisan policy advisors appeared in 1989, and the number had increased to 12 by 1997 (Temmes 2001). These developments have led to a decline in the connection between parties and policy formulation and have strengthened the technocratic and legalistic nature of the administration. They are part of broader reforms introduced in line with New Public Management thinking. The reforms have been carried out since the early 1990s, and the goal is to promote a more managerial and cost-effective organization of central state bureaucracy, including ministries, public agencies, and state-owned companies (Temmes 2003; Tiihonen 2006).

In recent years, Finnish governments have invested resources in improving coordination and strategic planning inside the cabinet and the entire executive branch. These efforts go back to a report the government commissioned from three foreign experts, according to which the key problem was the sectorized way of managing the central government (Bouckaert, Ormond, and Peters 2000; see also Tiili 2008). Hence the cabinets appointed since 2003 have tried to improve horizontal coordination inside the executive, mainly through the government's intersectoral policy programs and other coordination instruments, such as the government strategy document. While these reforms have undoubtedly improved central coordination of government decision making, it is very difficult to evaluate the extent to which the PM and other ministers are effectively in control of the policy processes and their ministries. After all, the establishment of these steering mechanisms was mainly a response to the cabinet's observed weaknesses in ensuring central coordination of public policy-making.

External Constraints

The most significant external constraint on the parliamentary chain of delegation in Finland has traditionally been the president (Arter 1999; Nousiainen 2001; Paloheimo 2001; Raunio and Wiberg 2003; Raunio 2004). As the president's role in cabinet formation and the dissolution of the parliament has been discussed in the previous sections, the analysis here focuses on the other traditionally important areas of presidential influence: foreign policy leadership, the passage of legislation, and appointment powers.

Finland is the oldest semi-presidential regime in Europe, with a directly elected president coexisting alongside a cabinet that is accountable to the parliament. This formal division of powers is stated in Section 3 of the constitution: "The legislative powers are exercised by the Parliament, which shall also decide on State finances. The governmental powers are exercised by the President of the Republic and the Government, the members of which shall have the confidence of the Parliament." Under the old constitution, the president was recognized as the supreme executive power, but the text of the constitution left room for interpretation, which the presidents, particularly Urho Kekkonen, used to their advantage. The balance between cabinet and president was therefore both constitutionally and politically strongly in favor of the president until the constitutional reforms of the 1990s, which were partly a response to the excesses of the Kekkonen era. A period of parliamentarization started in 1982, when President Koivisto took office after a quarter of a century of politics dominated by Kekkonen. President Koivisto and the political elite in general favored strengthening parliamentarism and curtailing the powers of the president. Table 4.8 summarizes the development of presidential powers during Finland's independence.

Apart from constitutional regulations, the widely acknowledged priority of maintaining amicable relations with the Soviet Union concentrated power in the hands of the president. Thus, additional impetus for downgrading presidential powers came as a result of the end of the cold war, since the dissolution of the Soviet bloc reduced the importance of personalized foreign policy leadership. Under the old constitution, foreign policy was the exclusive domain of the president. According to Section 93 of the new constitution, "the foreign policy of Finland is directed by the President of the Republic in co-operation with the Government. However, the Parliament accepts Finland's international obligations and their denouncement and decides on the bringing into force of Finland's international obligations in so far as provided in this Constitution. The President decides on matters of war and peace, with the consent of the Parliament. The Government is responsible for the national preparation of the decisions to be made in the European Union, and decides on the concomitant Finnish measures, unless the decision requires the approval of the Parliament. The Parliament participates in the national preparation of decisions to be made in the European Union, as provided in this Constitution."

In short, the president directs foreign policy but does so together with the cabinet and through the government's ministerial committee. However, it can be argued that the text of the constitution does not reflect reality (Raunio 2008). The president is expected to lead foreign policy without any

TABLE 4.8. Finland: Balance of Power by Constitutional Period

Division of Power According to the Constitution	Old Constitution (1919 until late 1980s)	Period of Constitutional Change (late 1980s–90s)	New Constitution (2000–)
General authority in executive decision making	President	President/Cabinet	Cabinet
Appointment of the cabinet	President has autonomous powers	President, after hearing parliamentary party groups	Parliament; president's role purely formal
Resignation of the cabinet	Parliament, or prime minister, or president indirectly by dissolving parliament	Parliament, or prime minister	Parliament, or prime minister
Dissolution of the parliament and the calling of an early election	President	President after an initiative by the prime minister	President after an initiative by the prime minister
Legislation: power of veto	President may delay the adoption of a law until after the next election	President may formally delay the adoption of a law until the next parliamentary session. Parliament may then override the president's veto.	President may formally delay the adoption of a law for up to three months. Parliament may then override the president's veto.
Legislation: decrees	President and cabinet	President and cabinet	Cabinet
Leadership in foreign policy	President	President	President in cooperation with cabinet
EU policy	Not Applicable: Finland not a member of the EU	Cabinet	Cabinet
Commander in chief of the armed forces	President	President	President
Appointment of senior civil servants	President appoints quite a large proportion of senior civil servants; other civil servants are appointed by cabinet or ministries	The number of senior civil servants appointed by the president is reduced.	President appoints only a very limited group of the highest civil servants.

Source: Adapted from Paloheimo 2003, 225.

administrative resources of his or her own, with basically all foreign policy matters prepared under the auspices of the cabinet. Intentionally or not, this arrangement clearly weakens the ability of the president to lead foreign policy. Without any doubt, the biggest challenge is the difficulty of drawing a clear line between European policy and other foreign policy matters. This applies in particular to the development of the EU's foreign and security policy. The problem is more political than administrative or legal by nature—that is, legal experts can always ultimately decide whether an issue is a foreign policy (requiring coleadership) or an EU matter (in the competence of the cabinet). However, the strong links between EU policy and foreign affairs make such categorizations inherently difficult, as national foreign and security policies are increasingly influenced by European coordination processes and policy choices. Hence it is completely logical that the current president has tried to legitimize her role in EU matters through the strong linkage between European and foreign policy, with the cabinet (supported by the Eduskunta) in turn safeguarding its territory.

With regard to the passage of legislation, the president has traditionally held both constitutionally and politically strong powers. New laws generally originate in legislative proposals from the government.[11] According to the constitution (Section 58), the president, in a presidential session of the government, determines that a bill shall be introduced in parliament.[12] The Eduskunta plenary session first sends the bill to a committee for preparation. Once the report of the committee has been issued, the proposal is considered in two readings in the plenary session. In the first reading, the committee report is debated, and a decision on the contents of the legislative proposal is made. In the second reading, which occurs no earlier than three days after the conclusion of the first reading, the parliament decides by simple majority whether to accept or reject the legislative proposal.[13]

Prior to a 1987 constitutional amendment, the president could delay legislation until overridden by a newly elected parliament. Provided that there was no early dissolution, the delay could be several years. Between 1987 and 2000 the president could delay laws until the next parliamentary session and under the new constitution this period was shortened to three months, with the parliament having the right to override the president's veto. According to the new constitution, bills adopted by the Eduskunta are submitted to the president for confirmation. If the president fails to confirm a law within three months, it is returned to the parliament. If the Eduskunta then readopts the bill "without material alterations," it enters into force without presidential confirmation (Section 77). Since a proposal can become a law without the president's approval, he or she has only a suspensive veto. It must be emphasized that, in practice, presidents have not challenged cabinet proposals or parliamentary decisions.

The president enjoyed very strong appointment powers until the new constitution entered into force. Until 1998, the president even appointed university presidents and professors. Although the new constitution reduced presidential powers by narrowing the list of offices the president appoints, these appointment powers are still fairly extensive and thus form, at least theoretically, a major constraint on the relationship between the government and the state bureaucracy. The president decides on these appointments in the government plenary session and on the recommendation of the cabinet.

While the president's powers have been significantly curtailed, the move to direct elections may give rise to a countertendency. The president is elected for no more than two consecutive six-year terms. Until 1982, the president was elected by an electoral college of 300 members (301 in 1982), who were elected by the same proportional system as MPs. A onetime experiment was conducted in the 1988 election, involving a mixed two-ticket system of direct and indirect voting. To be elected by a direct vote, a candidate needed to receive 50 percent of the votes. As no candidate reached this share, the election was passed on to a simultaneously elected electoral college. A new direct-election system for choosing the president was first used in 1994. If a candidate receives more than half of the votes, he or she is elected president. If none of the candidates receives the majority of the votes, a new election is held on the third Sunday after the first election. In the second round, the two persons who received the most votes in the first round run against each other. The candidate who receives the majority of votes is then elected president. In the three direct elections held so far (in 1994, 2000, and 2006), basically all candidates emphasized that, if elected, they would exercise the powers vested in the presidency, thus signaling that they had no plans to remain in the background. Turnout has been higher in presidential elections than in Eduskunta elections (in 2006, 73.9 percent voted in the first round and 77.2 percent in the second round). Also, the public seems to favor strong leadership. The system of dual executives may therefore result in tensions between the cabinet and the president, particularly in foreign policy issues and if the PM and the president represent different parties or have otherwise conflicting preferences (Isotalus and Borg 2007).

Corporatism is the second significant national constraint on parliamentary democracy. In comparative studies, Finland is usually ranked as having one of the most corporatist systems of governance. However, organized interests—such as labor, industry, and farmers—have traditionally not been as strong in Finland as in the other Nordic countries. Corporatism was particularly prevalent in the 1970s and 1980s, but there was a temporary weakening in the early 1990s, caused mainly by the economic recession that followed the dissolution of the Soviet Union. From the mid-1990s, the Lipponen cabinets (1995–2003) emphasized the importance of collective wage bargaining and corporatism, not least because the cooperation of the trade unions was seen as essential in order to meet the criteria of the Economic and Monetary Union and to maintain economic discipline once in the eurozone. While the system of collective wage talks is not as comprehensive as before, many labor market agreements and laws are effectively decided in tripartite negotiations between the employers' federations, the trade unions, and the government. Moreover, key interest groups are still actively involved in preparing new policies, and hence their voice is routinely heard in policymaking (Kauppinen 2003).

Trade union density has also risen over the decades, and over 80 percent of the workforce now belongs to trade unions. This is reflected in the memberships of the four main unions—the Central Organization of Finnish Trade Unions (SAK), the Confederation of Unions for Academic Professionals in Finland (AKAVA), the Finnish Confederation of Salaried Employees (STTK), and the Central Union of Agricultural Producers and Forest Owners (MTK). The decline in the membership of MTK is due to the simple fact that a smaller share of the population derives its income from agriculture. For example, the number of farms declined quite rapidly in recent decades.

While municipal governments are responsible for much of total government spending, the subnational level does not constitute an important constraint on national government. The spending of the local governments is mainly related to delivering core welfare state policies (primarily education, health care, and social security policies), and, overall, the municipal councils have relatively little freedom of maneuver when implementing such laws. Despite the introduction of reforms since the 1990s that have somewhat strengthened regional administration, Finland remains a unitary state, without any democratically elected regional bodies.

The increasing judicialization of politics—for example, through the European Convention on Human Rights and the European Court of Justice—has become a more important constraint on Finnish parliamentarianism. Finland has no actual constitutional court, but the parliamentary ombudsman and the chancellor of justice control the activities of the courts of law and other authorities and monitor civil servants and other persons responsible for public affairs, in order to ensure that they uphold the law and fulfill their responsibilities. Citizens make more active use of these channels than before. In 1945, the parliamentary ombudsman received a total of 971 complaints. It had risen modestly to 1,037 by 1970. Since then, complaints have become much more common. There were 1,747 in 1990, and citizens submitted 3,352 complaints to the ombudsman in 2005. The chancellor of justice received 250 complaints in 1945. The figure was 726 in 1970 and 976 in 1990. In 2005, citizens' complaints to the chancellor of justice totaled 1,186 (Wiberg 2006, 143).

National referendums, which are only consultative, have been used twice in Finland: on the prohibition of alcohol in 1931 and on EU membership in 1994. Examining the media, we find a radical decline in the share of newspapers that are officially or publicly affiliated with political parties. Immediately after World War II, in 1946, just above one-third (34.8 percent) of all newspapers issued between three and seven days a week were unaffiliated with political parties. Almost half (49.8 percent) were affiliated with the non-left parties, and 15.4 percent with leftist parties. The share of "neutral" newspapers had risen to 68.3 percent by 1986 and was as high as 96.6 percent in 2000 (Jyrkiäinen and Savisaari 2003). The concentration of media ownership together with the decline of party-affiliated newspapers means that the news content of the media (excluding the Internet) has become increasingly similar, with fewer alternative views offered to the citizens (Nieminen, Aslama, and Pantti 2005).

While European integration is undoubtedly a major external constraint on national political systems (see chapter 3), EU membership has in fact strengthened parliamentary democracy in Finland by consolidating the political leadership of the cabinet and strengthening the PM. Most notably, with the exception of treaty amendments, EU matters belong almost exclusively to the jurisdiction of the cabinet. The cabinet dictates national EU policy, with the president intervening mainly when questions related to Finland's foreign policy are on the agenda. The PM is the primary representative of Finland in the EU, but the president has also participated in most summits of the European Council. In practice, the president now focuses on what is left of so-called traditional foreign policy matters, that is, Finland's relations with countries outside the EU that are not handled via the EU (Raunio and Tiilikainen 2003, 96–112; Raunio 2008).

With respect to the impact of EU membership on the Eduskunta, while the Eduskunta has lost power to the EU, it has subjected the cabinet to relatively tight scrutiny in EU matters. Between 1995 and 2003, 12 percent of the laws enacted by the Eduskunta contained a reference to EU law (Wiberg 2004a). The most likely explanation for this relatively low share of

EU-related domestic laws is that most of the legislation adopted by the Eduskunta (and other national parliaments) deals with policy issues over which the EU has no legislative competence. At the same time, the Eduskunta (2005) itself has estimated that EU matters comprise as much as almost half of all the items processed by the parliament. Also, the workload of parliamentary committees has increased substantially as a result of EU membership. However, European matters are seldom debated in plenary session, with only more far-reaching EU decisions inspiring plenary debates.

Comparative studies indicate that the Eduskunta has one of the strongest scrutiny systems of the national parliaments of the EU countries (Raunio 2005b). The scrutiny model of the Eduskunta has four main strengths: the position of the parliament is regulated in the constitution, the Eduskunta gets involved relatively early in the processing of EU legislation, the parliament enjoys unlimited access to information from the government, and the responsibility for monitoring European matters is delegated downward to specialized committees (Jääskinen 2000). The Grand Committee is responsible for coordinating the Eduskunta's positions on EU issues, while the Foreign Affairs Committee deals with matters related to EU's foreign and security policy. The minister appears in the Grand Committee in person before and, when required, after the meeting of the Council of State. The standing committees are closely involved in the scrutiny of EU matters from an early stage in the policy process, and the final position of the Grand Committee is based on guidelines from the standing committees.

The constitutionally regulated access to information from the government reduces informational asymmetries in EU affairs. The rules encourage the government to provide the Eduskunta with information of its own accord, without any specific requests by MPs. Moreover, the active scrutiny of European matters has improved the overall dialogue between the cabinet and the Eduskunta. The regular appearance of ministers before the Grand Committee has led to improved policy coordination within the cabinet and between the ministries and has forced ministers to study the issues more thoroughly than might otherwise be the case. An often-mentioned feature of the EU policy process is bureaucratization, the shift of power from directly elected officeholders to civil servants. Likewise, in Finland, civil servants perform a central role at all stages of the process, from the initial formulation of the national position in the ministries in Helsinki to negotiations among the permanent representatives in Brussels. However, the autonomy of civil servants is at least partially counteracted by the active scrutiny of the Eduskunta in EU matters (Raunio 2007).

Conclusion

Developments in Finland point in two directions. As a result of constitutional amendments and the dissolution of the Soviet Union, the chain of delegation from voters to civil servants is now simpler than before and subject to fewer external constraints. Finland is therefore one of the few West European countries in which parliamentary democracy has become less constrained since the 1980s. At the same time, Finnish political parties are facing similar challenges as parties in the majority of West European countries.

The second step of delegation, from parliament to cabinet, is better designed to contain agency loss. Cabinet formation is now based on partisan negotiations. Free from presidential interference or the need to take foreign policy imperatives into account, it is also more responsive to the election result than before. The investiture vote requires that party groups of the cabinet parties in the Eduskunta actively support the cabinet from the beginning, and the cabinet program has, not surprisingly, become more important in guiding government action. The abolition of the deferment rule makes the division between the cabinet and the opposition clearer, and dissolving the parliament is now, in practice, in the hands of the PM. The information rights of the Eduskunta have become stronger, and MPs also make more use of control instruments such as interpellations and parliamentary questions. Above all, reflecting the parliamentarization of the political system, the Eduskunta is, at least formally, more in the center of things, as illustrated by the fact that the PM is far more actively present in the chamber than during the era of president-dominated politics.[14] Yet prospective as well as retrospective electoral accountability remains weaker than in the other Nordic countries; that is, it is harder for Finnish voters to influence which coalitions form in the first place, and it is more difficult for them to reward or punish particular parties for their performance in office.

Foreign policy excluded, Finland is effectively now a standard parliamentary democracy. While the president still enjoys quite significant powers, particularly regarding appointments, the political culture, at least among the elites, seems to be developing toward the consolidation of parliamentary government, with the president in the background in domestic politics. The direct election of the president may create problems in the future, particularly when the president and the PM represent different parties. But with the exception of the effects of European integration and corporatism, Finnish politics is much less subject to significant external constraints than previously.

Leadership by presidents has effectively been replaced with leadership by strong majority cabinets, which have ruled without much effective opposition since the early 1980s. While Finnish parties have by and large behaved in unitary fashion, the strongly decentralized system of candidate selection does constrain the ability of party leaders to reward and punish their MPs. That political parties do not align preferences as well as they used to is more worrisome. The strengthening of the parties in the Eduskunta stands in contrast to the weakening of the parties among the electorate. The cleavage structure is undergoing gradual transformation, and the ideological moderation inherent in cabinet formation and in formulating national EU policies widens the gap between citizens and elected officeholders. Moreover, fewer citizens turn out to vote or hold party membership cards. Nevertheless, for those who value parliamentary democracy, it is preferable to have strong working channels of delegation and accountability through the parliament—even with weakened electoral ties—than to have powerful but less accountable domestic constraints, such as a strong president, or nondemocratic external constraints, such as the Soviet Union.

NOTES

1. Constitution of Finland, 11 June 1999 (731/1999), Sections 16 and 19. These provisions are largely based on amendments that entered into force in 1995, and they include, for the first time, economic, social, and cultural rights.

2. The Center Party and the Swedish People's Party boast higher membership figures than the other parties. The grassroots organization of the Center Party has traditionally been very strong. As regards the Swedish People's Party, given its strong presence in Swedish-speaking municipalities, it is often quite difficult to draw the line between party members and nonparty members (Sundberg 1985, 119–72; Raunio 2006b).

3. Within electoral alliances, the distribution of seats is determined by the plurality principle regardless of the total number of votes won by the respective parties forming the alliance. No account is taken of the relative vote shares of the alliance partners, so smaller parties have tended to enter electoral alliances with larger parties. The Christian Democrats have particularly benefited from electoral alliances, with two-thirds of all the seats won by the party attributable to them (Paloheimo and Sundberg 2009).

4. The exception is the Social Democratic Party, which employs a system in which the placing of the candidates on the list is determined by their success in the membership ballots, with the candidate winning the most votes heading the list.

5. Despite the strong constituency connection, Finnish MPs primarily focus on national-level politics in their daily work. The traditionally strong role of the state, in terms of both legislative powers and identity, means that MPs focus first and foremost on influencing national legislation (Raunio 2005a).

6. For an informative analysis of the role of the opposition in Finland, see Arter 2006, 177–237, 262–66.

7. According to Section 64 of the constitution, "the President of the Republic grants, upon request, the resignation of the Government or a Minister. The President may also grant the resignation of a Minister on the proposal of the Prime Minister. The President shall in any event dismiss the Government or a Minister, if either no longer enjoys the confidence of Parliament, even if no request is made."

8. This does not necessarily apply to all policy sectors contained in the program or mean that the program would be a coherent document. While the programs contain detailed and specific objectives for some policy areas, they have been more vague on other matters, with much depending on the ability of the coalition partners to find agreement on the questions (Tiili 2008).

9. The binding nature of the cabinet program and the resulting lack of discussion inside the cabinet have attracted criticism from some leading politicians. The current minister for foreign trade and development, Paavo Väyrynen, who has served in the government during every decade since the 1970s, commented in an interview that "the most important change concerns the detailed nature of the government program. The real bargaining occurs during the government formation process. When the cabinet begins its work on the basis of the program, there is not much room for discussion" (Hautamäki 2007).

10. According to Paloheimo (2003), "this is a cost for the premier's party of the trend towards prime-ministerial governance" (240). Paloheimo also shows that "between 1950 and 1979 no party leader in the four biggest parties (Social Democrats, Center Party, Conservative Party, People's Democrats) resigned or was dismissed because of their party's poor electoral performance or their poor image as a leader. Since the 1980s, five out of twelve changes of party leader have owed to the party suffering a poor electoral result or to the poor image of the party leader" (239).

11. Individual MPs can also submit initiatives on legislative bills, budget motions, and petitionary motions, but these motions do not normally proceed any further than the committee stage. Between 1945 and 2002, 1.4 percent of such legislative initiatives tabled by individual MPs were successful (Wiberg 2004b, 19).

12. "The President of the Republic makes decisions in Government on the basis of proposals for decisions put forward by the Government. If the President does not make the decision in accordance with the proposal for a decision put forward by the Government, the matter is returned to the Government for preparation. Thereafter, the decision to submit or to withdraw a government proposal shall be made in accordance with the Government's new proposal for a decision."

13. Amending the constitution requires larger majorities in the Eduskunta. According to Section 73 of the constitution, "a proposal on the enactment, amendment or repeal of the Constitution or on the enactment of a limited derogation of the Constitution shall in the second reading be left in abeyance, by a majority of the votes cast, until the first parliamentary session following parliamentary elections. The proposal shall then, once the Committee has issued its report, be adopted without material alterations in one reading in a plenary session by a decision supported by at least two thirds of the votes cast. However, the proposal may be declared urgent by a decision that has been supported by at least five sixths of the votes cast. In

this event, the proposal is not left in abeyance and it can be adopted by a decision supported by at least two thirds of the votes cast."

14. As late as the early 1980s, the annual number of plenary speeches made by the prime minister could be as low as one or two. However, their number has increased rapidly since the Holkeri governments (1987–1991). For example, Lipponen spoke as prime minister in the parliament 605 times between the 1999 and 2003 elections (Wiberg 2006, 218; Paloheimo 2002, 210–11; Aula 2003, 96–97).

REFERENCES

Arter, David. 1999. "Finland." In Robert Elgie, ed., *Semi-presidentialism in Europe*. Oxford: Oxford University Press.
Arter, David. 2006. *Democracy in Scandinavia: Consensual, Majoritarian, or Mixed?* Manchester: Manchester University Press.
Arter, David. 2008. *Scandinavian Politics Today*. 2nd ed. Manchester: Manchester University Press.
Aula, Maria Kaisa. 2003. "Eduskunta Suomen poliittisessa järjestelmässä." In Pasi Saukkonen, ed., *Paikkana politiikka: Tietoa ja tulkintoja Suomen poliittisesta järjestelmästä*. Acta Politica 26. Helsinki: Yleisen valtio-opin laitos, Helsingin yliopisto.
Borg, Sami. 2006. "Osallistuminen vaali-ja puoluedemokratiaan." In Sami Borg, ed., *Suomen demokratiaindikaattorit*. Oikeusministeriön julkaisuja 2006:1. Helsinki: Oikeusministeriö.
Borg, Sami. 2008. "Kansalaisten jäsenyys ja toiminta puolueissa." In Heikki Paloheimo and Tapio Raunio, eds., *Suomen puolueet ja puoluejärjestelmä*. Helsinki: WSOY.
Bouckaert, Geert, Derry Ormond, and B. Guy Peters. 2000. *A Potential Governance Agenda for Finland*. Helsinki: Ministry of Finance.
Eduskunta. 2005. *EU-menettelyjen kehittäminen: EU-menettelyjen tarkistustoimikunnan mietintö*. Eduskunnan kanslian julkaisu 2. Helsinki: Eduskunta.
Esaiasson, Peter. 2000. "How Members of Parliament Define Their Task." In Peter Esaiasson and Knut Heidar, eds., *Beyond Westminster and Congress: The Nordic Experience*. Columbus: Ohio State University Press.
Forestiere, Carolyn. 2008. "New Institutionalism and Minority Protection in the National Legislatures of Finland and Denmark." *Scandinavian Political Studies* 31 (4): 448–68.
Forsten, Timo. 2005. *Valiokuntapeli eduskunnassa: Valiokuntajäsenyydet 1945–2002*. Turun yliopiston julkaisuja C:223. Turku: Turun yliopisto.
Grönlund, Kimmo, Heikki Paloheimo, Jan Sundberg, Risto Sänkiaho, and Hanna Wass. 2005. "Kiinnittyminen politiikkaan." In Heikki Paloheimo, ed., *Vaalit ja demokratia Suomessa*. Helsinki: WSOY.
Hautamäki, Jaakko. 2007. "Paavo Väyrynen: Hallitus käy varsin vähän sisäisiä keskusteluja." *Helsingin Sanomat*, June 11.
Heidar, Knut. 2000. "Parliamentary Party Groups." In Peter Esaiasson and Knut Heidar, eds., *Beyond Westminster and Congress: The Nordic Experience*. Columbus: Ohio State University Press.

Helander, Voitto. 1997. "Finland." In Pippa Norris, ed., *Passages to Power: Legislative Recruitment in Advanced Democracies*. Cambridge: Cambridge University Press.
Helander, Voitto, and Guy-Erik Isaksson. 1994. "Interpellations in Finland." In Matti Wiberg, ed., *Parliamentary Control in the Nordic Countries: Forms of Questioning and Behavioural Trends*. Jyväskylä: Finnish Political Science Association.
Holmberg, Sören. 2000. "Issue Agreement." In Peter Esaiasson and Knut Heidar, eds., *Beyond Westminster and Congress: The Nordic Experience*. Columbus: Ohio State University Press.
Isotalus, Pekka, and Sami Borg, eds. 2007. *Presidentinvaalit 2006*. Helsinki: WSOY.
Jääskinen, Niilo. 2000. "Eduskunta—Aktiivinen sopeutuja." In Tapio Raunio and Matti Wiberg, eds., *EU ja Suomi: Unionijäsenyyden vaikutukset suomalaiseen yhteiskuntaan*. Helsinki: Edita.
Jensen, Torben K. 2000. "Party Cohesion." In Peter Esaiasson and Knut Heidar, eds., *Beyond Westminster and Congress: The Nordic Experience*. Columbus: Ohio State University Press.
Jungar, Ann-Cathrine. 2002. "A Case of Surplus Majority Government: The Finnish Rainbow Coalition." *Scandinavian Political Studies* 25 (1): 57–83.
Jyrkiäinen, Jyrki, and Eero Savisaari. 2003. "Sanomalehdistön nykytila." In Kaarle Nordenstreng and Osmo Wiio, eds., *Suomen mediamaisema*. Helsinki: WSOY.
Karvonen, Lauri. 2004. "Preferential Voting: Incidence and Effects." *International Political Science Review* 25 (2): 203–26.
Karvonen, Lauri. 2009. "Politiikan henkilöityminen." In Sami Borg and Heikki Paloheimo, eds., *Vaalit yleisödemokratiassa: Eduskuntavaalitutkimus 2007*. Tampere: Tampere University Press.
Kauppinen, Timo. 2003. "Suomen työmarkkinamalli." In Pasi Saukkonen, ed., *Paikkana Politiikka: Tietoa ja tulkintoja Suomen poliittisesta järjestelmästä*. Acta Politica 26. Helsinki: Yleisen valtio-opin laitos, Helsingin yliopisto.
Kestilä, Elina. 2006. "Is There Demand for Radical Right Populism in the Finnish Electorate?" *Scandinavian Political Studies* 29 (3): 169–91.
Kuitunen, Soile. 2002. "Finland: Formalized Procedures with Member Predominance." In Hanne Marthe Narud, Mogens N. Pedersen, and Henry Valen, eds., *Party Sovereignty and Citizen Control: Selecting Candidates for Parliamentary Elections in Denmark, Finland, Iceland, and Norway*. Odense: University Press of Southern Denmark.
Kuusela, Kimmo. 1995. "The Finnish Electoral System: Basic Features and Developmental Tendencies." In Sami Borg and Risto Sänkiaho, eds., *The Finnish Voter*. Tampere: Finnish Political Science Association.
Laver, Michael, and W. Ben Hunt. 1992. *Policy and Party Competition*. New York: Routledge.
Lijphart, Arend. 1984. *Democracies*. New Haven: Yale University Press.
Mattila, Mikko. 1997. "From Qualified Majority to Simple Majority: The Effects of the 1992 Change in the Finnish Constitution." *Scandinavian Political Studies* 20 (4): 331–45.
Mattila, Mikko, and Tapio Raunio. 2002. "Government Formation in the Nordic Countries: The Electoral Connection." *Scandinavian Political Studies* 25 (3): 259–80.
Mattila, Mikko, and Tapio Raunio. 2004. "Does Winning Pay? Electoral Success

and Government Formation in 15 West European Countries." *European Journal of Political Research* 43 (2): 263–85.
Mattila, Mikko, and Tapio Raunio. 2005. "Kuka edustaa EU:n vastustajia? Euroopan parlamentin vaalit 2004." *Politiikka* 47 (1): 28–41.
Mattila, Mikko, and Risto Sänkiaho. 2005. "Luottamus poliittiseen järjestelmään." In Heikki Paloheimo, ed., *Vaalit ja demokratia Suomessa*. Helsinki: WSOY.
Müller, Wolfgang C., and Kaare Strøm, eds. 2003. *Coalition Governments in Western Europe*. 2nd ed. Oxford: Oxford University Press.
Nieminen, Hannu, Minna Aslama, and Mervi Pantti. 2005. *Media ja demokratia Suomessa: Kriittinen näkökulma*. Oikeusministeriön julkaisuja 2005:11. Helsinki: Oikeusministeriö.
Nousiainen, Jaakko. 1996. "Finland: Operational Cabinet Autonomy in a Party-Centered System." In Jean Blondel and Maurizio Cotta, eds., *Party and Government*. Basingstoke: Macmillan.
Nousiainen, Jaakko. 2000. "Finland: The Consolidation of Parliamentary Governance." In Wolfgang C. Müller and Kaare Strøm, eds., *Coalition Governments in Western Europe*. Oxford: Oxford University Press.
Nousiainen, Jaakko. 2001. "From Semi-presidentialism to Parliamentary Government: Political and Constitutional Developments in Finland." *Scandinavian Political Studies* 24 (2): 95–109.
Nousiainen, Jaakko. 2003. "Finland: The Consolidation of Parliamentary Governance." In Wolfgang C. Müller and Kaare Strøm, eds., *Coalition Governments in Western Europe*. 2nd ed. Oxford: Oxford University Press.
Nousiainen, Jaakko. 2006. "Suomalainen parlamentarismi." In *Eduskunnan muuttuva asema: Suomen eduskunta 100 vuotta, osa 2*. Helsinki: Edita.
Pajala, Antti. 2006. "Eduskunnan täysistuntoäänestykset vuosien 1945–2005 valtiopäivillä." *Politiikka* 48 (1): 64–75.
Pajala, Antti, and Aleks Jakulin. 2007. "Eduskuntaryhmien äänestyskoheesio vuosien 1991–2006 valtiopäivillä. *Politiikka* 49 (3): 141–54.
Paloheimo, Heikki. 2001. "Divided Government in Finland: From a Semi-presidential to a Parliamentary Democracy." In Robert Elgie, ed., *Divided Government in Comparative Perspective*. Oxford: Oxford University Press.
Paloheimo, Heikki. 2002. "Pääministerin vallan kasvu Suomessa." *Politiikka* 44 (3): 203–21.
Paloheimo, Heikki. 2003. "The Rising Power of the Prime Minister in Finland." *Scandinavian Political Studies* 26 (3): 219–43.
Paloheimo, Heikki. 2005a. "Finland: Let the Force Be with the Leader—but Who Is the Leader?" In Thomas Poguntke and Paul Webb, eds., *The Presidentialization of Politics: A Comparative Study of Modern Democracies*. Oxford: Oxford University Press.
Paloheimo, Heikki. 2005b. "Puoluevalinnan tilannetekijät." In Heikki Paloheimo, ed., *Vaalit ja demokratia Suomessa*. Helsinki: WSOY.
Paloheimo, Heikki. 2008. "Ideologiat ja ristiriitaulottuvuudet." In Heikki Paloheimo and Tapio Raunio, eds., *Suomen puolueet ja puoluejärjestelmä*. Helsinki: WSOY.
Paloheimo, Heikki, and Tapio Raunio, eds. 2008. *Suomen puolueet ja puoluejärjestelmä*. Helsinki: WSOY.

Paloheimo, Heikki, and Jan Sundberg. 2005. "Puoluevalinnan perusteet." In Heikki Paloheimo, ed., *Vaalit ja demokratia Suomessa*. Helsinki: WSOY.
Paloheimo, Heikki, and Jan Sundberg. 2009. "Vaaliliitot eduskuntavaaleissa 1945–2007." In Sami Borg and Heikki Paloheimo, eds., *Vaalit yleisödemokratiassa: Eduskuntavaalitutkimus 2007*. Tampere: Tampere University Press.
Pesonen, Pertti, and Risto Sänkiaho. 1979. *Kansalaiset ja kansanvalta: Suomalaisten käsityksiä poliittisesta toiminnasta*. Helsinki: WSOY.
Pesonen, Pertti, Risto Sänkiaho, and Sami Borg. 1993. *Vaalikansan äänivalta: Tutkimus eduskuntavaaleista ja valitsijakunnasta Suomen poliittisessa järjestelmässä*. Helsinki: WSOY.
Raunio, Tapio. 2004. "The Changing Finnish Democracy: Stronger Parliamentary Accountability, Coalescing Political Parties, and Weaker External Constraints." *Scandinavian Political Studies* 27 (2): 133–52.
Raunio, Tapio. 2005a. "Finland: One Hundred Years of Quietude." In Michael Gallagher and Paul Mitchell, eds., *The Politics of Electoral Systems*. Oxford: Oxford University Press.
Raunio, Tapio. 2005b. "Holding Governments Accountable in European Affairs: Explaining Cross-National Variation." *Journal of Legislative Studies* 11 (3–4): 319–42.
Raunio, Tapio. 2006a. "Poliittinen järjestelmä: Konsensusta kansallisen edun hengessä." In Tapio Raunio and Juho Saari, eds., *Eurooppalaistuminen: Suomen sopeutuminen Euroopan integraatioon*. Helsinki: Gaudeamus.
Raunio, Tapio. 2006b. "The Svenska Folkpartiet: The Gradual Decline of a Language Party." In Lieven De Winter, Marga Gómez-Reino, and Peter Lynch, eds., *Autonomist Parties in Europe: Identity Politics and the Revival of the Territorial Cleavage*. Barcelona: ICPS.
Raunio, Tapio. 2007. "The Finnish Eduskunta: Effective Scrutiny, Partisan Consensus." In Olaf Tans, Carla Zoethout, and Jit Peters, eds., *National Parliaments and European Democracy: A Bottom-up Approach to European Constitutionalism*. Groningen: Europa Law Publishing.
Raunio, Tapio. 2008. "Parlamentaarinen vastuu ulkopolitiikkaan: Suomen ulkopolitiikan johtajuus uuden perustuslain aikana." *Politiikka* 50 (4): 250–65.
Raunio, Tapio, and Teija Tiilikainen. 2003. *Finland in the European Union*. London: Frank Cass.
Raunio, Tapio, and Matti Wiberg. 2003. "Finland: Polarized Pluralism in the Shadow of a Strong President." In Kaare Strøm, Wolfgang C. Müller, and Torbjörn Bergman, eds., *Delegation and Accountability in Parliamentary Democracies*. Oxford: Oxford University Press.
Raunio, Tapio, and Matti Wiberg. 2008. "The Eduskunta and the Parliamentarisation of Finnish Politics: Formally Stronger, Politically Still Weak?" *West European Politics* 31 (3): 581–99.
Reunanen, Esa, and Pertti Suhonen. 2009. "Kansanedustajat ideologisella kartalla." In Sami Borg and Heikki Paloheimo, eds., *Vaalit yleisödemokratiassa: Eduskuntavaalitutkimus 2007*. Tampere: Tampere University Press.
Ruostetsaari, Ilkka. 2000. "From Political Amateur to Professional Politician and Expert Representative: Parliamentary Recruitment in Finland since 1863." In Heinrich Best and Maurizio Cotta, eds., *Parliamentary Representatives in Europe*,

1848–2000: Legislative Recruitment and Careers in Eleven European Countries. Oxford: Oxford University Press.
Ruostetsaari, Ilkka. 2003. *Valta muutoksessa.* Helsinki: WSOY.
Strøm, Kaare. 1990. *Minority Government and Majority Rule.* Cambridge: Cambridge University Press.
Stubb, Alexander, Heidi Kaila, and Timo Ranta. 2001. "Finland: An Integrationist Member State." In Eleanor E. Zeff and Ellen B. Pirro, eds., *The European Union and the Member States: Cooperation, Coordination, and Compromise.* Boulder: Lynne Rienner.
Sundberg, Jan. 1985. *Svenskhetens dilemma I Finland: Finlandssvenskarnas samling och splittring under 1900-talet.* Bidrag till kännedom av Finlands natur och folk, H. 133. Helsingfors: Societas Scientiarum Fennica.
Sundberg, Jan. 1994. "Finland: Nationalized Parties, Professionalized Organizations." In Richard S. Katz and Peter Mair, eds., *How Parties Organize.* London: Sage.
Sundberg, Jan. 1995. "Organizational Structure of Parties, Candidate Selection, and Campaigning." In Sami Borg and Risto Sänkiaho, eds., *The Finnish Voter.* Tampere: Finnish Political Science Association.
Sundberg, Jan. 1996. *Partier och partisystem i Finland.* Esbo: Schildts.
Sundberg, Jan. 1999. "The Enduring Scandinavian Party System." *Scandinavian Political Studies* 22 (1): 221–41.
Sundberg, Jan. 2002a. "The Electoral System of Finland: Old, and Working Well." In Bernard Grofman and Arend Lijphart, eds., *The Evolution of Electoral and Party Systems in the Nordic Countries.* New York: Agathon.
Sundberg, Jan. 2002b. "The Scandinavian Party Model at the Crossroads." In Paul Webb, David Farrell, and Ian Holliday, eds., *Political Parties in Advanced Industrial Democracies.* Oxford: Oxford University Press.
Sundberg, Jan. 2004. "Finland." In "Political Data Yearbook," special issue, *European Journal of Political Research* 43 (7–8): 1000–1005.
Temmes, Markku. 2001. *Määräaikaisen valmistelun kehittäminen.* Hallinnon kehittämisosasto, Tutkimukset ja selvitykset 6. Helsinki: Valtiovarainministeriö.
Temmes, Markku. 2003. "Valtionhallinto—jatkuvuutta ja muutosta." In Pasi Saukkonen, ed., *Paikkana Politiikka: Tietoa ja tulkintoja Suomen poliittisesta järjestelmästä.* Acta Politica 26. Helsinki: Yleisen valtio-opin laitos, Helsingin yliopisto.
Tiihonen, Seppo. 2006. *Ministeriön johtaminen: Poliittisen ja ammatillisen osaamisen liitto.* Tampere: Tampere University Press.
Tiili, Minna. 2008. *Strategic Political Steering after NPM reforms in Finland.* Acta Politica 34. Helsinki: Department of Political Science, University of Helsinki.
Wiberg, Matti. 1991. "Public Financing of Political Parties as Arcana Imperii in Finland." In Matti Wiberg, ed., *The Public Purse and Political Parties: Public Financing of Political Parties in Nordic Countries.* Jyväskylä: Finnish Political Science Association.
Wiberg, Matti. 1994. "To Keep the Government on Its Toes: Behavioural Trends of Parliamentary Questioning in Finland, 1945–1990." In Matti Wiberg, ed., *Parliamentary Control in the Nordic Countries: Forms of Questioning and Behavioural Trends.* Jyväskylä: Finnish Political Science Association.

Wiberg, Matti. 2000. "The Partyness of the Finnish Eduskunta." In Knut Heidar and Ruud Koole, eds., *Parliamentary Party Groups in European Democracies*. London: Routledge.
Wiberg, Matti. 2004a. "Lainsäädäntömme EU-vaikutteisuus luultua oleellisesti Pienempää." *Oikeus* 33 (2): 200–206.
Wiberg, Matti. 2004b. *Lainsäädäntötuotos Suomessa valtiopäivillä 1945–2002: Peruskartoitus*. Turun yliopiston valtio-opin laitoksen tutkimuksia 58. Turku: Turun yliopisto.
Wiberg, Matti. 2006. *Politiikka Suomessa*. Helsinki: WSOY.

INTERNET SOURCES

Eduskunta. Accessed February 2, 2008. http://www.eduskunta.fi/triphome/bin/tixhaku.sh?lyh=hex8110?kieli=ru?lomake=tix5050_ru
Keesing's Record of World Events. 2003. "June 2003—Finland." Vol. 49 (June, 2003 Finland): 45478. http://www.keesings.com
Statsrådet. Accessed February 2, 2008. http://www.vn.fi/hallitus/sv.jsp
Zárate's Political Collections (ZPC). Accessed May 17, 2008. http://www.terra.es/personal2/monolith/ooeuropa.htm

5 ✦ Iceland

Dramatic Shifts

SVANUR KRISTJÁNSSON AND INDRIDI H. INDRIDASON

There is a tendency to emphasize the commonalities of politics in the Scandinavian countries, which often are characterized as consensual and deliberative, allowing their parliaments substantial influence in policy-making. Iceland fits this model rather poorly. All the Nordic countries have a mix of Westminster and Madisonian features. Yet, comparatively, Iceland bears perhaps a greater resemblance to the Westminster parliamentary system than do the other four countries. For one thing, the near absence of minority cabinets in the postwar period suggests that Iceland differs in significant ways from its Scandinavian neighbors, and as argued elsewhere in this volume, minority cabinets have been a linchpin for the Scandinavian coincidence of strong parties and active, deliberative parliaments. However, there are also important similarities—for example, as regards formal political institutions— not least because the Danish constitution served as blueprint for the Icelandic constitution adopted in 1944.

This volume's foci on deparliamentarization and party decline are a useful guide for our examination of Icelandic parliamentary democracy. To foreshadow our findings, Iceland exhibits neither a clear trend toward stronger parliamentary institutions nor one of decline. The same is true for political parties. This is not to say that Icelandic politics have been immune to change. Indeed, the strength of parliamentary government in Iceland has varied greatly. In the 1990s, parliamentary government reigned supreme, managing to provide not only great coherence to the parliamentary chain of delegation and accountability but also freedom from effective external constraints. Early in the new millennium, parliamentary governance seems to face insurmountable obstacles. These include serious problems within the parliamentary chain of democratic policy-making, as well as the growth of external constraints that can effectively nullify its decisions. However, Icelandic parliamentary democracy has been pronounced dead before, only to rebound in spectacular fashion. We should therefore be careful in proclaiming a permanent decline of parliamentary democracy in Iceland. Nevertheless, something new is going on, and students of democracy must seek to understand it.

When the first draft of this chapter was written, its title—"Dramatic Shifts"—was intended to have a double meaning, referring both to the dramatic transitions between political regimes in Iceland and to the shifts within the current regime, as the forces of parliamentary government reached their zenith of power only to suffer several humiliating defeats. After the spectacular collapse of the economy in the fall of 2008, however, the title has acquired a third meaning—one that will quite possibly overshadow any of the previous political developments in the republic's history. The political repercussions of the economic collapse have yet to be played out fully, but the events following the collapse of the Icelandic banking system in October 2008 exposed many flaws in the country's process of parliamentary governance.

After a brief period of shock and disbelief, citizens took to the streets in what has been dubbed "the housewares revolution," demanding explanations and that someone accept responsibility for the crisis. Not surprisingly, the cabinet preferred to blame the international credit crunch, while conceding that the Icelandic banking system might have been overextended. The governor of the Central Bank claimed, however, that he had repeatedly warned the cabinet of the impending disaster. While the sources of Iceland's troubles will undoubtedly be debated for years to come, the episode highlighted worrisome aspects of Icelandic politics. First, Icelandic politicians confuse political with legal responsibility. Cabinet ministers repeatedly refused political responsibility, on the grounds that there was no proof that they had made mistakes and, moreover, that such proof could only be produced, in due time, by a proper investigative commission. In other words, the great majority of Icelandic politicians subscribe to the view that they only have an obligation to resign (political accountability) if they have been caught with their hands in the cookie jar (legal responsibility). Second, the crisis highlighted the fact that seats on the board of the Central Bank and other executive agencies have been dispensed as political patronage, with the result that an atmosphere of distrust permeates the relationship between the cabinet and many of its agencies. Even if the governor of the Central Bank, former prime minister Davíð Oddsson, did warn the cabinet about the dangers facing the banking sector, his warnings may not have been considered credible, because Oddsson was widely perceived to have a political agenda. While the crisis of confidence undoubtedly had something to do with the personalities involved, the underlying problem was a systematic one. Third, opposition parties largely avoided being held accountable by the public, which suggests that parliament really was as impotent as the pundits would have us believe. Not only was the opposition marginalized in lawmaking, but it was no longer expected even to keep a watchful eye on the executive or to demand answers to tough questions. Each of these problems has resulted in calls for reform, and while there are some hopeful signs, "politics as usual" has returned with almost alarming speed. Given the degree of unrest in the months following the economic collapse, one might have expected a watershed in Icelandic politics. However, rather than cleaning up the government and ushering in fresh faces, the call for an early election resulted in only limited renewal within the political parties.

In terms of party politics, however, the election results were historic and provided a number of "firsts." The parties on the left won a majority of the vote for the first time. The Independence Party lost one-third of its support and its place as the country's largest party (to the United Front). The Progressive Party, although posting a gain from the previous election, lost its position as the median party in the legislature. Thus, the party landscape was fundamentally altered, which will possibly pave the way for important changes to the Icelandic political system.

A Brief History

Let us first go back to the beginnings of modern Icelandic politics with a brief history, since Iceland is arguably the least well-known Nordic country. Icelandic parliamentary democracy was established gradually. The process began with the reestablishment of the Althingi (in Icelandic, *Alþingi*) in 1845. Parliamentary government was introduced in 1874, when Iceland was granted a constitution under Danish sovereignty. Executive power was placed in the hands of a single minister, who remained part of the Danish administration until Iceland gained home rule in 1904, at which point the minister of Iceland became accountable to the Althingi. From the start, the minister of Iceland had considerable powers, allowing the holder of the office to determine the scope of its activities without any clear boundaries. The first coalition government in 1917 represented a new regime that lasted through a period of transition from sovereignty to independence. In 1918, Iceland became a sovereign state under the Danish king, with government authority resting with the Icelandic parliament.

Another transformation took place between 1941 and 1944. Within a short period of time following Iceland's declaration of domestic autonomy in 1940, the political system changed from one of unlimited parliamentary government to semi-presidentialism (Kristjánsson 2002, 2005). In 1941, the Althingi elected the first head of state, or regent of Iceland, Sveinn Björnsson, who declared his intent to respect the supreme power of parliament. However, difficulties in forming a majority cabinet led to the rejection of pure parliamentarism in favor of a formally semi-presidential system.

The semi-presidential constitution adopted in 1944 established a dual executive, with the president holding substantial powers. The president appoints ministers (and can also remove them), while the Althingi can only dismiss the president by a three-fourths majority decision that must then be ratified in a national referendum. The constitution also places (negative) legislative powers in the hands of the executive. A presidential legislative veto triggers a national referendum. While the semi-presidential constitution remains Iceland's legal political framework, the system functions in practice much like a parliamentary system characterized by a high degree of "partyness."

Political Parties

The formation of the Icelandic political parties took place in a different environment than parties faced in the other Western European democracies. In the first years of the twentieth century, executive power rested with the king of Denmark. As a result, the Althingi took on many of the roles of the executive, blurring the line between legislative and executive powers. In addition, as Icelanders gained control over their own affairs, no clearly defined boundaries demarcating the role of the state existed—politicians and their parties had free rein to use the government for political and economic rent seeking. Thus, the Icelandic political parties were born in an environment that provided a wealth of opportunities for clientelism (Kristinsson 1996, 2001).

Three main parties existed during the interwar years: the Progressive Party (a farmers' party), the Independence Party (created through a merger of the old Conservative and Liberal parties), and the Social Democratic Party. Although the parties were formed in the parliamentary arena, they soon organized themselves as mass parties. Grímsson (1978) argues, however, that the Icelandic parties are better characterized as "network parties." These deviate from the hierarchical organization characteristic of mass parties, in that local party leaders maintain complex networks of influence outside and inside their parties. In the latter half of the interwar period, a fourth party, the Communist Party (later the Socialist Party and then the People's Alliance), emerged. The four-party system proved stable, and not until the 1980s did it undergo significant change. From the end of World War II until 1983, the effective number of electoral parties remained below four (see table 5.1 for election results).

Socioeconomic issues form the main cleavage in Icelandic politics, but two additional cleavages have had a significant role. On foreign policy, the Socialist Party/People's Alliance opposed Iceland's NATO membership and the presence of a U.S. military base (see chapter 9). Until the end of the cold war, this ruled out a coalition between the Independence Party and

TABLE 5.1. Elections to the Icelandic Parliament (Alþingi), 1946–2008

Election Year	SP	LM	PA	WA	NPP	ULL	ÞPM	UF	SDA	SDP	AESJ	PP	LP	CP	IP	Other
1946	19.5									17.8		23.1			39.4	
1949	19.5									16.5		24.5			39.5	
1953	16.1								6.0	15.6		21.9			37.1	3.3
1956			19.2		4.5					18.3		15.6			42.4	
1959a			15.3		2.5					12.5		27.2			42.5	
1959			16.0		3.4					15.2		25.7			39.7	
1963			16.0							14.2		28.2			41.4	0.2
1967			17.6							15.7		28.1			37.5	1.1
1971			17.1				8.9			10.5		25.3			36.2	2
1974			18.3				4.6			9.1		24.9			42.7	0.4
1978			22.9							22.0		16.9			32.7	5.5
1979			19.7							17.4		24.9			35.4	2.5
1983			17.3	5.5					7.3	11.7		19			38.7	0.5
1987			13.3	10.1					0.2	15.2	1.2	18.9		10.9	27.2	2.9
1991			14.4	8.3						15.5		18.9			38.6	4.3
1995			14.3	4.9				7.2		11.4		23.3			37.1	1.9
1999		9.1								26.8		18.4	4.2		40.7	0.8
2003		8.8								31.0		17.7	7.4		33.7	1.4
2007		14.3								26.8		11.7	7.3		36.6	3.3

Source: Data from Indridason 2005; Statistics Iceland, http://www.statice.is (accessed May 13, 2009).
Notes: Numbers in table represent vote shares in percentages. Party abbreviations are as follows: SP = Socialist Party (Sósíalistaflokkurinn); LM = Left Movement—Greens (Vinstri-hreyfing—grænt framboð); PA = People's Alliance (1995 PA and independents) (Alþýðubandalagið); WA = Women's Party (Kvennalistinn); NPP = National Preservation Party (Þjóðvarnarflokkurinn); ULL = Union of Liberals and Leftists (Samtök frjálslyndra og vinstri manna); ÞPM = Thjodvaki—People's movement (Þjóðvaki—Fylking fólksins); UF = United Front-Social Democratic Alliance (Samfylkingin); SDA = Social Democratic Alliance (Bandalag jafnaðarmanna); SDP = Social Democratic Party (includes Jafnaðarmannaflokkur Íslands in 1995 (Alþýðuflokkurinn); AESJ = Association for Equality and Social Justice (Samtök um jafnræði og félagshyggju); PP = People's Party (includes BB-list in 1995) (Framsóknarflokkurinn); LP = Liberal Party (Frjálslyndi flokkurinn); CP = Citizen's Party (Borgaraflokkurinn); IP = Independence Party (Sjálfstæðisflokkurinn).
aTwo elections were held in 1959.

the Socialist Party/People's Alliance—the only cabinet constellation that appears to have been off the table. The second dimension is the urban-rural divide. The Progressive Party represents the interests of rural areas, although the Independence Party also has substantial rural support. In contrast, the Social Democratic Party support is largely concentrated in urban areas (Harðarson 1995).

Before the 1980s, the parties on the left were less stable than those on the right, and a couple of short-lived new/splinter parties emerged (see table 5.1). The first election of the 1980s represented a more serious challenge to the four-party system, with two new parties (the Women's Party and the Social Democratic Alliance) each gaining over 5 percent of the vote. Both parties sought to mobilize voters disillusioned with the "old" parties, seeing them as both undemocratic and unable to manage the economy. Although neither party was particularly long-lived and the party system appears to be returning to the familiar pattern of four-party competition, the turmoil of the 1980s left its mark.

The four-party equilibrium was restored with the merger of the left parties, including the Women's Party, into the United Front (Social Democratic Alliance) before the 1999 election. The aim was to provide an effective counterweight to the more cohesive right. The left wing of the People's Alliance (successor of the Socialist Party) refused to go along with the merger and formed a new party, the Left Movement–Greens. There is, however, an important difference between the current four-party system and the previous one. The United Front has substantially greater support than any of the left parties ever achieved, opening up the possibility of a two-party center-left majority coalition after the May 2003 elections.

The party configuration on the right of the political spectrum has been more stable. Unlike in the other Nordic countries, where social democratic parties have traditionally been the strongest, the Independence Party has been Iceland's strongest party, usually winning 35 to 40 percent of the vote (Arter 1999). In fact, until the 2003 election, every potential two-party majority coalition included the Independence Party. The Liberal Party, albeit small, has created competition on the right side of the political spectrum since 2000. Prior to this, the only notable challenge to the traditional right parties occurred in the 1987 election, when the Citizen's Party garnered 11 percent of the vote.

The parties have retained the formal structure of mass parties. Accurate figures on party membership are hard to come by. Official party figures (see fig. 5.1) indicate that membership has been stable or increasing since the 1980s, but these numbers are probably inflated. Other than the Left

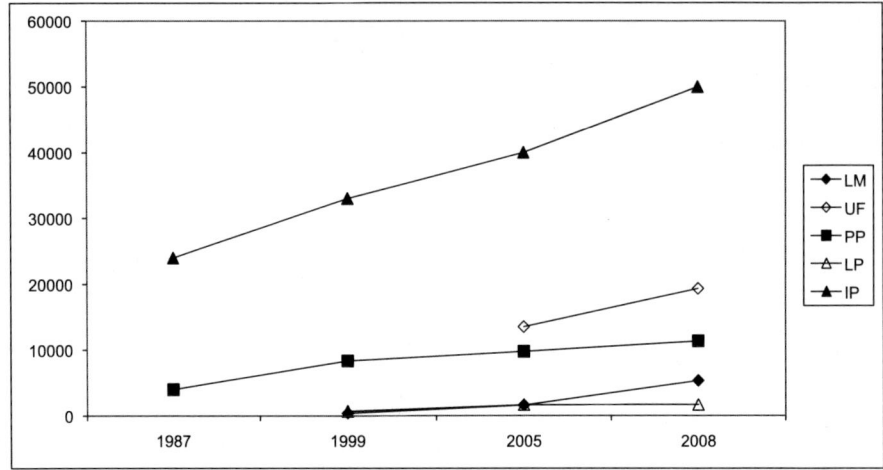

Fig. 5.1. Party membership in Iceland, 1987–2008. See table 5.1 for explanation of party labels. For presentational reasons, the PA, SDP, and WA are not included in figure 1. For these parties, we only have data from 1987. At that time, the parties had 4,300, 3,600, and 1,700 members, respectively. However, the membership numbers of these parties are included in the total party membership in chapter 8.

Movement–Greens, the parties do not charge membership fees, and many voters join in order to vote in a party's primary elections. In fact, official numbers are almost 50 percent higher than estimates obtained from voter surveys (Harðarson 1995).

Despite their formal organizations, the political parties do not operate as mass parties. In practice, they have adopted many of the characteristics of cartel parties, with a relatively small group of members being active within the parties. The main purpose of the political parties is to contest elections. Most Icelandic parties have adopted primaries for the selection of candidates, which essentially removes two of the most important functions of a mass party from party control. Since most of the primaries are effectively open, party members no longer play a privileged role in selecting the parties' candidates. In addition, primaries reduce the role of the parties in formulating party policy. The need to compete in primaries means that policy formulation is increasingly in the hands of candidates, which reduces the ability of the party to formulate a cohesive policy platform (Kristjánsson 1998).

There is some evidence to suggest that voters' ties with the political parties have weakened (see table 5.2). Turnout in parliamentary elections has remained comparatively high, although the last four elections show a modest drop. Since 1991, turnout has been lower than in any previous year since 1946, but the drop in turnout might be explained by the fact that the four most recent elections (prior to 2009) took place during a long, uninterrupted period of economic growth and low unemployment.

TABLE 5.2. Strength of Party Attachment in Iceland, 1946–2008

Election Year	Turnout (%)[a]	Share of Voters Changing Party between Elections (%)	Share of Voters Changing Bloc between Elections (%)	Share of Voters Deciding Which Party to Vote for during the Election Campaign (%)[b]	Party Supporter (%)	Close to a Party (%)	Independent (%)	Distrust of Politicians (%)[c]
1946	87.4							
1949	89.0							
1953	89.9							
1956	92.1							
1959[d]	90.6							
1959[d]	90.4							
1963	91.1							
1967	91.4							
1971	90.4							
1974	91.4							
1978	90.3							
1979	89.3							
1983	88.3	23.3	13.9	50	49.6	31.4	19.0	64.2
1987	90.1	36.4	16.1	62	45.7	30.7	23.6	69.2
1991	87.6	31.6	17.0	53	40.4	27.3	32.3	79.5
1995	87.4	34.0	19.6	61	39.0	30.1	31.0	72.4
1999	84.1	36.6	14.3	54	36.1	31.7	32.2	68.3
2003	87.7	30.5	15.7	60	39.0	33.1	27.9	61.7
2007	83.6							

Source: Data from *Statistics Iceland,* turnout data, http://www.statice.is/Statistics/Elections (accessed May 13, 2009); Ólafur Þ. Harðarson (survey data).

Notes: There are no available data on class voting for Iceland. The United Front, a merger of the Social Democratic Party, the Women's Party, the People's Alliance (splinter), and Þjóðvaki, ran for the first time in 1999. United Front voters voting for the four "old" parties were considered to be voting for the same party. It should be noted that only 33% of the supporters of the People's Alliance in 1995 voted for the United Front in 1999.

[a]Preliminary results indicate that the turnout in the April 25, 2009, elections was 85.1% (http://www.ipu.org/parline/reports/2143_E.htm accessed on May 13, 2009).

[b]The Island surveys define deciding during the election campaign as voters deciding less than a month before the election.

[c]Respondents answered the question about whether politicians can be trusted with "None," "Few," and "Some." Other possible answers were "Many" and "Usually."

[d]Two elections were held in 1959.

Turning to other measures of the ties between parties and voters, the number of self-identified party supporters fell from just under 50 percent to 39 percent between 1983 and 2003. This is a substantial drop, although it must be kept in mind that this occurred during a period of transition in which parties appeared, disappeared, and merged. Such changes are likely to influence the degree to which voters consider themselves party supporters, especially if party attachments form over time. Because electoral surveys have only been conducted since 1983, we must use electoral results to evaluate the long-term development of party attachment in Iceland. These results also suggest that party attachment has decreased. Comparing the periods before and after 1970, aggregate volatility—that is, the sum of changes in parties' vote shares from one election to the next—has more than doubled, from 6.5 percent to 14.1 percent (Pétursson 2005).[1] Survey data suggests that in the six elections between 1983 and 2003, between 14 and 20 percent of all voters switched blocs (see table 5.2).[2] This fits with the decline in class voting that has occurred in Iceland. Instead, a considerable gender gap has become apparent in party alignments (Styrkársdóttir and Kristjánsson 2005). Overall, however, the willingness of a substantial share of the voters to cross bloc lines in every election has had little perceptible effect on the balance of power between the blocs. Rather, these swings are more likely to influence the bargaining positions of the parties within each bloc in the coalition formation process.

The Parliamentary Chain of Delegation

From Voters to Parliament

Let us now examine the evidence of deparliamentarization or party decline in each link of the parliamentary chain of delegation in Iceland. Consider first the delegation from voters to parliamentarians. One peculiar aspect of the Icelandic electoral system is the fact that until the 1980s, the system favored not the largest party, the Independence Party, but the second largest party, the Progressive Party. This was due to a considerable malapportionment in favor of rural constituencies, where the Progressive Party is strong. In the 1949 election, for example, the Independence Party received 39.5 percent of the vote and 19 MPs, while the Progressive Party got 24.7 percent and 17 MPs. Behind every Progressive Party MP were a little over 1,000 votes, while the corresponding numbers for the Independence Party and the Socialist Party were around 1,500, with more than 1,700 votes for the Social Democratic Party. Thus, the electoral system created a serious interparty conflict that cut across the left-right dimension. In both 1942 and 1959, the Independence Party and the two socialist parties united behind electoral reform. The Progressive Party bitterly opposed it. Further electoral reforms were adopted unanimously in 1987 and 2003. Today, any party that obtains more than 5 percent of the national vote wins parliamentary seats roughly in proportion to its national vote.

At least three times, voters have sent the established parties strong signals of dissatisfaction by supporting new parties. This occurred in 1953, when the National Preservation Party received 6 percent of the national vote. The party placed itself on the democratic left and called for the expulsion of American armed forces from Iceland and for a return to the traditional foreign policy of neutrality. The Progressives and Social Democratic Party responded by forming an electoral alliance at the next parliamentary election in 1956, demanding the closing of the American military base.

In 1971, a new party, the Union of Liberals and Leftists, received five MPs. The party's main issue was the extension of the exclusive economic zone beyond 12 miles out to sea. The cabinet parties lost their majority, and a new cabinet, which included the Union of Liberals and Leftists, extended the fishing limits unilaterally. The new Women's Alliance received three MPs in the 1983 election. Until that time, a maximum of three women had been MPs during any given term of parliament. In 1983, nine women were elected to the Althingi, including three from the Women's Alliance and two from another new party, the Social Democratic Alliance. The representation of women has gradually risen, reaching 32 percent in 2007.

The purpose of this discussion is not to leave the impression that small parties have an overwhelming importance in Icelandic politics. Examples of small parties entering and leaving parliament without much of a trace can easily be cited. However, the three examples previously discussed are intended to highlight an important point: there is more to the role of voters as principals than meets the eye.

The importance and viability of minor parties depends on the electoral system. Iceland has had a two-tier system since 1934. In the first tier, 8 to 10 seats are allocated proportionally in each of the six districts. Nine supplementary seats are distributed in the second tier, in order to obtain proportionality at the national level. In the past, one district seat was sufficient for a party to be eligible for supplementary seats. The current electoral system adds another obstacle to minor party representation: the requirement that a party has to receive at least 5 percent of the national vote to qualify for supplementary seats.

A series of electoral reforms in Iceland have largely reflected ongoing compromises between the interests of incumbent MPs and responses to urban demands for less regional disparity. This has had several effects on parliamentary representation, some unintended. First, the impact of the personal vote has steadily decreased as multimember districts have replaced single- and two-member districts. Second, electoral outcomes have become increasingly proportional. Third, malapportionment has been reduced substantially, although the most advantaged electoral district still elects twice as many MPs as it would if there were no overrepresentation. Fourth, the electoral system has become much less hospitable to small parties. In fact, under the current system, the Women's Alliance would not have received any representation in 1983 and 1995.

In some ways, electoral reforms have distanced the voters from their representatives—for example, because the personal vote has been almost eliminated over time. In principle, this should strengthen political parties and increase their ability to present voters with cohesive policy platforms. But the advent of party primaries to select candidates has reinforced the personal vote and, at the same time, reduced the importance of the party in formulating policy. In addition, the most recent trend is to allow voters to influence a candidate's place on the party list at the time of the election (through semi-open lists) and not only at the candidate nomination stage. In the 2007 election, this affected the ranking of the candidates for the first time since 1946.

From Parliament to Cabinet

Legislatures serve two primary roles in parliamentary systems. First, they delegate executive power to the cabinet; that is, the executive needs the legislature's confidence. Second, legislatures legislate. We here address these two functions in turn.

Table 5.3 lists the 30 cabinets formed between 1944 and 2008. The Independence Party (due to its size) and the Progressive Party (because of its median location) have been the prime contenders for forming and leading coalitions, although coalition formation has generally been complicated and has resulted in a variety of different solutions. The Independence Party has held the position of prime minister 18 times; the Progressive Party, 8 times; and the Social Democratic Party, 4 times. The remaining cabinet was formed by the vice chairman of the Independence Party, Gunnar Thoroddsen. The majority of his party refused to support the cabinet and remained bitterly opposed.

The formation of coalitions has alternated between periods of stability and instability. Four periods can be identified. During 1944–58, coalition bargaining was complicated and lasted up to 167 days. From 1959 to 1971, the so-called restoration government, composed of the Independence Party and the Social Democratic Party, governed Iceland. Before the 1963 election, the two parties declared their intention to continue the coalition after the election. At no other parliamentary election have sitting cabinet parties formed a preelectoral pact. The period from 1971 to 1991 was one with several short-lived coalition formations. The coalition cabinets were of every possible permutation, and one (the Thoroddsen cabinet of 1980) was unimaginable until it actually formed. Each of the nine cabinets had a unique composition.

The last period, 1991–2007, largely corresponds with the prime ministerial career of Davíð Oddsson, chairman of the Independence Party. In 1991, Oddsson formed a cabinet with the Social Democratic Party. After the 1995 election, he changed partners. The Progressive Party, led by Halldór Ásgrímsson, then minister of foreign affairs, replaced the Social Democrats. This coalition remained in place following the 1999 and 2003 elections. In 2004, Oddsson and Ásgrímsson switched cabinet posts. Ásgrímsson resigned from his post as prime minister in 2006, and the Independence Party and the Progressive Party formed a new cabinet, this time with the Independence Party in the driver seat and with Haarde as prime minister. The coalition retained its majority in the 2007 election, but the Independence Party opted to change partners and formed a cabinet with the United Front. As a whole, this period exhibited a great deal of stability compared to previous years, although the years following Oddsson's departure appear more tumultuous than the period of his premiership.

The size of the Independence Party has structured the coalition formation game in an important way. No two-party majority-coalition cabinet excluding the Independence Party could be formed in the period 1942–2003. As soon as a two-party majority coalition excluding the Independence Party became possible (in 2003), the bargaining leverage of the Progressive Party increased, and it became the pivotal actor in coalition formation. This triggered the transfer of the prime minister's post from the Independence Party to the Progressive Party.

Generally, coalition theorists have found that policy preferences and the size of potential coalitions are important predictors of which coalition forms (Martin and Stevenson 1999; Mitchell and Nyblade 2008). In Iceland, the second factor is of paramount importance. Only majority cabinets are considered proper executives (Jóhannesson 2005). Minority cabinets have only

TABLE 5.3. Cabinets in Iceland, 1944–2008

Cabinet Number	Prime Minister	Date (yymmdd)	Cabinet Share (%) of Parliamentary Seats	Effective Number of Legislative Parties[a]	Median Legislator Party	Parties in Cabinet	Majority Cabinets[b] Single-Party	Majority Cabinets[b] Coalition	Minority Cabinets[c] Single-Party	Minority Cabinets[c] Coalition
1	Thors II	441021	71.2	3.49	PP	IP, SP, SDP		X		
2	Thors III	460630	75.0	3.61	PP	IP, SP, SDP		X		
3	Stefánsson	470204	80.8	3.61	PP	SDP, PP, IP		X		
4	Thors IV	491206	36.5	3.47	PP	IP			X	
5	Steinþórsson	500314	69.2	3.47	PP	PP, IP		X		
6	Thors V	530911	71.2	3.44	PP	IP, PP		X		
7	Jónasson III	560724	63.5	3.48	PP	PP, PA, SP		X		
8	Jónsson I	581223	15.4	3.48	PP	SDP			X	
9	Jónsson II	590628	11.5	3.20	PP	SDP			X	
10	Thors VI	591120	55.0	3.44	PP	IP, SDP		X		
11	Thors VII	630609	53.3	3.32	PP	IP, SDP		X		
12	Benediktsson I	631114	53.3	3.32	PP	IP, SDP		X		
13	Benediktsson II	670611	53.3	3.48	PP	IP, SDP		X		
14	Hafstein[d]	700710	53.3	3.48	PP	IP, SDP		X		
15	Jóhannesson I	710714	53.3	3.85	PP	PP, PA, ULL		X		
16	Hallgrímsson	740828	70.0	3.38	PP	IP, PP		X		
17	Jóhannesson II	780901	66.7	3.85	PP	PP, PA, SDP		X		
18	Gröndal	791015	23.3	3.85	PP	SDP			X	
19	Thoroddsen	800208	81.7	3.78	PP	IP, PA, PP		X		

20	Hermannsson I	830526	61.7	4.06	PP	PP, IP	X
21	Pálsson	870708	65.1	5.34	PP	IP, SDP, PP	X
22	Hermannsson II	880928	50.8	5.34	PP	PP, PA, SDP	
23	Hermannsson III	890910	60.3	5.34	PP	PP, PA, SDP, CP	X
24	Oddsson I	910430	57.1	3.78	PP	IP, SDP	X
25	Oddsson II	950423	63.5	3.94	PP	IP, PP	X
26	Oddsson III	990528	58.7	3.48	PP	IP, PP	X
27[e]	Oddsson IV	030523	54.0	3.71	PP	IP, PP	X
28	Ásgrímsson	040915	54.0	3.71	PP	PP, IP	X
29	Haarde I	060615	54.0	3.71	PP	IP-PP	X
30	Haarde II	070523	68.3	3.62	PP	IP-UF	X

Source: Data from Indridason 2005; newspapers (*Morgunblaðið, Þjóðviljinn*); Alþingi's Web site, http://www.althingi.is; Hardarson and Kristinsson 2007, 975; *Keesing's Record of World Events*, vol. 52 (June, 2006 Iceland): 47332; vol. 53 (May, 2007 Iceland): 47946; *Statistics Iceland*.

Note: See table 5.1 for explanation of party labels.

[a] Effective number of legislative parties: This index was developed by Markku Laakso and Rein Taagepera and is a measure of party system size. Both the number of parties and their relative size are taken into account. For an accessible introduction, see Lijphart 1984.

[b] Majority cabinet coalitions can be either a minimal winning coalition (mwc—a coalition that cannot lose a party and still be "winning") or a surplus coalition (a coalition that can lose one or more parties and still be winning). Except for the four minority cabinets, all but the first three postwar coalitions were minimal winning. Note that Thoroddsen effectively split the IP in forming his cabinet in 1980, thus leaving the majority of the IP's members in opposition.

[c] Minority cabinets control 50% or less of all seats in parliament.

[d] In 1970, Haftstein (cabinet number 14) became prime minister when Benediktsson died July 10.

[e] During the formation of Oddsson IV (cabinet number 27) an agreement was made that the post of prime minister would be transferred to Ásgrímsson (PP) on September 15, 2004.

been considered short-term solutions, to be replaced as soon as practical. Ideology seems to have little relevance, and cabinet formation is an open-ended game. Every parliamentary party in Iceland is a possible coalition partner to any other party. Comparing cabinet coalitions in the Nordic countries, Indridason (2005, 451) finds that "Iceland has the lowest frequency of ideologically connected coalitions (46.2 percent) by far, with Finland coming second (79.5 percent)." Under these circumstances, the outcome of cabinet formation is at once highly predictable and highly unpredictable. After each election, a majority cabinet will be formed, but which parties will comprise that majority is impossible to predict. With everybody "dating" everybody else, it is impossible to anticipate the next "wedding."

The patterns of coalition formation in Iceland provide a stark contrast with experience in the other Nordic countries (with the possible exception of Finland) where minority coalitions are common. Our explanation for why majority coalitions dominate in Iceland centers on the nature of the political parties and the role of the president in defining the rules of cabinet formation. First, Icelandic political parties are rooted in clientelism, defined as "the particularistic allocation of state resources aimed at maximizing a political actor's probability of election" (Indridason 2005, 440). As noted previously, the clientelistic nature of Icelandic political parties can be traced back to the circumstances surrounding the origins of the Icelandic state. As Shefter (1977) argued, two factors prevented political parties in Western countries from pursuing clientelistic politics: an independent civil service and the monarchy, both of which represent preexisting institutional structures that constrain politicians' access to state resources. Political parties faced neither of these obstacles in Iceland, and the state was a vehicle for providing particularistic benefits. As a result, the parties value cabinet participation highly.

Second, the president formally appoints the cabinet. If the party leaders fail to duly form a majority cabinet, the president steps in and threatens to unilaterally appoint a nonpartisan cabinet. We can date precisely when a head of state first translated his formal power of cabinet appointment into a leading role in cabinet formation. Faced with a disintegration of the sitting coalition cabinet in the fall of 1941, Björnsson refused to accept the prime minister's request for dissolution, instructing him to repair the cracks in the coalition and to continue in office. At the same time, he turned to a personal friend and asked him to be prepared to form a nonpartisan cabinet. These actions turned out to be decisive for the choice of a semi-presidential constitution and the conduct of subsequent presidents. When faced with party leaders unable to form a majority cabinet, all presidents have followed Björnsson's lead. They issue a time-specific ultimatum to party leaders, instructing them to form a majority-coalition cabinet. Meanwhile, they prepare a nonpartisan cabinet, headed by someone personally close to themselves, to be used in the event that no majority solution is forthcoming.[3]

Together, the nature of the political parties in Iceland and the role of the president have ensured that majority cabinets have formed. In fact, they have done so with increasing ease since the political parties shed the last remains of traditional left-right ideology and it became clear that all presidents make the same demand—that there be a majority cabinet or political parties are out of the government business. The 2007 election highlights this tendency, as any of the potential majority coalitions could be considered to have been on the table.

The delegation of executive power to the cabinet affords the cabinet a great deal of influence over legislation. Table 5.4 shows the number of cabinet and individual members' bills from 1944 to 2008. Until about 1970, a majority of legislative bills were introduced by individual MPs, but since then, the cabinet has introduced the majority (see also Arter 1984). This change primarily reflects increased activity on the part of the cabinet, as the number of individual members' bills remained fairly constant throughout the period. A great majority of cabinet bills become laws. Most cabinet bills that fail do so because the parliamentary session ends and the bills expire. Not surprisingly, private members' bills fare far worse. In the first years of the republic, the parliament adopted more than half the individual members' bills. This number has steadily declined, and in recent years, it has generally been less than one-tenth (see also Þórleifsson 2006).

These trends suggest that the cabinet has become increasingly important in policy-making and that the Althingi's role is declining. Magnússon (2005) reports that private members' bills are not only less successful but also tend to be substantively less important—for example, amendments of existing laws. Thus, formulation of policy primarily takes place within the cabinet and in the ministries. It is difficult to say whether these trends reflect a change in the relationship between the cabinet and the parliament or simply the fact that with an increase in the scope and complexity of legislation, the executive is better positioned to formulate policy, because it has better resources that include a larger staff and better information. Whatever the cause, these trends are consistent with the thesis of deparliamentarization. Parliament's influence on policy has clearly declined.

Of course, introducing legislation is not the only way parliament exerts influence. Legislative bills are debated and amended on the floor of the

TABLE 5.4. Parliamentary Activities, Iceland, 1944–2008

Session	Year	Cabinet Bills[a]	Cabinet Bills Approved	Individual Member Bills[b]	Individual Member Bills Approved	Cabinet Resolutions[c]	Cabinet Resolutions Approved	Individual Member Resolutions	Individual Member Resolutions Approved
63	1944	47	36	121	90			109	81
64	1945	18	16	139	76			84	27
65	1946	7	6	2	1			4	3
66	1946	27	26	141	78			85	22
67	1947	39	31	75	37			72	20
68	1948	46	35	96	50			51	9
69	1949	42	29	77	35			48	19
70	1950	61	53	74	35			54	19
71	1951	38	34	91	33			41	16
72	1952	48	41	108	38			52	24
73	1953	51	44	103	38			46	19
74	1954	51	47	85	31			60	25
75	1955	57	40	69	23			62	36
76	1956	55	48	67	23			56	29
77	1957	34	31	86	27			67	38
78	1958	47	25	68	29			49	24
79	1959	2	2	4	1			5	1
80	1959	43	35	57	18			65	27
81	1960	65	55	73	17			73	31
82	1961	84	75	57	18			75	23
83	1962	72	49	74	25			90	22
84	1963	55	39	67	16			91	33
85	1964	74	66	60	18			55	14
86	1965	66	60	74	22			47	11
87	1966	59	49	74	14			52	13
88	1967	67	55	63	18			48	18
89	1968	75	69	84	20			67	17
90	1969	66	54	81	19			69	21
91	1970	79	61	105	16			108	33
92	1971	82	67	64	25			116	46
93	1972–73	92	71	44	13			69	25
94	1973–74	109	68	70	16			101	21
95	1974	8	7	0	0			2	1
96	1974–75	74	59	75	16			93	32
97	1975–76	122	94	58	14			74	18
98	1976–77	71	50	51	13			87	26
99	1977–78	115	88	76	21			85	18
100	1978–79	92	63	80	22			88	30
101	1979	17	0	9	0			11	0
102	1979–80	88	52	35	11			61	15
103	1980–81	98	84	84	15			96	47
104	1981–82	87	70	83	15			90	35
105	1982–83	76	36	84	17			70	15
106	1983–84	120	94	67	17			109	26
107	1984–85	107	87	87	15			139	27
108	1985–86	86	74	68	6			101	23

TABLE 5.4—(Continued)

Session	Year	Cabinet Bills[a]	Cabinet Bills Approved	Individual Member Bills	Individual Member Bills Approved	Cabinet Resolutions[c]	Cabinet Resolutions Approved	Individual Member Resolutions[b]	Individual Member Resolutions Approved
109	1986–87	91	71	64	8	10		103	28
110	1987–88	82	66	78	11	2		121	31
111	1988–89	107	89	75	15	0		110	26
112	1989–90	113	75	92	15	0		125	31
113	1990–91	107	65	83	8	0		96	32
114	1991	0	0	2	2	1	1	0	0
115	1991–92	114	65	50	8	7	6	80	15
116	1992–93	154	97	62	10	19	17	97	17
117	1993–94	132	93	81	18	20	20	93	18
118	1994–95	116	81	68	15	14	10	66	8
119	1995	20	14	9	5	2	2	7	1
120	1995–96	131	109	76	18	16	12	71	10
121	1996–97	132	106	86	17	13	13	98	19
122	1997–98	135	111	113	8	17	14	104	20
123	1998–99	114	82	86	14	11	10	94	18
124	1999	1	1	2	0	2	2	3	0
125	1999–2000	145	127	84	11	20	19	82	8
126	2000–2001	141	118	100	12	31	28	104	9
127	2001–2	135	111	80	8	25	25	106	14
128	2002–3	130	115	75	13	27	26	107	13
129	2003	0	0	0	0	1	1	1	0
130	2003–4	126	109	94	13	24	24	115	6
131	2004–5	105	93	93	8	18	18	128	2
132	2005–6	138	115	93	2	19	19	99	6
133	2006–7	125	103	81	5	20	18	89	12
134	2007–8	7	7	2	1	0	0	0	0
135	2007–8	136	114	79	2	16	16	79	8

Source: Data from Ársskýrsla Alþingis (1999–2002); *Alþingistíðindi* (various issues); Alþingi's Web site, http://www.althingi.is.
Note: Because of missing data, this table does not include questions and interpellations.
[a] Bills are specific proposals for legislation.
[b] The Althingi's records do not distinguish between individual member resolutions and cabinet resolutions until the 109th session. The number of resolutions prior to the 109th session includes cabinet resolutions.
[c] Resolutions are policy initiatives requesting the cabinet to take (some) action in a particular policy area.

legislature and in its committees. The committee system is often considered a venue where parliament can scrutinize bills and exert influence by offering amendments. The Althingi has permanent committees whose jurisdictions largely correspond with the executive departments. These allow the development of a higher degree of specialization among MPs and give them a greater opportunity to more thoroughly scrutinize legislative bills. Committee meetings are held behind closed doors, which allows committee members to give the bills an impartial reading with some degree of freedom from the normal party politics. But committees have no way to protect their compromises once the legislation goes to the floor of the Althingi for debate. All bills are considered under open rules, and compromises can unravel. The committees' importance in the legislative process is greatest on technical or legal issues of limited political significance.[4]

Two committees have special status. The cabinet is obliged to confer with the foreign affairs committee on important foreign policy issues and legislation, and the budgetary committee scrutinizes the cabinet's proposed budget. Whether the special status of these committees enhances their influence is unclear.[5] For example, the cabinet's decision to support the U.S. invasion of Iraq, which was controversial at the time, drew renewed attention when serious doubts were raised about how much the cabinet conferred with the foreign affairs committee before making this decision. Although this is only one case where the cabinet seems to have largely bypassed the foreign affairs committee, the importance of the case suggests that the committee does not greatly constrain the cabinet. By contrast, the budgetary committee's reputation suggests that it wields considerable influence over the eventual shape of the budget. In fact, the Althingi has often been blamed for unraveling carefully constructed budgets, although a comparison of the initial budget proposal with the final result suggests that the Althingi's influence is modest. Kristinsson (1999) examined budgets between 1970 and 1998 and concluded that the Althingi's influence has been decreasing. Between 1998 and 2006, the average increase in expenditures between the original proposal and the final bill was 1.6 percent. However, the Althingi cannot be blamed for having behaved irresponsibly during this period, because the change in government receipts was highly correlated with the change in expenditures ($r = .92$). While it is difficult to estimate how important the Althingi is in shaping the budget, this result suggests that it has some influence. Of course, aggregate numbers do not capture the salience of specific amendments in appropriations. Nor do they reveal whether the amendments originated in the parliament or the executive branch. In fact, a National Audit Office examination of budget bills over the 1990–2000 period shows that most amendments came from the cabinet (National Audit Office 2001).

The number of amendments is another indication of how much influence the Althingi has on legislation. Magnússon (2005) finds that 65 percent of all legislative bills are amended. At the same time, he also points out that these amendments rarely constitute major changes to the legislation. When they do, it is typically on issues that cut across the parties' platforms. The work of the Althingi revolves around the parliamentary parties. Any effort on behalf of the cabinet to pass legislation concentrates not on reaching a compromise with the opposition parties but on making sure that the coalition's parliamentary parties will provide the necessary support, which is achieved by a combination of compromise and party discipline. The parliamentary parties have been strikingly successful in this respect. Jensen (2000) finds that in the 1995–96 parliamentary session, an index of party cohesion (the Rice index) rated it as 96.9 (out of 100). Given that most political parties employ open primaries, which require MPs to make a name for themselves, such high levels of party cohesion are somewhat surprising. They suggest that the Althingi functions much like a legislature in a Westminster system. The emphasis is on delivering support for the governing coalition's legislative program and shutting the opposition out of the decision-making process.

That the Althingi delegates most of its legislative powers as well as executive power to the cabinet does not necessarily imply that the parliamentary chain of delegation is broken. It simply means that the system functions more like a majoritarian democracy than a consensual or Madisonian one. However, accountability becomes more important when parliament delegates many of its powers to the executive. The Althingi's ability to exercise oversight has increased in the last two decades. The National Audit Office became an agency under the Althingi's control in 1986. This arrangement provides the Althingi with greater access to information and increases the credibility of the National Audit Office, which no longer answers to the executive. Until 1991, the Althingi was organized into two functional divisions (as was long the case with the Norwegian Storting), each with its own permanent committees. When the Althingi became an ordinary unicameral legislature, the number of permanent committees was reduced by half, thus reducing the number of committee assignments held by the average MP. This, in turn, allowed for greater specialization. The committees were also given the freedom to meet outside parliamentary sessions, providing (at least potentially) constant oversight. In the last few years, the working conditions of the MPs have improved—for example, by expansion of the professional staff of the Althingi (Magnússon 2005).[6] However, while MPs' access to information and expertise has improved, there have also been setbacks. The National Economic Institute, an important source of economic data and independent research, was abolished in 2001, when its functions were assigned to the Ministry of Finance and the Bureau of Statistics (which had the status of a ministry at the time).

The MPs' right to put questions concerning public matters to ministers serves an important oversight function. MPs can submit a written request that a minister answer a question either orally or in writing, and the interpellation must be placed on the parliamentary agenda within eight workdays.

A minister is required to produce a report on a public matter if one is requested by nine MPs and approved by parliament. The right of MPs to put questions to ministers was expanded in 1991 to include questions asked in parliament that the minister does not receive in writing in advance. Since 1999, it has been customary for the speaker to allow questions on the floor at the beginning of each meeting (Magnússon 2005).

Opposition MPs are more likely to ask questions, and they account for 70 to 80 percent of the oral and written questions (see table 5.5a). Not surprisingly, their fondness for unprepared questions is even greater. They account for approximately 85 percent of such questions, which present an opportunity to put the minister on the spot. The general increase in the use of interpellations and questions (see tables 5.5a and 5.5b) raises questions about the purpose of these queries. One interpretation is that the questions are used for political, rather than policy, purposes—that is, that the opposition uses them in an attempt to catch the ministers off guard, in the hope it will demonstrate the cabinet's incompetence, rather than using them to solicit information for the purpose of producing better policy. An alternative explanation is that the disproportionate number of questions from the opposition stems from an informational asymmetry that occurs because cabinet-party MPs have closer contact with the executive and are consulted on policy during meetings of the parliamentary party. That unprepared questions constitute only 10 to 15 percent of all questions would appear to support this latter view.

TABLE 5.5a. Interpellations and Questions to Cabinet Ministers, Iceland, 1999–2008

Year	Parties in Cabinet	Oral Questions	Oral Questions from Opposition (%)	Written Questions	Written Questions from Opposition (%)	Unprepared Questions	Unprepared Questions from Opposition (%)
1999–2000	IP, PP	165	72.7	123	70.7	49	81.6
2000–2001	IP, PP	177	74.0	168	62.5	56	82.1
2001–2	IP, PP	177	74.0	189	79.9	44	88.6
2002–3	IP, PP	158	64.6	197	75.6	33	84.8
2003–4	IP, PP	310	84.8	307	81.8	47	93.6
2004–5	IP, PP	249	82.7	197	87.8	46	83.0
2005–6	IP, PP	247	87.8	186	72.6	49	85.7
2006–7	IP, PP	194	82.5	161	71.4	34	91.2
2007–8	IP, UP	188	79.3	130	78.5	188	80.3

Source: Data from *Ársskýrsla Alþingis*, 1999–2004.
Note: See table 5.1 for explanation of party labels.

Whatever role parliamentary questions play, their total number has increased (see table 5.5b) since the 1988–89 parliamentary session. Most of this increase is due to a greater number of written questions, which can be assumed to concern more detailed information. The number of oral questions has been much more stable. These findings could be interpreted as evidence of parliamentary oversight and as evidence against deparliamentarization. The more plausible explanation, in our view, is that the increasing number of questions is a response to the deparliamentarization of Icelandic politics. The opposition parties have largely been shut out of the policy-making process and are grasping at straws. Asking questions has become the only way for the opposition to hold the cabinet accountable. The general tenor among opposition MPs suggests frustration with the limited opportunities to influence policy.

In sum, the evidence about Iceland favors the deparliamentarization thesis—especially if "parliamentarization" implies an active role in policy-making. The role of the Althingi has been reduced to providing support for the legislative program of the cabinet parties. There is little to suggest that the Althingi, as a whole, has much influence on legislation. The level of voting

TABLE 5.5b. Interpellations and Questions to Cabinet Ministers, Iceland, 1988–2008

Sessions	Year	Parties in Cabinet	Oral Questions	Written Questions	Written Replies
111	1988–89	PP, PA, SDP	148	59	57
112	1989–90	PP, PA, SDP, CP	158	72	69
113	1990–91	PP, PA, SDP, CP	124	38	36
115	1991–92	IP, SDP	183	88	82
116	1992–93	IP, SDP	142	104	98
117	1993–94	IP, SDP	171	107	104
118 and 119	1994–95	IP, SDP	92	91	88
120	1995–96	IP, PP	121	105	103
121	1996–97	IP, PP	127	130	128
122	1997–98	IP, PP	137	179	173
123 and 124	1998–99	IP, PP	130	159	158
125	1999–2000	IP, PP	170	117	119
126	2000–2001	IP, PP	177	168	160
127	2001–2	IP, PP	177	189	173
128	2002–3	IP, PP	158	198	182
130	2003–4	IP, PP	308	301	293
131	2004–5	IP, PP	258	188	187
132	2005–6	IP, PP	247	186	180
133	2006–7	IP, PP	194	161	158
134 and 135	2007–8	IP, UP	188	130	126

Source: Data from Alþingi's Web site, http://www.althingi.is.
Note: See table 5.1 for explanation of party labels.

cohesion is high, the success rate of opposition legislative bills is low, and the opposition has no means to constrain the cabinet's majority. That said, however, not all MPs are created equal. To enact its legislative program, the cabinet must consult with its parliamentary parties to ensure their support. Although the intraparty politics remain largely a black box, cabinet-party MPs appear to exert at least a modicum of policy influence. Thus, while it remains true that the Althingi delegates legislative powers to the cabinet, these powers cannot be exercised without the Althingi's consent. Nonetheless, parliamentary consent implies only the consent of a majority of the Althingi's members, which leaves the opposition out in the cold.

Within the Cabinet

Conflict within the cabinet is managed by leaders of the coalition parties. Sometimes a larger subset of cabinet ministers will handle important and sensitive tasks; for example, a cabinet committee supervised the privatization of government enterprises. Coalition discipline is generally very high with regard to policies outlined in the coalition agreement but can vary on other issues. Ministers sometimes disagree publicly on important issues. For example, in Oddsson's cabinets, the prime minister and the foreign minister frequently clashed publicly on the question of Iceland's membership in the European Union.

The formation of executive cabinets is usually accompanied by public coalition agreements that are primarily concerned with policy. Until 1991, coalition partners also agreed on a negative election rule: the prime minister would not ask the president to dissolve parliament unless supported by the whole cabinet. By contrast, none of Oddsson's cabinets (1991–2004) were based on such an agreement; in that case, the prime minister publicly claimed for himself the exclusive right to dissolve parliament.[7]

The coalition parties do not make formal agreements about appointments to noncabinet posts. However, appointments to the boards of directors of state banks were traditionally based on an informal but strict quota system, in which one seat was allocated to each party at each state bank. This system still operates at the Central Bank, which has three governors to accommodate the parties. Former prime minister Oddsson became chief governor of the Central Bank upon retiring from party politics. His predecessor as prime minister, Hermannsson, also became governor of the Central Bank when he retired from politics. Ministers have considerable autonomy in making appointments—for example, to positions in the upper ranks of executive agencies and various executive committees. Ministers normally clear major appointments with their party leaders, and the most important positions, such as governors of the Central Bank and director of the state broadcasting company, are allocated by the leaders of the coalitions.

The size of the cabinet has grown from 6 to 12 ministers since 1944, while the number of ministries (portfolios) has increased more slowly. The Bureau of Statistics was a ministry from 1988 to 2007, and the Ministry of the Environment was created in 1989. The increase in the number of ministers and ministries is directly related to facilitating the formation of coalition cabinets. By turning the Bureau of Statistics into a ministry and by creating the Ministry of the Environment, leaders of coalitions sought to broaden the parliamentary support of a weak coalition cabinet. The number of ministers has been temporarily scaled down in times of short-lived minority cabinets (1958–59 and 1978–79). When the number of parties in a coalition increases, so does the number of ministers. When a two-party coalition between the Independence Party and the Progressive Party forms, there is a tendency to appoint an even number of ministers (as occurred in 1950, 1974, and 1999).

An interesting consequence of the increase in the number of ministers is that MPs from the (junior) coalition parties become ministers with relative ease. Five of the Social Democratic Party's 10 MPs became ministers in 1991, and 6 of the Progressive Party's 12 MPs did so in 1995. Iceland has a long tradition of cabinet ministers being MPs (except in nonpartisan cabinets), which helps explain both the aversion MPs have toward nonpartisan cabinets and the tendency to increase the number of cabinet ministers. The ratio of cabinet ministers to MPs has almost doubled from 1944 (11 percent) to 2004 (19 percent). The positions of speaker of parliament and chairs of the Althingi's 12 standing committees are all reserved for MPs of cabinet parties.[8] As a result, nearly all MPs directly reap power and/or material benefits from their own parties' cabinet participation. In addition, it is quite common for cabinet ministers to appoint MPs from cabinet parties, especially from their own party, to salaried working committees in the executive branch. In fact, few, if any, MPs from cabinet parties receive only their basic MP salary. The opposite is true of opposition MPs. Almost none of them have an income outside their pay as MPs.

Certain rules have evolved regarding the distribution of the ministerial portfolios. The post of prime minister usually goes to either the Independence Party or the Progressive Party, and it is usually a point of friction. Oddsson dealt very successfully with this issue in 1991 and made Ásgrímsson his replacement as prime minister. In Oddsson's absence, the office of prime minister moved from the Independence Party to the Progressive

Party. Later, the two leaders added another twist to the art of coalition bargaining when they agreed—after the 2003 election—to rotate the post of prime minister. Oddsson continued as prime minister until the fall of 2004, at which point Ásgrímsson took over. In return, the Independence Party got the Ministry of the Environment and the Ministry of Foreign Affairs, increasing its number of ministers to seven while the Progressive Party's share dropped to five.

The post of prime minister is clearly the most important portfolio. The Ministry of Foreign Affairs is second in importance, and the Ministry of Finance is third. The Ministry of the Environment is considered the least important. Each party is normally autonomous in selecting ministers to fill its own portfolios. When it comes to the distribution of portfolios, almost everything, with a few exceptions, is on the negotiation table. One of the exceptions is that the People's Alliance never holds the Ministry of Foreign Affairs, nor do they seek it. It was opposed to Iceland's membership of NATO and the stationing of American troops in the country. When in the cabinet, the Progressive Party almost always holds the Ministry of Agriculture.

Thus far, we have discussed the relationship between parliament and cabinet largely in general terms and in terms of the rules structuring delegation and accountability. It is interesting to supplement this with information about the people occupying key ministerial positions. The leadership style of successful prime ministers has differed from those who failed to hold a coalition cabinet together until the end of their term. Of course, it is possible that leaders who are successful in keeping their coalitions together might nonetheless fail to make much of an impact on policy. We believe, however, that these factors tend to go together; that is, leaders who are capable of keeping a coalition together are also more effective in governing.

Table 5.6 provides information about the background of individuals who have held the three most important ministerial posts—prime minister, finance minister, and foreign minister—as well as the post of justice minister, which is not considered a key ministry in Iceland. As shown in the table, the typical cabinet minister is a middle-aged, male MP with a university degree who worked in the public sector prior to entering parliament. His career in politics did not necessarily start with the party's youth organization, but virtually all prime ministers, foreign ministers, and finance ministers have served many years in parliament and held a high-ranking position in the party before they were appointed.

The first woman to hold one of the top cabinet offices, Valgerður Sverrisdóttir, took office as Minister of Foreign Affairs in June 2006. Her successor was also a woman, Ingibjörg Gísladóttir. Two women have also held the post of justice minister, in 1970–71 and 1999–2003 respectively. The latter incumbent, Sólveig Pétursdóttir, suffered the rare fate of not retaining her cabinet post—and not getting another cabinet office—even though the ruling coalition stayed in power after the 2003 election and her party held on to the Ministry of Justice. The most important ministers are drawn from an exclusive group, which rules out almost all women and most men, too. This club is even more narrowly based than table 5.6 suggests. In particular, the majority of cabinet ministers and two-thirds of prime ministers have held law degrees, and most have been employed in the public sector before entering parliament.

A few differences in the backgrounds of persons appointed to the four ministerial posts are evident in table 5.6. Compared to the positions of prime minister and foreign minister, it is much less likely that persons appointed to the posts of finance or justice minister have held prior cabinet positions. Justice ministers have also, on average, had less parliamentary experience and are much less likely to have worked for the party or in the private sector. They are also less likely to have held high party office. Those appointed foreign minister or justice minister are less likely to have held high rank in the youth party. Those appointed finance minister are less likely than other ministers to have been elected to local or regional office.

On the surface, it appears that political parties recruit about half of the most important ministers from within—from the party's youth organization and/or elected officials at the local level. In reality, however, the party does not act as an effective gatekeeper to a political career, because most politicians enter politics through the open primary and rely on their own personal and political network. The party does, however, screen candidates for top ministerial positions in the sense that party leadership is usually a requisite for becoming prime minister, finance minister, or foreign minister. As we shall see, this does not amount to ex ante party control by party leaders, because parties throw out leaders who do not keep the party in office.

The background of the ministers holding core portfolios has not changed much over time, although a few changes bear mentioning. It has become more common for ministers with core portfolios to have prior experience in cabinet. This is likely due, at least in part, to an increase in the number of portfolios, as well as greater coalition durability. Prior high-rank positions in the youth party has also become more important, suggesting that the parties function less like mass parties than cadre parties. If the period since 1945 is split in two, prior employment in the party has become more important. However, it has declined considerably since 1990.

TABLE 5.6. Ministerial Background, First Appointment, by Portfolio, Iceland, 1944–2008

Portfolio within Cabinet	Age (mean years)	Female Ministers (%)	Prior Cabinet Position (%)	Parliamentary Experience (mean years)[a]	Prior Party High-Rank Position (%)[b]	Prior Youth Party High-Rank Position (%)[c]	Major Prior Appointment within Parliament (%)[d]	Major Prior Elected Offices at Local/Regional Level (%)[e]	Formal Education Level[f]	Any Prior Employment within the Public Sector (%)[g]	Any Prior Employment within the Private Sector (%)	Any Prior Salaried Employment in Party (%)	Member of Parliament at the Time of Minister Appointment (%)[h]	N (unique number of ministers)
Prime minister	52.1	0	69	14.8	88	50	88	63	4.0	88	75	19	100	16
Finance minister[i]	47.4	0	26	10.7	84	47	84	32	3.6	84	79	32	95	19
Foreign minister	52.9	13	60	13.1	87	27	73	60	3.9	87	87	13	87	15
Justice minister[j]	48.0	12	12	8.1	41	41	88	59	3.7	88	53	6	100	17
1944–2007 Mean	50.1	6	42	11.7	74	41	83	54	3.8	87	73	18	95	67
1945–75 Mean	49.5	3	29	12.0	74	29	84	65	3.6	90	74	13	97	31
1991–2007 Mean	49.6	21	71	12.5	79	75	86	36	4.1	79	86	0	100	14

Source: Data from Þingmannatal Alþingis, http://www.althingi.is.

Note: All of the calculations presented in this section are based on a data set that contains data on ministers who got portfolios at the beginning of a new cabinet. A new cabinet is defined here as a cabinet that fulfills at least one of three conditions: any change in the set of parties holding cabinet membership, any change in the identity of the prime minister, or any general election (see Müller and Strøm 2003, 12).

[a] Prior parliamentary experience (in full years) does not include years that a person has been in cabinet. That is, for systems that allow for the holding of simultaneous cabinet and parliamentary positions, we only count "parliamentary experience" for the years that the MP does not also have a cabinet position. (The latter is coded as prior cabinet experience: yes or no.) If the total parliamentary experience (service as MP) sums to less than six months, it is counted as zero (0) years of experience.

[b] Prior party high-rank position refers to any of the following: party leader, party secretary, member of the party national board, or head of local or regional board.

[c] Prior youth party high-rank position refers to the positions in a youth organization corresponding to the prior party high-rank positions.

[d] Major prior appointment within parliament refers to any of the following: Speaker (president of parliament or chamber/subdivision), group leader, vice group leader, committee chairman, or vice committee chairman.

[e] Major prior elected offices at local/regional level refers to any of the following: head of municipality, head of region, member of local parliament, or member of regional parliament.

[f] Formal education level: 1 = primary (or less); 2 = secondary (high school, Swedish gymnasium); 3 = any enrollment in postsecondary education (such as technical college, nursing school, college, university) but no degree; 4 = any undergraduate degree at technical college, nursing school, college, or university (2–4 years in length) that is post-high school or postgymnasium; 5 = postgraduate degree (licensiat, huvudfag, PhD).

[g] Prior employment refers to the employer, that is to say, the one paying the salary. Salary by the party does not include elected offices, only jobs (such as party ombudsman). The three categories (public, private, party) are not mutually exclusive categories (as they, in combination, speak to a minister's general career pattern). Private employment includes people employed in trade unions and other nongovernmental organizations.

[h] The coding "Member of parliament at the time of minister appointment" only has one possible answer (yes or no).

[i] Finance minister is defined as the minister heading the ministry in control of the state budget.

[j] Justice minister is defined as the minister heading the ministry in control of the police force.

Coalition governance in Iceland has become simpler in some ways. The simplicity stems from the fact that the president has not played a decisive role in cabinet formation since 1980, while politicians have shown great skill in providing stable cabinet coalitions. Until very recently, a stable economic situation also contributed to a less stressful environment in which to conduct cabinet formation and maintenance. The presidents' insistence on majority cabinets has also focused the efforts of party leaders on a subset of potential cabinets.

At the same time, the methods of operating parliamentary government have changed as party leaders have extended the scale of governing techniques at their disposal. Icelandic politics is still characterized by "clientelism," but that term should not divert our attention away from a fundamental transformation from societal and party-based clientelism to individual clientelism. This refers to the fact that individual political leaders have been known to distribute public resources, public property, and public benefits to individuals and firms favorable to them.[9]

One difficulty in assessing whether deparliamentarization or party decline has taken place in Iceland is that coalition cabinets have been very stable for the better part of the past two decades. Moreover, for most of that time, the coalitions have been led by Oddsson as prime minister. Oddsson was frequently characterized as a charismatic and forceful leader able to rein in his party. It is thus possible that the cabinets' success during these special circumstances can be mistaken for deparliamentarization or party decline.

However, it is clear that the PM does not govern alone. As he stated in an interview, Oddsson clearly saw the position and function of the PM to be very different from the office of the mayor of Reykjavík, a post he held for nine years (1982–91).

> The job of the Prime Minister as a leader is completely different from that of the mayor. It is mostly concerned with coordinating the views of individuals with different backgrounds. I do not have the supreme power, I mean the direct power to command, which I possessed as mayor. Each cabinet minister has full power over his department. Formally the Prime Minister cannot command him to do anything. Consequently my power as Prime Minister consists of influence rather than the power to command, although both types clearly coexist. (Hauksson 1996)

In the same interview, Oddsson also emphasized the importance of personal contact with his cabinet ministers, of making himself accessible to them at all times. This allows the PM to coordinate and influence. It also "forces" cabinet ministers to consult with the PM, because they cannot hide behind the cover of not being able to reach the PM.

The Oddsson cabinet, like previous cabinets, avoided majority voting. Consensus usually emerged before cabinet meetings, although the PM made the final decision in cases of serious disagreement over ministerial jurisdiction. Oddsson also made a sharp distinction between the powers of the PM as such and the position of the PM as his or her party leader. The PM does not select his or her coalition partners' ministers, nor is the PM politically responsible for the conduct of those ministers while they are in office. In practice, ministers are delegates of their respective parties, and they are not politically accountable to the PM.

Successful PMs appear to display political skills in three arenas. They are successful in forming and maintaining coalition cabinets, preserving a strong position in the parliamentary party, and winning parliamentary elections. For Icelandic PMs, the first two of these skills can be the most important. When they fall short, it is often because of a lack of skill in coalition management and maintenance.

The cabinet is not a collective body dominated by the PM but, rather, a council of highly independent ministers. The prevalence of coalition cabinets further complicates the PM's role, although it also absolves the PM of political responsibility for his or her coalition partners' ministers. The successful PM adjusts to the formal and informal rules of the game by carefully learning on the job rather than by establishing a clear chain of delegation and accountability. Those who approach the PM's role in a purely formal fashion quickly fail.

At the end of the day, the performance of the PM and his or her coalition partners is judged by voters in legislative elections. Political systems in which coalition cabinets are the norm are not ideally suited to enhance accountability. This is because voters face uncertainty about whether the government as a whole or individual parties in the cabinet are responsible for policy failures. This, in turn, creates an incentive for coalition parties to pass the buck to their coalition partners in order to avoid being held accountable or losing popularity. Strøm (1990) argues that the tendency of cabinet parties to lose votes in elections helps explain the formation of minority coalitions, since the expectation of such losses might temper the parties' desire for executive office. In light of the prevalence of majority coalitions in Iceland, it is interesting to consider whether cabinet parties have in fact fared badly in elections. Table 5.7 shows that cabinet parties (in office at time of election) have lost an average of 4.3 percent of the vote in legislative elections since

1946, which suggests that the scarcity of minority cabinets is due to constitutional norms enforced by the president rather than to positive electoral incentives for parties to form majority coalitions. However, there is an interesting difference between the Progressive Party, which has lost an average of 3 percent, and the Social Democratic and Independence parties, which have lost an average of only 1.4 percent. Elections in which voters have heavily punished cabinet parties include those of 1978, 1987, and 1991.

Delegation from Ministers to Civil Servants

Icelandic ministers enjoy considerable autonomy from the cabinet when it comes to running their ministries. However, they face substantial constraints that limit the degree to which they can delegate to civil servants. In-

TABLE 5.7. Electoral Performance of Incumbent Cabinet Parties, Iceland, 1944–2008

Cabinet Number	Cabinet Composition	Election Year following Cabinet	PA	SP	ULL	SDP	PP	IP	CP	Cabinet Total
1	IP, SP, SDP 1944	1946		+1.0		+3.6		+1.0		+5.6
3	SDP, PP, IP 1947	1949				−1.3	+1.4	0.0		+0.1
5	PP, IP 1950	1953					−2.6	−2.4		−5.0
6	IP, PP 1953	1956					−6.3	+5.3		−1.0
8	SDP 1958	1959				−5.8				−5.8
9	SDP 1959	1959				+2.7				+2.7
10	IP, SDP 1959	1963				−1.0		+1.7		+0.7
12	IP, SDP II 1963	1967				+1.5		−3.9		−2.4
14	IP, SDP 1970	1971				−5.2		−1.3		−6.5
15	PP, PA, ULL 1971	1974	+1.2		−4.3		−0.4			−3.5
16	IP, PP 1974	1978					−8.0	−10.0		−18.0
18	SDP 1979	1979				−4.6				−4.6
19	IP, PA, PP 1980	1983	−2.4				−5.9	+3.3		−5.0
20	PP, IP 1983	1987					−0.1	−11.5		−11.6
23	PP, PA, SDP, CP 1989	1991	+1.1			+0.3	0.0		−10.9	−9.3
24	IP, SDP 1991	1995				−4.1		−1.5		−5.6
25	IP, PP 1995	1999					−4.9	+3.6		−1.3
26	IP, PP 1999	2003					−0.7	−7.0		−7.7
29	IP, PP 2006	2007					−6.0	+2.9		−3.1
Mean gains/losses			−0.03	+1.0	−4.3	−1.4	−3.0	−1.4	−10.9	−4.3

Source: Data from Indridason 2005; *Statistics Iceland.*

Notes: See table 5.1 for explanation of party labels. Numbers in table represent percentages of national vote.

stead of delegating, Icelandic ministers actively run interference on behalf of their clients, even in routine administrative matters. In fact, anyone can make an appointment with a minister, and this undercuts the civil service hierarchy and decreases its autonomy. Moreover, the adoption of (open) primary elections has added to the minister's incentive to intervene on behalf of his or her constituency in an effort to build the minister's personal vote (Kristjánsson 2003).

For most of the postwar period, ministers have wielded the power of appointing civil servants. This power has proven to be a double-edged sword. Civil servants enjoyed secure tenure until the mid-1990s. The combination of political appointments and lifelong tenure was likely to place limits on how much power ministers were willing to delegate to civil servants, especially senior civil servants that had been appointed by opposition parties.

To some degree, of course, delegating powers to the civil service cannot be avoided. As a result, the minister is forced to monitor his or her civil servants. One type of response to this situation has been the establishment of numerous boards to monitor and control the actions of civil servants (Kristinsson 2006a). Ad hoc committees, often composed of bureaucrats, interest groups, and party members, are also used to deal with special issues or to formulate policy (Kristinsson 1994a).

While it is possible to debate whether political appointments and lifelong tenure in the civil service are desirable, one is hard pressed to find an argument in favor of combining the two. However, there is a reason why this system emerged and was sustained for so long. Kristinsson (1994b) points out that Iceland inherited (literally) the Danish bureaucratic model, in which bureaucrats enter the civil service and work their way up the hierarchy as they gain experience. Bureaucrats also enjoyed secure tenure and a generous pension system. There was, however, never any political support for an autonomous bureaucracy. Icelandic politicians quickly discovered that public employment could be turned into political spoils by offering jobs to their supporters. Thus, politicians kept the aspects of the Danish administrative tradition that proved to be valuable to them and discarded the rest.

The use of the civil service as spoils appears to have declined in recent years, in part because public employment has become less lucrative. The new Civil Service Act may have had an influence as well, although its adoption might also have been a result of the declining importance of the civil service for clientelistic purposes. This does not mean that political appointments have disappeared. Analyzing 111 major administrative and judicial appointments between 2001 and 2005, Kristinsson (2006b) finds that 44 percent of them can be classified as political appointments. Each appointment could also be classified as bureaucratic (the appointee was a career bureaucrat) or professional (the appointee had professional qualifications); that is, the categories are not mutually exclusive. Even so, 16 percent of the cases could only be classified as political appointments.

The principal-agent problems are quite apparent when it comes to the management of executive agencies and companies. Despite the reforms of the past decade, ministers appear unable to exert control over executive agencies. Executive agencies are required by law to keep their spending within budget. Despite this, Másson and Indridason (2005) found that half the executive agencies exceeded their budgets every year between 1998 and 2004. Even though recent reforms have eliminated lifetime tenure, not a single head of agency has been removed from his or her post. A reasonable conclusion is that cabinet ministers have failed to hold the heads of the executive agencies accountable. In addition, the remnants of the ministers' control and oversight mechanisms, the agency boards, have not enabled them to exert control. Instead of controlling agency spending, they often provide ready access for special interests and have become cheerleaders for further spending. The heads of executive agencies are formally accountable to their ministers, but the presence of a board provides the head of the agency with an additional principal whose demands he or she must also satisfy. In fact, Másson and Indridason (2005) find that executive agencies with boards are significantly more likely to go over budget.

In sum, the delegation from ministers to civil servants is problematic at best. Secure tenure for civil servants increases the likelihood of diverging preferences between the principal and the agent. Ministers must therefore devote time and energy to keeping a watchful eye on civil servants and must adopt institutional mechanisms for oversight. The use of the civil service for spoils also risks sacrificing the public benefit for political gain, because the most qualified candidates might be rejected in favor of lesser ones.

External Constraints

Icelandic parliamentary democracy faces several external constraints. First, the president has considerable formal powers that constrain the delegation of power from voters to parliament. While accounts of Icelandic politics have tended to deemphasize the role of the president, events in this decade have demonstrated that the president is a force to be reckoned with. The most important power of the president is his or her ability to veto legislation, which forces a referendum on the law.[10] In 2004, President Grímsson used the presidential legislative veto for the first time. His veto of a bill on media ownership led to a constitutional crisis, with the cabinet arguing that the president's actions were unconstitutional. In the end, the cabinet backed down, but rather than acknowledge the constitutionality of the president's veto, it had parliament repeal the law. This was clearly a victory for the president, and future cabinets would be unwise to ignore presidential veto threats, especially when the legislation in question is widely opposed by the public, as was true in this case.[11]

This was not the first time the president had been called on to veto legislation. Some previous presidents, however, emphasized the symbolic, ceremonial role of the head of state and refrained from taking political stances (Kristjánsson 2004). In this sense, 2004 may constitute a breaking point in the history of the republic—as the year Iceland ceased to operate as a parliamentary system and moved toward a semi-presidential practice closer to the letter of the constitution. Only time can tell whether the political system has thus been permanently transformed. However, President Grímsson's exertion of power may not go unchallenged. The cabinet did not sit idly by but began a process of constitutional review by appointing an executive commission charged with reconsidering several articles of the constitution. Not surprisingly, Article 26, which grants the president legislative veto power, was one of these articles.

The presidency limits the authority of the legislature via the veto and, perhaps, via the president's role as *informateur*, which arguably helps alleviate some of the problems inherent in the delegation of powers from voters to parliament. Agency relationships generally need some degree of oversight for the principal to achieve his or her objectives. The presidential veto performs exactly such a function by keeping a check on parliament and alerting the public when the president believes that the parliament is not acting in the public's best interest. The presidential veto may thus make parliament more accountable to its voters.[12]

Corporatism is another external constraint on parliamentary governance. Icelandic unions have historically been strong, and union membership increased until the early 1990s, when it reached over 95 percent of the labor force. Unionization rates remain very high comparatively—around 85 percent. Corporatism gained increased prominence in the early 1990s, with the employers' associations and the trade unions reaching an agreement, the National Consensus, outlining various labor market issues, including wage-increase policies. The cabinet and the parliament were marginalized in the making of the National Consensus but passed the necessary legislation and let the agreement guide its negotiation with the unions in the public sector (Kristjánsson 2003). Members of the cabinet even went so far as to declare that they thought some of the legislation was bad policy but that they would vote for it to maintain the consensus.[13] The importance of corporatist arrangements has, however, declined since the late 1990s.

The most recent decade has also witnessed the rise of new external constraints on parliament. Iceland's membership in the European Economic Area (EEA) has profoundly influenced Icelandic politics. EEA membership implies that Iceland must adopt all European Union (EU) legislation pertaining to areas covered by the EEA treaty, even though it has little influence over its content. Thirteen percent of the legislation adopted in the last four sessions of the Althingi (2001–5) was adopted to satisfy requirements of the EEA treaty (Magnússon 2005). This has not only limited parliament's authority in certain areas but also reduced the authority of the cabinet to engage in particularistic politics. Indeed, Gwartney, Lawson, and Gartzke (2005) count Iceland among the countries in the world that have made the greatest gains in economic freedom since 1985.[14]

Another external constraint is created by the courts, which have increasingly asserted their independence. In recent years, the Supreme Court, historically almost deferential to the executive, has struck down several laws and regulations every year on the grounds that they are unconstitutional. In 2003, for example, the Supreme Court struck down legislation on public assistance to the disabled, much to the cabinet's consternation.

In sum, the importance of external constrains has grown substantially in recent years. While some constraints, such as the EEA treaty, might be seen as hampering the representational role of parliament, it can also be argued that increasingly activist courts and the presidential veto have provided the citizens with agents that are formally external to the parliamentary chain of delegation but that can help hold elected politicians accountable.

Parliamentary Democracy: An Assessment

The Voters-Parliament Link

We here evaluate parliamentary democracy in Iceland by going through the three main steps in the parliamentary chain of democracy, beginning with the link from voters to parliamentarians. The sovereignty of the voter is strongly protected in the sense that all elections are conducted according to strict legal standards. The open primary gives voters an additional opportunity to reward and punish politicians. However, the open primary has taken the role of recruiting MPs away from the political parties. In giving up power over nominations, the political parties have undermined their ability to offer meaningful alternatives to voters.

The parties enter elections without making commitments about post-electoral coalitions. Following an election, each parliamentary party is in the position of a free agent, without any kind of covenant with voters about carrying out specific policy alternatives or forming a particular coalition cabinet. The theory of parliamentary democracy assigns political parties the task of asserting the position of voters as the ultimate principal to parliament. In Iceland, MPs are elected without a specific mandate binding them to voters. In this sense, parliamentary democracy is rather weak. The open primary also gives MPs an overriding incentive to cultivate personal ties with their constituency and various special interests on the basis of clientelistic relations. In fact, as an institution, the Althingi often functions as a kind of regional administration. All MPs from each electoral district work together, providing a link between local governments in their district and the central government.

The political parties organize the work of the Althingi. The strength of each parliamentary party is determined by its relationship to the cabinet, not by its ties to voters. Cabinet-party MPs are part of a majority coalition involved in the task of running the government, including passing necessary legislation. Opposition MPs use parliament mainly as a forum for criticism of the cabinet, general political debate, and public relations. None of the parliamentary parties has an effective, organized connection to voters or to its formal party organization.

The Parliament-Cabinet Link

From the early 1980s until very recently, party leaders showed great skill in forming and maintaining cabinet coalitions. The parliamentary parties formed and terminated cabinets without much intervention by the president, who had a more active role in the making and unmaking of coalition cabinets in earlier periods. Thus, a cohesive parliamentary majority and capable party leaders—with the cooperation of the president—have been able to pull a parliamentary rabbit out of the semi-presidential constitutional hat. In this period, the Althingi was also strengthened in various ways as an institution. Its professional staff was expanded, and the chairmanship of some standing committees was turned over, briefly, to opposition MPs.

The stronger position of parliament turned out to be a short-term reversal of the strong Icelandic tradition of cohesive governing parties. After the 1999 election, the supremacy of the cabinet over parliament was de facto established by the combination of two factors: the unwillingness of cabinet-party MPs to protect the autonomy of parliament and the ability and will of two government leaders—Oddsson and Ásgrímsson—to take personal command of the executive branch while relegating parliament to a supporting role. This development has turned the theory of parliamentary government on its head. Parliament has largely become an agent of the cabinet. In fact, almost all cabinet-party MPs work in both parliament and the executive branch, either directly, through being both MPs and ministers, or indirectly, by serving on salaried executive committees.

The Cabinet–Civil Service Link

Icelandic cabinet ministers are the masters of their respective departments. If a minister chooses to run a professional ministry, including hiring people on merit, he or she can do so. Likewise, if a minister wants to pursue clientelistic politics, including employing his or her political allies, the minister can do that.

For a while, it seemed that some cabinet ministers were leading the way in creating a more independent civil service. In recent years, however, it has been revealed that this is not the case. Political clientelism appears rampant at the top, with cabinet ministers repeatedly being accused of violating public trust by appointing their clients to the highest positions, including directors of the Central Bank, ambassadors, and Supreme Court justices. More qualified applicants to public offices are passed over in favor of less qualified but "connected" people. Some of those treated unfairly have successfully sued the government for damages. To avert the threat of lawsuits, the most recent tactic of cabinet ministers has been to fill the posts temporarily and then extend the appointments, rather than opening up the positions for applications from all qualified candidates. Three people now filling a position of permanent secretary are currently serving temporary appointments.

Conclusion

We find signs of decay at every step of the parliamentary chain of delegation and accountability, because political parties have lost much of their ability to give coherence to the chain. The unusual turn of events in the fall of 2008 makes it especially difficult to predict the future of parliamentary democracy in Iceland. It represents a rare opportunity for institutional reform as well for the creation of new political norms.

In the spring of 2009, the Althingi was considering a constitutional amendment that would establish an elected constitutional assembly with a largely unrestricted mandate to rewrite the constitution. Many of the expected institutional reforms are intended to strengthen voter sovereignty. The governing parties, as of 2009, have shown interest in changing the electoral law to an open-list proportional representation system. This proposal is intended to increase the MPs' responsiveness to voter demands and to ease the stranglehold of the parties on parliamentary business. The means chosen may, however, endanger the opportunity to set new standards for informal political practices.

Political patronage is one of the fundamental problems of Icelandic politics. The problem is likely to be especially acute when it is time for the government to (re)privatize the banks. When the banks, in their previous incarnation, were privatized, the process was reportedly riddled with irregularities and political favoritism. The present awareness concerning the costs of political patronage and of close ties between business and politics provides an opportunity to impose new standards, but those might be undermined by an electoral system that creates incentives for politicians to build a personal vote. Norms are far more difficult to change than institutions, and they develop in a complex interaction between politicians, the public, and the media. Still, there have been hopeful signs. The minister of trade resigned in January 2009, citing the need for someone to accept responsibility for the banking collapse. The uproar surrounding major financial contributions to the Independence Party, which happened just before a new law restricting such contributions took effect, may also help tip the scales toward a clearer separation between politics and business.

Regardless of what the final outcome will be, politicians will still face some of the same constraints that were in place before the financial collapse. Judicial review by the courts is not likely to fade away, nor will the constraints imposed by membership in the European Economic Area. Indeed, the question of whether to join the EU was propelled onto the political agenda in the aftermath of the collapse, although public support for the idea has since declined. The president is likely to continue to be a relevant political actor, which reflects a long Icelandic tradition of regarding popular election as superior to the indirect representation found in parliamentary democracy. However, the constitutional assembly may well reduce the powers of the president—for example, replacing his veto by allowing referenda to be called by a parliamentary minority or a citizen initiative. Such a change seems even more likely as, in hindsight, many consider the president to have gone too far in championing those who led Iceland's economic expansion.

The current state of parliamentary democracy in Iceland is characterized by a threefold paradox. First, parliament is accountable to voters by providing majority coalition cabinets. At the same time, parliamentary parties act as free agents, not bound to voters by any preelection commitment. Second, by bypassing the president and making the cabinet completely dependent on the support of a parliamentary majority, the Althingi's ability to hold the cabinet accountable is enhanced. More recently, however, cabinet leaders have turned the tables and made parliament serve the executive branch. Third, the majority of the public administration is free of political clientelism, but the top levels of the civil service are plagued by clientelistic practices. In sum, two opposite forces are operating at each link of the parliamentary chain of delegation and accountability, one strengthening parliamentary democracy and the other undermining it. The future of Icelandic parliamentarism depends on which of these forces will prevail.

NOTES

1. We have added the 2003 election to the Pétursson (2005) data. The 1999 election is excluded because only part of the People's Alliance merged with the other left parties.

2. Bloc volatility measures the degree to which voters switch their votes from left-wing parties to right-wing parties. The right bloc is assumed to include the Independence Party, the Progressive Party, the Liberal Party, and the Citizen's Party. The Women's Party was not included among the left bloc parties.

3. See Jóhannesson 2005, 2006. The first three presidents of Iceland all threatened the formation of a nonpartisan cabinet when the parties had difficulty forming a majority coalition. Finnbogadóttir was reluctant to use this option, though Jóhannesson points out that it was rumoured that a nonpartisan cabinet might have been in the works. Since 1991, government formation has proceeded smoothly, thus minimizing the role of the president.

4. Þorleifsson (2006) finds that holding committee chairs has a small but statistically insignificant effect on the influence of the opposition parties.

5. *Morgunblaðið* 2004.

6. As an example, the Althingi's budget increased by about 43 percent between 1998 and 2006.

7. *Morgunblaðið* 1994.

8. The government parties experimented briefly with allowing the opposition to chair parliamentary committees in the 1990s.

9. For example, the privatization of the state banks has come under criticism

for cheaply transferring state property into the hands of politically connected individuals.

10. The law goes into effect even if the president vetoes it. Technically, therefore, the president cannot veto legislation but can only subject the law to a referendum.

11. A poll conducted by Gallup in July 2004 indicated that 62 percent of respondents were against the legislation while 31 percent supported it (IMG Gallup 2004).

12. This conclusion depends naturally on the motives of the president. Presidential vetoes could also lead to logrolling between the president and the legislature that could make the public worse off.

13. See, e.g., the Althingi's record of parliamentary debates on bill 485/1993, available at http://althingi.is/dba-bin/ferill.pl?ltg=117&mnr=251 (accessed September 17, 2006).

14. Note that Iceland has usually been ranked as one of the least corrupt countries in the world according to Transparency International's Corruption Perceptions Index (CPI). The CPI measures corruption disproportionally in the form of bribes in the public and political sectors. Clientelism or particularism, however, does not necessarily involve bribes. It may simply constitute favorable or preferential treatment of individuals or firms loyal to the party. In other words, while corruption involves the misuse of public office for private gain, clientelism involves the misuse of public office for political gain.

REFERENCES

Arter, David. 1984. *The Nordic Parliaments*. London: Hurst.
Arter, David. 1999. *Scandinavian Politics Today*. Manchester: Manchester University Press.
Eggertsson, Dagur B. 1999. *Steingrímur Hermannsson—Ævisaga 1*. Reykjavík: Vaka-Helgafell.
Eggertsson, Dagur B. 2000. *Steingrímur Hermannsson—Ævisaga 2*. Reykjavík: Vaka-Helgafell.
Grímsson, Ólafur Ragnar. 1978. *Network Parties*. Oútgefið rit: Háskól: Íslands.
Gwartney, James, Robert Lawson, and Erik Gartzke. 2005. *Economic Freedom of the World*. Vancouver, BC: Fraser Institute.
Harðarson, Ólafur Þ. 1995. *Parties and Voters in Iceland*. Reykjavík: Háskólaútgáfan.
Harðarson, Ólafur, and Gunnar Helgi Kristinsson. 2007. "Iceland." In "Political Data Yearbook," special issue, *European Journal of Political Research* 46 (7–8): 974–79.
Hauksson, Jón G. 1996. "Stjórnandinn Davíð: Ítarlegt viðtal við Davíð Oddsson forsætisráðherra um hann sem stjórnanda." *Frjáls verslun* 57 (1): 32–39.
IMG Gallup. 2004. *Þjóðarpúlsinn*. July.
Indridason, Indridi H. 2005. "A Theory of Coalitions and Clientelism: Coalition Politics in Iceland, 1945–2000." *European Journal of Political Science* 44 (3): 439–64.
Jensen, Torben. 2000. "Party Cohesion." In Peter Esaiasson and Knut Heidar, eds., *Beyond Westminster and Congress: The Nordic Experience*. Columbus: Ohio State University Press.

Jóhannesson, Guðni Th. 2005. *Völundarhús valdsins: Stjórnarmyndanir, stjórnarslit og staða forseta Íslands í embættistíð Kristjáns Eldjárns, 1968–80*. Reykjavík: Mál og Menning.
Jóhannesson, Guðni Th. 2006. "Leikstjóri, leikari eða áhorfandi? Forsetinn og stjórnarmyndanir." *Stjórnmál og Stjórnsýsla* 2:75–98.
Kjartansson, Helgi Skúli. 2006. "Forveri forseta: Konungur Íslands 1904–1944." *Stjórnmál og Stjórnsýsla* 2:57–74.
Kristinsson, Gunnar Helgi. 1994a. *Embættismenn og stjórnmálamenn*. Reykjavík: Mál og Menning.
Kristinsson, Gunnar Helgi. 1994b. *Þróun íslensku stjórnarskrárinnar*. Reykjavík: Félagsvísindastofnun.
Kristinsson, Gunnar Helgi. 1996. "Parties, States, and Patronage." *West European Politics* 19 (3): 433–57.
Kristinsson, Gunnar Helgi. 1999. *Úr digrum sjóði: Fjárlagagerð á Íslandi*. Reykjavík: Félagsvísindastofnun-Háskólaútgáfan.
Kristinsson, Gunnar Helgi. 2001. "Clientelism in a Cold Climate: The Case of Iceland." In Simona Piattoni, ed., *Clientelism, Interests, and Democratic Representation*. Cambridge: Cambridge University Press.
Kristinsson, Gunnar Helgi. 2006a. "Patronage and Public Appointments in Iceland." Manuscript.
Kristinsson, Gunnar Helgi. 2006b. "Pólitískar stöðuveitingar á Íslandi." *Stjórnmál og Stjórnsýsla* 2:5–29.
Kristjánsson, Svanur. 1994. *Frá flokksræði til persónustjórnmála*. Reykjavík: Háskólaútgáfan.
Kristjánsson, Svanur. 1998. "Electoral Politics and Governance: Transformation of the Party System in Iceland, 1970–1995." In Jan Erik Lane and Paul Pennings, eds., *Comparing Party System Change*. London: Routledge.
Kristjánsson, Svanur. 2002. "Stofnun lýðveldis—Nýsköpun lýðræðis." *Skírnir* 176: 7–45.
Kristjánsson, Svanur. 2003. "Iceland: A Parliamentary Democracy with a Semi-Presidential Constitution." In Kaare Strøm, Wolfgang C. Müller, and Torbjörn Bergman, eds., *Delegation and Accountability in Parliamentary Democracies*. Oxford: Oxford University Press.
Kristjánsson, Svanur. 2004. "Iceland: Searching for Democracy along Three Dimensions of Citizen Control." *Scandinavian Political Studies* 27 (2): 153–74.
Kristjánsson, Svanur. 2005. "Forseti Íslands og utanríkisstefnan." *Ritið* 2:141–68.
Lijphart, Arend. 1984. *Democracies*. New Haven: Yale University Press.
Líndal, Sigurður. 2004. "Forseti Íslands og synjunarvald hans." *Skírnir* 178:203–37.
Magnússon, Þorsteinn. 2005. "Alþingi í ljósi samþættingar löggjafarvalds og framkvæmdavalds." *Stjórnmál og Stjórnsýsla* 1:25–49.
Martin, Lanny W., and Randolph T. Stevenson. 2001. "Government Formation in Parliamentary Democracies." *American Journal of Political Science* 45 (1): 33–50.
Másson, Arnar Þór, and Indridi H. Indridason. 2005. "Enginn kann tveimur herrum að þjóna: Stofnanir, stjórnir og halli." *Rannsóknir í Félagsvísindum* 6:513–24.
Mitchell, Paul, and Benjamin Nyblade. 2008. "Government Formation and Cabinet Type." In Kaare Strøm, Wolfgang C. Müller, and Torbjörn Bergman, eds.,

Cabinets and Coalition Bargaining: The Democratic Life Cycle in Western Europe. Oxford: Oxford University Press.

Morgunblaðið. 1994. "Valta ekki yfir Samstarfsflokkinn." August 10.

Morgunblaðið. 2004. "Bandaríkin birtu 'lista hinna staðföstu' eftir að stuðningsyfirlýsingar bárust." December 9.

Müller, Wolfgang C., and Kaare Strøm, eds. 2003. *Coalition Governments in Western Europe.* 2nd ed. Oxford: Oxford University Press.

National Audit Office. 2001. *Fjárlagaferlið: Um útgjaldastýringu ríkisins.* Reykjavík: Ríkisendurskoðun.

Pétursson, Sigtryggur. 2005. "Electoral Instability in Iceland, 1931–1995." *Stjórnmál og Stjórnsýsla* 1:159–86.

Shefter, Martin. 1977. "Party and Patronage: Germany, England, and Italy." *Politics and Society* 7:403–51.

Strøm, Kaare. 1990. *Minority Government and Majority Rule.* Cambridge: Cambridge University Press.

Styrkársdóttir, Auður, and Svanur Kristjánsson. 2005. "Des moyens hors de l'ordinaire pour changer les choses: Le parcours des Islandaises vers la citoyenneté politique." In Manon Tremblay, ed., *Femmes et Parliament: Un regard international.* Montréal: Remue-Menage.

Þórleifsson, Eiríkur. 2006. "Dagskrárvald, stjórnarandstaða og samráð á Alþingi." BA thesis, University of Iceland.

INTERNET SOURCES

Alþingi's Web site. http://www.althingi.is

Keesing's Record of World Events. 2006. "June 2006—Government Changes." Vol. 52 (June, 2006 Iceland): 47332. http://www.keesings.com

Keesing's Record of World Events. 2007. "May 2007—Legislative Elections—Resignation of PP Leader." Vol. 53 (May, 2007 Iceland): 47946. http://www.keesings.com

Statistics Iceland. http://www.statice.is

Statistics Iceland. Turnout data. Accessed May 13, 2009. http://www.statice.is/Statistics/Elections

Transparency International. 2005. *Corruption Perceptions Index 2005.* http://www.transparency.org

6 ◆ Norway
From Hønsvaldian Parliamentarism Back to Madisonian Roots

HANNE MARTHE NARUD AND KAARE STRØM

Norwegian democracy was born Madisonian, and it is returning to its roots. James Madison was president of the United States when Norway got its radically democratic constitution in 1814. Although there is no evidence that Madison personally influenced the drafting of the constitution, his ideas and the example of the American Revolution certainly did. The Norwegian constitution, which is now the oldest codified constitution in Europe and second in the democratic world only to that of the United States, was intended to be a separation-of-powers document, with a broad and inclusive franchise, a multitude of checks and balances, and no provisions for political parties to play any significant role.

Yet Norwegian democracy did not always remain Madisonian. Over the course of its close to 200 years of constitutional history, the Norwegian parliament has run the gamut from constitutional assertion to submissiveness. For about a century and a half after 1814, Norway moved ever closer to a parliamentary and largely Westminsterian system of government, by simple and unconstrained political delegation through cohesive parliamentary parties to a cabinet with extensive agenda control. The constitutional preeminence of the Storting was a rallying cry for the constitutional reformers of the 1880s. "All power in this assembly!" was the slogan of Liberal leader and later prime minister Johan Sverdrup, and Sverdrup succeeded in his aims. The right of the parliamentary majority to dismiss the cabinet was first established in the constitutional crisis of 1884, when the Liberal Party gained control of parliament and impeached the members of the incumbent Conservative cabinet. The parliamentary principle remained somewhat contested until Norwegian independence in 1905, but since then, there has been a clear and unambiguous convention that individual ministers or cabinets must resign if they lose confidence votes in the Storting (Andenæs 1981; Hansen and Mo 1994, 118; Nordby 2000).

After 1884, the power of the monarch gradually eroded, international and judicial constraints weakened, and the autonomy of local government was reduced through a series of centralized reforms in the policies on education and social welfare. Sustained by a system of strong and cohesive political parties that first emerged in the critical decade of the 1880s, the cabinet increasingly came to dominate national policy-making, especially after World War II, while the parliamentary majority appeared willing to delegate itself into oblivion. Thus, in 1959, at the height of his party's predominance, the Labor Party's parliamentary leader Nils Hønsvald proclaimed that parliamentary control of the executive had effectively been transferred from the floor of parliament to the internal organs of his party. Party government had eclipsed parliamentary deliberation. Around 1960, Norway had thus reached a constitutional form that, apart from some party fragmentation on the center-right caused by proportional representation, looked much like a Westminster system.

From that point on, however, Norwegian democracy has generally moved away from this model. A series of weaker minority governments has given rise to parliamentary reassertion. The Norwegian party system has further fragmented and changed in character, and the individual parties have atrophied as mass membership organizations. In addition, a heightened assertiveness on the part of the judiciary has helped contain parliamentary power. Two hotly contested European Union membership referendums in 1972 and 1994 have firmly established the role of direct democracy in critical political decisions, and despite the results of these two popular consultations, international constraints have become more significant. The erosion of parliamentary democracy is indeed a prominent concern in the Norwegian Power and Democracy Study, 1998–2003. In that study, Østerud and his colleagues argue that de facto transfer of constitutional sovereignty has weakened the national chain of democratic governance (Østerud, Engelstad, and Selle 2003, 116–26).

In this chapter, we will show that even though Norwegian parliamentary democracy has changed substantially since its birth in the nineteenth century, it is not obvious that these changes overall or specifically the more recent ones have weakened popular sovereignty or political accountability. Norwegian democracy has always had Madisonian as well as Westminsterian features. The former were prominent at the founding of Norwegian democracy, but the intentions of the "founding fathers" notwithstanding, Norway had very closely approached the ideal type of parliamentary democracy by the 1950s. This happened largely because of the force of political parties, which changed the contents of Norwegian democracy decisively. Parties attained this preeminence because they led the three most important mass movements of the nineteenth and early twentieth centuries: the political emancipation of the rural population (the "peasants," as Eckstein called them in 1966), the movement for national independence and political reform, and the mobilization of a rapidly growing industrial working class. The parliamentary institutions gradually came to accommodate and sustain the parties.

Over the past half century, however, a number of developments have progressively challenged the party cohesion, parliamentary supremacy, and extensive delegation to the executive branch that used to characterize Norwegian politics. These features have not simply disappeared but, instead, have largely been supplanted by a novel series of constraints on political power, many of which function as ex post checks on those who govern Norway. Thus, the early twenty-first century finds Norway closer to its Madisonian roots than it has been for a long time. Many factors have contributed to this development, among them a growing voter detachment from political parties and the increasing willingness of Norwegian citizens and politicians to create and use a series of accountability mechanisms outside partisan control. Nonetheless, despite such visible challenges to their power, Norwegian parties remain cohesive and comparatively healthy.

Political Parties and the Party System

Until the early 1970s, Norway had one of the most stable party systems in Western Europe. It was defined around six dimensions of political cleavage rooted in economic, geographical, and cultural circumstances (see Rokkan 1967, 1970; Valen and Rokkan 1974). The major division, however, has traditionally been between socialists and nonsocialists located along a left-right axis.

From left to right, the present parties are the Socialist Left (Sosialistisk Venstreparti, or SV), The Labor Party (Arbeiderpartiet, or A/DNA), the Center Party (Senterpartiet, or SP), the Christian People's Party (Kristelig Folkeparti, or KRF), the Liberals (Venstre, or V), the Conservatives (Høyre, or H), and the Progress Party (Fremskrittspartiet, or FRP).[1] Only the first and last of these parties were formed after 1970. The Socialist Left emerged as a result of a union between the Socialist People's Party (formed in 1961), the Communist Party, and an anti–European Community (EC) faction of the Labor Party (Arbeiderbevegelsens informasjonskomité mot norsk medlemskap i EF [AIK]), while the Progress Party was originally founded as a protest party against high taxes and public expenditures.[2] The electoral returns are presented in table 6.1.

Policy Dimensions

The policy dimensions of Norwegian politics have traditionally been shaped largely by the dominant social cleavages. The socioeconomic class cleavage is expressed through the ideological left-right dimension, whereas territorial and sectoral cleavages are reflected in the center-periphery and the urban-rural dimensions, respectively. Cultural cleavages in Norway have given rise to a moral-religious dimension. While different studies of Norwegian policy dimensions yield somewhat different spatial representations, they leave no doubt that the dominant dimension of political contention

TABLE 6.1. Elections to the Norwegian Parliament (the Storting), 1945–2008

Election Year	NKP	RV	SF/SV	A	V	DLF	KRF	SP	H	FRP	CST	Others
1945	11.9			41.0	13.8		7.9	8.1	17.0			0.3
1949	5.8			45.7	13.5		8.5	7.9	17.8			0.7
1953	5.1			46.7	10.0		10.5	9.0	18.8			
1957	3.4			48.3	9.7		10.2	9.3	18.9			0.2
1961	2.9		2.4	46.8	8.9		9.6	9.3	20.0			0.1
1965	1.4		6.0	43.1	10.4		8.1	9.9	21.1			
1969	1.0		3.5	46.5	9.4		9.4	10.5	19.6			
1973	—	0.4	11.2	35.3	3.5	3.4	12.3	11.0	17.4	5.0		0.5
1977	0.4	0.6	4.2	42.3	3.2	1.4	12.4	8.6	24.8	1.9		0.2
1981	0.3	0.7	5.0	37.1	3.9	0.6	9.4	6.6	31.8	4.5		0.1
1985	0.2	0.6	5.5	40.8	3.1	0.5	8.3	6.6	30.4	3.7		0.3
1989		0.8	10.1	34.3	3.2		8.5	6.5	22.2	13.0		1.4
1993		1.1	7.9	36.9	3.6		7.9	16.7	17.0	6.3		2.6
1997		1.7	6.0	35.0	4.5		13.7	7.9	14.3	15.3	0.4	1.2
2001		1.2	12.5	24.3	3.9		12.4	5.6	21.2	14.6	1.7	2.6
2005		1.2	8.8	32.7	5.9		6.8	6.5	14.1	22.1	0.8	1.1

Source: Data from Bernt Aardal, http://home.online.no/~b-aardal.

Notes: Numbers in table represent vote shares in percentages. Dash (—) indicates that the NKP did not contest the election in 1973 as an independent party. Party abbreviations are as follows:
NKP = Communist Party (Norges Kommunistiske Parti); RV = Red Election Alliance/Communist (Rød Valgallianse); SF/SV = Socialist Left Party (Sosialistisk Venstreparti), 1961–1973—Socialist Peoples Party, 1973–1977—Social Electoral Alliance, 1977—Socialist Left Party (founded 1975); A = Labor (Det Norske Arbeiderparti); V = Liberals (Venstre); DLF = Liberal Peoples Party (Det Liberale Folkeparti); KRF = Christian People's Party (Kristelig Folkeparti); SP = Center Party (Senterpartiet); H = Conservatives (Høyre); FRP = Progress Party (Fremskrittspartiet); CST = Coast Party (Kystpartiet); Others = Others (Andre partier).

over the past half century has been the left-right axis.[3] In the 1990s, the predominance of this dimension lessened somewhat, but it rose again after the turn of the millennium (Aardal and Valen 1995; Narud 1996, 2007).

As the majority party, Labor controlled the median position on Laver and Hunt's (1992) left-right dimension, as well as the cabinet, between 1945 and 1961.[4] After the party lost its majority in 1961, it continued to hold the median legislator until 1965. The Liberal Party occupied the median position from 1965 until 1973, when Labor again regained it. The Christian People's Party controlled the median position from 1981 to 2005, when the Liberal Party captured it. Thus, the pivotal position in Norwegian politics has shifted from the Labor Party to the more centrist parties of the nonsocialist bloc.[5]

Two other important dimensions in Norwegian politics are strongly correlated: the urban-rural dimension and the center-periphery axis. The policy positions of the various parties tend to be highly consistent across these two dimensions, as the parties that most favor rural interests are also the strongest defenders of the peripheries, and vice versa. On each of these dimensions, the ordering of the parties' policy positions differs considerably from the left-right axis.[6] The Progress Party is the most pro-urban party, and the Center Party is the most pro-rural one. The Conservatives are fairly close to the Progress Party, whereas the Christian People's Party is adjacent to the Center Party on the anti-urban side. All other parties hold more centrist positions on this dimension (see, e.g., Valen and Narud 2007a; Narud and Rasch 2007). Thus, the traditional allies in the bourgeois camp, who are fairly close neighbors on the left-right axis, are highly polarized along the urban-rural dimension. Moreover, Labor has consistently controlled the median legislator on the urban-rural dimension since 1945. This dimension is therefore particularly inimical to nonsocialist cooperation.

This secondary dimension has been mobilized in dramatic ways at particular times in the postwar period, notably during the EC and European Union (EU) campaigns in the early 1970s and again in the 1990s. On these occasions, the left-right dimension declined in significance, and the established patterns of left-right opposition were weakened. Indeed, the saliency of the urban-rural dimension has led to the termination of two coalitions (Narud 1995) and inhibited the formation of others. It has also caused great internal strain on several parties, and both of the significant new parties that have emerged since World War II were born during the first EC membership campaign. The nearly identical results of the EC/EU struggles of the 1970s and the 1990s indicate that these conflicts are neither coincidental nor likely to change quickly. Instead, they reflect traditional conflict dimensions that are likely to constrain future coalition bargaining in predictable ways and that may pose serious future challenges to several of the major parties, most likely, perhaps, the Labor Party and the Progress Party.

The postwar Norwegian party system has, in Laver and Schofield's (1990) terms, changed from a unipolar, through a bipolar, to a multipolar format and is possibly now shifting back toward bipolarity. From World War II until 1961, Labor was predominant. The 1961 emergence of the Socialist People's Party caused some erosion of Labor's support, while the nonsocialist parties gained in strength and cohesion. Yet until the 1990s, the socialist and nonsocialist blocs were extremely evenly balanced, and minority Labor governments alternated with bourgeois coalitions (see Groennings 1961; Rommetvedt 1984). The party system could best be described as alternational (see chapter 1).

The formation of a three-party centrist coalition government in 1997 represented an important step away from the two-bloc format of the past. In 2001, a massive loss for the incumbent Labor Party paved the way for a minority government of the Conservatives with the Christian People's Party and the Liberals, while their former ally, the Center Party, stayed in opposition. The 2005 election once again brought about massive changes in party support and a new coalition formula. The Labor Party regained some of its former strength, even though the result was the second worst in its postwar history. Two of the coalition parties, the Conservatives and the Christian People's Party, suffered severe losses, whereas the Progress Party increased its vote share by almost 8 percentage points. The resulting center-left coalition of Labor, the Center Party, and the Socialist Left meant a departure from Labor's long-standing anticoalition stance (Valen and Narud 2007b; Aardal 2007). The massive electoral shifts in 2001 raised the effective number of parties to a record high of 5.5 (see table 6.3). In 2005, the party system returned to a more "normal" size of 4.6 effective parties, although with the Progress Party as the dominant nonsocialist party.

Party Membership and Identification

As the party system has thus changed, the parties have also collectively weakened. Their decline is most significant with regard to membership and party identification. Traditionally, Norwegian parties on the left as well as the right had strong membership organizations. For many years, according to party reports, a full 15 percent of the voters were dues-paying members (Svåsand, Strøm, and Rasch 1997; Heidar and Saglie 2002). In some smaller

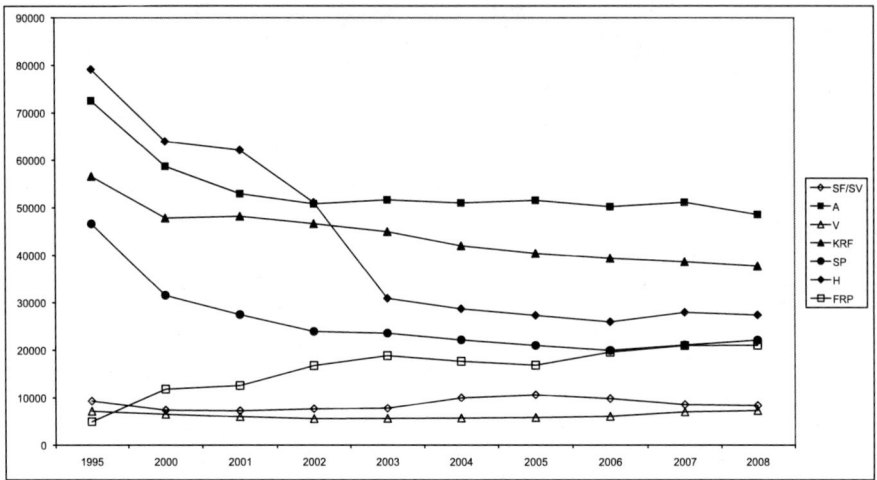

Fig. 6.1. Party membership in Norway, 1995–2008. See table 6.1 for explanation of party labels.

parties, particularly the Center Party, the ratio of members to voters has been as high as one in three.

From the 1980s on, this picture began to change dramatically. Party records show an extraordinary membership decline after 1985, particularly for the larger parties. Both the Labor Party and the Conservatives (the two largest organizations) lost about two-thirds of their gross membership numbers between 1985 and 2001 (Heidar and Saglie 2002, 34–35). This negative trend has continued, especially for the Conservatives. As is clear from figure 6.1, only the Progress Party has seen membership figures rise over the last decade. Between 1995 and 2008, that party more than quadrupled its number of members, a tendency that runs parallel to the party's growing electoral fortunes.[7] Yet even these gains have left the Progress Party with a comparatively low membership density. Even the Liberals and the Socialist Left (in the mid-2000s) have experienced some minor growth in membership numbers, but these small increases are in no way enough to offset the membership losses in the larger parties. National election surveys confirm the general trend previously reported. During the 1990s, reported party membership declined to around 10–11 percent, whereas only 8 percent of respondents in 2001 and 2005 reported being members of a political party (Aardal 2003, 2007).

Declining party identification runs parallel to the slumping membership figures. The share of voters identifying themselves with a particular political party has fallen substantially and almost monotonically since the first election surveys in the 1950s (see table 6.2). In 2001, the number of strong identifiers (a subcategory of all identifiers) was just over 18 percent, although it had rebounded somewhat by 2005, to about 26 percent

TABLE 6.2. Strength of Party Attachment in Norway, 1945–2008

Election Year	Turnout (%)	Class Voting (Alford index)[a]	Party Identification (%)	Share of Voters Changing Party between Elections (%)	Share of Voters Changing Bloc between Elections (%)	Share of Voters Deciding Which Party to Vote for during the Election Campaign (%)	Distrust of Politicians (%)[b]
1945	76.4						
1949	82.0						
1953	79.3						
1957	78.3	43					
1961[c]	79.1						
1965	85.4	43	72	13[d]		15	
1969	83.8	40	60	24	5.8	14	58
1973	80.2	38	62	32	7.9	24	74
1977	82.9	36	70	31	9.9	20	
1981	83.2	29	71	31	6.7	22	
1985	84.0	29	69	29	8.9	21	
1989	83.2	18	62	38	11.9	42	64
1993	75.8	15	57	44	15.7	42	65
1997	78.3	13	53	43	12.2	51	55
2001	75.5	6	41	44	14.2	47	68
2005	77.4	−2	48	47	16.4	44	53

Source: Data on turnout from Bernt Aardal, http://home.online.no/~b-aardal. Data on changing party, party id, and deciding late from Aardal 2003, 34, 13, 214; Aardal 2007. Data on changing bloc from Aardal and Valen 1995, 33. Numbers for 1997 and 2001 from National Election Survey 1997 and 2001. Guro Stavn, Institute for Social Research, provided valuable assistance. Data on class voting from Knutsen 2004, 72, fig. 4.2.

Note: The numbers for changing party, changing bloc, and party id include respondents who did not vote.

[a]The Alford index is based on the difference between the vote share for the parties on the left (in this case the Left and Social Democratic Parties) among the working class (measured by occupation) and the vote share for the same parties among the middle class. A higher index implies that working-class voters vote for the parties on the left to a greater extent than do middle-class voters.

[b]Distrust in politicians was measured as follows. 1969–93—Index based on survey items in which voters were asked whether they agreed or disagreed with the following statement: "The parties are only interested in people's votes, not their opinions" and "The MPs do not take ordinary people's thoughts much into consideration." 1997–2001—Placement on scale on basis of the following statement: "Some say that political parties in Norway care what ordinary people think. Others say that political parties in Norway don't care what ordinary people think."

The numbers are based on the index "Tillit til partier og folkevalgte" (Trust in parties and politicians), Aardal 2003, 214, fig. 9.4.

[c]No election survey was conducted in 1961.

[d]Data for 1965 in column share of voters changing party between elections is based on recall data.

(Berglund 2003, 2007; for cross-national comparisons, see Dalton and Wattenberg 2000). In 2001, almost 60 percent of voters characterized themselves as "independents," a huge increase since the early years of election surveys, although the corresponding number in 2005 showed a decline to just over 50 percent. Nonetheless, in the longer run, the role of parties as vehicles for mobilization and identification has clearly been weakened.

This loosening of popular attachment to political parties corresponds with a new trend in electoral behavior. Until the end of the 1960s, the parties tended to appeal to voters' class identification and other group affiliations. In recent years, they have been less concerned with social background, focusing instead on individual issues, a development that Henry Valen (1999) has characterized as a change "from class struggle to a struggle over the political agenda."

Another striking development is the rise of electoral volatility—voters changing parties between elections (see table 6.2). Through the 1960s, Norway had one of the most stable party systems in Western Europe, with volatility rates of 15 to 25 percent. From the early 1970s, however, about one out of three voters began changing parties from one election to the next. In 1993, volatility reached almost 44 percent, a proportion that remained virtually unchanged in 1997 and 2001. It rose again in 2005, to a record high of 47 percent. In addition, the number of "late deciders" has increased substantially since the mid-1980s. In the elections in 1997 and 2001, about half of all voters reported that they had decided which party to support during the election campaign itself (Aardal 2007). While this number declined in the most recent election, it remains much higher than it was until the late 1980s.

One area in which Norwegian parties are not hurting is in financial support. Public support for the parties' extraparliamentary organizations was first introduced in 1970, under the nonsocialist Borten government. The size of these subsidies has increased steadily and more rapidly than the overall growth in public spending. In 2004, controlling for inflation, the volume of support for the national party organizations had increased to almost three times the level of 1970 (NOU 2004, 39). New forms of subsidies have also been introduced, so that there are separate appropriations for the parties' parliamentary and extraparliamentary organizations and for their regional and municipal organizations, as well as for their youth organizations. The level of support a party receives is closely tied to its support among the voters. Some parties, such as the Socialist Left, have virtually no other significant sources of income, whereas such parties as the Christian People's Party, the Conservatives, and Labor still receive significant funds from private donations. Nonetheless, all Norwegian parties currently receive the majority of their income from government subsidies (NOU 2004, 53).

These public subsidies allow Norwegian parties to run very expensive operations by international standards. On a per capita basis, Norwegian party expenditures are significantly larger than those of any other Nordic country. Norwegian parties also spend more than 10 times as much per capita as German ones, 11 times as much as their Canadian counterparts, 14 times as much as the Australians, and more than 25 times as much as the British parties (NOU 2004, 37).

The way in which Norwegian parties increasingly have been able to feed themselves at the public trough is the most compelling evidence that these organizations have transformed themselves into something akin to cartel parties (Katz and Mair 1995). However, they clearly do not fit all of the characteristics of this party model (Allern 2007). For example, they have not ceased to vigorously compete with one another for the favor of Norwegian voters, and there is little evidence that they have colonized the state for clientelistic purposes.

The Democratic Constitutional Chain of Governance

The constitutional chain of governance in Norway is comparatively simple. Under the constitution, all legislative authority is exercised by the people through parliament: "The people exercise the Legislative Power through the Storting" (Article 49). Like all major Western European states except Switzerland, Norway is a parliamentary democracy, albeit a peculiar one. Norway conforms to Westminster parliamentarism in the sense that members of parliament (the Storting) are the only national agents elected by the people. Although national direct democracy has been employed on six occasions since national independence in 1905, it fell into disuse from the 1920s to the 1970s. In its heyday in the 1950s, Norway came very close to the Westminster ideal of a singular chain of democratic delegation, running through parliament and controlled by political parties. Since then, however, it is increasingly clear that Norway is moving back toward a more Madisonian separation-of-powers system.

The place to look for these important changes is rarely in the formal constitution itself. The Norwegian constitution has become an increasingly archaic and often ambiguous document. It gives scant guidance to such important questions as the reach of judicial review, and it was not until 2007 that the constitution was amended fully to include parliamentary provisions. The parliamentary system became a part of the constitution through the new Article 15 (Amendment 364), and the old division of parliament into an upper quasi-chamber (Odelstinget) and a lower one (Lagtinget) was abolished (Amendment 365).[8] In addition, changes were introduced to the Court of Impeachment, which played a critical role in launching parliamentarism in the 1880s but has been of little political consequence since the 1920s. Thus, for a good century, there were major discrepancies between formal constitutional provisions and prevailing political practice. In this sense, Norwegian parliamentary democracy has a long history but only a tenuous place in the formal constitution.

Norwegian parties remain critical players at most stages of the policy process. They control the selection of candidates for parliamentary office to a greater extent than in any other Nordic country. In parliament, party cohesion is very high, as is also the case in the cabinet. In coalition governments, the most serious disagreements have tended to be handled through party leaders, rather than through formal cabinet channels. It is only in the civil service that party control is significantly less prominent, which is again consistent with the Westminster model. While Norwegian voters have, in recent years, become less enamored of their parties, there is as yet little evidence that the parties have lost much control of the democratic chain of delegation.

Delegation from Voters to Parliament

The most critical way in which citizens delegate democratic authority is through the simple act of voting. Whereas much of the Norwegian living constitution has evolved organically and without much prior debate or discernible political intent, the delegation from voters to parliamentary representatives has been subject to frequent and often blatantly strategic institutional tinkering. Some rules by which members of parliament are selected and held accountable are contained in the constitution; others are spelled out in ordinary legislation (Aardal 2002). Unlike most parliamentary systems, legislative terms are constitutionally fixed, and there is no provision for early parliamentary dissolution. The constitution also provides no recall or expulsion mechanism. There is no term limit or mandatory retirement age, although parties rarely nominate or renominate candidates who will turn 70 during the parliamentary term. Thus, the independence of the elected representatives is very strongly protected.

Since parliamentary terms are fixed, Norwegian election dates are perfectly predictable (the second Monday in September every fourth year), and no legislation is needed to regulate the length of election campaigns. There are few other explicit regulations of electoral competition. Though political parties enjoy generous public subsidies, there is no official regulation of campaign spending. The parties do not enjoy free broadcasting access. Commercial television is relatively new in Norway, so TV advertising has only recently become an issue. In July 1999, the Storting passed a law permitting political advertising on radio but not on television. Since that time, the prohibition against political and religious advertising on television has been upheld.

Other features of the electoral system have been designed by and for the major political parties. Since 1952, the country has used a modified Sainte-Laguë system of proportional representation (PR), and over the second half of the twentieth century, Norway saw a series of electoral reforms aimed at greater proportionality in representation. Yet Norwegian electoral results have ranked among the least proportional in Western Europe (Lijphart 1999, 162), and the main beneficiaries have been the Labor Party and rural regions. Several factors explain the comparative disproportionality: malapportionment, small district magnitude, and, until 1989, the lack of any pool of supplementary seats (for higher-tier adjustment). Complex districting was introduced in 1989, first with 157 first-tier seats and a pool of 8 national second-tier seats. The system was amended in 2005, when the number of adjustment seats was raised to 19, while the number of first-tier seats was reduced to 150. Consequently, the overrepresentation of peripheral areas has been considerably reduced, and the overall partisan proportionality has been enhanced.[9]

At different times, Norwegian electoral laws have included provisions for *apparentement*, so that different parties could benefit from forming electoral alliances by sharing their "excess" votes. The 1989 electoral reform banned these provisions, which were mainly used by nonsocialist parties, particularly the centrist ones. Even at times when *apparentement* has not been feasible or interesting, these parties have occasionally engaged in various forms of electoral cooperation, such as joint lists, though this practice has been much more common in local elections than in national ones. The introduction of supplementary seats has lessened the incentives for electoral alliances, and their incidence has correspondingly declined.

Norwegian citizens have traditionally voted with great regularity and in substantial numbers. As in most of Western Europe, however, turnout in Norwegian national elections has declined (see table 6.2). From a rate of about 83 percent in 1989, turnout in Storting elections fell to 76 percent in 1993. After recovering a bit in 1997—to 78 percent—it fell back to 75.5 percent in 2001. In 2005, turnout rose again to 77.4 percent, probably because of the presence of two clear-cut government alternatives (Valen and Narud 2007b). The same declining trend is even more evident in local elections. During the 1980s, the average turnout in local elections hovered around 70 percent. Over the 1990s, it dropped steadily, falling from 66 percent in 1991 to 59 percent in 2003 (Saglie and Bjørklund 2005, 328).

To some extent, Norwegian citizens can also participate in the selection of candidates within their respective parties. There are two important dimensions to the extent of citizen control of parliamentary candidate selection (Narud, Pedersen, and Valen 2002). One is inclusiveness—the number of individuals allowed to participate in the selection of candidates. The other dimension is centralization—whether power over candidate selection is embodied in the central, the regional, or the local party branches.

Norwegian nominations are highly decentralized but take place in a closed-list system. The candidates on each list are ranked in the order in which their party wishes to see them elected. The voters are permitted to change the list by crossing out the name of one or more candidates. In practice, however, such changes have no impact, because in order to overrule the default ranking, a very large number of voters must cross out the same name. In fact, voters have never successfully changed the rank ordering of the candidates of any party in a Storting election (Valen 1988, 211). Proposals to introduce more meaningful personal preference votes in national elections have failed to win a parliamentary majority.

Although candidate selection takes place at a level close to the individual voters, it is not simple or costless for ordinary citizens to participate, and most do not. The more inclusive method of holding primary elections among members or voters has never been employed in Norway. The Norwegian reliance on a closed-list PR system also means that voters can only influence candidate selection at the time that the party lists are drawn up, which is several months before the election.

There is ample evidence that political parties play a critical role in ex ante screening of candidates for the Norwegian parliament. These screening devices are largely similar across parties. Until June 2002, Norway was one of the few countries in which nominations were regulated by law. The law stipulated that in each of the 19 constituencies, electoral lists were to be decided by party conventions, in which only dues-paying party members were allowed to participate. Of these members, about one in three actually participated in the nomination process. Their selection decisions were final and could not be overruled by public authorities or national party bodies.[10] The law was not mandatory but was supported, instead, by financial incentives, and the parties tended, in general, to comply. Based on experience from the 2005 election, there is no indication that the abolition of this law has had any serious consequences for the parties' nomination procedures (Narud and Valen 2007).

All parties report that local organizations carry a great deal of weight when the committees draw up their lists (Valen 1988, 213). The process of candidate selection in Norway is decentralized, and the ultimate decision lies with the convention of the constituency party organizations at the regional level. The Progress Party is a notable exception in that the national party leadership has greater control. Data from the 2001 Storting election suggests that the party's national leader played an active role in the nomination process in several constituencies (Valen, Narud, and Skare 2002, 181). All in all, parties retain firm control of the selection of their parliamentary representatives, albeit in a geographically decentralized manner.

As in most parties in other countries (Ranney 1981; Gallagher and Marsh 1988), incumbency is an important selection criterion. Service in local government has also traditionally been an important credential for Norwegian parliamentarians. In addition, Norwegian parties strive for and attain a high degree of social representativeness, which has been reflected, traditionally, in a comparatively high proportion of working-class parliamentarians and, more recently, in a high percent of women, approximately 40 percent (Raaum 1995; Skjeie 1997; Narud and Valen 2007). The predominant long-term trend has been the replacement of farmers and blue-collar workers with career politicians and public-sector employees. In addition, the legislature has been intellectually professionalized through increased levels of education (Eliassen and Pedersen 1978; Matthews and Valen 1999; Eliassen and Sjøvaag Marino 2000; Narud 2003; Narud and Valen 2007). However, the "talking professions," particularly lawyers, have been remarkably poorly represented. In the elections of 1993 and 1997, for example, not a single lawyer was elected to parliament.

The record of parliamentary turnover has traditionally been kind to Norwegian politicians, as long as they have been loyal partisans. Their major obstacle has been getting their party's support, and most parties have let interested parliamentarians accumulate up to three or four (four-year) terms of seniority. Legislative turnover reached an all-time high in 1969, largely due to generational turnover, and again in 1993, in large part because of dramatic changes in partisan vote shares. In the 2001 election, the overall rate of turnover was 38 percent, of which 12 percent was due to the election result (Valen, Narud, and Skare 2002; Narud 2003). Elections of particularly high turnover have tended to coincide with high electoral volatility and corresponding changes in the partisan vote shares (Matthews and Valen 1999).

Delegation from Parliament to Cabinet

The Norwegian cabinet is still officially known as the King's Council, and the constitution formally gives the monarch broad discretion to appoint its members. In practice, however, the king has exerted no influence on the composition of any cabinet since 1928.[11] When he formally calls on someone to form a new government, the king always follows the advice of the leaders of the parliamentary parties. In practice, the choice of a prime minister designate has rarely been difficult or involved much bargaining. The initial attempt at cabinet formation has been inconclusive on only four occasions, each time due to a serious policy conflict among the nonsocialist parties over foreign policy, specifically EU membership, or over abortion. Because of the absence of formal rules and mechanisms, Norwegian government formation is best described as "free-style bargaining" among the parliamentary parties. The use of *informateurs* has no codified place in the Norwegian constitution and has occurred only once in the postwar period.[12]

Until 2005, all Norwegian cabinets were either socialist or nonsocialist. In fact, for a long time, the Norwegian Labor Party was the only major social democratic party in Western Europe never to have entered a cabinet coalition with any bourgeois party. Labor also eschewed coalitions with any of the smaller parties to its left. Thus, a socialist government meant a cabinet of Labor alone and therefore, between 1961 and 2005, also a minority cabinet. However, Labor's massive 2001 electoral losses provoked a change in the party's attitudes. In the general election of 2005, Labor joined the Center Party and the Socialist Left in a preelectoral alliance. This alliance formalized into the first majority cabinet since 1985, as the three parties gained a parliamentary (though not a popular) majority and formed a "red-green" coalition.

As table 6.3 demonstrates, nonsocialist cabinets have tended to be coalitions (Rommetvedt 1984, 1991), and all but one have included at least three parties.[13] There have been three types of nonsocialist coalitions: six broad center-right governments, one center-right government excluding the Center Party, and two centrist coalitions consisting of the Christian People's Party, the Center Party, and the Liberals. Both of the latter (Korvald and Bondevik I) formed under circumstances in which dissent over European integration precluded coalescence between Conservatives and the other nonsocialist parties, specifically the Center Party. Both were led by a prime minister from the Christian People's Party.

The postwar period has seen 18 single-party administrations and 11 coalitions. Ten cabinets have included representatives of parties that collectively controlled a majority of the seats in the Storting, while 19 have been minority cabinets, including many of the nonsocialist coalitions. Most minority governments have relied on ad hoc parliamentary support. Only one (Willoch I, 1981–83) had stable and prenegotiated support from two parties outside the cabinet—namely, the Christian People's Party and the Center Party.

Parliamentary Deliberation and Coalitions

The Storting is an active working parliament, which stays in session from the beginning of October to the end of June. Its activity is fairly continuous, occupied with budget deliberations during much of the fall session and legislation during much of the spring. Over time, there has been a continuous and fairly monotonic increase in the measurable activity level in the Storting. This is reflected in table 6.4, which provides data reflecting interparty controversy. The number of private members' bills increased from 15 in 1984–85 to 79 in 1993–94 and 156 in 2001–2 (see also Rommetvedt 2003, 47). It has since then plateaued at a higher level than in the early 1990s. Measured in terms of separate proposals, the increase in private members' bills has been even greater. Similarly, the number of dissenting remarks in committee reports (data not shown) climbed from 948 in the 1945–49 parliament to 5,273 for 1973–77 and 21,790 for 1989–93 (Rommetvedt 2003, 57). Some of the sharpest increases followed electoral gains by the Progress Party, the Socialist Left, and the Center Party (in 1993). Thus, some of the growth in formal parliamentary activity is probably due to a more confrontational political climate promoted by the growth of these parties.

Given the frequency of minority governments, most Norwegian cabinets have needed to attend carefully to their relationships with the formal opposition parties (Strøm 1990). The simple calculus of parliamentary decision making has required most of these governments to seek outside support for their most important decisions. Contrary to Denmark, where formal—though often substantively limited—accommodations have been common, most majority building in Norway has been ad hoc. Labor minority governments in particular have felt relatively secure in being able to play their leftist opposition against the "bourgeois" parties in order to reach

TABLE 6.3. Cabinets in Norway, 1945–2008

				Effective			Majority Cabinets[b]		Minority Cabinets[c]	
			Cabinet	Number of	Median					
Cabinet		Date	Share (%) of Parliamentary	Legislative	Legislator		Single-		Single-	
Number	Prime Minister	(yymmdd)	Seats	Parties[a]	Party	Parties in Cabinet	Party	Coalition	Party	Coalition
1	Gerhardsen II	451105	50.7	3.2	A	A	X			
2	Gerhardsen III	491010	56.7	2.7	A	A	X			
3	Torp I	511119	56.7	2.7	A	A	X			
4	Torp II	531012	51.3	3.1	A	A	X			
5	Gerhardsen IV	550122	51.3	3.1	A	A	X			
6	Gerhardsen V	571007	52.0	3.0	A	A	X			
7	Gerhardsen VI	610911	49.3	3.2	A	A			X	
8	Lyng	630828	49.3	3.2	A	H, SP, V, KRF				X
9	Gerhardsen VII	630925	49.3	3.2	A	A				X
10	Borten I	651012	53.3	3.5	V	SP, H, V, KRF		X		
11	Borten II	690907	50.7	3.2	V	SP, H, V, KRF		X		
12	Bratteli I	710313	49.3	3.2	V	A			X	
13	Korvald	721018	31.3	3.2	V	KRF, SP, V				X
14	Bratteli II	731016	40.0	4.1	A	A			X	
15	Nordli I	760115	40.0	4.1	A	A			X	
16	Nordli II	770911	49.0	3.0	A	A			X	
17	Brundtland I	810204	49.0	3.0	A	A			X	
18	Willoch I	811014	34.2	3.2	KRF	H			X	
19	Willoch II	830608	51.0	3.2	KRF	H, KRF, SP		X		
20	Willoch III	850908	49.7	3.1	KRF	H, KRF, SP				X

#	Cabinet	Date	%	ENLP	Party	Coalition		
21	Brundtland II	860509	45.2	3.1	KRF	A		X
22	Syse	891016	37.6	4.2	KRF	H, KRF, SP			X
23	Brundtland III	901103	38.2	4.2	KRF	A		X
24	Brundtland IV	930913	40.6	4.0	KRF	A		X
25	Jagland	961025	40.6	4.0	KRF	A		X
26	Bondevik I	971017	25.5	4.4	KRF	KRF, SP, V		
27[d]	Stoltenberg	000317	39.4	4.4	KRF	A		X
28[e]	Bondevik II	011019	37.6	5.5	KRF	KRF, H, V		X
29	Stoltenberg II	051017	51.5	4.6	V	A, SV, SP	X	

Source: Data from Comparative Parliamentary Democracy Project—Data Archive, which builds on Müller and Strøm 2003; Narud and Strøm 2003, updated from 1999 onward by Hanne Marthe Narud. Data for 2005 from Kommunal- og Regionaldepartmentet (2005), http://odin.dep.no/krd/html/valgresultat2005/frameset.html.

Notes: See table 6.1 for explanation of party labels. NKP/RV: The figures from 1945 to 1961 are the electoral results of the Communist Party (NKP), whereas the 1993 results apply to the Red Election Alliance (RV). SF/SV: 1961–73—Socialist Peoples Party; 1973–77—Social Electoral Alliance, 1977—Socialist Left Party (founded 1975). Other: This category consists of the following parties: 1973–77—Lib.P.P. = *Det Liberale Folkeparti* (Liberal People's Party); 1989–93—FFF = *Folkeaksjonen Fremtid for Finmark* (the Popular Movement for the Future of Finnmark); 1997–2005—TF: *Tverrpolitisk Folkevalgte*, also called *Kystpartiet* (the Coastal Party).

[a] Effective number of legislative parties: Index developed by Markku Laakso and Rein Taagepera that is a measure of party system size. Both the number of parties and their relative size are taken into account. For an accessible introduction, see Lijphart 1984.

[b] Majority cabinet coalitions can be either a minimal winning coalition (mwc—a coalition that cannot lose a party and still be "winning") or a surplus coalition (a coalition that can lose one or more parties and still be winning).

[c] Minority cabinets control 50% or less of all seats in parliament.

[d] Cabinet 27: Stoltenberg's cabinet did not resign immediately after the election, because the cabinet to be (Bondevik II) needed time for negotiations. For cross-national comparison, we count the election day as the end of the cabinet.

[e] Cabinet 28: Bondevik's cabinet II did not resign immediately after the election, because the cabinet to be (Stoltenberg II) needed time for negotiations. For cross-national comparison, we count the election day as the end of the cabinet.

TABLE 6.4. Parliamentary Activities, Norway, 1984–2008

Year	Number of Government Bills[a]			Number of Private Member Bills (Dokument 8)[b]	Number of Separate Proposals in the Private Member Bills (Dokument 8)[c]	Percentage of Private Member Bills (Dokument 8) Approved or Partly Approved by Parliament[d]		Number of Recorded Votes Counting Individual MPs[e]
	St.prp.	Ot.prp.	Total			Approved or Partly Approved	Referred to Government	
1984–85	133	90	223	15	24	0	13.3	456
1985–86	113	74	187	21	74	0	23.8	449
1986–87	124	86	210	28	61	3.6	32.1	329
1987–88	148	79	227	51	89	0	3.9	549
1988–89	137	90	227	51	175	7.8	11.8	784
1989–90	115	77	192*	51	153	9.8	17.6	1,307
1990–91	104	73	177	63	200	6.3	9.5	1,706
1991–92	130	100	230	46	94	8.7	13.0	1,458
1992–93	99	108	207	42	47	11.9	21.4	1,296
1993–94	67	90	157	79	122	11.4	12.7	1,176
1994–95	76	78	154	103	198	12.6	12.6	1,235
1995–96	90	77	167	115	178	6.1	8.7	1,374
1996–97	83	86	169	111	199	15.3	2.7	1,456
1997–98	88	87	175	124	187	19.4	5.6	516
1998–99	98	99	197	74	120	8.1	1.4	603
1999–2000	88	82	170	92	143	12.0	2.2	536
2000–2001	103	108	211	133	201	15.0	0.8	789
2001–2	81	117	198	156	275	12.8	2.6	705
2002–3	85	107	192	136	289	9.6	4.4	1,001
2003–4	83	94	177	95	215	6.3	0	735
2004–5	74	103	177	103	222	7.8	2.9	910
2005–6	87	103	190	113	320	1.8	0	390
2006–7	90	79	169	114	496	3.5	0.9	639
2007–8	87	83	170	146	512	4.8	3.4	671

Source: Pre-2001—Number of government bills, number of private member bills, number of separate proposals (1984–85): "Stortingstidende." Separate proposals approved, recorded votes pre-1998–99—Data from Norsk Samfunnsvitenskapelig Datatjeneste (NSD).
Separate proposals approved/referred to government from 1998 to 1999: "Stortingets Forhandlinger" for the relevant parliamentary period. 2001–8—Number of government bills, number of private member bills: Stortinget, http://www.stortinget.no/no/Saker-og-publikasjoner/Statistikk-over-saker (accessed February 5, 2009). 2005–8—Number of separate proposals: "Stortingets Forhandlinger" for the relevant parliamentary period.

Note: This table does not include questions and interpellations.
[a]Number of government bills: Entries represent *Stortingsproposisjoner* (finance bills) and *Odelstingsproposisjoner* (non-finance bills). Government bills in any given year are numbered consecutively. The entries here represent the number assigned to the last Ot.prp. introduced in the given year, as reported in "Stortingets Forhandlinger." There may be minor discrepancies, because occasionally a number is assigned to a bill that is not in the end introduced. However, such occurrences are rare.
[b]Number of private member bills: Entries represent private motions (*Private forslag*, also known as *Dokument 8 forslag*).
[c]Number of separate proposals in the private member bills: Entries represent the number of separate proposals in each bill, as coded by a researcher on the basis of the text contained in "Stortingstidende"/"Stortingets Forhandlinger." The counting rules are as follows. (1) Every paragraph or item proposing a change counts as one proposal; likewise with every paragraph in the proposed legislation. Proposals on when to implement the bill do not count as separate proposals. (2) In less specific proposals each guideline, or suggested measure to be taken to reach the desired end, counts as a separate proposal. (3) For

TABLE 6.4—Continued

budget bills, the counting rules are as follows: (a) If the bill proposes that money be moved from item A to item B, this counts as one proposal. (b) If the bill proposes to increase expenditure under a specific item, but does not specify where the money is to be taken from, this counts as one proposal. (c) If the bill proposes increased spending on several items and the source of money is not specified, every supplementary spending item counts as one proposal. (d) If the bill proposes increased spending fully covered by proposed revenue increases, the suggested increases in revenues and expenditure each count as one proposal. In the latter part of the 1980s, budget proposals were not uncommon, but from the onset of the 1990s and onward they became few and far between. Furthermore, nearly all of them are of the type described under (b). Thus, the counting rules other than (b) will be of little consequence for the larger picture.

^dPercentage of all separate proposals approved or partly approved by parliament: Entries represent the percentage of private member bills (*Private forslag*) approved or partly approved by parliament, as well as the percentage of such bills referred to the government. These are alternative and mutually exclusive procedures. The data up to 1997–98 were provided by NSD. From 1998 to 1999: Ole Søe Eriksen has coded the data from "Stortingets Forhandlinger" for the relevant parliamentary period. On average for the period 1998–2008, 27.5% of all proposals were rejected immediately in parliament, 70.2% of all Dokument 8 proposals were transferred to a relevant committee, 0.5% of all proposals were withdrawn, and 1.5% were treated immediately in parliament based on special regulations in Stortingets Forretningsorden §28 (due to the urgency of certain matters). Only 2 of 1,161 proposals in the period were transferred directly to government. Of the proposals reaching a relevant committee, 32.7% were rejected when discussed in parliament, and 11.6% were approved/partly approved. The remainder were primarily attached to Stortingets protocol or not processed. Possible differences in coding patterns might affect the comparability of data pre-/post-1998.

^eNumber of recorded votes counting individual MPs: Entries represent all non-unanimous plenary votes in the Storting recorded in the archives of parliament. Note that on June 19, 1997, the Storting adopted a reform of its budget proceedings. This reform caused the number of recorded votes to be reduced by more than half. Note that the column has very limited comparability over time, as voting rules, routines, and the impact of continuous rationalizations in Storting votes affect the figures markedly in different years.

acceptable agreements. Nonsocialist governments have often needed to reach an accommodation with the Progress Party, which has been at times a truculent, unpredictable, or opportunistic partner (Strøm 1994). The often uneasy relationship between the Progress Party and the centrist parties has been further exacerbated by the latters' strong opposition to many of the populist appeals of the Progress Party.

Bourgeois coalitions have therefore made use of a number of different coordination mechanisms to avoid overt conflict in parliament. Much intracoalition policy coordination takes place in parliamentary committees. Since Norwegian parliamentary committees are relatively small and conduct their business behind closed doors, they are arenas conducive to legislative compromise (Mattson and Strøm 1995). Parliamentary committee members are in close communication with their respective parliamentary leaders, whose coordination and supervision are critical to coalition decision making.

Bargaining over the budget typically goes on more or less continuously through the fall session, with budget agreements typically reached under severe time pressure just before the Christmas recess. From the early 1970s to 2005, budget negotiations were particularly challenging and high-profile. Especially in the early part of this period, minority governments would often solve their budget problems through the so-called slalom method, which meant darting from one legislative coalition to another on different budget issues. This form of budget making often meant little overall coordination and rendered the government unable to maintain fiscal discipline. To avoid these problems, the Storting imposed on itself a series of procedural reforms aimed at streamlining the process and imposing a commitment to a specific budget ceiling. While these reforms have met with some success, they have (predictably) not solved such underlying problems as the inherent parliamentary weakness of many minority governments or weakness of will on the part of politicians.

While there is a fair amount of variation in budget coalitions (for an overview, see Narud and Valen 2007, 223), they highlight one interesting feature of Norwegian budgetary politics: governments often form on the left (or in the center) but typically prefer to negotiate their budgetary support on the right. Thus, Labor governments have reached budget agreements with the centrist parties (especially the Christian People's Party) much more often than with the Socialist Left. Nonsocialists have tended not to reciprocate this favor. Centrist coalitions have tended to coalesce with the Conservatives, center-right coalitions (including the Conservatives) with the Progress Party. Deviations from this regularity appear to have been driven more by the government's need to maintain credibility ("we are open to cooperation with any opposition party") than by the true inclinations of the incumbents.

Parliamentary Oversight and Questions

Parliamentary oversight takes place through a variety of means. The most prominent such mechanisms in the Storting are the standing committees and various forms of parliamentary questions. All matters requiring substantive Storting decisions are referred to a standing committee for scrutiny, discussion, and negotiation. Each representative is a member of only one standing committee, with a fixed membership and jurisdiction. Under normal circumstances, members serve on the same committee throughout the four-year parliamentary term,[14] and reelected representatives often retain their committee assignments. In general, the jurisdictions of parliamentary committees tend to mirror those of the ministerial departments, though exceptions to this rule have become increasingly common (Rommetvedt 2003, chap. 3).

Each standing committee engages in various forms of oversight of the executive agencies under its jurisdiction. For most of the post-1945 period, the Storting has had one standing committee with more general oversight functions. Until 1972, this was the Protocol Committee, which was established as early as 1814 and authorized to read and audit cabinet minutes. Under the early separation-of-powers constitution, this was a powerful committee, but it gradually faded into obscurity under parliamentarism. By the 1950s, members complained publicly that committee service gave them stomachaches (Sejersted 2000, 176). The committee was therefore abolished in 1972, and its oversight functions were divided between the other permanent committees. This reform turned out to impede coordination, so in 1981, another centralized oversight committee was established—the Control Committee, which also took over responsibility for constitutional affairs (Hansen and Mo 1994, 28–30). However, the fact that the members had their primary committee assignments elsewhere weakened this new committee, and in 1992, it was reorganized once again and made equal to other committee assignments. This latest reorganization ushered in a renaissance for the Control Committee during the 1993–97 parliamentary term, when the committee vigorously scrutinized a string of executive "scandals" (Sejersted 2000).

Parliamentary questions have long played an important role in Norwegian parliamentarism, and their importance has tended to increase over time. Questions have been asked in the Storting as far back as 1885 (the year after the introduction of parliamentary government), and interpellations found their way into the Rules of Procedure in 1908. A regular question time, held every Wednesday beginning at 11:00 am, was established in 1949 (Rasch 1994, 254–55).

Several other types of parliamentary questions have since evolved. For many years, "long" questions (which allowed the questioner and the responding minister five minutes of debating time each) coexisted with short ones, but the former were abolished in 1989. An October 1996 reform instituted two additional forms of parliamentary questions: (1) a spontaneous question time (up to one hour in duration) and (2) written questions to be answered in writing (Rasch 1998). The former allows for the most immediate and spontaneous debate between cabinet members and MPs, because the questions are not known in advance. Finally, the parliamentary standing orders permit representatives to raise urgent questions during the daily adjournment debate. Known as "questions at the conclusion of the meeting," such inquiries are rare. Ordinary questions remain, by far, the most numerous (Rasch 1998, 9).

As Rasch notes, "Parliamentary questions are in fact used quite extensively as a means of controlling the executive. This is not because the legislators necessarily intend to control. Rather, control is realized as a by-product of behavior motivated primarily by an attempt to reach other (less collective) aims related to—or derived from—the electoral arena" (Rasch 1994, 247–48; see also Kuhnle and Svåsand 1984). Overall, questions are a large and important part of the activities of the Norwegian parliament, and they are particularly useful to opposition parties, who tend to account for 80–90 percent of all questions. By all accounts, as shown in table 6.5, this activity has become quantitatively more important since the 1970s—particularly ordinary questions and written ones.

Outside their own ranks, members of the Storting can turn to more specialized vehicles of third-party oversight. One of these is the Auditor General's Office (Riksrevisjonen), which has a staff of approximately 500 and is headed by five auditors appointed by parliament. This office was traditionally engaged in more technical review of the government's expenditures and financial dispositions. During the 1980s, however, these audits became more comprehensive and often critical. From 1993 on, these more incisive audits were increasingly seized on by the reformed and emboldened parliamentary Control Committee, to which the Auditor General's Office reports. At the same time, the Auditor General's Office began issuing separate reviews of particularly important and controversial government agencies. Thus, there have, in recent years, been strong synergies between the Storting's Control Committee and the Auditor General's Office, and their simultaneous emergence as important forums of ex post scrutiny of the executive branch is no coincidence (Sejersted 2000).

Other oversight vehicles include parliamentary ombudsmen for specific issue areas and commissions of inquiry. The parliamentary ombudsman for civilian affairs was established in 1962 to investigate administrative abuses against ordinary citizens. This office is a quasi-judicial institution that reports to parliament. The ombudsman cannot assess penalties but does report on inappropriate practices and may propose reforms and various forms of redress. Since its inception, this office has virtually displaced parliament itself as a forum for petitions and individual case work concerning government agencies. The Norwegian Parliamentary Intelligence Oversight Committee (Stortingets kontrollutvalg for etterretnings-, overvåkings- og sikkerhetstjeneste, EOS-utvalget), which scrutinizes the secret (intelligence) services, was established in 1995 and reports to parliament. Finally, the Storting may appoint independent commissions of inquiry. Until recently, most investigative commissions were actually appointed by the cabinet, though often after consultation with parliament. Between 1985 and 2000, however, there were at least four important commissions of inquiry established by the Storting itself (Sejersted 2000, 178).

Thus, there is no doubt that parliamentary scrutiny of the Norwegian executive has become more intense in recent years, perhaps particularly so during the 1990s, or that the parliament has found an increasing number of effective institutional vehicles. Sejersted (2000, 179) argues that compared to its counterpart in Denmark, the Norwegian parliament has focused less strictly and stringently on legal criteria. It has more and more jealously defended its right to be properly informed by executive agencies, and critical scrutiny of individual ministers has often focused on whether they have neglected to inform parliament properly about executive actions under their respective jurisdictions. Through this growing activism, the Norwegian parliament has also increasingly focused on ex post, rather than ex ante, control of the executive branch. The main factor that limits the effectiveness of such parliamentary scrutiny is the bluntness (and hence lack of credibility) of the ultimate sanctions: no-confidence votes and impeachment.

The Confidence Relationship and Impeachment

Since 1905, Norway has seen the evolution of the constitutional convention that individual ministers or cabinets that lose confidence votes must resign (Hansen and Mo 1994, 118; Nordby 2000). Yet this basic feature of parliamentary democracy was only inserted into the constitution in 2007. Motions that may lead to the resignation of the cabinet can be introduced by the government itself (confidence motions) or by any member of parliament, typically representing the opposition and offering a motion of no confidence. No-confidence motions may be brought against individual ministers or against the cabinet collectively. They can be introduced by any member at any time and need no second sponsor. They are voted on in plenary sessions. To be adopted, a no-confidence motion needs a simple majority (50 percent plus one) of those present and voting (as long as these constitute a quorum).

Confidence motions may be presented by individual ministers or by the prime minister on behalf of the cabinet as a whole. As in the case of no-confidence motions, there are few specific regulations in the parliamentary standing orders. While Norwegian governments must resign if a parliamentary majority adopts an unambiguous motion of no confidence, they may choose to stay in office in case of a "negative majority"; that is, if two or more different motions of no confidence collectively gain the votes of a parliamentary majority but no single motion has majority support, the government is under no obligation to resign (Stavang 1968, 1971; Hansen and Mo 1994, 118–19). Thus, although the formal constitution recognizes no

TABLE 6.5. Interpellations and Questions to Cabinet Ministers, Norway, 1970–2008

Year	Parties in Cabinet	Interpellations	Interpellations from Opposition (%)[a]	Ordinary Questions	Ordinary Questions from Opposition (%)[b]	Long Questions	Written	Spontaneous
1970–71	(a) SP, H, V, KRF							
	(b) A	35		171		68		
1971–72	A	40		199		97		
1972–73	KRF, SP, V	25		309		90		
1973–74	A	16		389		79		
1974–75	A	30		432		56		
1975–76	A	19		383		50		
1976–77	A	32		339		64		
1977–78	A	11		320		41		
1978–79	A	20		355		77		
1979–80	A	19		408		56		
1980–81	A	22		391		44		
1981–82	H	15		566		28		
1982–83	H	17		527		43		
1983–84	H, KRF, SP	17		547		42		
1984–85	H, KRF, SP	19		592		24		
1985–86	(a) H, KRF, SP							
	(b) A	13		542		10		
1986–87	A	11		763		24		
1987–88	A	10		755		10		
1988–89	A	15		854		12		
1989–90	H, KRF, SP	9		888				

1990–91	A	19		748			
1991–92	A	31		745			
1992–93	A	25		501			
1993–94	A	9	66.7	576	90.6		
1994–95	A	20	70.0	521	92.0		
1995–96	A	16	87.5	617	90.0		
1996–97	A	47	89.4	409	94.0	161	209
1993–97		**92**	**82.6**	**2,123**	**91.4**		
1997–98	KRF, SP, V	49	92.9	670	91.2	296	213
1998–99	KRF, SP, V	52	85.5	606	91.7	402	232
1999–2000	KRF, SP, V	36	88.9	604	86.1	476	188
2000–2001	A	23	87.0	544	93.0	554	194
1997–2000	KRF, SP, V	**147**	**89.1**	**1,880**	**89.7**		
2000–2001	A	**23**	**87.0**	**544**	**93.0**		
2001–2	KRF, SP, V	32	71.9	467	93.1	590	170
2002–3	KRF, SP, V	22	90.9	430	91.2	782	170
2003–4	KRF, SP, V	46	76.6	369	91.9	974	131
2004–5	KRF, SP, V	36	80.6	277	94.2	991	115
2001–5		**137**	**78.8**	**1,543**	**92.5**		
2005–6	A, SP, SV	55	70.9	257	97.7	1,243	103
2006–7	A, SP, SV	70	68.6	229	94.8	1,415	124
2007–8	A, SP, SV	72	90.3	317	96.8	1,607	127

Source: Pre-2001—Rasch 2005. 2001–8—Stortinget, *Spørsmål*, http://stortinget.no/Stortinget-og- demokratiet/Arbeidet/Sporreinstituttene/ (accessed February 5, 2009).

Notes: See table 6.1 for explanation of party labels. Bold indicates summary results for the given range of years.

[a]Interpellations from opposition calculated by researcher by counting the number of interpellations from parties not in cabinet, using "Stortingets Forhandlinger" for the relevant parliamentary period.

[b]Ordinary questions from opposition calculated by researcher by counting the number of ordinary questions (Spørsmål til spørretimen) from parties not in cabinet, using "Stortingets Forhandlinger" for the relevant parliamentary period.

such rule, the government may in practice choose to interpret its relationship to the Storting as governed by a "constructive" vote of no confidence. There is, however, no requirement of an investiture vote when a new cabinet takes office.

The government is not expected to hand in its resignation in the event of a parliamentary defeat unless the bill has been made the subject of a motion of confidence or no confidence. Even defeats on major legislative initiatives (e.g., parts of the budget) need not lead to the cabinet's resignation, and Norwegian governments (especially minority cabinets) have, over time, tolerated a greater number of parliamentary defeats. Motions of confidence or no confidence are by no means exceptional. Between 1945 and 1999, more than 50 no-confidence motions were introduced, as were 16 motions of confidence (Strøm and Narud 2003, 536–37). Only once, in the case of the Gerhardsen cabinet in 1963, has a no-confidence motion introduced by the opposition actually succeeded and forced the government to resign. Two cabinets have died at their own hands, after losing confidence votes they introduced themselves: Lyng in 1963 and Willoch III in 1986.

The use of no-confidence motions has been cyclical. The Kings Bay vote of 1963 (over the Gerhardsen government's handling of a mining tragedy) was the eighteenth motion of no confidence after 1945 and the first successful one. Fourteen of these votes occurred prior to 1961, when the Labor Party held a parliamentary majority and there was virtually no chance that a no-confidence motion would succeed. During the 10 years that followed Kings Bay, there were very few no-confidence votes, though their incidence increased substantially after the Socialist Left and the Progress Party gained parliamentary representation in 1973. In contrast, Brundtland's (minority) cabinets between 1986 and 1996 attracted a relatively large number of such motions, 13 in total. Confidence motions have been much less frequent, particularly under Labor governments. Nonsocialist cabinets have used this procedure somewhat more liberally, but confidence votes remain a rare occurrence in the Norwegian parliament. After Willoch's defeat in 1986, for example, there was no such vote until June 1998.

Impeachment is a venerable procedure established by Articles 86 and 87 of the constitution of 1814. Charges can be brought against members of parliament, the cabinet, or the Supreme Court for criminal abuses of their office. Until 2007, charges would be brought by the lower division of the Storting (Odelstinget), while the Court of Impeachment would be constituted by five members of the Supreme Court and 10 members of the upper division of the Storting (Lagtinget). The Court of Impeachment would thus have a majority of politically, rather than judicially, appointed members. In its most famous case, the Selmer cabinet trial of 1884, the political members of the Court did indeed overrule the judicial members.

Even though the Selmer case is not unique, impeachment has been a rare occurrence in Norwegian politics, with no more than eight cases in all. Besides the Selmer case, the most politically interesting case was the unsuccessful impeachment of the prime minister Abraham Berge in 1926–27. Since then, the procedure has essentially fallen into disuse (see Smith 1997).

The constitutional amendment of 2007 represents an interesting attempt to reform this institution. According to the new rules, members of parliament will no longer serve on the Court of Impeachment but will be replaced by six lay judges appointed by parliament for a six-year term. The Supreme Court will continue to be represented by five justices, and the chief justice of the Supreme Court will be the presiding judge. To the extent that the new impeachment procedure becomes politically meaningful, it will thus diminish the power of parliament in this ultimate sanction, which will likely be a more judicial and less political institution than previously.

Delegation within the Cabinet

Once a coalition government has been formed, the cabinet meets regularly, normally several times per week. There are two forms of cabinet meetings: the meetings of the Council of State (Statsråd), in which the king presides, and cabinet conferences. Only Council of State decisions are official. The cabinet conferences are considered to be informal gatherings, and no constitutional rule exists for their decision making or for their agenda. However, even cabinet conferences may reach decisions that bind individual ministers (Berggrav 1994). Occasionally the parliamentary leaders of coalition parties are invited to take part in cabinet conferences, which can thus serve as vehicles for conflict management. Conflicts within the coalition government are discussed at the cabinet conferences, and if no agreement can be reached, individual ministers have the opportunity to dissent (Berggrav 1994).

Coalition Discipline in Cabinet

Norwegian coalition governments have had no formal or explicit rules concerning parliamentary votes on legislative proposals or other parliamentary behavior. This should not be read as acquiescence in legislative indiscipline, however. Generally, party cohesion is very strong in parliament (Svåsand, Strøm, and Rasch 1997), and coalition governments are founded on the expectation of such cohesion. However, it is up to each of the coalition parties to control its own parliamentary group. Interviews with central party actors involved in coalition politics suggest that enforcement has not been highly institutionalized. As a result, coalition enforcement procedures must be sought largely in internal party mechanisms. Strict party control over ballot access and political finance are surely among the factors that facilitate party discipline, although some control over these resources is decentralized to the district level.

Cabinet Members' Backgrounds

Norwegian cabinet members are not required to have any parliamentary experience, much less a current seat, and since World War II, only about half have claimed such prior experience—one of the lowest proportions in Western Europe. Yet the cabinet members occupying the most central portfolios, especially the prime minister and the finance minister, have had more extensive parliamentary experience (see table 6.6). Prime ministers and foreign ministers have usually also had prior cabinet experience. Many politicians in Norway have reached cabinet rank at a comparatively early age (say, before the age of 40), because the parties have seen the appointment of young cabinet members as a way to project a youthful image. This is particularly true for relatively "light" cabinet portfolios, such as the Ministry for Development Assistance, as well as for cabinet members who handle policy issues that appeal predominantly to younger voters, such as environmental affairs or family affairs. Even other portfolios have attracted remarkably young politicians.

Table 6.6 reports extensive information on the cabinet members' background for four ministries (the justice, foreign, finance, and prime ministries). The mean age of these four cabinet ministers between 1945 and 2005 has been a bit short of 49 years. On average, the ministers of finance and justice have been about 46 years old, whereas the prime minister and the minister of foreign affairs have been about 52. Of the 19 justice ministers who have served since 1945, only six have been older than 50 at the time of their first appointment, and three of the five most recent ones have been below 40 (data not shown). There are exceptions. For understandable reasons, foreign ministers have tended to be among the most senior cabinet members, and young appointees have been rare.

Since Gro Harlem Brundtland's first cabinet was formed in 1981, Norwegian cabinets have been characterized by (and at least initially famous for) their virtual gender parity, and a reshuffle in 2007 resulted in the first female-majority cabinet. In the 1980s, this high proportion of women coexisted with rather "traditional" appointment patterns, with female cabinet members assigned to portfolios such as family affairs, social affairs, development assistance, and, increasingly, justice. Thus, table 6.6 shows that over the whole postwar period, the majority of ministers of justice have been female, whereas relatively few women have served in the other positions. Indeed, no woman has yet served as minister of foreign affairs. However, since the 1990s, women have been appointed to such "untraditional" portfolios as defense and energy, and in 2005, Kristin Halvorsen (Socialist Left) became the first female minister of finance.

The Labor Party in particular has had a tradition of appointing cabinets comprising a broad social mix, including individuals of humble social origins and few educational credentials. Thus, for example, Trygve Bratteli served as finance minister and later prime minister without even a secondary education. Even in 1998, an international study found that Norway ranked at the very bottom in the educational credentials of the cabinet members, with fewer than 40 percent having earned a university degree (*Aftenposten* 1998).

Table 6.6 reveals some interesting differences between the various ministries in this regard. On average, Norwegian prime ministers have had significantly lower education levels than the other three types of ministers, with the minister of foreign affairs and justice on top. However, together with the ministers of foreign affairs, they have had more experience in prior cabinet positions. Prime ministers have also had considerably more parliamentary experience than any of the others. Hence, a combination of political experience and parliamentary training seems to be more important for the post of prime minister than for other cabinet positions. For foreign minister candidates, cabinet experience and a high-ranking position in the party are key credentials, while finance ministers have strong party credentials. Those appointed justice minister have much less party and parliamentary experience but considerably more experience of elected office at subnational levels and of previous employment (both inside and outside the public sector).

Table 6.6 also presents the means for different time periods. Not surprisingly, the proportion of female ministers is much greater between 1991 and 2005 than before 1975. There are also a number of substantial differences between the two periods as regards professional experience. Between 1945 and 1975, only one-third were members of parliament at the time of their appointment, but since 1975, two out of three have been recruited from parliament. In addition, length of parliamentary experience of the cabinet members has increased, and more appointees have had major prior appointments within parliament. Just as notably, the proportion of cabinet members with experience from a high-ranking office in their party's youth organization increased from 25 to 55 percent.

TABLE 6.6. Ministerial Background, First Appointment, by Portfolio, Norway, 1945–2008

Portfolio within Cabinet	Age (mean years)	Female Ministers (%)	Prior Cabinet Position (%)	Parliamentary Experience (mean years)[a]	Prior Party High-Rank Position (%)[b]	Prior Youth Party High-Rank Position (%)[c]	Major Prior Appointment within Parliament (%)[d]	Major Prior Elected Offices at Local/Regional Level (%)[e]	Formal Education Level[f]	Any Prior Employment within the Public Sector (%)[g]	Any Prior Employment within the Private Sector (%)	Any Prior Salaried Employment in Party (%)	Member of Parliament at the Time of Minister Appointment (%)[h]	N (unique number of ministers)
Prime minister	51.8	8	62	10.4	100	54	85	69	3.7	69	31	31	921	13
Finance minister	46.0	5	29	6.9	62	57	38	48	4.1	67	57	14	57	21
Foreign minister[i]	52.4	0	63	6.5	63	38	50	56	4.8	75	56	38	44	16
Justice minister[j]	45.3	53	26	1.2	37	5	11	74	4.7	95	74	16	26	19
Mean 1945–2005	48.9	17	45	6.2	66	39	46	62	4.3	77	55	25	55	69
Mean 1945–75	49.8	6	34	3.8	63	25	28	63	4.4	81	53	25	34	32
Mean 1991–2005	47.0	25	45	6.7	65	55	55	45	4.5	65	50	30	65	20

Source: Data from Nordby 1985; Torp 1986, 1990, 1994; Stortinget, home page, http://www.stortinget.no; Arntzen and Helle 1999–; Aschehoug and Gyldendal 1990; Arbeiderpartiet, http://arbeiderpartiet.no/.

Note: All of the calculations presented in this section are based on a data set that contains data on ministers who got portfolios at the beginning of a new cabinet. A new cabinet is defined here as a cabinet that fulfills at least one of three conditions: any change in the set of parties holding cabinet membership, any change in the identity of the prime minister, or any general election (see Müller and Strøm 2003, 12).

[a] Prior parliamentary experience (in full years) does not include years that a person has been in cabinet. That is, for systems that allow for the holding of simultaneous cabinet and parliamentary positions, we only count "parliamentary experience" for the years that the MP does not also have a cabinet position. (The latter is coded as prior cabinet experience: yes or no.) If the total parliamentary experience (service as MP) sums to less than six months, it is counted as zero (0) years of experience.

[b] Prior party high-rank position refers to any of the following: party leader, party secretary, member of the party national board, or head of local or regional board.

[c] Prior youth party high-rank position refers to the positions in a youth organization corresponding to the prior party high-rank positions.

[d] Major prior appointment within parliament refers to any of the following: Speaker (president of parliament or chamber/subdivision), group leader, vice group leader, committee chairman, or vice committee chairman.

[e] Major prior elected offices at local/regional level refers to any of the following: head of municipality, head of region, member of local parliament, or member of regional parliament.

[f] Formal education level: 1 = primary (or less); 2 = secondary (high school, Swedish gymnasium); 3 = any enrollment in postsecondary education (such as technical college, nursing school, college, university) but no degree; 4 = any undergraduate degree at technical college, nursing school, college, or university (2–4 years in length) that is post–high school or post-gymnasium; 5 = postgraduate degree (licensiat, huvudfag, PhD).

[g] Prior employment refers to the employer, that is to say, the one paying the salary. Salary by the party does not include elected offices, only jobs (such as party ombudsman). The three categories (public, private, party) are not mutually exclusive categories (as they, in combination, speak to a minister's general career pattern). Private employment includes people employed in trade unions and other nongovernmental organizations.

[h] The coding "Member of parliament at the time of minister appointment" only has one possible answer (yes or no).

[i] Finance minister is defined as the minister heading the ministry in control of the state budget.

[j] Justice minister is defined as the minister heading the ministry in control of the police force.

There is thus little evidence to suggest that the centrality that either political parties or the parliamentary arena have held in cabinet recruitment has declined, as the presidentialization thesis might suggest. On the contrary, if we compare the past 15 years with the earlier postwar period, it is clear that the parliamentary as well as the youth party experience of key cabinet members have increased. If anything, Norwegian cabinet ministers have thus become more, rather than less, partisan, and the extent of parliamentary vetting has seemingly also increased. These background factors appear to have been prioritized at the expense of experience in subnational executive offices and professional expertise.

Electoral Performance

Since the 1970s, it has become common in Norwegian journalism and political parlance to refer to governments as suffering "wear and tear" (*slitasje*). While this term is hardly defined in any precise way, loss of popular support and, more specifically, anticipated electoral losses are surely a major part of this concern. The general recognition of this phenomenon has developed along with—and, no doubt, partly as a result of—a growing tendency for incumbent parties to suffer at the polls. Table 6.7 shows the electoral gains and losses of incumbent parties between 1949 and 2005.

Overall, there is a moderate tendency toward an adverse incumbency effect: a slight tendency for governing parties to lose votes. The mean net loss amounts to 1.9 percent of the total national poll. Yet there are differences across parties and cabinet types. Labor actually gained votes in its first three postwar elections but has since lost ground six of the eight times it has been in office at election time. In coalition cabinets, it is rare for all parties to suffer the same fate. This has happened only in 1985, when all three nonsocialist governing parties suffered minor setbacks. However, all four coalition governments have experienced net losses in subsequent elections.

In the period, two of the centrist parties, the Christian People's Party and the Center Party, actually benefited more often than they lost from taking government responsibility. But the Conservatives and, to a lesser extent, the Liberals show a fairly consistent pattern of losing votes as incumbents. The notable exception occurred in 2005, when the Christian People's Party suffered badly while the Liberals gained. The results indicate that the two traditionally large parties with clearly defined left-right placements (Labor and the Conservatives) suffer electoral liabilities from holding office, whereas the two smaller parties with programmatic commitments most clearly related to alternative policy dimensions (the Christian People's Party and the Center Party) have faced less of a dilemma, at least until the Christian

People's Party's debacle in 2005. Public opinion polling data confirm that the Conservative Party tends to be more popular with the voters when they are out of government than when they are in, whereas the other coalition parties are less affected by incumbency (Narud 1996).

It is not clear whether these differences in electoral fortunes are due to policy profiles, size, or historical accident. However, consistent with results from other countries (e.g., Powell and Whitten 1993), the evidence from Norway may suggest that the effect of economic performance varies by ideological leanings. Voters most commonly evaluate Labor more favorably on unemployment and social policies, while nonsocialist coalitions do better on the issue of inflation (Aardal and Listhaug 1986). How these assessments figure into the voters' retrospective judgments seems to be related to the ideological distinctiveness of the parties (Narud and Valen 2007).

There is no doubt, however, that incumbency losses have increased over time. Over the past 30 years, the election of 1993 is the only one in which incumbents gained ground. The two most dramatic losses have occurred in 2001 and 2005. In each case, the governing parties jointly slipped more

TABLE 6.7. Electoral Performance of Incumbent Cabinet Parties, Norway, 1945–2008

Cabinet Number	Cabinet Composition	Election Year following Cabinet	A	H	SP	KRF	V	Cabinet Total
1	A 1945–49	1949	+4.7					+4.7
3	A 1951–53	1953	+1.0					+1.0
5	A 1955–57	1957	+1.6					+1.6
6	A 1957–61	1961	−1.5					−1.5
9	A 1963–65	1965	−3.6					−3.6
10	SP, H, V, KRF 1965–69	1969		−1.5	+0.6	+1.3	−1.0	−0.6
13	KRF, SP, V 1972–73	1973			+0.5	+2.8	−5.9	−2.6
15	A 1976–77	1977	+7.0					+7.0
17	A 1981	1981	−5.1					−5.1
19	H, KRF, SP 1983–85	1985		−1.3	−0.1	−0.6		−2.0
21	A 1986–89	1989	−6.5					−6.5
23	A 1990–93	1993	+2.6					+2.6
25	A 1996–97	1997	−1.9					−1.9
27	A 2000–2001	2001	−10.7					−10.7
28	KRF, H, V 2001–5	2005		−7.1		−5.6	+2.0	−10.7
Mean gains/losses			−1.1	−3.3	+0.3	−0.5	−1.6	−1.9

Source: Data from Müller and Strøm 2003; Strøm and Bergman 2005.
Notes: See table 6.1 for explanation of party labels. Numbers in table represent percentage of national vote.

than 10 percentage points in the popular vote. By national or international standards, these are huge losses.

Delegation from the Cabinet to Civil Servants

The initial structure and organization of the Norwegian civil service was an inheritance from Denmark. As one of the few social organizations with professional expertise, it played a major role in the political and economic development of Norway in the nineteenth century. Throughout its history, there has been an ongoing debate over whether the civil service should be organized around a smaller set of hierarchical departments under strong political control (traditionally known as the "Danish model," although Denmark itself has deviated somewhat from these principles in recent decades) or in the form of a larger set of more autonomous and professional agencies under less direct political control (the "Swedish model"). In practice, the Norwegian administration has become a hybrid. The former principle is embodied in a structure of departments, the latter in a set of directorates (*direktorater*). There are currently 18 departments and approximately 70 directorates in the Norwegian central administration (Christensen and Egeberg 1994; Svardal 1994).

Since the early 1980s, the total number of civil servants in the central administration has been between 3,000 and 4,000. Most of the longer-term growth has occurred in the directorates. Thus, between 1945 and 1991, the number of departmental positions increased by 70 percent, whereas the corresponding growth in the directorates amounted to no less than 210 percent (Christensen and Egeberg 1994).

There are two classes of Norwegian civil servants: higher civil servants (*embetsmenn*) and ordinary civil servants (*tjenestemenn*). According to Article 28 of the constitution, higher civil servants must be appointed by the king in a formal cabinet meeting. Their tenure is also strictly protected, in that they can only be dismissed if found guilty of malfeasance by a court of law. Ordinary civil servants have lesser protections. In practice, Norwegian civil servants of both categories have always tended to be professional and nonpartisan.

Under professional civil service systems such as the Norwegian one, politicians have very little ex post control over the civil servants to whom they delegate. Certainly, civil servants cannot typically be hired or fired at will. Accountability takes place in two ways. First, civil servants have explicitly designed contracts that prevent them from taking various types of hidden or arbitrary action. Second, all decisions taken in the executive branch explicitly carry the authorization of the head of the department. A great deal of formal authority is therefore placed in this minister's hands. Ex ante controls, however, are quite strong, in that the credentials that are required of civil servants tend to be quite substantial.

Over the past 15 years, agencies in the central administration have gained more managerial autonomy through a process of structural delegation, partly inspired by the doctrine of New Public Management (NPM), but also as a result of Norway's adaption to the EU (Christensen et al. 2007, 55–61; Christensen and Lægreid 2007, 507). Until the mid-1990s, major public sectors like railways and telecommunications were organized as integrated government services under unified political control. Since then, the commercial parts of these enterprises have become corporate, in an effort to promote competition and openness to the market. At the same time, the regulatory parts have been streamlined into separate agencies, creating a more fragmented and disintegrated model. This development was furthered by a 2003 reform initiated by the center-right government that upgraded competition policy to a main regulatory concern. To date, the red-green coalition formed in 2005 has formally kept the new model, although it has attempted to downplay the market orientation and give more emphasis to government ownership and sectoral coordination.

Christensen and Lægreid (2007, 507) question the effects of these NPM reforms, pointing to the complex trade-offs between political control and agency autonomy. They argue that the transformation from an integrated state model to a management-inspired one with more autonomous agencies has weakened the ministries' ability to control subordinate agencies. It has made the agencies less susceptible to political signals, and it has become more difficult for the political executive to obtain information from them. Consequently, Christensen and Lægreid (2002) argue that NPM-related reforms have limited cabinet members' political discretion and control.[15]

Rune J. Sørensen (2005) paints a rather different and more positive picture, emphasizing the strengthening of ex post and often third-party controls. Since the late 1960s, ex post control has been facilitated by legislation designed to open up the administration to third-party oversight. For example, the Administrative Procedures Act (Forvaltningsloven) of 1967 gave affected interests the right to be consulted before the administration adopts general rules that significantly impact them. The Freedom of Information Act (Offentlighetsloven) of 1970 gave citizens a general right of access to administrative documents. Such reforms have detracted from the simplicity and singularity of the Norwegian chain of delegation, because they allow interest groups, media, and ordinary citizens to become increasingly engaged in the oversight of public agencies. It seems reasonable to see these trends as an evolution toward a different and specifically more Madisonian, though not necessarily weakened, form of parliamentary democracy. For representative democracy in general and for the political parties in particular, the obvious challenge is to find a balance between autonomy and professional independence, on the one hand, and political accountability, democratic transparency, and responsiveness, on the other.

External Constraints

Norway is a fairly pure parliamentary democracy. Although some constraints exist on delegation and accountability through the parliamentary chain, these are modest compared to many other European nations. However, the evolution of the parliamentary model in Norway toward Madisonianism is partly due to the increasing importance of external checks (constraints) on the sovereignty of parliament and other agents directly or indirectly elected by the voters. Such constraints may come in many forms. In the case of Norway, two constraints have become especially important: judicialization and Europeanization.

Judicialization

More decisively than either Denmark or Sweden, Norway has established a doctrine of judicial review. In fact, the Norwegian tradition of judicial review postdates only that of the United States, and in developing this practice, Norwegian legal authorities relied heavily on American doctrines (Smith 1993, 32). Judicial review was not explicitly established in the 1814 constitution but evolved gradually through a series of Supreme Court decisions. Smith (1993, 158–59) argues that the practice can be traced back to the 1840s, that it is clearly evident from 1866 on, and that it is first explicitly articulated in a Supreme Court decision in 1890. The latter decision inaugurated the "golden age" of judicial activism in Norway. Activism declined from about 1930 until the mid-1970s, a period during which courts were extremely reluctant to challenge the constitutionality of government decisions.

In a widely recognized majority decision in 1976—the "Kløfta-saken"— which upheld private property rights against government regulation, the Norwegian Supreme Court ushered in an era of increased judicial activism. In two additional cases in the mid-1990s, the Court protected social insurance benefits against the retroactive effects of new legislation (Broch 2003).

Nonetheless, Norway has not followed the present tendency in Europe to develop a "constitutional court."[16]

Judicial independence in Norway was long constrained by appointment procedures. Members of the Supreme Court have traditionally been recruited in a more politicized manner in Norway than in most other European countries. Norway never established a formalized judicial career system, and court appointments are made by the cabinet on the advice of the minister of justice. Parliament's role is limited to the possibility of reviewing appointments ex post. This practice gives the Ministry of Justice considerable agenda powers (Smith 2003, 179). To constrain this ministry, a 2001 reform established an independent administrative authority to evaluate judicial candidates for any vacancy and to propose three of them to the government. De facto, however, the Ministry of Justice still holds the key to court appointments, and although judicial independence is growing, it is still modest by European standards.

Domestic courts are not the only judicial constraints on the Norwegian parliament. Parliamentary power can also be constrained when international agreements impact on—or even conflict with—ordinary domestic legislation. Over the last few years, EU laws (through the European Economic Area [EEA] agreement) and the European Convention on Human Rights have become a more important concern in Supreme Court practice. Although the Supreme Court has the competence to decide how far the EEA treaty integrates Norway into the EU system, the treaty gives EU regulations priority above national law. Moreover, the final authority to settle the terms of Norwegian legal obligations within the EEA relationship rests with the European courts. In the case of the European human rights regime, the same logic applies. If it conflicts with Norwegian legislation, human rights law has priority.

Such judicial and international constraints figure prominently among the concerns in the Norwegian Power and Democracy Study, 1998–2003 (Østerud, Engelstad, and Selle 2003, 116–26). By their progressive case-by-case interpretations of treaties with broad and imprecise clauses, international courts bind national courts and legislatures. In addition—as a consequence of extensive legislation conferring positive (welfare) rights—domestic power is transferred from elected assemblies to administrative and legal institutions dealing with popular complaints. This conferment of rights, it is argued, is on a collision course with the authority of local governments acting within tight budget constraints (Østerud 2002, 14–15). Nonetheless, the judicialization of Norwegian politics certainly has had many positive aspects, as good government implies individual rights and the rule of law as well as popular sovereignty. In any event, whether popular sovereignty has been weakened or reinforced, parliamentary institutions have certainly become increasingly constrained.

Europeanization

The second important contemporary constraint on the parliamentary chain of governance lies in Norway's international commitments and especially in the effects of European integration. This statement may sound paradoxical since Norway is not a member of the European Union and thus has not transferred sovereignty to this transnational organization. Nonetheless, Norway's membership in the European Economic Area has entailed serious constraints on parliamentary authority and particularly on its access to critical information.

In the Storting, European issues have traditionally been and remain the domain of the Foreign Affairs Committee. Since May 1994, the Storting has decided to locate the government's consultation with the Storting on EEA matters within the European Consultative Organ (ECO)—also named the EEA Commission—which consists of all the members of the Foreign Affairs Committee, supplemented by the six Norwegian representatives to the EEA Joint Parliamentary Committee (Myhre-Jensen and Fløistad 1997). In reality, of course, EEA issues affect Norwegian domestic politics in a variety of policy areas that are not represented in this organ. Moreover, the government has been criticized for giving too little information to the Storting on EU issues (Christensen 1997). Critics have pointed to the short deadlines within which the Storting has to deal with matters related to the EEA agreement. Deliberations on EEA matters are rather impenetrable, since the documents from the meetings are not made public. Overall, the Storting's capacity to control government activities in this area is limited.

Sejersted (1996, 125) argues that the Storting has been weakened in two ways. First, the EEA agreement means a massive transfer of real, if not always formal, power from the Storting, through the EEA organs, to EU institutions. Second, it has led to a shift in the national balance of power, weakening parliament and strengthening the cabinet and the central administration, as well as the courts. Sejersted contends that it is primarily the legislative function of the Storting, rather than its financial and budgetary authority, that has been weakened by Europeanization. Unlike parliaments in the member states, the Storting has not transferred any formal legislative powers. However, Sejested argues that compared to full membership, the EEA agreement has created less favorable conditions for parliamentary oversight, because the formal status of the agreement camouflages the real transfer of power. This keeps the Storting from introducing necessary reforms.

In these ways, the judicialization and Europeanization of Norwegian politics have weakened the parliamentary model by placing increasingly important constraints on the authority of the Storting. However, Norwegian parliamentarism, especially the agenda power of the cabinet, have been weakened at least as much by an erosion of authority *within* the parliamentary chain of delegation.

Corporatism

A historically prominent constraint that is less constitutionally entrenched lies in the Norwegian version of corporatism. In cross-national surveys (e.g., Lijphart 1999), Norway is typically ranked among the most corporatist countries in the world. One foundation for corporatism can be found in Norway's high unionization rate. For almost the entire period since World War II, this rate has exceeded half of the labor force, and unionization has extended well into white-collar and private-sector occupations. The foremost factor that has contributed to this high and stable unionization rate is social democratic hegemony. Other contributing factors are the large public sector, which accounts for 37 percent of all employment, and the predominance in the industrial sector of heavy production based in raw materials.

Norwegian corporatism has two main institutional manifestations: a practice of remiss (*høring*), that is, of consulting affected interests in legislative and administrative matters; and a structure of permanent and temporary boards and committees on which such interests are represented. The remiss procedure provides a right for affected interests—such as government agencies, institutions, and interest organizations—to be consulted when legislative initiatives of significant concern to them are prepared. Interestingly, guaranteed access for affected interests and freedom of information were embedded in ordinary legislation passed under a nonsocialist coalition government (led by Borten) in 1967 and 1970 (mentioned earlier in this chapter). Thus, although corporatist practices were most vigorously advanced by social democratic governments, such forms of decision making enjoyed fairly broad cross-partisan support from the 1950s through the 1970s. The appointment of government boards and committees with interest group representation became a regular feature of Norwegian politics in the years following World War I and expanded greatly during the social democratic era from the mid-1930s on. The 261 committees (192 permanent and 69 temporary) that existed in 1936 gradually grew to 1,141 by 1976 (912 permanent and 229 temporary), the high point of Norwegian corporatism.

Today, the foundations of Norwegian corporatism are less solid than they once were. Unionization rates began to drop in the early 1980s. Moreover, quite critically, the union movement has begun not only to decline in numbers but also to fragment. In the heyday of social democracy, from the 1950s through the 1970s, the great majority of union members were organized under the umbrella of the Landsorganisasjonen, which has always retained extremely close ties with the Labor Party. Increasingly, however, the labor movement has split into several partly competing peak associations, as groups of skilled labor have broken away from the Landsorganisasjonen and from the direct influence of the Labor Party. Today, the Landsorganisasjonen comprises only about half of organized labor, compared to about 80 percent at its peak.

The institutional manifestations of corporatism have not gone unchallenged. As the countercyclical expansionary economic policies of the late 1970s failed, the governing Labor Party began to have doubts about the wisdom of strengthening the "iron triangles" of Norwegian politics through corporatist practices. Such doubts were much more openly articulated when the Conservative Willoch cabinet came to power in 1981 and began to dismantle many of the organizational forms of corporatism (Nordby 1994, 71). By 1994, the number of government committees had declined to 673 (611 permanent and 62 temporary), even though the practice of creating new such bodies has never been totally abandoned.

Thus, it makes sense to see Norwegian corporatism both as a historical phenomenon rather than a permanent feature and as a delegative instrument chosen by political parties rather than an alternative to them. Finally, although corporatism has its roots in the pre-Labor era, its heyday coincides with the period of social democratic ascendancy.

Other Constraints

Norway is a unitary state. Although local government was established as early as 1837 and enjoys broad support and participation, it is weakly entrenched in the constitution. Local governments have weak taxation powers, and much of their revenue comes in the form of transfers from the national government. Although some of their responsibilities have remained fairly constant since the early nineteenth century, others have changed, and the central (national) government has frequently done the changing. Provincial governments, of which there are 19, are even weaker. Following a reform in the 1970s, each province now has an elected government, but their jurisdiction is narrow. In recent years, several parties have called for reductions in their authority or for their abolition altogether. Thus, subnational government is largely dependent on authority and funds delegated by the national government and poses no significant constraint on the latter.

The same is true of direct democracy. Since Norwegian independence in 1905, only six national referendums have been held: two in 1905, on national independence and the form of the new Norwegian state (monarchy vs. republic); two during the interwar period, over prohibition; and, most recently, the 1972 and 1994 EU membership referendums. The constitution does not require that referendums be held on any particular issue (including constitutional amendments), nor is there any mechanism by which any authority except parliament can call such an event. Because the constitution does not mention national referendums, they can only be consultative, although parliament has, in practice, always followed the will of the majority.[17] Nonetheless, parliament is constrained by direct democracy only to the extent that it decides to submit itself to this mechanism.

Finally, there is no strong tradition in Norway according to which particular agencies of the executive branch or even nationalized industries can enjoy autonomy from political control. Thus, the Norwegian Broadcasting Corporation, whose acronym is NRK, was known to its detractors (including Carl I. Hagen of the Progress Party) as ARK, which translates as "the Labor Party's Broadcasting Corporation." In recent years, however, the NRK has gained political autonomy, at least from the Labor Party (a recent chief executive was a former Conservative politician). Similarly, there has been a dramatic increase in the political independence of the print media, which used to be closely identified with particular political parties. Within the government itself, the autonomy granted to the Bank of Norway in 2001 has been an important development, although it is still sorely resented by the Socialist Left.

Conclusion

Norway is not the epitome of parliamentary democracy. In fact, the 1814 constitution was drawn up to establish a very different kind of regime, a separation-of-powers system. Only gradually and informally was the constitution transformed into a parliamentary one. Central parliamentary principles, such as the duty to inform the Storting and the cabinet's duty to resign after a vote of no confidence, were not included in the constitution until 2007. In addition, the constitution still lacks some of the typical features of parliamentarism, such as parliamentary dissolution powers. Nonetheless, delegation of authority seems to follow the parliamentary pattern fairly closely. This is largely due to two interrelated factors: the strength of party government and a strong reliance on ex ante controls over agents. Ex post controls, though increasingly important over the past decade, have historically been much less well developed.

The performance of Norwegian democracy has traditionally kept most of its citizens happy. In the 1985 election survey, 89 percent of Norwegian respondents claimed to be satisfied or very satisfied with the way democracy worked in their country, a percentage that rose to 90 percent in 1997, declined to 77 percent in 2001, and rebounded to 88 percent in 2005 (Aardal 2003, 2007). Similarly, confidence in politicians has quite consistently been higher than in such societies as Sweden and the United States, and cynicism has been comparatively low (Aardal and Valen 1989, 276–81; Miller and Listhaug 1990).

Whether this happy outcome can be maintained is an entirely different matter. Both main features of Norwegian parliamentarism—party government and ex ante controls—have been eroded by recent developments. Though political parties so far maintain effective control of candidate selection as well as over policy-making in the Storting, they are rapidly declining as vehicles of mass participation, and their previously high level of popular support is slipping (Heidar and Saglie 2002; Strøm and Svåsand 1997). Given these developments and the clear trend toward more open processes of candidate selection in other Nordic countries, it is unclear how long Norwegian parties can maintain their strict control of parliamentary politics and recruitment. The weakening of ex ante controls has occurred simultaneously with the decline of parties, and the two phenomena are interrelated in many ways. This weakening is also in part the reflection of the rise of new parties (e.g., the Progress Party and the Socialist Left) that have rejected many traditional forms of social control.

The increasing difficulty of relying on ex ante control mechanisms is also driven in part by the emergence of a more diverse, competitive, and less transparent society. The extensive efforts at civil service reform only add to this picture. However, Norwegian politicians seem to recognize these developments and have responded to them by strengthening mechanisms of ex post control (e.g., committee hearings and more rigorous audits), particularly in the parliamentary arena. Their success or failure in these endeavors could have a major effect on the future trajectory of Norwegian democracy.

In sum, compared to most others in Europe, Norway is still a relatively unconstrained polity with a strong parliament and cohesive parties. There are few important ways in which the citizenry is partitioned into multiple democratic principals, and the country fairly closely resembles the parliamentary ideal type of an unfettered hierarchy controlled by the median voter. Despite this, there is substantial evidence that the parties are declining in their ability to capture the loyalty of most Norwegian voters. Although parties are still well placed institutionally, they are becoming empty shells organizationally, enjoying less and less loyalty. It would, however, be unfair to characterize them as cartel parties, as collusion, clientelism, and corruption are not typical features of Norwegian party politics. But the share of the population that harbors such suspicions about the parties is probably growing.

What is even more obvious, however, is that there is an unmistakable trend toward greater policy-making complexity and increasing constraints on policymakers. Norway's reluctant but seemingly inevitable incorporation into a larger Europe is the greatest and most decisive of these constraints, but it is not the only one. Judicial institutions are likely to play an increasingly important political role, and direct democracy will perhaps do likewise. Although central bank independence has met with greater skepticism than in most other European countries, it is not likely to be reversed. All in all, then, Norway is clearly becoming more Madisonian and less Westminsterian.

NOTES

The authors thank Sunniva E. Holberg, Magnus Opsahl, Magnus R. Ruud, and Ole Søe Eriksen for excellent research assistance and Torbjörn Bergman for helpful comments.

1. In addition to parties listed in the text, three parties have gained parliamentary representation in recent decades: a Marxist-Leninist party, the Red Election Alliance (renamed "Red" in 2007), in one parliamentary term (1993–97); and two largely regional lists, Folkeaksjonen Fremtid for Finmark (Popular Movement for the Future of Finnmark) (1989–93) and Tverrpolitiske Folkevalgte, also called Kystpartiet (the Coastal Party) (1997–2005).

2. The Progress Party was originally Anders Lange's Party, named after its founder.

3. The policy dimensions of Norwegian politics have been analyzed through voter and/or elite surveys (Narud 1996; Valen 1981, 1990), content analysis of party programs (Narud and Valen 2004; Strøm and Leipart 1989, 1993), "expert" judgments (Laver and Hunt 1992; Ray and Narud 2000), and records of parliamentary behavior (Rommetvedt 1984; Shaffer 1998).

4. Laver and Hunt (1992) provide no information on the Communist Party (NKP). For this reason, and because a major faction of the party merged with the Socialist People's Party in 1973, we have, in identifying the median party, given the Communists the same ordinal rank on the urban-rural dimension as the Socialist People's Party. Note that the position of the Communist Party is only relevant for the years the party was represented in the Storting (i.e., 1945–61) and that it never affects the identity of the median party.

5. Laver and Hunt's (1992) left-right placement probably misrepresents the Center Party from the 1980s on. Laver and Hunt place this party to the right of the Christian People's Party, as was the conventional ordering for the early postwar period. Since the 1980s, however, these two parties have swapped places on the left-right axis (Narud 2007; Aardal and Valen 1995). This reflects the leftward drift of the Center Party, as the party's opposition to European integration has gradually generalized into a greater skepticism toward market economics. This more "leftist" orientation of the Center Party is reflected in the party's entry into a "red-green" coalition with Labor and the Socialists in 2005. Another discrepancy is that since the 1990s, the Liberals have been considered to be to the right of both the Christian People's Party and the Center Party, whereas Laver and Hunt place the party to the left of these two competitors (Valen and Narud 2007a).

6. The urban-rural (cum center-periphery) dimension has on several occasions influenced coalition politics as well as party competition. For this reason, we have defined it as the second most important dimension. The third most important dimension may be the moral-religious axis, on which the Christian People's Party is at one pole and the parties of the left-right extremes (the Socialist Left and the Progress Party) are at the other.

7. Observe that in the case of the Progress Party, the reports on membership figures until 1994 are not entirely reliable.

8. These two amendments will take effect after the 2009 general election.

9. From 2005 on, the constitution specifies only the principles of seat allocation, not the number elected in each district. Prior to every second Storting election, the allocation will be adjusted for population changes.

10. The law permitted the conventions to submit the list to a vote among party members, in which case this vote would be final. However, such a vote has never been held (Valen, Narud, and Skare 2002).

11. In 1928, King Haakon VII, against the advice of the outgoing prime minister, called on the leader of the Labor Party to form a new government. This led to the formation of the first socialist government in Norwegian history (Björnberg 1939). The government proved short-lived, but the king's behavior did much to solidify his support among Norwegian Social Democrats.

12. In 1971, when a bourgeois majority coalition had just broken down over the EC issue, Storting president Bernt Ingvaldsen, a Conservative, was asked to investigate the feasibility of another nonsocialist coalition. Ingvaldsen's role was purely that of an *informateur*.

13. The exception, Willoch I (1981–83), nevertheless enjoyed consistent parliamentary support from the Christian People's Party and the Center Party.

14. Members of the Storting who are appointed to the cabinet must relinquish their seats to their respective deputies as long as they serve in the cabinet. If they

return to the Storting before the end of the term, however, they are not guaranteed reassignment to the same committees on which they served before their cabinet appointments.

15. Christensen and Lægreid (2007, 515) nevertheless note that in specific cases, as studies of immigration and hospital policies demonstrate, the political leadership is still able to assert control.

16. Smith (2003, 186) claims that the prestige that the Westminster parliamentary system enjoys, as well as its doctrine of parliamentary sovereignty, would most likely mean that Norwegian MPs "would not easily accept someone 'above parliament.'"

17. Before the EU membership referendum in 1994, representatives of several anti-EU organizations suggested that they would not feel obligated by a narrow pro-EU majority. However, the popular response to this stance was largely negative, so that it is unclear whether the anti-EU representatives would in fact have followed through on their threat to disregard the popular vote.

REFERENCES

Aardal, Bernt. 2002. "Electoral Systems in Norway." In Bernard Grofman and Arend Lijphart, eds., *The Evolution of Electoral Systems and Party Systems in the Nordic Countries*. New York: Agathon.
Aardal, Bernt, ed. 2003. *Velgere i villrede . . . : En analyse av Stortingsvalget 2001*. Oslo: Damm forlag.
Aardal, Bernt, ed. 2007. *Norske velgere. En studie av stortingsvalget i 2005*. Oslo: Damm forlag.
Aardal, Bernt, and Ola Listhaug. 1986. "Economic Factors and Voting Behavior in Norway, 1965–1985." Working Paper 4, Institute for Social Research, Oslo.
Aardal, Bernt, and Henry Valen. 1989. *Velgere, Partier og Politisk Avstand*. Oslo: Central Bureau of Statistics.
Aardal, Bernt, and Henry Valen. 1995. *Konflikt og opinion*. Oslo: NKS-Forlaget.
Allern, Elin. 2007. "Parties, Interest Groups, and Democracy: Political Parties and Their Relationship with Interest Groups in Norway." PhD diss., University of Oslo.
Andenæs, Johs. 1981. *Statsforfatningen i Norge*. Oslo: Tanum-Nordli.
Arntzen, Jon Gunnar, and Knut Helle, eds. 1999–. *Norsk biografisk leksikon*. Oslo: Kunnskapsforlaget.
Aschehoug and Gyldendal. 1990. *Store norske leksikon*. Oslo: Kunnskapsforlaget.
Berggrav, Dag. 1994. *Slik styres Norge: Kongen, regjeringen og Stortinget i norsk statsliv*. Oslo: Schibsted.
Berglund, Frode. 2003. "Valget i 2001—skillelinjemodellens endelikt?" In Bernt Aardal, ed., *Velgere i villrede*. Oslo: Damm forlag.
Berglund, Frode. 2007. "Nye sosiale skiller og deres betydning for valgatferden." *Norske velgere: En studie av stortingsvalget i 2005*. Oslo: Damm forlag.
Björnberg, Arne. 1939. *Parlamentarismens utveckling i Norge efter 1905*. Uppsala: Almqvist och Wiksell.
Aftenposten. 1998. "Bondevik-regjeringen dårligst utdannet." 17 September.

Broch, Lars Oftedal. 2003. "'Strict' or 'Liberal' Interpretation? Comments on Norway." In Eivind Smith, ed., *The Constitution as an Instrument of Change*. Stockholm: SNS Förlag.

Christensen, Dag Arne. 1997. "Europautvala i Danmark, Sverige og Noreg." *Nordisk Administrativt Tidsskrift* 78 (2): 143–62.

Christensen, Tom, and Morten Egeberg. 1994. "Sentraladministrasjonen—en oversikt over trekk ved departement og direktorat." In Tom Christensen and Morten Egeberg, eds., *Forvaltningskunnskap*. 2nd ed. Oslo: TANO.

Christensen, Tom, Morten Egeberg, Helge O. Larsen, Per Lægreid, and Paul G. Roness. 2007. *Forvaltning og politikk*. Oslo: Universitetsforlaget.

Christensen, Tom, and Per Lægreid. 2002. *Reformer og lederskap: Omstilling i den utøvende makt*. Oslo: Universitetsforlaget.

Christensen, Tom, and Per Lægreid. 2007. "Regulatory Agencies: The Challenges of Balancing Agency Autonomy and Political Control." *Governance* 20 (3): 499–520.

Dalton, Russell J., and Martin P. Wattenberg, eds. 2000. *Parties without Partisans: Political Change in Advanced Industrial Democracies*. Oxford: Oxford University Press.

Demker, Marie, and Lars Svåsand, eds. 2005. *Partiernas århundrade: Fempartimodellens uppgång och fall i Norge och Sverige*. Stockholm: Santèrus Förlag.

Eliassen, Kjell, and Mogens N. Pedersen. 1978. "Professionalization of Legislatures: Long-Term Change in Political Recruitment in Denmark and Norway." *Comparative Studies in Society and History* 20 (2): 286–318.

Eliassen, Kjell, and Marit Sjøvaag Marino. 2000. "Democratization and Parliamentary Elite Recruitment in Norway, 1848–1996." In Heinrich Best and Maurizio Cotta, eds., *Parliamentary Representatives in Europe, 1848–2000*. Oxford: Oxford University Press.

Gallagher, Michael, and Michael Marsh, eds. 1988. *Candidate Selection in Comparative Perspective: The Secret Garden of Politics*. London: Sage.

Groennings, Sven. 1961. "Cooperation among Norway's Non-Socialist Political Parties." PhD diss., Stanford University.

Hansen, Guttorm, and Erik Mo. 1994. *Om Stortingets arbeidsordning*. Oslo: Stortinget.

Heidar, Knut, and Jo Saglie. 2002. *Hva skjer med partiene?* Oslo: Gyldendal Norsk Forlag.

Katz, Richard S., and Peter Mair. 1995. "Changing Models of Party Organization and Party Democracy: The Emergence of the Cartel Party." *Party Politics* 1 (1): 5–28.

Knutsen, Oddbjørn. 2004. "Voters and Social Cleavages." In Knut Heidar, ed., *Nordic Politics: Comparative Perspectives*. Oslo: Universitetsforlaget.

Kuhnle, Stein, and Lars Svåsand. 1984. "Spørreordningene og politiske profiler i Stortinget 1977–1981." In Ole Berg and Arild Underdal, eds., *Fra valg til vedtak*. Oslo: Aschehoug.

Laver, Michael, and W. Ben Hunt. 1992. *Policy and Party Competition*. London: Routledge.

Laver, Michael, and Norman Schofield. 1990. *Multiparty Government*. Oxford: Oxford University Press.

Lijphart, Arend. 1984. *Democracies*. New Haven: Yale University Press.

Lijphart, Arend. 1999. *Patterns of Democracy.* New Haven: Yale University Press.
Matthews, Donald, and Henry Valen. 1999. *Parliamentary Representation: The Case of the Norwegian Storting.* Columbus: Ohio State University Press.
Mattson, Ingvar, and Kaare Strøm. 1995. "Parliamentary Committees." In Herbert Döring, ed., *Parliaments and Majority Rule in Western Europe.* New York: St. Martin's Press.
Miller, Arthur H., and Ola Listhaug. 1990. "Political Parties and Confidence in Government: A Comparison of Norway, Sweden, and the United States." *British Journal of Political Science* 20 (3): 357–86.
Müller, Wolfgang, and Kaare Strøm, eds. 2003. *Coalition Governments in Western Europe.* Oxford: Oxford University Press.
Myhre-Jensen, Kjell, and Brit Fløistad. 1997. "The Storting and the EU/EEA." In Matti Wiberg, ed., *Trying to Make Democracy Work.* Stockholm: Bank of Sweden Tercenary Foundation and Gidlunds Förlag.
Narud, Hanne Marthe. 1995. "Coalition Termination in Norway: Models and Cases." *Scandinavian Political Studies* 18 (1): 1–24.
Narud, Hanne Marthe. 1996. *Voters, Parties, and Governments.* Report 96:7. Oslo: Institute for Social Research.
Narud, Hanne Marthe. 2003. "Norway: Professionalization—Party-oriented and Constituency-based." In Jens Borchert and Jürgen Zeiss, eds., *The Political Class in Advanced Democracies.* Oxford: Oxford University Press.
Narud, Hanne Marthe. 2007. "Fra mindretallsregjering til flertallsregjering." In Bernt Aardal, ed., *Norske velgere: En studie av stortingsvalget i 2005.* Oslo: Damm forlag.
Narud, Hanne Marthe, Mogens N. Pedersen, and Henry Valen, eds. 2002. *Party Sovereignty and Citizen Control.* Odense: University Press of Southern Denmark.
Narud, Hanne Marthe, and Bjørn Erik Rasch. 2007. "Koalisjonsdannelser og ideologiske avstander." In Per Kristen Mydske, Dag Harald Claes, and Amund Lie, eds., *Politikkens vilkår i det nyliberale samfunn.* Oslo: Universitetsforlaget.
Narud, Hanne Marthe, and Kaare Strøm. 2003. "Norway: A Fragile Coalition Order." In Wolfgang C. Müller and Kaare Strøm, eds., *Coalition Governments in Western Europe.* 2nd ed. Oxford: Oxford University Press.
Narud, Hanne Marthe, and Henry Valen. 2004. "Partiprogram og velgerappell." In B. Aardal, A. Krogstad, and H. M. Narud, eds., *I valgkampens hete.* Oslo: Universitetsforlaget.
Narud, Hanne Marthe, and Henry Valen. 2007. *Demokrati og ansvar: Om politisk representasjon i et flerpartisystem.* Oslo: Damm forlag.
Narud, Hanne Marthe, and Henry Valen. 2008. "Coalition Membership and Electoral Performance." In Kaare Strøm, Wolfgang C. Müller, and Torbjörn Bergman, eds., *Cabinet and Coalition Bargaining: The Democratic Life Cycle in Western Europe.* Oxford: Oxford University Press.
Nordby, Trond, ed. 1985. *Storting og regjering 1945–1985: Biografier.* Oslo: Kunnskapsforlaget.
Nordby, Trond. 1994. *Korporatisme på norsk 1920–1990.* Oslo: Universitetsforlaget.
Nordby, Trond. 2000. *I politikkens sentrum: Variasjoner i Stortingets makt 1814–2000.* Oslo: Universitetsforlaget.
NOU [Norges offentlige utredninger]. 2004. *Penger teller, men stemmer avgjør: Om*

partifinansiering, åpenhet og partipolitisk fjernsynsreklame. Report 2004:25. Oslo: Statens Forvaltningstjeneste.

Østerud, Øyvind. 2002. "Judicialization and Parliamentary Democracy." Paper presented at the Nordic-Scottish Seminar on Democracy, Aberdeen, May.

Østerud, Øyvind, Fredrik Engelstad, and Per Selle. 2003. *Makten og demokratiet.* Oslo: Gyldendal Norsk Forlag.

Powell, G. Bingham, Jr., and Guy D. Whitten. 1993. "A Cross-National Analysis of Economic Voting: Taking Account of the Political Context." *American Journal of Political Science* 37 (2): 391–414.

Raaum, Nina C. 1995. "The Political Representation of Women: A Bird's Eye View." In Lauri Karvonen and Per Selle, eds., *Women in Nordic Politics: Closing the Gap.* Aldershot: Dartmouth.

Ranney, Austin. 1981. "Candidate Selection." In David Butler, Howard R. Penniman, and Austin Ranney, eds., *Democracy at the Polls.* Washington, DC: American Enterprise Institute.

Rasch, Bjørn Erik. 1994. "Question Time in the Norwegian Storting: Theoretical and Empirical Considerations." In Matti Wiberg, ed., *Parliamentary Control in the Nordic Countries: Forms of Questioning and Behavioural Trends.* Jyväskylä: Finnish Political Science Association.

Rasch, Bjørn Erik. 1998. "Electoral Incentives to Control Government Ministers." Paper presented at the International Conference on the Significance of the Individual Parliamentary Member in Parliamentary Politics, Budapest, July 1–5.

Rasch, Bjørn Erik. 2005. *Electoral Incentives to Control Government Ministers: Questions from Individual Members of the Norwegian Parliament.* Paper presented at the Nordic Political Science Association Conference, Reykjavik, Iceland, August 11–13.

Ray, Leonard, and Hanne Marthe Narud. 2000. "Mapping the Norwegian Political Space: Some Findings from an Expert Survey." *Party Politics* 6 (2): 225–39.

Rokkan, Stein. 1967. "Geography, Religion, and Social Class: Crosscutting Cleavages in Norwegian Politics." In Seymour Martin Lipset and Stein Rokkan, eds., *Party Systems and Voter Alignments.* New York: Free Press.

Rokkan, Stein. 1970. *Citizens, Elections, Parties.* New York: David McKay.

Rommetvedt, Hilmar. 1984. *Borgerlig samarbeid.* Stavanger: Universitetsforlaget.

Rommetvedt, Hilmar. 1991. *Partiavstand og partikoalisjoner,* Doktoravhandling. Universitet i Bergen.

Rommetvedt, Hilmar. 2003. *The Rise of the Norwegian Parliament.* London: Frank Cass.

Saglie, Jo, and Tor Bjørklund, eds. 2005. *Lokalvalg og lokalt folkestyre.* Oslo: Gyldendal Akademisk.

Sejersted, Fredrik. 1996. "The Norwegian Parliament and European Integration: Reflections from Medium Speed Europe." In Eivind Smith, ed., *National Parliaments as Cornerstones of European Integration.* London: Kluwer.

Sejersted, Fredrik. 2000. "Stortingets kontrollfunksjon." *Nytt Norsk Tidsskrift* 17 (2): 173–85.

Shaffer, William R. 1998. *Politics, Parties, and Parliaments: Political Change in Norway.* Columbus: Ohio State University Press.

Skjeie, Helge. 1997. "A Tale of Two Decades: The End of a Male Political Hege-

mony." In Kaare Strøm and Lars Svåsand, eds., *Challenges to Political Parties: The Case of Norway*. Ann Arbor: University of Michigan Press.
Smith, Eivind. 1993. *Høyesterett og folkestyret*. Oslo: Universitetsforlaget.
Smith, Eivind, ed. 1997. *Makt uten ansvar: Om Riksretten i vår tid*. Oslo: TANO.
Smith, Eivind. 2003. "Courts and Parliament: The Norwegian System of Judicial Reviews of Legislation." In Eivind Smith, ed., *The Constitution as an Instrument of Change*. Stockholm: SNS Förlag.
Sørensen, Rune J. 2005. "Et folkestyre i fremgang: Demokratisk kontroll med brannalarmer og autopiloter." *Nytt Norsk Tidsskrift* 22 (3): 258–70.
Stavang, Per. 1968. *Parlamentarisme og maktbalanse*. Oslo: Universitetsforlaget.
Stavang, Per. 1971. "Negativt fleirtal i norsk parlamentarisme." *Lov og rett*, 145–66.
Strøm, Kaare. 1990. *Minority Government and Majority Rule*. Cambridge: Cambridge University Press.
Strøm, Kaare. 1994. "The Presthus Debacle: Intraparty Politics and Bargaining Failure in Norway." *American Political Science Review* 88 (1): 112–27.
Strøm, Kaare, and Torbjörn Bergman. 2005. "Partierna och regeringsmakten." In Marie Demker and Lars Svåsand, eds., *Partiernas århundrade: Fempartimodellens uppgång och fall i Norge och Sverige*. Stockholm: Santèrus Förlag.
Strøm, Kaare, and Jørn Leipart. 1989. "Ideology, Strategy, and Party Competition in Post-war Norway." *European Journal of Political Research* 17 (3): 263–88.
Strøm, Kaare, and Jørn Leipart. 1993. "Policy, Institutions, and Coalition Avoidance: Norwegian Governments, 1945–1990." *American Political Science Review* 87 (4): 870–87.
Strøm, Kaare, and Hanne Marthe Narud. 2003. "Norway: Virtual Parliamentarism." In Kaare Strøm, Wolfgang C. Müller, and Torbjörn Bergman, eds., *Delegation and Accountability in Parliamentary Democracies*. Oxford: Oxford University Press.
Strøm, Kaare, and Lars Svåsand, eds. 1997. *Challenges to Political Parties: The Case of Norway*. Ann Arbor: University of Michigan Press.
Svardal, G. 1994. "Stortinget, regjeringen og statsadministrasjonen." In Tom Christensen and Morten Egeberg, eds., *Forvaltningskunnskap*. 2nd ed. Oslo: TANO.
Svåsand, Lars, Kaare Strøm, and Bjørn Erik Rasch. 1997. "Party Organization." In Kaare Strøm and Lars Svåsand, eds., *Challenges to Political Parties: The Case of Norway*. Ann Arbor: University of Michigan Press.
Torp, Olaf Chr. 1986. *Stortinget i navn og tall: Høsten 1985–våren 1989*. Oslo: Universitetsforlaget.
Torp, Olaf Chr. 1990. *Stortinget i navn og tall: Høsten 1989–våren 1993*. Oslo: Universitetsforlaget.
Torp, Olaf Chr. 1994. *Stortinget i navn og tall: Høsten 1993–våren 1997*. Oslo: Universitetsforlaget.
Valen, Henry. 1981. *Valg og Politikk*. Oslo: NKS-Forlaget.
Valen, Henry. 1988. "Norway: Decentralization and Group Representation." In Michael Gallagher and Michael Marsh, eds., *Candidate Selection in Comparative Perspective: The Secret Garden of Politics*. London: Sage.
Valen, Henry. 1990. "Coalitions and Political Distances." In Risto Sänkiaho, ed., *People and Their Polities*. Helsinki: Finnish Political Science Association.
Valen, Henry. 1999. "Fra klassekamp til kamp om dagsorden." *Nytt Norsk Tidsskrift* 16 (4): 271–84.

Valen, Henry, and Hanne Marthe Narud. 2007a. "The Conditional Party Mandate. A Model for the Study of Political Representation." *European Journal of Political Research* 46 (3): 293–318.

Valen, Henry, and Hanne Marthe Narud. 2007b. "The Storting Election in Norway, September 2005." *Electoral Studies* 26 (1): 219–23.

Valen, Henry, Hanne Marthe Narud, and Audun Skare. 2002. "Norway: Party Dominance and Decentralized Decision-Making." In Hanne Marthe Narud, Mogens N. Pedersen, and Henry Valen, eds., *Party Sovereignty and Citizen Control*. Odense: Odense University Press.

Valen, Henry, and Stein Rokkan. 1974. "Norway: Conflict Structure and Mass Politics in a European Periphery." In Richard Rose, ed., *Electoral Behavior: A Comparative Handbook*. New York: Free Press.

INTERNET SOURCES

Aardal, Bernt. Home page. http://home.online.no/~b-aardal
Arbeiderpartiet. Accessed February 5, 2009. http://www.arbeiderpartiet.no/dna.no/Aps-historie/Organisasjonen/Arbeiderpartiets-medlemstall-1890-2008
Arbeiderpartiet. Home page. http://www.dna.no
Kommunal-og Regionaldepartmentet. 2005. *Valg 2005: Stortingsvalget*. http://odin.dep.no/krd/html/valgresultat2005/frameset.html
Stortinget. Home page. http://www.stortinget.no
Stortinget. *Spørsmål*. Accessed February 5, 2009. http://stortinget.no/Stortinget-og-demokratiet/Arbeidet/Sporreinstituttene
Stortinget. "Statistikk over saker." Accessed February 5, 2009. http://www.stortinget.no/no/Saker-og-publikasjoner/Statistikk-over-saker

7 ✦ Swedish Democracy
Crumbling Political Parties, a Feeble Riksdag, and Technocratic Power Holders?

TORBJÖRN BERGMAN AND NIKLAS BOLIN

Swedish democracy is changing once again. The parliamentary democracy originated with a separation-of-powers system that was far from democratic, but the "working constitution" (in Swedish, "den levande författningen"; see, e.g., Mattson and Petersson 2008) gradually became quite similar to the parliamentary democracy ideal type and the Westminster model. Today, Sweden is on the way back to a separation-of-powers system, but in a new Madisonian form (see chapter 1).

The separation-of-powers constitution, from 1809, remained in force through 1974. It was based on a formal division between, on the one hand, the king and his cabinet and, on the other hand, the Swedish parliament, the Riksdag. However, by 1917, the principle that the political survival of the cabinet rested with the parliamentary majority was firmly established. Over the years that followed, the disparity between the letter of the constitution and constitutional practice continued to grow (Bergman 2003, 2004). The new constitutional practice was eventually further reformed and codified in a new constitution that came into force on January 1, 1975.

The new constitution, the Instrument of Government, proclaims that all public power proceeds from the people (Article 1:1), and it declares that the parliament, the Riksdag, is the foremost representative of the people (Article 1:4). The Riksdag legislates and approves the national budget, and it is the political basis for the cabinet. In this constitutional design, there are few constraints on nationally elected politicians and the political parties that are central to representative democracy.

Since the mid-1970s and increasingly during the last two decades, a new separation-of-powers (or Madisonian) system has emerged. However, this time, the separation and the ongoing power struggle are not between the cabinet and the Riksdag. Rather, the new division of power is between the national center and both the supranational and subnational levels of decision making. It is also between elected politicians and "experts," such as those in the courts or at the central bank. These new divisions function in a way that questions and limits the ability of nationally elected politicians to govern the realm. Yet these developments are not in any direct sense forced on the national political center, as was the case when the king lost out to the parliament almost a century ago. Instead, elected politicians at the national level have actively promoted these developments. In this chapter, we focus on the national political chain in the context of such changes.

The Party System

We start with the party system. The Swedish parties have traditionally been split into two competing blocs—one socialist (left), the other nonsocialist. The left bloc has consisted of the Communist (now Left) Party and the Social Democrats, while the right bloc has included the Liberal, Center, and Conservative (literally, the "Moderate") parties. In 1988, these five established parties were joined in the Riksdag by the Greens. In 1991, the Green Party lost their seats in the parliament, but two other newcomers were elected, the Christian Democratic Party and the populist New Democracy Party. By the 1994 elections, the New Democracy Party had disintegrated, and it lost all its seats in parliament. The Greens returned to parliament, and the Christian Democrats retained their presence in the Riksdag. Table 7.1 shows the vote share of each party over time. The parties are presented according to their position on the left-right scale (pro or con to public ownership), as established in an expert study by Laver and Hunt (1992, 305).

Since 1994, there have been seven parties in the parliament. But beneath the surface, the seven-party system is not perfectly stable (or "frozen"). The Left, Green, Center, Christian Democratic, and Liberal Parties have all, at times, been close to the national threshold of 4 percent of the vote that is needed for a party to get Riksdag seats. In 2008, what most observers label as a populist, right-wing party with anti-immigrant connotations, the Swedish Democrats (Sverigedemokraterna), hovered around this national threshold. Another very important change in the party system is the relative weakening of the previously dominant Social Democratic Party. Including the 2006 election, where they gained only 35 percent of the vote, the Social Democrats have not won over 40 percent in the last three elections. The move from a stable five-party system (until 1988) to a seven- or eight-party system and the decline in the Social Democrats' average vote share has made both legislative politics and government formation more complex. Yet there are both patterns of change and patterns of stability.

Understanding the relative stability of Swedish party politics in the face of the expansion of the party system requires noting some characteristics that remain largely in place. From a comparative perspective, the Swedish political parties are quite centralized, well organized, and unitary (Laver and Schofield 1990, 241). With the exception of the Left Party, they have managed to avoid party splintering. Another characteristic is that some of the parties have close ties to organized interests. In general, the Conservative

TABLE 7.1. Elections to the Swedish Parliament (Riksdagen), 1944–2008

Election Year	Left	SD	Green	Ce	CD	Li	New Dem	Co	Others
1944	10.3	46.7		13.6		12.9		15.9	0.7
1948	6.3	46.1		12.4		22.8		12.3	0.1
1952	4.3	46.1		10.7		24.4		14.4	0.1
1956	5.0	44.6		9.4		23.8		17.1	0.1
1958	3.4	46.2		12.7		18.2		19.5	0.0
1960	4.5	47.8		13.6		17.5		16.5	0.1
1964	5.2	47.3		13.2	1.8	17.0		13.7	1.8
1968	3.0	50.1		15.7	1.5	14.3		12.9	2.6
1970	4.8	45.3		19.9	1.8	16.2		11.5	0.4
1973	5.3	43.6		25.1	1.8	9.4		14.3	0.6
1976	4.8	42.7		24.1	1.4	11.1		15.6	0.4
1979	5.6	43.2		18.1	1.4	10.6		20.3	0.8
1982	5.6	45.6	1.7	15.5	1.9	5.9		23.6	0.2
1985[a]	5.4	44.7	1.5	12.4	—	14.2		21.3	0.5
1988	5.8	43.2	5.5	11.3	2.9	12.2		18.3	0.7
1991	4.5	37.7	3.4	8.5	7.1	9.1	6.7	21.9	1.0
1994	6.2	45.3	5.0	7.7	4.1	7.2		22.4	2.3
1998	12.0	36.4	4.5	5.1	11.7	4.7		22.9	2.6
2002	8.4	39.9	4.6	6.2	9.1	13.4		15.3	3.1
2006	5.9	35.0	5.2	7.9	6.6	7.5		26.2	5.7

Source: Data from *Allmänna valen* (2003); Valmyndigheten 2006b, http://www.val.se.

Notes: The Swedish parliament was bicameral until 1969. The results presented here are the results for the second chamber until 1968 and for the unicameral parliament in the following elections. Numbers in table represent vote shares in percentages. Dash (—) indicates that the CD did not contest the election in 1985 as an independent party. Party abbreviations are as follows: Left = Left Party (Vänsterpartiet); SD = Social Democrats (Arbetarepartiet—Socialdemokraterna); Green = Green Party (Miljöpartiet de gröna); Ce = Center Party (Centern); CD = Christian Democratic Party (Kristdemokraterna); Li = Liberal Party (Folkpartiet liberalerna); New Dem = New Democracy (Ny Demokrati); Co = Conservative Party (Moderata samlingspartiet); Others = Other parties.

[a]The election result in 1985 includes a technical electoral alliance between the Center Party (Ce) and the Christian Democratic Party (CD), and so the percentage vote share for Ce in 1985 presents the *joint* results for the two parties.

Party has been close to organized business, and the Center Party remains strong among organized farmers. Most of the editorial pages of the daily press support the Liberal Party (Birgersson and Westerståhl 1992). Since the 1960s, however, this support has usually exceeded the party's popularity as measured in terms of electoral strength. In terms of membership and organization, the closest link has been between the Social Democratic Party and organized labor, particularly the national federation for blue-collar workers, the Swedish Trade Union Confederation (Landsorganisationen).

The continued relevance of the left-right split is sometimes questioned, but it remains the most dominant party conflict in party politics. Crosscutting cleavages based on language, religion, or regions are less significant in Sweden than in most other West European countries. To the extent that there has been a single, stable, and important alternative dimension, its poles are perhaps best labeled economic growth versus green politics. This dimension has manifested itself differently over time. Its roots go back to an urban-agrarian conflict, with agrarian interests represented by the Center Party. In the 1960s and 1970s, it broadened to become a more general center-periphery dimension that included issues such as decentralization, particularly of the public sector (Back and Berglund 1978). Over time, the alternative dimension also came to reflect a growing concern for green or environmental values. Typically, both the Left and the Center parties have been seen as representatives of the ecology position in Swedish politics (Vedung 1979, 170). Nowadays there is also a party in parliament (the Greens) that claims particular ownership of "sustainable development," but all parties argue that they have good environmental programs. Similarly, all Swedish parliamentary parties proclaim themselves to be "feminist" in some fashion.

While dominant, the content of the left-right dimension has also changed over time. Early on, in the late 1940s, the left-right debate was about the benefits and drawbacks of centralized economic planning. Since then, it has focused on mandatory public pension funds (late 1950s–early 1960s) and the buyout of private stocks using union-controlled funds, the so-called wage-earner funds debate from the late 1970s and early 1980s. The size of the public sector and the (high) level of taxation are issues that currently split left and right into two distinct blocs. This line of conflict has been salient in election campaigns, in general political rhetoric, and in cabinet formation. At the same time, parliamentary decision making and day-to-day politics are often carried out under the banner of consensus, and the Social Democrats and the Conservatives, the two main competitors, often and perhaps increasingly find that they agree on economic growth, military defense, and the proper Swedish relationship toward the European Union.

On the basis of developments that include new parties, a changing left-right dimension, and a weakening of the Social Democrats, one could perhaps expect that the two-bloc split would fade away. But formalized cooperation between the Social Democrats and its support parties, the Left and the Greens, from 1998 and 2006 reaffirmed the applicability of Ruin's (1968) modified two-party system model, which is akin to the Westminster model.[1] In 2006, the two-bloc split got additional nourishment from the preelectoral alliance formed by the four center-right parties (Aylott and Bolin 2007). For the first time ever, the nonsocialist parties worked out a *detailed* joint program and campaigned on it. In the name of the "Alliance," the Conservative Party even refrained from issuing its own election manifesto and instead ran on the Alliance manifesto.

But while the national party system is alive and well at the level of the cabinet and the parliament, its foundations in the citizenry are weakening. The picture is not all gloomy, but there are areas of concern for those who favor the Westminster model. For one thing, the political parties rely on the taxpayers for their funding. Swedish political parties have received public financing since 1966 (Gidlund 1983; Pierre and Widfeldt 1992). For a few years, only parties with seats in parliament were eligible for such funding. However, since 1972, all parties that get more than 2.5 percent of the national vote also receive public support, as do parties that have recently lost all their seats in the Riksdag (regardless of election performance). The increase in public support has been dramatic in recent years but has also tended to favor elected representatives and party groups rather than the party organization itself (Bolin 2007). In 2005, the parties at the national level received just over 362 million Swedish kronor (SEK),[2] a figure that includes support for assistants to MPs. In 2006, total public subsidies at the regional level were slightly lower, while local-level funding was at least 100 million kronor higher (Lantto 2008, 7). This means that the combined financial support for political party organizations, MP assistants, and other support for elected representatives at all three levels of government is a sizable expense for the taxpayers.

Despite this generous funding, political parties have run into problems. One indicator of this is declining party membership. The share of the population holding party membership used to be very high. In the mid-1980s, the political parties had more than 1,600,000 members. The Social Democratic Party alone reported more than 1,200,000 members out of a population of a little more than eight million, in part because of the party's practice

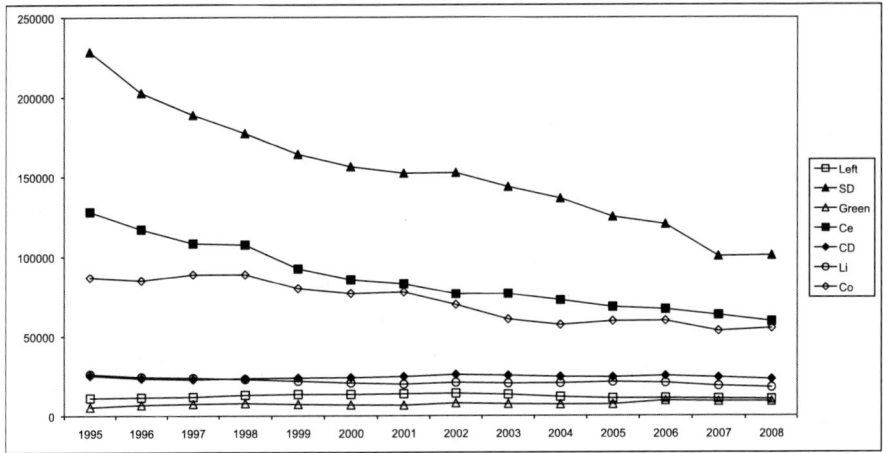

Fig. 7.1. Party membership in Sweden, 1995–2008. See table 7.1 for explanation of party labels.

of allowing local unions to register their members collectively as party members. Unsurprisingly, membership in political parties declined dramatically in the early 1990s, when the Social Democratic Party, under pressure from opposition parties and union members, abolished this practice of collective party membership. But the decline has also continued beyond that event. As figure 7.1 shows, all parties have continued to lose members. Some of the parties manage to maintain basically the same number of party members, at least in election years, but the three parties that have had the most members—the Social Democrats, the Center Party, and the Conservatives—continue to suffer losses.

Membership decline is not the only way in which the relationship between parties and citizens has changed. The problems of party democracy have also been reflected in electoral turnout (see table 7.2, column 2). Although voting is not mandatory, turnout levels were over 90 percent in the four elections between 1973 and 1982. The highest turnout was in 1976, when 91.8 percent of eligible voters cast votes. Turnout has tended to decline in recent elections, falling from 86.8 percent in 1994 to 81.4 percent in 1998 and 80.1 percent in 2002. This is the lowest for any election since the extra election in 1958, when turnout was 77.4 percent ("Allmänna valen" 2003). The trend was slightly reversed in 2006, when turnout rose to 82 percent. Interestingly, turnout has not declined if compared to the 1950s. Turnout began to rise around 1960, just after the parties split into two distinct blocs over the issue of mandatory public pension funds (see Molin 1965).

Other common indicators of party-based democracy also show a weakening of the ties between voters and parties. Since the 1960s, there has been a decline in the extent to which parties of the left attract primarily working-class votes (the Alford index). Initially, the drop was drastic. Since the 1970s,

TABLE 7.2. Strength of Party Attachment in Sweden, 1944–2008

Election Year	Turnout (%)	Class Voting (Alford index)[a]	Share of Voters with Party Identification as a "Supporter" of a Particular Party (%)	Share of Voters that Changed Party from the Last Election (%)	Share of Voters Changing Bloc between Elections (%)	Share of Voters Deciding Which Party to Vote for during the Election Campaign (%)	Distrust of Politicians (%)[b]
1944	71.9						
1948	82.7						
1952	79.1						
1956	79.8	51					
1958	77.4						
1960	85.9	55		11.4	5.3		
1964	83.9	46		12.8	5.2	18	
1968	89.3	38	65	13.7	5.5	23	46
1970	88.3	35	64	16.0	5.9	26	
1973	90.8	46	60	16.0	6.6	27	53
1976	91.8	36	61	19.1	7.2	28	58
1979	90.7	38	59	18.1	5.4	29	63
1982	91.4	37	60	19.5	6.2	33	60
1985	89.9	34	53	19.2	5.6	39	63
1988	86.0	30	51	20.2	6.8	40	65
1991	86.7	25	48	30.0	11.8	51	70
1994	86.8	30	47	29.2	12.5	49	72
1998	81.4	29	42	30.7	8.3	57	75
2002	80.1	26	40	31.8	8.7	57	65
2006	82.0	25	31	37.1	11.8	58	61

Source: Data from *Allmänna valen* (2003); *Allmänna valen* (2008), http://www.scb.se; Holmberg and Oscarsson 2004, 249; Oscarsson and Holmberg 2008, 22, 25, 39, 225, 239; Valmyndigheten 2006b, http://www.val.se. Distrust of Politicians percentage for 2006: E-mail correspondence with the Swedish Election Studies Program, April 19, 2009.

[a] The Alford index is based on the difference between the vote share for the parties on the left (in this case the Left and Social Democratic Parties) among the working class (measured by occupation) and the vote share for the same parties among the middle class. A higher index implies that working-class voters vote for the parties on the left to a greater extent than do middle-class voters.

[b] Distrust of politicians = Voters answering "yes" to the statement "MPs do not pay much attention to the views of ordinary people." ("De som sitter i riksdagen och beslutar tar inte mycket hänsyn till vad vanligt folk tycker och tänker.") The question about distrust was not included in the 1970 election survey.

there has been more of a steady decline in class-based voting. For all parties, the decline in party identification is more recent. A first drop occurred in the mid-1980s and another one in the late 1990s.

Adding to the picture is the increase in the share of voters who wait to decide what party to vote for until the final weeks leading up to the election. Also noteworthy is that most of the volatility occurs within the two blocs rather than across them. Based on available survey data, it seems that bloc switching reached double-digit numbers only three times: during the large electoral swings in favor of the right in 1991, back to the left in 1994, and again in favor of the right (the Alliance) in 2006. In other elections, fewer than 10 percent of voters have switched from one bloc to another between two consecutive elections. The long trend of increasing distrust of politicians is another cause for concern. However, on both accounts, turnout and distrust, the 2006 election went against the general trend, as turnout went up while the level of distrust went down (for the second election in a row).

At the same time, surveys indicate that citizen activities outside the political parties seem to be on the rise. Although people have become less inclined to join a party, a greater share of the population reports having been active on a particular issue and/or having participated in a demonstration or some other form of civic participation. Less positively, the group of citizens who say they do nothing "political" and who do not associate themselves with a political party has been growing over the years (Holmberg 2000, 52–55).

Some observers argue that there has been an "Americanization" of election campaigns. While there seems to be no precise definition of this concept, it refers to such developments as a popularization of political content that emphasizes a few individuals, the rise in use of public relations consultants, a more candidate-based electoral system, and the increased use of mass media for political communication. A sign of this may be the television commercials for political parties that appeared on national broadcast TV for the first time in the campaign for the upcoming European Parliament elections in the spring of 2009. Nonetheless, in most respects, Sweden still conforms more to a traditional style of party-based, rather than individualistic, campaigning (Petersson et al. 2006).

Overall, despite some problematic trends, party decline should not be exaggerated. The parties remain well organized and open to membership influence, at least in cross-national comparison. Their organizations outside of parliament are far from being only a "transmission belt" for elected politicians (Sannerstedt and Sjölin 1994; Widfeldt 1997; Aylott 2003). At the same time, current challenges to political parties are many and profound (see also, e.g., Petersson et al. 2000).

The Democratic Chain

In this section, we take a closer look at the national democratic chain from voters to the state bureaucracy. We conceptualize the chain in terms of four relationships of delegation and accountability: between voters and parliament, between parliament and cabinet, within the cabinet, and between the cabinet and civil servants. In each section, we discuss constitutional rules as well as other closely related laws—for example, the election law. We begin the analysis by introducing how votes are transposed into party seats and voting power in parliament.

From Voters to Parliament

The constitution and the separate election law specify electoral rules and procedures rather than how parties are to organize and behave. Political parties are free to regulate themselves in many areas. For example, there is no legislation covering primaries, term limits, or mandatory retirement age. Similarly, there are no regulations about the length of electoral campaigns or any legal limits on campaign spending (Bergman 2003; Pierre and Widfeldt 1992; Bäck and Möller 2003).

Swedish parties nominate candidates at local and regional party conferences. They can also use nonbinding primaries (*provval*) in which members vote on a preliminary list of candidates. This method was rather unusual 30 years ago but is quite common today (SOU 1972; Back and Berglund 1978, 103–8; Pierre and Widfeldt 1992, 817–18; Bäck and Möller 2003). Generally, the national party level has had little say in candidate selection. Although party elites sometimes ask regional-level party organizations to place a particular candidate high on the party's list of candidates, such requests are not always granted. One general exception to the regional constituency's autonomy in candidate selection is that, in the last two decades, all national parties have begun to promote gender equality on the party lists. The proportion of women elected to the Riksdag has been above 30 percent since 1985 and above 40 percent since the 1994 election. In 2006, more than 47 percent of elected MPs were women (Riksdagen 2006b). But since this norm is firmly established at both the constituency level and at the level of the central party in most parties, the general calls to promote female candidates does not seem to promote much dissonance between different levels of the political parties.

When regional party organizations select candidates, other social background characteristics are also important. These include long service in the local and regional party and place of residence (geographic location) within the regional constituency. In addition, parties often try to obtain balanced lists with regard to characteristics such as age and ethnicity (Aylott 2005a). Parties also have their own traditions and principles for candidate selection. For example, a trade union career has been meritorious for Social Democrats (Andrén 1968, 70–74; Birgersson and Westerståhl 1992). Once elected, members of parliament are held accountable at the regional and local levels of the party organization. If regional or local party members and party boards are displeased with the performance of a particular MP, they can demote or remove this person from the (regional) constituency list in the next election. In practice, however, a candidate who is highly ranked in one election tends to remain at the top of her or his party's constituency list.

A recent development, discernible from the 1980s and growing in strength, is the emergence of a debate about the need to and benefits of opening up candidate nominations to individuals who are not formally party members but who sympathize with the party. This issue has mainly received attention within a few parties (notably within the Left Party and the Liberals), but the argument has had a larger following. The support apparently stems from a growing belief that the parties are closed, stagnant organizations that need new, fresh blood.

Since the 1998 parliamentary election, in addition to casting a vote for a party, voters can also choose (check) a candidate on that party's list. If a particular candidate's individual preference vote is 8 percent or more of the party's total vote share in one of the 29 constituencies, that candidate moves to the top of the party's list in that constituency (the list otherwise remains unchanged). If more than one candidate gets more than 8 percent, the one with the most preference votes moves to the top of the list and fills the party's first seat in that constituency. In the 1998 elections, about 30 percent of voters used the preference vote, but most of them went to candidates already at the top of the party list. In 2002, somewhat fewer voters used the preference vote (26 percent). Moreover, of those elected on preference votes, almost all would otherwise have been elected on the basis of the party list. Data from the 1998 elections show that the direct effect of preference voting was that 12 (of 349) members of parliament were elected instead of candidates ranked higher on their parties' lists (SOU 1999). The corresponding number for 2002 was ten MPs (Blomgren 2003, 107). In the 2006 election, only 22 percent of voters used the opportunity to vote for a particular candidate (Valmyndigheten 2006b), and only six candidates won seats as a consequence of preference voting (*Riksdag & Departement* 2006a). Preference votes are fairly equally distributed among men and women. In 2002,

43 percent of these votes were cast for female candidates, and the corresponding figure for 2006 was 41 percent ("Allmänna valen" 2003; Valmyndigheten 2006a).

Based on the results of the three national elections since preference voting was introduced, it thus appears that the reform has not been all that popular among voters. A study by Davidsson (2006) also raises questions about the usefulness of reforms that can further weaken the political party organizations. Davidsson argues that the preference vote makes it harder for voters to hold the politicians accountable for their actions. The preference vote encourages candidates to cultivate a distinct political profile, one not necessarily in line with their party. Such a development calls for the creation of mechanisms for personal accountability, something that the Swedish electoral system presently lacks.

Davidsson (2006) also found that while reforms such as preference voting for individual candidates have had little effect on parliamentary behavior, there is an important generational effect. Younger MPs tend to have less respect for party discipline and are more inclined to vote or propose bills that are not entirely in keeping with the party's position on an issue. One might suspect that this has something to do with being a newly elected MP, but the relationship holds up even when controlling for tenure. In other words, younger MPs who have served longer are more freewheeling than older MPs in their first or second term.

From the perspective of the voters, another drawback of the new system may be that it gives the formal party hierarchy full control over the party list. In previous elections, competing lists with the same party label could determine MP selection. Today, if political parties register to protect their names (something that all the major parties do), only the formal party organization at the relevant level can nominate candidates (i.e., present party lists). In addition, the new electoral system does not allow voters to add or cross out candidates, which was allowed under the previous system (albeit with no practical effect at the national level). Consequently, although it gives voters a greater role in choosing candidates from parties' lists, the new rule also gives party organizations stricter control over ballot access in the first place.

Nonetheless, the overall behavior of MPs has not changed much (yet). Once elected, they primarily see themselves more as party representatives than as representatives of their constituency. The main concern of MPs is national-level policy-making, and constituency interests are seen as a complementary concern (Esaiasson and Holmberg 1996; Bäck and Möller 2003, 112). In practice, the parliamentary party groups are both cohesive and influential in shaping the policies that MPs promote (Hagevi 1999; Isberg 1999). Thus, MP behavior is shaped more firmly by interparty competition and parliamentary (group) procedures than by the constituency link. However, in this context, it is also interesting to note that since the early 1990s, there has been a dramatic increase in MP turnover. Both during mandate periods and at general elections, more parliamentarians choose to leave the Riksdag. One reason might be the extension of the mandate period from three to four years starting with the 1994 elections. However, another, more important reason is a change in the attitude about the role of a parliamentarian. Many MPs refer to problems they have experienced with regard to party discipline and describe their frustration with having to toe the party line on so many issues (Hermansson, Ahlbäck Öberg, and Wängnerud 2007, 211).

Linking Parliament to Cabinet

We now turn to an examination of the rules and activities that link parliament to cabinet formation and of the role of both the legislature and the executive in national level policy-making.

The Formation Process

Before 1975, the Swedish cabinet formation rules were an example of classic "negative parliamentarism" (Bergman 1993), and a new cabinet could come to power even if it was only tolerated by a parliamentary majority rather than actively supported by one. It was common that the Social Democrats simply remained in power after a mandatory election. No bargaining process was initiated; no votes were held. The end result was usually a foregone conclusion—the Social Democratic party leader retained the post as prime minister. The process was made even easier by the fact this was the same person—Tage Erlander—during the entire period from 1946 to 1969.

Compared to other countries with negative parliamentarism, Swedish formation rules since 1975 have been unusual in two ways. First, the head of state (the monarch) is excluded from the cabinet formation process (Bergman 1999). Second, Sweden has a "negative" investiture vote in the Riksdag. The speaker proposes a candidate for PM, and before a new cabinet can assume power, a vote must be held. The speaker's candidate succeeds unless more than half of the members of the Riksdag (175 MPs) vote against her or him. In fact, all candidates proposed by the speaker since 1975 have been approved on the first vote.

Partly as a result of its institutional context of negative parliamentarism,

Sweden has a long tradition of minority cabinets. From World War II through 2009, there were a total of 28 different cabinets. Only six of these excluded the Social Democrats, and in 19 of the remaining 22 cabinets, the Social Democratic Party governed alone. The only single-party cabinet that did not include the Social Democrats was a short-lived cabinet formed by the Liberal Party in 1978–79. Two minority coalitions led by Fälldin (Center, Liberal), in 1981, and Bildt (Conservative, Liberal, Center, and Christian Democratic), in 1991, make the list of minority cabinets even longer (see table 7.3).

Table 7.3 demonstrates the crucial importance of the median legislator. Its electoral support and its frequent position as the median legislator party on the dominant (left-right) dimension explains much of the Social Democratic Party's success in winning and holding on to political power. Taken together, the rules of the game of cabinet formation, the seat distribution among the parties (especially the size of the Social Democratic Party), the importance of the median legislator (which stems from the predominantly unidimensional party system), and strong competition for votes between and within the blocs help explain the historical record of cabinet formation in Sweden. In the 1990s and 2000s, however, changes in the party system and parliamentary procedures have provided incentives for the "opposition" parties within the socialist bloc (a bloc that, in practice, has turned out to include the Greens) to assume a new role. This spurred developments that probably helped facilitate the four-party alliance in 2006.

Support Parties

The most important basis for cabinet formation is party size (in terms of seats) and strategic position on the most important policy dimension within the parliament. However, there is no immediate correspondence between this and the outcome of the bargaining process. An additional crucial element is institutional design. An important part of the explanation for why the median legislator party can often form a cabinet without controlling a majority of seats in the Riksdag is that negative parliamentarism facilitates the existence of support parties. A support party is one that behaves in a way that directly contributes to the existence of a minority cabinet, whether its behavior favors a cabinet by vote or abstention (Bergman 1995).

In the context of negative parliamentarism, the votes of support parties are not needed to reach a constitutionally defined majority threshold. Because of this, support parties will often find themselves in a situation of having to choose not between whether or not to join a cabinet but between whether or not to vote against a proposed cabinet that includes the median

TABLE 7.3. Cabinets in Sweden, 1945–2008

Cabinet Number	Prime Minister	Date (yymmdd)	Cabinet Share (%) of Parliamentary Seats	Effective Number of Legislative Parties[a]	Median Legislator Party	Parties in Cabinet	Majority Cabinets Single-Party	Majority Cabinets Coalition[b]	Minority Cabinets[c] Single-Party	Minority Cabinets[c] Coalition
1	Hansson	450731	50.0	3.1	SD	SD			X	
2	Erlander I	461011	50.0	3.1	SD	SD			X	
3	Erlander II	480919	48.7	3.1	SD	SD			X	
4	Erlander III	511001	61.7	2.1	SD	SD, Ce		X		
5	Erlander IV	520921	59.1	3.1	SD, Ce	SD, Ce		X		
6	Erlander V	560926	54.1	3.2	Ce	SD, Ce		X		
7	Erlander VI	571031	45.9	3.2	Ce	SD			X	
8	Erlander VII	580601	48.1	3.2	SD	SD			X	
9	Erlander VIII	600918	49.1	3.1	SD	SD			X	
10	Erlander IX	640920	48.5	3.2	SD	SD			X	
11	Erlander X	680915	53.6	2.8	SD	SD	X			
12	Palme I	691014	53.6	2.8	SD	SD	X			
13	Palme II	700920	46.6	3.3	SD	SD			X	
14	Palme III	730916	44.6	3.4	SD, Ce	SD			X	
15	Fälldin I	761007	51.6	3.5	Ce	Ce, Li, Co		X		
16	Ullsten	781013	11.2	3.5	Ce	Li			X	

#	Cabinet	Date	%	ENP[a]	Party	Coalition	Majority[b]	Minority[c]	Surplus
17	Fälldin II	791011	50.1	3.5	Ce	Ce, Li, Co	X		
18	Fälldin III	810519	29.2	3.5	Ce	Ce, Li		X	
19	Palme IV	821007	47.6	3.1	SD	SD		X	
20	Palme V	850915	45.6	3.4	SD	SD		X	
21	Carlsson I	860312	45.6	3.4	SD	SD		X	
22	Carlsson II	880918	44.7	3.7	SD	SD		X	
23	Bildt	911003	48.7	4.2	Ce	Co, Ce, CD, Li			X
24	Carlsson III	941006	46.1	3.5	SD	SD		X	
25	Persson I	960321	46.1	3.5	SD	SD		X	
26	Persson II	980920	37.5	4.3	Green	SD		X	
27	Persson III	020915	41.3	4.2	Green	SD		X	
28	Reinfeldt	061005	51.0	4.1	Ce	Co, Ce, CD, Li	X		

Source: Data from Bergman 2003; Valmyndigheten 2005, http://www.val.se, and 2006b, http://www.val.se; Widfeldt 2007, 1121. Data on Cabinet Persson III and Cabinet Reinfeldt from authors' own calculations.

Note: See table 7.1 for explanation of party labels.

[a] Effective number of legislative parties: This index was developed by Markku Laakso and Rein Taagepera and is a measure of party system size. Both the number of parties and their relative sizes are taken into account. For an accessible introduction, see Lijphart 1984.

[b] Majority cabinet coalitions can be either minimal winning (mwc—a coalition that cannot lose a party and still be "winning") or a surplus coalition (a coalition that can lose one or more parties and still be winning).

[c] Minority cabinets control 50% or less of all seats in parliament.

legislator party. To strengthen its bargaining position, a support party must be able to credibly threaten to actively vote against the median legislator party. If it cannot, then the cabinet party can rely on the support party without granting any concessions. The weak bargaining position of support parties helps explain why political parties in Sweden, compared to those in many other countries, take less time to form a cabinet and more often form minority cabinets.

Note that support arrangements can vary. Before the 1990s, the Social Democrats could trust the Left Party to keep them in power without the latter raising specific demands for policy concessions. The Social Democrats often governed by forming ad hoc legislative coalitions with one or more of the nonsocialist parties on particular policy decisions. The Left Party grew increasingly frustrated with the assumption that it would never actively reject a Social Democratic government. In 1982, after the Social Democrats had returned to power, the Left Party occasionally threatened to sink Social Democratic proposals in parliament. At the same time, the Left Party was explicitly committed to oppose the formation of any nonsocialist cabinet. This meant that the Social Democrats still could always count on the Left Party votes if their position as government party was threatened. However, a Left Party refusal to support an austerity package in the early 1990s put a huge dent in that belief and prepared the way for a decade of "contract parliamentarism," a topic that we will return to after we consider the reform of the budget process that also took place in the 1990s.

Budget Reform

A new set of rules and principles for the handling of the state budget was introduced in 1996 (Mattson 2000). A serious problem with state finances in the early 1990s was a major reason behind the reform. The national budget process in parliament was widely seen as prolonged and badly coordinated. It also encouraged increased spending, since the parliament never actually took a decision on the whole budget but, rather, decided on each spending item in a separate vote, making it susceptible to piecemeal changes (particularly increases). Since the reform, the Riksdag has used a top-down budget process in which it first sets spending targets for total central government expenditures and then, several months later, holds one final vote on the budget. This generally means that if the opposition parties are split but control a majority of the seats, they must agree on one single budget alternative in order to prevail over the government proposal. In practice, this has given minority cabinets better control over the budget process. It also means that a government that loses a vote on the budget suffers a significant loss of prestige and will have a difficult time continuing in office (Mattson 2008). This has encouraged cabinets to secure budget agreements with one or more opposition parties well in advance of the final vote. This, in turn, contributed to the emergence of a decade (1995–2006) of "contract parliamentarism" (Aylott and Bergman 2004).

The Decade of Contract Parliamentarism

Across-bloc parliamentary cooperation between the Social Democrats and the Center Party from 1995 to 1998 stabilized the Swedish budget and helped ensure budget reform in parliamentary procedures. However, both parties suffered a major loss of votes and seats in the 1998 elections, and the Social Democrats subsequently turned to the Left and the Green parties for support. Without forming a formal cabinet coalition, the three parties agreed to cooperate on economic and financial issues. In a media release dated October 5, 1998 (Statsrådsberedningen 1998), they announced that they had reached agreement on a support arrangement for five specific policy areas: the economy (the state budget), employment, distributive justice, gender equality, and the environment. They did not formally commit to cooperating on other issues but stated their intention to work together for the full electoral period.

In the run-up to the next election, in 2002, both the Left Party and the Greens were highly critical of these support arrangements. These parties complained that the situation disadvantaged them relative to the Social Democrats, not least because it left too much of the agenda-setting power (and media coverage) to the cabinet ministers. Both parties demanded cabinet positions after the 2002 election (Olsen 2007). But the Social Democrats refused, and the support parties backed down. Instead, the new deal became known as the "121-points program" (Finansdepartementet 2003). Organized under eleven headings, the parties listed 121 items that they planned to implement together. In a move reminiscent of the Center Party's cooperation with the Social Democrats in 1995 and different from the three parties' first agreement for 1998–2002, both the Left Party and the Greens were allowed to appoint a limited number (eight each) of high-ranking political appointees to government ministries. This method of ensuring cabinet support from support parties through the use of formal agreements is quite different from support arrangements used prior to the 1994 elections.

The existence of a minority cabinet with solid support from two parties ensured a stable majority in parliament. This cabinet was replaced by a majority coalition in 2006. This means that Sweden has not had an old-fashioned ("pure") minority cabinet since shortly after the 1994 elections.

TABLE 7.4. Parliamentary Activities, Sweden, 1979–2008

Year	Number of Bills Sent from the Cabinet to Parliament (*propositioner*)	Number of Bills Submitted from Members of Parliament (*motioner*)[a]	Number of Individual Proposals in the Bills Submitted from Members of Parliament	Number of Decided Individual Proposals in the Bills Submitted from Members of Parliament (regardless when submitted)	Number of Individual Proposals in the Bills Submitted from Members of Parliament Approved or Partly Approved by the Riksdag[b]	Number of Plenary Hours in Parliament	Number of Votes That Actually Involved the Counting of Individual MP Votes[c]
1979–80	179	2,080				597	1,010
1980–81	207	2,218				586	1,378
1981–82	229	2,572				658	1,664
1982–83	177	2,439				591	934
1983–84	202	2,985				631	1,015
1984–85	225	3,245				634	894
1985–86	178	3,329				567	932
1986–87	168	3,767	9,500			609	1,058
1987–88	179	4,029	8,985			650	1,285
1988–89	153	4,429	10,088			610	1,148
1989–90	159	4,849	12,488	15,446	1,014	688	1,275
1990–91	183	4,989	13,102	16,454	1,222	668	1,294
1991–92	165	3,095	6,591	8,418	387	560	739
1992–93	246	3,667	8,371	9,622	534	633	1,038
1993–94	227	3,029	7,808	9,295	692	618	1,055
1994–95	203	2,969	9,268	7,867	485	525	790
1995–96	207	735	2,777	4,414	164	461	684
1996–97	147	2,951	9,604	8,879	262	609	1,044
1997–98	153	3,272	11,035	11,569	359	638	1,232
1998–99	147	2,513	7,966	7,164	287	524	792
1999–2000	149	3,211	8,892	8,640	224	615	844
2000–2001	151	3,675	10,055	9,948	243	652	843
2001–2	190	4,231	12,420	14,230	372	652	1,059
2002–3	151	3,538	10,366	8,273	115	551	835
2003–4	181	3,991	12,045	11,968	189	602	884
2004–5	178	4,167	11,734	11,095	215	730	766
2005–6	215	4,824	14,794	17,834	287	681	912
2006–7	133	2,617	5,914	5,282	18	645	529
2007–8	168	3,577	7,555	6,876	11	758	n.d.

Source: Data from Riksdagen 2003, 2006a, 2008a; Riksdagen (2002, 2005b, 2005c, 2008b, 2008c: http://riksdagen.se) e-mail correspondence with the Riksdag Research Service (Riksdagens utredningstjänst [RUT]), March 11, 2009.

Note: This table does not include questions and interpellations. n.d. = "no data."

[a] Private member bills (*motioner*) can either be in the form of amendments to government proposals (and must then be clearly related to the government proposal) or submitted during a period of "any bill goes" when the MPs can propose anything they like, as long that the subject matter falls under the jurisdiction of the parliament. This period takes place for a few weeks at the beginning of the parliamentary session. There was no such general period for private member bills during 1995–96 (because of a large-scale reform of the budget process), which helps account for the low number of *motioner* in that period.

TABLE 7.4—Continued

[b]For comparison, note also that very few government bills do not pass through parliament; e.g., in 2002–3 only 9 individual proposals from a few government bills did not make it all the way (see Riksdagen 2003, 76). That parliamentary year, 151 government bills were submitted, and a very rough estimate (mostly a guess) is that each such cabinet bill includes on average of something like 10 proposals. That implies that more than 99% of all government proposals were approved by parliament that same year. This is probably a conservative figure for that year.

[c]Most Riksdag decisions (votes) are made through a simplified process in which the Speaker simply asks the chamber if the MPs approve or disapprove of the proposal at hand. Individual votes are not counted unless a MP requests such a count. It is only when a vote count is requested (by any MP) that the positions of the individual MPs are recorded. Thus, the column "Number of votes that actually involved the counting of individual MP Votes" only applies to a subset of all parliamentary "votes."

This raises the question of how parliamentarians can control and monitor minority and majority cabinets.

Parliament and Cabinet in the National Policy-Making Process

For most parliaments and cabinets in most periods, cabinet proposals (*propositioner*) dominate the parliamentary decision-making process. This is also true in Sweden. Table 7.4 shows that the numbers of such proposals have remained fairly stable over the last two decades. The number of private bills (*motioner*) has fluctuated, largely due to increases the year before an election and increases when the cabinet has held a less stable majority in parliament. A similar pattern of flux is visible in the number of private member bills that are approved and the number of parliamentary voting rounds that are decided by a vote count. The number of plenary hours of the chamber has fluctuated somewhat, but there is no trend up or down. What has changed the most is the number of interpellations and questions that MPs put to cabinet ministers (see table 7.5). This is one of the ways in which MPs can hold cabinet ministers accountable (Andrén 1968; Holmberg and Stjernquist 1980; Sterzel 1998, 220–23).

The constitution gives an MP the right to ask the cabinet questions and to inquire about government affairs. In the 1990s, attempts were made to make the debates livelier, and there are now three types of questions. One form of scrutiny by questioning, introduced in 1991, is the weekly, televised session in which oral questions are answered directly by a subset of ministers. Members of parliament also have the right to ask written questions and interpellations. Since 1996, written questions are only answered in writing, while an interpellation might prompt a debate in parliament. If so, an MP has the right to debate with a minister on any issue that falls within the latter's area of responsibility (Holmberg and Stjernquist 2000, 201–2; see also Riksdagen 1991, 20–23; Konstitutionsutskottet 1996, 18).

Table 7.5 presents separate data on MP interpellations and questions from the government parties, as distinct from those from opposition parties. The interest and energy that MPs demonstrate in this type of parliamentary scrutiny activity usually vary depending on whether the MP belongs to a government or opposition party. Opposition MPs are much keener to show that they are active. However, a fair share of the MPs from the government party (or parties) also finds this a useful way to perhaps influence policy and/or to show the voters back home that they are active on their behalf. There has been an increase in such questioning from MPs from cabinet parties during periods of coalition cabinets relative to periods of single-

TABLE 7.5. Interpellations and Questions to Cabinet Ministers, Sweden, 1979–2008

Year	Parties in Cabinet	Interpellations	Interpellations from Opposition (%)	Questions	Questions from Opposition (%)
1979–80	Ce, Li, Co	197	109 (55)	540	311 (58)
1980–81	Ce, Li, Co	138	77 (56)	443	240 (54)
1981–82	Ce, Li	187	164 (88)	426	313 (73)
1982–83	SD	138	120 (87)	559	499 (89)
1983–84	SD	154	140 (91)	609	555 (91)
1984–85	SD	151	140 (93)	624	564 (90)
1985–86	SD	216	200 (93)	613	541 (88)
1986–87	SD	253	230 (91)	618	n.d.
1987–88	SD	260	245 (94)	535	481 (90)
1988–89	SD	235	216 (92)	690	632 (92)
1989–90	SD	169	151 (89)	681	622 (91)
1990–91	SD	206	180 (87)	691	618 (89)
1991–92	Ce, CD, Li, Co	195	108 (55)	858	523 (61)
1992–93	Ce, CD, Li, Co	180	116 (64)	774	407 (53)
1993–94	Ce, CD, Li, Co	149	115 (77)	580	328 (57)
1994–95	SD	154	133 (86)	736	624 (85)
1995–96	SD	261	227 (87)	718	544 (76)
1996–97	SD	372	336 (90)	839	619 (74)
1997–98	SD	313	295 (94)	1,103	924 (84)
1998–99	SD	370	337 (91)	991	848 (86)
1999–2000	SD	415	384 (93)	1,413	1,182 (84)
2000–2001	SD	457	409 (89)	1,698	1,464 (86)
2001–2	SD	497	453 (91)	1,643	1,495 (91)
2002–3	SD	417	395 (95)	1,375	1,118 (81)
2003–4	SD	551	423 (77)	1,616	1,071 (66)
2004–5	SD	688	655 (95)	2,197	1,900 (86)
2005–6	SD	479	391 (82)	2,144	1,599 (75)
2006–7	Ce, CD, Li, Co	695	596 (86)	1,658	1,019 (61)
2007–8	Ce, CD, Li, Co	844	787 (93)	1,655	1,111 (67)

Source: Data from Riksdagen 1986, 2008a; Riksdagen (2005b, 2008c: http://www.riksdagen.se); e-mail correspondence with the Riksdag Research Service (Riksdagens utredningstjänst [RUT]), March 11, 2009.
Note: See table 7.1 for explanation of party labels. n.d. denotes missing data.

party cabinets. Taken together, the results indicate that if deparliamentarization of Swedish politics is occurring, it is doing so simultaneously with an increase in scrutinizing activities by MPs.

Delegation within the Cabinet

In this section, we take a look inside the cabinet, at such matters as the distribution of authority and the recruitment patterns of ministers.

Cabinet Rules and Personnel

The constitution grants the prime minister broad powers of appointment and dismissal as well as authority over ministerial jurisdiction (Persson 2003). In coalition cabinets, this authority to select particular individuals is constrained and largely delegated to the party leaders of the coalition partners (Bergman 2000). In the postwar period, the cabinet has had between 16 and 22 ministers (Hadenius, Molin, and Wieslander 1993, 372–80; Holmberg and Stjernquist 2000, 109). After the 2006 elections, there were 22 cabinet ministers, including the PM. The number of ministers has increased a little over time, and no cabinet since 1982 has had fewer than 20 ministers (including the PM). This level was first reached with the nonsocialist three-party cabinet in 1976, but the Social Democratic cabinets have also maintained roughly the same number until recently, when there seems to have been another slight increase. The increased number of cabinet ministers has not been mirrored by a similar increase in the number of ministries (or departments). After a slight increase in the 1980s, the number of ministries has now returned to levels characteristic of the 1940s and 1950s. In 2008, there were 13 ministries, when the PM's office (Statsrådsberedningen) is included.

Cabinet-level decisions are made only at formal cabinet meetings. Formally, all ministers, including the PM, have the same weight in cabinet decision making. Unless individual ministers explicitly reserve themselves against a particular decision, they are all formally responsible for all cabinet decisions. In practice, however, heads of individual ministries are in charge of them, constrained only by law and general cabinet procedures. Individual ministers prepare many decisions that are never discussed but simply accepted by their fellow ministers at the formal cabinet meetings (Andrén 1968, 299–311; Holmberg and Stjernquist 1980; T. Larsson 1986, 181–86).

In addition, while ministers are formally equal at the moment of decision making, the actual decision rule within the cabinet is best described as consensus defined by the PM. Under the old 1809 constitution, the king formally made all cabinet decisions, which is one explanation for the traditional lack of a formal rule for cabinet decisions. Establishing a decision rule was discussed during the constitutional reforms of the 1970s, but in the end, it was left to individual cabinets to decide such matters (Holmberg and Stjernquist 2000, 120–21; for a case study, see S.-E. Larsson 1986, 185–208).

A question that has received a fair amount of attention in recent years is whether the role of the PM has increased over time. This is a central claim of the presidentialization argument, which holds that prime ministers in parliamentary democracies have gained almost presidential status (see chapter 1). In support of this claim, it is clear that the Swedish prime minister has considerable agenda-setting power. This is not a particularly new development, but in recent years, the PM has had a larger staff to initiate and coordinate policy-making. Since the 1960s, the prime minister's resources for monitoring the activities of other ministers have increased quite dramatically,[3] although the speed of the increase has declined in the last decade (Bäck et al. 2007).

The 1975 constitution allows the PM to appoint a deputy (Article 7:8), but the position is primarily honorary. After the PM, the Ministry of Finance has a dominant role relative to other departments (Larsson 1994; Mattson 2000). In fact, the finance minister, who is responsible for preparing the state budget, has generally had a better capacity to monitor other ministries than even the PM (Larsson 1990, 154). It is only since the late 1980s and early 1990s that there has been a major shift in resources and monitoring capacity in favor of the PM's office.

Another important claim of the presidentialization thesis is that the importance of party and parliamentary experience has declined, while characteristics such as compatibility with mass media and name recognition have increased. A comparative examination of the backgrounds of persons given important minister portfolios—the PM and the ministers of finance, foreign affairs, and justice—reveals a number of interesting facts about career patterns (see table 7.6). For example, parliamentary experience and prior high-ranking position within the party and Riksdag are particularly important for prime ministers. Ministers of justice have had the least political experience when first appointed to office. However, they and finance ministers have the highest level of formal education, while PMs have the least.

Looking at developments over time, a discernible trend is toward a more equal gender distribution. In the first period, 1945–75, there were no female ministers in these four portfolios. Looking exclusively at the last fifteen years, the distribution has been 60–40 in favor of men. Another prominent feature is the difference in prior cabinet experience. Between 1945 and 1975, almost all of those appointed to these minister posts (92 percent) had such experience. In contrast, in the period 1991–2006, not even half of all new ministers in these four portfolios had prior cabinet experience. In part, this can probably be explained by the fact that all cabinets in the first period (1945–75) were Social Democratic, either in coalition with the Center Party or by themselves, while the second period begins with a new nonsocialist cabinet in which none of the four officeholders had previous cabinet experience.

Obviously the data is sensitive to such cutoff points, but it is still possible to recognize some general trends, and it appears that the evidence for the presidentialization thesis is mixed. Prior high-ranking party position has become more important. Having begun a political career early, in the youth party, is another factor that seems to help those who aspire to the highest echelons of government. Having held local or regional elected office has also become more important.

On the basis of a different but similar set of data, Bäck and colleagues (2007) conclude that while the share of ministers with national parliamentary experience seems to have decreased, those who are chosen have a higher average length of time as MP. They also suggest that the lack of Riksdag experience might be compensated for by greater subnational parliamentary experience. Our own results support this argument, which implies that the presidentialization thesis should be qualified. With a few exceptions, both then and now, most of those selected for high cabinet portfolios have clear partisan ties and have proved their loyalty to their party prior to being appointed. To the extent that presidentialization implies that cabinet ministers have less prior partisan experience today than they used to, it is probably exaggerated. However, it is true that fewer cabinet members are recruited directly from the parliament, and those who are recruited have, on average, served longer in the Riksdag than was typical of their colleagues during the first part of the postwar period. Bäck and colleagues (2009) also find that European integration works in favor of the selection of ministers that have some "expert" background beyond their partisan connections and their parliamentary careers.

Considering all the evidence previously discussed, there are signs of increased power for the Swedish PM, but the picture is neither unambiguous nor simple. The resources available to the PM have expanded, media attention has intensified (Aylott 2005b), and the recruitment pattern of ministers has changed. While ministers tend to have less prior cabinet experience, they still have partisan experience. In addition, the importance of coalition politics must be kept in mind. To the extent that some PMs have acted "more

TABLE 7.6. Ministerial Background, First Appointment, by Portfolio, Sweden, 1945–2008

Portfolio within Cabinet	Age (mean years)	Female Ministers (%)	Prior Cabinet Position (%)	Parliamentary Experience (mean years)[a]	Prior Party High-Rank Position (%)[b]	Prior Youth Party High-Rank Position (%)[c]	Major Prior Appointment within Parliament (%)[d]	Major Prior Elected Offices at Local/Regional Level (%)[e]	Formal Education Level[f]	Any Prior Employment within the Public Sector (%)[g]	Any Prior Employment within the Private Sector (%)	Any Prior Salaried Employment in Party (%)	Member of Parliament at the Time of Minister Appointment (%)[h]	N (unique number of ministers)
Prime minister	47.3	0	67	9.7	100	56	89	56	3.6	67	11	67	100	9
Finance minister[i]	50.8	9	64	6.4	82	36	55	45	4.0	91	55	55	55	11
Foreign minister	53.6	33	67	8.5	75	67	33	50	3.8	67	42	50	67	12
Justice minister[j]	50.5	23	46	2.0	23	15	8	23	4.1	92	15	0	23	13
Mean 1945–2006	50.6	16	61	6.7	70	42	46	44	3.9	79	31	43	61	45
Mean 1945–75	54.0	0	92	4.9	62	31	54	31	3.9	69	54	31	77	13
Mean 1991–2006	47.2	40	47	8.0	80	47	47	67	3.7	80	33	53	47	15

Source: Data from Asker 1996; *Fakta om folkvalda* (various years); Larsson 2003; Norberg 1992; Riksdag & Departement 2006b.

Note: All of the calculations presented in this section are based on a data set that contains data on ministers who got portfolios at the beginning of a new cabinet. A new cabinet is defined here as a cabinet that fulfills at least one of three conditions: any change in the set of parties holding cabinet membership, any change in the identity of the prime minister, or any general election (see Müller and Strøm 2003, 12).

[a] Prior parliamentary experience (in full years) does not include years that a person has been in cabinet. That is, for systems that allow for the holding of simultaneous cabinet and parliamentary positions, we only count "parliamentary experience" for the years that the MP does not also have a cabinet position. (The latter is coded as prior cabinet experience: yes or no.) If the total parliamentary experience (service as MP) sums to less than six months, it is counted as zero (0) years of experience.

[b] Prior party high-rank position refers to any of the following: party leader, party secretary, member of the party national board, or head of local or regional board.

[c] Prior youth party high-rank position refers to the positions in a youth organization corresponding to the prior party high-rank positions.

[d] Major prior appointment within parliament refers to any of the following: Speaker (president of parliament or chamber/subdivision), group leader, vice group leader, committee chairman, or vice committee chairman.

[e] Major prior elected offices at local/regional level refers to any of the following: head of municipality, head of region, member of local parliament, or member of regional parliament.

[f] Formal education level: 1 = primary (or less); 2 = secondary (high school, Swedish gymnasium); 3 = any enrollment in postsecondary education (such as technical college, nursing school, college, university) but no degree; 4 = any undergraduate degree at technical college, nursing school, college, or university (2–4 years in length) that is post–high school or post-gymnasium; 5 = postgraduate degree (licensiat, huvudfag, PhD).

[g] Prior employment refers to the employer, that is to say, the one paying the salary. Salary by the party does not include elected offices, only jobs (such as party ombudsman). The three categories (public, private, party) are not mutually exclusive categories (as they, in combination, speak to a minister's general career pattern). Private employment includes people employed in trade unions and other nongovernmental organizations.

[h] The coding "Member of parliament at the time of minister appointment" only has one possible answer (yes or no).

[i] Finance minister is defined as the minister heading the ministry in control of the state budget.

[j] Justice minister is defined as the minister heading the ministry in control of the police force.

equal" than the others, this applies more to single-party (Social Democratic) cabinets than to coalition cabinets. In the latter, PMs spend much time and effort consulting with the other party leaders in the coalition and ensuring cabinet coordination (Premfors and Sundström 2007).

Cabinet Electoral Performance

If ministers and the cabinet perform poorly in the eyes of the citizens, MPs also suffer. As shown in table 7.7, parties who are in cabinet during the preceding electoral period usually suffer a loss of electoral support, on average 2 percent at every election. When measured in terms of election losses/gains for parties in cabinet, only Erlander's cabinets in the 1958, 1960, and 1968 elections, the Conservatives (Bildt) in the 1994 election, and Persson in the 2002 election increased their vote support while in office. Generally, come election day, it does not pay to be a cabinet party in Sweden. Elections since 1991 have reinforced this trend.

TABLE 7.7. Electoral Performance of Incumbent Cabinet Parties, Sweden, 1946–2008

Cabinet Number	Cabinet Composition	Election Year following Cabinet	SD	Ce	CD	Li	Co	Cabinet Total
2	SD 1946	1948	−0.6					−0.6
4	SD, Ce 1951	1952	0	−1.7				−1.7
5	SD, Ce 1952	1956	−1.5	−1.3				−2.8
7	SD 1957	1958	1.6					1.6
8	SD 1958	1960	1.6					1.6
9	SD 1960	1964	−0.5					−0.5
10	SD 1964	1968	2.8					2.8
12	SD 1969	1970	−4.8					−4.8
13	SD 1970	1973	−1.7					−1.7
14	SD 1973	1976	−0.9					−0.9
16	Li 1978	1979				−0.5		−0.5
18	Ce, Li 1981	1982		−2.6		−4.7		−7.3
19	SD 1982	1985	−0.9					−0.9
21	SD 1986	1988	−1.5					−1.5
22	SD 1988	1991	−5.5					−5.5
23	Co, Ce, CD, Li 1991	1994		−0.8	−3	−1.9	0.5	−5.2
25	SD 1996	1998	−8.9					−8.9
26	SD 1998	2002	3.5					3.5
27	SD 2002	2006	−4.9					−4.9
Mean gains/losses through 2006			−1.4	−1.6	−3	−2.4	0.5	−2.0

Source: Bergman 2003; Valmyndigheten 2006b, http://www.val.se.
Notes: See table 7.1 for explanation of party labels. Numbers in table represent percentage of national vote.

Cabinet and Civil Servants

So far, we have mainly examined the "upstream" process of delegation and accountability in the national policy-making chain. Before we draw any conclusions, we need to take a look "downstream," at what takes place after the parliament and cabinet have made a decision on a law or a budget. This turns our attention to the relation between the cabinet and the state bureaucrats in ministries and agencies.

Constitutionally, state agencies fall under the authority of the cabinet rather than an individual minister responsible for a particular policy area (Article 7:3). There has traditionally been broad support for this system among the political parties (Wockelberg 2003). Ministers have been known to complain about their inability to direct agencies and about occasional resistance among ministerial civil servants and state agencies to cuts in funding or major policy shifts. For example, the 1976 shift from a Social Democratic cabinet to a three-party (nonsocialist) coalition cabinet faced resistance from some highly placed civil servants (Pierre 1995). At the same time, high civil servants usually come from high-income backgrounds, and most tend to vote for nonsocialist parties (Bäck and Larsson 2006, 210). In general, individual ministers "talk to," "consult with," and "exchange information with" the agencies that implement policy in their area. In practice, they control the preparation of policy decisions and agency budgets within the framework decided by the Riksdag. Ministers also control nominations to the highest positions in the agencies. All of this gives them ample opportunity to influence civil servants (Petersson and Söderlind 1993). It is worth noting, however, that the scope and appropriateness of informal steering continue to be a matter of debate among constitutional scholars (Bull 1999).

As regards government bureaucrats, they overwhelmingly see themselves as loyal administrators in service of the cabinet. In surveys, they also report that they increasingly work with international contacts and affairs, not least those in policy areas such as agriculture, environment, and commerce and trade (Premfors and Sundström 2007). In more general terms, civil servants probably exercise more influence over policy today than they did in the early postwar period. For example, in a survey in the mid-1990s, when asked what group in society had increased its power most, MPs mentioned civil servants second only to the mass media (Esaiasson and Holmberg 1996, 200–202). Initiated observers also suggest that civil servants now take more policy initiatives, and their influence over public policy has been increasing in both the proposal and implementation stages (Wallin et al. 1999).

Fortunately, state civil servants are generally capable and professional

(Bäck and Larsson 2006, 222). In comparative perspective, the Swedish bureaucracy at all levels of government also remains largely free of corruption (Andersson 2002). Nevertheless, the bureaucracy is a constant concern for politicians and other observers. For one thing, in Sweden, as in other European countries, the bureaucracy has undergone a period of reformation in the name of New Public Management (NPM) thinking. The reforms have been ongoing since the early 1980s and include both privatization of services, the use of administrative principles borrowed from the private sector, and an emphasis on cost-efficiency and strong leadership (Christensen et al. 2005).

The implementation of NPM principles has not meant a decreased interest in further reforms. One important example involves the cabinet agencies in charge of public audits, which formerly, until July 2003, were better funded and staffed than the Riksdag's Parliamentary Audit Office (Riksdagens Revisorer) (Petersson and Söderlind 1993). The main auditor, the National Audit Office, was both under the control of the cabinet and dependent on a budget allocated via the cabinet. It was also suggested to be more sensitive to ministerial interests than was the Riksdag's Parliamentary Audit Office. The Parliamentary Audit Office had constitutional protection (Article 12:7), but the Riksdag did not have well-developed routines for utilizing its findings (Ahlbäck 1999). In July 2003, these two audit offices were replaced by one major audit office under the Riksdag. While it is too early to evaluate the independence, efficiency, and relevance of the reform (Ahlbäck Öberg 2008), a general impression seems to be that while the audits themselves work reasonably well, the reform has created more problems for the Riksdag than for the government. The parliamentary majority that supports the cabinet (regardless of whether it is left or right) seems unsure about how to use audit reports that criticize the very same cabinet and its civil servants.

While parliamentarians certainly keep busy and do scrutinize cabinet ministers, MPs probably have less capacity to monitor civil servants and society at large (Tarschys 2002, 97–98). The new Audit Office could probably be of great help, but for a parliament such as the Swedish Riksdag, which is still focused more on law production than on holding the state administration accountable, it has been difficult to develop effective reforms for this purpose.

External Constraints

Corporatism

Parliamentary democracy is embedded in a context in which organized interests influence the democratic policy-making chain. In Sweden, as in other small West European nation-states, a system of democratic corporatism has been very important (see, e.g., Katzenstein 1985). As mentioned earlier, the particularly strong ties between the Social Democrats and the blue-collar union federation, the Landsorganisationen (LO), are an often-noted feature of Swedish politics (see, e.g., Back and Berglund 1978; Feldt 1991; Petersson 1994; Bäck and Möller 2003; Teorell 1998). More generally, although the literature often has focused on the organizations representing labor and capital, a broad variety of organized interests have been influential through their close ties with state administration.

LO is still a Social Democratic stronghold, partly because of its economic support, partly because of the number of volunteers that LO can mobilize at election time. If LO decreases in size, this will also strain the Social Democratic Party. In fact, although LO remains a very influential organization, there are signs of stagnation. For one thing, after its 2006 victory, the Alliance government cut subsidies for the unemployment schemes that are run by the unions. Shortly afterward, as union dues for unemployment insurance became more expensive, some LO unions (the ones with the highest fees) began experiencing a significant drop in membership numbers. This strengthened an already existing negative trend. Membership numbers have declined steadily from a peak in the late 1980s. In 2006, if the affiliated student associations are included, the combined membership numbers for the two other major trade union federations, Tjänstemännens Centralorganisation (TCO) and Sveriges akademikers centralorganisation (SACO), both white-collar, were reported to exceed LO's (*Dagens Nyheter* 2006).

The corporatist system and close cooperation between parties and organized interests was long seen as a natural and uncontroversial aspect of partisan politics. Nonetheless, corporatism deviates from the ideal democratic chain of delegation and accountability. It is probably also the one external constraint that has become weaker during the last two decades. It has declined in importance partly as a consequence of new relations between the major organized interests in the labor market (Lewin 1994; Petersson 1994, 162–65). These new relations, in turn, are very much a consequence of the fact that groups representing business have opted out of the system by refusing to appoint representatives to the commissions that prepare cabinet proposals or to the boards that implement public policy (Rothstein and Bergström 1999). Decreasing importance is not, however, the same as the complete passing away of the system. Indeed, more recent studies point to the continued importance of corporatism, despite its decline since its heyday (Svensson and Öberg 2002). In addition, other interest groups have strengthened their access; for example, from the 1990s on, organized pensioners have been granted direct access to the PM in regularly scheduled meetings (Feltenius 2004).

Vertical Separation of Powers

While the impact of corporatism as a constraint has weakened, the importance of other constraints has increased. The direct and single chain of parliamentary democracy has been affected by increased local government spending and by the new power relations between central and local governments that have accompanied this expansion (Petersson 1994, 122–40; Häggroth and Peterson 1999; Stjernquist 1999). The importance of local governments in welfare spending has roots going back to before World War II. Since the early 1970s, it has also been national policy to give local (and regional) governments increasingly greater responsibility and autonomy for welfare provision in the social sector (schools, health, etc.). In terms of social expenditure and personnel, Swedish social welfare provision is very much a function performed by local governments. In fact, about 70 percent of total government consumption occurs at these levels. Over time, the national government has shifted from steering by detailed instructions to a system of general policy targets. In the process, it has become increasingly difficult for the national government to deliver on promises about services and public-sector reforms. Today, it is very much up to local governments to actually decide and implement these promises. Recent attempts to recentralize decisions to the national level can be seen in that light (Lidström and Kolam 2003).

The vertical separation of powers is not only a delegation downward to the local level; it also involves delegation of powers upward to the supranational EU level. Membership in the EU fundamentally reshapes national-level politics. In fact, today, the de facto constitution exhibits a "dualism" between the ideal-typical national constitution and the treaties of the EU (Algotsson 2000). This, in turn, has prompted a partial reorganization of the Riksdag. The European Affairs Committee (EU-Nämnden) was created for the purpose of monitoring the cabinet when the latter represents Sweden in the EU Council of Ministers. This committee allows the Riksdag to scrutinize ministers, but it does not have the full formal status of a regular Riksdag committee. Although it does not have the right to put forth policy initiatives on its own or to refer issues to the full chamber, both parliamentarians and cabinet ministers view it as quite important.[4]

Hegeland and Mattson (2000) show that in many policy areas, EU membership has transferred information and influence toward the government and away from parliament, but they also make clear that this is not the full picture. In areas where negotiations between member states determine policy outcomes, the Riksdag tends to get more information than it did before membership. This is the case in some areas of foreign policy and, for example, in agricultural policy. The EU impact on national-level democracy is thus complex and includes both a constraining and an enabling impact.

The EU impact on the working constitution has been noted in a few constitutional statutes. In 2002, a constitutional reform abolished the restrictions on transfers of power to the EU, as long as they do not involve basic constitutional principles of the Swedish state or reductions in protection for civil and human rights. As a result of the reform (of Article 10:5), which attracted some debate but was supported by an overwhelming majority of MPs, any other transfer of power to the EU can be decided by a three-quarters majority among voting MPs.

Constitutionally, Sweden has comparatively strict and elaborate rules for transfers of power to the EU (Isberg 2008). At the same time, the effect of recent reforms is to reduce the need for further constitutional changes or even referendums on EU matters. If it chooses to do so, a qualified majority in the Riksdag can transfer encompassing powers to the EU. The EU Court of Justice further complicates the matter of delegation upward to the EU. With its authority over EU law and with the precedent that EU law supersedes national law, the EU Court of Justice is already a supreme court (something of a principal) in policy areas under the EU domain.

Horizontal Separation of Powers

Constitutional adherence to the ideal type of parliamentary democracy assigns only a limited role to local and regional governments and hardly any for supranational organizations. It also assumes a particular role for the courts. Although few would dispute the importance of autonomous courts that are able to resist pressure from powerful politicians, an ideal parliamentary democracy assumes that they have a more limited role than they do in an ideal-typical separation-of-powers system.

Traditionally, the distinction between state administration and the court system has been weak. This is at least partly because the system has roots that can be traced back to an arrangement under which the king's rule over the country involved both having power over the state administration and being the administrative appeal authority (Brunsson, Sonneby, and Wittenmark 1990). Both courts and judges have been reluctant to play an active role relative to party politics. Courts have a constitutional authority to prohibit the implementation of laws that they find unconstitutional (Article 11:14), but this power was hardly ever used until the 1980s. Courts and judges did not want to appear political in a system where democratic politics had priority over legalism (Board 1991; Petersson et al. 1999).

Today, there is more of a constitutional debate over the proper role of the courts. Much of the impetus for an increase in judicial activism seems to stem from developments outside Sweden, such as the role of courts in European integration. The EU Court of Justice is obviously an important case in point. Another important European development is associated with the European Convention on Human Rights and the European Court of Human Rights in Strasbourg (Petersson 1994, 120–21). This court has questioned the traditional Swedish system of cabinet appeal rather than court appeal in administrative matters: for example, the appeals process for professional licensing and procedural rules concerning the expropriation of property. Following decisions of the European Court of Human Rights, appeals on such matters have been transferred from the cabinet to administrative courts of justice (Petersson and Söderlind 1993, 262–64; Holmberg and Stjernquist 2000, 195–96).

Following an international and certainly European trend, another horizontal separation of powers has taken place during the last decade. Since 1999, the Riksdag has delegated responsibility for monetary and currency politics to the Swedish central bank, the *Riksbank*. In essence, it has been given an independent position from the Riksdag and the government. This means that power over monetary and currency policies rests with members of the Riksbank's governing board, and this increases its autonomy from the government (Halvarson, Lundmark, and Staberg 2003).

Democratic Constraints

Direct democracy is another deviation from the representative ideal-typical parliamentary democracy. Direct democracy can be a way to ensure that important decisions are legitimate. Alternatively, the people can constrain the parliamentary chain of delegation through referendums. However, referendums can also be a way for the parties to abdicate responsibility. The history of Swedish referendums illustrates all sides of the argument. Advisory referendums were held both in 1955 (left- or right-hand traffic) and in 1957 (public and mandatory pension funds). Before this, the referendum had only been used in 1922 (prohibition of alcohol). The national nuclear power program was put to a national referendum in 1980. Membership in the EU was decided in a referendum in 1994, as was nonmembership in the European Monetary Union in 2003.

Formally, these referendums have all been advisory. Despite this, the political parties have always promised to follow the wishes of the majority—at least for some time. Referendums can have both positive and negative consequences, but, in general, a mix of direct and representative democracy tends to make political power more diffuse than is implied by the ideal type of parliamentary democracy.

Media

The media in Sweden is mentioned and protected by three fundamental laws (Halvarson, Lundmark, and Staberg 2003).[5] Also, as mentioned earlier, members of parliament see media (TV, radio, newspapers) as the most influential force outside the democratic chain that shapes what goes on within the chain. Media communication also impacts on political participation patterns among citizens. A citizenry more inclined to read newspapers tends to have more political knowledge. It has also been shown that TV watching is negatively correlated with voting turnout. In an international comparison, Sweden fits this pattern perfectly. Swedes often read newspapers but watch comparatively little television, and despite recent declines, Sweden still has among the highest levels of voter turnout among wealthy, democratic countries (Milner 2002).

Swedish newspapers have historically had close ties to the political parties, something that is reflected on editorial pages. Moreover, it is not unusual that journalists have held political positions or gone from a career in journalism to one in politics (Hadenius 2003). While the Social Democrats have dominated both government and parliament, it is interesting to note that about 70 percent of the daily newspapers that express a political point of view actually support the nonsocialist parties. Corresponding support for the Social Democrats is only about 20 percent (Hadenius and Weibull 2003). In addition, an increasing share of total newspaper production is controlled by privately owned media. In 1978, 59 percent of the total was published by media with private ownership, while the corresponding figure for 2003 was 73 percent. Above all, newspapers that are affiliated via ownership with the labor movement have lost market shares. Their share was 20 percent in 1973 but dropped to only 3 percent by 2003. This is partly due to a loss in circulation but is primarily a result of the continued privatization of newspapers that were previously owned by the labor movement or by farmers associations and the Center Party (Petersson et al. 2005). Although the ownership structure of Swedish newspapers is not evenly distributed among the different parties and although most editorial pages have a nonsocialist profile, actual research on how the news is reported shows little systematic and general bias in favor of either bloc over time (Petersson et al. 2006).

Conclusion

The parties in Sweden are losing members, and fewer voters have strong attachments to a particular party. Electoral turnout has been falling. As for the future of the parties, turnout figures for the 2006 election suggest a temporal halt in downward trends. Any early predictions of a turnout rate below 80 percent for the first time since 1958 proved false. Nonetheless, party membership numbers are decreasing, and other measures of party health are, from the point of view of the parties, worrisome. We can also note that the opening up of candidate nominations beyond party members to a broader circle of sympathizers and the introduction of a preference vote has not done much to reverse the main trends of weakening support for parties and politicians.

At the same time, 80 percent turnout levels and a critical but still largely interested electorate are perhaps not all that bad. Proponents of nomination and preference vote reforms can probably argue that (a) things could have been worse without the reforms and (b) the reforms are fairly popular among the electorate even if they have not had much of the intended effect. Indeed, proponents of the individual preference vote claim that its limited success stems from the fact that the preference vote threshold is too high and that it should be lowered or simply removed. Perhaps this is all that is needed, but we remain skeptical that such a reform can reverse the general trend. It is more likely that party competition over important and different agendas, close elections, public subsidies for parties, and a continued link between organized interests and the parties tend to keep the latter in business and account for some of the resilience that is also evident with regard to the party-in-the-electorate. The stronger trend, however, is decline.

While the party-in-the-electorate is weakening, party control of the upstream component of the national chain of public policy-making remains firm. After the crisis in state finances in the early 1990s, two things happened. First, working together, the Social Democrats and the nonsocialist parties reformed the budget process to ensure that cabinet budget proposals will pass more easily, as long as there is no coherent majority opposing it. Second, the Social Democrats made sure that they had one or two reliable support parties in order to manage the economy and the budget. Over time, this evolved into the contract parliamentarism that characterized the late 1990s and early 2000s. It demonstrates that in a parliamentary system, a major reason behind variation in the relative power and influence of the cabinet versus the parliament is coalitional politics. Some coalitions (including those that maintain one-party cabinets) have stable support in the parliament, and in such cases, power over day-to-day decision making shifts away from the parliament and toward the cabinet. Other cabinets have a more precarious relationship with the parliamentary opposition, and such cabinets might have less influence over politics. Either way, at the top level of government, the chain is party controlled.

Also in general, political parties remain essential for the democratic chain. The parties nominate candidates for elections and make authoritative decisions in the cabinet and Riksdag. They also select representatives to other bodies that participate in the preparation and implementation of public policy. Indeed, Sweden actually seems to have been only moderately affected by the ills of declining parties in contemporary Western democracy. Falling levels of turnout and party membership are perhaps the biggest signs that something is not well, but the dramatic changes that have occurred in the two indicators on which Sweden used to be uniquely high (turnout and party membership) have made Sweden more like other common West European countries and do not represent (nor ought they to be interpreted as) a complete crumbling of the party system.

As for the thesis of decline of parliament, within the chain, we can note that parliament is, in some aspects, more active than two decades ago. Data presented earlier in this chapter indicate that MPs have become increasingly more inclined to scrutinize both the cabinet and individual cabinet members. Parliamentary committee scrutiny as well as the number of individual MP bills and the number of questions asked of cabinet ministers has increased. In Sweden, it seems that parliament and MPs are doing more, not less. At the same time, "President" Persson, as he sometimes was called, was a powerful prime minister, and contract parliamentarism and a new budget procedure have shifted the power balance in favor of the government. We have also seen (although evidence is scarce) that cabinet ministers less often work their way up by serving in parliament and usually have a background that is closely associated with parties that they end up representing in cabinet. The size and the budget of the government ministries have also been growing. In sum, within the domestic chain, there is evidence both for and against the decline thesis.

Downstream from the cabinet and parliament, available information is scarce. The extent to which the cabinet and cabinet ministers are in charge and steer the work of the state administration is uncertain. Available evidence does not seem to indicate significant change, but the verdict is still out on the effects of the recent audit reform, and the results are not in yet for a number of government commissions on state bureaucracy and regional administration reforms. It is this aspect of the changing role of parties and parliaments that is perhaps least understood today.

Questions about the overall role of the democratic chain and especially the role of parliament relative to external constraints can be answered more straightforwardly. When we place the constitutional chain of parliamentary democracy in a broader context, we can see that powerful external constraints such as the EU (in some policy areas) overshadow the (formerly) sovereign Riksdag. At the same time, external constraints such as supranational authority and direct democracy can also enable citizens. Some of the constitutional debates, such as the referendums on membership in the EU and the Economic and Monetary Union, have led to participation levels close to those that occur in connection with general elections. The EU also provides some hope of better effectiveness in dealing with problems such as environmental pollution and trade barriers within Europe.

In any case, the Westminster model is losing much ground as a model by which Swedish politics should be understood. This is primarily because of the problems in the party-electorate link and the growing importance of constraints that are external to the chain itself. The overall trend is that delegation to experts (technocrats), such as judges and national bank officials and officials in the EU, has become more common. In contrast to the early 1970s, when the constitution was written, it is now often seen as positive to isolate these experts as much as possible from the alleged shortsightedness and private interests of elected politicians. In principal-agent terms, the dominant trend in constitutional practice is that democratically elected principals should delegate widely and be less able to hold experts accountable. As a consequence, we should perhaps expect political parties to lose more ground, the Riksdag to delegate further, and constraints to grow even stronger. In other words, in practice if not formally, politics in Sweden is moving further away from the Westminster system and toward a more Madisonian model. Such a move has many implications, but a core aspect is that it weakens the possibility for accountability through cohesive political parties. The party system might not be completely crumbling, the Riksdag is far from feeble, and while technocrats (experts) have gained political power, they have not taken over; nevertheless, Swedish democracy has changed and quite dramatically so.

NOTES

1. According to Ruin (1968, 1985), competition dominates during electoral campaigns and in government formation, but consensus and cooperation characterize much of the everyday proceedings in the Riksdag.
2. The steep rise in 2005 had to do with two policy changes. First, the amount allocated to parties per MP increased rather dramatically. Second, from 2005, the Riksdag would finance one secretary for every MP. In the years immediately before that, the policy was one secretary for every two MPs (Riksdagen 2005a).
3. When Tage Erlander became prime minister in 1946, his entire staff consisted of a secretary and an assistant. From the mid-1950s, he had an advisory support staff of his own. However, it was not until 1964 that he began to build a formal office that included a junior minister (or *statssekreterare*). This followed a 1963 incident in which the PM learned about the capture of a Soviet spy only after some of his ministers had already been informed. In 1976, when the first postwar nonsocialist coalition came to power, the PM's office became an arena for coalition coordination and problem solving (T. Larsson 1986, 181–95). During the 1991–94 coalition, the PM's office included, in addition to civil servants and the PM's personal staff, a separate coordinating unit for each of the four coalition partners, and it played a central role as a conflict-resolution mechanism (Bergman 2000). The 2006 coalition uses a similarly elaborate coordinating organization within the PM's office.
4. For more on the Swedish committee, see Hegeland 1999 and Hegeland and Mattson 1997; for a comparison with the Danish committee, see Hegeland and Mattson 1996; for a broad EU comparison, see Bergman 1997. For a study of the impact of the EU on national democracy in Sweden and the other Nordic countries, see the other country studies in Bergman and Damgaard 2000.
5. In this chapter, all the specific individual articles that are mentioned come from the Instrument of Government, which is the act that defines the main state institutions and the relationship between these institutions. There are three other fundamental laws. These are the Act of Succession, the Freedom of the Press Act, and the Fundamental Law of Freedom of Expression. The Act of Succession does not include media and citizen rights.

REFERENCES

Ahlbäck, Shirin. 1999. *Att kontrollera staten: Den statliga revisionens roll i den parlamentariska demokratin*. PhD diss., Department of Political Science, Uppsala University.

Ahlbäck Öberg, Shirin. 2008. "Förvaltning och revision." In Ingvar Mattson and Olof Petersson, eds., *Svensk författningspolitik*. 2nd ed. Stockholm: SNS Förlag.

Algotsson, Karl-Göran. 2000. *Sveriges författning efter EU-anslutningen*. Stockholm: SNS Förlag.

"Allmänna valen 2002: Del 1: Riksdagen den 15 september 2002." 2003. Stockholm: Statistiska Centralbyrån.

Andersson, Staffan. 2002. "Corruption in Sweden: Exploring Danger Zones and Change." PhD diss., Umeå University.
Andrén, Nils. 1968. *Svensk statskunskap.* Stockholm: Liber.
Asker, Björn. 1996. *Enkammarriksdagen 1971–1993/94: Ledamöter och valkretsar.* Vols. 1–2. Stockholm: Sveriges Riksdag.
Aylott, Nicholas. 2003. "After the Divorce: Social Democrats and Trade Unions in Sweden." *Party Politics* 9 (3): 369–90.
Aylott, Nicholas. 2005a. "De politiska partierna." In Magnus Blomgren and Torbjörn Bergman, eds., *EU och Sverige—ett sammanlänkat statsskick.* Malmö: Liber.
Aylott, Nicholas. 2005b. "'President Persson'—How Did Sweden Get Him?" In Thomas Poguntke and Paul Webb, eds., *The Presidentialization of Politics: A Comparative Study of Modern Democracies.* Oxford: Oxford University Press.
Aylott, Nicholas, and Torbjörn Bergman. 2004. "Almost in Government, but Not Quite: The Swedish Greens, Bargaining Constraints, and the Rise of Contract Parliamentarism." Paper presented in panel 6 at the European Consortium for Political Research joint sessions of workshops, Uppsala, April 2004.
Aylott, Nicholas, and Niklas Bolin. 2007. "Towards a Two-Party System? The Swedish Parliamentary Election of September 2006." *West European Politics* 30 (3): 621–33.
Bäck, Hanna, Patrick Dumont, Henk Erik Meier, Thomas Persson, and Kåre Vernby. 2009. "Does European Integration Lead to a 'Presidentialization' of Executive Politics? Ministerial Selection in Swedish Postwar Cabinets." *European Union Politics* 10:226–52.
Bäck, Hanna, Thomas Persson, Kåre Vernby, and Lina Westin. 2007. *Från statsminister till president? Sveriges regeringschef i ett jämförande perspektiv.* SOU 2007:42. Stockholm: Fritzes.
Bäck, Henry, and Torbjörn Larsson. 2006. *Den svenska politiken: Strukturer, processer och resultat.* Malmö: Liber.
Bäck, Mats, and Tommy Möller. 2003. *Partier och organisationer.* 6th ed. Stockholm: Nordstedts Juridik.
Back, Pär-Erik, and Sten Berglund. 1978. *Det svenska partiväsendet.* Stockholm: Almqvist och Wiksell.
Bergman, Torbjörn. 1993. "Formation Rules and Minority Governments." *European Journal of Political Research* 23 (1): 55–66.
Bergman, Torbjörn. 1995. "Constitutional Rules and Party Goals in Coalition Formation: An Analysis of Winning Minority Governments in Sweden." PhD diss., Umeå University.
Bergman, Torbjörn. 1997. "National Parliaments and EU Affairs Committees: Notes on Empirical Variation and Competing Explanations." *Journal of European Public Policy* 4 (3): 373–87.
Bergman, Torbjörn. 1999. "Trade-offs in Swedish Constitutional Design: The Monarchy under Challenge." In Wolfgang Müller and Kaare Strøm, eds., *Policy, Office, or Votes? How Political Parties in Western Europe Make Hard Decisions.* Cambridge: Cambridge University Press.
Bergman, Torbjörn. 2000. "Sweden: When Minority Cabinets Are the Rule and Majority Coalitions the Exception." In Wolfgang Müller and Kaare Strøm, eds., *Coalition Governments in Western Europe.* 2nd ed. Oxford: Oxford University Press.

Bergman, Torbjörn. 2003. "Sweden: From Separation of Power to Parliamentary Supremacy—and Back Again?" In Kaare Strøm, Wolfgang Müller, and Torbjörn Bergman, eds., *Delegation and Accountability in Parliamentary Democracies*. Oxford: Oxford University Press.

Bergman, Torbjörn. 2004. "Sweden: Democratic Reforms and Partisan Decline in an Emerging Separation of Powers System." *Scandinavian Political Studies* 27 (2): 203–25.

Bergman, Torbjörn, and Erik Damgaard. 2000. *Delegation and Accountability in European Integration: The Nordic Parliamentary Democracies and the European Union.* London: Frank Cass.

Birgersson, Bengt Ove, and Jörgen Westerståhl. 1992. *Den svenska folkstyrelsen.* Stockholm: Publica.

Blomgren, Magnus. 2003. "Cross-Pressure and Political Representation in Europe: A Comparative Study of MEPs and the Intra-party Arena." PhD diss., Umeå University.

Board, Joseph B. 1991. "Judicial Activism in Sweden." In Kenneth M. Holland, ed., *Judicial Activism in Comparative Perspective.* London: Macmillan.

Bolin, Niklas. 2007. "Established Parties and Their Measures against New Parties: The Case of Sweden." Paper presented at the Fourth European Consortium for Political Research General Conference, Pisa, September 6–8.

Brunsson, Karin, Claes Sonneby, and Lars Wittenmark. 1990. *Beslutsmaskinen—en bok om regeringskansliet.* Lund: Studentlitteratur.

Bull, Thomas. 1999. "Självständighet och pluralism—om vertikal maktdelning i Sverige." In Lena Marcusson, ed., *Dessa studier i offentlig rätt tillägnas Fredrik Sterzel med anledning av hans avgång från professuren i konstitutionell rätt 1999 av kollegor och vänner.* Uppsala: Iustus Förlag.

Christensen, Tom, Per Lægreid, Paul G. Roness, and Kjell Arne Røvik. 2005. *Organisationsteori för offentlig sektor.* Malmö: Liber.

Dagens Nyheter. 2006. "TCO och Saco har fler medlemmar än LO." February 2.

Davidsson, Lars. 2006. *I linje med partiet? Maktspel och lojalitet i den svenska riksdagen.* Stockholm: SNS Förlag.

Esaiasson, Peter, and Sören Holmberg. 1996. *Representation from Above: Members of Parliament and Representative Democracy in Sweden.* Aldershot: Dartmouth.

Fakta om folkvalda. 1985–88, 1988–91, 1991–94, 1994–98, 1998–2002. Stockholm: Riksdagens Förvaltningskontor.

Feldt, Kjell-Olof. 1991. *Alla dessa dagar . . . i regeringen 1982–1990.* Stockholm: Norstedts.

Feltenius, David. 2004. "En pluralistisk maktordning? Om pensionärsorganisationernas politiska inflytande." PhD diss., Umeå University.

Gidlund, Gullan. 1983. *Partistöd.* Lund: Liber CWK Gleerup.

Hadenius, Stig. 2003. *Modern svensk politisk historia—konflikt och samförstånd.* Stockholm: Hjalmarson och Högberg.

Hadenius, Stig, Björn Molin, and Hans Wieslander. 1993. *Sverige efter 1900: En modern politisk historia.* Stockholm: Bonnier Alba.

Hadenius, Stig, and Lennart Weibull. 2003. *Massmedier—en bok om press, radio & TV.* Stockholm: Bonnier.

Hagevi, Magnus. 1999. "Parliamentary Party Groups in the Swedish Riksdag." In

Knut Heidar and Ruud Koole, eds., *Parliamentary Party Groups in European Democracies.* London: Routledge.
Häggroth, Sören, and Carl-Gunnar Peterson. 1999. *Kommunalkunskap: Så fungerar din kommun.* Stockholm: Hjalmarsson och Högberg.
Halvarson, Arne, Kjell Lundmark, and Ulf Staberg. 2003. *Sveriges statsskick—fakta och perspektiv.* Stockholm: Liber.
Hegeland, Hans. 1999. *Riksdagen, Europeiska unionen och demokratin.* Lund: Statsvetenskapliga Institutionen, Lunds Universitet (Licenciatavhandling).
Hegeland, Hans, and Ingvar Mattson. 1996. "To Have a Voice in the Matter: A Comparative Study of the Swedish and Danish European Committees." *Journal of Legislative Studies* 2:198–215.
Hegeland, Hans, and Ingvar Mattson. 1997. "The Swedish Riksdag and the EU: Influence and Openness." In Matti Wiberg, ed., *Trying to Make Democracy Work: The Nordic Parliaments and the European Union.* Stockholm: Bank of Sweden Tercentenary Foundation and Gidlunds Förlag.
Hegeland, Hans, and Ingvar Mattson. 2000. "Another Link in the Chain: The Effects of EU Membership on Delegation and Accountability in Sweden." In Torbjörn Bergman and Erik Damgaard, eds., *Delegation and Accountability in European Integration: The Nordic Parliamentary Democracies and the European Union.* London: Frank Cass.
Hermansson, Jörgen, Shirin Ahlbäck Öberg, and Lena Wängnerud. 2007. "Framväxten av en ny politikertyp och en ny sorts demokrati." In Shirin Ahlbäck Öberg, Jörgen Hermansson, and Lena Wängnerud, eds., *Exit riksdagen.* Malmö: Liber.
Holmberg, Erik, and Nils Stjernquist. 1980. *Grundlagarna med tillhörande författningar.* Stockholm: PA Norstedts & Söners Förlag.
Holmberg, Erik, and Nils Stjernquist. 2000. *Vår författning.* Stockholm: Norstedts juridik.
Holmberg, Sören. 2000. *Välja Parti.* Stockholm: Norstedts juridik.
Holmberg, Sören, and Henrik Oscarsson. 2004. *Väljare: Svenskt väljarbeteende under 50 år.* Stockholm: Norstedts juridik.
Isberg, Magnus. 1999. *Riksdagsledamoten i sin partigrupp: 52 riksdagsveteraners erfarenheter av partigruppernas arbetssätt och inflytande.* Stockholm: Gidlunds Förlag.
Isberg, Magnus. 2008. "Lagstiftningsmakten—om delegation och maktdelning." In Ingvar Mattson and Olof Petersson, eds., *Svensk författningspolitik.* 2nd ed. Stockholm: SNS Förlag.
Katzenstein, Peter. 1985. *Small States in World Markets: Industrial Policy in Europe.* Ithaca: Cornell University Press.
Konstitutionsutskottet. 1996. "Granskning av statsrådens tjänsteutövning och regeringsärendenas handläggning." 1995/96:KU30. Riksdagstryck.
Lantto, Johan. 2008. "Utvärdering av det kommunala partistödet." In *Rapport från Riksdagen 2007/08:RFR23.* Stockholm: Riksdagen.
Larsson, Sven-Erik. 1986. *Regera i koalition: Den borgerliga trepartiregeringen 1976–1978 och kärnkraften.* Stockholm: Bonnier.
Larsson, Torbjörn. 1986. *Regeringen och dess kansli.* Lund: Studentlitteratur.
Larsson, Torbjörn. 1990. "Regeringens och regeringskansliets organisationsstruk-

tur, berednings och beslutsformer under 150 år." In *Departementshistoriekommittén, Att styra riket—regeringskansliet 1940–1990*. Stockholm: Allmänna Förlaget.
Larsson, Torbjörn. 1994. "Cabinet Ministers and Parliamentary Government in Sweden." In Michael Laver and Kenneth Shepsle, eds., *Cabinet Ministers and Parliamentary Government*. Cambridge: Cambridge University Press.
Larsson, Ulf. 2003. *Sveriges regeringar 1840–2003*. Stockholm: Regeringskansliet.
Laver, Michael, and W. Ben Hunt. 1992. *Policy and Party Competition*. New York: Routledge.
Laver, Michael, and Norman Schofield. 1990. *Multiparty Government: The Politics of Coalition in Europe*. Oxford: Oxford University Press.
Lewin, Leif. 1994. "The Rise and Decline of Corporatism: The Case of Sweden." *European Journal of Political Research* 26 (1): 59–79.
Lidström, Anders, and Kerstin Kolam. 2003. "Kommunal självstyrelse i förändring—ansvarsfördelningen mellan stat och kommuner 1974–2002." In *Förslag till riksdagen 2002/03:RR21, bilaga 6*. Stockholm: Riksdagen.
Lijphart, Arend. 1984. *Democracies*. New Haven: Yale University Press.
Mattson, Ingvar. 2000. *Den statliga budgetprocessen—rationell resursfördelning eller meningslös ritual?* Stockholm: SNS Förlag.
Mattson, Ingvar. 2008. "Finansmakten." In Ingvar Mattson and Olof Petersson, eds., *Svensk författningspolitik*. 2nd ed. Stockholm: SNS Förlag.
Mattson, Ingvar, and Olof Petersson, eds. 2008. *Svensk författningspolitik*. 2nd ed. Stockholm: SNS Förlag.
Milner, Henry. 2002. *Civic Literacy*. London: University Press of New England.
Molin, Björn. 1965. *Tjänstepensionsfrågan: En studie i svensk partipolitik*. Göteborg: Akademiförlaget.
Müller, Wolfgang C., and Kaare Strøm. 2003. "Coalition Governance in Western Europe: An Introduction." In Wolfgang Müller and Kaare Strøm, eds., *Coalition Governments in Western Europe*. Oxford: Oxford University Press.
Norberg, Anders. 1992. *Tvåkammarriksdagen 1867–1970: Ledamöter och valkretsar.* Vols. 1–5. Stockholm: Almqvist och Wiksell.
Olsen, Lennart. 2007. *Rödgrön reda: Regeringssamverkan 1998–2006*. Stockholm: Hjalmarsson och Högberg.
Oscarsson, Henrik, and Sören Holmberg. 2008. *Regeringsskifte: Väljarna och valet 2006*. Stockholm: Norstedts juridik.
Persson, Thomas. 2003. "Normer eller nytta? Om de politiska drivkrafterna bakom Regeringskansliets departementsindelning." PhD diss., Uppsala University.
Petersson, Olof. 1994. *Swedish Government and Politics*. Stockholm: Publica.
Petersson, Olof, Klaus von Beyme, Lauri Karvonen, Birgitta Nedelmann, and Eivind Smith. 1999. *Democracy the Swedish Way*. Stockholm: SNS Förlag.
Petersson, Olof, Monika Djerf-Pierre, Jesper Strömbäck, and Lennart Weibull. 2005. *Mediernas integritet*. Stockholm: SNS Förlag.
Petersson, Olof, Monika Djerf-Pierre, Sören Holmberg, Jesper Strömbäck, and Lennart Weibull. 2006. *Mediernas valmakt*. Stockholm: SNS Förlag.
Petersson, Olof, Gudmund Hernes, Sören Holmberg, Lisa Togeby, and Lena Wängnerud. 2000. *Demokrati utan partier?* Stockholm: SNS Förlag.
Petersson, Olof, and Donald Söderlind. 1993. *Förvaltningspolitik*. Stockholm: Publica.

Pierre, Jon. 1995. "Governing the Welfare State: Public Administration, the State, and Society in Sweden." In Jon Pierre, ed., *Bureaucracy in the Modern State: An Introduction to Comparative Public Administration*. Cheltenham: Edward Elgar.
Pierre, Jon, and Anders Widfeldt. 1992. "Sweden." In Richard S. Katz and Peter Mair, eds., *Party Organizations*. London: Sage.
Premfors, Rune, and Göran Sundström. 2007. *Regeringskansliet*. Malmö: Liber.
Riksdag & Departement. 2006a. "Få riksdagsledamöter vann på kryss." *Riksdag & Departement*. September 25.
Riksdag & Departement. 2006b. "Sveriges nya regering." October 9.
Riksdagen. 1986. *Riksdagens årsbok 1985/86*. Stockholm: Riksdagen.
Riksdagen. 1991. *Riksdagens årsbok: Riksmötet 1990/91*. Stockholm: Riksdagen.
Riksdagen. 2003. *Riksdagens årsbok 2002/03*. Stockholm: Riksdagen.
Riksdagen. 2005a. *Riksdagens årsbok: Riksmötet 2004/05*. Stockholm: Riksdagen.
Riksdagen. 2006a. *Riksdagens årsbok 2005/06*. Stockholm: Riksdagen.
Riksdagen. 2008a. *Riksdagens årsbok 2007/08*. Stockholm: Riksdagen.
Riksdag Research Service. 2009. E-mail correspondence. March 11.
Rothstein, Bo, and Jonas Bergström. 1999. *Korporatismens fall och den svenska modellens kris*. Stockholm: SNS Förlag.
Ruin, Olof. 1968. *Mellan samlingsregering och tvåpartisystem: Den svenska regeringsfrågan 1945–1960*. Stockholm: Bonnier.
Ruin, Olof. 1985. "Tvåpartisystem, samlingsregering eller vad?" In *Makten från folket. 12 uppsatser om folkstyrelsen*. Stockholm: Allmänna Förlaget.
Sannerstedt, Anders, and Mats Sjölin. 1994. "Folkstyrets problem." In Anders Sannerstedt and Magnus Jerneck, eds., *Den moderna demokratins problem*. Lund: Studentlitteratur.
SOU [Statens offentliga utredningar]. 1972. "Nomineringsförfarande vid riksdagsval." SOU 1972:17. Stockholm: Justitiedepartementet.
SOU. 1999. "Personval 1998—en utvärdering av personvalsreformen." SOU 1999:136. Stockholm: Justitiedepartementet.
Statsrådsberedningen. 1998. "Pressmeddelande: Samarbete mellan regeringen, vänsterpartiet och miljöpartiet." October 5.
Sterzel, Fredrik. 1998. *Författning i utveckling*. Uppsala: Iustus Förlag.
Stjernquist, Nils. 1999. "Huruledes särskilda menigheter må för egna behov sig beskatta." In Lena Marcusson, ed., *Festskrift till Fredrik Sterzel*. Stockholm: Iustus Förlag.
Svensson, Torsten, and PerOla Öberg. 2002. "Labour Market Organisations' Participation in Swedish Public Policy-Making." *Scandinavian Political Studies* 25 (4): 295–315.
Swedish Election Studies Program. 2009. E-mail correspondence. April 19.
Tarschys, Daniel. 2002. "*Huru skall statsverket granskas?*"—*Riksdagen som arena för genomlysning och kontroll: Rapport till ESO Ds 2002:58*. Stockholm: Regeringskansliet Finansdepartementet.
Teorell, Jan. 1998. *Demokrati eller fåtalsvälde? Om beslutsfattande i partiorganisationer*. PhD diss., Department of Political Science, Uppsala University.
Vedung, Evert. 1979. *Kärnkraften och regeringen Fälldins fall*. Stockholm: Raben och Sjögren.

Wallin, Gunnar, Peter Ehn, Magnus Isberg, and Claes Linde. 1999. *Makthavare i fokus.* Stockholm: SNS Förlag.
Widfeldt, Anders. 1997. "Linking Parties with People? Party Membership in Sweden, 1960–1994." PhD diss., Göteborg University.
Widfeldt, Anders. 2007. "Sweden." In "Political Data Yearbook," special issue, *European Journal of Political Research* 46 (7–8): 1118–26.
Wockelberg, Helena. 2003. "Den svenska förvaltningsmodellen: Parlamentarisk debatt om förvaltningens roll i styrelseskicket." PhD diss., Uppsala University.

INTERNET SOURCES

"Allmänna valen 2006: Del 4: Specialundersökningar." 2008. Accessed August 9. http://www.scb.se/statistik/_publikationer/ME0106_2006A01_BR_00_ME04BR0801.pdf
Finansdepartementet. 2003. Finansplan. Accessed June 2, 2010. http://www.regeringen.se/content/1/c4/30/92/eea92a86.pdf
Regeringskansliet. 2005. "The Government Offices Including Ministries." Accessed March 2. http://www.sweden.gov.se/sb/d/576
Riksdagen. 2002. "Redogörelse till Riksdagen 2001/02:RS2: Riksdagsförvaltningens årsredovisning för verksamhetsåret 2001." Accessed March 15, 2009. http://www.riksdagen.se
Riksdagen. 2005b. "Antal propositioner, motioner, interpellationer och frågor." Accessed October 10, 2006. http://www.riksdagen.se
Riksdagen. 2005c. "Redogörelse till Riksdagen 2005/06:RS2: Riksdagsförvaltningens årsredovisning för verksamhetsåret 2005." Accessed March 15, 2009. http://www.riksdagen.se
Riksdagen. 2006b. "Fördelning kvinnor och män vid Riksdagsvalet 2006." Accessed November 14. http://www.riksdagen.se
Riksdagen. 2008b. "Antal propositioner, motioner, interpellationer och frågor." Accessed March 15, 2009. http://www.riksdagen.se
Riksdagen. 2008c. "Redogörelse till Riksdagen 2007/08:RS2: Riksdagsförvaltningens årsredovisning för verksamhetsåret 2007." Accessed March 15, 2009. http://www.riksdagen.se
Valmyndigheten. 2005. "Val 2002." Accessed August 16. http://www.val.se
Valmyndigheten. 2006a. "Personröster." Accessed November 14. http://www.val.se
Valmyndigheten. 2006b. "Val 2006." Accessed October 10. http://www.val.se
Wikipedia. 2006. Various pages. Accessed October 9. http://sv.wikipedia.org

COMPARATIVE CONCLUSIONS

8 ✦ Parties and Party Systems in the North

NICHOLAS AYLOTT

As discussed in chapters 1 and 2, political parties are absolutely central to the chains of delegation and accountability by which citizens exercise their sovereignty in parliamentary democracies. Parties have frequently been seen as essential mechanisms for communication between state and society—perhaps especially in times of crisis, such as the severe economic downturn that struck the Nordic countries, and many others, in 2008–9. The country chapters in this volume (chapters 3–7) have examined each of the Nordic policy processes in detail. The purpose of this chapter is twofold: to outline the basic ways in which parties have contributed to Nordic democracy and to assess their roles in contemporary Nordic politics. Put another way, it offers an assessment of the "crisis-of-party" thesis, or at least one of its variants, "the redundancy of party" thesis (Daalder 1992). This suggests, inter alia, that parties have atrophied organizationally and been marginalized in the promulgation of public policy. As so often in political science, the chapter's conclusions are mixed. Nordic parties are in many ways weaker than they were, but they remain fundamental to political life in our five countries.

In what follows, I concentrate on the first link in the chain of delegation and accountability that underpins this volume's analytical framework—that is, the link that connects electorates and parliamentarians. With an eye to Key's (1964) distinction, mentioned in chapter 1, between the party in the electorate, the party organization, and the party in government, this chapter addresses the first two aspects.[1] In other words, although this chapter will consider interparty relations in parliament, it will not examine the party in government—in the sense of how parties manage the work of their affiliates within the cabinet, within ministries, and among the top-level civil service.

The analysis is divided into two parts, inspired by Müller's (2000) suggestion that parties play a double role in delegation within parliamentary democracy. On one hand, they enhance voters' scope to select politicians to act on their behalf, thanks to the parties' capacity to screen would-be candidates, and then synchronize the preferences and interests of public-office holders, thus allowing voters to judge the performance of a coherent body of representatives. This can be seen as the constitutional track of delegation. At the same time, delegation also occurs *within* the parties. Through some mechanism, a party needs to decide, first, which aspiring politicians it will endorse through formally associating them with the party label; and, second, who among the party's ranks will lead its policy-making work. These collective choices are likely to produce considerable overlap in the agents selected. Public-office holders, then, can often be said to have two principals: the electorate that voted them in and the partisans who presented them to the electorate in the first place.

Of course, this conception of double-track delegation is a central part of the ideal-typical Westminster model. In the model, political competition is channeled through a simple electoral system that favors just two main parties, both of which are long-established, with "brand names" (as distinct policy-preference packages) that are well known to electors. The parties have plenty of connections to the electorate through mass-membership organizations. These organizations offer a wellspring of potential election candidates for the parties to recruit from. After an election, under the Westminster model, government is controlled by a single winning party, which thus dominates policy output. This enables the electorate to hold its agents directly responsible for what they do; no other parties or institutions blur this clear line of accountability. Parties are strong, while parliament, as an institution in its own right, is weak. If we assume that one party wins a majority of seats, and that its MPs act in a disciplined way, then the leadership of this parliamentary party decides the legislative agenda. Parliament as an institution becomes little more than a rubber stamp, in which the main constraint on the governing party leadership is the need to keep its own backbenchers happy (King 1976).

How well does this model capture politics in the Nordic countries? In fact, not particularly well. The parties are—or have been—strong in various ways. At the same time, parliaments have also been strong, which is a deviation from the Westminster model. Because a single party rarely wins its own majority, the party leadership that heads the government must negotiate constantly about legislation with other party leaderships in order to secure parliamentary majorities. Interparty bargaining is thus the dominant mode of operation. Sometimes negotiation occurs within the more or less stable framework of majority coalition government, in which two or more parties share control of the cabinet and collectively command a parliamentary majority. As chapter 2 showed, however, governing parties in some Nordic countries often control only a minority of the parliamentary seats, which makes parliament the main arena in which interparty negotiation takes place (Damgaard 2000, 278–80). If these negotiations fail, the cabinet cannot legislate as it wants. Even if they succeed, the cabinet will probably have to compromise on its basic preferences. The need for constant interparty bargaining is seen as making parliament "strong." Strong parties and strong parliaments are an unusual combination, but it became the norm in Denmark, Finland, Iceland, Norway, and Sweden.

The chapter develops as follows. In the next section, I begin with a brief overview of the origins of the party systems and individual parties' historical association with specific segments of society. This provides a platform for the following two sections, which follow Müller's distinction between tracks of delegation. In the first of those, I examine patterns of cooperation and competition between parties—that is, the party systems—and their potential for abetting democratic delegation. There is then a review, based on data aggregated from the earlier country chapters, of the extent to which those electorates have felt willing to avail themselves of this potential. This is followed by a look at developments within the party systems to assess the clarity with which rival government constellations have been presented to the Nordic electorates over time. In the subsequent section, I look at the party track of delegation. In effect, this means party organization, particularly the extent to which the Nordic parties traditionally resembled the classic models of organization used in the academic literature, and the implications that this might have had for democratic delegation.

Cleavages, Blocs, and the Nordic Party Systems

I next review research on the origins of the Nordic party systems.[2] What are the origins of the parties, and how did they contribute to the formation of party systems? That common factors were at work is suggested by the similarities of the five systems. Nonetheless, they have never been identical.

The most influential account of the development of West European party systems is offered by Lipset and Rokkan (1967). Their explanation rests on the concept of political "cleavages," shaped by prevailing social conflicts that may have originated as far back as the sixteenth and seventeenth centuries. For instance, in Finland and Norway, resistance to the dominant foreign cultures imposed by (respectively) Swedish- and Danish-speaking elites influenced the domestic political constellations. Later, after the wars of the early nineteenth century had reshuffled various European territorial sovereignties, the pursuit of national independence in Finland (from Russia), Iceland (from Denmark), and Norway (from Sweden) also affected the alignment of political forces. Furthermore, the strong Nordic peasantries accentuated two other dimensions of political conflict. The first was a center-versus-periphery cleavage. The second dimension was an urban-versus-rural cleavage, as peasants responded to the industrial revolution by mobilizing politically to defend their interests.

As mass politics became established, the industrial revolution shaped the main cleavage in all the Nordic political systems (as in most of Europe), namely, that between labor and capital. It was most evident in Sweden, where late and rapid industrialization created a strong working-class identity. In response, conservative forces organized to try to preserve the privileges of the old elites and, to a lesser but increasing extent, to defend the institutions of private property and free markets. This latter cause was also taken up by bourgeois liberalism, although, in the struggle for democratization, Nordic liberals had more in common with labor than with the conservatives. In addition, the emergence of the Soviet Union intensified class conflict and prompted the formation of communist parties, thus dividing labor. In Finland, this process led to civil war.

Historically, then, all five electorates were left with three poles: labor, business, and farmers. Each pole was represented primarily by one party: a labor party, a conservative party, and an agrarian party, respectively.[3] This triangular model had three fronts along which the pole parties competed for the votes of specific classes within the electorates (Rokkan 1999, 376).

From Three Fronts to Five Parties

In comparing party systems, it is helpful to distinguish between format, which captures the nature of the individual parties involved, and mechanics, which describe the ways in which these parties compete and cooperate with each other (Sartori 1976). Table 8.1 summarizes the formats of party systems in the five Nordic countries as they appeared in 1960. It is based on Berglund and Lindström's (1978) five-party model, which is in many ways an elaboration of Lipset and Rokkan's three-front schema. The model adds two more party types, liberal and communist, to the three pole parties.

As early as 1916, and for decades thereafter, Sweden fit the five-party model almost perfectly. Norway also adhered closely to it, although its

TABLE 8.1. The Five-Party Model and the Nordic Party Systems, 1960

	Party Families					
	Communist	Social Democratic	Agrarian	Liberal	Conservative	Additional Parties
Denmark		Social Democrats (39)	Liberals (23)	Radical Liberals (8)	Conservatives (17)	Socialist People's Party (0), Schleswig Party (1), Justice Party (4)
Finland	Finnish People's Democratic League (22)	Social Democrats (26)	Agrarian League (26)	Finnish People's Party (5)	National Coalition (14)	Swedish People's Party (7)
Iceland	People's Alliance (16)[a]	Social Democrats (14)	Progressive (32)		Independence (38)	
Norway	Communists (3)	Labor (53)	Center (9)	Liberals (12)	Conservatives (17)	Christian People's Party (7)
Sweden[b]	Communists (2)	Social Democrats (48)	Center (12)	Liberals (21)	Conservatives (17)	

Source: Data from Berglund and Lindström 1978; Esaiasson and Heidar 2000; Einhorn and Logue 2003; party Web sites.

Notes: The parties included are those with parliamentary representation in 1960 or the latest election prior to that year. The figure in parentheses after each party indicates its average percentage of national parliamentary seats in elections in which it competed between and including 1945 and 1960 (percentages may not sum to 100). This figure does not include the percentages previously attained by parties that subsequently merged to form a new party. Very small parties and independents are excluded, as are the parties holding seats reserved for the Faroes and Greenland in the Danish parliament and for Åland in the Finnish parliament. The Communists (5) and the Justice Party (5) both lost their parliamentary representation in Denmark in the 1960 election.

[a]The classification of the Icelandic People's Alliance as a communist party could be questioned, but its communist heritage is clear.

[b]For Sweden, the figures are for the lower chamber only.

Communists gained parliamentary representation only intermittently, and its Christian People's Party, which campaigned nationally from 1945, did constitute a deviation. And in Denmark, besides the five "old" ones, a few other parties, including the Socialist People's Party (formed in 1959 by moderates expelled by the Communist Party), achieved parliamentary representation fairly consistently. Finland's liberals found representation mainly in several small parties, while the Swedish People's Party represented Finland's Swedish-speaking minority (frequently through participation in coalition governments). Iceland's parties, meanwhile, had already undergone numerous splits and mergers by the late 1950s, yet basic elements of the five-party model were visible even there.[4] Its main deviation from the other Nordic countries was that its right was dominated by the Independence Party, formed in 1929 through the merger of conservative and liberal parties. As its name suggested, national independence from Danish rule was the issue that united the party's components. This meant that the liberal category was vacated in the Icelandic case.

When looking comparatively at party-system mechanics, cross-country differences become more significant (cf. Arter 1999, 71–76). One feature commonly associated with Nordic, or at least Scandinavian, systems is social democratic dominance. This historical tendency is often associated with the timing and social context of industrialization and working-class organization (e.g., Castles 1978, 15–22), plus the social democrats' subsequent decision "to subordinate class purity to the logic of majority politics" (Esping-Andersen 1985, 8), which exploited the political division of the bourgeois political forces. By 1960, social democracy was certainly dominant in Norway, where the Labor Party had won a majority of parliamentary seats in every election since 1945. It was also true of Sweden. However, Swedish Social Democrats won their own parliamentary majority only once after 1945, in 1969. More commonly, when they fell just short of a majority, the Social Democrats' de facto control of parliament was underwritten by the Communists.

To some extent, social democratic dominance could also be observed in Denmark, especially in the 1920s and 1930s. However, the Social Democrats never won their own parliamentary majority, and it was only once, in 1966, that, together with the party to their left, they managed to muster a joint majority. Social democracy was weaker still in the other two Nordic countries. Finnish Social Democrats could never quite attain a parliamentary majority even together with the communists. Once, in 1958, the communists actually won more seats than the Social Democrats. The Icelandic Social Democrats frequently had fewer mandates than the party to their left—a scenario that would be unthinkable in Denmark, Norway, or Sweden.

Parties, Party Systems, and Delegation

The party systems described above were, by the 1960s, long-established and remarkably stable. As Lipset and Rokkan (1967, 51) put it, they were "frozen." Voters had come to know the parties and their policy preferences well, which enhanced voters' ability to make informed choices between the parties' candidates at election time. Party identification throughout the Nordic region was high. A large proportion of voters perceived that they belonged to a particular social group and saw a particular party as its representative. Accordingly, electoral turnout was also high, as was party membership. Thus, in principal-agent terms, I infer that such voters had a strong faith in these sectorally based parties' capacity to screen candidates, because those candidates' social backgrounds and preferences would usually be rooted in particular group identities. It is thus arguable that, from the perspective of constitutional and party-based delegation, democracy in the Nordic countries was in pretty good shape—at least when judged by the yardstick of the Westminster model.

Of course, Scandinavia was not Westminster. The existence of multiparty systems did make it harder for Nordic voters to wrest prior commitments from aspiring MPs about which prime ministerial candidates they preferred, and thus also about their preferred governments and public policies. However, in some countries and at some points in time, this ambiguity was tempered by the existence of informal party blocs, which offered reliable predictors of MPs' preferences. This was especially the case in Norway and Sweden, in whose "alternational" systems (see chapter 1) parties on the left were clearly distinguished from the "bourgeois" or "nonsocialist" parties on the right.[5]

In Finland and Iceland, the median legislator—the crucial, centrally placed member of parliament on the left-right dimension—was frequently controlled by parties able to exploit this powerful position to the fullest, due to the fact that they were not bound by bloc identity in the way that Norwegian and Swedish parties were. In Finland, the Center Party was prepared to build minority and majority coalitions with parties to its left and its right, sometimes at the same time. In Iceland, the Progressive Party consistently held the median position. In this case, however, this strategic advantage was undermined by the looser ideological constraints in the Icelandic system—that is, by the ability of parties to the left and right to cooperate with each other, without the Progressive Party. While Finland and Iceland could thus, by around 1960, be characterized as having "pivotal" party systems (again, see chapter 1), Denmark was something of a hybrid.

Its party system was largely alternational, but it had a pivotal party, the Radical Liberals, that was willing to cooperate both to its right and left.

In sum, the challenges that multiparty systems and minority parliamentarism posed to a clear delegation of power from parliamentarians to prime ministers and from voters to parliamentarians were limited in Norway, Sweden, and, to a slightly lesser extent, Denmark, because bloc politics imposed a reasonably predictable constraint on party behavior. In Finland and Iceland, voters had more difficulty predicting what relationships between parties would develop after an election.

Parties and Voters: Weakening Ties

In the next section, I examine the development of the Nordic party systems from the perspective of their delivering effective means for electorates to weigh the merits of clearly defined alternative governments. Before that, though, I assess evidence that—for whatever reasons—voters were, indeed, becoming less enamored of their party-dominated systems of political representation.

By Western standards (Dalton 2000; Schmitt and Holmberg 1995), electoral turnout in the Nordic states remains high, with the partial exception of Finland. Nonetheless, and notwithstanding a modest rise across the region from the late 1990s, three of the Nordic countries have experienced a long-term decline in turnout over the postwar period, and all five have seen a fall since the late 1980s (see figure 8.1). The trend has been particularly dramatic in Finland and Norway, with Sweden not far behind. Even Denmark has experienced some decline since the high point of the 1970s.

One of the reasons why Nordic citizens have become less likely to vote is surely linked to their flagging identification with particular political parties. There is a clear and nearly monotonic downward trend in self-reported party identification in all the Nordic countries (see figure 8.2), with the partial exception of Denmark, where the decline has been only modest since the late 1970s. The downturn is particularly strong in Sweden (where it is virtually unbroken over 35 years) and Norway (where there have been a couple of reverses, but where the overall decline has been dramatic). In Finland, the decline began later, in the early 1990s, but since then it has been significant. Iceland has had the lowest level of party identification in the Nordic region since survey data became available in the 1980s, and there has been a clear decline.

This decline in party identification is neatly paralleled by a steady increase in electoral volatility—vote switching from one election to the next.

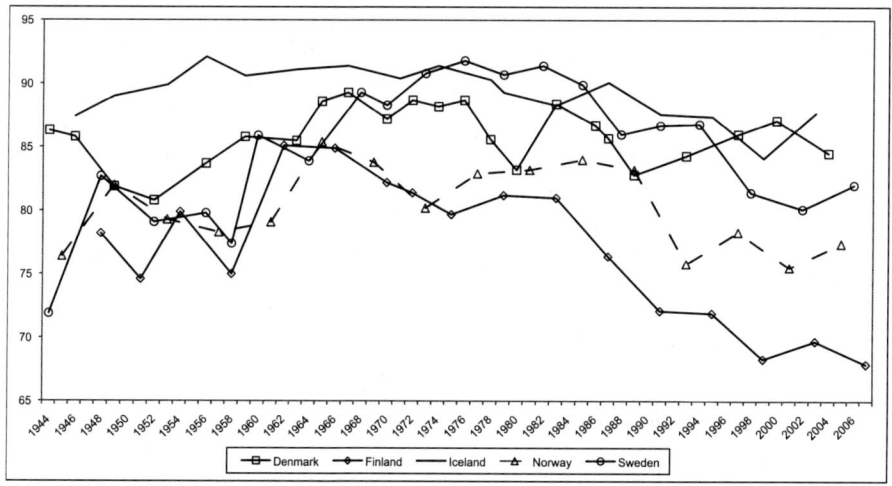

Fig. 8.1. Voter turnout, 1944–2008 (%). Data from tables 3.2, 4.2, 5.2, 6.2, 7.2 (column: Turnout).

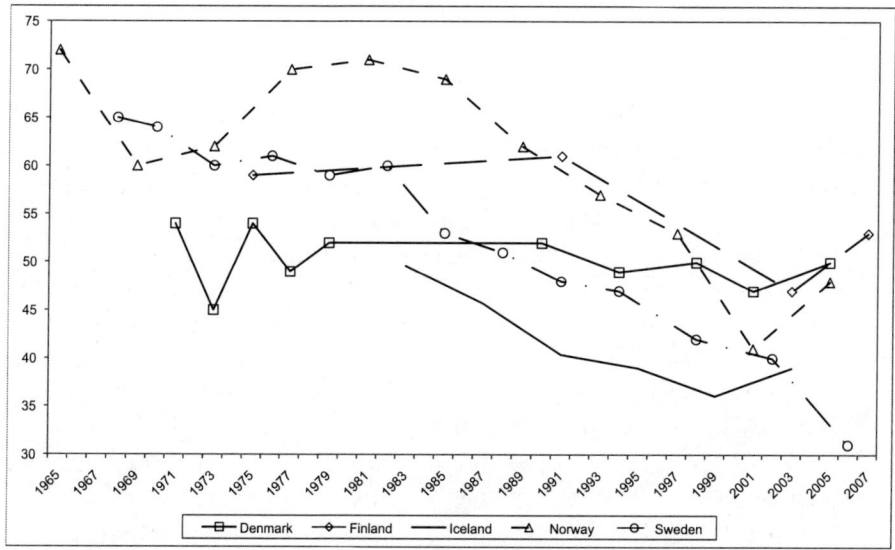

Fig. 8.2. Identifying with party, 1965–2007 (%). Data from tables 3.2 (column: Share of Voters Identifying with Party), 4.2 (column: Party Attachment), 5.2 (column: Party Supporter), 6.2 (column: Party Identification), 7.2 (column: Share of Voters with Party Identification as a "Supporter" of a Particular Party).

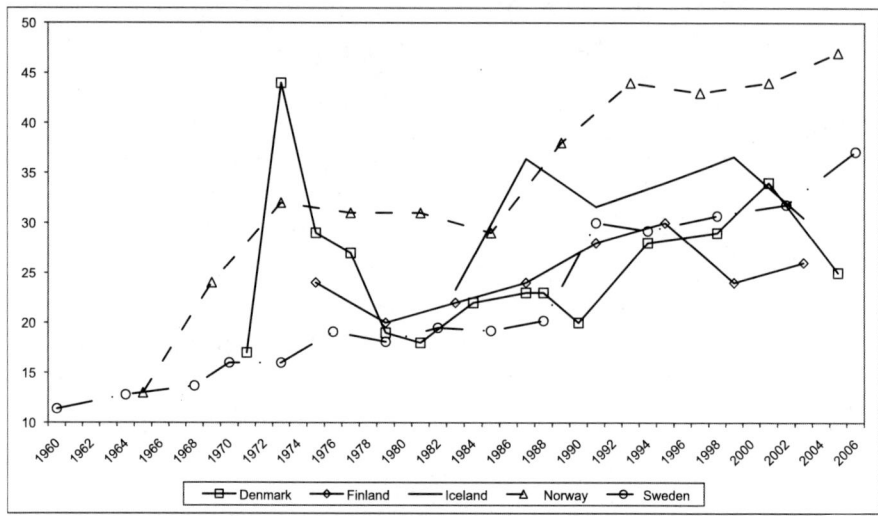

Fig. 8.3. Changing party between elections, 1960–2006 (%). Data from tables 3.2, 4.2, 5.2, 6.2 (column: Share of Voters Changing Party between Elections) and 7.2 (column: Share of Voters That Changed Party from the Last Election).

The data presented in figure 8.3 show survey estimates of gross electoral volatility between consecutive parliamentary elections. Again, the deviant data come from Denmark. Figure 8.3 demonstrates that Danish parties experienced an "earthquake" election in 1973, when about 45 percent of voters opted for a party they had not supported in the previous parliamentary election. Volatility in Denmark then gradually declined, but from the early 1990s it once again increased. Finland has a fairly flat trajectory, with only a modest increase in volatility since its time-series began in the early 1970s.

The upward trend is more noticeable in Iceland and especially in Norway and Sweden, where volatility has increased almost monotonically from very modest initial levels. In Norway, it is now even higher than in the Danish earthquake election of 1973—despite there having been no significant new parties in Norway over the past few elections. Thus, the entire increase in Norwegian volatility is due to voters changing their preferences between existing parties, rather than having new parties to have preferences about. Norwegian voters seem to have become particularly detached political consumers, looking for the best offer without much concern about their choice in the previous election.

This picture of fickleness is supported by data about when respondents

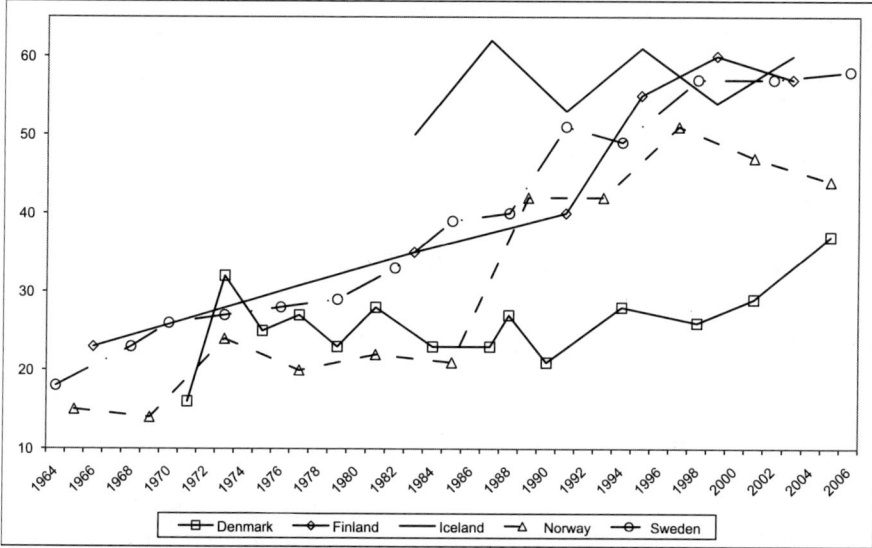

Fig. 8.4. Deciding during election campaign, 1964–2006 (%). Data from tables 3.2, 4.2, 5.2, 6.2, 7.2 (column: Share of Voters Deciding Which Party to Vote for during the Election Campaign).

make their electoral choices. Figure 8.4 shows the percentage of voters reporting that they decided which party to vote for during the electoral campaign (which typically lasts only a few weeks). There is an unmistakable upward trend, consistent for all countries. In Iceland, the less striking results are due in part to a shorter time-series and perhaps also to Icelandic voters having almost always (with one exception) settled on a party later than voters in any other Nordic country. In Denmark, there was the familiar spike in 1973 and a subsequent decline, but since the early 1990s the trend has once again been upward. In Norway, Finland, and Sweden the upward trend has been dramatic and long-term.

One obvious inference is that these quite dramatic Nordic trends might be indicative of weakening structural bonds between political parties and particular social subcultures. Figure 8.5 displays the Alford index of class voting, a measure of what, as mentioned above, has commonly been considered the most salient political cleavage in Nordic politics: social class. Data are missing for Finland and Iceland. Nevertheless, for the three countries for which there is time-series evidence, there is a consistent trend. Class voting has slowly but surely declined, but the trend is dramatic only in Norway, where the Alford index actually turned negative in the 2005

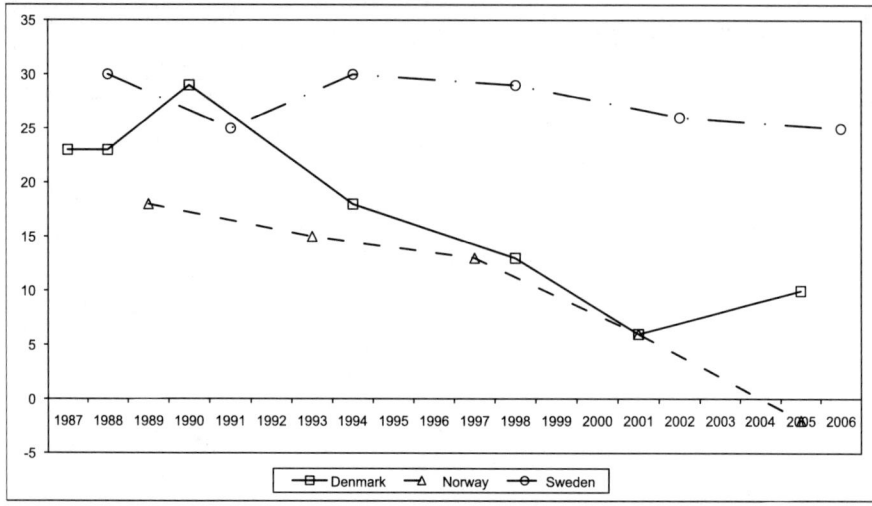

Fig. 8.5. Alford index, 1987–2006. Data from tables 3.2, 6.2, 7.2 (column: Class voting (Alford index)). No data is available for Iceland. Only broad survey data is available for Finland. This data indicates a decline but not a drastic one. For Finnish class voting, see table 4.2.

election, indicating that voters from working-class households were more likely than those from middle- and upper-class families to vote for nonsocialist parties. First and foremost, the Norwegian results reflect the strength of the appeal of the Progress Party among working-class voters (see below). Denmark exhibits a trend much like that of Norway, except that it began from a higher level in the 1980s and then witnessed a rise in class voting in 2005.

In sum, there is little doubt that Nordic voters have become increasingly detached from their political parties. Across the Nordic region, citizens vote less regularly than they used to, they feel less identification with particular parties, they are more inclined to switch support between parties, and they make up their minds later in the campaign. Their voting patterns are also somewhat less closely tied to their social backgrounds. Some of these trends, such as that in party identification, hold more strongly and consistently across the region than others. In general, Denmark has seen less consistent long-term change. This is interesting not least because Denmark is precisely the country where the trend toward party detachment was first and most dramatically evident. Over the longer haul, though, Norway and Sweden stand out as the countries in which political parties' relationships with the voters have most thoroughly weakened. In most respects,

Finland is more similar to Sweden and Norway than to Denmark. Iceland is in many ways a case unto itself, because parties in that country never had the coherence that they used to have elsewhere in the region (and perhaps because our data are more spotty).

Delegation: The Constitutional Track

As might be expected, the looser relationship between parties and voters has been reflected in the party systems of the Nordic countries. Partisan dealignment and increased electoral volatility may well have provided openings for new parties (Arter 1999, 101–12). Also quite plausible is that the process worked in reverse, with new parties encouraging voters to reject old partisan ties and try new electoral options. Whatever the flow of causality, by the 1990s, the Nordic party systems were far more populated, and therefore more complex, than they had been in 1960. Without going too deeply into the details of each party system, some general features can be discussed. Again, the overview covers both format and mechanics.

Party Choice and Government Choice: Thawing Party Systems?

Various types of new parties arrived between 1960 and 1990. As the earlier country-specific chapters in this volume make clear, the customary left-right spectrum of political competition was augmented by the emergence or reemergence of manifest political conflicts on other dimensions. One such was that between old and new politics, which gave scope especially for new competitors to the left of the social democrats (Inglehart 1977; Kitschelt 1994, 8–39). In Norway, for example, Labor left-wingers formed their own party in 1961. Following the bitterly contested referendum on EC membership a dozen years later, they joined with other Labor defectors and far-left groups to form what became, in 1975, the Socialist Left. In Finland, Social Democratic defectors won parliamentary seats in 1962, but a reunion with the Social Democrats in 1973 prompted some of them to join the Communist-run front.

On the radical right, the ferment in at least two party systems has been more significant. In 1973 both Denmark and Norway saw the breakthrough of a new type of party, often called right-wing populist. The Danish one came first and called itself the Progress Party. The Norwegian party adopted the same name in 1977. Much has been written about these new parties (e.g., Andersen and Bjørklund 2000; Svåsand 1998), which combined economic liberalism—especially opposition to high Scandinavian taxes and skepticism toward government intervention—with, from the 1980s, increasing opposition to immigration.

Changes also occurred among the more mainstream Nordic parties. Some of the older ones renamed themselves. Following the example of Norwegian and Swedish parties, in 1965 the Finnish Agrarians became the Center Party. Both developments signaled the intention of parties with rather narrow social constituencies to branch out and seek votes from across the electorate—to become, in other words, catchall parties (see below).

New parties also competed for the middle ground, albeit sometimes for delimited parts of it. The Norwegian Liberals split in the early 1970s over the issue of EC membership. In Denmark, the earthquake election of 1973 not only brought three old parties back into parliament, but also two debutants, including the Christian People's Party, which became the second confessional party represented in the Nordic parliaments, following its long-established Norwegian namesake. Two years later a third arrived on the scene, in Finland. In 1983 a Women's List won seats in Iceland, and that same year the Finnish Green League became the first party of its type to break into the Nordic parliaments. In 1988 the Greens entered the Swedish parliament, the first new party to do so since 1932.

The significance of all these new parties becomes clear when we consider the mechanics of the systems by 1990. The newcomers on the left probably had the least impact. With the exception of the Icelandic People's Alliance, which was a frequent participant in coalition governments, especially from the mid-1970s, these parties did not break the isolation of their communist antecedents in coalition formation. On the right, the Progress parties in Denmark and Norway found themselves in a similar situation. Their coalition potential was nonexistent because the bourgeois parties viewed them with the same disdain that the social democrats had traditionally shown the communists. On the other hand, the new parties attracted support from traditional social democratic social constituencies, especially the urban working class. Thus, in both Denmark and Norway, the arrival of the Progress parties on the far right weakened the social democrats and pushed the mainstream bourgeois parties toward the median legislator.

The new middle parties in Denmark had an additional impact. Previously, the Radical Liberals had almost monopolized the role of pivot between the left and right blocs. After 1973 they had two rivals for that powerful position: the Center Democrats and the Christian People's Party. In 1988 the Radical Liberals, having frequently governed with the Social Democrats, joined a coalition with the Conservatives and the Liberals, again confusing bloc identity.

Party-System Change since 1990: Back to the Future?

With noncommunist radical-left parties, greens, Christians, and right-wing populists all having established durable footholds in party politics, the Nordic five-party model was obsolete by 1990 (Demker and Svåsand 2005, 386). As for the parties' collective capacity to present the electorates with clear government alternatives, that too seemed to have waned by the early 1990s. The arrival of the Danish and Norwegian Progress parties may have weakened the left wing electorally, but they had also robbed the mainstream right parties of any realistic hopes of winning their own collective parliamentary majorities. As Narud and Strøm observe in this volume, the extremely narrowly based centrist coalition that was formed in Norway after the 1997 election was only the most striking illustration of this trend. Norway's system thus became multipolar or "diffuse" in character (Heidar 2005, 830).

In 1991 Sweden seemed likely to join the same club, as its own right-wing populist party, New Democracy, burst into parliament and ensured that the new center-right government was precariously dependent on its whims—so precariously, in fact, that the government chose to go hat in hand to the Social Democrats for policy agreements when economic crisis struck. (Indeed, the 1991 election can be seen as a belated equivalent to Denmark's 1973 earthquake. New Democracy was joined by the much-longer-established Christian Democrats in making their parliamentary debuts.) In 1995–97, the Center Party further reduced the predictability of bloc boundaries in Sweden by formalizing parliamentary cooperation with a Social Democratic minority government.

In Finland, meanwhile, although bloc politics had never been very significant, the idea that elections might present the electorate with clear alternative governments seemed to expire completely in 1995.[6] In that year the remarkable "rainbow coalition" was formed, in which two parties with long experience of government, the Social Democrats and the Swedish People's Party, were joined in office by others as diverse as the former communists, the Greens and the conservative National Coalition (Jungar 2002). Although few parties or voters could have envisaged such a government in advance, the rainbow coalition stayed in power, more or less intact, for eight years.

Since the late 1990s, however, an intriguing trend back toward fewer, simpler, more coherent government alternatives has occurred—most strongly in the three countries with traditions of alternational party systems, but even in those with customarily pivotal systems. Some parties with relatively flexible government preferences have disappeared (see table 8.2), while formerly untouchable fringe parties have been drawn into the mainstream.

TABLE 8.2. The Nordic Party Systems, 2009

	Party Families									
	(Ex-) Communist	Radical Left	Social Democratic	Greens And New Politics	Ethno-Regional	Agrarian Origins	Liberal	Confessional	Conservative	Radical Right
Denmark	Red-Green Alliance (3)	Socialist People's Party (8)	Social Democrats (30)			Liberals (27)	Radical Liberals (6), Liberal Alliance (3)		Conservatives (11)	Danish People's Party (12)
Finland	Left Alliance (10)		Social Democrats (24)	Green League (8)	Swedish People's Party (5)	Centre (23)		Christian Democrats (4)	National Coalition (20)	True Finns (2)
Iceland		Left Movement (13)	United Front (30)	Citizens Movement (6)		Progressive (18)	—[a]		Independence (37)	
Norway		Socialist Left (9)	Labor (32)			Centre (9)	Liberals (4)	Christian Democrats (10)	Conservatives (17)	Progress (15)
Sweden	Left (7)		Social Democrats (39)	Greens (5)		Centre (7)	Liberals (8)	Christian Democrats (8)	Conservatives (22)	

Source: See table 8.1 for data sources.

Note: The parties included are those with parliamentary representation in May 2009 or the latest election prior to that date. The figure in parentheses after each party indicates its average percentage of national parliamentary seats in the elections in which it competed between and including 1990 and 2009 (percentages may not sum to 100). This figure does not include the percentages previously attained by parties that subsequently merged to form a new party. Very small parties and independents are excluded, as are the parties holding seats reserved for the Faroes and Greenland in the Danish parliament and for Åland in the Finnish parliament.

[a] The Icelandic Liberals lost their seats in 2009.

Perhaps the first steps in this direction occurred in Sweden. The format of the party system had already settled down in 1994, when New Democracy's electoral support vanished. But the mechanics of the system, too, became more rigid in 1998, when a Social Democratic government established formal cooperation with the two other left-of-center parties, the Greens and the Left. This contract (Bale and Bergman 2006) fell short of a full coalition, but it coordinated the left wing as never before. Comparable developments then occurred in Denmark. Two potentially pivotal middle parties, the Center Democrats and the Christian People's Party, lost their parliamentary seats in 2001 and 2005, respectively, which simplified the options open to would-be coalition builders. Still more significant, after the 2001 election, the Conservatives and the Liberals, who took office together, struck a deal with the right-wing populist Danish People's Party (which had just muscled aside the Progress Party, from which it had earlier broken away). This agreement brought a measure of unity to the broad Danish right.

The revival of alternational politics then gathered pace with the increasing occurrence of a rare, if not entirely new, Nordic phenomenon: pre-electoral coalitions, in which parties bind themselves to an alliance in advance of election day, without waiting to see what bargaining power the electorate bestows on them. The historic decision of the Norwegian Labor Party, after its electoral disaster of 2001, to commit itself to a future coalition with the Socialist Left and Center parties united the broader left wing and presented Norway's voters in 2005 with a clear connection between party choice and preferred government. The choice for Swedish voters a year later was even clearer. The four right-of-center parties had formed an "Alliance for Sweden" and even composed a joint policy platform. In Denmark, meanwhile, the slow steps of the Socialist People's Party toward the political mainstream accelerated so markedly that, by early 2009, the Social Democrats and even the Radical Liberals were prepared to work for a coalition that included it.

Of the traditionally pivotal party systems, even Finland saw a step toward bloc politics in 2007, when a largely right-of-center government was formed, and in which neither the Social Democrats nor the Left Wing Alliance was represented. And although Iceland's government after the 2007 election was cross-bloc in character, that government collapsed in early 2009, in the aftermath of the country's economic catastrophe. As noted in Kristjánsson and Indridason's chapter, it was succeeded by Iceland's first broad-left cabinet, as the Left Movement—originally refuseniks from the various groups that had formed the social democratic United Front a decade earlier—stepped up to replace Independence as the United Front's coalition partner. The two-party government soon won a landslide victory in an early parliamentary election.[7]

The reasons for this rediscovery of bloc politics in the Nordic countries are not entirely clear. Although party-specific circumstances induced strategic departures in various individual cases, which in turn facilitated new cross-party alliances (Allern and Aylott 2009), the similarity of developments across the Nordic region do suggest at least some common factors. These might include changes in the 1990s to parliamentary procedure for formulating national budgets (Christiansen and Damgaard 2008, 62–69). Alternatively, such strategic innovations might simply have spread through conscious emulation. Whatever the causes, the effect has been a striking revival of clearly defined, reasonably coherent alternative governments—especially in Denmark, Norway, and Sweden, but even, to a lesser extent, in Finland and Iceland. From the perspective of democratic delegation, then, the party systems have actually been working more effectively.

Moreover, the parties collectively still dominate the provision of candidates for voters to choose between. There have been the odd exceptions, but independent or nonparty candidates have seldom made it into parliament. In Sweden, it is unheard of (Strøm 2000, 204).

Delegation: The Party Track

The ideal-typical, five-party Nordic party system may be largely gone, but whether the same can be said of the three-front model is a more contentious question. We have seen how the Nordic countries had become more electorally volatile, while class voting, at least in some Nordic countries, almost disappeared (see also Knutsen 2004, 65–73). Yet, Sundberg (2003, 46–54) argues that the three pole parties—labor, agrarian, and conservative—have retained a fairly stable collective share of the vote in Denmark, Norway, Finland, and Sweden since 1945. The inference, according to Sundberg (2003, 60), is that "the three pole parties have managed to incorporate . . . new [generations of] voters into the prevailing cleavage structure." That, in turn, implies a certain adaptability in the parties as political actors—a suggestion that I now examine more closely by looking at party organizations. In this section, then, I address the second way in which Müller (2000) envisages parties as contributing to effective democratic delegation: through allowing voters to hold politicians accountable, not just as public officials (or aspiring ones), mandated and removable through public elections, but also as party agents, mandated and removable by *internal party mechanisms.* I thus examine three aspects of party organization: membership, finance, and candidate selection.

Models of Party

In his classic work, Duverger (1964, 62–71) distinguished between two types of party that had developed in Western Europe. The cadre party, he explained, depended on the "quality" of the politicians who were affiliated to it. It was an elite grouping without much in the way of organization or, especially, membership. The mass party, on the other hand, relied on a large, well-organized membership, because the resources needed to fund its activity could only be raised through membership dues from a large number of people. Before the advent of mass democracy, cadre parties were dominant. Social groups outside the system, such as the industrial working class, then formed mass parties to gain access to the system. The older, cadre-type parties soon realized that mass parties were much better equipped to compete for votes, and started to emulate the latter's organizational features—what Duverger called "contagion from the left" (1964, xxvii).

This idealized picture of party-organizational development fits the Nordic cases quite well. The first protoparties were those aligning either conservative elements or liberal, prodemocratic forces. These were then challenged by what are often described in the Nordic countries as "people's movement" parties—those representing preexisting social organizations, often from the working class and the farmers. The cadre parties then reorganized themselves in order to enhance their campaigning capacity, and one way in which they did this was to promote internal party democracy. As Strøm and Müller (1999, 16–18) have argued, intraparty democracy—the chance for grassroots members to influence the party's policy platform and to choose the individuals who lead and represent it—is one of the main privileges that party leaders offer in return for members' dues and efforts during campaigning. By joining a party, an individual voter can both influence its platform and influence the screening of its agents.

Thus, with numerous small variations, plus the rather more significant Icelandic exceptions (Kristjánsson and Indridason, in this volume, refer to "network parties"), party organization in the Nordic countries converged toward a fairly standard pattern by the 1960s. As the mass-party model suggests, the party congress, to which delegates were elected by local party branches, became the highest decision-making organ. Individual membership of the party was via the municipal branch (or even more basic units), rather than via the national central office.

To be sure, two distinct power centers have always existed at the national level within each party. First, there is the leadership of the party organization, elected by its congress. Second, there are its MPs, who, once mandated in public elections, enjoy the Burkean freedom to vote as conscience (or any other personal interest) directs—regardless, in theory, of any instruction from their parties.

However, in practice, the relationship between the party's organization and its parliamentarians has usually been ordered and straightforward. There are institutional reasons for this. First, in a parliamentary system, aspiring politicians understand that, for their pledges to the electorate to be credible, these pledges must be coordinated through affiliation to a party.[8] Thus, once elected, any MP with a desire to serve more than a single parliamentary term has a strong interest in retaining the favor of her party, since it decides whether she will be renominated as one of its candidates at the next election.[9] Second, there has always been plenty of overlap of individuals between the Nordic parties' organizations and parliamentary groups. Indeed, the leader of the organization, elected by congress, and the leader of the parliamentary group, elected by the party's MPs, have very often been the same person.[10] On the whole, then, and although there have been exceptions, solid internal party unity has been the norm. As Berglund and Lindström (1978, 157) noted, "members of the parliamentary parties act as though they were one single individual most of the time."

Because their memberships were relatively large, a case could thus be made that the Nordic parties were collectively representative of the wider electorate's preferences. It could even be argued that an additional influence on certain parties made them still more representative. Parties resembling the "people's movement" type could be found across the spectrum, but their foremost exemplars were the social democratic parties. These parties' relationships with the trade-union movements were especially strong in Scandinavia proper. In Norway and Sweden, the organizational ties between them were preserved in a system of collective party membership. Municipal union branches could affiliate with municipal social democratic party branches, and in so doing the union branches' members would automatically become party members. In highly unionized workforces, this naturally inflated social democratic membership figures enormously, especially in Sweden. Arguably, it linked the social democrats even more closely to their core electoral constituency.

However, for reasons that I will examine in more detail below, the halcyon days of mass, internal party democracy are widely seen as gone. Political scientists have long since proposed new models of party that were more appropriate for contemporary Europe. As early as the 1960s, Kirchheimer (1966) suggested that the mass parties of Western Europe had turned into "catchall parties." This party type had fewer ties to a particular class or segment of the electorate, but instead sought out votes wherever it could find them. It also featured a diminished role for ideology; a freer hand for leadership at the expense of grassroots influence; and looser relationships with a variety of interest groups, rather than a privileged relationship with just one type (such as trade unions). Two decades later Panebianco (1988, 262ff) proposed an extension of the catchall model with his "electoral-professional party," in which the party organization had become staffed by specialist professionals rather than partisans.

Later still, Katz and Mair (1995) suggested that European parties had moved from being components of civil society toward being a part of the state. Instead of being mouthpieces for specific social interests, they had become comfortable vehicles for office- and benefit-seekers. A system of competing social movements had become a cozy cartel of political elites. Because it is open-ended and not very specific, this "cartel party" thesis (see chapter 2) is difficult to operationalize and research empirically. At the same time, it is intuitively appealing to many observers of modern politics, because it might help to explain part of the growing political mistrust and cynicism that many observers have identified (Norris 1999)—even if those trends have been relatively modest in the Nordic countries. After all, the very term *cartel* suggests agency loss: when they act as a cartel, politicians that are supposed to be agents of the citizens in fact collude to feather their own nests. Thereby, these politicians undersupply the collective goods that their principals, the citizens, rely on them to deliver.

Some aspects, at least, of the general claims of the electoral-professional and cartel-party theses are observable. On what empirical grounds, then, were these new models of party organization predicated? I now examine three: membership, finance, and candidate selection.

Decline of Mass Memberships

On the face of it, there seems ample evidence to suggest that the Nordic parties have become much less suited to assist the democratic-delegation process than they were previously. Their broad memberships, arguably the main reason for seeing parties as an additional track of delegation, declined (see table 8.3). This occurred first in Denmark, where quite significant drops in party membership were evident as early as the 1970s. It was less marked in Finland and Norway, but by 1990 it was clearly visible. The connection to the detachment of voters from the parties, reviewed earlier, is obvious.

The fall in Swedish party membership during the 1980s looks spectacular, and it can be attributed to a particular cause. In 1987, the Social Democratic congress agreed to phase out the system of collective party membership for members of affiliated trade-union branches by 1991 (Aylott 2003). In Norway, too, the number of union branches affiliating to the party had been in decline for some years (Allern and Heidar 2001, 116–20), and Labor soon followed its Swedish sister party in abolishing collective membership. Even after these major changes to the political organization of the Norwegian and Swedish labor movements, however, party membership throughout the Nordic region continued to decline (see figure 8.6). Indeed, except for Iceland, where available data are limited and known to be problematic, party membership levels have been declining in all countries and all recent periods for which there is evidence.

How injurious has citizens' increasing reluctance to commit themselves to party membership been for the functioning of the party track of democratic delegation? Although it is hard to interpret the decline of party membership as a positive development for popular governance, the negative effects can be exaggerated. Many of the collectively affiliated members of the Swedish Social Democrats and the Norwegian Labor Party, for example, were entirely passive, never participating in party meetings or ballots. Some were apparently unaware that they were members at all. It is at least arguable that the Swedish and Norwegian social democrats lost little with the departure of such passive members (Elvander 1979, 18). Evidence from Denmark, moreover, suggests that local-branch-level activism has not declined in step with overall party membership, even if it has declined overall (Pedersen 2003, 465–75). While they might penetrate the electorate less than they used to, Nordic party organizations are not yet dead.

TABLE 8.3. Membership Density in Political Parties by Country and Decade

	1960s	1970s	1980s	1989–90	1997–98
Denmark	21.0	13.5	7.6	5.9	5.1
Finland	18.3	17.2	14.0	13.5	9.7
Norway	15.5	13.4	15.6	13.1	7.3
Sweden	22.0	19.6	23.7	8.0	5.5

Source: Sundberg 2002, 196.
Note: Membership density is the proportion of the electorate that belongs to one of the political parties.

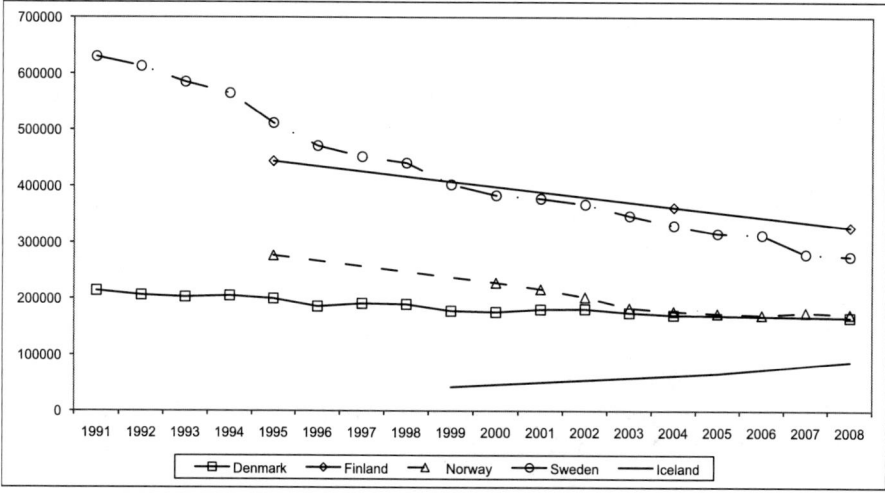

Fig. 8.6. Total party membership, 1991–2008, absolute numbers. Numbers come from the raw data for figure 1 in each country chapter. This data is available on the book's home page, the Nordic Parliamentary Democracy Data Archive, http://www.erdda.se.

Party Finance

One thing that the parties did lose with their declining memberships were the dues that those lost members had previously paid. Probably not coincidentally, political parties increasingly turned to the state for the resources they needed (Sundberg 2003, 135–38). Denmark was the last of the five Nordic countries to introduce public subsidies for parties, in 1987, and they subsequently expanded rapidly. Indeed, the cartel thesis lays considerable emphasis on how parties have become more detached from their social constituencies and more attached to the spoils that the public sector provides. Cartel parties also secure benefits for their leaders through the pursuit of various offices in the public sector. Although these spoils of office are not so clearly pursued in the four bigger states as they are in Iceland, the country chapters in this volume observed that party patronage in public appointments is by no means unknown in the Nordic region.

Figure 8.7 demonstrates how the relationship between the number of party members and public subsidies has changed for the Swedish parties. Adjusting for inflation but not (slight) population growth, the figure shows that in the late 1980s a party member "cost" taxpayers about 160 Swedish

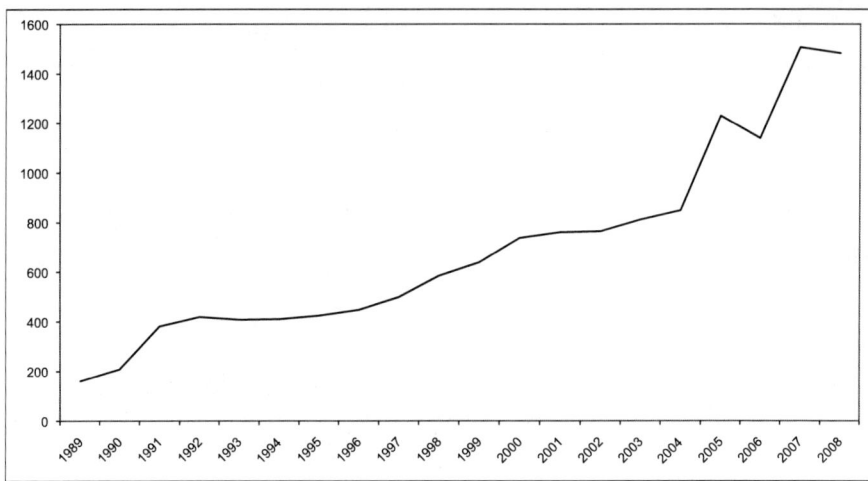

Fig. 8.7. SEK per party member (Sweden), 1989–2008, in 2008 prices. Data from fact sheets from the Swedish Riksdag (1989–2008); *Statistics Sweden* (2008), http://www.scb.se/Pages/PricesCrib__258649.aspx (accessed May 25, 2009). The dip in 2006 is caused by the fact that the Riksdag fact sheet only reports expenses up to the election in September of that year.

kronor per year. Two decades later, each member costs almost 1,500 kronor per year. This is an effect of the simultaneous drop in party memberships and the increase in public subsidies to parties. There are no comparable data for the other Nordic countries, but similar trends are very likely. In Norway, for example, party membership levels have experienced a similar drop, while public party subsidies have greatly and steadily increased (NOU 2004).

It is difficult to judge whether the electoral detachment that Nordic parties have suffered is due to their transformation into cartel parties, but there is at least partial evidence that is consistent with this thesis. At the very least, it is reasonable to say that as they have lost some of the steadfast allegiance among the voters, Nordic parties have found other ways to generate income for themselves and perhaps to retain their organizational effectiveness in government. Party leaders may have become lonelier, but they have not become poorer.

Candidate Selection: Where Iceland Led, Have Others Followed?

In the 1970s Iceland's political parties underwent a transformation so profound that their basic democratic role was brought into question (Kristjánsson 2002, 131). Faced with calls to "democratize" the process of choosing electoral candidates, Icelandic parties adopted a system of internal primary elections. Prior to this, candidate selection had been the preserve of regional party conventions, and, because there was little scope for voters to change the lists through personal-preference voting, the parties' rank-ordering of their candidates decisively determined which of them occupied the seats that each party won. Advisory primary ballots were not the norm in other Nordic countries, though they were not unheard of. The difference in Iceland was that the distinction between party member and nonmember, a fairly obvious one in other European countries, was often unclear, due to poorly maintained membership lists and the absence of a system of individual membership fees. Without such membership registers, it was impossible for the parties to restrict who could take part in candidate selection. In effect, the primaries became "open"—and the parties, in consequence, became almost "empty shells" (Kristjánsson 2004, 165). Their role in screening aspiring politicians was fundamentally undermined.

Yet, other Nordic parties have shown only limited signs of following their Icelandic counterparts. Outside Iceland, Nordic party membership lists are much more rigorously maintained, which preserves each party's control over its selection of candidates. True, as this volume's country chapters have shown, voters at large have acquired increased scope to shape, if not the *composition* of the lists, then at least the *order* in which a party's candidates will be awarded the mandates that the party wins. Denmark's parties have increasingly used the possibility provided by the country's complex electoral system to allow voters to determine the ranking of candidates. This is in effect a move toward the Finnish system of open lists, in which a party's candidates are elected, not in an order established by the party prior to the election, but rather according to the individual preference votes that they attract among the voters. Such a system may reduce the power of the party over the candidate, because the candidate has an incentive to pursue her own personal campaign to win voters' support.

In 1995 Sweden took a small step toward more open lists. But it was only a small step; being highly ranked by the party is still much the most effective way for a candidate to secure election in Sweden. Party lists in Norway remain in effect closed, with party ranking decisive. In fact, much the same applies in Iceland, with the important caveat that party rankings are established through primary elections. Even in the tumultuous election of 2009, when record numbers of Icelandic voters took the chance to cross out disfavored candidates from their preferred party's list, no MPs lost their seats as a consequence (*Iceland Review Online*, May 27).

Within the parties, rank-and-file party members do appear to have become more influential in candidate selection, at the expense of partisans higher up the intraparty hierarchy. As described by Raunio in this volume, Finnish law pretty much requires internal primaries before candidate selection is completed in the larger parties, and it restricts the scope of the party district's leadership to amend the primary's outcome. Indeed, throughout the Nordic countries, national party leaderships rarely get involved in any direct way in candidate selection, which is conducted, even for parliamentary elections, at the level of the local and regional party branches.[11] In fact, if any trend is noticeable across the Nordic parties, it is that candidate selection, which was already relatively decentralized (Bille 2001), has become even more so (Narud, Pedersen, and Valen 2002, 218). This development, at least, is difficult to square with the cartel thesis. At the same time, however, parties as a whole retain their control of the supply of election candidates. As we saw earlier, independent candidates remain rare. In the three Scandinavian countries at least, few parties are prepared to allow nonpartisans, even well-known and popular ones, on their lists.

Conclusion

The nature of party life in the Nordic countries has undoubtedly changed. Research about the politics of Denmark, Finland, Iceland, Norway, and Sweden, particularly in political economy, often refers to a golden age that occurred around 1960. Much the same is suggested by a review of democratic "performance" of the Nordics' parties and party systems at about that time. The five-party model offered a good description of party competition and cooperation, albeit with some deviations outside Sweden. More important, in each country, these five parties (and a few others) were deeply rooted in their respective electorates. This was especially true of the three pole parties, whose origins could frequently be found in social conflicts that originated back in the nineteenth century. Such longevity made them relatively reliable guides to the policy choices on offer to the electorates. Even when no single party won its own parliamentary majority, bloc politics in Norway, Sweden, and (depending on the mood of the pivot parties) Denmark made it possible to foresee reliably the government formation process even before the election.

Since then, much has changed. The party systems have become more populated, with new parties emerging across the respective political spectrums. This has complicated the patterns of competition and cooperation between the parties, which in turn has complicated the process of democratic delegation for the electors, the ultimate principals. Common to all the Nordic countries has been an accelerating decline in electoral stability, party identification, and party membership, as well as, in the Scandinavian trio, a looser relationship between parties and other social organizations. Public trust in parties, especially in Sweden, has fallen markedly. As measured by some indicators of effective political delegation, the Nordic region has become somewhat less distinct among the democracies of Western Europe. The sharp recession of 2008–9 appears to have exacerbated these trends, at least in Iceland. As Kristjánsson and Indridason show in this volume, voters' faith in their parties—particularly the one that has usually won the most votes, the Independence Party—was dealt a savage blow by the economic meltdown of 2008–9.

Yet, bloc politics lives on, especially in Norway and Sweden. And, intriguingly, coherent constellations of office-seeking parties have reemerged in recent years throughout the Nordic countries, some of which have welcomed formerly radical parties into the mainstream. Such coherence has emerged, albeit to a limited degree, even in Finland and Iceland, where bloc politics had been almost consigned to history. From a delegation perspective, the Nordic party systems have arguably never worked so well.

Moreover, developments since the golden age also illustrate the adaptability of the parties. Arguably, the enduring share of the vote won by the pole parties shows how successfully they integrated new voter cohorts into the structure of competition forged many years previously—even if certain issues, such as European integration, have proved enduringly troublesome to, for example, social democratic parties. Moreover, the parties have responded to a variety of profound changes in their domestic societies, which have made it harder to recruit party members, by turning to the state for economic sustenance.

As societies have diversified and group identity has declined, parties no longer play a prominent role in many people's everyday lives, as some of them once did. Parties have shifted their operations away from civil society and toward the state (van Biezen 2004). In most (if not all) respects, their decisive power centers have ascended up their organizational structures, and into their central offices and parliamentary groups. The ideological competition between parties, which must also have invigorated their members and sympathizers (either through positive inspiration or fear of their opponents' plans), has certainly diminished in intensity. Radical socialism lost much of its appeal in the economic troubles of the 1970s and 1980s. An even more radical alternative, communism, was largely discredited as it collapsed throughout Soviet-controlled Europe.

Yet the very logic of parliamentarism requires intermediary institutions to coordinate communication between electors and candidates, and subsequently between different parliamentarians, and parties are as yet the only institutions capable of filling these functions. In some ways, Nordic parties, like others in Europe, have indeed declined; membership is the most striking indicator of that. But in other ways, they are stronger than ever (Strøm 2000, 183). Thanks to subsidies, they are well resourced; they still control the supply of candidates for elective public office; and they determine the power structures within parliaments and cabinets. Even if some regret, on normative grounds, the changes that they have undergone, parties remain at the heart of Nordic democracy.

NOTES

Many thanks to the authors of the country chapters and the editors of this volume for their invaluable help in preparing this chapter. Without these original, empirical foundations, such a comparative overview could not have been written.

1. A comparable "morphology" of party life is offered by Katz and Mair (2002), who distinguish between the party on the ground, the party in central office, and the party in public office. This chapter deals with the first two of these "faces."

2. Note that the English-language names of the parties are used, as they are translated in Müller and Strøm 2003. The names are not always the same as that which a Nordic party may itself prefer, according to its or the national parliament's Web site.

3. While nearly all West European countries have equivalents to the labor- and conservative-pole parties, Heidar (2004, 59) argues that it is the presence of the third, agrarian pole that really makes the Nordic party systems distinct. Very few other West European countries had or have significant agrarian parties.

4. Iceland was not covered by Berglund and Lindström's (1978) original survey.

5. Indeed, Heidar (2004, 41) calls the bloc system a third way of describing the Nordic party systems, in addition to the three-front and five-party models.

6. This was despite the constitutional steps away from semipresidentialism and toward parliamentarism that Raunio describes in his chapter for this volume.

7. Indeed, an ideologically "connected" coalition in Iceland complemented what had become, perhaps a little ironically, the Nordic party system that most closely resembled the old five-party model.

8. This necessity is sharpened when the electoral system requires parties to draw up lists of their candidates, as all those in the Nordic countries do.

9. Of course, an MP could reject the party on whose platform she was elected and, at the next election, seek instead nomination by another party. But such defection could confer on that MP a reputation for unpredictability, which both the electors and other parties might not appreciate. In the Nordic countries, defections have only rarely occurred.

10. In Denmark, the existence of a third, "political" leader could further complicate internal coordination.

11. Leaderships in Denmark, Finland, and Sweden, the three Nordic EU member states, have, on the other hand, had more direct involvement in candidate selection before elections to the European Parliament. But even then, the leadership's discretion is often tempered by an advisory intraparty primary.

REFERENCES

Allern, Elin Haugsgjerd, and Nicholas Aylott. 2009. "Overcoming the Fear of Commitment: Pre-Electoral Coalitions in Norway and Sweden." *Acta Politica* 44 (3): 259–85.
Allern, Elin Haugsgjerd, and Knut Heidar. 2001. "Partier och intresseorganisasjoner i Norge." In Jan Sundberg, ed., *Partier och intresseorganisationer i Norden*. Copenhagen: Nordic Council of Ministers.
Andersen, Jørgen Goul, and Tor Bjørklund. 2000. "Radical Right-Wing Populism in Scandinavia: From Tax Revolt to Neo-Liberalism and Xenophobia." In Paul Hainsworth, ed., *The Politics of the Extreme Right: From the Margins to the Mainstream*. London: Pinter.
Arter, David. 1999. *Scandinavian Politics Today*. Manchester: Manchester University Press.
Aylott, Nicholas. 2003. "After the Divorce: Social Democrats and Trade Unions in Sweden." *Party Politics* 9 (3): 369–90.
Bale, Tim, and Torbjörn Bergman. 2006. "Captives No Longer, but Servants Still? Contract Parliamentarism and the New Minority Governance in Sweden and New Zealand." *Government and Opposition* 41 (3): 449–76.
Berglund, Sten, and Ulf Lindström. 1978. *The Scandinavian Party System(s)*. Lund: Studentlitteratur.
Biezen, Ingrid van. 2004. "Political Parties as Public Utilities." *Party Politics* 10 (6): 701–22.
Bille, Lars. 2001. "Democratizing a Democratic Procedure: Myth or Reality? Candidate Selection in Western European parties, 1960–1990." *Party Politics* 7 (3): 363–80.
Castles, Francis G. 1978. *The Social Democratic Image of Society: A Study of the Achievements and Origins of Scandinavian Social Democracy in Comparative Perspective*. London: Routledge and Kegan Paul.
Christiansen, Flemming Juul, and Erik Damgaard. 2008. "Parliamentary Opposition under Minority Parliamentarism: Scandinavia." *Journal of Legislative Studies* 14 (1–2): 46–76.
Daalder, Hans. 1992. "A Crisis of Party?" *Scandinavian Political Studies* 15:269–88.
Dalton, Russell J. 2000. "The Decline of Party Identifications." In Russell J. Dalton and Martin P. Wattenberg, eds., *Parties Without Partisans: Political Change in Advanced Industrial Democracies*. Oxford: Oxford University Press.
Damgaard, Erik. 2000. "Parliament and Government." In Peter Esaiasson and Knut

Heidar, eds., *Beyond Westminster and Congress: The Nordic Experience*. Columbus: Ohio State University Press.

Demker, Marie, and Lars Svåsand. 2005. "Partisystemenes utviklingslinjer." In Marie Demker and Lars Svåsand, eds., *Partiernas århundrade*. Stockholm: Santérus.

Duverger, Maurice. 1964. *Political Parties: Their Organization and Activity in the Modern State*. 3rd ed. London: Methuen.

Einhorn, Eric S., and John Logue. 2003. *Modern Welfare States: Scandinavian Politics and Policy in the Global Age*. Westport, CT: Praeger.

Elvander, Nils. 1979. "Scandinavian Social Democracy: Its Strengths and Weaknesses." Skrifter rörande Uppsala universitet. Uppsala University, Acta Universitatis Upsaliensis.

Esaiasson, Peter, and Knut Heidar, eds. 2000. *Beyond Westminster and Congress: The Nordic Experience*. Columbus: Ohio State University Press.

Esping-Andersen, Gøsta. 1985. *Politics Against Markets: The Social Democratic Road to Power*. Princeton: Princeton University Press.

Gidlund, Gullan. 1991. "Public Investments in Swedish Democracy." In Matti Wiberg, ed., *The Public Purse and Political Parties*. Jyväsklä: Gummerus.

Heidar, Knut. 2004. "Parties and Party Systems." In Knut Heidar, ed., *Nordic Politics: Comparative Perspectives*. Oslo: Universitetsforlaget.

Heidar, Knut. 2005. "Norwegian Parties and the Party System: Steadfast and Changing." *West European Politics* 28 (4): 807–33.

Inglehart, Ronald. 1977. *The Silent Revolution*. Princeton: Princeton University Press.

Jungar, Ann-Cathrine. 2002. "A Case of Surplus Majority Government: The Finnish Rainbow Coalition." *Scandinavian Political Studies* 25 (1): 57–83.

Katz, Richard S., and Peter Mair. 1995. "Changing Models of Party Organization and Party Democracy: The Emergence of the Cartel Party." *Party Politics* 1 (1): 5–28.

Katz, Richard S., and Peter Mair. 2002. "The Ascendancy of the Party in Public Office: Party Organizational Change in 20th-Century Democracies." In Richard Gunther, José Rámon Montero, and Juan L. Linz, eds., *Political Parties: Old Concepts and New Challenges*. Oxford: Oxford University Press.

Key, V. O. 1964. *Politics, Parties, and Pressure Groups*. New York: Crowell.

King, Anthony. 1976. "Modes of Executive-Legislative Relations: Great Britain, France, and West Germany." *Legislative Studies Quarterly* 1:11–16.

Kirchheimer, Otto. 1966. "The Transformation of the West European Party Systems." In Joseph LaPalombara and Myron Weiner, eds., *Political Parties and Political Development*. Princeton: Princeton University Press.

Kitschelt, Herbert. 1994. *The Transformation of European Social Democracy*. Cambridge: Cambridge University Press.

Knutsen, Oddbjørn. 2004. "Voters and Social Cleavages." In Knut Heidar, ed., *Nordic Politics: Comparative Perspectives*. Oslo: Universitetsforlaget.

Kristjánsson, Svanur. 2002. "Iceland: From Party Rule to Pluralist Political Society." In Hanne Marthe Narud, Mogens N. Pedersen, and Henry Valen, eds., *Party Sovereignty and Citizen Control: Selecting Candidates for Parliamentary Elections in Denmark, Finland, Iceland, and Norway*. Odense: University Press of Southern Denmark.

Kristjánsson, Svanur. 2004. "Iceland: Searching for Democracy along Three Dimensions of Citizen Control." *Scandinavian Political Studies* 27 (2): 153–74.
Lipset, Seymour Martin, and Stein Rokkan. 1967. "Cleavage Structures, Party Systems, and Voter Alignments: An Introduction." In Seymour Martin Lipset and Stein Rokkan, eds., *Party Systems and Voter Alignments: Cross-National Perspectives*. New York: Free Press.
Müller, Wolfgang C. 2000. "Political Parties in Parliamentary Democracies: Making Delegation and Accountability Work." *European Journal of Political Research* 37 (3): 309–33.
Müller, Wolfgang C., and Kaare Strøm, eds. 2003. *Coalition Government in Western Europe*. Oxford: Oxford University Press.
Narud, Hanne Marthe, Mogens N. Pedersen, and Henry Valen, eds. 2002. *Party Sovereignty and Citizen Control: Selecting Candidates for Parliamentary Elections in Denmark, Finland, Iceland, and Norway*. Odense: University Press of Southern Denmark.
Norris, Pippa, ed. 1999. *Critical Citizens: Global Support for Democratic Governance*. Oxford: Oxford University Press.
NOU. 2004. *Penger teller, men stemmer avgjør. Om partifinansiering, åpenhet og politisk tv-reklame*, 2004:25. Oslo: Ministry of Modernisation.
Panebianco, Angelo. 1988. *Political Parties: Organization and Power*. Cambridge: Cambridge University Press.
Pedersen, Karina. 2003. *Party Membership Linkage: The Danish Case*. Copenhagen: Department of Political Science, University of Copenhagen.
Rokkan, Stein. 1999. "Notes." In Peter Flora, with Stein Kuhnle and Derek Urwin, eds., *State Formation, Nation-Building, and Mass Politics in Europe: The Theory of Stein Rokkan*. Oxford: Oxford University Press.
Sartori, Giovanni. 1976. *Parties and Party Systems: A Framework for Analysis*. Cambridge: Cambridge University Press.
Schmitt, Hermann, and Sören Holmberg. 1995. "Political Parties in Decline?" In Hans-Dieter Klingemann and Dieter Fuchs, eds., *Citizens and the State*. Oxford: Oxford University Press.
Strøm, Kaare. 2000. "Parties at the Core of Government." In Russell J. Dalton and Martin P. Wattenberg, eds., *Parties Without Partisans? Political Change in Advanced Industrial Democracies*. Oxford: Oxford University Press.
Strøm, Kaare, and Wolfgang C. Müller. 1999. "Political Parties and Hard Choices." In Wolfgang C. Müller and Kaare Strøm, eds., *Policy, Office, or Votes? How Political Parties in Western Democracies Make Hard Choices*. New York: Cambridge University Press.
Sundberg, Jan. 2002. "The Scandinavian Party Model at the Crossroads." In Paul Webb, David Farrell, and Ian Holliday, eds., *Political Parties in Advanced Industrial Democracies*. Oxford: Oxford University Press.
Sundberg, Jan. 2003. *Parties as Organized Actors: The Transformation of the Scandinavian Three-Front Parties*. Helsinki: Finnish Society of Sciences and Letters.
Svåsand, Lars. 1998. "Scandinavian Right-Wing Radicalism." In Hans-Georg Betz and Stefan Immerfall, eds., *The New Politics of the Right: Neo-Populist Movements and Parties in Established Democracies*. New York: St. Martin's Press.

INTERNET SOURCES

Statistics Sweden. 2008. Accessed May 25, 2009. http://www.scb.se/Pages/Prices Crib____258649.aspx

Sveriges riksdag. 2008. "Financial Support to the Political Parties," Factsheet 10. Stockholm: Riksdagen. www.riksdagen.se/upload/Dokument/bestall/engelska/Faktablad_E10.pdf

9 ✦ East-West Conflict and Europeanization
International Effects on Democratic Politics in the Nordic States

CYNTHIA KITE

On January 26, 2009, the government of Iceland led by Prime Minister Geir Haarde resigned. The resignation came a week after a crowd of at least 2,000 broke windows and threw eggs and yogurt at Iceland's parliament building to protest the country's growing economic crisis. The events that led to the fall of the government can be traced to the collapse of the subprime mortgage market in the United States in the fall of 2008. This developed into a global financial crisis, and Iceland's banks, heavily indebted, immediately had problems borrowing money. In contrast to the United States, the government lacked the resources needed to bail out the banks. The currency plummeted. The banking system collapsed. Haarde's government was forced to nationalize banks, fix the value of the currency, and turn to the IMF for a loan. Others, notably Sweden and Britain, also provided help. In the end, however, none of this saved the government. As one protester explained, "We've lost all faith in our leaders" (Moody 2009; see also chapter 5, this volume).

What is surprising in this story is not that a government was forced out of office by events that originated beyond its borders. Rather, it is that the impact of international developments on the domestic policy process, the authority of national actors and institutions, and the national democratic chain of delegation and accountability is often overlooked. And when it is acknowledged, it is seen as a deviation from politics "as usual." This chapter seeks to correct this view by considering how, over time, democratic politics in the Nordic countries have been influenced by the international environment.

This chapter is brief, but the overall message is that international developments can influence democratic politics in a variety of ways, sometimes rather predictably, other times unexpectedly. In addition, the analysis will show that these five countries have not necessarily been affected in the same way or to the same degree. Rather, it is the interaction of internal and international conditions that determines how the international environment matters across the Nordic region. The Nordic states have been subject to similar (but far from identical) international pressures, but the ways in which governments, parliaments, and political parties have responded and the impact they have had on democratic politics have differed.

Together with chapter 8, this chapter sets the stage for the final analysis in chapter 10. In particular, since this chapter analyzes the international origins of some of the changes in and constraints on parliamentary democracy, the final chapter can focus on changes and constraints that are commonly understood as domestic. The issue of the impact of international environment on national democratic politics is, however, a potentially unwieldy topic. To make it manageable I have limited my focus to two empirical topics, which I use to explore the consequences of international developments on the national policy process. These topics are security and regional integration (EU) policy. I do not discuss developments in North-South relations, global trade and finance, or the United Nations. Although obviously important in their own right, they have generally had less impact on parliamentary politics in the Nordic states than security and regional integration. Moreover, relations of friendship and enmity are fundamental characteristics of the international system. It is difficult to understand other aspects of the external environment without knowledge of them.

The years since the mid-1980s are of particular interest. However, we must briefly consider the way in which international developments impacted on democratic politics in the Nordic states before this period. This provides a useful backdrop for understanding the current period. In addition, it is a healthy reminder that the intrusion of international politics into the democratic policy process is not a new phenomenon.

East-West Rivalry, Security Policy, and Domestic Politics

There is nothing new about the fact that the international environment affects domestic politics, as noted above. At the end of World War II many people around the world hoped that the postwar period would be dominated by peaceful conflict resolution through the United Nations and by international economic cooperation for prosperity and development. During this optimistic period, Nordic political elites articulated a common commitment to pursuing friendly relations with all states and to supporting the expansion of international trade and investment (Tammes 1991; Lundestad 1980; Haskel 1976; Dau 1969). Finland's emphasis on the importance of bilateral relations of accommodation and trust with the Soviet Union (USSR) was the exception.

Relations between the West and the USSR became increasingly confrontational throughout 1945–46, and a number of events and subsequent foreign policy responses in 1947 and early 1948 contributed to a sense of deepening crisis.[1] As a result of this deterioration in the external environment, the Nordic states faced new challenges, opportunities, and constraints. Of fundamental importance was the institutionalization of the East-West conflict into competing alliances—first the North Atlantic Treaty Organization (NATO) and then the Warsaw Pact.

Confronted with superpower rivalry, the Nordic states were forced to reevaluate their security policies. Three policy options were seriously considered (except in Finland): some form of neutralism, NATO membership, and a Nordic defense pact. Norway rejected the latter as insufficient, which effectively killed it. Denmark, Iceland, and Norway abandoned neutralism in favor of NATO. Sweden reaffirmed its commitment to neutrality. Finland, under duress, signed a bilateral treaty with the USSR. These policy choices created some political disagreement, but overwhelming majorities supported them. In some of the Nordic countries, the disagreement that did exist tended to follow, and therefore reinforced, the dominant left-right dimension (see chapter 8). Denmark and Iceland were partial exceptions to this, so security policy occasionally disrupted normal politics.

Throughout the Nordic region, the East-West rivalry, due to its implications for security policy, impacted in various ways on policies and the domestic policy process. Its effect was greatest in Finland. In Finland, it impacted directly by closing off security-policy options and strengthening the power of the president and by influencing government formation. Finland had fought against the Soviet Union in the Winter War (1939–40) and Continuation War (1941–44), before signing an armistice agreement committing itself to opposing Germany. Its situation was precarious, and President Paasikivi made it clear that Finland's only hope of retaining political independence was to seek friendship and accommodation with the Soviet Union. He refused Marshall Plan aid from the United States and ordered the conviction and punishment of Finns deemed guilty of bring the country into the war against the USSR in 1941. This approach to bilateral relations, which became known as the Paasikivi-Kekkonen line, was formally articulated in the 1948 Treaty of Friendship, Cooperation, and Mutual Assistance. The treaty was controversial in Finland, and Paasikivi's success in getting parliamentary approval for it reinforced his status with Moscow and thus his authority at home. This and subsequent incidents solidified the status of the president as the guardian of Finnish independence and authoritative interpreter of what Moscow was prepared to tolerate. Naturally, this gave the Finnish president strong political powers, including a voice in government formation.[2]

In the other Nordic states, the East-West rivalry had its greatest impact when it tapped into latent (or secondary) conflict dimensions in the party system. Swedish freedom of action was constrained due to its need to maintain credibility for neutrality policy, but there is little evidence that this directly influenced the functioning of democratic politics. Political tussles about what credibility actually required Sweden to do (or refrain from doing) occasionally erupted, but they tended to follow the left-right dimension and were thus part of the normal pattern of Swedish politics.

For Norway, Denmark, and Iceland, NATO membership seems to have imposed rather limited policy demands. Iceland was not required to maintain any military strength at all. While the U.S. base was controversial among nationalist-neutralists, it provided significant economic benefits. In addition, despite opposition from Britain, NATO membership had no impact on Iceland's decision to expand its fishing zone in 1958 and then again in the early and mid-1970s.[3] Denmark and Norway kept the alliance at least partly out of the Scandinavian region by refusing nuclear weapons and foreign troops in peacetime. In addition, their defense spending declined during the Cold War, often against the wishes of the United States (which was nonetheless unable to reverse the trend).

NATO membership occasionally disrupted democratic politics. In Denmark the Radical Liberals retained a strong pacifist/neutralist sentiment throughout the Cold War. This had the potential to split the right and push the Radical Liberals and the left together, something that became particularly visible in the 1980s, when rising tensions brought the disagreement into the open (see also chapter 3, this volume, and Damgaard and Svensson 1989).[4] The four-party minority cabinet that held power from 1982 to 1988 was repeatedly defeated on NATO policy proposals by an alternative majority that was nonetheless unable to cooperate to bring the government down.[5]

The U.S. military presence in Iceland had a similar effect because it tapped into a rural-urban conflict in Icelandic politics.[6] Norway had no such problem because opposition to NATO was concentrated on the left, thus reinforcing the left-right dimension. However, in 1961 an anti-NATO group quit the Labor Party to form the Socialist People's Party (Christensen 1998; Elvander 1980). In 1963 the new party won enough votes to end 28 years of social democratic government. More broadly, it created competition for voters to the left of the social democrats. This forced the Social Democrats to pay greater attention to this segment of voters and their representatives within the party whenever security issues were (or could become) politicized.

European Integration, Security, and Sovereignty in the Nordic States

A second fundamental development in the international environment of the post–World War II period has been the establishment of supranationalist European cooperation. Security was also a driving force behind supranationalism—elites believed that by tying states together in powerful political institutions future war in Europe could be prevented. With the exception of Finland, the process of regional integration in Europe has in some respects been (and continues to be) more disruptive of the democratic chain of delegation and accountability in the Nordic states than the East-West rivalry ever was.

The first successful step in regional integration based on supranationalist ideas was the creation of the European Coal and Steel Community (ECSC) in 1952. After failing to reach agreement on a European Defense Community, the six ECSC members established Euratom and the European Economic Community (EEC) in 1957. These developments split the states of Western Europe into two groups—those committed to supranationalism and far-reaching political unity (the "inner six") and those who favored intergovernmental cooperation (the "outer seven"). The UK spearheaded efforts to create a Europe-wide free-trade arrangement including both groups, but when this failed it supported the creation of the European Free Trade Agreement (EFTA) as an alternative to the EEC.

Nordic attitudes to the EEC were influenced by a variety of factors, not least an overall skepticism or opposition to supranationalism because of its perceived negative consequences for national political autonomy. Neutralist foreign policy sentiments, ideologically rooted commitments to far-reaching political control of the economy, a sense of cultural distinctiveness, and—in Norway and Iceland—relatively recent national independence contributed to the Nordic attachment to autonomy.[7] On the other hand, as small, economically open states, all the Nordics needed reliable access to export markets on equal terms as other exporters, although their specific economic interests with respect to the European Community (EC) varied.

Over the years, the question of how to respond to European integration caused considerable political disruption in the Nordic states—considerably more than security policy. This is because the issue often cuts across the left-right dimension, weakens party unity (especially for social democratic parties), and unleashes direct democratic processes. These developments are particularly easy to identify at times when European integration emerges on the active political agenda. Three clear examples of this are Britain's decision in 1961 to abandon EFTA and apply for EEC membership, the EEC decision at the 1969 Hague summit to open membership negotiations with all interested states, and the revitalization of the EC from the mid-1980s. Each of these developments threatened to reduce the benefits of the preferred policy of the Nordic states—EFTA membership—and increase the costs of remaining outside of the EC. As a result they pushed the issue of the country's relationship with the EC to the top of the political agenda throughout the region.[8] The same was true for Sweden and Finland, but it was the end of the Cold War in 1989–90 that marked a genuine turning point for them. In addition, as chapters 3–7 have made clear (and as will be discussed in the next section), the deepening of European cooperation since the 1990s has significant implications for national democratic politics insofar as it gives actors external to the national democratic chain considerable political authority as well as influences the relative authority of actors within the chain itself.

Sweden

During the Cold War, the question of how to respond to European integration occasionally created policy problems and some political controversy in Sweden. These periods coincided with external developments mentioned above, and in each case the policy problem was that an external event threatened to undermine the economic benefits of EFTA.

Between the 1960s and 1989, the Social Democrats and the Center Party maintained the view that membership was incompatible with neutrality policy because the EC's supranationalism meant giving up independent political authority to an organization whose members all belonged to NATO, and thus unequivocally to the western bloc. Whenever external developments pushed the question of EC membership to the top of the political agenda these parties repeated this position, while the (smaller) Conservative and Liberal parties argued that the economic consequences of remaining outside a deeper or larger EC would be much greater than the Social Democrats admitted (or understood). They criticized the government for unilaterally ruling out membership, and, when Denmark and Norway applied for membership, called for applying for membership with a neutrality reservation, arguing that the problems membership posed for neutrality could be resolved with special protocols (Miljan 1977). They were unable, however, to do more than this. One reason was because the government retained authority over foreign policy. It informed the Riksdag of its decision not to seek membership in the 1960s and early 1970s; it did not ask for a mandate to do so. Another reason was that the Center Party agreed with the Social Democrats. Thus, the government had broad parliamentary support for its position, and there was no united nonsocialist support for an alternative policy. Nor was there any internal party conflict to exploit. Finally, public opinion was overwhelmingly supportive of neutrality and thus skeptical toward EC membership.

In the late 1970s and early 1980s, when the nonsocialists were in government, the Conservative and Liberal parties had no incentive to raise the issue of Sweden's relationship with the EC. The opposition of the Center Party and the potential loss of voter support was sufficient reason for the nonsocialists to shy away from the question. Moreover, and perhaps fortunately for them, these years were also a period when the EC was struggling with its own problems and the benefits of membership compared to the free trade agreement that governed Swedish-EC relations seemed rather limited. Thus, no external developments forced the nonsocialists to deal with the question.

Finland

Finland's challenge was similar to Sweden's. It was anxious to avoid winding up outside of regional economic agreements that included the Nordic states and Britain, but unable to apply for membership—even in EFTA. The Soviet Union's opposition ruled out both and thus clearly constrained the authority of the Finnish Eduskunta in the area of foreign trade policy.

Finland adopted a wait-and-see approach to promoting its interests—working outside of the public eye to get Soviet support before taking any action (Rehn 2003; Hakovirta 1981). This approach led to the FINNEFTA solution in 1961, which enabled Finland to participate in EFTA's economic cooperation while remaining outside its political arrangements; to the successful negotiation of a free trade agreement with the EC in 1973; and to Finnish participation in the EEA in the 1980s (Kinnunen 2003). In the

1970s, to reassure Moscow of Finland's continued friendship and neutrality, Finland scuttled plans for a Nordic customs union after Soviet officials expressed concerns about it and extended to the USSR's eastern European allies the same free-trade benefits it had granted to EC members.

Denmark

Denmark and Norway never had security objections to joining the EC, so their relationships with it reflected political struggles between domestic actors who disagreed about the economic, political, and cultural consequences of joining or remaining outside. Economic arguments emphasized the costs and benefits of membership for the economy in general and for particular sectors. Arguments about the political consequences were similar in the two countries and reflected Nordic aversion to supranationalist schemes and preference for national autonomy and democracy. Much of the opposition to membership was located on the left and, in Norway, among representatives of protected primary sectors, while support came from conservatives and social democrats. The views of agrarian and other middle parties varied across the Nordic states, in part due to different economic interests, but also because of different patterns of neutralist foreign policy sentiments.

Because attitudes to EC membership and other EC-related questions did not always follow the left-right dimension nor unite parties behind a single position, the EC repeatedly disrupted politics as usual in Denmark and Norway (although more so in the latter). They created internal party conflict; undermined government coalitions; created disagreement between party elites, rank-and-file members, and sympathizers; and promoted grass-roots oppositional politics and direct democracy at the expense of parliamentary procedures. The latter, direct democracy, emerged because party elites—sometimes reluctantly, sometimes in an effort to preserve party unity, sometimes tactically—agreed to allow referenda to decide the issue once negotiations were completed.

Initially, there was broad support for membership among Danish political parties—from the Conservatives on the right to the Social Democrats on the left (Kite 1996). The Liberal Party, with its socioeconomic base of support in the export-oriented agricultural sector, was strongly in favor of joining. Denmark's Radical Liberal Party favored negotiations, although it was otherwise rather lukewarm to the EC. The only party formally opposed to membership was the Socialist People's Party.

From the early 1970s, however, the question became more problematic for the parties and thus for democratic politics. When the Hague summit opened the door to UK membership in the EC, the Danish government quickly announced its intention to join. Most Radical Liberal Party supporters continued to support membership, but by this time many party members and elites opposed it as contrary to their preferred foreign policy, which was one rooted in neutralism and strong Nordic ties. Given this dilemma, the party opted to accept negotiations but refused to take a position on membership, even after negotiations were completed. The question created even greater difficulties for the Social Democrats. There was strong opposition to EC membership among left-wing members of the party. Moreover, traditional trade union rank-and-file skepticism toward the "capitalist" EC and the radicalizing effect of New Left ideology led most party sympathizers to oppose it, despite the promembership stance of the party.

Under the Danish Constitution, decisions to transfer authority to international organizations must be subject to a referendum if they are supported by fewer than five-sixths of the members of the Folketing. However, in light of their internal party difficulties, and fearing significant losses in the upcoming elections, the Social Democratic Party—hoping to lift the issue out of ordinary representative politics—announced in early May 1971 that they would force a referendum to decide the issue of membership, regardless of the outcome of the Folketing vote (Petersen and Elklit 1973; Miljan 1977). The Radical Liberals quickly supported the decision. Negotiations with the EC were completed by December 1971. The Folketing voted to support membership in December 1971 and again in September 1972. The membership referendum was held October 2, 1972. During the referendum campaign, a mix of forces that included the Socialist People's Party, splinter groups of Social Democrats and Radical Liberals, as well as some trade unions opposed membership. The outcome was nonetheless a clear victory for membership, with 63 percent voting in favor of joining. Despite this, anti-EC sentiments in Denmark did not disappear. They reflect the alternative foreign-policy conflict dimension discussed above and have continued to manifest themselves in Danish EC politics.

Denmark has held five referenda about extending and deepening the EC's scope and authority—the Single European Act (SEA) (1986), the Maastricht Treaty (1992), Edinburgh (Maastricht with opt-outs) (1993), the Amsterdam Treaty (1998), and the EMU (2000). The outcomes show a significant, stable level of Euroskepticism among Danish voters (Damgaard and Nørgaard 2000). In some cases, they also reveal considerable disagreement among political elites and voters. In the first postmembership referendum, the SEA, a majority (56 percent) of parliamentarians—the alternative majority (Radical

Liberals, Social Democrats, Socialists, and Left Socialists)—voted against. In the subsequent referendum, voters (also 56 percent!) sided with the government, and approved the SEA despite parliamentary opposition. In 1992 the situation was reversed. Among parliamentarians, 85 percent supported the Maastricht Treaty, but a (very small) majority of voters (50.7 percent) rejected it.

Danish rejection of the Maastricht Treaty led to the negotiation of the Edinburgh Agreement, which allowed Denmark to opt out of the final phase of the EMU, defense cooperation outside of NATO, EU citizenship, and cooperation on justice and home affairs. Danish voters approved the agreement (56.7 percent) in May 1993. About the same share of voters (55.1 percent) approved the Amsterdam Treaty five years later. Danish voters have not, however, given up their independent thinking on EU matters. In 2000, they rejected EMU membership by 53.3 to 46.7 percent. In this case, even voters from Denmark's most pro-European parties voted no—including a third of the Liberal Party voters and a quarter of Conservative Party voters (Qvortrup 2001). This serves as a good illustration of the fact that the left-right character of Danish EU opinion has weakened over time. Denmark's membership referendum campaign in the early 1970s largely followed and thus reinforced the left-right dimension (Petersen and Elklit 1973). This is much less true today, given the establishment of the EU-skeptical Danish People's Party in 1995, the anti-EU attitudes of the (now largely defunct) Progress Party, and evidence of issue-specific EU skepticism even among conservative voters.

Norway

In contrast to Denmark, Norway's anti-EU sentiment was broader and included established, nonextremist parties. It weakened established bloc politics and turned otherwise antagonistic groups and parties into temporary allies. Because nonextremist parties were also opposed to membership, it made this position more "respectable" and thus more attractive to ordinary voters. The EU membership question hurt the Labor Party. By activating the urban-rural dimension in Norwegian politics, it undermined nonsocialist government coalitions. In short, in Norway, the EU created serious problems for everybody.

From the 1960s to the 1990s the only consistently promembership parties were the Conservatives and Labor. Conservative voters agreed with their party's position. By contrast, prominent Labor Party members, the party's youth organization, many trade unions, and large numbers of Labor sympathizers opposed the party's promembership position. In 1994, the National Confederation of Labor Unions even voted against membership and thus refused to participate in the promembership campaign.

Because the Socialist People's Party strongly rejected membership, whenever the EC issue is on the active political agenda, Labor elites worry about losing support on the left. In an effort to prevent this, despite the promembership views of top party elites, the party moved slowly in both the 1970s and 1990s, appointing commissions to study potential consequences of membership and seeking party-congress and parliamentary-group approval before applying for membership (Allen 1979; Kite 1996). Not reassured, in both the 1970s and 1990s Labor Party members established antimembership organizations to mobilize public opinion and defeat membership.

The political confrontation in the 1970s significantly damaged the party. Opponents conducted an anti-EC campaign that largely ignored the wider interests of the party, while party elites excluded them from participating in intraparty forums focused on EC matters (Aylott 2002). The prime minister staked the future of the government on the outcome of the referenda, and one of the party slogans was "A Labor Voter is a Yes Voter" (Aylott 2002, 453). When voters rejected membership in September 1972 (53.5 percent voted no), the government kept its promise and resigned. It was replaced by a minority coalition of opponents of membership—the Christian People's Party, the Center Party, and some Liberal Party members—who otherwise had rather little in common, although they did succeed in negotiating the free trade agreement that regulated Norwegian relations with the EU until the European Economic Area Agreement (EEA) came into effect in the 1990s. The party seemed to learn from these mistakes, and in the 1990s opponents campaigned against the EU without attacking the party's leadership and opponents were not excluded from intraparty EU forums. The government did not tie its future to the outcome of the referendum and did not resign when voters again rejected membership by a vote of 52.5 to 47.8 percent in November 1994. The government withdrew its request that Parliament support the treaty of accession and announced that Norway's relations with the EU would continue to be governed by the EEA.

Norway's nonsocialist parties suffered their own EC-related difficulties, including both interparty conflict and coalition-building problems. The strong opposition to membership from agriculture and fishing—both of which relied on government subsidies and other discriminatory legislation deemed incompatible with membership—helped reinforce a culturally rooted antipathy to the EC in rural and peripheral regions. The Liberals and Christian People's Party, neither of whom had economic bases of support that clearly pushed them in one direction or the other, suffered serious internal disagreement because their urban and rural wings had very different views of the EC.[9] Although both parties supported membership negotiations in the 1960s, they came out against membership from the 1970s. The Liberal Party's decision to oppose membership was made at the 1972 Party Congress, and it prompted the pro-EC group to quit the party and form the New People's Party. The party reunited in the 1990s, on the basis of an agreement that included a commitment to oppose membership.

The membership question not only created intraparty conflicts but also undermined the cohesion of the nonsocialist bloc. In addition to the opposed but internally split Christians and Liberals, the bloc included the firmly promembership Conservatives and emphatically antimembership Center Party. When membership became a real possibility in the early 1970s, Norway was being governed by a four-party, nonsocialist coalition led by the Center Party. Efforts to hold the government together despite disagreement on EC membership failed, and it fell in March 1971. The same thing occurred in 1990, when the Conservative-led Syse government fell due to sharp disagreement about membership.

The anti-EC coalition in Norway did not have the same antiestablishment character as it did in Denmark. Perhaps paradoxically, this allowed it to have more severe effects on parliamentary democracy because it made it stronger—both in terms of numbers and in terms of other resources. In both the 1970s and 1990s, the promembership coalition was a mix of Social Democrats, Conservatives, employers, urban voters in the south, and some trade unions. Opposition came from a mix of left and radical liberal groups (both traditional labor as well as New Left postmaterialism groups were very active in the antimembership campaign), but also rural and peripheral communities, particularly farmers and fishermen. The Center Party, along with primary sector groups, played a significant role in the antimembership campaign, which gave it organizational and financial support as well as increased its credibility among groups outside the radical left.

Norway's current relationship with the EU (regulated in the EEA agreement) has been called "quasi-membership" (Eliassen and Sitter 2003). The EEA agreement makes Norway a part of the single market but exempts it from the common agriculture and fisheries policies and regional policy. Norway has also sought to expand its relationship with the EU beyond EEA-regulated matters on an issue-by-issue basis—for example, education, research, and border control. Although the EEA agreement allows Norway to participate in early phases of the EU policy process, it has no formal role in decision making. It retains formal sovereignty to adopt or reject new EU legislation. However, if the parliament refuses to adopt measures related to the single market, the EU has the right to suspend the parts of the EEA agreement that are relevant to the new legislation. Given the importance of the EEA agreement for the Norwegian economy, in effect this means that Norway has little choice but to adopt EU legislation that it has little ability to influence. This must be seen as a potentially serious external constraint on Norway's democratic chain of delegation and accountability.

After the Cold War—EU Referenda in Sweden and Finland

With the end of the Cold War in the early 1990s, membership in the EU became a real option for Sweden and Finland. As a result, debates about their relations with the EU came to resemble those of Denmark and Norway. Security considerations receded, and arguments about the economic and political costs and benefits came to the fore. In Sweden, opinions largely followed the left-right dimension, although it also tapped into a postmaterial sentiment in the Green Party and Center. Agriculture, as well as business and industry, supported membership. Trade union leaders tended to be in favor, though there was considerable opposition among blue-collar workers (Kite 1996).

Among the Swedish political parties, the Conservatives, Liberals, Center, and the Social Democrats supported membership and voted, in December 1990, in favor of applying while retaining neutrality policy, which was seen as compatible with membership in a post–Cold War environment. Only the Socialists and Greens opposed, thus giving Sweden's opposition the antiestablishment character of Denmark's. EU membership created the same intraparty conflict for Swedish Social Democrats as it did for their Danish and Norwegian counterparts. It also created difficulty for Center. Its anti-EU sentiment was particularly strong in the youth and women's organizations, and had similar roots as opposition within the Greens—that is, the EU's democratic deficiencies and membership's negative consequences for regional development, environmentalism, decentralization, and Sweden's political autonomy to decide these issues itself (Kite 1996; Jahn and Storsved 1995).

A variety of pressures led to Sweden's decision in 1991 to bypass the institutions of representative democracy in favor of a referendum on membership after negotiations were completed. These included the perceived importance of the question, precedent in Denmark and Norway, disagreement within political parties (particularly among Social Democrats and

Center), and strategic calculations. The outcome of the November 1994 referendum was a modest majority—52.2 percent—in favor of membership. Support for membership declined quickly after the referendum, and Euroskepticism remains stronger in Sweden than in many other member states, although the most recent Eurobarometer data show that almost 60 percent now agree that membership is a "good thing." However, only about 50 percent think the country has "on balance benefited" from membership (Eurobarometer 2008).[10]

One reflection of Swedish skepticism toward the benefits of EU membership, as well as the particular difficulty that additional integrationist developments pose for the Social Democrats and Center, was the government's decision not to join the EMU from the start (Aylott 2005a). The issue was decided in a referendum in September 2003, which was in many ways a repeat of 1994. This time, however, the opposition successfully avoided appearing antiestablishment. This was due in part to its own efforts, but also because the Center Party opposed EMU and the central organization of the blue-collar labor unions (*Landsorganisationen*, LO) remained neutral. A decisive majority (55.9 percent) voted no.

Finnish political elites began raising the possibility of EU membership in internal discussions in 1990 (Raunio and Tiilikainen 2003). The National Coalition, Swedish People's Party, and Social Democrats came out in favor of applying the following year. The Center Party was more ambivalent. Its basis of support was agriculture and rural areas, where attitudes to the EU were negative due to fears that membership would force Finland to replace its more generous support program with the EU's Common Agriculture Policy (CAP). The Finnish political economy was therefore similar to that of Norway, with membership pitting business and industry against agriculture. A crucial difference, however, was that the Finnish Center Party led the government that applied for membership negotiations and it retained a promembership, if reserved, attitude (Jahn and Storsved 1995; Raunio and Tiilikainen 2003).

Finland's Social Democratic party did not suffer the level of internal conflict characteristic of its sister parties in the other Nordic states, and the trade union movement was also less divided and more favorable than those in Sweden and Norway. In general, opposition to membership in Finland was more like Denmark's and Sweden's—that is, antiestablishment—than Norway's broader coalition of anti-EC forces (Jahn and Storsved 1995). The antimembership campaign brought together nationalists on the far right with leftists, environmentalists, and agriculture. However, the Left Alliance and Greens did not formally oppose membership (Raunio 2007). On the promembership side, in addition to the familiar economic arguments made by proponents in the other Nordic states, Finnish proponents began to link membership and security, as fears rose late in the campaign that developments in Russia were moving in the wrong direction. The security benefits of membership were initially presented in general terms, but as time went on supporters began to suggest that EU membership would enhance Finnish national security by providing protection against Russia (Raunio and Tiilikainen 2003). Among ordinary voters, opinions about EU membership displayed a strong center-periphery divide (Pesonen, Jenssen, and Gilljam 1998b). However, in contrast to Norway, the Finnish Center Party remained firmly in favor of membership, so popular opposition to membership in rural areas did not undermine the government. In the October 1994 referendum, Finnish voters decisively supported membership by a vote of 57 to 43 percent.

Since joining the EU Finland has developed a reputation as the least reluctant Nordic member. There is a fair amount of popular skepticism toward the EU and some skepticism among most parties, but the only fully Eurosceptic party in the Finnish parliament is the very small True Finns (Raunio 2007). Moreover, unlike the other Nordic members, Finland has held no subsequent referenda on the EU. It has no Danish-like opt-outs and was a founding member of the EMU.

Iceland

Iceland is the only Nordic state that has never applied for membership in the EU (although the 2009 economic crisis has reactualized the question and increased support for membership). While there were numerous debates about relations with Europe between 1960 and the early 1990s, no party or group seriously pursued it (Thorhallsson 2004). Iceland's core interest was protecting and expanding its access to export markets for fish while maintaining control over marine resources. It was not clear that membership in the EEC or EFTA would promote this interest, and there were concerns that it would undermine other economic interests, including those of agriculture and industry. Iceland responded to this uncertainty by following developments but otherwise adopted a wait-and-see attitude. There was no serious political confrontation about the country's relationship with the EC. In general, the Independence Party and Social Democrats have pursued closer relations to the EC than the Progressives and People's Alliance have been willing to support. Thus, at the level of political parties, this pattern of policy preference is the same as the pattern of support and opposition to the U.S. military presence in the country.

In response to Britain's application for EEC membership in 1961, and in anticipation of applications from Denmark and Norway, a coalition government composed of the Independence and Social Democrat parties applied for association status (Thorhallsson and Vignisson 2004b). No party or group supported membership, while the Progressives and People's Alliance came out against association on the grounds that it was economically harmful and for nationalist-cultural reasons. The issue of association faded away when De Gaulle vetoed Britain's application, and in the late 1960s the question of EFTA membership replaced it.[11] The political lineup was similar, with the Independence Party and Social Democrats in favor of membership, and the Progressives and People's Alliance opposed. The opposition of agriculture heavily influenced the former, while the Alliance rejected membership on the grounds that it would harm industry, increase unemployment, and undermine national control of the economy (Thorhallsson and Vignisson 2004b). Despite this, the government's parliamentary majority enabled it to win approval for the treaty of accession, and Iceland joined EFTA in 1970. Two years later, a new coalition government composed of the Progressives, People's Alliance, and the Union of Liberals and Leftists successfully negotiated an industrial free-trade agreement with the EC. All parties supported the agreement, which provided significant benefits to the fishing industry without undermining Icelandic control of its newly expanded fishing limits (Thorhallsson and Vignisson 2004b).

Only in 1989, when commission president Jacques Delors proposed the EEA, did Iceland's relationship with Europe again become an important political issue. At the time, Iceland was ruled by a three-party coalition composed of the Progressives, Social Democrats, and People's Alliance. While all three parties formally supported negotiations, only the Social Democrats were strongly committed to it (Thorhallsson and Vignisson 2004a). The cabinet had only a one-seat lead in the Althingi, and the Social Democrats worried about defections from their coalition partners. This precarious situation helped convince the Social Democrats to switch partners and form a coalition government with the Independence Party after the 1991 election (Thorhallsson and Vignisson 2004a). Both the People's Alliance and a large number of Progressive Party parliamentarians came out against the EEA.

The EEA issue aroused considerable attention, greater-than-usual interest-group activity, and considerable grassroots campaigning,[12] but the basic operation of ordinary representative politics was maintained. The government maintained control of the issue. There was no referendum, and the government's majority in the Althingi was sufficient to win passage.

The EEA came into effect in 1994. As noted above with regard to Norway, the agreement is a potentially serious constraint on democratic politics because it requires the country to implement policies related to the free movement of goods, services, people, and capital even though it has not formally participated in the decision-making process that produced them. The Social Democratic Party has made applying for EU membership a formal party position, and in the wake of the financial crisis of 2008, the issue has emerged on the active political agenda and has gained additional support.

External Environment and Present Challenges

The country chapters and chapter 8 provide numerous examples of how domestic parliamentary processes are influenced by external developments. In both security and European integration policy, external developments closed off certain options, including ones that Nordic majorities (both voters and parties in parliament) seem to have preferred—for example, neutralist security policy and intergovernmental free-trade cooperation. At times, these developments also had significant impacts on domestic politics and democratic delegation and accountability. This penultimate section provides further details on how domestic politics has been linked to the developments outlined above. It also shows that the impact continues to exist today.

In Denmark in the 1980s, NATO's missile deployment policy was strongly opposed by a parliamentary majority that repeatedly thwarted the government's conduct of foreign policy, though it could not hold together to bring down the government. Security policy was less disruptive in Norway. While opposition to NATO membership led to the creation of the Socialist People's Party by a breakaway left-wing faction of the Labor Party, security policy did not create significant political controversy. This contrasts with the political response to the question of Norway's relationship to the EC, which was a difficult issue for the Labor Party, undermined nonsocialist cooperation, and brought down two governments. It also had significant (if temporary) impacts on parliamentary elections. In 1973, a year after the first membership referendum, Labor went from 72 seats (45.6 percent) to 62 (35.2 percent), while the Socialist People's Party gained 16 seats. In 1993, in the middle of the most recent Norwegian struggle for membership, the Center Party gained 21 seats, although it lost them again four years later. Disagreement over EC membership caused the Liberal Party to split in 1972, which led to its falling out of government for more than 20 years.

Sweden and Finland were largely spared internal conflict over security policy, and therefore EC policy, during the Cold War. For Sweden these were largely self-made choices. Finland's rather precarious situation toward the Soviet Union meant that its lack of political conflict was partly a reflection of its limited political autonomy and self-censorship. Once the Cold War ended, consensus on European policy broke down, and debates similar to those in the other Nordic countries developed. The issue did not create difficulties like those suffered by Norway, although individual parties experienced difficulties.

In all four of these states relations with Europe have become a matter for direct democracy. Thus, even where national relations with the EU did not create deep and lasting political divisions and disruptions of political life, it has significantly disrupted the normal functioning of representative democracy in the Nordic states and led to referendum campaigns dominated by unusual alliances and characterized by massive grassroots mobilization. The reason for this seems to be considerable uncertainty and disagreement among the political parties. These, in turn, undermine the ability of parties to control the political process and create an opportunity and incentive for mobilization (Kite 1996).

As early as 1962, in its report on the question of EEC membership, the Norwegian Storting's Committee on Foreign and Constitutional Affairs recommended holding a referendum after the completion of negotiations in order to allow citizens to express their views. The report revealed considerable disagreement about membership, not least because it contained a majority recommendation and two minority recommendations. Moreover, the majority recommendation did not actually include a policy preference—calling only for negotiations as a way to clarify the conditions under which the country could join. Having promised to allow the citizens to express their views in a referendum in 1962, it was impossible to refuse to hold a referendum 10 years later.

Similarly, in Denmark in the 1970s, the Social Democrats called for a referendum in an effort to protect the party from being weakened, or even split, due to intraparty conflict. The Danish constitution makes it easy for a minority to force a referendum on transferring political power to international organizations, and doing so has thus become the norm. It gives Danish citizens considerable political clout in certain kinds of EU questions, but it disrupts representative democracy. In general, then, the precedent established by Norway and Denmark has made direct democracy the "ordinary" process of decision making for a certain class of European regional integration questions—not just membership across the Nordic states.

In the 1990s, there was barely any resistance to holding membership referenda in Sweden and Finland. On the other hand, there is variation across the Nordic states. Finland has successfully refused to hold any other referenda, while Sweden has thus far limited the use of referendum to membership and the EMU. Iceland stands out as the most different Nordic. This is because its security policy, in particular the presence of the U.S. military base, has been rather contentious, but—since it has not sought membership—it has not experienced serious political controversy over European integration. Whether or not this will change if (or when) the government applies for membership remains to be seen.

The impacts of Nordic security and EU policy choices on national autonomy are complicated. In general, NATO membership seems to have left the Nordics with considerable room to maneuver, as illustrated by Danish and Norwegian decisions not to accept foreign bases or nuclear weapons in their territories in peacetime, and by Danish parliamentary behavior in the 1980s (see note 5). Although Sweden refused to take sides during the Cold War, the credibility of neutrality policy forced the country to anticipate superpower reactions to a variety of international and defense policies and to act accordingly. Despite disagreement about exactly how much impact the USSR had on Finnish policy and politics during the Cold War, Finland's need to reassure the USSR in order to protect national independence clearly limited national autonomy.

EU integration has been a more significant external constraint on Nordic policy autonomy than NATO membership, both because of the supranationalist structure of the EU and the greater scope of cooperation. This is true for both members and nonmembers. In general, of course, for member states, what is lost in formal autonomy is partly compensated for by influence on the EU policy-making process. However, there is also interesting variation in the opportunities that member states' voters and political parties have to influence national action in EU forums; such opportunities are probably greatest in Denmark, least in Finland.

In Denmark, as noted above, constitutional requirements and political praxis have led to the emergence of an EU-referenda politics that allows Danish voters to retain a degree of control over larger questions. Moreover, the Danish parliament's EU Committee forces the government to take account of domestic interests and policy preferences in day-to-day policy-making in the EU. The EU skepticism among Swedish voters and parties has fewer outlets than Denmark's but more than Finland's. The differences here have less to do with the formal powers of EU committees in the national parliaments than with the lack of EU-skeptic parties in the Finnish parliament and the more elitist tradition of Finnish foreign policy. Perhaps ironically, Norwegian nonmembership seems to be a greater external constraint than membership. Norway is largely forced to adopt EU legislation without having any formal role in the EU decision-making process, despite the fact that voters have rejected membership twice. Iceland is in a similar situation, albeit less dramatically because it is more satisfied with the EEA agreement and thus less concerned about being shut out of European cooperation.

As the EU continues to expand and evolve, it will continue to have an impact on both Nordic politics and autonomy. One development already under way is the challenge of European Security and Defense Policy (ESDP). Since the late 1990s the issues of security policy and European integration have begun to merge. During the Cold War and throughout much of the 1990s the two were formally distinct insofar as NATO was the organization and arena for security cooperation, while the EU was the regional integration arena. In the past decade this has changed. A key decision was made at the Helsinki Summit in 1999, when the European Council decided to establish military institutions and defense capability for crisis management to support the already agreed-upon Petersberg Tasks—humanitarian intervention, crisis management, and peacemaking. The Helsinki Headline Goal established a specific target—that by 2003 member states would be able to deploy a military force, capable of carrying out the Petersberg Tasks, of up to 60,000 persons within 60 days and sustainable for at least one year (Quille 2006). In June 2004, the Headline Goal 2010 broadened the Petersberg Tasks, created new institutions (including a European Defense Agency), and established new operational ambitions, including battle groups.

The merger of European regional integration and security is ongoing, but it has already created a number of issues that the Nordic states will have to resolve. Some of these have to do with democratic politics and as-yet-unresolved questions about the future of security policy and the role of national and EU actors and institutions in the policy process. What is clear is that in some states these questions create intraparty disagreements and/or disagreements between elites and voters.

Finland and Sweden have been active supporters of ESDP efforts, as well as willing participants in ESDP missions (Bailes 2006). This is due in large part to their interests in promoting the development of security and defense cooperation in directions that do not directly compromise their national security policies and do not compete with NATO. Although they no longer use the word *neutrality*, both retain a policy of military nonalignment. In practice this means that they remain outside NATO, though they participate in Partnership for Peace (PFP) and have moved rapidly toward interoperational ability with NATO. In both Finland and Sweden there is still considerable domestic support for neutrality, so the fact that the EU still has no authority over intra-European territorial defense allows them to keep more fundamental security policy debates about EU developments and neutrality off the political agenda. Nonetheless, the EU's 2004 solidarity clause, which states that members have a responsibility to mobilize all instruments, including military ones, to prevent terrorist threats in other member states' territories, as well as the rising operational demands of ESDP suggests that it cannot be avoided indefinitely. In Sweden, EU skepticism tends to be strongest among those who are most attached to neutrality. It is therefore likely that when the question rises to the top of the political agenda it will be accompanied by a repeat of the politics of the membership and EMU debate and referenda. Since security policy arguments tend to increase support for the EU in Finland, developments there may be quite different.

Denmark has been much less involved in ESDP due to its Edinburgh opt-out. While Danish political elites are in favor of opting back in, they have not yet called for a referendum to do so. When they do, it will unleash another round of EU decision making by direct democracy, and the outcome remains unclear. The left and Radical Liberals oppose what they refer to as the militarization of the EU, and, more generally, there is still considerable Euroskepticism in the Danish parliament (Raunio 2007; Kite 2006). On the other hand, there is more support for common defense policy in Denmark than Finland and Sweden, and some observers argue that it is unlikely the opt-out will be retained much longer (Pedersen 2006).

For Norway and Iceland, ESDP creates different problems and raises the potential cost of nonmembership. As outsiders, they have no real ability to influence decisions and developments. While eligible to participate in joint EU-NATO missions, their inclusion in purely EU efforts depends on what the EU itself decides. Both Finland and Sweden favor their inclusion and promote this view within EU institutions and by supporting integrated Nordic crisis response units (Bailes 2006). Both Norway and Iceland have participated in several ESDP missions. More problematic in the long run (as is true for Finland and Sweden, albeit for different reasons) is the impact that EU security and defense policy will have on NATO's role in European defense and global crisis and peace missions. As NATO insiders and EU outsiders, the weakening of the former due to the emergence of the latter will put further pressure on these states to reconsider joining the EU.

Thus far, the focus of the chapter has been the impact of international developments, holding domestic political institutions constant. That is, the emphasis has been on how particular developments impact on national democracy by enabling or forcing voters and parties to reconsider policy choices. In doing so, external developments also have the potential to shift voter support or the ability of parties to work together. We have also seen examples of external actors having veto power over certain policies or government formations (most notably the Soviet Union toward Finland).

At a deeper level, we need also to consider whether external developments can actually transform the institutional context in which domestic actors operate. Both the decline of the power of parliaments and the increasing power of chief executives—referred to by some scholars as "presidentialization"—are two institutional changes that have been observed broadly throughout Europe (Poguntke and Webb 2005; Peters, Rhodes, and Wright 2000). While there is certainly national variation, with a number of factors behind these changes, there can be little doubt that they are also linked to the broadening and deepening of European integration—that is, changes in the external environment. The establishment of parliamentary committees to oversee and exert control over the government's behavior in EU decision making is a clear example of this. All the Nordic states have such committees, and while they are among the strongest in the EU (Bergman 2000), they have not prevented a loss of power of parliaments compared to the executive branch (Börzel and Risse 2006). The strengthening of the role of the European Council has also contributed to the relative strengthening of chief executives, not only toward parliaments but also at the expense of other government ministers (Johansson and Tallberg 2009). In Finland, because EU matters are lodged with the prime minister rather than the president, this development can be said to have strengthened the parliamentary chain of delegation and accountability. In Sweden, the growing power of the prime minister (Aylott 2005b) is better understood as a redistribution of power among institutions in the existing policy process.

The Lisbon Treaty, which came into force on December 1, 2009, brought about a number of significant changes in the way the EU operates. In particular, a greater number of decisions are decided by qualified majority voting in the Council; the European Parliament (EP) has a stronger role in policy-making; and two new posts, EU president and EU foreign minister, have been created. It is reasonable to expect that the relative power of actors in the chain of delegation and accountability will shift in favor of those with presence and authority in European institutions. It is also likely that the Lisbon Treaty will expand the opportunity for increasingly powerful actors external to the domestic chain, for example, the more supranationalist European Council and the European Parliament, to change the way in which democratic politics operate.

Conclusion

This chapter began by noting that the impact of the international environment on the democratic chain of delegation and accountability varies across the Nordic states. Despite similarities, there have been significant differences in how international developments have impacted on public opinion, party fortunes, and government formation and stability. But they have clearly had an impact! Moreover, they have also led to institutional changes (e.g., the establishment of new committees and parliamentary procedures as a consequence of EU membership) and changes in the relative power of actors within the chain.

At the same time, the fact that the international environment impacts on states and sometimes acts as an external constraint does not necessarily mean that parliaments and parties are largely helpless in the face of external pressures. Nor can it be concluded that the domestic chain of delegation and accountability has been undermined everywhere and in similar ways, or that membership in organizations reduces autonomy more than nonmembership. The next chapter addresses the contemporary variation in the mix of parties, parliaments, and constraints in the Nordic parliamentary democracies as well as the ways in which the theses of decline do and do not apply in these countries.

NOTES

1. These included the U.S. declaration of the Truman Doctrine (March 1947) amid fears that communist insurgencies would otherwise gain the upper hand in Greece and Turkey, Soviet reactions to the U.S. Marshall Plan to rebuild Europe (June 1947), the establishment of Cominform (September 1947), the breakdown of talks about the future of Germany (December 1947), the Communist coup in Czechoslovakia (March 1948), and the Berlin blockade (June 1948). For a good introduction to the history of the Cold War, see Gaddis 2006.

2. For more information on how the East-West conflict impacted on Finnish domestic policy see Hakovirta 1981, Arter 1987, and Rehn 2003.

3. Iceland's actions were strongly opposed by Britain and led to a series of confrontations known as the "cod wars." The conflict escalated in the mid-1970s, when Britain sent military ships to protect British fishermen defying Icelandic law. Clashes erupted, and Iceland threatened to close the Keflavik base. The importance of the base prompted NATO to act as mediator, and the conflict was resolved largely in Iceland's favor, with an agreement recognizing Iceland's authority but granting British fishermen some limited right to fish in Icelandic waters.

4. After a relative warming in superpower relations from the late 1960s, relations soured again in the 1980s in the wake of the Soviet invasion of Afghanistan, the Reagan administration's decision to fund research into space-based missile defense (the Strategic Defense Initiative, widely referred to as *Star Wars*), and NATO plans to deploy new intermediate-range missiles in Europe in response to Soviet deployment of a new generation of missiles.

5. In 1982, the Radical Liberals supported the formation of a four-party minority coalition cabinet, because it favored its economic policy. However, it rejected the cabinet's foreign policy. The Radical Liberals voted with the cabinet on economic policy and refused to bring it down. At the same time, it formed an "alternative majority" with the Social Democrats, Socialists, and Left Socialists on matters of foreign and security policy. The cabinet was repeatedly forced to decide whether to implement a foreign policy it opposed, stall and refuse to comply with the expressed will of parliament, or call new elections. In some cases the cabinet submitted reservations to NATO decisions that it did not actually oppose (for example, on intermediate-range nuclear missiles in Europe and missile defense), leading some observers to refer to Danish NATO policy in this period as the "footnote policy." Finally, in 1988, the cabinet called new elections, stating that it would interpret the vote as an expression of popular sentiment about NATO membership (Damgaard and Svensson 1989). The outcome was interpreted as a show of support for NATO, and a new coalition cabinet including the Radical Liberals was formed.

6. For more on this see Grímsson 1982 and Ingimundarson 2001.

7. This sense of distinctiveness was rooted in the belief that the history, values, and aspirations of the Nordic states set them apart from France, Germany, and Italy, who were the dominant forces in the EEC.

8. EEC member states also agreed at the Hague Summit to rename the organization the European Community. The EC became the EU in 1992. The revitalization of the EC in the 1980s began with the resolution of a budget dispute with Britain, the decision to complete the internal market, and the negotiation of the Single European Act (SEA).

9. While opposition in the Christian People's Party was largely a rural phenomenon, in the Liberal Party opposition was originally concentrated in its radicalized urban wing.

10. By comparison, 48 percent of Finns and 64 percent of Danes report that membership is a "good thing" (EU27 average is 53 percent). On the other hand, 57 percent of Finns say their country has benefited from EU membership, and fully 76 percent of Danes agree that membership benefits their country (EU27 average 56 percent).

11. Britain refused to accept Icelandic membership in EFTA in 1959 due to a dispute over fishing rights.

12. Groups representing industry, manufacturing, and fisheries expressed support for the EEA, while agriculture opposed it. The Labor Federation argued in favor of special provisions to protect employment, and civil society groups argued against membership on the grounds that it would undermine Icelandic democracy and culture. A petition campaign collected 34,000 signatures against the EEA (Thorhallsson and Vignisson 2004a).

REFERENCES

Allen, Hillary. 1979. *Norway and Europe in the 1970s.* Oslo: Universitetsforlaget.
Arter, David. 1987. *Politics and Policy-Making in Finland.* Sussex and New York: Wheatsheaf Books and St. Martin's Press.
Åström, Sverker. 1990. "Kommentarer till Karl Molin och Yngve Möller." In Bo Huldt and Klaus Misgeld, eds., *Socialdemokratin och den svenska utrikespolitiken.* Stockholm: Utrikespolitiska institutet.
Aylott, Nicholas. 2002. "Let's Discuss This Later: Party Responses to Euro-division in Scandinavia." *Party Politics* 8 (4): 441–61.
Aylott, Nicholas. 2005a. "Lessons Learned, Lessons Forgotten: The Swedish Referendum on EMU of September 2003." *Government and Opposition* 40 (4): 540–64.
Aylott, Nicholas. 2005b. "'President Persson'—How Did Sweden Get Him?" In Thomas Poguntke and Paul Webb, eds., *The Presidentialization of Politics: A Comparative Study of Modern Democracies.* Oxford: Oxford University Press.
Bailes, Alyson J. K. 2006. "The European Defence Challenge for the Nordic Region." In Alyson J. K. Bailes, Gunilla Herolf, and Bengt Sundelius, eds., *The Nordic Countries and the European Security and Defence Policy.* Stockholm: SIPRI, Oxford University Press.
Bergman, Torbjörn. 2000. "The European Union as the Next Step of Delegation and Accountability." *European Journal of Political Research* 37 (3): 415–29.
Blidberg, Kersti. 1987. *Just Good Friends: Nordic Social Democracy and Security Policy, 1945–50.* Oslo: Forsvarshistorisk Forskningssenter.
Börzel, Tanja A., and Thomas Risse. 2006. "Europeanization: The Domestic Impact of European Union Politics." In Knud Erik Jørgensen, Mark A. Pollack, and Ben Rosamond, eds., *Handbook of European Union Politics.* London: Sage.
Christensen, Dag Arne. 1998. "Foreign Policy Objectives: Left Socialist Opposition in Denmark, Norway, and Sweden." *Scandinavian Political Studies* 21 (1): 51–70.
Damgaard, Erik, and Asbjørn Sonne Nørgaard. 2000. "The European Union and Danish Parliamentary Democracy." In Torbjörn Bergman and Erik Damgaard, eds., *Delegation and Accountability in European Integration: The Nordic Parliamentary Democracies and the European Union.* London: Frank Cass.
Damgaard, Erik, and Palle Svensson. 1989. "Who Governs? Parties and Policies in Denmark." *European Journal of Political Research* 17 (6): 731–45.
Dau, Mary. 1969. *Danmark og Sovjetunionen: 1944–49.* Copenhagen: Dansk Udenrigspolitisk Institut.
Eliassen, Kjell A., and Nick Sitter. 2003. "Ever Closer Cooperation? The Limits of the 'Norwegian Method' of European Integration." *Scandinavian Political Studies* 26 (2): 125–44.
Elvander, Nils. 1980. *Skandinavisk arbetarrörelse.* Stockholm: LiberFörlag.
Eriksen, Knut Einer. 1972. *DNA og NATO.* Oslo: Gyldendal Norsk Forlag.
Gaddis, John Lewis. 2006. *The Cold War: A New History.* New York: Penguin.
Grímsson, Ólafur. 1982. "Iceland: A Multilevel Coalition System." In Eric C. Browne and John Dreijmanis, eds., *Government Coalitions in Western Democracies.* New York: Longman.

Hakovirta, Harto. 1981. *Neutral Countries in East-West Economic Relations.* Tampere: University of Tampere, Institute of Political Science.
Haskel, Barbara. 1976. *The Scandinavian Option: Opportunities and Opportunity Costs in Postwar Scandinavian Foreign Policies.* Oslo: Universitetsforlaget.
Ingimundarson, Valur. 2001. "The Role of NATO and the U.S. Military Base in Icelandic Domestic Politics, 1949–99." In Gustav Schmidt, ed., *A History of NATO—the First Fifty Years.* New York: Palgrave.
Jahn, Detlef, and Ann-Sofie Storsved. 1995. "Legitimacy through Referendum? The Nearly Successful Domino-Strategy of the EU-Referendums in Austria, Finland, Sweden, and Norway." *West European Politics* 18 (4): 18–37.
Johansson, Karl Magnus, and Jonas Tallberg. 2009. "Explaining Chief Executive Empowerment: European Union Summitry and Domestic Change." Stencil, Department of Political Science, University of Stockholm.
Kinnunen, Jussi. 2003. "Managing Europe from Home: The Europeanisation of the Finnish Core Executive." Occasional Paper 3.1—09.03. University of Helsinki: Centre for European Studies.
Kite, Cynthia. 1996. *Scandinavia Faces EU: Debates and Decisions on Membership, 1961–1994.* Umeå University, Department of Political Science.
Kite, Cynthia. 2006. "The Domestic Background: Public Opinion and Party Attitudes towards Integration in the Nordic Countries." In Alyson J. K. Bailes, Gunilla Herolf, and Bengt Sundelius, eds., *The Nordic Countries and the European Security and Defence Policy.* Stockholm: SIPRI, Oxford University Press.
Lundestad, Geir. 1980. *America, Scandinavia, and the Cold War, 1945–49.* New York: Columbia University Press.
Miljan, Toivo. 1977. *The Reluctant Europeans: The Attitudes of the Nordic Countries towards European Integration.* London: C. Hurst.
Möller, Yngve. 1990. "Östen Undén's Utrikespolitik." In Bo Huldt and Klaus Misgeld, eds., *Socialdemokratin och den svenska utrikespolitiken.* Stockholm: Utrikespolitiska institutet.
Pedersen, Klaus Carsten. 2006. "Denmark and the European Security Defence Policy." In Alyson J. K. Bailes, Gunilla Herolf, and Bengt Sundelius, eds., *The Nordic Countries and the European Security and Defence Policy.* Stockholm: SIPRI, Oxford University Press.
Pesonen, Pertti, Anders Todal Jenssen, and Mikael Gilljam. 1998a. "Postscript: Developments after the EU Referendums." In Anders Todal Jenssen, Pertti Pesonen, and Mikael Gilljam, eds., *To Join or Not to Join: Three Nordic Referendums on Membership in the European Union.* Oslo: Scandinavian University Press.
Pesonen, Pertti, Anders Todal Jenssen, and Mikael Gilljam. 1998b. "To Join or Not to Join." In Anders Todal Jenssen, Pertti Pesonen, and Mikael Gilljam, eds., *To Join or Not to Join: Three Nordic Referendums on Membership in the European Union.* Oslo: Scandinavian University Press.
Peters, B. Guy, R. W. Rhodes, and Vincent Wright, eds. 2000. *Administering the Summit: Administration of the Core Executive in Developed Countries.* Basingstoke: Macmillan.
Petersen, Nikolaj, and Jørgen Elklit. 1973. "Denmark Enters the European Communities." *Scandinavian Political Studies* 8:198–213.

Poguntke, Thomas, and Paul Webb, eds. 2005. *The Presidentialisation of Politics: A Comparative Study of Modern Democracies.* Oxford: Oxford University Press.
Quille, Gerrard. 2006. "The Impact of EU Capability Targets and Operational Demands on Defence Concepts and Planning." In Alyson J. K. Bailes, Gunilla Herolf, and Bengt Sundelius, eds., *The Nordic Countries and the European Security and Defence Policy.* Stockholm: SIPRI, Oxford University Press.
Qvortrup, Mads H. 2001. "How to Lose a Referendum: The Danish Plebiscite on the Euro." *Political Quarterly* 72 (2): 190–96.
Rasmussen, Morton. 2006. "The Political Economy of Danish European Policy, 1950–1973." Paper prepared for the Fourteenth International Economic History Congress, Helsinki, August 21–25, 2006.
Raunio, Tapio. 2007. "Softening but Persistent: Euro-scepticism in the Nordic EU Countries." *Acta Politica* 42 (2–3): 191–210.
Raunio, Tapio, and Teija Tiilikainen. 2003. *Finland in the European Union.* London: Frank Cass.
Rehn, Olli. 2003. "Can a Neutralist Nordic Become a Core European? Historical Trajectory and Political Culture in the Making of Finland's EU Policy." Paper prepared for the ECPR Joint Session of Workshops, Edinburgh, March–April 2003.
Tammes, Rolf. 1991. *The United States and the Cold War in the High North.* Oslo: Ad Notam.
Thorhallsson, Baldur. 2004. "Approaching the Question: Domestic Background and Conceptual Framework." In Baldur Thorhallsson, ed., *Iceland and European Integration on the Edge.* London: Routledge.
Thorhallsson, Baldur, and Hjalti Thor Vignisson. 2004a. "A Controversial Step: Membership of the EEA." In Baldur Thorhallsson, ed., *Iceland and European Integration on the Edge.* London: Routledge.
Thorhallsson, Baldur, and Hjalti Thor Vignisson. 2004b. "The First Steps: Iceland's Policy on European Integration from the Foundation of the Republic to 1972." In Baldur Thorhallsson, ed., *Iceland and European Integration on the Edge.* London: Routledge.
Viklund, Daniel. 1977. *Spelet om frihandelsavtalet: En kritisk studie i svensk europapolitik 1959–72.* Stockholm: Rabén & Sjögren.

INTERNET SOURCES

Eurobarometer. 2008. *Eurobarometer 70: Public Opinion in the European Union.* http://ec.europa.eu/public_opinion/archives/eb/eb70/eb70_first_en.pdf
Moody, Jonas. 2009. "Global Financial Crisis Claims Iceland." *Time* January 26. Downloaded April 19, 2009. http://www.time.com/time/world/article/0,8599,1874036,00.html

10 ✦ The Nordics
Demanding Citizens, Complex Polities

TORBJÖRN BERGMAN AND KAARE STRØM

On the surface, there seems to be little reason to worry about the fate of parliamentary democracy in Northern Europe or indeed anywhere else. Parliamentary government is the most common of all democratic regime types, at least in the sense that more people live under this form than under any other. Since World War II, parliamentary democracies have been remarkably stable, and they have won praise from many political scientists. By many accounts, parliamentary systems also constitute the most stable democratic regime type, and they are commonly praised for their "kinder and gentler" features such as relative income equality and the virtual elimination of extreme poverty under such regimes in Western Europe (Lijphart 1999; Linz 1994). Moreover, parliamentary systems seem less susceptible than other democracies to executive abuses of power. Thus, in Europe the most democratically deficient states (such as Belarus and Russia) tend to be among those whose constitutions deviate most from the parliamentary norm.

Yet, even for parliamentary democracies, there are potential trouble spots to consider, and the skeptics are not necessarily confined to the paranoid and the perennial wolf-criers. One such curious and disconcerting fact is that, especially outside Europe, few of the new democracies that have emerged over the past 30 or 40 years have chosen the parliamentary model. As a proportion of all states, the share of parliamentary democracies has remained remarkably flat at just under 30 percent. In fact, there were proportionally more parliamentary democracies in the world in the 1950s (largely because most of Africa had not yet been decolonized) than there are today. Yet, the low rate at which parliamentary systems have since then been introduced and taken root is reflected most dramatically in the fact that as a proportion of all democracies, parliamentary regimes have fallen from about 70 percent in the 1970s to 45 percent in 2002 (Cheibub 2007). And in some ways, even established parliamentary systems do not seem to be inoculated against popular protest and disenchantment. Thus, the rise of radical populist protest parties has been especially dramatic in parliamentary systems, and such parties have taken a far larger share of the vote in some such regimes, such as Austria, Belgium, Italy, and the Netherlands, than they have in most presidential regimes.

Also, as we have seen, even in the most entrenched and secure parliamentary democracies, such as the Nordic countries, citizens and observers harbor concerns about the future of their democratic institutions. A cold wind—a Nordic chill—has swept over the region, manifest as a simultaneous decline of its particular mix of "working" (strong) parliaments and cohesive mass parties. In macroinstitutional terms, most of these countries have moved from relatively unconstrained Westminster democracies with proportional features toward a more Madisonian model of parliamentary democracy, with more checks and balances and constitutional constraints on elected public officials. Yet, there is no challenge to parliamentary democracy as a basic constitutional choice. And within these new parameters, the elected parliaments continue to function well. The downside, however, is to be found in the state of political parties, which have atrophied as mass membership organizations and in their ability to mobilize voters. This erosion of party strength has consequences for the status of parliamentary institutions as well. The distance of the political class from ordinary citizens has increased, as the mechanisms of political recruitment and accountability have withered. This picture becomes even more complex as we consider the intraregional differences, as the fate of parties and parliaments looks more diverse across the region than the conventional picture of Nordic homogeneity would suggest.

In this chapter, we bring together the various pieces of the puzzle that the Nordic countries thus constitute. We begin by analyzing the effectiveness of parliamentary governance in contemporary Nordic politics. Next we turn to the evidence on the functions and health of Nordic political parties. And by bringing together these two critical aspects of representative democracy, we can then more fully capture the contemporary state of popular governance in the Nordic region.

Three Transformations

Before we can flesh out this picture, however, let us recall the societal transformations that parliamentary democracies face today (see chapter 1). We have in this volume considered contemporary challenges to the Nordic parties and parliaments that stem from changes in three different aspects of their polities: (1) the voters, (2) the politicians, and (3) the policy process. Across the advanced industrial democracies, there has been pervasive change in each of these features. Citizens have been empowered and hence have come to take a less deferential attitude toward politicians than ever before. Politicians have become increasingly separated from the social groups from which they used to be drawn, which may make them less faithful agents of their constituents than they once were. And the democratic policy process has increasingly been constrained by judicial intervention, technological demands, and supranational integration. These are the social and political forces that have changed the face of politics not just in the Nordic region but in virtually all advanced democracies.

A More Demanding Electorate

Ultimately, the fate of politicians depends on their ability to please the voters, not just intermittently and specifically on election day, but over the entire course of the parliamentary life cycle (see Strøm, Müller, and Bergman 2008). Yet, there are clear indications in many contemporary parliamentary democracies that ordinary citizens are becoming less deferential toward, and even less tolerant of, parliamentarians and other politicians. Fewer voters identify with any political party, and this trend is most noticeable among younger and more educated voters. Concomitantly, electoral volatility has increased, and more voters make up their minds late in the election campaign or simply fail to vote at all. Moreover, voters in many countries have turned in large numbers from the mass integration parties of the past (such as Social Democrats or Christian Democrats) to protest parties of the left or right, parties that often show little respect for the established institutions and practices of representative democracy. And ordinary citizens across the world are extraordinarily critical in their attitudes toward existing political parties.

There are many reasons why politicians are facing growing skepticism and an increasingly detached electorate. New information technology offers enormous opportunities for enhanced communication and the spread of knowledge and opinions. Citizens of contemporary advanced democracies are therefore better educated than ever before and less dependent on political parties for information or guidance. At the same time, popular culture has become more individualistic and more skeptical toward social traditions and authorities. And the ability of political parties to control or influence the dominant media has rapidly decreased. The combination of these changes has resulted in a much less deferential attitude toward politicians.

Declining Parties, Growing Agency Problems?

Contemporary challenges to parliamentary democracies do not all have their roots among the voters. The political parties themselves, and the politicians within them, have also changed. Parties have traditionally had a privileged place in parliamentary systems because of their importance as mechanisms of accountability. In parliamentary democracies, the holders of virtually all important political offices were traditionally party politicians, or at least politicians sympathetic to and appointed by a particular political party. The task of ensuring that these politicians acted in accordance with the will of the voters thus fell heavily on the political parties. And as long as parties remained beholden to their respective social constituencies, and these constituencies were cohesive and mobilized, their elected representatives also more or less faithfully represented these voters' preferences.

But to the extent that these conditions ever held, they no longer do, in part because parties have lost capacity, in part because traditional communities based on class or faith have disintegrated, and in part because the preferences of party politicians have shifted. In many contemporary democracies, parties have lost control over political appointments that used to be within their domain, so that it has become possible for more independent contenders to emerge and prevail. This is probably most obviously true of managerial positions in public enterprises, but it has also affected judicial and executive branch appointments. Even cabinet appointees without strong partisan credentials have become more common.

At the same time, parties may also have become less faithful agents of their supporters. The cartel party thesis (Katz and Mair 1995) suggests that parties have shifted their attention away from representing broad social constituencies and that they have instead turned to capturing and exploiting the machinery of state and the benefits (especially financial ones) that flow from it. Not only have parties become more detached from their social bases and the rest of civil society, but they have also become more predatory. In other words, according to this thesis the preference gulf between party politicians and their supporters has widened, causing greater agency losses in this essential relationship between politicians and social interests.

An Increasingly Constrained Policy Process

Yet another major challenge facing parliamentary democracies is an increasingly constrained policy process. In European states, this is due in part to the increasing scope of supranational legislation and the growing complexity and empowerment of the European Union (EU). And as chapter 9 has shown, the Cold War and the European integration process have over time greatly constrained the domestic decision-making process in many of the member states and shaped the political parties that work within it. At the same time, the growing power of the EU has made it increasingly important for national policymakers to oversee and control the policy process within that supranational organization. Yet it is difficult for national parliaments to scrutinize their respective governments in EU affairs because of informational asymmetries. The EU policy process is very complex and often far from transparent. National parliaments also lack authority and capacity; they do not have the means or the right to intervene in internal policy-making processes in the EU.

But this is only one way in which parliamentary authority has been progressively constrained. There are other constraints, of growing importance, that are external to the chain of parliamentary governance but still domestic in character. They include *democratic* provisions such as abrogative referenda, federalism, and other constitutional devolutions of power. European integration has, through the various EU treaties adopted since the 1980s, indirectly yet greatly contributed to the rise of referendum democracy across much of Europe. All the Nordic countries but Iceland have held important EU-related referenda since 1990, and in the region as a whole European integration has contributed to making direct democracy a more important part of the national policy process. Federalism and regional devolution have proceeded in countries such as Belgium, Spain, and the United Kingdom, which have become models for aspiring regional politicians in other European countries. And although federalism is not a live option in the Nordic countries, decentralization of power has many champions. Finally, a wave of new *technocratic* constraints has removed political authority from the national parliament and assigned it to nonelective institutions, such as independent central banks and courts, that are not subject to majority rule. Again, European integration has contributed significantly to both of these developments. Within the countries of the Euro Zone (including Finland), the European Central Bank has of course greatly reduced the influence of national parliamentarians over monetary affairs. And the European Court of Justice has similarly promoted the judicialization of politics within the entire EU as well as the EEA states (including Iceland and Norway). The judiciary has indeed been one of the most obvious beneficiaries of the growth of external constraints, as both international, European, and national developments have empowered courts and judges in matters of human rights and European law.

Adaptive Parliaments

For proponents of the ideal-typical parliamentary democracy with cohesive and centralized parties (the Westminster model), these are troubling trends. In the previous chapters our contributors have examined the severity of these challenges to the Nordic model of parliamentary governance. We shall now summarize and analyze that evidence. To what extent has the parliamentary policy process been altered? Have Nordic parties lost much of their ability to control this process? Is the picture different from one polity to the next?

The last of these questions requires us to discuss the Nordic countries separately and not just in aggregate. Analyses of Nordic politics have generally overplayed the similarities and ignored the differences between these countries. They are indeed similar in a number of ways, but as we shall show, there are also important ways in which the Nordic countries differ from one another. In the sections that follow, drawing on themes that we introduced in chapter 1, we note the distinction between alternational party systems (in Scandinavia proper) and pivotal party systems (in Finland and Iceland). The more pivotal countries also differ from the rest in their semipresidential constitutions. Iceland and Norway long differed from the other Nordics (and Europeans) in their quasi-bicameral parliaments, although this institutional peculiarity lost its real-world significance a long time ago and has since been abandoned (though in Norway only very recently). Denmark has the most traditionally Westminsterian parliament but combines it with the most established use of referendum devices. Of course, the five Nordics differ in their relationships with the EU as well, and until 1991 Finland was unique in its special (and not entirely self-imposed) relationship with the Soviet Union.

Coalition Bargaining

Let us now consider how the national parliaments have fared across the Nordic region. As students of parliamentary democracy have known since Bagehot (1867), the first function of parliament is elective: to generate a stable and effective executive. Hence, in our scrutiny of parliamentary performance, we begin with the record of coalition bargaining and cabinet formation. It is commonly noted that the Scandinavian countries proper (though Finland and Iceland less so) have had a remarkably high incidence of minority government. In most parliamentary democracies, and especially in the Westminster model, majority governments are the rule and minority governments the exception. In Scandinavia, it has often been the other way around. Moreover, Scandinavian minority governments have typically formed in situations of high transparency and predictability. Given the restrictions on early parliamentary dissolution in Sweden and the absence of any possibility of early elections in Norway, politicians know that once a cabinet is formed there is little incentive for renegotiation during the rest of the parliamentary term. As the country chapters have shown, minority governments have rarely resulted from protracted, difficult, or confrontational bargaining episodes. Nor have they on the whole been short-lived. Thus, it makes little sense to think of Scandinavian minority cabinets as emergency solutions formed in response to some unexpected parliamentary crisis (Strøm 1986, 1990). Clearly, these cabinets are not simply short-term stopgap solutions, but rather Madisonian adaptations that allow more fluid parliamentary coalitions to form.

As our data show (see table 3 in each of the country chapters), the Nordic incidence of minority cabinets has been high throughout the postwar period, never slipping below 40 percent in any decade prior to the 2000s. The three Scandinavian countries resorted to minority solutions with even greater frequency from the early 1970s on. Thus, the overall Nordic share of governments without majority support in parliament (discounting a small number of nonpartisan cabinets in Finland) went from 50 percent in the 1940s, to 45 percent in the 1950s and 43 percent in the 1960s, but then rose markedly to 58 percent in the 1970s and an astonishing 68 percent in the 1980s. This upturn in minority cabinets occurred because party leaders adapted to party system changes that were beginning to take place. Growing electoral volatility and party system fragmentation were at least partly responsible.

The high frequency of minority governments also reflected a forward-looking strategy on the part of party leaders, especially Social Democrats. Politicians, especially those with experience from the executive branch, became increasingly aware that voters tend to punish, rather than reward, those who have recently been in office, and that those punishments were increasing in severity. Coalition governments, in which each party must typically make visible and often painful policy concessions up front, were taking particularly heavy electoral losses. As the electoral costs of government incumbency rose (see Narud and Valen 2008), parties became more reluctant to govern with strange bedfellows, especially in coalitions that would imply visible and significant policy concessions up front. These considerations led social democrats in all three countries to prefer single-party minority cabinets to majority coalitions.

Yet, in the late 1990s and early 2000s, this strategy changed in several countries simultaneously. The Swedish Social Democrats have experimented with unorthodox coalitions since the 1990s (Bale and Bergman 2006), and in Norway the Labor Party abandoned its long-standing anticoalition strategy and in 2005 gave Norway its first majority government in 20 years. This coalition was returned to power by a very narrow margin in the September 2009 election. And the Danish Liberal Party (Venstre) has led the construction of a stable center-right coalition that since 2001 has secured a stable majority in the parliament, even though the cabinet has remained minoritarian.

Overall, the Nordic incidence of minority governments dropped to 57 percent in the 1990s and further to 38 percent in the 2000s up through 2008. Neither Finland nor Iceland has in fact seen a single minority cabinet form since the 1980s. Thus, the parties' calculus of electoral and policy benefits seems to have shifted back in favor of majority governments. This trend may have had various causes, including, on one hand, institutional changes in all three Scandinavian countries' parliamentary budgetary processes that raised the bar for fiscal coordination (Christiansen and Damgaard 2008) and, on the other hand, the incentives for national governments anticipating negotiations within the EU to build strong domestic majorities in support of their positions. These incentives apply even to EEA members Iceland and Norway, though surely more so to Denmark, Finland, and Sweden.

Cabinet Performance

The best measure of cabinet performance, however, is less its membership or majority than its record in office, especially as reflected in the implicit judgments that parliamentarians and voters pass at later stages in the parliamentary game. In any parliamentary system, the governing parties are accountable to two masters: the parliamentary majority and, ultimately, the voters. Successful cabinets meet these responsibilities in such ways that we do not observe dramatic sanctions on the part of either of their democratic principals. In other words, successful cabinets, especially in the Westminster model, tend to serve out their parliamentary terms rather than being defeated or retired before that time, and they do not lose a large number of votes in parliament. Similarly, while in a well-functioning parliamentary system there is at least the potential of alternation at election time, voters do not routinely and predictably savage successful incumbents.

Figure 10.1 turns our attention to the first of these accountabilities, the chief executive's responsibility to the parliamentary majority, by examining

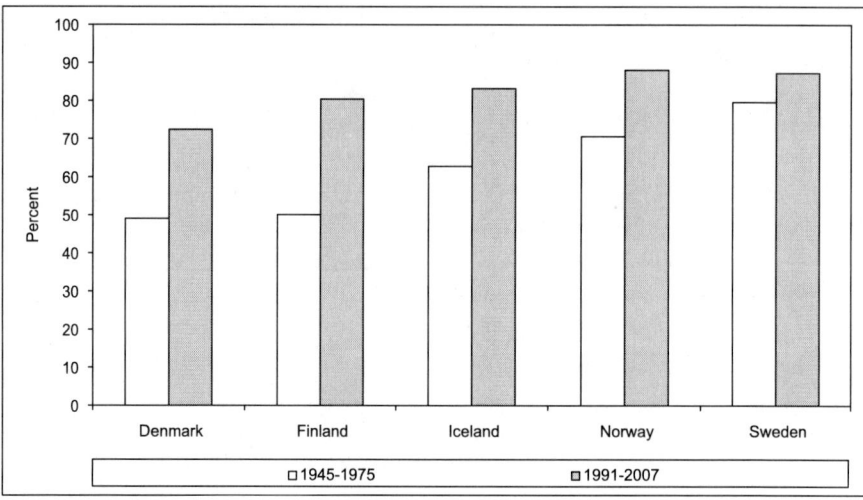

Fig. 10.1. Cabinet duration, as share of maximum potential duration, by country and period. Each column represents the mean duration for cabinets formed in that period. (Data from the book's home page, the Nordic Parliamentary Democracy Data Archive, http://www.erdda.se.)

cabinet duration by country and over time. Keep in mind, however, that the duration of a given cabinet is bounded by the point in the cycle of parliamentary elections at which it was formed. If a cabinet is formed immediately after a general election, then it may serve the entire regular parliamentary term (which in most of our cases is four years). If a cabinet forms halfway through the parliamentary term, however, then the cabinet's maximum potential duration is only half as long. To control for these differences, we measure the proportion of the remaining term that each cabinet served, rather than the raw number of months or days. The results are displayed in figure 10.1, which shows us the average share of the maximum potential term that cabinets have served, in two different parts of the post–World War II era: 1945–75 versus 1991–2007. (For simplicity of presentation, we have left out the middle period.)

The lesson of figure 10.1 is simple and straightforward: cabinet stability has increased in every one of the Nordic countries since the early postwar period. And it has increased most in those countries where it was previously low, that is, Denmark and Finland. In the first 30 years of the postwar period, the average Danish or Finnish cabinet served only about half of its maximum potential tenure. Since 1991, however, average duration has topped 70 percent in every one of the Nordic countries and 80 percent in all but Denmark. Thus, in terms of executive stability, the Nordic experience over the past couple of decades is an unqualified success story. In this respect, the Nordic countries resemble the Westminster model more closely today than they did 20 years ago.

Yet, executives in parliamentary systems answer not only to the members of parliament but also to the voters. And the way in which voters control these executives is in large part by passing a retrospective judgment on the incumbents on election day. To get a sense of the voters' judgment, we therefore examine the electoral fortunes of political parties in office at the time of parliamentary elections. Figure 10.2 displays the relevant data, but note that due to the limited number of observations, we split the postwar period in two and compare the early postwar years (1945–75) with the entire period that has succeeded them (1976–2007).

The results displayed in figure 10.2 are much more divergent than those presented in the previous figure. Thus, while in both Denmark and Finland incumbent parties now lose fewer votes than in the 1945–75 period, in Norway and Sweden incumbency losses have mounted substantially in recent elections. In Iceland, the picture is even more striking, as voters have taken to punishing their incumbents with severity. Yet, in this case our periodization exaggerates the differences between the Nordic countries. There is in fact no Nordic country in which the recent electoral record has been benign compared with the early postwar years. It is just that in some countries the incumbency costs began rising earlier, so that some particularly punitive elections are captured in our 1945–75 period. Thus, in Denmark and Finland, the election in which the incumbents took the most severe beating occurred in the early 1970s. In Sweden, in contrast, the date was 1998, and in Norway the elections of 2001 and 2005 tie for this honor. Finally, since the 1970s Iceland has witnessed a series of elections in which incumbents have been severely punished. In fact, between 1963 and 2008, no single election has resulted in gains for the Icelandic parties in power.

In the Nordic region as a whole, the record of electoral accountability is thus very different from that of parliamentary accountability. Whereas governments in all countries have become better at satisfying their parliamentary principals, they have generally gotten worse at pleasing the voters. To the extent that there is reason to worry about the parliamentary chain of delegation in these countries, our attention should thus be focused on the relationship between politicians and the voters, rather than on relations between the executive and the legislative branches of government. To some extent, though, this picture varies from country to country. Iceland, Norway, and Sweden all fit the general Nordic pattern quite closely. Cabinets

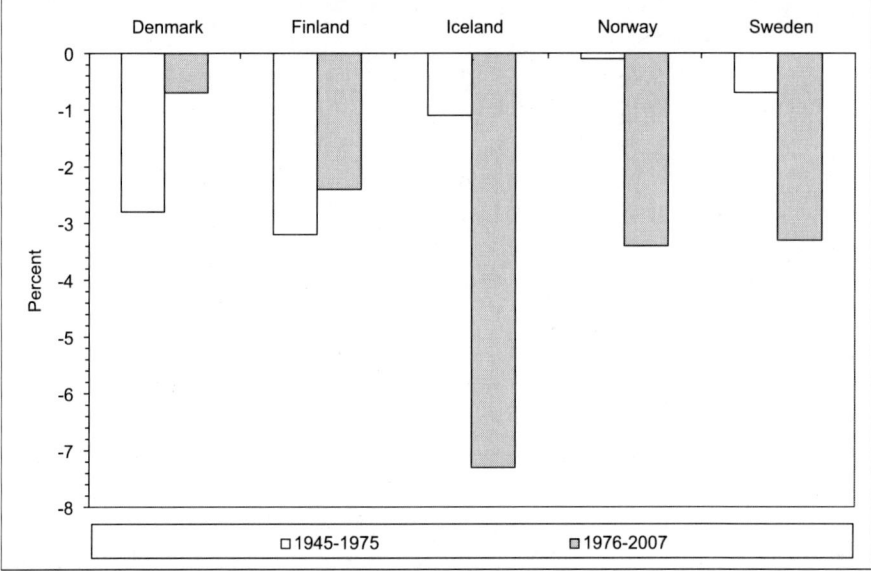

Fig. 10.2. Electoral performance of incumbent cabinet parties, by country and period. Each column represents the mean (loss) for cabinets formed in that period. (Data from tables 3.7, 4.7, 5.7, 6.7, and 7.7 [column: Cabinet Total].)

have become more stable at the same time that voters have become more restive. Finland and especially Denmark, in contrast, exhibit a happier combination of increasing cabinet durability and more modest incumbency losses. Thus, Denmark stands out as the Nordic case in which recent trends in executive accountability seem most benign.

Legislative Activity

While "making and breaking governments" is clearly a key function of parliaments (see Laver and Shepsle 1996), coalition bargaining is only one part of the role that the representatives of the people play in the process of parliamentary governance. In the Nordic countries, cabinets are typically made and unmade only every four years or so. Needless to say, many critical policy decisions must be made in the intervals, and the national parliaments are certainly important arenas in these policy processes.

In previous chapters we have examined patterns of legislative activity in each of the Nordic countries. Since there are so many measures of parliamentary activity, and since parliamentary procedures and data availability differ considerably from one country to another, these data are not easily summarized. Yet, at the very least the evidence does not support a picture of decaying parliaments. The number of bills deliberated on in parliament in each country has tended either to be fairly stable or to trend upward. In Finland, legislative activity by these counts has ebbed and flowed over the post–1945 period, with peaks in private members' bills in the 1970s and government bills in the 1990s. In the Scandinavian countries (Denmark, Norway, and Sweden), in contrast, there has been a broad increase in the frequency of private members' bills or resolutions. Only in Iceland has the trend gone in the opposite direction, presumably because the country's party system has been consolidated, and parliamentary politics has become more national and less parochial in orientation. Yet, the Nordic region as a whole has seen a gradual increase in the number of parliamentary bills and other legislative activity.

Where we have reliable evidence (Denmark, Finland, and Sweden), legislative activity as measured in the annual number of hours parliament is in session has also increased. In Denmark, for example, the number of sitting hours increased from 496 in 1998–99 (the first year for which we have data) to 724 in 2003–4, an increase of 46 percent in just five years. Over the longer span from 1979–80 to 2004–5, Swedish sitting hours similarly increased from 597 to 730, or a gain of 22 percent. The Nordic parliaments have traditionally been considered "working parliaments," and there is thus nothing in our data to suggest that that characterization is less true today than it was in the past. On the contrary, our data suggest that the level of parliamentary activity has increased.

One MP prerogative is to ask questions of cabinet ministers. Parliamentary questions come in a variety of forms and serve many purposes, but typically such inquiries are a weapon wielded by the parliamentary opposition and a way for individual MPs (particularly those from opposition parties) to grab the limelight and demonstrate their commitment to their respective constituencies (Wiberg 1994). Questions can thus be an important mechanism of parliamentary accountability. Figure 10.3 reports the number of parliamentary questions asked per country per year relative to the number asked in 1990. For ease of presentation, we have standardized the incidence for each country in 1990 at 1. At first glance, figure 10.3 suggests a somewhat divergent picture. In Finland the pattern of activity has been quite stable, except for a spurt of legislative inquiries between 1996 and 1998, shortly after the country joined the European Union. In contrast, MPs in Denmark, Iceland, and Sweden asked a lot more questions in the early 2000s than they did only a decade or two previously. In Denmark,

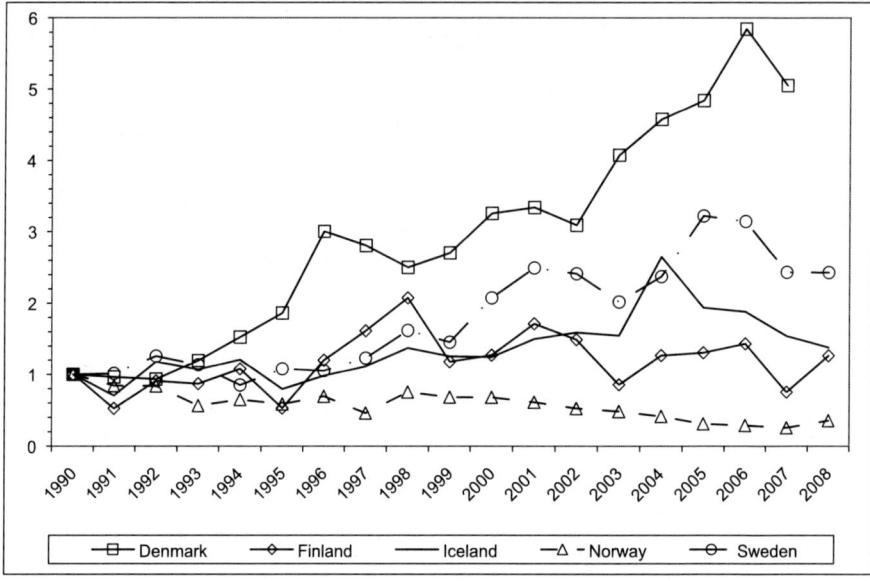

Fig. 10.3. Questions to cabinet ministers by country, 1990–2008. The index year is 1990, and all changes are relative to that year. (Data from tables 3.5 [column: Questions], 4.5 [column: Written Questions], 5.5b [columns: Written Questions and Oral Questions], 6.5 [column: Ordinary Questions], and 7.5 [column: Questions].)

the volume of parliamentary questions thus quadrupled between 1990 and the early 2000s. In Norway, on the other hand, the number of parliamentary questions has gradually declined from a peak around 1990. Yet, this picture is misleading in the Norwegian case, since figure 10.3 includes only so-called ordinary questions. As chapter 6 notes, two new forms of parliamentary questions ("written" and "spontaneous") were introduced in 1996 and have since gained a great deal of currency in the Storting. If we therefore discount the apparent decline in the Norwegian case, the data point to a substantial and continuous increase in the volume of parliamentary questions in most of the Nordic countries.

There may be many ways to interpret this trend, particularly when the institutional rules change, as has happened frequently in the Nordic countries. But it is plausible to ascribe some part of this trend to heightened electoral competition. Green-Pedersen (2010) suggests that as parties all across Western Europe increasingly have had to engage in competition over issues, rather than basing their appeal on left-right structural cleavages, the incentives have been growing for MPs to devote time and energy to nonlegislative matters. This trend enhances the utility of parliamentary questions. Moreover, the country chapters bear evidence that national MPs feel that they have less and less influence over national policy and government activities through the regular lawmaking channels. As a consequence, they may have become more inclined to try to capture the attention of ministers and media through parliamentary questions. The long-term increase in parliamentary questions may also reflect a genuine strengthening of parliamentary oversight, which would be consistent with a situation of frequent minority government (which provides motivation for more parliamentarians to scrutinize the executive), high electoral volatility (which may add to that motivation), and enhanced parliamentary resources (which provide opportunity).

Cabinet Recruitment

Under parliamentary government, the cabinet is the critical arena of top-level policy-making. Cabinet ministers are therefore key decision makers, and any decline in the importance of the parliamentary channel of policy-making might therefore be reflected in the personnel at the cabinet level. It has indeed been argued that contemporary trends have weakened the status and influence of regular "line ministers" in the cabinet with respect to the prime minister (PM). This alleged decline is associated with the relative shift of power and influence toward the national executive and the increased attention and power (presidentialization) vested in the PM (see Poguntke and Webb 2005). The media—not least the new electronic forms—have sharpened their focus on the prime minister and thereby heightened the importance of intracabinet coordination. For EU member states, and even for states affected by EU decision making through the EEA agreement, the preeminence of the prime minister has been further enhanced by the PM's critical role in EU negotiations. At the same time that the focus on the prime minister has increased, however, there has been sharp media focus on the demographic patterns of recruitment to all cabinet positions, particularly concerning the representation of women and younger politicians. Thus, the background characteristics of ordinary cabinet ministers have become more salient, even as they have arguably become increasingly subordinated to the prime minister.

We examine the credentials and background characteristics of the core Nordic cabinet members in order to consider two hypotheses concerning the putative effects of presidentialization. The first hypothesis is that if parliament has diminished in importance as a political arena, we should see declining levels of prior parliamentary experience among core cabinet members. The second hypothesis is that to the extent that elected politicians have become detached from their social constituencies, we should see less attention being paid to social representation than previously.

Let us consider the latter proposition first. The country chapters have presented comparative data on the occupants of four core ministries in each of the Nordic countries: the prime minister, the minister of finance (budget), the minister of foreign affairs, and the minister of justice. This set of ministries represents the core functions of modern states: public finance, law enforcement, external relations, and overall policy coordination. We begin by examining these data with respect to social representation. Our focus will be first on the representation of women in core cabinet portfolios, since gender equality has surely been the most salient issue of demographic representation in the Nordic region over the past generation. Figure 10.4 thus reports on the representation of women in key ministerial positions in the Nordic countries in two temporal slices: 1945–75 versus 1991–2007. Note that for simplicity of presentation, we do not report the middle period, 1976–90.

Not surprisingly, there has been a large and rapid increase in the percentage of female cabinet members in these four core portfolios. The magnitude of the change is due in part to the fact that until the 1970s female representation was so minimal. In Finland and Sweden, there were no female cabinet members at all in the core portfolios prior to 1975. But although there has been a healthy increase in the share of female cabinet ministers in all five countries, Norway and Sweden have seen much greater increases than the others. In Denmark, Finland, and Iceland, the proportion of female core cabinet members has gone up, but only to a level of 15 to 20 percent in the most recent period. In contrast, in Norway, women have surpassed the 25 percent threshold, and the country had a female prime minister as early as 1981. The Swedish percentage has virtually skyrocketed, taking Swedish women from total absence from the cabinet table prior to 1975 to near parity with men after 1990. Thus, Sweden is a front-runner worldwide in the representation of women in core cabinet positions. And at least as far as gender is concerned, the Nordic countries have not abandoned concerns with social representation.

Whether that lesson can be generalized to other social background characteristics is less obvious, however. Immigrants and ethnic minorities, for example, remain very poorly represented in Nordic parliaments. And whereas these assemblies were once noted for their high representation of members from modest economic and educational backgrounds, over the past generation the Nordic parliaments have become dominated by well-

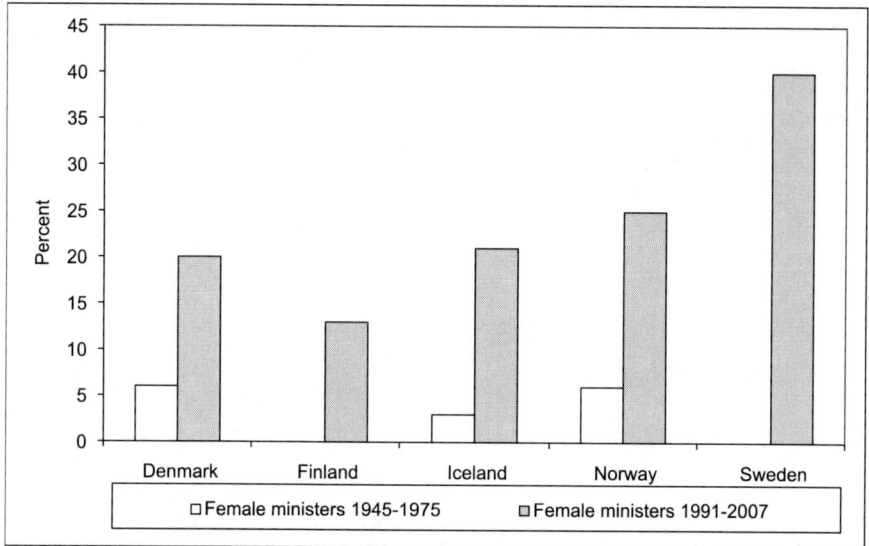

Fig. 10.4. Female ministers in key ministerial portfolios, by country and period. Key ministerial portfolios include prime minister, finance minister, foreign minister, and minister of justice. (Data from tables 3.6, 4.6, 5.6, 6.6, and 7.6.)

educated middle-class representatives. Yet, there are differences within the Nordic region. In Sweden, the average level of formal education among cabinet members has actually declined slightly. In Finland and Norway, it has increased, but only marginally. It is in Iceland and Denmark that we see the most substantial increase in educational attainment, in Denmark to the extent that every single occupant of the core cabinet portfolios since 1991 has had a postgraduate degree.

Similar cross-national differences show up in the representation of different economic sectors. In Denmark (90 percent) and Iceland (86 percent), the vast majority of core cabinet members in recent years have had some professional experience from the private sector, and if anything these numbers have trended upward. Finland occupies a middle ground, with a stable proportion around 75 percent. In Norway (50 percent) and Sweden (33 percent), in contrast, the percentages are much lower and in both cases declining. Given the fact that about two-thirds of the workforce in these two countries is in the private sector, this of course means that this sector is significantly to grossly underrepresented in the core political executive.

This bias in representation appears to be a more general phenomenon.

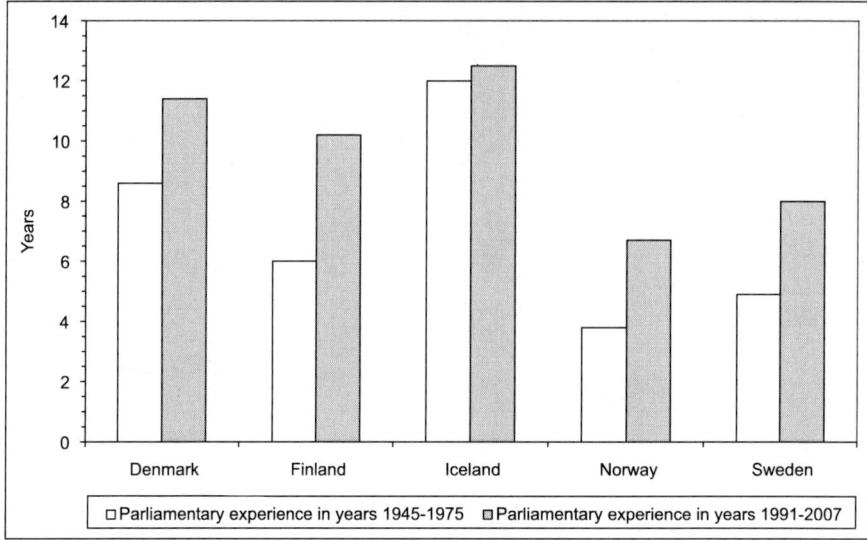

Fig. 10.5. Average prior parliamentary experience for four key ministerial portfolios, by country and period. Key ministerial portfolios include prime minister, finance minister, foreign minister, and minister of justice. (Data from tables 3.6, 4.6, 5.6, 6.6, and 7.6.)

Thus, among the 55 newly elected members of the Norwegian Parliament in 2009, only 8 came directly from the private sector. In contrast, 31 of the Storting freshmen were professional politicians who previously held a full-time position in public office or in the political parties (*Aftenposten* 2009). In sum, social representation presents a more complex picture than when we simply consider women's representation. Whereas the Nordic countries have had remarkable success in boosting the representation of women in the executive, they have seemingly paid less attention to the status of other underrepresented groups. There are indeed some indications that the political class has become more biased and insular in its recruitment patterns with respect to educational credentials and economic sector. But these trends also vary substantially across the Nordic region, with Denmark for example diverging sharply from its Scandinavian neighbors.

Turning now to the importance of parliament as an arena for executive recruitment, consider the data in figure 10.5 on cabinet members' prior parliamentary experience as evidence concerning our second hypothesis of parliamentary decline. Again, for clarity of presentation, we show only the first and last of the three temporal cuts: 1945–75 versus 1991–2007. (This

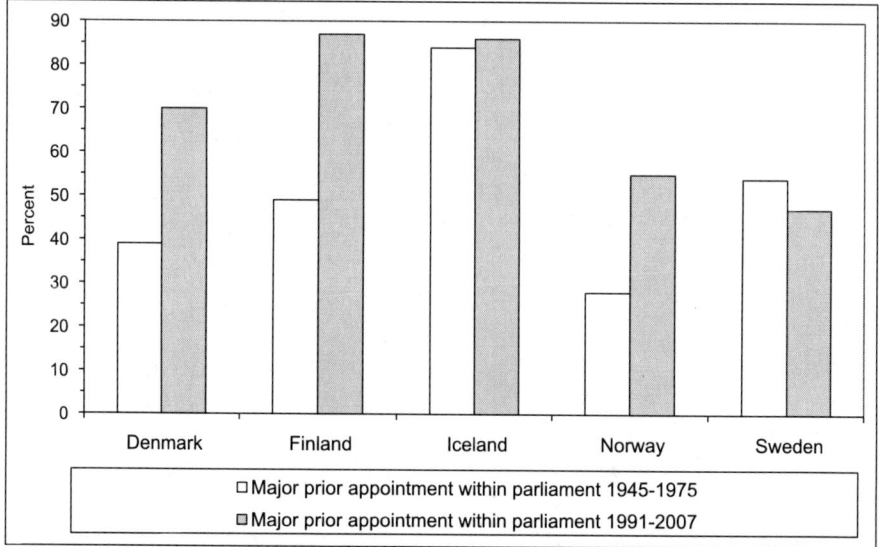

Fig. 10.6. Major prior appointment within parliament for four key ministerial portfolios, by country and period. Key ministerial portfolios include prime minister, finance minister, foreign minister, and minister of justice. (Data from tables 3.6, 4.6, 5.6, 6.6, and 7.6.)

does not change our interpretation; the median period follows the same overall trend.) Figure 10.5 demonstrates that to get appointed to core ministerial portfolios, parliamentarians in all five countries have recently had to serve longer in parliament than did their counterparts prior to 1975. In Iceland, this difference is negligible, as Icelandic cabinet members have always tended to have extensive parliamentary experience. In the other countries, however, recent ministers have had significantly more parliamentary experience than previous generations. These data clearly contradict the hypothesis that parliament has become less important for recruitment to top cabinet positions. Rather, it suggests that if you serve long enough in parliament, a ministerial position can still await you.

Finally, figure 10.6 exhibits the relationship between major parliamentary appointments and core cabinet office by presenting the share of key cabinet members who have held important legislative offices before their cabinet appointment. Again, our analysis of trend averages gives no support to the proposition that parliamentary office has become a less important credential for cabinet ministers. On the contrary, our data show that a growing share of cabinet members have held high-ranking positions in the parliament prior to their entry into high executive office. In two countries, Iceland and Sweden, there is no significant difference in the proportion of cabinet members with prior high office in the two periods. In our three remaining countries, however, such background has become significantly more common in the most recent period.

On the basis of these data, we can therefore confidently say that there is no evidence of any cross-national decline in the importance of parliamentary experience for top executive-level positions—rather the contrary. Unquestionably, parliamentary experience remains important for politicians with ministerial ambitions. The presidentialization thesis must therefore be qualified. Most of those selected for high cabinet portfolios have previously served in the parliament, and many have held a high-ranking legislative office before being elevated to cabinet positions. If anything, this kind of experience has become more common, rather than less, over the past couple of decades. However, as is the case with the cartel party thesis (see below), the presidentialization argument surely captures at least one significant recent trend. The office of prime minister does seem to have increased in importance and media salience in the Nordic countries. That development is likely to have consequences for cabinet recruitment, but at least so far this has not led to a clear and stable erosion in the importance of the parliamentary arena.

A Plague on the Parties?

Political parties have long had a privileged place in parliamentary systems because of their importance as mechanisms of accountability. Across parliamentary democracies, the strength of parliaments is systematically related to the strength of political parties. Westminster parliamentary democracy indeed relies on extensive delegation of power from the legislative to the executive branch. Parties facilitate such delegation by securing stable parliamentary majorities. One of the payoffs to politicians willing to submit to party discipline is a high "partyness" in the executive branch. Top executive offices are controlled and filled by partisan politicians. And parties protect their electoral stability by acting on the interests of broad and well-defined social constituencies. Under such conditions, strong parties sustain orderly parliaments and stable executives. In order for parliaments to delegate successfully to the political executive, political parties thus have to be cohesive and effective. When they are not, parliamentary government may mean "surviving without governing" (Di Palma 1977). Occasionally, such systems do not even survive, as evidenced by the French Fourth Republic in the 1950s or Italy in the 1990s.

In contemporary parliamentary democracies as well as elsewhere, however, political parties seem to be on the wane (chapter 1). Peter Mair (2007, 22) puts the matter in stark and direct terms: "Never before in the history of postwar Europe have governments and their political leaders—at the national level—been held in such low regard." Mair goes on to argue:

> First, it is my contention that parties are failing. Having gone through a lengthy process of organizational and strategic adaptation, political parties now find themselves increasingly unable to legitimate their governance. Second, precisely because parties have formed such a core and constitutive element within representative democracy in Europe, their failings have led to various reconsiderations about what democracy entails, and about how it might be developed. Third, these reconsiderations are tending to converge on the notion that democracy is about rights rather than voice, about output rather than input, and about a process that need not involve a substantial emphasis on popular involvement and control. That is, they converge on a notion of democracy that prioritises constitutional democracy over popular democracy. (23)

Mair thus suggests that the decline of political parties in parliamentary Europe has to do with the judicialization of European politics, with the growing importance of external constraints on the parliamentary policy-making process. But parties may also be in trouble because they have become less faithful agents of their respective constituencies. The cartel party thesis (Katz and Mair 1995) thus suggests that parties have turned their attention away from representing broad social constituencies to capturing and exploiting the machinery of the state and the benefits that flow from it. And presidentialization may have weakened the party's control over executive office and thus their standing among parliamentarians.

Do any of these developments threaten the status of Nordic parties? Let us first consider the point at which parties most directly structure the parliamentary policy process: their control of executive recruitment. Figure 10.7 reports the record of core Nordic cabinet members with respect to prior experience in leading party offices. The figure thus compares the proportions of core cabinet members that have held high party office before their appointment to the cabinet. The results are surprising in that, in four of the five Nordic countries, core cabinet members are more likely to have had a prior party career now than a generation ago. The exception is Denmark, where the incidence of such backgrounds was already low by Nordic

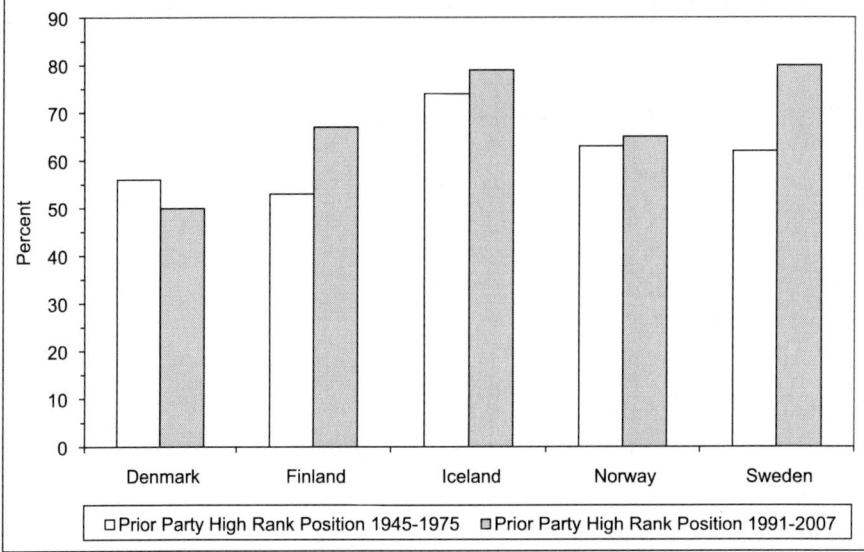

Fig. 10.7. Prior high-ranking position in party for four key ministerial portfolios, by country and period. Key ministerial portfolios include prime minister, finance minister, foreign minister, and minister of justice. (Data from tables 3.6, 4.6, 5.6, 6.6, and 7.6.)

standards. In the most recent period, it stands at 50 percent, as opposed to about 65 to 80 percent in the other Nordic countries. Yet the results for the other Nordic countries are directly contrary to what we would expect on the basis of the presidentialization thesis, according to which the value of a partisan background should have declined over time. One possible explanation for these results is that the recruitment of cabinet members without strong partisan ties may have occurred disproportionately outside our core ministries. Nevertheless, there is thus little evidence that presidentialization has weakened the importance of parties for executive recruitment in the Nordic region.

Consider also the share of key cabinet members that have previously held salaried employment within their respective parties, which is reported in the various country chapters. For the 1991–2008 period, this proportion varies significantly, from 0 percent in Iceland to 20 percent in Denmark, 27 percent in Finland, 30 percent in Norway, and a remarkable 53 percent in Sweden. Over time, this proportion has declined in Iceland, seen little change in Denmark and Finland, and increased in Norway and Sweden. In sum, there is surely no evidence that Nordic parties have lost their hold on executive recruitment. Rather, the picture that emerges is again one of divergence, with parties maintaining or even strengthening their control in Norway and Sweden, whereas in Denmark and Iceland their position appears considerably more tenuous (and Finland finds itself in an intermediate position).

Voter Turnout and Detachment

While parties in most of the Nordic countries maintain solid control of the executive branch and political recruitment, the picture is quite different when we consider their standing among the Nordic voters. For one thing, parties have been less successful in simply bringing the voters to the polls. The cross-national data presented in chapter 8 show that electoral turnout has indeed been falling in the Nordic region since about the 1980s. This drop-off has been particularly dramatic in Finland and Norway, with Sweden not far behind. In the late 1990s and early 2000s, this decline seems to have leveled off (at least temporarily so), but there has been no return to the high participation levels that used to characterize these countries. Turnout in Iceland has been more stable, though a modest downward trend was noticeable in the 1990s. Denmark is the only country in which electoral participation has remained relatively stable, but even here there has been some decline since the high point of the 1970s. Yet by Western standards, voter turnout in the Nordic states remains comparatively high, with the partial exception of Finland.

One of the reasons why Nordic citizens have become less likely to vote is surely linked to their flagging identification with particular political parties. There is a clear and close to monotonic downward trend in self-reported party identification in all of the Nordic countries, with the partial exception of Denmark, where the decline has been only modest since the late 1970s.

This downturn in party identification is neatly paralleled by a steady increase in electoral volatility—vote switching from one election to the next. Again, the deviant case is Denmark. In terms of "unfaithful" voters, Danish parties experienced an earthquake election in 1973, when about 45 percent of voters opted for a party they had not supported in the previous parliamentary election. Of course, this was partly because there were several significant parties on the ballot in 1973 that had not existed at the time of the previous election. Over the next four elections, volatility in Denmark gradually declined and returned to "conventional" Nordic levels. Since the early 1990s Danish volatility has once again increased, though it fell off somewhat in the most recent election (2005). Finland has seen no earthquake election and has a fairly flat trajectory, with only a modest increase in volatility since its time-series began in the early 1970s.

The upward trend in volatility is more pronounced in Iceland and especially in Norway and Sweden, where it has steadily increased from modest initial levels. In Norway volatility is now even higher than it was in the Danish earthquake election of 1973. This is all the more remarkable in light of the fact that there have been no significant new parties in Norway since the 1970s. Thus, the entire increase in Norwegian volatility is due to voters changing their preferences among existing parties, rather than having new parties to choose from. In this way, Norwegian voters in particular seem to have become detached political consumers, looking for the best offer without being much constrained by their previous choices.

In sum, there is little doubt that Nordic voters have become increasingly detached from their political parties. Across the Nordic region, a higher share of citizens vote less regularly than they used to, they feel less identification with particular parties, they are more inclined to switch support between parties, and they make up their minds later in the process. Their voting patterns are also less closely tied to their social background and most specifically to their class membership. Some of these trends, for example, with regard to party identification, are stronger and more consistent than others.

We also note consistent differences among the Nordic countries. In general, Denmark has seen less consistent long-term change than the rest. This is interesting not least because Denmark is precisely the country where party detachment was first and most dramatically evident. Over the longer haul, though, Norway and Sweden stand out as the countries in which the political parties' relationships with the voters have been most thoroughly weakened. Recall that these are precisely the countries where parties maintain the tightest control of the executive arena. Thus, where parties have been most exclusive and controlling, they have also seen the greatest erosion in popular support. In most respects Finland is more similar to Sweden and Norway than to Denmark. Iceland is in many ways a case unto itself, because the early postwar parties in that country never had the coherence that they had elsewhere in the region (and perhaps because our data are more spotty).

Lonely but Rich Parties?

The evidence we have considered thus far tells a story of voter detachment, as shown cross-nationally by Dalton and Wattenberg (2000) and Mair

(2007). But this is not the full story, and in some ways our data support a picture of adaptive rather than dying parties. The cartel party thesis suggests that contemporary political parties, specifically in Europe, have become more detached from their social constituencies and more attached to the spoils that the public sector provides. Political parties, according to this thesis, have gone from being mouthpieces for specific social interests to becoming comfortable cartels of office and benefit seekers. As they have made this transition, parties have downplayed their mass membership organization in favor of strategies that yield better financial returns with fewer policy constraints. Chief among them has been the pursuit of public subsidies. Cartel parties also secure benefits for their leaders through the pursuit of various offices in the public sector.

Because it is open-ended and not very specific (see chapter 1), the cartel party thesis is difficult to put to a single empirical test. At the same time, it is intuitively appealing to many observers of modern politics, and some manifestations of its general claims are readily observable. For example, a straightforward implication of the cartel party thesis is that we should expect mass party membership organizations to atrophy. The cross-national membership data presented in chapter 8 helps us consider that proposition in light of the Nordic evidence. While this evidence is not always striking, it is quite consistent with the thesis. Except for Iceland, where available data are limited and known to be problematic, party membership levels have been declining in all countries and recent periods for which we have evidence. And the countries in which the parties have most successfully "colonized" political offices (Norway and Sweden) are also the countries where the voters have most decisively deserted them. In absolute numbers, the Norwegian and the Swedish parties have suffered the heaviest membership losses. Danish parties have fared better, with much more modest losses, whereas Finland falls somewhere in between.

The cartel party thesis also suggests that parties get richer as they get lonelier. This proposition is more difficult to evaluate, in part because the data are so qualitative and country-specific. Nonetheless, there is at least some country-specific evidence on the payoff to party leaders in public subsidies. Chapter 8 shows how the ratio between public subsidies and the number of party members has dramatically increased for the Swedish parties. This is an effect of a simultaneous drop in party members and an increase in public party subsidies. Though there is no comparable data for the other Nordic countries, we know that, in Norway, party membership levels have experienced a similar drop, while public party subsidies have greatly and steadily increased (NOU 2004, 25).

While it is difficult to judge whether the electoral detachment that Nordic parties have suffered is due to their transformation into cartel parties, there is evidence that is consistent with this thesis. At the very least, it is reasonable to say that as they have lost some of the steadfast allegiance among the voters, Nordic parties have found other ways to generate income for themselves and perhaps to retain their organizational effectiveness in government. Party leaders may have gotten lonelier, but at least they have not become poorer.

Trust in Government

There is thus little doubt that Nordic citizens have become more fickle and demanding in their political decisions. But the implications for system support are more ambiguous. Compared with the rest of Europe, all the Nordic countries score above the European average in political trust and satisfaction (see chapter 2). And these attitudes appear to be robust, in the sense that the results are very similar whether one asks about satisfaction with democracy in general, satisfaction with specific institutions such as parliament, or trust in the politicians that populate these institutions. Characteristically, one institution in which the Nordic populations do not put high levels of trust is the European Parliament.

There are many possible explanations for these sentiments, and beliefs in government can have many sources. For example, they might reflect long-standing attitudes of deference or communitarianism that have little to do with current politics. Nevertheless, it is noteworthy that there also seem to be clear differences among the Nordic countries. While they all display higher levels of trust than the Western European average, Norwegian and especially Swedish citizens are noticeably less trustful than those of the other Nordic countries. The main divergence in terms of trust seems to be within the alternational group of Nordic democracies, between Denmark on the one hand and Norway and Sweden on the other, and not between the alternational and pivotal groups of countries. As it turns out, this is a distinction that runs through much of our data on parties and parliamentary institutions. The lower levels of trust in Norway and Sweden may reflect a lower level of trust in politicians rather than a lack of confidence in political institutions. Thus, while Norwegians and Swedes still score very high on trust in the national parliament, they express less trust in politicians.

More reassuringly, temporal trends show that outright distrust has generally declined throughout the Nordic region in recent years. This improvement is most consistent in Denmark, but there is no country in the region in which reported distrust has actually increased in election surveys since the turn of the millennium (although recent data are missing for Finland). The trends in Denmark in fact are quite remarkable. Since about 1990, Danish parties and politicians have been the most trusted in the Nordic countries, and the level of distrust has continuously declined since the early 1980s at least. After the earthquake election of the early 1970s, Danish citizens have regained much of their faith in the party system and in the parliament.

Conclusion

Parliamentary democracy is a form of government that has found much favor among students of democratic institutions. Historically, this form of government has also been warmly embraced in the Nordic countries. Even though two of them have popularly elected presidents (and are thus semi-presidential at least in formal terms), all adhere to the parliamentary norm of cabinet accountability to the legislative majority. And this form of government seems to have served these countries well and long. The Nordic countries are among the most stable and politically successful parliamentary countries anywhere in the world.

We have examined the extent to which these countries have nevertheless experienced challenges to their form of government, stemming from changes among the voters, among politicians, or in the features of the policy process. Our aim has been to judge whether such challenges have weakened the governing role of parliament or the pivotal role of political parties for which parliamentary systems, and especially Westminster democracies, are known.

Our results can now be summarized. The Nordic countries have certainly experienced change, and some forms of change have been dramatic. Voters have become much more volatile and detached. The social cleavage pattern has become much less predictable. Politicians have changed greatly, most notably perhaps in their gender composition. Parties have transformed themselves from mass membership organizations financed by dues to much more skeletal networks financed by the taxpayers. Despite all this, most voters have not become cynical, and coalition politics has not become chaotic or anarchic.

Institutionally, Nordic democracy has changed. The Nordic countries, or at least some of them, are in varying ways moving away from the Nordic version of the Westminster model of democracy toward one that is more Madisonian. Iceland, Norway, and especially Sweden have clearly moved in this direction. On the other hand, freed from its "special relationship" with the Soviet Union, Finland has moved away from its previous semi-presidentialism toward a more traditional parliamentary model. And Denmark is now the country that best resembles the Westminster model.

The Madisonian turn is most evident in the larger constitutional environment in which parliamentary politics is played out. Though much lawmaking capacity remains at home, and national politicians still control the critical purse strings (taxes and public spending), significant political powers have moved to EU institutions of political decision making. The Nordic democracies are all heavily affected by joint decision making in the European Union (even though only three of these countries are voting members). They all exhibit trends toward multilevel governance that involve decision-making processes that span from the European (and sometimes the global), through the national, and down to the local level (e.g., in environmental policy). In other domains of decision making, Nordic politicians have witnessed important encroachments by the courts, both domestic and international (especially the European Court of Justice). An increase in the use of direct democracy and the removal of such policy areas as monetary decision making from partisan control have driven these polities in the same direction. During the last two decades the Nordics have all yielded more autonomy to their central banks. Thus, Europeanization and judicialization have surely imposed substantial constraints on the parliamentarians of the Nordic countries and brought these countries closer to a Madisonian model of checks and balances and further away from the Westminster ideal of parliamentary sovereignty. To this we can add, not least, the diminishing importance of neocorporatist arrangements. In sum, the Nordic democracies have become more constrained and more complex (Madisonian) and hence more difficult to reconcile with the classical model of Westminster parliamentary democracy.

Table 10.1 illustrates and spells out our two conceptions of parliamentary democracy: the Westminster and Madisonian models. The Westminster model relies heavily on *ex ante* controls for political accountability. Strong and cohesive political parties with deep social roots have secured stable and effective government. Through extensive screening, they have found suitable candidates for office and if necessary removed nonperforming incumbents from office through tight ballot control. In the Madisonian model, the control logic is much more external and *ex post*. This model relies much more on external constraints to scrutinize what politicians do and decide. This means a greater dependence on courts and other independent auditors rather than political parties.

Characteristics	Westminster Ideal Type	Madisonian Ideal Type	Nordic Region 1990	Nordic Region 2010
Authority of parliament in policy process	Parliamentary sovereignty	Parliament is one among other bodies with legislative functions; dispersion of agenda and veto powers	All but sovereign parliaments; president has specific powers in Finland	Parliaments coshare legislative powers with EU institutions, especially in member countries; presidential power has been reduced in Finland.
Nationalization of policy process	Centralized at national level	Dispersed over a number of levels of government through federalism	Unitary states but with elements of "fiscal federalism" and growing decentralization toward local government	Unitary states; multilevel governance with elements of "fiscal federalism"
Domestic constraints on parliamentary authority	None	Important domestic constraints, e.g., independent central banks and courts with judicial review	Autonomous courts reluctant to be "politicized"; central banks controlled by parliament and cabinet	More autonomous central banks and greater judicial independence
Civil society and interest representation in national policy process	Pluralistic and noninstitutionalized interest group influence channeled through parliament and political parties	Pluralistic and noninstitutionalized interest representation through a variety of channels	Strong neocorporatist institutions involving labor and capital in centralized public policy-making	Neocorporatist interest group representation has weakened (Denmark, Norway, and Sweden); mass media have become more important and diversified and less partisan.
Government formation	Cohesive, single-party government; alternation in government only after elections	Shifting legislative coalitions reflected in minority or coalition government; occasional midterm alternation in government	Frequent minority governments; most alternations occur after elections	Declining but still high incidence of minority governments; declining incidence of midterm alternations
Partisan control of executive recruitment	Very high	Low	Very high	Very high, but occasional appointments of nonpartisans to cabinet office
Party cohesion, centralization, and capacity	Parties are centralized and cohesive; high organizational capacity	Parties are decentralized and not cohesive; lower organizational capacity	Parties are very cohesive and fairly centralized; high organizational capacity	Parties are very cohesive and fairly centralized; declining organizational capacity
Parties and social interests	Parties represent well-defined social interests with a strong presence in civil society.	Parties represent diverse and fluid social interests.	Parties mostly represent well-defined social interests with a strong presence in civil society.	Parties increasingly represent diverse and fluid social interests.

Table 10.1 maps the major institutional developments in the Nordic countries over the past two decades in light of these models. All the Nordic countries have been moving toward more Madisonian characteristics in the sense that their parliaments have been reined in by judicialization, European integration, and the emergence of other external constraints. Similarly, civil society and interest representation have evolved toward more fluid and diverse forms that have eroded the influence of political parties and their allies in their interest group community. Thus, there have been powerful Madisonian trends in the recent evolution of the Nordic polities.

The Nordic version of Westminster democracy throughout the twentieth century was one that differed from the British model in one critical aspect in particular: its multiparty system. Yet, in much of the Nordic region, and especially in Scandinavia, that difference could in large part be reduced to the fact that the Nordic democracies featured a bloc of mostly coalescent center-right parties in lieu of the encompassing British Conservatives. As traditional bloc divisions in the Nordic region have become less clear-cut, the Nordic party systems have also drifted away from the Westminster model. While they have retained much of their policy cohesion and their control of executive recruitment, parties have changed most at the electoral level, becoming looser and more transitory coalitions of voters more akin to the Madisonian model. This is partly a trend driven by strategy and electoral opportunism, and partly a necessity given the parties' reduced capacity to mobilize significant core constituencies such as the working class or a community of believers.

In many ways, the Nordic country that has most successfully met the challenges we have examined is Denmark. Like the rest of the Nordic countries, Denmark has experienced growing external constraints on its parliamentary policy process. But at the same time, Danish parties have responded effectively to the electoral shocks that they experienced in the 1970s. Cabinet stability has been growing and incumbency losses diminishing. Denmark currently also has the highest level of political trust. It has experienced the smallest decrease in electoral turnout over the past couple of decades. And it now has the highest level of party identification and a fairly modest level of electoral volatility. Danish parties have also lost fewer members than those in Norway and Sweden. Altogether, Denmark seems to have the most vital political parties and the most intact chain of parliamentary delegation.

Why, then, is Denmark a success story among the Nordic countries? Is this perhaps because the country has a more flexible party system than some of its neighbors, less moored to the cleavage structure of the industrial and preindustrial era? Seemingly, this party system flexibility enables new parties representing anti-EU and anti-immigration sentiments to surface without seriously disrupting the party system, and it has allowed a party previously tied to the agrarian sector (the Liberals) to redefine its role and constituency in Danish politics. Perhaps the Danes have also more successfully learned how to deal and live with the new multilevel Europe. Yet another and reasonable explanation found in the Danish Power Study is that the Danish parties themselves have allowed and encouraged their members to exercise influence in a way that if anything seems to have strengthened the intraparty organization relative to the party leadership (Togeby et al. 2003, 183–85). In Sweden, and perhaps in Norway, ordinary party members may instead have been crowded out by their own party elites and by civil servants.

But Denmark's experience is not the only interesting trajectory that our study has brought to our attention. Our study also shows that political parties can decline in cohesiveness and voter attachment, and yet at the same time the chain of parliamentary delegation and accountability can be strengthened. To see how this seeming paradox can manifest itself, look at Finland. Even though Finnish parties have experienced some organizational atrophy, the role of parliament in the national policy process has been enhanced, as the presidency has declined in role and influence. Cabinets have become increasingly stable, and the incumbency losses imposed by the voters have diminished somewhat. Moreover, the large and sometimes menacing shadow of the Soviet Union no longer constrains Finnish parliamentary politics in the way that it did until the early 1990s.

Still, there is reason to be concerned about the standing of Nordic parties among the voters and particularly about their apparent trajectory toward some facets of the cartel party model. There is also more reason to worry about the accountability of Nordic parties to ordinary citizens than about the ways in which the parties function in the parliamentary arena. At the same time, the political parties are where they are today precisely because they have shown such powers of adaptation and resilience. While it is prudent to point out the challenges they face, it would be folly to predict their demise. Many contemporary trends in Nordic politics are worrisome, but it would be a monumental misunderstanding to claim that their parliaments and parties have all failed. They are instead being transformed, both actively and passively. And the trend toward more Madisonian democracy in the Nordic countries may well offer a broader range of political opportunities for a wider range of citizens and organizations.

REFERENCES

Aftenposten. 2009. "Næringslivet på Stortinget." September 19.
Bagehot, Walter. 1867. *The English Constitution*. London.
Bale, Tim, and Torbjörn Bergman. 2006. "Captives No Longer, but Servants Still? Contract Parliamentarism and the New Minority Governance in Sweden and New Zealand." *Government and Opposition* 41 (3): 449–76.
Cheibub, Jose Antonio. 2007. *Presidentialism, Parliamentarism, and Democracy*. Cambridge: Cambridge University Press.
Christiansen, Flemming J., and Erik Damgaard. 2008. "Parliamentary Opposition under Minority Parliamentarism: Scandinavia." *Journal of Legislative Studies* 14 (1–2): 46–76.
Dalton, Russell J., and Martin P. Wattenberg, eds. 2000. *Parties without Partisans: Political Change in Advanced Industrial Democracies*. Oxford: Oxford University Press.
Di Palma, Giuseppe. 1977. *Surviving without Governing: The Italian Parties in Parliament*. Berkeley: University of California Press.
Gidlund, Gullan. 1991. "Public Investments in Swedish Democracy." In Matti Wiberg, ed., *The Public Purse and Political Parties*. Jyväskylä: Gummerus Printing.
Green-Pedersen, Christoffer. 2010. "Bringing Parties into Parliament: The Development of Parliamentary Activities in Western Europe." *Party Politics* 16 (3): 347–69.
Katz, Richard S., and Peter Mair. 1995. "Changing Models of Party Organization and Party Democracy: The Emergence of the Cartel Party." *Party Politics* 1 (1): 5–28.
Laver, Michael, and Kenneth A. Shepsle. 1996. *Making and Breaking Governments*. Cambridge: Cambridge University Press.
Lijphart, Arend. 1999. *Patterns of Democracy: Government Forms and Performance in Thirty-six Countries*. New Haven: Yale University Press.
Linz, Juan J. 1994. "Presidential or Parliamentary Democracy: Does It Make a Difference?" In Juan Linz and Arturo Valenzuela, eds., *The Failure of Presidential Democracy*. Baltimore: Johns Hopkins University Press.
Mair, Peter. 2007. "Policy-Scepticism and Party Failings." In *The Challenge to European Democracy*. Wassenaar: Netherlands Institute for Advanced Study in the Humanities and Social Sciences.
Narud, Hanne Marthe, and Henry Valen. 2008. "Coalition Membership and Electoral Performance." In Kaare Strøm, Wolfgang C. Müller, and Torbjörn Bergman, eds., *Cabinets and Coalition Bargaining: The Democratic Life Cycle in Western Europe*. Oxford: Oxford University Press.
NOU. 2004. *Penger teller, men stemmer avgjør. Om partifinansiering, åpenhet og politisk tv-reklame*, 2004:25. Oslo: Ministry of Modernisation.
Poguntke, Thomas, and Paul Webb, eds. 2005. *The Presidentialization of Politics: A Comparative Study of Modern Democracies*. Oxford: Oxford University Press.
Strøm, Kaare. 1986. "Deferred Gratification and Minority Government in Scandinavia." *Legislative Studies Quarterly* 11:583–605.
Strøm, Kaare. 1990. *Minority Government and Majority Rule*. Cambridge: Cambridge University Press.

Strøm, Kaare, Wolfgang C. Müller, and Torbjörn Bergman, eds. 2008. *Cabinets and Coalition Bargaining: The Democratic Life Cycle in Western Europe.* Oxford: Oxford University Press.
Togeby, Lise, Jørgen G. Andersen, Peter M. Christiansen, Torsten B. Jørgensen, and Signild Vallgårda. 2003. *Magt og Demokrati i Danmark-Hovedresultater fra Magtudredningen.* Aarhus: Aarhus Universitetsforlag.
Wiberg, Matti, ed. 1994. *Parliamentary Control in the Nordic Countries: Forms of Questioning and Behavioural Trends.* Jyväskylä: Finnish Political Science Association.

INTERNET SOURCES

"Financial Support to the Political Parties." *Fact Sheets from the Swedish Riksdag.* Year 1991–2005. http://www.riksdagen.se/upload/Dokument/bestall/engelska/Faktablad_E10.pdf

Contributors

NICHOLAS AYLOTT is associate professor of political science at Södertörn University, Stockholm, Sweden. His main interest is comparative European politics, with a special focus on Scandinavia and political parties. He has authored and coauthored various books and journal articles in these fields. Much of his most recent work focuses on party organization.

TORBJÖRN BERGMAN is research professor of political science at Södertörn University, Stockholm, and at Umeå University. He has also recently been professor of political science at Luleå University of Technology. He has been a visiting researcher at the University of California, San Diego, and at the University of North Carolina, Chapel Hill. His most recent publications include two books with Oxford University Press, *Delegation and Accountability in Parliamentary Democracies* (2003) and *Cabinets and Coalition Bargaining* (2008), both coedited with Kaare Strøm and Wolfgang C. Müller.

NIKLAS BOLIN is a graduate student in political science at Umeå University, Sweden. His dissertation examines new political parties and the conditions under which they enter national parliaments. His most recent publication is "Towards a Two-Party System? The Swedish Parliamentary Election of September 2006" in *West European Politics* (2007), coauthored with Nicholas Aylott.

ERIK DAMGAARD is professor emeritus of political science at Aarhus University, Denmark. His professional interests include legislative studies, parliamentary government, coalition studies, and democratic theory. Over the past several decades he has published widely in both books and journals about Danish and Nordic parliaments. His most recent publications include articles in *Journal of Legislative Studies* with Henrik Jensen (in 2005 and 2006) and Flemming Juul Christiansen (2008).

INDRIDI H. INDRIDASON is assistant professor of political science at the University of California, Riverside. His current research is in the areas of comparative political institutions and applied game theory with a focus on electoral systems, electoral behavior, coalition formation, and cabinet management strategies. His recent work has been published in journals such as *Journal of Politics*, *British Journal of Political Science*, *Electoral Studies*, *Economics and Politics*, and *Journal of Peace Research*.

CYNTHIA KITE is assistant professor of political science at Umeå University. Her main interests are comparative politics and international relations. She has authored and coauthored book chapters and has published in the *European Journal of Political Research*.

SVANUR KRISTJÁNSSON is professor of political science at the University of Iceland, Reykjavik. He has mainly published on theories of democracy and the development of democracy in Iceland. His most recent research contribution in English is "Iceland: Searching for Democracy along Three Dimensions of Citizen Control" in *Scandinavian Political Studies* (2004).

HANNE MARTHE NARUD is professor of political science at the University of Oslo, Norway. Her academic work has been in the fields of elections, parties, coalition governance, and political representation. She has been a visiting scholar at the University of Leiden, the Netherlands; the University of California, San Diego; the University of Gothenburg, Sweden; the Netherlands Institute for Advanced Study (NIAS), Wassenaar; and the University of Auckland, New Zealand. She has been a member of the Executive Committee of the European Consortium of Political Research (2003–9) and is a fellow of the Norwegian Academy of Science and Letters (DNVA).

TAPIO RAUNIO is professor of political science at the University of Tampere. His research interests include the role of national legislatures and parties in European integration, the European Parliament, Europarties, and the Finnish political system. He has published articles in journals such as the *European Journal of Political Research*, *European Union Politics*, *Journal of Common Market Studies*, *Party Politics*, and *Scandinavian Political Studies*. He has also recently coedited, with John O'Brennan, the volume *National Parliaments within the Enlarged European Union: From "Victims" of Integration to Competitive Actors?* (2007).

KAARE STRØM is Distinguished University Professor of Political Science at the University of California, San Diego, and senior research fellow at the

Centre for the Study of Civil War, International Peace Research Institute in Oslo (PRIO), Norway. He has authored or edited a large number of scholarly articles and books on political parties, parliamentary democracy, and coalition bargaining, including most recently *Cabinets and Coalition Bargaining*, with Wolfgang C. Müller and Torbjörn Bergman (2008). Strøm is a fellow of the Norwegian Academy of Science and Letters (DNVA) and of the Royal Norwegian Society for Science and the Arts.

Name Index

Note: Page numbers in italic indicate tables.

Aardal, Bernt, *203*, 204, 205, 206, *207*, 208, 210, 233, 242, 244n5
Aghion, Phillipe, 9
Ahlbäck Öberg, Shirin, 262, 278
Aldrich, John A., 12
Algotsson, Karl-Göran, 280
Alivizatos, Nicos C., 101
Allen, Hillary, 339
Allern, Elin Haugsgjerd, 55, 209, 314, 318
Andenæs, Johs, 201
Andersen, Johannes, 73
Andersen, Jørgen Goul, *73*, 75, 79 (Togeby et al. 2003), 105, 309, 385
Andersson, Staffan, 278
Andeweg, Rudy, 15
Andrén, Nils, 260, 269, 271
Anton, Thomas J., 41
Arter, David, 35, 42, 56, 83, 113, 125, 141, 151n6, 163, 173, 302, 309, 351n2
Aslama, Minna, 147
Aten, Bettina, 52
Aula, Maria Kaisa, 121, 152n14
Aylott, Nicholas, 255, 258, 260, 267, 273, 314, 318, 339, 342, 350

Bäck, Hanna, 272, 273
Bäck, Henry, 277, 278
Bäck, Mats, 259, 261, 279
Back, Pär-Erik, 254, 259, 279
Bagehot, Walter, 11, *15*, 16, 361

Bailes, Alyson J. K., 348, 349
Bale, Tim, 313, 363
Berger, Suzanne, 26, 31n12
Berggrav, Dag, 227
Berglund, Frode, 208
Berglund, Sten, 254, 259, 279, 300, 316, 324n4
Bergman, Torbjörn, 3, 5, 6, 7, 9, 13, *13* (Strøm et al. 2003), 19, 20, 25, 26, 27, 30n4, 40, 50, 52, 59n4, 68, 90, 233, 251, 259, 262, 263, 267, 271, 276, 287n3, 287n4, 313, 350, 358, 363
Bergström, Jonas, 42, 279
Bernhard, William, 102
Biezen, Ingrid van, 18, 232
Bille, Lars, 71, 79, 322
Birgersson, Bengt Ove, 254, 260
Björklund, Tor, 212, 309
Björnberg, Arne, 244n11
Blom-Hansen, Jens, 42, 100
Blomgren, Magnus, 9 (Bergman et al. 2003), 20 (Bergman et al. 2003), 260
Blyth, Mark, 25
Board, Joseph B., 282
Bogdanor, Vernon, 40, 56
Bolin, Niklas, 255
Borg, Sami, 114, 115, *116*, 118, 145
Borre, Ole, *73*, 75
Börzel, Tanja A., 350
Bouckaert, Geert, 141

393

Name Index

Broch, Lars Oftedal, 236
Brunsson, Karin, 281
Bryce, James, 15, 16
Bull, Thomas, 277

Castles, Francis B., 302
Cheibub, Jose Antonio, 357
Christensen, Dag Arne, 238, 333
Christensen, Jens Peter, 102
Christensen, Jørgen Grønnegård, 99, 103
Christensen, Tom, 16, 234, 235, 245n15, 278
Christiansen, Flemming Juul, 98, 314, 363
Christiansen, Peter Munk, 55, 79 (Togeby et al. 2003), 100, 103, 105, 106, 385
Cox, Gary W., 11, 12, 19, 56

Daalder, Hans, 297
Dahl, Robert A., 5, 22
Dalton, Russell J., 3, 17, 18, 208, 304, 378
Damgaard, Erik, 3, 6, 26, 27, 28, 54, 59n4, 68, 71, 74, 78, 79, 80, 83, *84*, 85, *86*, *87*, 90, *95*, 96, 97, 98, 99, 100, 101, 102, 104, 105, 287n4, 299, 314, 332, 337, 352n5, 363
Dau, Mary, 331
Davidsson, Lars, 261
Demker, Marie, 311
Di Palma, Giuseppe, 374
Djerf-Pierre, Monika, 258 (Petersson et al. 2006), 284 (Petersson et al. 2005; Petersson et al. 2006)
Dumont, Patrick, 273
Duverger, Maurice, 56, 315

Eckstein, Harry, 42, 202
Egeberg, Morten, 234, 235 (Christensen et al. 2007)
Ehn, Peter, 277 (Wallin et al. 1999)
Einhorn, Eric S., 35
Elder, Neil, 42
Elgie, Robert, 16
Eliassen, Kjell A., 213, 340

Elklit, Jørgen, 71, 72, 78, 337, 338
Elvander, Nils, 318, 333
Engelstad, Fredrik, 237
Epstein, David, 9
Eriksen, Ole Søe, *219*
Ersson, Svante, 23
Esaiasson, Peter, 3, 79, 119, 261, 277
Esping-Andersen, Gøsta, 41, 302

Farrell, David, 17, 18
Feldt, Kjell-Olof, 279
Feltenius, David, 280
Fløistad, Brit, 238
Forestiere, Carolyn, 139
Forsten, Timo, 132

Gaddis, John Lewis, 351n1
Gallagher, Michael, 213
Gartzke, Erik, 192
Gidlund, Gullan, 255
Gilljam, Mikael, 343
Green-Pedersen, Christoffer, 43, 85, 368
Greve, Carsten, 103
Grímsson, Ólafur, 161, 352n6
Groennings, Sven, 205
Grönlund, Kimmo, 115, *116*
Gwartney, James, 192

Hadenius, Stig, 271, 283
Hagevi, Magnus, 262
Häggroth, Sören, 280
Hague, Rod, 72
Hakovirta, Harto, 335, 351n2
Halvarson, Arne, 282, 283
Hansen, Bernhard, 71, 79
Hansen, Guttorm, 201, 221, 223
Hansen, Martin E., 87
Harðarson, Ólafur Þ., 163, 164, *165*
Harrop, Martin, 72
Haskel, Barbara, 331
Hauksson, Jón G., 186
Hautamäki, Jaakko, 151n9
Hegeland, Hans, 280, 287n4
Heidar, Knut, 3, *39*, 205, 206, 242, 311, 318, 324n3, 324n5
Helander, Voitto, 118, 127

Herman, Valentine, 68
Hermansson, Jörgen, 262
Hernes, Gudmund, 258 (Petersson et al. 2000)
Heston, Alan, 53
Hirschman, Albert O., 22
Hix, Simon, 27
Hjarvard, Stig, 104
Holliday, Ian, 17, 18
Holmberg, Erik, 269, 271, 272, 282
Holmberg, Sören, 116, 257, 258, 258 (Petersson et al. 2000; Petersson et al. 2006), 261, 277, 284 (Petersson et al. 2006), 304
Hooghe, Liesbet, 26
Hunt, W. Ben, 74, 138, 204, 243n3, 244n4, 244n5, 252

Indridason, Indridi, H., 42, *162*, 172, *188*, 190, 314, 315, 323
Ingimundarson, Valur, 352n6
Inglehart, Ronald, 309
Isaksson, Guy-Erik, 127
Isberg, Magnus, 277 (Wallin et al. 1999), 281
Isotalus, Pekka, 145
Iversen, Torben, 42

Jääskinen, Niilo, 148
Jahn, Detlef, 341, 342
Jakulin, Aleks, 119
Jensen, Henrik, 71, 85, 88
Jensen, Jesper Bo, 102
Jensen, Katrine N., 104
Jensen, Torben K., 71, 79, 83, 119, 177
Jenssen, Anders Todal, 343
Jóhannesson, Guðni Th., 169, 196n3
Johansson, Karl Magnus, 350
Jørgensen, Torben Beck, 79 (Togeby et al. 2003), 105, 385
Jungar, Ann-Cathrine, 121, 311
Jyrkiäinen, Jryki, 147

Kaila, Heidi, 140
Karvonen, Lauri, 55, 118, 119, 126, 282 (Petersson et al. 1999)

Katz, Richard S., 24, 25, 30n9, 209, 317, 324n1, 359, 375
Katzenstein, Peter, 41, 42, 279
Kauppinen, Timo, 146
Kautto, Mikko, 43
Kenworthy, Lane, 41
Kestilä, Elina, 114
Key, V. O., 17, 18, 30n9, 57, 297
Kiewiet, D. Roderick, 9
King, Anthony, 17, 97, 298
Kinnunen, Jussi, 335
Kirchheimer, Otto, 317
Kite, Cynthia, 336, 339, 341, 346, 349
Kitschelt, Herbert, 309
Kjær, Ulrik, 79, 80
Klemmensen, Robert, 87
Knutsen, Oddbjørn, 57, 58, 207, 314
Kolam, Kerstin, 280
Korpi, Walter, 41
Krehbiel, Keith, 30
Kristinsson, Gunnar Helgi, 161, 176, 189
Kristjánsson, Svanur, 161, 164, 166, 189, 191, 192, 313, 315, 320–21, 321, 323
Krogh, Torben, 104
Kuhnle, Stein, 222
Kuitunen, Soile, 118
Kurrild-Klitgaard, Peter, 87
Kuusela, Kimmo, 117

Lægreid, Per, 16, 235, 235 (Christensen et al. 2007), 245n15, 278 (Christensen et al. 2005)
Lane, Jan-Erik, 23
Lantto, Johan, 255
Larsen, Helge O., 235 (Christensen et al. 2007)
Larsson, Sven-Erik, 272
Larsson, Torbjörn, 271, 272, 277, 278, 287
Laver, Michael, 68, 74, 138, 204, 205, 243n3, 244n4, 244n5, 252, 253, 366
Lawson, Robert, 192
Leipart, Jørn, 243n3
Lewin, Leif, 40, 42, 279
Lidström, Anders, 280

Lijphart, Arend, 3, 10, 28, 30n5, 30n6, 30n7, 42, 52, 53, 102, 211, 239, 356
Lindbeck, Assar, 44
Linde, Claes, 277 (Wallin et al. 1999)
Lindström, Ulf, 41, 300, 316, 324n4
Linz, Juan J., 3, 356
Lipset, Seymour Martin, 299, 300, 303
Listhaug, Ola, 233, 242
Logue, John, 35
Lund, Anker Brink, 104
Lundestad, Geir, 331
Lundmark, Kjell, 282, 283
Lupia, Arthur, 8, 9

Madison, James, 14
Magnússon, Þorsteinn, 173, 176, 177, 178, 192
Mair, Peter, 14, 18, 24, 25, 30n9, 209, 317, 324n1, 359, 375, 378
Manin, Bernard, 7, 9
Marcussen, Martin, 102
Marino, Marit Sjøvaag, 213
Marks, Gary, 26
Marosi, Kalle, 104
Marsh, Michael, 213
Martin, Lanny W., 169
Másson, Arnar Þór, 190
Matthews, Donald, 213, 214
Mattila, Mikko, 113, 116, *116*, 121, 126, 139
Mattson, Ingvar, 219, 251, 266, 267, 272, 280, 287n4
McCubbins, Mathew D., 9, 12
Meier, Henk Erik, 273
Metcalf, Michael, 40
Miles, Lee, 35
Miljan, Toivo, 335, 337
Miller, Arthur H., 242
Milner, Henry, 54, 283
Mitchell, Paul, 68, 169
Mo, Erik, 201, 221, 223
Molander, Per, 44
Molin, Björn, 257, 271
Møller, Birgit, 72 (Elklit et al. 2005), 79
Möller, Tommy, 259, 261, 279
Moody, Jonas, 329
Müller, Wolfgang C., 3, 5, 6, 7, 9

(Bergman et al. 2003), 12, 13, 13
(Strøm et al. 2003), 19, 20 (Bergman et al. 2003), 23, 25, 30n4, 50, 52, 59n5, *233*, 298, 299, 314, 315, 324n2, 358
Myhre-Jensen, Kjell, 238

Narud, Hanne Marthe, 23, 79, 204, 205, 212, 213, 220, 226, 233, 243n3, 244n5, 244n10, 311, 322, 362
Nedelmann, Birgitta, 282 (Petersson et al. 1999)
Nielsen, Hans Jørgen, 73
Nieminen, Hannu, 147
Nijzink, Lia, 15
Nordby, Trond, 201, 223, 240
Nørgaard, Asbjørn Sonne, 78, 100, 101, 337
Norris, Pippa, 3, 22, 317
Nousiainen, Jaakko, 115, 121, 127, 131, 137, 138, 139, *139*, 141
Nyblade, Benjamin, 13 (Strøm et al. 2003), 169

Öberg, PerOla, 279
O'Halloran, Sharyn, 9
Olsen, Lennart, 267
Ormond, Derry, 141
Oscarsson, Henrik, 257
Østerud, Øyvind, 201, 237

Pade, Anne Birte, 78
Pajala, Antti, 119, 126, *129*
Pallesen, Thomas, 103
Palmer, Matthew, 11
Paloheimo, Heikki, 113, 115, 115 (Grönlund et al. 2005), *116*, *116* (Grönlund et al. 2005), 118, 121, 126, 136, 137, 138, 141, *143*, 150n3, 151n10, 152n14
Paltiel, Khayyam Z., 25
Panebianco, Angelo, 317
Pantti, Mervi, 147
Pedersen, Karina, 55, 71, 79, 318
Pedersen, Klaus Carsten, 349
Pedersen, Mogens N., 69, 79, 80, 212, 213, 322

Persson, Thomas, 271, 272 (Bäck et al. 2007), 273 (Bäck et al. 2007)
Persson, Torsten, 44
Pesonen, Pertti, 115, *116*, 118, 343
Peters, B. Guy, 141, 350
Petersen, Nikolaj, 337, 338
Peterson, Carl-Gunnar, 280
Petersson, Olof, 44, 251, 258, 277, 278, 279, 280, 282, 284
Pétursson, Sigtryggur, 166, 196n1
Pierre, Jon, 29n3, 255, 259, 277
Poguntke, Thomas, 25, 27, 350, 369
Pontusson, Jonas, 41
Pope, John, 68
Powell, G. Bingham, Jr., 233
Premfors, Rune, 276, 277
Przeworski, Adam, 7, 9

Quille, Gerrard, 348
Qvortrup, Mads H., 338

Raaum, Nina C., 213
Ranney, Austin, 12, 213
Ranta, Timo, 140
Rasch, Bjørn Erik, 204, 205, 221, 222, 227
Raunio, Tapio, 27, 113, 116, 117, 121, 126, 127, 139, *139*, 140, 141, 143, 147, 148, 150n2, 150n5, 322, 324n6, 342, 343, 349
Ray, Leonard, 243n3
Rehn, Olli, 335, 351n2
Reunanen, Esa, 115
Rhodes, R. W., 350
Riddell, Peter, 31n13
Risse, Thomas, 350
Rokkan, Stein, 202, 299, 300, 303
Rommetvedt, Hilmar, 54, 205, 214, 215, 220, 243n3
Roness, Paul G., 16, 235 (Christensen et al. 2007), 278 (Christensen et al. 2005)
Rothstein, Bo, 21, 42, 279
Røvik, Kjell Arne, 278 (Christensen et al. 2005)
Ruin, Olof, 41, 255, 287n1
Ruostetsaari, Ilkka, 119, 140

Saglie, Jo, 205, 206, 212, 242
Sandmo, Agnar, 44
Sänkiaho, Risto, 115, 115 (Grönlund et al. 2005), *116*, *116* (Grönlund et al. 2005), 118
Sannerstedt, Anders, 41, 258
Sartori, Giovanni, 20, 300
Savisaari, Eero, 147
Scarrow, Susan, 18
Schlesinger, Joseph A., 12
Schmitt, Hermann, 304
Schofield, Norman, 68, 205, 253
Schumpeter, Joseph A., 8
Sejersted, Fredrik, 221, 222, 223, 238
Selle, Per, 201, 237
Shaffer, William R., 243n3
Shefter, Martin, 21, 172
Shepsle, Kenneth A., 366
Sitter, Nick, 340
Siune, Karen, 73
Sjöblom, Gunnar, 56
Sjölin, Mats, 41, 54, 258
Skare, Audun, 213, 244n10
Skjæveland, Asbjørn, 75, 91
Skjeie, Helge, 213
Smith, Eivind, 227, 236, 237, 245n16, 282 (Petersson et al. 1999)
Söderlind, Donald, 277, 278, 282
Sonneby, Claes, 281
Sørensen, Max, 67
Sørensen, Mette H., 102
Sørensen, Rune J., 235
Staberg, Ulf, 282, 283
Stapleton, John, 16
Stavang, Per, 223
Stephens, John D., 41
Sterzel, Fredrik, 269
Stevenson, Randolph T., 169
Stjernquist, Nils, 55, 59n1, 269, 271, 272, 280, 282
Stokes, Susan, 7, 9
Storsved, Ann-Sofie, 341, 342
Strandberg, Urban, 55
Strøm, Kaare, 3, 5, 6, 7, 9 (Bergman et al. 2003), 13, 19, 20 (Bergman et al. 2003), 23, 25, 30n4, 50, 52, 59, 68, 138, 187, 205, 215, 219, 226, 227,

Strøm, Kaare (*continued*)
 233, 242, 243n3, 311, 314, 315, 324,
 324n2, 358, 362
Strömbäck, Jesper, 258 (Petersson et
 al. 2006), 284 (Petersson et al. 2005;
 Petersson et al. 2006)
Stubager, Rune, 75
Stubb, Alexander, 140
Styrkársdóttir, Auður, 166
Suhonen, Pertti, 115
Summers, Robert, 52
Sundberg, Jan, 113, 114, 115
 (Grönlund et al. 2005), *116*, *116*
 (Grönlund et al. 2005), 117, 119,
 150n2, 150n3, 314, *318*, 319
Sundström, Göran, 276, 277
Svardal, G., 234
Svåsand, Lars, 205, 222, 227, 242, 309,
 311
Svensson, Palle, 71, 72 (Elklit et al.
 2005), 96, 332, 352n5
Svensson, Torsten, 279
Swedenborg, Birgitta, 44
Swindle, Stephen M., 50

Tallberg, Jonas, 350
Tammes, Rolf, 331
Tarschys, Daniel, 278
Taylor, Michael, 68
Temmes, Markku, 141
Teorell, Jan, 279
Thomas, Alastair H., 42
Thomsen, Søren Risbjerg, 73
Thorhallsson, Baldur, 343, 344, 352n12
Thygesen, Niels, 44
Tiihonen, Seppo, 141
Tiili, Minna, 137, 141, 151n8
Tiilkainen, Teija, 147, 342, 343
Tirole, Jean, 9
Togeby, Lise, 55, 72 (Elklit et al. 2005),
 79, 105, 106, 258 (Petersson et al.
 2000), 385
Tonsgaard, Ole, 73

Valen, Henry, 23, 79, 202, 204, 205,
 207, 208, 212, 213, 214, 220, 233,
 242, 243n3, 244n5, 244n10, 322,
 362
Vallgårda, Signild, 79, 105 (Togeby et
 al. 2003), 385
van Biezen, Ingrid, 18, 323
Vedung, Evert, 254
Vernby, Kåre, 272 (Bäck et al. 2007),
 273 (Bäck et al. 2007)
Vignisson, Hjalti Thor, 344, 352n12
von Beyme, Klaus, 282 (Petersson et al.
 1999)
von Sydow, Björn, 41

Wallin, Gunnar, 277
Wängnerud, Lena, 79, 258 (Petersson
 et al. 2000), 262
Wass, Hanna, 115 (Grönlund et al.
 2005), *116* (Grönlund et al. 2005)
Wattenberg, Martin P., 17, 18, 208,
 378
Webb, Paul D., 17, 18, 25, 27, 350,
 369
Weibull, Lennart, 258 (Petersson et al.
 2006), 283, 284 (Petersson et al.
 2005; Petersson et al. 2006)
Weldon, Steven A., 17
Westerståhl, Jörgen, 254, 260
Westin, Lina, 272 (Bäck et al. 2007),
 273 (Bäck et al. 2007)
Wheare, K. C., 15
Whitten, Guy D., 233
Wiberg, Matti, 115, *116*, 117, 119,
 127, 137, 139, 141, 147, 151n11,
 152n14, 367
Widfeldt, Anders, 255, 258, 259
Wieslander, Hans, 271
Wittenmark, Lars, 281
Wockelberg, Helena, 277
Wright, Vincent, 350

Þórleifsson, Eiríkur, 173, 196n4

Subject Index

Note: Page numbers in italic indicate tables or figures.

abortion policy, 214
absolutism, 36; in Denmark, 67
accountability, administrative: in Iceland, 190; in Norway, 234–36; in Sweden, 278
accountability, cabinet, 30n4, 30n10, 187, 363, 365, 366, 367, 381; in Denmark, 67, 80, 366; in Finland, 112, 132, 126, 142; in Iceland, 177, 179, 187, 196
accountability, electoral, 298, 365; in Finland, 149; in Iceland, 160
accountability, member of parliament (MP): in Denmark, 79; in Norway, 210; in Sweden, 260, 261
accountability, ministerial, 58, 367; in Denmark, 86, 88, 97–98, 99, 103; in Finland, 127, 148; in Iceland, 159, 160, 177–78, 187; in Norway, 201, 223; in Sweden, 269, 278, 280
accountability, political, 7–10, 298, 314–15, 357, 382, 385 (*see also* chain of delegation and accountability); in Denmark, 105; in Iceland, 159, 191, 192, 196; impact of European integration on, 27, 333, 341, 350; mechanisms of, 8–9, 359, 374 (*see also* contract design; control instruments; screening; selection); in Norway, 201, 202; in Sweden, 261, 286; under the Westminster model, 10–11, 13, 56, 382

activity, legislative. *See* activity, parliamentary
activity, parliamentary, 15, 16, 58, 366–69. *See also* cabinet bills; interpellations; parliamentary oversight; parliamentary questions; private members' bills
administration, public, 6, 9, 21, *44*; in Denmark, 98–99, 100; in Finland, 140–41, 145; in Iceland, 160, 189, 193, 196; in Norway, 222, 234–35, 237–38, 239; in Sweden, 277–78, 279, 281–82, 286. *See also* agencies, executive; civil servants; civil service
Administrative Procedures Act of 1967 (Norway), 235
Afghanistan, 352n4
Africa, 37, 356
"Age of Liberty," 40
agencies, executive: in the chain of delegation, 6, 12; in Denmark, 98; in Finland, 140–41; in Iceland, 159, 180–81, 189–90; in Norway, 220, 222, 223, 234–36, 239, 241; in Sweden, 277–78. *See also* administration, public; civil servants; civil service
agency loss, 8–9, 14, 51, 149, 317
agency problems, 8–10, 23–25, 27, 359. *See also* agency loss; moral hazard; selection, adverse
agenda-setting power, 298; in Denmark, 88, 90, 104; in Finland, 137;

399

agenda-setting power (*continued*) in Norway, 200, 208, 227, 237, 239; in Sweden, 267, 272
agrarian movement, in Finland, 42
agrarian party, 300, 314, 324n3, 336; in Denmark, 385; in Finland, 310; in Sweden, 254
Agrarian Union (Finland), *114*. See also Center Party (Finland)
agricultural interests: in Denmark, 42, 336; in Finland, 146, 342; in Iceland, 343, 344, 352n12; in Norway, 339; in Sweden, 341
agriculture policy, *48*, 59n4, 100; in Denmark, 100; in Norway, 340; in Sweden, 277, 281
Åland Islands, *114*, 117
Alford index, 57–58, 72, 73, *116*, 207, 257, *257*, 307–8, *308*
Alliance (Sweden), 255, 258, 279, 313
alliances, electoral, 313, 346; in Finland, 113, 117, 126, 150n3; in Iceland, 167; in Norway, 211, 214, 313; in Sweden, *253*, 255
alternative majority, 304, 311, 314; in Denmark, 86, *86*, *87*, 96, 332, 337, 352n5; in Finland, 125. See also opposition, political
Althingi (Iceland). See parliament
amendment, constitutional: in Denmark, 78, 80, 103; in Finland, 120, *129*, 133, 142, 144, 149, 150n1, 151n13; in Iceland, 195; in Norway, 209–10, 227, 241, 244n8
amendment, legislative: in Denmark, 85, 88; in Iceland, 173, 175, 176; in Sweden, *269*
"Americanization," 258
appointment powers, 319, 359; in Denmark, 98, 99, 102, 106; in Finland, 136, 140, 142, *143*, 145, 149; in Iceland, 172, 180–81, 189–90, 194; in Norway, 234, 237, 239; in Sweden, 271, 277
Ásgrímsson, Halldór, 169, 181–82, 194
association of local governments (Denmark), 100

Audit Office (Sweden), 278
audit reform, in Sweden, 286
Auditor General's Office (Norway), 222
auditors, independent, 382
audits: in Denmark, 97, 99; in Iceland, 176–77; in Norway, 221, 222, 242; in Sweden, 278, 286
Australia, 209
Austria, 42, *44*, *46*, *47*, *48*, *52*, *53*, 357
autonomy, local, 53, 55; in Norway, 201; in Sweden, 280
autonomy, national political, 333, 336, 351; in Finland, 346, 347; in Iceland, 40; impact of European integration on, 27, 347, 348; in Sweden, 341

bank, central, 26, 28, 360, 382; in Denmark (*Nationalbanken*), 68, 102, 104, 106; in Iceland, 159, 180–81, 194; in Norway (Bank of Norway), 241, 243; in Sweden (*Riksbank*), 252, 282, 286
banking system, in Iceland, 159, 195, 196n9, 329
Belarus, 356
Belgium, 17, *44*, *46*, *47*, *48*, *52*, 357, 360
Berge, Abraham, 227
bicameralism: in Sweden, 253; quasi-, 361
Bildt cabinet, 263, 276
Björnsson, Sveinn, 161, 172–73
bloc politics, 20, 30n10, 299, 303–4, 313–14, 322–23, 324n5, 384; in Denmark, 73, 87, 310; in Finland, *116*, 121, 311, 313; in Iceland, *165*, 166, 196n2, 313; in Norway, 204, 205, 207, 338, 340; in Sweden, 252, 254, 255, 257, *257*, 258, 263, 267, 284, 311
boards, executive, 42, 43; in Denmark, 103; in Iceland, 159, 180, 189, 190; in Norway, 239, 279, 282
Bondevik I cabinet, 214
Borten cabinet, 208, 239
Bratteli, Trygve, 229
Britain, 10, 11, 19, 54, 209, 329, 332,

Subject Index • 401

334, 335, 344, 351n3, 352n8, 352n11, 384. *See also* United Kingdom (UK)
Brundtland cabinets, 226, 228
Brussels, 140, 148. *See also* European Union (EU)
budget process, 15, 58, 314, 363; in Denmark, 87–88, 96, 105; in Finland, 125, 126–27, *128*, *129*, 132, 151n11; in Iceland, 176, 190, 196n6; in Norway, 215, *219*, 219–20, 226, *231*, 237, 238; in Sweden, 251, 266–67, *268*, 272, 277, 278, 284–85
Bureau of Statistics (Iceland), 177, 181
bureaucracy. *See* administration, public; agencies, executive; civil servants; civil service
business, 41, 54, 75, 91, 195, 254, 279, 300, 341, 342. *See also* capital; industry

cabinet, caretaker, in Finland, 120, 121
cabinet, definition of new, 59n5
cabinet, nonpartisan: in Finland, 362; in Iceland, 172–73, 181, 196n3
cabinet, nonsocialist, 43; in Denmark, 71; in Norway, 208, 214, 215, 219, 226, 232, 233, 239, 244n12, 338, 340; in Sweden, 266, 271, 273, 277, 335
cabinet accountability. *See* accountability, cabinet
cabinet bills, 367; in Denmark, 81, 82, *82*, 83, *84*, 85, 86, *86*, 87, 88, 332; in Finland, 127, *128*–29, 144, 151n12; in Iceland, 173, *174*–75, 175–76, 180; in Norway, *218*–*19*, 226; in Sweden, 266, *268*–*69*, 269, 277, 280, 284. *See also* budget process; private members' bills
cabinet duration, 81, 105, 136, 183, 364–66
cabinet electoral performance, 23, 362, 363, 365–66, *366*; in Denmark, 94–95, *95*, 384; in Finland, 138, *139*, 151n10, 385; in Iceland, 187–88, *188*; in Norway, 205, 232–33, *233*; in Sweden, 255, 276, 276

cabinet formation, 50–51, 58, 322, 350, 351, 361–63; in Denmark, 67, 68, 69, 80–81, 105, 322, 352n5; in Finland, 112, 117, 119–26, 142, 149, 150, 151n9, 331, 332, 350; in Iceland, 168–72, 180–81, 186, 187, 193, 196n3, 310; in Norway, 204, 205, 214, 244n11; in Sweden, 40, 253, 254, 262–66, 287n1
cabinet governance: in Denmark, 90–91, 94; in Finland, 133, 136–38, 139–40; in Iceland, 180–82, 186–88; in Norway, 227–28; in Sweden, 271–72, 273, 276, 287n3
cabinet ministers. *See* ministers, cabinet
cabinet program, 25; in Finland, 119–20, 137–38, 141, 149, 151n8, 151n9; in Iceland, 179–80; in Norway, 243n3; in Sweden, 255, 268
cabinet proposals. *See* cabinet bills
cabinet recruitment, 369–74, 375, 376–77, 384; in Denmark, 94; in Iceland, 183; in Norway, 229, 232; in Sweden, 271, 273
cabinet stability, 51, 58, 299, 351, 362, *364*, 364–65, 366–67, 374, 382; in Denmark, 68, 81, 106, 363, 384; in Finland, 121, 125, 385; in Iceland, 169, 186; in Sweden, 285. *See also* cabinet duration
cabinet termination, 58; in Denmark, 94; in Finland, 138; in Iceland, 193; in Norway, 204
Canada, 37, 209
candidate selection. *See* selection, candidate
candidates, nonpartisan, 19, 314, 322
capital, 41, 42, 279, 300, 345
cartel-party thesis, 25, 317, 319, 322, 359, 374, 375, 379–80, 385
Center Democrats (Denmark), 69, 70, 70, 74, 75, 81, 84, 310, 313
Center Party (Finland), 113, *114*, 120, 121, 125, 126, *139*, 150n2, 151n10, 303, 310, 342, 343

402 ♦ Subject Index

Center Party (Norway), 202, *203*, 204, 205, 206, 214, 215, 232, 244n5, 244n13, 313, 339, 340, 345
Center Party (Sweden), 252, *253*, 254, 256, 262, 263, 267, 273, 284, 311, 334, 335, 341, 342
center-periphery cleavage. *See* cleavage structure
Central Organization of Finnish Trade Unions (SAK), 146
Central Union of Agricultural Producers and Forest Owners (MTK), 146
chain of delegation and accountability: constraints on, 14, 25, 36, 51, 360, 365; definition of, 6, 7, 8, 56; in Denmark, 68–69, 71, 78, 91, 94, 100, 104, 105, 106, 384; in Finland, 113, 117, 141, 149, 350; in Iceland, 158–59, 166, 177, 187, 192, 194, 196; impacts of European integration on, 330, 333, 334, 350, 351; in Norway, 201, 209, 210, 235, 236, 238, 239, 341; role of parties in, 18, 297, 385; strength of, 351, 365; in Sweden, 252, 259, 277, 278, 279, 280, 282, 283, 284–86
chain of governance. *See* chain of delegation and accountability
chancellor of justice (Finland), 146–47
Christian Democratic Party (Finland), *114*, 125, 150n3
Christian Democratic Party (Sweden), 252, *253*, 263, 311
Christian People's Party (Denmark), 69, 70, *70*, 74, 81, 84, *84*, 310, 313
Christian People's Party (Norway), 202, *203*, 204, 205, 208, 214, 215, 220, 232–33, 244n5, 244n6, 244n13, 302, 310, 339–40, 352n9
citizen participation, 5, 45, 72, 318, 377; in Norway, 212, 240, 242; in Sweden, 258, 283
Citizen's Party (Iceland), *162*, 163, 196n2
civil rights, in Sweden, 281
civil servants, 5, 6, 15, 27, 56, 58, 59n6, 385; in Denmark, 90, 98–99, 100,
106; in Finland, 120, 137, 140–41, *143*, 146, 148, 149; in Iceland, 188–90; in Norway, 234–35; in Sweden, 277–78, 287n3. *See also* administration, public; agencies, executive; civil service
civil service, 12, 297; Danish model, 189, 234; in Iceland, 172, 189–90, 194, 196; in Norway, 210, 234, 242; Swedish model, 234. *See also* administration, public; agencies, executive; civil servants
Civil Service Act (Iceland), 189
civil society, 24, 26, 53, 317, 323, 352n12, 359, 384
civil war, in Finland, 40, 42, 300
class conflict. *See* class struggle
class dealignment, 113, 208, 310, 317, 359, 378. *See also* class voting
class struggle, 41–42, 208, 300
class voting, 57–58, 300, 307–8, 314, 378; in Denmark, 72, 73, 105; in Finland, 113, *116*; in Iceland, *165*, 166; in Norway, *207*; in Sweden, 257–58, *257*. *See also* Alford index; class dealignment
cleavage structure, 57, 299–300, 303, 307, 309, 314, 331, 334, 343, 368, 381; in Denmark, 74–75, 81, 91, 336, 338, 384–85; in Finland, 112, 113, 115–16, 150; in Iceland, 162–63, 167, 173, 333, 338; in Norway, 202, 203–4, 233, 244n4, 244n5, 244n6, 333, 336, 339–40; in Sweden, 252, 254–55, 263, 332, 341. *See also* party system, dimensionality
clientelism, 21, 42; in Iceland, 161, 172, 186, 189, 193, 194, 196, 197n14; in Norway, 209, 243. *See also* patronage; spoils
coalition: ad hoc legislative, 30, 51, 215, 266; agreements, 25, 91, 138, 180, 267, 313; bourgeois, 125, 205, 219, 244n12; cross-bloc, 121, 267, 313; discipline, 90, 91, 180, 227–28; ideologically connected, 81, 172, 324n7; majority (*see* majority

cabinet); nonsocialist, 214, 215, 233, 239, 244, 271, 277, 340; oversized, 121, 125, 139; pre-electoral (*see* alliances, electoral); rainbow, 120, 121, 311; red-green, 214, 235, 244n5
Coast Party (Norway), *203*, 243n1
"cod wars," 351n3
Cold War, 29, 112, 140, 142, 162, 332, 334, 341, 345, 346, 347, 348, 351n1, 360
collusion, 243, 317
commissions, 41, 42; in Denmark, 97, 99, 100; in Iceland, 159, 191; in Norway, 222, 339; in Sweden, 279, 286
Committee on Foreign and Constitutional Affairs (Norway), 346
committees, cabinet: in Denmark, 98, 99; in Finland, 137, 141, 143; in Iceland, 180, 181, 189, 194; in Norway, 239–40. *See also* commissions; committees, consultative
committees, consultative, 43; in Denmark, 99, 100–101; in Finland, 141; in Iceland, 189; in Norway, 239–40. *See also* commissions; committees, cabinet
committees, parliamentary, 27, 350, 351; in Denmark, 82, 88, *89*, 96–97, 105, 287n4, 346; in Finland, 126, 132, 138, 144, 148, 151n11, 151n13; in Iceland, 175–77, 181, 193, 196n4, 196n8; in Norway, 215, 219, 220–21, 222, 238, 242, 245n14, 346; specialization, 82, 88, 148, 175, 177; in Sweden, 280, 285, 287n4
Common Course Party (Denmark), 69, 70
Communist Party (Denmark), 69, *70*, 74, 302
Communist Party (Finland), *114*, 302, 309, 311, 312
Communist Party (Iceland), 162. *See also* People's Alliance (Iceland); Socialist Party (Iceland)
Communist Party (Norway), 203, *203*, 244n4, 302. *See also* Socialist Left Party (Norway)
Communist Party (Sweden), 252, 302. *See also* Left Party (Sweden)
companies, state. *See* corporations, public; enterprises, state-run
Confederation of Unions for Academic Professionals in Finland (AKAVA), 146
Congress. *See* United States (U.S.), Congress
consensual politics, 28, 30n6, 30n7, 36, 41–42, 59; in Denmark, 90; in Finland, 139–40; in Iceland, 58, 177; in Sweden, 59n1, 255, 271–72, 287n1
Conservative Party (Denmark), 69, *70*, *70*, 71, 74, 75, 81, 83, 84, *84*, 85, 86, 86, 87, *87*, 88, 91, 102, 310, 313, 336, 338
Conservative Party (Finland), 151n10
Conservative Party (Iceland), 161, 302. *See also* Independence Party (Iceland)
Conservative Party (Norway), 200, 202, *203*, 204, 205, 206, 208, 214, 220, 232, 233, 240, 241, 244n12, 338, 340
Conservative Party (Sweden), 252, *253*, 253–54, 255, 256, 263, 276, 334, 335, 341
constitution: of 1809 (Sweden), 251, 272; of 1814 (Norway), *39*, 40, 200, 226, 236, 241, 244n8; of 1849 (Denmark), 67, 158; of 1944 (Iceland), *39*, 158, 161; of 1919 (Finland), 119, 142; of 1953 (Denmark), *39*, 40, 67, 78, 80, 101, 337, 346; of 1975 (Sweden) (*see* instrument of government (Sweden)); of 2000 (Finland), *39*, 112, 113, 120, 132, 133, 136, 139, 143, 144–45, 148, 150n1, 151n7, 151n13
constitution, working, 56, 59n6, 251, 281
constitutional crisis: in Iceland, 191; in Norway, 200

404 • Subject Index

Constitutional Law Committee (Finland), 132
constraints, types of, 25–26, 31n11, 54
Continuation War of 1941–44 (Finland), 331
contract design, 9, 235
contract parliamentarism, in Sweden, 266, 267, 285
Control Committee (Norway), 221, 222
control instruments, 10, 11, 12, 13, 24, 27, 365, 382; in Denmark, 96–97, 99, 101; in Finland, 127, 132–33, 149; in Iceland, 183, 190; in Norway, 202, 221–22, 223, 234–35, 242. *See also* accountability, political, mechanisms of
corporations, public: in Denmark, 103; in Finland, 140; in Norway, 235. *See also* enterprises, state-run
corporatism, 26, 36, 42–43, 382; in Denmark, 100; in Finland, 112, 145–46, 149; in Iceland, 191–92; in Norway, 239–40; in Sweden, 278–80
corruption, 20, 52, 54, 197n14, 243, 278
Council of the European Union, 101, 280, 350
Court, Supreme: in Denmark, 102; in Iceland, 192, 194; in Norway, 226, 227, 236–37
Court Administration (Denmark), 102
Court of Impeachment (Norway), 210, 226–27
courts, 26, 28, 59, 67, 68, 360, 382; in Denmark, 101–2, 104, 106; in Finland, 146; in Iceland, 192, 194, 195; in Norway, 210, 226–27, 234, 236–37, 238; in Sweden, 252, 281–82, 286
Council of Ministers. *See* Council of the European Union
Council of State, 59n5; in Finland, 119, 127, 129, *130*, *131*, 140, 148; in Norway, 214, 227. *See also* cabinet
"crisis-of-party" thesis. *See* party decline, thesis of

culture, political, 41, 59; in Finland, 140–41, 149; in Sweden, 41
culture, popular, 358
Czechoslovakia, 351n1

Danish People's Party (Denmark), 70, 71, 75, 84, 85, 313, 338
Danish Power and Democracy Project, 55, 79, 385
de Gaulle, Charles, 344
declaration of independence (Finland), 39, *39*, 113, 117
declaration of independence (Iceland), 39, 40, 161, 302
defense policy. *See* security policy
deferment rule, in Finland, 138–39, 149
delegation: definition of, 4–7, 7; in Westminster model, 11–12. *See also* chain of delegation and accountability
Delors, Jacques, 344
democracy, definitions of, 4–6
deparliamentarization: in Denmark, 105; in Iceland, 158, 166, 173, 179–80, 186; in Sweden, 271; thesis of, 14–17. *See also* parliamentary decline
devolution of power, regional, 360
direct democracy, 5, 51, 334, 336, 346, 382; in Denmark, 67, 336, 346, 349; in Norway, 201, 209, 241, 243, 336, 346; in Sweden, 282, 286. *See also* referendums
dismissal power, 5, 31n10, 50; in Denmark, 67, 96; in Finland, 136, 140, 151n7, 151n10; in Iceland, 161, 234; in Norway, 200–201; in Sweden, 271
dissolution power, 50; in Denmark, 96; in Finland, 133, 136, 142, *143*, 144, 149; in Iceland, 172, 180; in Norway, 210, 242, 362; in Sweden, 40, 362

earthquake election of 1973 (Denmark), 82, 306, 310, 311, 377, 378, 381
economic crisis, 3, 41, 43, 55, 323; in

Denmark, 75, 102; in Finland, 146; in Iceland, 159–60, 313, 323, 329, 343; in Sweden, 297, 311. *See also* economic performance

economic performance, 3–4, *38*, 43–45, *44*, 322; in Denmark, 68; in Iceland, 165, 186, 195, 332; in Norway, 233, 234; in Sweden, 334–35. *See also* economic crisis

economic policy, 23, 26, 42, 323, 333–34; in Denmark, 102, 103, 104, 336, 352n5; in Finland, 146, 335, 341, 342–43; in Iceland, 163, 167, 192, 343, 344; in Norway, 240, 244n5, 341, 342; in Sweden, 254, 267, 285, 334, 341

education: levels of attainment by politicians, 94, 213, 229, 272, 370, 371, 372; policy, 22, 112, 146, 201, 340; political consequences of, 18, 22, 358

Eduskunta (Finland). *See* parliament

efficacy, voter, 22

electoral acts of 1969 and 1975 (Finland), 118

electoral campaigns, 8, 13, 315, 321, 346, 368; in Denmark, 337, 338; in Finland, 114–15, 118–19, 125, 126, 342–43; in Iceland, 344; in Norway, 204, 210–11, 339, 340; in Sweden, 254, 255, 258, 259, 287n1

electoral institutions, 20, 56, 298; apparentement, *211*; candidate-based (*see* electoral institutions, preference vote); closed-list system (*see* electoral institutions, party lists); d'Hondt method, 117; direct election for president in Finland, 112, 145, 149; district magnitude, 117, 167–68, 211, 244n9; electoral college, 145; majoritarian, 10, 56, 177; malapportionment, 166, 168, 211; method of largest remainders, 117; open-list system (*see* electoral institutions, party lists; electoral institutions, preference vote); party lists, 78, 105, 117–18, 151n4, 168, 195, 211, 212–13, 244n10, 259–61, 321, 322, 325n8; personal vote (*see* electoral institutions, preference vote); preference vote, 72, 78–79, 105, 117–19, 168, 189, 195, 212, 258, 260–61, 284, 321; preferential vote (*see* electoral institutions, preference vote); primary, 164, 168, 177, 183, 189, 192–93, 212, 259, 321–22, 325n11; proportional representation (PR), 56, 72, 78, 79, 117, 145, 167–68, 195, 201, 211, 212, 357; reform, 118, 167, 168, 195, 211, 261, 284; Sainte-Laguë system, 211; supplementary seats, 167, 211; two-tier system, 167; vote threshold, 72, 167, 252, 284

electoral volatility, 18, 23, 57, 304, 306–7, *307*, 308, 309, 314, 323, 358, 362, 369, 377–78, 381; in Denmark, 72–74, *73*, 377–78, 384; in Finland, 113–14, 115, *116*; in Iceland, *165*, 166, 196n2; in Norway, *207*, 208, 213–14, 378; in Sweden, *257*, 258

enterprises, state-run, 359; in Denmark, 68, 103, 104, 106; in Iceland, 180; in Norway, 235. *See also* corporations, public

Erlander, Tage, 262, 287n3

Erlander cabinets, 276

Euratom, 333

Eurobarometer, 342

Europe, 18, 21, 22, 26, 36, 43, 45, 51, 54, 142, 200, 237, 243, 286, 300, 317, 323, 333, 343, 344, 346, 350, 351n1, 352n4, 352n5, 356, 360, 385; Northern, 4, 36, 356; Southern, 54; Western, 13, 36, 37, 43, *44*, 45, *46*, 47, 48, *48*, 51–52, *52*, 202, 208, 211, 214, 228, 243, 315, 317, 323, 324, 333, 356, 368, 375, 379, 380. *See also* European Union (EU)

European Affairs Committee (Sweden), 280

European Central Bank, 360

European Coal and Steel Community (ECSC), 333

European Community (EC), 333–34, 352n8; and Denmark, 101, 103, 336–37; and Finland, 335–36, 345; and Iceland, 344; and Norway, 203, 204, 245n12, 309, 310, 338–39, 340, 345; and Sweden, 334–35, 345. *See also* European Union (EU)

European Consultative Organ (Norway), 238

European Convention on Human Rights, 102, 146, 237, 282

European Council, 90, 147, 348, 350

European Council of Ministers. *See* Council of the European Union

European Court of Justice (ECJ), 146, 281, 282, 360, 382

European Defense Agency, 348

European Defense Community, 333

European Economic and Monetary Union (EMU), 53, 102, 146, 283, 286, 337, 338, 342, 343, 347, 349. *See also* Eurozone

European Economic Area (EEA), 27, 49, 59n4, 192, 195, 237, 238, 335, 339, 340–41, 344–45, 348, 352n12, 360, 363, 369; EEA Commission (Norway) (*see* European Consultative Organ (Norway)); EEA Joint Parliamentary Committee (Norway), 238

European Economic Community (EEC), 333, 334, 343, 344, 346, 352n7, 352n8

European Economic Community Protocol, 55

European Free Trade Agreement (EFTA), 333, 334, 335, 343, 344, 352n11

European integration, 23, 26–27, 29, 42, 53, 55, 59, 67, 323, 330, 333–34, 341, 345–51, 351, 360, 384; and Denmark, 90, 101, 103–4, 105, 336–38; and Finland, 113, 143, 144, 147, 149, 335–36, 342–43, 346; and Iceland, 59n4, 195, 333, 343–45, 347, 348; and Norway, 53, 59n4, 201, 204, 214, 237, 238–39, 241, 244n5, 244n12, 245n17, 309, 310, 333, 338–41, 345, 347–48; and Sweden, 273, 280–81, 282, 286, 334–35, 341–42

European Monetary Union. *See* European Economic and Monetary Union (EMU)

European Parliament, 47, 48, 49, 78, 258, 325n11, 350, 380

European Security and Defense Policy (ESDP), 348–49

European Social Survey (ESS), 45, 47, 48

European Union (EU), 26–27, 28, 36, 48, 49, 53, 333–51, 352n8, 360, 361, 363, 369, 375, 382; Amsterdam Treaty, 337, 338; Constitutional Treaty, 101; democratic deficit, 27, 341; and Denmark, 36, 55, 68, 101, 103–4, 105, 106, 325n11, 352n10, 385; Edinburgh Agreement, 337, 338, 349; and Finland, 112, 115, 125, 129, 132–33, 140, 142, 143, 143, 144, 147–48, 150, 325n11, 352n10, 368; and Iceland, 36, 59n4, 180, 192, 195; Lisbon Treaty, 101, 350; Maastricht Treaty, 26, 102, 337, 338; and Norway, 36, 55, 59n4, 201, 204, 214, 235, 237, 238–39, 241, 340–41; and Sweden, 255, 280–81, 283, 286, 287n4, 325n11; Treaty of Rome, 26. *See also* European Community (EC); European integration

European Union Committee (Denmark), 347

European Union Common Agriculture Policy (CAP), 342

Europeanization, 236, 238–39, 382

Euroskepticism, 49, 53, 333, 335, 337, 338, 342, 343, 347, 349

Eurozone, 146, 360. *See also* European Economic and Monetary Union (EMU)

executive, dual: in Finland, 145; in Iceland, 161. *See also* monarch, dual

experience, political, 362, 369–74, 372, 373, 375; in Denmark, 92–93, 94; in

Finland, 119, 133, *134–35*, 136; in Iceland, 183, *184–85*, 189, 373; in Norway, 228–29, *230–31*, 232; in Sweden, 272, 273, *274–75*
experts: in Denmark, 97, 99; in Finland, 141, 144; in Sweden, 252, 274, 286

Fagerholm III cabinet, 138
Fälldin cabinet, 263
farmers, 24, 41, 91, 145, 146, 161, 213, 254, 283, 300, 315, 340. See also peasants
federalism, 14, 25, 30n7, 52, 53, 360
Federalist Papers, 13, 14
Finance Committee (Finland), 132
finance policy, 330, 370; in Finland, 132, 142; in Norway, *218;* in Sweden, 266, 285
Finnbogadóttir, Vigdís, 196n3
Finnish Confederation of Salaried Employees (STTK), 146
fishing policy, 59n4; in Iceland, 167, 332, 343, 344, 351n3, 352n11, 352n12; in Norway, 339, 340
Foreign Affairs Committee (Finland), 132, 148
Foreign Affairs Committee (Norway), 238
foreign policy, 27, 331, 333, 336; in Denmark, 83, 336, 337, 345, 352n5; in Finland, 126, 138, 139–40, 142–44, 145, 147, 149, 335, 347; in Iceland, 162, 167, 176; in Norway, 214; in Sweden, 281, 335
formateur, in Finland, 119. See also informateur
formulation, policy, 16; in Denmark, 100; in Finland, 140–41, 144, 146, 148, 150, 151n12; in Iceland, 164, 168, 173, 189; in Norway, 239; in Sweden, 271, 272, 277, 279, 285
France, 20, 37, *44, 46, 47, 48*, 50, 52, 101, 352n7, 374
Freedom of Information Act of 1970 (Norway), 235
Folketing (Denmark). See parliament

gender distribution, 3, 94, 136, 166, 228, 229, 259, 261, 267, 272, 370, 381
Gerhardsen cabinet, 226
Germany, 20, 37, 40, *44, 46, 47, 48*, 50, 52, 53, 97, 209, 331, 351n1, 352n7
Gísladóttir, Ingibjörg, 182
globalization, 23, 26, 27, 31n12, 35, 115
governance, 29n3; cabinet, 50–51, 58, 71, 105, 186; chain of, 14, 68, 78, 100, 105, 201, 209, 238; coalition, 186; corporatist system of, 145; democratic, 5, 10, 53, 318, 357; market, 103; multilevel, 26, 382; parliamentary, 56, 158, 159, 192, 357, 360, 361, 366; party, 54, 69, 375; prime-ministerial, 151n10
government, 30n8; parliamentary, 5, 30n4, 356–57; subnational, 100, 133, 140, 146, 183, 193, 201, 211–12, 213, 237, 240–41, 273, 280, 281, 286, 360, 382, 385. See also cabinet, caretaker; cabinet, definition of new; cabinet, nonpartisan; cabinet, nonsocialist
Grand Committee (Finland), 132, 148
Great Nordic War, 39
Greece, *44, 46, 47, 48*, 52, 351n1
Green League (Finland), 113, *114*, 121, 125, 310, 311, 342
Green Party (Sweden), 252, 253, 254, 255, 263, 267, 310, 313, 341
Greenland, 37, *38*
Grímsson, Ólafur Ragnar, 190–91

Haakon VII, 244n11
Haarde, Geir, 169, 329
Hagen, Carl I., 241
Hague Summit, 334, 336–37, 352n8
Halvorsen, Kristin, 229
head of state. See monarch, president
Helsinki, 148
Helsinki Headline Goal, 348
Helsinki Summit, 348
Hermannsson, Steingrímur, 180
Holkeri cabinets, 152n14

home rule, 40; in Finland, 39; in Greenland, 37; in Iceland, 160; in Norway, 39
Hønsvald, Nils, 201
House of Commons. *See* United Kingdom (UK)
House of Representatives. *See* United States (U.S.)
"housewares revolution," 159
human rights, 237, 281, 360; in Denmark, 68, 102; European Convention on, 146, 237, 282; European Court of, 282; in Sweden, 281

immigration, 37, *48*, 75, 245n15, 371; anti-immigration, 75, 252, 310, 385
impeachment, in Norway, 200, 210, 223, 226–27
incumbency effect. *See* cabinet electoral performance
Independence Party (Iceland), 160, 161, 162, *162*, 163, 166, 167, 168, 169, 181, 182, 188, 195, 196n2, 302, 314, 323, 343, 344
Independent Party (Denmark), 70, 71, 74
individual members' bills. *See* private members' bills
industrialization, 300, 302
industry interests, 100, 145, 241, 341, 342, 343, 344, 352n12
informateur: in Denmark, 80; in Iceland, 191; in Norway, 214, 244n12
information, access to, 8–9, 22, 25, 358; in Denmark, 97, 104; in Finland, 131–33, 148, 149; in Iceland, 174, 177–78; in Norway, 223, 235, 238, 239; in Sweden, 277–78, 280–81, 285–86. *See also* formateur
information asymmetry, 8, 26, 148, 174, 178, 235, 360
information technology, 22, 358
Ingvaldsen, Bernt, 244n12
instrument of government (Sweden), 15, *39*, 40, 251, 262, 272, 287n5
interest organizations, 42, 51, 317, 384; in Denmark, 97, 99, 100–101, 104,
106; in Finland, 140, 145, 146; in Iceland, 189, 190, 193, 344; in Norway, 235, 239; in Sweden, 253, 278–80, 284
intergovernmentalism, 90, 333, 345
International Monetary Fund (IMF), 329
interpellations: in Denmark, 86, 88–89, *89*, 96; in Finland, 127, *129*, 149; in Iceland, 177–78, *178*, *179*; in Norway, 221, 269, 270. *See also* parliamentary questions
Inuits, 37
investiture vote, 49; in Finland, 120–21, 149; in Norway, 226; in Sweden, 262
Iraq, 176
Ireland, 37, 38, *44*, 46, *46*, 47, *48*, 49, 52
iron triangles, 240
Italy, 17, 19, 37, *44*, *46*, 47, *48*, *52*, 53, 59n3, 121, 199, 352n7, 357, 374

Jäätteenmäki, Anneli, 125
judicial activism, 358; in Denmark, 102; in Norway, 236; in Sweden, 282
judicial review, 14, 26, 52, 53; in Denmark, 102, 236; in Iceland, 195; in Norway, 209, 236; in Sweden, 236
judicial system, 260, 360; in Denmark, 67, 102; in Norway, 201, 237, 243. *See also* courts
judicialization, 360, 375, 382, 384; in Finland, 146; in Norway, 236, 237, 239
Justice Party (Denmark), 69, 70, *70*, 74

Kalmar Union, 39
Karl XII, 39
Keflavik base, 351n3
Kekkonen, Urho, 142, 332
king. *See* monarch
King's Council (Norway), 214. *See also* cabinet, nonsocialist, in Norway; cabinet bills, in Norway; cabinet electoral performance, in Norway; cabinet formation, in Norway;

cabinet governance, in Norway;
cabinet program, in Norway; cabinet
recruitment, in Norway; cabinet
termination, in Norway
Kløfta-saken decision, 236
Koivisto, Mauno, 120, 142
Korvald cabinet, 214
Kremlin, 138. *See also* Moscow; Russia;
Soviet Union

labor, 42, 43, 45, 57, 138, 145, 191,
239, 240, 254, 279, 300, 314, 324n3,
340; market, 100, 146, 191, 279;
movement, 240, 283, 318. *See also*
parties, labor; unions
Labor Federation (Iceland), 352
Labor Party (Norway), 201, 202, 203,
203, 204, 205, 206, 208, 211, 214,
215, 220, 226, 229, 232, 233, 240,
241, 244n5, 244n11, 302, 309, 313,
318, 333, 338–39, 345, 363
Lagtinget, 210, 226
Landsorganisasjonen (Norway), 240
Lange, Anders, 243n2
Left Alliance (Finland), *114*, 121, 125,
313, 342
Left Movement–Greens (Iceland), *162*,
163, 164, 313
Left Party (Sweden), 252, 253, *253*,
254, 255, 257, 260, 266, 267, 313
left-right cleavage. *See* cleavage
structure
Left Socialist Party (Denmark), 69, *70*,
73, 338, 352n5
legislator. *See* members of parliament
(MPs)
legislature. *See* parliament
Liberal Alliance Party (Denmark), *70*
Liberal Center Party (Denmark), *70*,
70, 74
Liberal Party (Denmark), 69, *70*, *70*,
71, 74, 75, 81, 83, 84, *84*, 85, 86, *86*,
87, *87*, 88, 91, 94, 95, 102, 310, 313,
336, 338, 363, 385
Liberal Party (Finland), *114*, *139*. *See
also* Center Party (Finland)
Liberal Party (Iceland), 161, *162*, 163,

196n2. *See also* Independence Party
(Iceland)
Liberal Party (Norway), 200, 202, *203*,
204, 205, 206, 214, 232, 244n5, 310,
339–40, 345, 352n9
Liberal Party (Sweden), 252, *253*, 254,
260, 263, 334, 335, 341
liberalism: bourgeois, 300; economic,
102, 309; political, 5, 42
Liechtenstein, 36
Liinamaa cabinet, 120
Lipponen, Paavo, 120, 152n14
Lipponen cabinets, 146
logrolls: in Finland, 125; in Iceland,
197n12
Luxembourg, *44*, *46*, *47*, *48*, 52, 54
Lyng cabinet, 226

Maastricht Treaty, 26, 102, 337, 338
Madison, James, 14, 200
Madisonian model, 4, 10, 13–14, 19,
28, 29, 30n6, 30n7, 357, 362, 382,
384, 385; in Denmark, 67, 69; in
Iceland, 158, 177; in Norway, 200,
201, 202, 209, 236, 243; in Sweden,
251, 252, 286
majority cabinet, 15, 30n10, 58, 299,
361–63; in Denmark, 68, 71, 75, 80–
81, 84, 95, 97–98, 105, 106; in
Finland, 51, 97–98, 120, 121, 138,
150, 303; in Iceland, 51, 97–98, 160,
161, 163, 167, 169, 172–73, 180,
186, 187–88, 193, 196, 196n3, 344;
in Norway, 98, 204, 214–15, 226,
244n12, 302, 363; in Sweden, 98,
267, 269, 278, 299, 302
majority coalition government. *See*
majority cabinet
majority government. *See* majority
cabinet
Marshall Plan, 331, 351n1
media, 22, 25, 52, 53, 68, 358, 369,
374; in Denmark, 91, 97, 99, 104,
106; in Finland, 147; in Iceland, 191,
195; in Norway, 235, 241; in
Sweden, 258, 267, 272, 273, 277,
283–84, 287n5

median legislator, 20, 30; in Denmark, 74–75, 310; in Finland, 121, 303; in Iceland, 160, 168, 303; in Norway, 204, 244n4, 310; in Sweden, 263–66
median party. *See* median legislator
median voter, 30–31, 243
members of parliament (MPs), 6, 10, 12, 16, 18, 19, 20, 30n10, 298, 303, 316, 324n9, 367, 368–69; in Denmark, 79, 80, 83, 97, 100, 103, 104, 106; in Finland, 116, 117, 119, 120, 126, 127, 129, 131, 136, 138, 145, 148, 149, 150, 150n5, 151n11; in Iceland, 166, 167, 168, 173, 175, 177–78, 179, 180, 181, 192–94, 195, 321; in Norway, 209, 210, 213, *218–19*, 220, 221, 222, 223, 245n16; in Sweden, 255, 259, 260, 261–62, *268–69*, 269–71, 276, 277, 278, 281, 285, 287n2
Middle Ages, 36
Miettunen I cabinet, 138
minister, finance, 370, *371, 372, 373, 376*; in Denmark, 91, *92, 93,* 94; in Finland, 133, *134–35,* 136; in Iceland, 182, 182–83, *184–85*; in Norway, 228–29, *230–31*; in Sweden, 272–73, *274–75*
minister, foreign, 370, *371, 372, 373, 376*; in Denmark, 90, 91, *92–93,* 94; in Finland, 133, *134–35,* 136, 151n9; in Iceland, 169, 180, 182–83, *184–85*; in Norway, 228–29, *230–31*; in Sweden, 272–73, *274–75*
minister, foreign affairs. *See* minister, foreign
minister, justice, 370, *371, 372, 373, 376*; in Denmark, 91, *92–93,* 94; in Finland, 133, *134–35*; in Iceland, 182, 182–83, *184–85*; in Norway, 228–29, *230–31,* 237; in Sweden, 272–73, *274–75*
minister, prime (PM), 5, 6, 25, 27, 30n4, 40, 49, 50, 58, 59n5, 303, 304, 369, 370, *371, 372, 373, 374, 376*; in Denmark, 78, 80, 83, 90, 91, *92–93,* 94, 96, 102; in Finland, 120, 125, 126, 132, 133, *134–35,* 136–38, 141, *143,* 145, 147, 149, 151n7, 151n10, 152n14, 350; in Iceland, 159, 160, 168, 169, 172, 180, 181–83, *184–85,* 186–87, 329; in Norway, 200, 214, 215, 223, 227, 228–29, *230–31,* 244n11, 339, 370; in Sweden, 262, 271, 272–73, *274–75,* 276, 280, 285, 287n3, 350
minister, trade, in Iceland, 195
ministers, cabinet, 6, 19, 27, 350, 367, 368, 369, 370, *371, 372, 373, 373, 374, 376*; in Denmark, 86, 88, *89, 90–91, 92–93,* 94, 97–98, 99, 103, 104, 106; in Finland, 120, 127, 129, 132–33, *134–35,* 136–38, 140, 141, *143,* 151n7; in Iceland, 159, 161, 177, 178, 180–83, *184–85,* 186–87, 188–89, 190, 194; in Norway, 221, 223, 227, 228–29, *230–31,* 232, 235; in Sweden, 267, 269, *270,* 271–73, *274–75,* 276, 277, 278, 280, 285, 286, 287n3. *See also* cabinet, nonpartisan; cabinet, nonsocialist; cabinet formation; cabinet governance; cabinet program; cabinet recruitment; cabinet stability
ministers, junior: in Denmark, 91, 98, 99; in Finland, 91; in Iceland, 91; in Sweden, 287n3
ministers, line. *See* ministers, cabinet
ministers, nonpartisan, 19, 120. *See also* cabinet, nonpartisan
ministries, cabinet, 6, 27, 91, 297, 370, 376; in Denmark, 81, 85, 90–91; in Finland, 127, 132, 133, 136, 137, 140–41, *143,* 148; in Iceland, 173, 181, 188, 194; in Norway, 220, 228, 229, 235, 237; in Sweden, 267, 271, 272, 277, 285
Ministry, Agriculture: in Denmark, 91; in Iceland, 182
Ministry, Development Assistance, in Norway, 228, 229
Ministry, Energy, in Norway, 229
Ministry, Environment: in Iceland, 181, 182; in Norway, 228

Ministry, Family Affairs, in Norway, 228, 229
Ministry, Finance: in Finland, 127; in Iceland, 177, 182; in Sweden, 272
Ministry, Foreign, 27; in Finland, 125; in Iceland, 182
Ministry, Justice: in Denmark, 102; in Finland, 133; in Iceland, 183; in Norway, 237
Ministry, Labor, in Denmark, 91
Ministry, Social Affairs, in Norway, 229
Ministry, Social Welfare, in Denmark, 91
Ministry, Trade and Industry, in Denmark, 91
minority cabinet, 20, 30n10, 50–51, 56, 58, 187, 299, 304, 361–63, 369; in Denmark, 55, 67, 68, 71, 80–81, 83, 84, 85, 88, 91, 94, 97, 105–6, 332, 352n5; in Finland, 121, 303; in Iceland, 158, 169, 172, 181, 187, 188; in Norway, 55, 97, 201, 205, 214, 215, 219–20, 226, 339; in Sweden, 97, 263, 266, 267, 269, 311
minority coalition cabinet. *See* minority cabinet
minority government. *See* minority cabinet
monarch, 21, 36, 40, 49–50, 172; in Denmark, 40, 67, 80, 160, 161; dual, 39; in Norway, 40, 201, 214, 234, 244n11; in Sweden, 40, 251, 252, 262, 272, 281
moral hazard, 8, 10, 24, 25
moral-religious cleavage. *See* cleavage structure
Moscow, 126, 332, 336. *See also* Kremlin; Russia; Soviet Union
motions of confidence. *See* vote of confidence
motions of no confidence. *See* vote of no confidence
multidimensional scaling (MDS), 75

Napoleonic Wars, 39

National Audit Office (Iceland), 176, 177
National Audit Office (Sweden), 278
National Auditing Office (Denmark), 97, 99
National Coalition (Finland), 113, 120, 121, 125, 126, 311, 342
National Confederation of Labor Unions (Norway), 339
National Consensus (Iceland), 191–92
National Economic Institute (Iceland), 177
National Preservation Party (Iceland), 167
"negative majority," 223
negative parliamentarism, 49, 50; in Denmark, 80, 81, 105; in Iceland, 180; in Sweden, 262–63, 266
Nelson, Horatio, 39
neocorporatism. *See* corporatism
Netherlands, *44*, 45, *46*, 47, *48*, 52, 101, 357
neutrality policy, 331, 333, 336, 337, 345; in Denmark, 332, 337; in Finland, 336, 348–49; in Iceland, 167, 332; in Sweden, 331, 332, 335, 341, 347, 348–49
New Democracy Party (Sweden), 252, *253*, 311, 313
New Left ideology, 337, 340
New People's Party (Norway), 340
New Public Management (NPM), 141, 156, 235, 278
Nordic customs union, 336
Nordic defense pact, 331
Nordic model, 3, 361
North Atlantic Treaty Organization (NATO), 162, 182, 331, 332, 333, 334, 338, 345, 347, 348, 349, 351n3, 352n4, 352n5
Norwegian Broadcasting Corporation (Norway), 241
Norwegian Parliamentary Intelligence Oversight Committee (Norway), 222
Norwegian Power and Democracy Study, 55, 201, 237
nuclear policy, 125, 282, 332, 347, 352

Oddsson, Davíð, 159–60, 169, 180, 181–82, 186–87, 194
Oddsson cabinets, 180, 187
Odelstinget (Norway), 210, 226
ombudsman, 16; in Denmark, 97, 99; in Finland, 146–47; in Norway, 222
opposition, political, 17, 20, 342, 343, 367; in Denmark, 81, 83, 85, 88, 96, 97, 106; in Finland, 125, 127, 138, 149, 151n6; in Iceland, 160, 177, 178, 179, 180, 181, 189, 193, 196n4, 196n8; in Norway, 204, 215, 219, 220, 222, 223, 226, 244n5; in Sweden, 256, 263, 266–67, 270, 285
opposition bills. *See* private members' bills
organized interests. *See* interest organizations

Paasikivi, Juho Kusti, 331, 332
Paasikivi-Kekkonen line, 332
parliament, functions of, 15–16. *See also* parliamentary decline; parliamentary democracy; parliamentary oversight; parliamentary questions; parliamentary strength; parliamentary system; parliamentary turnover
parliamentarization, in Finland, 113, 142, 149
Parliamentary Audit Office (Sweden), 278
parliamentary decline, 4, 16, 19–20, 28, 58, 59, 350, 357, 369, 373, 385 (*see also* deparliamentarization; parliamentarization); in Denmark, 69, 105–6; in Iceland, 158–59, 166, 173, 186; thesis of, 16, 31n13, 54, 285, 370, 372
parliamentary democracy. *See* democracy; parliamentary system
parliamentary oversight, 9–10, 15, 16, 19, 26–27, 58, 350, 360, 369, 383; in Finland, 147–48; in Iceland, 175–76, 177–79, 191; in Norway, 220–23, 235–36, 238–39; in Sweden, 269–71, 278, 280, 285. *See also* parliamentary questions

parliamentary questions, 57, 58, 367–68, *368*, 369; in Denmark, 88–89, *89*, 96–97, 99; in Finland, 127, 129, *130–31*, 149; in Iceland, 160, 177–79, *178*, *179*; in Norway, 220, 221–22; in Sweden, 269–70, 270, 285. *See also* interpellations; parliamentary oversight
parliamentary recruitment. *See* selection, candidate
parliamentary scrutiny. *See* parliamentary oversight
parliamentary strength, 4, 13, 14–15, 16, 19–20, 28, 298–99, 350, 357, 367, 369, 374, 381; in Denmark, 83; in Finland, 112, 121, 132, 142, 148, 149, 150, 385; in Iceland, 158, 193–94, 196; in Norway, 201, 215, 220, 235, 236, 238, 239, 242, 243; in Sweden, 286
parliamentary system, 5–6, 7, 13, 14, 19, 168, 285, 316, 356–57, 359, 363, 365, 374, 381
parliamentary turnover, 20, 213–14, 262
parties: bourgeois, 73, *116*, 204, 214, 215, 302, 303, 310 (*see also* parties, nonsocialist); cadre, 183, 315; cartel, 24, 25, 164, 209, 243, 317, 319, 320, 379, 380; catchall, 24, 310, 317; Christian, 311, 358; communist, 300, 310; confessional, 310; conservative, 120, 126, 300, 311, 314, 315, 324n3; effective number of, 75, 113, 162, 205; electoral-professional, 317; extremist, 114; fringe, 311; function of, 18–19; green, 311; labor, 300, 314, 324n3; liberal, 300, 302, 315, 340; mass, 24, 25, 79, 161, 163, 164, 183, 201, 242, 298, 300, 315, 316, 317, 357, 358, 379, 381; nationalist, 114, 342; network, 161–62, 315; nonsocialist, 73, 202, 204, 205, 211, 214, 215, 220, 232, 252, 255, 266, 277, 283, 284, 303, 335, 339, 340, 345 (*see also* parties, bourgeois); "people's movement," 315, 316;

pole, 300, 314, 322, 323, 324n3; populist, 219, 252, 309, 311, 313, 357; protest, 71, 203, 357, 358; protoparties, 315; radical, 309, 311, 323, 340, 357; right-wing, 71, 196n2, 252, 309, 311, 313; role of, 4, 10–12, 13, 14, 17, 28, 54, 297, 298, 323, 374, 381; social democratic, 41, 302, 309, 310, 316, 323, 334, 358, 362; social democratic, in Norway, 20, *207*, 214, 239–40, 244n11, 310, 318, 333, 340 (*see also* Labor Party (Norway)); support, 59n5, 86, *86*, 87, *87*, 255, 263, 266, 267, 285

Party Act of 1969 (Finland), 117

party attachment, 12, 18, 19, 24, 57, *305*, 308–9, 318, 319, 320, 358, 359, 370, 377–79, 380, 381; in Denmark, 71–74, *73*, 105, 385; in Finland, *116*; in Iceland, *165*, 166; in Norway, 202, *207*, 208, 306; in Sweden, *257*, 284

party cohesion, 4, 10, 11, 19, 28, 29n1, 30n10, 316, 357, 374, 382, 384, 385; in Denmark, 71, 75; in Finland, 119; in Iceland, 163, 177, 179–80, 193; in Norway, 200, 201, 202, 205, 210, 227, 243, 340; in Sweden, 261–62, 286

party congress, 315, 316, 318, 339

party decline, 4, 13, 17–19, 54, 56–57, 59, 158, 324, 357, 359, 375, 385; in Denmark, 55, 69, 71–72, 90, 105–6; in Finland, 114, 141, 150; in Iceland, 158, 164–65, 166, 186; in Norway, 55, 205, 208, 242, 243; in Sweden, 256, 258, 284; thesis of, 18, 56, 297. *See also* party organization; party strength

party detachment. *See* party attachment

party discipline, 11, 12, 18, 298, 374; in Denmark, 71, 90; in Finland, 119; in Iceland, 177; in Norway, 227–28; in Sweden, 261–62

party finance, 24–25, 315, 319–20, 323, 324, 379; in Denmark, 71, 105; in Finland, 117, 199; in Norway, 208–9, 211; in Sweden, 255, 284, 287n2

party fractionalization, 19, 69

party identification, 18, 303, 304, *305*, 308, 323, 358, 377, 378; in Denmark, 72, 105, 384; in Finland, 115; in Norway, 205, 206–8, *207*; in Sweden, *257*, 258

party loyalty, 18, 22, 23, 25, 104, 197n14, 213, 243, 273

party membership, 13, 17, 18, 24, 57, 298, 303, 315, 316, 317–18, *318*, 319–20, *319*, 321, 323, 324, 357, 379, 381; collective, 256, 316, 318; in Denmark, 55, 71, 72, 100; in Finland, 112, 114–15, 140, 150, 150n2; in Iceland, 163–64, 321; in Norway, 201, 205–6, 244n7; in Sweden, 254, 255–56, 258, 279, 284, 285

party organization, 11, 14, 18, 24–25, 57, 297–98, 314–22, 323, 357, 375, 379, 380, 381; in Denmark, 71, 78–79, 105, 385; in Finland, 114, 117, 118, 150n2, 385; in Iceland, 161, 164, 182, 193; in Norway, 201, 205–6, 208–9, 213, 243, 339, 340, 385; in Sweden, 253, 255, 258, 259–60, 261, 385

party strength, 4, 12, 13, 14, 19–21, 28, 42, 57, 297, 298–99, 307, 324, 334, 357, 374–77, 382, 385; in Denmark, 71, 85, 91, 106, 346; in Finland, 113, 115, 117, 150, 150n2; in Iceland, 158, 163, 166, 168, 193; in Norway, 201, 205, 206, 208, 227, 242, 308; in Sweden, 255, 261, 266, 284

party system: alternational, 20, 28, 30n10, 205, 303–4, 311, 313, 361, 380; in Denmark, 69–71, 74–78; dimensionality, 20, 30n10, 74–78, 81, 115–16, 163, 167, 202–5, 232, 243n3, 244n6, 254–55, 263, 300, 303, 309, 331, 332, 333, 334, 336, 337, 338, 341; expansion, 253; in Finland, 113–17; five-party model, 69, 252, 253, 300–302, 311, 314, 322, 324n5, 324n7; fragmentation,

party system (*continued*)
20, 56, 78, 113, 119, 121, 138, 201, 362; frozen, 252, 303 (*see also* party system, stable); in Iceland, 161–66; in Norway, 202–5; pivotal, 20–21, 28, 30n10, 303, 304, 311, 313, 361, 380; stable, 74, 113, 162, 163, 202, 208, 252, 253, 254, 303 (*see also* party system, frozen); in Sweden, 252–58; three-front model, 300–302, 314, 322, 323, 324n3, 324n5; three-pole model (*see* party system, three-front model); unstable, 29

party youth organization: in Denmark, *92–93*, 94; in Finland, *134–35*; in Iceland, 182–83, *184–85*; in Norway, 208, 229, *230–31*, 232, 338; in Sweden, 273, *274–75*, 341

patronage, 319; in Finland, 140; in Iceland, 159, 195. *See also* clientelism; spoils

peasants, 202, 300. *See also* farmers

People's Alliance (Iceland), *162*, 162, 163, *165*, 182, 196n1, 310, 343, 344. *See also* Communist Party (Iceland); Socialist Party (Iceland); United Front (Iceland)

People's Democratic Union (Finland), *114*, 151n10

Persson, Göran, 285

Persson cabinet, 276

Petersberg Tasks, 348

Pétursdóttir, Sólveig, 183

plenary hours. *See* sitting hours

pluralism, 100

policy-making process, 4, 11, 20, 26, 28, 36, 42, 298, 347, 350, 360, 369; in Denmark, 71, 97–98; in Finland, 112–13, 141, 146; in Iceland, 158, 173, 179; in Norway, 201, 242, 243; in Sweden, 261, 269–71, 272, 277, 278–79, 284

Popular Movement for the Future of Finnmark (Norway), 243n1

portfolios, ministerial, 17, 58, 59n5, 370–71, *371*, *372*, *373*, 373, 374, 376; in Denmark, 90–91; in Finland, 120, 133, 136; in Iceland, 181–82, 183; in Norway, 228, 229; in Sweden, 272–73. *See also* ministers, cabinet

poverty, 3, 356

preference vote. *See* electoral institutions, preference vote

preparation, policy. *See* formulation, policy

president: in Finland, 40, 49–50, 112, 113, 117, 119, 120, 121, 126, 133, 136, 138, 140, 141–42, *143*, 144, 145, 147, 149, 150, 151n7, 151n12, 331–32, 350, *383*, 385; in Iceland, 40, 49–50, 161, 172, 173, 180, 186, 188, 190–91, 192, 193, 195–96, 196n3, 197n10, 197n12

presidential government, 3, 5, 6, 7, 10, 13, 14, 17, 19, 357. *See also* semi-presidentialism

presidentialization, 25, 27, 58, 273, 285, 350, 369, 375, 376; thesis, 232, 272, 273, 374, 376

private members' bills, 367; in Denmark, 81, *82*, 83, 85, 86, *87*, 88, 105; in Finland, *128–29*, 151n11; in Iceland, 173, *174–75*, 180; in Norway, 215, *218–19*; in Sweden, 261, *268–69*, 269, 285

private members' resolutions. *See* private members' bills

privatization: in Denmark, 103; in Iceland, 180, 195, 196n9; in Sweden, 278, 283

Progress Party (Denmark), 69, *70*, 71, 309, 310, 311, 313, 338

Progress Party (Norway), 202, 203, *203*, 204, 205, 206, 213, 215, 219, 220, 226, 241, 242, 243n2, 244n6, 244n7, 308, 309, 310, 311

Progressive Party (Iceland), 160, 161, 163, 166, 167, 168, 169, 181–82, 188, 196n2, 303, 343, 344

proportional representation (PR). *See* electoral institutions, proportional representation (PR)

Protestant Reformation, 36

Protocol Committee (Norway), 221

questions. *See* parliamentary questions

Radical Liberal Party (Denmark), 20, 69, 70, *70*, 71, 74, 75, 81, 84, *84*, 85, 86, *86*, 87, *87*, 88, 304, 310, 313, 332, 336, 337–38, 349, 352n5
Rasmussen, Nyrup, 68
Reagan administration, 352n4
Red Election Alliance (Norway), 243n1
referendums, 26, 49, 51–53, 360, 361; in Denmark, 68, 102, 103–4, 105, 106, 337–38, 346, 347, 349; in Finland, 147, 343, 346–47; in Iceland, 161, 190, 194, 195, 197n10, 344, 346; in Norway, 49, 201, 241, 245n17, 309, 336, 339, 345, 346; in Sweden, 281, 282–83, 286, 341–42, 346–47, 349
regional integration. See European integration
remiss system, 42; in Norway, 239
republic, 14, 49, 241
"restoration government," 169
revolution, industrial, 300, 302
Reykjavík, Iceland, 186
Riksdag (Sweden). See parliament
roll-call data, 126
Roman rule, 36
Rules of Procedure of 1908 (Norway), 221
rural interests: in Finland, 342, 343; in Iceland, 163, 166; in Norway, 202, 204, 211, 339–40, 352n9
Rural Party (Finland), 113, *114*, 125, 126
rural-urban cleavage. See cleavage structure
Russia, 36, 37, 39, 40, 300, 343, 356. See also Kremlin; Moscow; Soviet Union

Samis, 37
scandal, 97, 99, 221
Scandinavia, 29n2, 35
Scandinavian dualism, 39
screening, 9. See also selection
screening, candidate. See selection, candidate
security policy, 330, 331–33, 334, 341, 345, 347, 348–49; in Denmark, 336;

in Finland, 130, 140, 144, 331–32, 343, 345, 346, 349; in Iceland, 347; in Norway, 333, 336, 345; in Sweden, 341, 345–46
selection, 9; adverse, 8–10, 24
selection, candidate, 8, 11, 12, 13, 16, 18, 19, 298, 303, 314, 315, 316, 320–22, 324, 324n8, 325n11, 357, 382; in Denmark, 78–80, 105, 321; in Finland, 117–19, 145, 150, 150n4; in Iceland, 164, 168, 183, 192–93, 320–21; in Norway, 210, 212–13, 242; in Sweden, 259–61, 284, 285
Selmer cabinet, 227
semi-presidentialism, 361, 381; in Finland, 112, 142, 324n6, 382; in Iceland, 161, 172, 191, 193
Senate. See United States (U.S.)
Single European Act (SEA), 26, 337–38, 352n8
sitting hours, *82*, *83*, *128*, *129*, 131, *268*, *269*, 367
Skåne, 35
slalom method, 219–20
Social Democratic Alliance (Iceland), 163, 167. See also United Front (Iceland)
Social Democratic Party (Denmark), 69–70, *70*, 71, *73*, 74, 75, 81, 83, 84, *84*, 85, 86, 87, *87*, 88, 91, 94, 102, 302, 310, 313, 336, 337, 338, 346, 352n5
Social Democratic Party (Finland), 113, *114*, 120, 121, 125, 126, 150n4, 151n10, 302, 309, 311, 313, 342
Social Democratic Party (Iceland), 161, *162*, 163, *165*, 166, 167, 168, 169, 181, 188, 302, 343, 344, 345. See also United Front (Iceland)
Social Democratic Party (Sweden), 20, 113, 252–53, *253*, 254, 255–56, *257*, 260, 262, 263, 266, 267, 271, 273, 276, 277, 279, 283, 284, 302, 311, 313, 316, 318, *334*, 335, 341, 342, 363
Socialist Left Party (Norway), 202–3, *203*, 205, 206, *207*, 208, 214, 215, 220, 226, 229, 241, 242, 244n5, 244n6, 309, 313

Socialist Party (Iceland), 162, *162*, 163, 166. *See also* Communist Party (Iceland); People's Alliance (Iceland)
Socialist People's Party (Denmark), 69, *70*, 75, 83, 302, 313, 336, 337, 338, 352n5
Socialist People's Party (Norway), 202, *203*, 205, 244n4, 333, 339, 345. *See also* Socialist Left Party (Norway)
Sorsa VI cabinet, 137
sovereignty: citizen (*see* sovereignty, voter); national, 67, 101, 160, 238, 300, 340; parliamentary, 10, 236, 245n16, 286, 382; political, 26, 201; popular (*see* sovereignty, voter); voter, 5, 6, 23, 67, 192, 195, 201, 238, 297
Soviet Union, 35, 40, 112, 138, 140, 142, 146, 149, 150, 287n3, 300, 323, 331, 335, 336, 346, 350, 351n1, 352n4, 361, 382, 385. *See also* Kremlin; Moscow; Russia
Spain, 37, *44*, *46*, *47*, *48*, *52*, 360
"special advisors," 91, 99, 137
spoils, 319, 379; in Finland, 141; in Iceland, 189, 190, 319. *See also* clientelism; patronage
Storting (Norway). *See* parliament
subsidies for parties. *See* party finance
suffrage, *39*, 40
supranationalism, 26–27, 30n7, 53, 252, 280, 281, 286, 333, 334, 336, 347, 350, 358, 359, 360
Sverdrup, Johan, 200
Sveriges akademikers centralorganisation (SACO), 279
Sverisdóttir, Valgerður, 182
Swedish Democrats (Sweden), 252
Swedish People's Party (Finland), *114*, 121, 125, 150n2, 302, 311, 342
Swedish Trade Union Confederation, *Landsorganisationen (LO)*, 254, 279, 342
Switzerland, 36, 209
Syse cabinet, 340

taxes, 43, *44*, 74, 75, 103, 203, 240, 254, 255, 309, 320, 381, 382

technocrats. *See* experts
term in office, 50, 364; in Finland, 117, 145; in Norway, 210, 220; in Sweden, 259, 262
Thoroddsen, Gunnar, 168
Thoroddsen cabinet, 169
threshold of representation: in Denmark, 72; in Sweden, 252
Tjänstemännens Centralorganisation (TCO), 279
trade policy, 277, 331, 333, 335–36, 339, 344, 345
transparency, 21, 24, 59, 362; in Finland, 126; in Norway, 236
Transparency International, 52, 54, 197n14
Treaty of Friendship, Cooperation, and Mutual Assistance (Finland), 332
True Finns (Finland), *114*, 343
Truman Doctrine, 351n1
trust, political, 3, 17, 45, *47*, 48–49, 57, 317, 323, 380–81; in Denmark, 72, 73, 74, 105, 384; in Finland, *116*; in Iceland, *165*; in Norway, 207, 242; in Sweden, 242, 257, 258
Turkey, 351n1

unemployment, 45, *46*; in Iceland, 165, 344; in Norway, 233; in Sweden, 279
unicameralism: in Denmark, 78; in Finland, 117; in Iceland, 177; in Sweden, 253
Union of Liberals and Leftists (Iceland), *162*, 167, 344
Union of University Graduates (Denmark), 100
Union of White-Collar Workers (Denmark), 100
unions, 41, 43, 316, 317, 318; in Denmark, 100, 337; in Finland, 146, 342; in Iceland, 191; in Norway, 231, 239, 240, 338–39, 340; in Sweden, 254, 256, 260, 279, 341, 342. *See also* labor
unitary government or state, 10, 14, 53, 104, 146, 240

United Front (Iceland), 160, *162*, 163, *165*, 169, 313–14
United Kingdom (UK), 11, *44*, *46*, *47*, *48*, 49, 50, *52*, 96, 97, 99, 333, 337, 360; House of Commons, 20. *See also* Britain
United Nations (UN), *47*, 48, 49, 330
United States (U.S.), 6, 7, 9, 13, 14, 19, 36, 162, 167, 176, 182, 200, 236, 242, 329, 331, 332, 343, 347, 351n1; American Revolution, 200; Congress, 9, 30n10; House of Representatives, 6; military presence in Iceland, 162, 332–33, 343, 347 (*see also* Keflavik base); Senate, 6
Unity List (Denmark), 69, *70*, 74
urban-rural cleavage. *See* cleavage structure
USSR, 331, 332, 336, 347. *See also* Soviet Union

Vanhanen, Matti, 125
Vanhanen cabinet, 125, 137–38
Väyrynen, Paavo, 151n9
Vennamo, Veikko, 126
veto, presidential: in Finland, *143*, 144; in Iceland, 161, 190–91, 192, 195, 197n10, 197n12
veto powers, 9, 14, 103, 350
Vikings, 37
vote of confidence, 50; in Denmark, 96; in Finland, 119, 120, 127, 142; in Iceland, 168; in Norway, 201, 223, 226
vote of no confidence, 9, 30n4, 50; in Denmark, 80, 88–89, 96; in Finland, 127, 151n7; in Norway, 223, 226, 242
voter attachment. *See* party attachment

voter turnout, 18, 303, 304, *305*, 377; in Denmark, 71–72, *73*, 105, 384; in Finland, 112, 114, 115, *116*, 145, 150; in Iceland, 165, *165*; in Norway, 207, 211–12; in Sweden, 256–57, *257*, 258, 283, 284, 285

wage bargaining, 43; in Finland, 146; in Iceland, 191
wage-earner funds, 254
War of Independence of 1918 (Finland), 40
Warsaw Pact, 331
welfare policy, 29, 36, 43–45, 53; in Finland, 146; in Norway, 201, 237; in Sweden, 280
Westminster model, 4, 10–15, 18, 20, 28, 30n5, 30n6, 50, 56, 298, 303, 357, 361, 363, 365, 374, 381–82, 384; in Denmark, 67, 69, 96, 97; in Iceland, 158, 177; in Norway, 200, 201, 209, 210, 243, 245n16; in Sweden, 251, 255, 286
Willoch, Kåre, 226
Willoch cabinets, 215, 226, 240, 244n13
Winter War of 1939–40 (Finland), 331
Women's Alliance (Iceland), 167, 168
Women's List (Iceland), 310
Women's Party (Iceland), *162*, 163, *165*, 196n2. *See also* United Front (Iceland)
working class, 24, 41, 42, 57, 300, 302, 308, 310, 315, 384; in Denmark, *73*; in Finland, *116*; in Norway, 202, 207, 213; in Sweden, 257, 257
World War I, 40
World War II, 40, 330